MARRIAGES and DEATH NOTICES
in
The Raleigh Register
and
North Carolina State Gazette
1826-1845

Carrie L. Broughton

HERITAGE BOOKS
2008

HERITAGE BOOKS
AN IMPRINT OF HERITAGE BOOKS, INC.

Books, CDs, and more—Worldwide

For our listing of thousands of titles see our website
at
www.HeritageBooks.com

A Facsimile Reprint
Published 2008 by
HERITAGE BOOKS, INC.
Publishing Division
100 Railroad Ave. #104
Westminster, Maryland 21157

Originally published as:
Bulletin of the
North Carolina State Library
Raleigh, North Carolina
1947

— Publisher's Notice —
In reprints such as this, it is often not possible to remove blemishes from the original. We feel the contents of this book warrant its reissue despite these blemishes and hope you will agree and read it with pleasure.

International Standard Book Numbers
Paperbound: 978-0-7884-1996-6
Clothbound: 978-0-7884-7164-3

We are very pleased
that you are reprinting
Carrie L. Broughton's
MARRIAGE AND DEATH NOTICES
FROM
THE RALEIGH REGISTER
AND
NORTH CAROLINA STATE GAZETTE
FROM 1826 - 1845.

◈

NORTH CAROLINA STATE LIBRARY

Philip S. Ogilvie,
State Librarian

Margaret B. Price,
Genealogy Reference Librarian

PREFACE

This index was prepared by Carrie L. Broughton, State Librarian. The information was compiled from a weekly paper founded October 22, 1799 by Joseph Gales, Sr., which was issued first as the Raleigh Register and North Carolina Weekly Advertiser, and later changed to the Raleigh Register and North Carolina Gazette.

The years 1799-1825 were embodied in the Biennial report of 1942-1944, but with this issue and in the future, the information will be published as a separate bulletin under the title Marriages and Death Notices Appearing in the Raleigh Register and North Carolina Gazette. It is the desire of the librarian to continue this publication until the entire file has been completed. On account of a small staff in the library, this work has been greatly retarded.

The material has been arranged in two parts: Part 1, Marriages; Part 2, Deaths. The entries have been made as brief as possible, listing each name alphabetically, giving date of marriage or death, the place of residence which the person resided, the paper and date of publication. The only abbreviations used is R.R. which stands for Raleigh Register and North Carolina Gazette.

The files possessed by the library is not entirely complete, and there are missing issues now and then, therefore this will explain occasional omissions.

CARRIE L. BROUGHTON.

1946.

PART I

MARRIAGES

1826

Adams, Allen to Elizabeth White, Mar. 29, Wake county. R. R. Apr. 21, 1826.
Adams, Capt. Andrew M. to Phoeba Rounsaville, Apr. 2, Iredell county, R. R. Apr. 14, 1826.
Adams, Meredith to Jane Clancey, Dec., Hillsboro. R. R. Dec. 15, 1826.
Alexander, Enoch to Frances Rew, Feb. 1, Newbern. R. R. Feb. 17, 1826.
Alexander, Capt. Isaac F. to Mary King, Apr. 2, Iredell county. R. R. Apr. 14, 1826.
Alexander, Oswald to Mary Moore, Oct. 26, Mecklenburg county. R. R. Nov. 3, 1826.
Allen, Sarah to Dr. George W. B. Robertson, Aug. 3, Milton. R. R. Aug. 18, 1826.
Alsobrooke, Lunsford L. of Alabama to Temperance B. Eaton, Je. 7, Warren county. R. R. Je. 23, 1826.
Armsted, Robert of Chatham county to Louisa Olive, Nov. Wake county. R. R. Nov. 10, 1826.
Arrington, Elizabeth to James R. Batrle of Nash county, Nov. 14, Halifax. R. R. Dec. 1, 1826.
Askin, Thos. of Maryland to Isabella Ingram, Mar., Fayetteville. R. R. Mar. 24, 1826.
Badger, Geo. E. to Mary Polk, Nov. 9, Raleigh. R. R. Nov. 17, 1826.
Baily, Miss to Henry Delamoth, Aug. 1, Montgomery county. R. R. Aug. 25, 1826.
Barber, Helen to Thos. B. Ives of Davidson county, Mar. 2, Onslow county. R. R. Mar. 24, 1826.
Bartlett, Elizabeth B. to Major Anthony G. Glynn of Raleigh, Jly. 24, Washington, D. C. R. R. Aug. 4, 1826.
Battle, Brice to Nancy Dudley, Aug., Newbern. R. R. Aug. 25, 1826.
Battle, Elizabeth H. to Wm. Drake of Chatham county, Jan. 12, Raleigh. R. R. Jan. 20, 1826.
Battle, James R. of Nash county to Elizabeth Arrington, Nov. 14, Halifax. R. R. Dec. 1, 1826.
Beall, Dr. Aza of Iredell county to Susan Ann Harriet Remson, Sept. 12, Lincolnton, Ga. R. R. Sept. 29, 1826.
Beaman, Parkes to Catharine M'Rae, Aug. 10, Anson county. R. R. Sept. 8, 1826.
Beamon, Mary to Isaac Lane, Aug. 17, Sampson county. R. R. Sept. 1, 1826.
Bears, Mrs. Maria E. to Salmon Hall, Jan., Newbern. R. R. Jan. 13, 1826.
Beasley, Isaac to Clarinda Price, Apr. 29, Wake county. R. R. My. 5, 1826.
Bell, Drusilla to William Sanders, Jan., Newbern. R. R. Jan. 13, 1826.
Bellamy, John to Mrs. Ann Patillo, Aug., Warrenton. R. R. Aug. 18, 1826.
Bennett, Elizabeth to Gideon B. Smith of Raleigh, Jan 22, Baltimore. R. R. Feb. 3, 1826.

Benton, Sarah to David B. Raymond, Apr. 30, Anson county. R. R. Je. 16, 1826.
Bishop, Mary to J. G. M'Kenzie of Scotland Neck, Aug. 17, Edgecombe county. R. R. Sept. 8, 1826.
Blackwell, Wealthy to Geo. Robinson, Feb. 2, Rowan county. R. R. Feb. 17, 1826.
Blair, Elizabeth to Joshua Skinner, Feb., Edenton. R. R. Feb. 24, 1826.
Bonner, Hannah N. to Matthew Shaw of Washington, Feb. 15, Beaufort county. R. R. March 3, 1826.
Booe, Mary to Isaac D. Jones, Apr. 30, Rowan county. R. R. Je. 16, 1826.
Boushall, Penelope to Dr. John D. Toy, Aug., Camden county. R. R. Sept. 1, 1826.
Boykin, Sarah to William Stevens, Feb. 28, Sampson county. R. R. Mar. 17, 1826
Bozman, Harriet to William L. Chesson, Feb., Plymouth. R. R. Feb. 24, 1826.
Bradley, Priscilla to M. West, Je., Halifax. R. R. Je. 9, 1826.
Brady, Mary to Allen Hodge of Kentucky, Nov. Edgecombe county. R. R. Nov. 24, 1826.
Bragg, Sarah to Thomas Rowe of Craven county, Jly., Newberne. R. R. Jly. 28, 1826.
Branton, Eliza S. to Chapel M'Churchill, Apr. 20, Greene county. R. R. My. 5, 1826.
Britton, Elizabeth Ann to Dr. Lewis M. Jiggats of Hertford, Sept., Bertie county. R. R. Sept. 22, 1826.
Brown, Moses L. to Letitia Hartman, Aug. 3, Rowan county. R. R. Aug. 25, 1826.
Bryan, Christopher to Rebecca Conner, Aug. 1, Trenton, Jones County. R. R. Aug. 4, 1826.
Bryan, Mary to William Hellen, Nov., Jones county. R. R. Dec. 1, 1826.
Bumgarner, Catharine to Alfred Martin, Oct. 5, Lincoln county. R. R. Nov. 3, 1826.
Burnett, John of Virginia to Susan Cardwell, Jan. 19, Granville county. R. R. Feb. 3, 1826.
Byrd, Elizabeth to Reuben Wallace, Jan., Lenoir county. R. R. Jan. 27, 1826.
Caldwell, Daniel to Isabella Shields, Jan. 19, Meckenburg county. R. R. Feb. 3, 1826.
Caldwell, David T. to Harriet Davidson, Apr., Charlotte. R. R. Apr. 14, 1826.
Calloway, Nancy to James M. Nye, Aug. 7, Ashe county. R. R. Sept. 22, 1826.
Camp, Sophia Weston to John S. Ford, Aug. 24, Rutherford county. R. R. Oct. 6, 1826.
Campbell, Miss E. to Elane Moore, Jan. 19, Mecklenburg county. R. R. Feb. 3, 1826.
Campbell, John Jr. tó Emily Pope, Je. 27, Halifax county. R. R. Jly. 21, 1826.
Campbell, Mary Elizabeth Ann to Robert Lanier, Jr., Feb. 16, Pitt county. R. R. Mar. 17, 1826
Caraway, Edward of Craven county to Abigail Ward, Aug. 15, Beaufort. R. R. Sept. 1, 1826.

Cardwell, Susan to John Burnett of Virginia, Jan. 19, Granville county. R. R. Feb. 3, 1826.
Carmott, Ann to Capt. Timothy Hunter, Nov., Newberne. R. R. Dec. 1, 1826.
Carter, Martha M. to William Collins, Nov. 28, Halifax county. R. R. Dec. 15, 1826.
Carter, Nancy to Philip Gatling, Aug. 10, Anson county. R. R. Sept. 1, 1826.
Carter, Susan of Caswell county to Robert Galloway, Apr. 30, Rockingham. R. R. Je. 16, 1826.
Carter, Turner to Sarah Watson, Aug. 6, Bertie county. R. R. Aug. 8, 1826.
Cartwright, Duke to Nancy Scott, Mar. 30, Elizabeth City. R. R. Apr. 14, 1826.
Chambers, Jas. to Carolina Fillyaw, Aug., New Hanover county. R. R. Aug. 25, 1826.
Chapman, Carolina to Henry Waring, Jr. of New York, Je. 17, Newbern. R. R. Je. 30, 1826.
Chapman, Marinda to Peter Kestler, Apr. 15, Rowan county. R. R. Je. 9, 1826.
Chesson, William L. to Harriet Bozman, Feb., Plymouth. R. R. Feb. 24, 1826.
Christian, Wm. to Sarah Terrel, Apr. 30, Montgomery county. R. R. Je. 9, 1826.
Clairborn, John H. to Sarah Hall, Aug. 2, Milton. R. R. Aug. 18, 1826.
Clancey, Jane to Meredith Adams, Dec., Hillsboro. R. R. Dec. 15, 1826.
Clifton, Henry Jr. to Miss Fort, Dec. 12, Wake county. R. R. Dec. 15, 1826.
Cobb, Hannah to David Wilson, Aug. 17, Guilford county. R. R. Sept. 1, 1826.
Collins, William to Martha M. Carter, Nov. 28, Halifax county. R. R. Dec. 15, 1826.
Colman, Sabria to Edward W. Tweford, Aug. 17, Guilford county. R. R. Sept. 1, 1826.
Connelly, Margaret C. to Smith Patterson, Je. Louisburg. R. R. Je. 9, 1826.
Conner, Eliza M. to W. S. Simonton, Jly. 27, Lincoln county. R. R. Aug. 18, 1826.
Conner, Rebecca to Christopher Bryan, Aug. 1, Trenton, New Jersey. R. R. Aug. 4, 1826.
Cook, Dr. Alfred to Sally Turrentine, Apr. 30, Rowan county. R. R. Je. 23, 1826.
Copes, Rebecca to John Smith, Mar. Smithville. R. R. Mar. 17, 1826.
Cornell, Paul to Catharine Mackey, Feb. 26, Plymouth. R. R. Mar. 17, 1826.
Cowan, Capt. Abel to Maria M'Kinsey, Feb. 2, Rowan county. R. R. Feb. 17, 1826.
Cowan, Joseph, Jr. to Sarah Young, Sept. 5, Rowan county. R. R. Sept. 22, 1826.
Crawford, Ann to Joseph Hodge, Feb. 23, Fayetteville. R. R. Feb. 24, 1826.
Crawford, Ann Maria to Raiford Hooks, Sept. 7, Wayne county. R. R. Oct. 15, 1826.

Crawford, John C. to Eliza Sasser, Sept. 7, Wayne county. R. R. Oct. 15, 1826.
Creecy, Robert to Parthenia Weston, Nov. 20, Edenton. R. R. Dec. 8, 1826.
Crowder, Robert A. of Mecklenburg county, Va. to Eleanor Robertson, Jly. 20, Caswell county. R. R. Aug. 4, 1826.
Curtis, David W. to Elizabeth B. Hart, Je. 29, Kinston. R. R. Jly. 28, 1826.
Curtis, Thomas J. to Martha J. Yarbrough of Franklin county, Jan. 11, Fayetteville. R. R. Jan. 13, 1826.
Cutlar, Frederick J. to Louisa Dubrutz, Je. 27, Fayetteville. R. R. Je. 30, 1826.
Cutler, Henry G. to Eliza Thorp, Jly. 27, Northampton county. R. R. Aug. 4, 1826.
Dancy, Hannah to Paul Turner, Aug. 24, Rowan county. R. R. Sept. 8, 1826.
Daniel, Chisley to Lucy Noblin, Jly. 6, Granville county. R. R. Jly 14, 1826.
Darden, Alfred to Sarah Moore, Jly. 5, Camden county. R. R. Jly. 7, 1826.
Davidson, Harriet to David T. Caldwell, Apr. Charlotte. R. R. Apr. 14, 1826.
Davidson, Dr. John M. to Mary J. Silvester, Apr. 5, Mecklenburg county. R. R. My. 5, 1826.
Davidson, Margaret Eliza to John E. Patton, Oct. 17, Buncombe county. R. R. Dec. 8, 1826.
Davis, Eliza to Robert M'Lure, Nov. 30, Mecklenburg county. R. R. Dec. 15, 1826.
Davis, Michael to Sally Trexler, Aug. 31, Salisbury. R. R. Sept. 15, 1826.
Davis, Thomas F. Jr. of Wilmington to Elizabeth Fleming, Nov. 16, Hillsboro. R. R. Nov. 17, 1826.
Dellamoth, Henry to Miss Baily, Aug. 1, Montgomery county. R. R. Aug. 25, 1826.
Delony, Dr. W. to Susan Sledge, Nov. 8, Warren county. R. R. Nov. 24, 1826.
DeRossett, Dr. M. J. of Wilmington to Sarah Waddell, Jan. 22, Brunswick county. R. R. Mar. 3, 1826.
Derring, Sallie to Holoman Gardner, Nov. Nash county. R. R. Dec. 1, 1826.
Dever, Eunice to Joseph Miller, Apr. 21, Rowan county. R. R. Je. 23, 1826.
Dinkins, Sarah C. C. to Nathaniel Greene of Warren county. Apr. Mecklenburg county. R. R. Apr. 28, 1826.
Dodge, Jas. R. of Lexington to Susan Williams of Surry county, Apr. 24, Surry county. R. R. Je. 9, 1826.
Dodson, Permelia T. to Gideon B. Turner, Mar. 9, Milton. R. R. Mar. 31, 1826.
Doughtery, Dr. Middleton to Davy A. Wilson, Aug. 18, Mecklenburg county. R. R. Sept. 1, 1826.
Drake, Wm. of Chatham county to Elizabeth H. Battle, Jan. 12, Raleigh. R. R. Jan. 20, 1826.
Drew, Lucy to Gabriel L. Holmes, Nov. 6, Halifax county. R. R. Nov. 17, 1826.
Dubrutz, Louisa to Frederick J. Cutlar, Je. 27, Fayetteville. R. R. Je. 30, 1826.
Dudley, Mary to Spence Harris, Feb. Craven county. R. R. Feb. 24, 1826.
Dudley, Nancy to Brice Battle, Aug., Newbern. R. R. Aug. 25, 1826.

Dunn, Thos. C. to Edy Hearne, Sept. 28, Montgomery county. R. R. Oct. 20, 1826.
Eaton, Temperance B. to Lunsford L. Alsobrooke of Alabama, Je. 7, Warren county. R. R. Je. 23, 1826.
Eccles, Janet to Williamson Whitehead, Jly. 31, Fayetteville. R. R. Aug. 4, 1826.
Elliott, Martin to Eliza M'Combs, Sept. 14, Rutherford county. R. R. Nov. 3, 1826.
Elliott, Safrona to Wm. Gray, Jan. 18, Burke county. R. R. Feb. 17, 1826.
Evans, David to Martha G. Jordan, Mar. 2, Person county. R. R. Mar. 31, 1826.
Fillyaw, Caroline to Jas. Chambers, Aug., New Hanover county. R. R. Aug. 25, 1826.
Fisher, Elizabeth to Levi Rowe, Je. Newbern. R. R. Je. 9, 1826.
Fisher, Samuel C. to Elizabeth Webber of Newbern, Feb. 6. R. R. Feb. 17, 1826.
Fleming, Elizabeth to Thomas F. Davis, Jr. of Wilmington. Nov. 16, Hillsboro. R. R. Nov. 17, 1826.
Fleming, Mary to Haynes Waddel, Jarr. 4, Wilmington. R. R. Jan. 27, 1826.
Fletcher, Ann J. to Shadrack H. Sedbury, Nov. 16, Fayetteville. R. R. Dec. 8, 1826.
Fletcher, Pamela to Russel H. Jones of Georgia, Sept. 21, Wilkes county. R. R. Oct. 20, 1826.
Ford, John S. to Sophia Weston Camp, Aug. 24, Rutherford county. R. R. Oct. 6, 1826.
Fort, Miss to Henry Clifton, Jr. Dec. 12, Wake county. R. R. Dec. 15, 1826.
Foster, Polly to Jeremiah Potts, Mar. 23, Rowan county. R. R. Apr. 14, 1826.
Fulenwider, Wm. to Martha E. Hayes, Oct. 26, Lincoln county. R. R. Nov. 3, 1826.
Gaines, Jas. L. of Moore county to Sarah Shaw, Sept. 13, Fayetteville. R. R. Sept. 15, 1826.
Gainey, Edsey to Lloyd West, Je. Fayetteville. R. R. Je. 30, 1826.
Galloway, Robert to Susan Carter of Caswell county, Apr. 30, Rockingham. R. R. Je. 16, 1826.
Gant, Jeremiah to Harriet Harden, Oct. 26, Hillsborough. R. R. Nov. 10, 1826.
Gardner, Holman to Sallie Derring, Nov. Nash county. R. R. Dec. 1, 1826.
Gardner, Martha to Guilford Tally, Jan. Warren county. R. R. Feb. 3, 1826.
Garrett, Henry W. to Sarah Sasnett, Oct. 26, Edgecombe county. R. R. Nov. 17, 1826.
Gatling, Philip to Nancy Carter, Aug. 10, Anson county. R. R. Sept. 1, 1826.
Giles, Arabella to John W. Norwood, Jan. 30, Hillsboro. R. R. Feb. 3, 1826.
Gillett, Dr. Bezaleel to Jane Henderson, Apr. 18, Raleigh. R. R. Apr. 21, 1826.
Glenn, Dr. James of Louisburg to Emily Yarbrough of Franklin county, Jan. 26. R. R. Jan. 27, 1826

Glynn, Major Anthong G. of Raleigh to Elizabeth B. Bartlett, Jly 24, Washington. R. R. Aug. 4, 1826.
Goldston, Jno. H. to Mary Smith, Je. 15, Newbern. R. R. Je. 30, 1826.
Graham, Dr. Geo. F. of Memphis, Tenn. to Martha Ann Harris, Mar. 28, Lincoln county. R. R. Apr. 14, 1826.
Graham, Jane of Newbern to William H. Haywood, Jr., of Raleigh, Feb. 1, Newbern. R. R. Feb. 10, 1826.
Granberry, Josiah T. to Sarah Ann Sawyer, Jan. Chowan county. R. R. Feb. 3, 1826.
Gray, Mrs. Deborah to Thomas Tillett, Je. 6, Camden county. R. R. Jly. 7, 1820.
Gray, Wm. to Safrona Elliott, Jan. 18, Burke county. R. R. Feb. 17, 1826.
Green, Capt. Samuel of Lexington to Mrs. Mary Owen of Jersey settlement, Aug. 15, Davidson county. R. R. Sept. 1, 1826.
Green, Nathaniel of Warren county to Sarah C. C. Dinkins, Apr., Mecklenburg county. R. R. Apr. 28, 1826.
Gregory, Claudia G. M. Hamilton to Rev. Philip Bruce Wiley, Nov. Elizabeth City. R. R. Nov. 10, 1826.
Gregory, Felix of Newport, R. I. to Sarah King, Mar. Elizabeth City. R. R. Mar. 31, 1826.
Guthrie, Caroline J. to Wm. T. Yeomans, Nov. 28, Washington, Beaufort county. R. R. Dec. 22, 1845.
Hall, Mrs. Mary to Seymour Penyear, Jan. Chatham county. R. R. Feb. 3, 1843.
Hall, Mary E. to Wm. S. Webb, Jan. Newbern. R. R. Feb. 3, 1826.
Hall, Salmon to Mrs. Maria E. Bears, Jan., Newbern. R. R. Jan. 13, 1826.
Hanes, Anna of Davidson county to Emanuel Shober of Stokes county, Mar. 30. R. R. Apr. 21, 1826.
Harden, Harriet to Zeremiah Gant, Oct. 26, Hillsborough. R. R. Nov. 10, 1826.
Harris, Rev. Eleazer of South Carolina to Jane Agnew Kirkpatrick of Mecklenburg county, Nov. 28. R. R. Dec. 15, 1826.
Harris, John T. to Mrs. Patience Lee, Mar 7, Wilmington. R. R. Mar. 17, 1826.
Harris, Martha Ann to Dr. Geo. F. Graham of Memphis Tenn. Mar. 28, Lincoln county. R. R. Apr. 14, 1826.
Harris, Spence to Mary Dudley, Feb. Craven county. R. R. Feb. 24, 1826.
Harrison, Mrs. to Col. Joseph Hawkins, Aug. 14, Northampton county. R. R. Aug. 25, 1826.
Hart, Elizabeth B. to David W. Curtis, Je. 29, Kinston. R. R. Jly. 28, 1826.
Hartman, Letitia to Moses L. Brown, Aug. 3, Rowan county. R. R. Aug. 25, 1826.
Hartman, Nancy to Alex Smith, Feb. 2, Rowan county. R. R. Feb. 17, 1826.
Hatch, Mrs. Alicia to Col. Edmund Hatch, Je. Jones county. R. R. Je. 9, 1826.
Hatley, Alfred to Barbara Rodgers, Jly. 30, Montgomery county. R. R. Sept. 1, 1826.
Haughton, Jonathan, Jr. to Mary Popelston, Mar. 2, Edenton. R. R. Mar. 17, 1826.

Hawkins, Col. Joseph to Fanny Minter, Sept. Chatham county. R. R. Sept. 15, 1826.
Hawkins, Col. Joseph to Mrs. Harrison, Aug. 14, Northampton county. R. R. Aug. 25, 1826.
Hawkins, Philemon to Miss J. B. Sherrod, Je. Louisburg. R. R. Je. 9, 1826.
Hawley, Francis of Hartford, Connecticutt to Mary M'Leod of Richmond county, Jan. 19, Laurel Hill. R. R. Feb. 3, 1826.
Hayes, Martha E. to Wm. Fulenwider, Oct. 26, Lincoln county. R. R. Nov. 3, 1826.
Haywood, Delia H. to General William Williams of Warren county, My. 9, Raleigh. R. R. My. 12, 1826.
Haywood, William H. Jr. of Raleigh to Jane Graham of Newbern, Feb. 1, Newbern. R. R. Feb. 10, 1826.
Hearne, Edy to Thos. C. Dunn, Sept. 28, Montgomery county. R. R. Oct. 20, 1826.
Heartt, Mary to Thomas Lyon, Nov. Edgecombe county. R. R. Nov. 24, 1826.
Heerman, John to Ferma Mitchell, Aug. 28, Elizabeth City. R. R. Sept. 1, 1826.
Hellen, William to Mary Bryan, Nov. Jones county. R. R. Dec. 1, 1826.
Henderson, Jane to Dr. Bezaleel Gillett, Apr. 18, Raleigh. R. R. Apr. 21, 1826.
Hicks, Christiana to Christopher Hill, Aug. 17, Guilford county. R. R. Sept. 1, 1826.
Hill, Christopher to Christiana Hicks, Aug. 17, Guilford county. R. R. Sept. 1, 1826.
Hinton, Isabella W. of Granville county to Henry M. Miller, Feb. 21, Granville county. R. R. Mar. 14, 1826.
Hodge, Allen of Kentucky to Mary Brady, Nov., Edgecombe county. R. R. Nov. 24, 1826.
Hodge, Joseph to Ann Crawford, Feb. 23, Fayetteville. R. R. Feb. 24, 1826.
Holmes, Gabriel L. of Sampson county to Lucy Drew, Nov. 6, Halifax county. R. R. Nov. 17, 1845.
Hooks, Raiford to Ann Maria Crawford, Sept. 7, Wayne county. R. R. Oct. 15, 1826.
Hoskins, Lemuel to Elizabeth Norcom, Jan., Chowan county. R. R. Feb. 3, 1826.
Hovey, Capt. Darius of Massachusetts to Sally Sawyer, Nov., Elizabeth City. R. R. Nov. 10, 1826.
Howell, Sarah to Samuel M'Longue, Aug. 17, Guilford county. R. R. Sept: 1, 1826.
Hunter, Capt. Timothy to Ann Carmott, Nov. Newbern. R. R. Dec. 1, 1826.
Ingram, Isabella to Thos. Askin of Maryland, Mar. Fayetteville. R. R. Mar. 24, 1826.
Irwin, Mary to Ezekiel M'Knight, My. 11, Rowan county. R. R. Je. 9, 1826.
Ives, Thos. B. of Davidson county to Helen Barber, Mar. 2, Onslow county. R. R. Mar. 24, 1826.

Jiggats, Dr. Lewis M. of Hertford to Elizabeth Ann Britton, Sept. Bertie county. R. R. Sept. 22, 1826.
Johnson, Gen'l. Robert R. to Mrs. Ann Russell, Je. 10, Warren county. R. R. Je. 23, 1826.
Johnson, Philip to Elizabeth Penny, Nov. 25, Wake county. R. R. Dec. 1, 1826.
Jones, E. to Elizabeth Stanly, Aug. Lenoir county. R. R. Sept. 15, 1826.
Jones, Isaac D. to Mary Booe, Apr. 30, Rowan county. R. R. Je. 16, 1826.
Jones, Russell H. of Georgia to Pamela Fletcher, Sept. 21, Wilkes county. R. R. Oct. 20, 1826.
Jones, Miss to Willey Pope, Je. 9, Wake county. R. R. Je. 16, 1826.
Jordan, Martha G. to David Evans, Mar. 2, Person county. R. R. Mar. 31, 1826.
Jordan, Mary Eliza to George B. Outlaw, Je. 13, Bertie county. R. R. Je. 23, 1826.
Jordan, Rev. Wm. H. to Elizabeth Watson, Feb. 9, Windsor. R. R. Feb. 24, 1826.
Joyner, Alice B. of Martin county to Joshua Watson of Martin county. Sept. 19. R. R. Sept. 29, 1826.
Kestler, Peter to Marinda Chapman, Apr. 15, Rowan county. R. R. Je. 9, 1826.
Kilpatrick, John L. of Green county to Sarah Tucker, Aug. 8, Lenoir county. R. R. Sept. 29, 1826.
Kimball, Short to Elizabeth Taylor, Nov. 22, Warren county. R. R. Dec. 1, 1826.
Kinchclow, Charles of Tennessee to Narcissa Stout of Randolph county, Mar. 5, Randolph county. R. R. Mar. 17, 1826.
King, John to Jane M. Philips, Aug. 14, Rowan county. R. R. Sept. 1, 1826.
King, Mary to Capt. Isaac F. Alexander, Apr. 2, Iredell county. R. R. Apr. 14, 1826.
King, Sarah to Felix Gregory of Newport, R. I. Mar., Elizabeth City. R. R. Mar. 31, 1826.
Kirkpatrick, Jane Agnew of Mecklenburg county to Rev. Eleazer Harris of South Carolina. Nov. 28. R. R. Dec. 15, 1826.
Knight, Nancy to Kinchen Mayo, Aug. 24, Edgecombe county. R. R. Sept. 8, 1826.
Knox, John to Hannah Nealey, Je., Mecklenburg county. R. R. Je. 9, 1826.
Kornegay, Jane to Dr: Levin B. Lane, Jan., Trenton. R. R. Jan. 27, 1826.
Krider, Catharine to James Dunn Smith, Feb. 2, Rowan county. R. R. Feb. 17, 1826.
Lane, Isaac to Mary Beamon, Aug. 17, Sampson county. R. R. Sept. 1, 1826.
Lane, Dr. Levin B. to Jane Kornegay, Jan. Trenton. R. R. Jan. 27, 1826.
Lanier, Robert Jr. to Mary Elizabeth Ann Campbell, Feb. 16, Pitt county. R. R. Mar. 17, 1826.
Lapsley, Lavinia Isabella to Nathaniel J. Palmer, Jly. 20, Orange county. R. R. Jly. 28, 1826.
Lee, Mrs. Patience to John T. Harris, Mar. 7, Wilmington. R. R. Mar. 17, 1826.
LeGrand, James of Montgomery county to Frances G. Marshall, Oct. Halifax. R. R. Oct. 20, 1826.
Long, Richard to Mary Yarbrough, Dec. Salisbury. R. R. Dec. 8, 1826.

Lourance, Lawson to Emeline Witherspoon, Jan. 5, Lincoln county. R. R. Feb. 3, 1826.
Lowe, Quinton to Elizabeth Williams, Aug. 24, Randolph county. R. R. Sept. 1, 1826.
Lynch, Daniel to Margam D. Morgan of Orange county, Aug. 17. R. R. Sept. 1, 1826.
Lyon, Thomas to Mary Heartt, Nov. Edgecombe county. R. R. Nov. 24, 1826.
M'Alister, John of Bladen county to Ferebe Williams, Nov. 8, Cumberland county. R. R. Nov. 17, 1826.
M'Churchill, Chapel to Eliza S. Branton, Apr. 20, Greene county. R. R. My. 12, 1826.
M'Combs, Eliza to Martin Elliott, Sept. 14, Rutherford county. R. R. Nov. 3, 1826.
M'Connaughey, Geo. to Elizabeth Partee, Je. 22, Rowan county. R. R. Jly. 7, 1826.
M'Ilwain, Sarah G. M. to Major Benjamin S. Tilman, Je., Craven county. R. R. Jly. 7, 1826.
M'Innis, Mrs. Ann to Kenneth M'Leod, Jly. 18, Bladen county. R. R. Aug. 4, 1826.
M'Innis, Sarah to Neil M'Kellar, Jan. 5, Richmond county. R. R. Feb. 3, 1826.
M'Kellar, Neil to Sarah M'Innis, Jan. 5, Richmond county. R. R. Feb. 3, 1826.
M'Kenzie, Ann to John Wilkinson, Jly. 20, Fayetteville. R. R. Jly. 21, 1826.
M'Kenzie, J. G. of Scotland Neck to Mary Bishop, Aug. 17, Edgecombe county. R. R. Sept. 8, 1826.
M'Kinsey, Maria to Capt. Abel Cowan, Feb. 2, Rowan county. R. R. Feb. 17, 1826.
M'Knight, Ezekiel to Mary Irwin, My. 11, Rowan county. R. R. Je. 9, 1826.
M'Knight, William to Carolina Taylor, Nov. 30, Mecklenburg county. R. R. Dec. 15, 1826.
M'Lean, L. H. to Mrs. Elizabeth Taylor, Sept. 7, Halifax county. R. R. Sept. 22, 1826.
M'Lean, Malcom to Ann Tailor Snow, Sept. 14, Fayetteville. R. R. Sept. 29, 1826.
M'Lennan, Alexander to Mary St. George, Mar. 4, Wilmington. R. R. Mar. 17, 1826.
M'Leod, Kenneth to Mrs. Ann M'Innis, Jly. 18, Bladen county. R. R. Aug. 4, 1826.
M'Leod, Mary of Richmond county to Francis Hawley of Hartford, Conn. Jan. 19, Laurel Hill. R. R. Feb. 3, 1826.
M'Longue, Samuel to Sarah Howell, Aug. 17, Guilford county. R. R. Sept. 1, 1826.
M'Lure, Robert to Eliza Davis, Nov. 30, Mecklenburg county. R. R. Dec. 15, 1826.
M'Master, Polly to John Truit, Mar. 5, Randolph county. R. R. Mar. 17, 1826.
M'Phail, Dougald to Catharine Taylor, Feb. 16, Cumberland county. R. R. Feb. 17, 1826.

M'Rae, Catharine to Parkes Beaman, Aug. 10, Anson county. R. R. Sept. 9, 1826.
M'Rae, John of Fayetteville to Mary Ann Shackelford, Jan. 18, South Carolina. R. R. Feb. 3, 1826.
Machen, Henry D. to Penelope Spearman, Dec. Newbern. R. R. Dec. 22, 1826.
Mackey, Catharine to Paul Cornell, Feb. 26, Plymouth. R. R. Mar. 17, 1826.
Mallett, Lallerstedt of Bladen county to Jane Smith, Aug. 2, Cumberland county. R. R. Aug. 4, 1826.
Mabry, Chas to Frances Staton, Nov. Edgecombe county. R. R. Nov. 24, 1826.
Marshall, Frances G. to James LeGrand of Montgomery county. Oct., Halifax. R. R. Oct. 20, 1826.
Marshall, Penelope to John Whitaker of Halifax, Nov. 28, Edgecombe county. R. R. Dec. 15, 1826.
Martin, Alfred to Catharine Bumgarner, Oct. 5, Lincoln county. R. R. Nov. 3, 1826.
Mayo, Kinchen to Nancy Knight, Aug. 24, Edgecombe county. R. R. Sept. 8, 1826.
Mikel, Nicholas to Mrs. Margaret Wethers, Aug. 17, Davidson county. R. R. Sept. 15, 1826.
Miles, Nancy of Guilford county to Absalom B. Paine of Davidson county, Aug. 31, R. R. Sept. 15, 1826.
Miller, Elizabeth to Joshua Riley, Apr. 21, Rowan county. R. R. Je. 23, 1826.
Miller, Henry M. of Raleigh to Isabella W. Hinton of Granville county. Feb. 21, R. R. Mar. 14, 1826.
Miller, Joseph to Eunice Dever, Apr. 21, Rowan county. R. R. Je. 23, 1826.
Minter, Fanny to Dr. Joseph Hawkins, Sept., Chatham county. R. R. Sept. 15, 1826.
Mitchell, Ferma to John Mitchell, Aug. 28, Elizabeth City. R. R. Sept. 1, 1826.
Mitchell, John to Rutha Ann Tunstall, Mar. 9, Nash county. R. R. Mar. 31, 1826.
Moore, Ann Hester to Jesse H. Powell, Nov. 28, Halifax. R. R. Dec. 15, 1826.
Moore, Elam to Miss E. Campbell, Jan. 19, Mecklenburg county. R. R. Feb. 3, 1826.
Moore, Mary to Oswall Alexander, Oct. 26, Mecklenburg county. R. R. Nov. 3, 1826.
Moore, Sarah to Alfred Darden, Jly. 5, Camden county. R. R. Jly. 7, 1826.
Morgan, Margam of Orange county to Daniel Lynch, Aug. 17. R. R. Sept. 1, 1826.
Morton, Jane A. to Alexander Watson of Nashville, Sept., New York. R. R. Sept. 29, 1826.
Nealey, Hannah to John Knox, Je. Mecklenburg county. R. R. Je. 9, 1826.
Noblin, Lucy to Chisley Daniel, Jly. 6, Granville county. R. R. Jly. 14, 1826.
Norcom, Elizabeth to Lemuel Hoskins, Jan., Chowan county. R. R. Feb. 3, 1826.
Norwood, John W. to Arabella Giles, Jan. 30, Hillsboro. R. R. Feb. 3, 1826.

Nye, James M. to Nancy Calloway, Aug. 7, Ashe county. R. R. Sept. 22, 1826.
Olivia, Louisa to Robert Armsted of Chatham county, Nov. Wake county. R. R. Nov. 10, 1826.
Osgood, Capt. John to Henrietta Prentiss, Nov., Newbern. R. R. Dec. 1, 1826.
Outlaw, George B. to Mary Eliza Jordan, Je. 13, Bertie county. R. R. Je. 23, 1826.
Owen, Mary of Jersey settlement to Capt. Samuel Green of Lexintgon, Aug. 15, Davidson county. R. R. Sept. 1, 1826.
Paine, Absalom B. of Davidson county to Nancy Miles of Guilford county, Aug. 31, R. R. Sept. 15, 1826.
Palmer, Nathaniel J. to Lavinia Isabella Lapsley, Jly. 20, Orange county. R. R. Jly. 28, 1826.
Parish, Catharine to D. L. Smith of Tennessee, Jan. Warren county. R. R. Feb. 3, 1826.
Parsons, James Jr. to Polly Thrift, Jly. 20, Guilford county. R. R. Aug. 10, 1826.
Partee, Elizabeth to Geo. M'Connaughey, Je. 22, Rowan county. R. R. Jly. 7, 1826.
Pasteur, Edward G. to Sarah Ann Torrance, My., Newbern. R. R. My. 5, 1826.
Patillo, Mrs. Ann to John L. Bellamy, Aug., Warrenton. R. R. Aug. 18, 1826.
Patrick, John Menan to Louisa Patrick, Apr. 18, Greene county. R. R. Apr. 28, 1826.
Patrick, Louisa to John Menan Patrick, Apr. 18, Greene county. R. R. Apr. 28, 1826.
Patterson, Smith to Margaret C. Connelly, Je., Louisburg. R. R. Je. 9, 1826.
Patton, John E. to Margaret Eliza Davidson, Oct. 17, Buncombe county. R. R. Dec. 8, 1826.
Pendleton, Mrs. Lovey to E. Weaver, Aug. 29, Lenoir county. R. R. Sept. 15, 1826.
Penny, Elizabeth to Philip Johnson, Nov. 25, Wake county. R. R. Dec. 1, 1826.
Penyear, Seymour to Mrs. Mary Hall, Jan. Chatham county. R. R. Feb. 3, 1826.
Peter, Susan E. to Neman Van Zevely, Aug. 20, Salem. R. R. Sept. 22, 1826.
Philips, Jane M. to John King, Aug. 14, Rowan county. R. R. Sept. 1, 1826.
Polk, Mary to Geo. E. Badger, Nov. 9, Raleigh. R. R. Nov. 17, 1826.
Pope, Emily to John Campbell, Jr., Je. 27, Halifax county. R. R. Jly. 21, 1826.
Pope, Wiley to Miss Jones, Je. 9, Wake county. R. R. Je. 16, 1826.
Popelston, Mary to Jonathan Haughton, Jr. Mar. 2, Edenton. R. R. Mar. 17, 1826.
Potts, Jeremiah to Polly Foster, Mar. 23, Rowan county. R. R. April 14, 1826.
Powell, Bridget to Benton Williams, Nov. 26, Wake county. R. R. Dec. 1, 1826.

Powell, G. W. to Mary Ramsay, Sept. 16, Northampton county. R. R. Sept. 22, 1826.
Powell, Jesse H. to Hester Ann Moore, Nov. 28, Halifax county. R. R. Dec. 15, 1826.
Prentiss, Henrietta to Capt. John Osgood, Nov. Newbern. R. R. Dec. 1, 1826.
Price, Clarinda to Isaac Beasley, Apr. 29, Wake county. R. R. My. 5, 1826.
Ramsay, Mary to G. W. Powell, Sept. 16, Northampton county. R. R. Sept. 22, 1826.
Raymond, David B. to Sarah Benton, Apr. 30, Anson county. R. R. Je. 16, 1826.
Reed, Lucy Ann to John Wiseman, Oct. Davidson county. R. R. Oct. 6, 1826.
Remson, Susan Ann Harriet to Dr. Aza Beall of Iredell county, Sept. 12, Lincolnton, Ga. R. R. Sept. 29, 1826.
Rew, Frances to Enoch Alexander, Feb. 1, Newbern. R. R. Feb. 17, 1826.
Riley, Joshua to Elizabeth Miller, Apr. 21, Rowan county. R. R. Je. 23, 1826.
Rish, Annie to Lewis Van Dyke, Aug. 8, Haywood county. R. R. Sept. 16, 1826.
Robertson, Eleanor to Robert A. Crowder of Mecklenburg county, Va. Jly. 20, Caswell county. R. R. Aug. 4, 1826.
Robertson, Dr. George W. B. to Sarah Allen. Aug. 3, Milton. R. R. Aug. 18, 1826.
Robinson, Geo. to Wealthy Blackwell, Feb. 2, Rowan county. R. R. Feb. 17, 1826.
Rodgers, Barbara to Alfred Hatley, Jly. 30, Montgomery county. R. R. Sept. 1, 1826.
Rogers, Matilda P. to Stephen M. Rum, Apr., Mecklenburg county. R. R. Apr. 28, 1826.
Rounsaville, Phoeba to Capt. Andrew M. Adams, Apr. 2, Iredell county. R. R. Apr. 14, 1826.
Rowe, Levi to Elizabeth Fisher, Je., Newbern. R. R. Je. 9, 1826.
Rowe, Thomas of Craven county to Sarah Bragg, Jly. Newbern. R. R. Jly. 28, 1826.
Rowzee, Paschall of Rowan county to Matilda Williams, Mar. Surry county. R. R. Apr. 14, 1826.
Ruffin, James H. to Susan A. Williamson, Jan. 24, Person county. R. R. Feb. 17, 1826.
Rum, Stephen to Matilda P. Rogers, Apr. Mecklenburg county. R. R. Apr. 28, 1826.
Russell, Mrs. Ann to Gen'l. Robert R. Johnson, Je. 10, Warren county. R. R. Je. 23, 1826.
St. George, Mary to Alexander M'Lennan, Mar. 4, Wilmington. R. R. Mar. 17, 1826.
Sanders, William to Drusilla Bell, Jan. Newbern. R. R. Jan. 13, 1826.
Sasnett, Sarah to Henry W. Garrett, Oct. 26, Edgecombe county. R. R. Nov. 17, 1826.
Sasser, Eliza to John G. Crawford, Sept. 7, Wayne county. R. R. Oct. 15, 1826.
Sawyer, Sally to Capt. Darius Hovey of Massachusetts, Nov. Elizabeth City. R. R. Nov. 10, 1826.

Sawyer, Sarah Ann to Josiah T. Granberry, Jan. Chowan county. R. R. Feb. 3, 1826.
Sawyer, William G. of Camden county to Eleanor L. Shannonhouse, Dec. Elizabeth City. R. R. Dec. 15, 1826.
Saxton, G. D. Parthenia to Capt. Joseph Wilburn, Je. 22, Randolph county. R. R. Jly. 7, 1826.
Scott, Nancy, to Duke Cartwright, Mar. 30, Elizabeth City. R. R. Apr. 14, 1826.
Sedbury, Shadrack, H. to Ann J. Fletcher, Nov. 16, Fayetteville. R. R. Dec. 8, 1826.
Shackelford, Eldah to Col. Eli W. Ward of Onslow county, Aug., Newbern. R. R. Aug. 25, 1826.
Shakelford, Mary Ann to John M'Rae of Fayetteville, Jan. 18, S. C. R. R. Feb. 3, 1826.
Shannonhouse, Eleanor L. to William G. Sawyer of Camden county, Dec., Elizabeth City. R. R. Dec. 15, 1826.
Shaw, Matthew of Washington to Hannah N. Bonner, Feb. 15, Beaufort county. R. R. Mar. 3, 1826.
Shaw, Sarah to Jas. L. Gaines of Moore county, Sept. 13, Fayetteville. R. R. Sept. 15, 1826.
Shelton, Ann W. to Dr. W. P. Young of Rockingham, Sept., Guilford county. R. R. Oct. 6, 1826.
Sherrod, Miss J. B. to Philemon Hawkins, Je., Louisburg. R. R. Je. 9, 1826.
Shields, Isabella to Daniel Caldwell, Jan. 19, Mecklenburg county. R. R. Feb. 3, 1826.
Shooer, Emanuel of Stokes county to Anna Hanes of Davidson county. Mar. 30. R. R. Apr. 21, 1826
Shuford, Catharine to Peter Warlick, Jan. 12, Lincoln county. R. R. Feb. 17, 1826.
Sill, Rebecca to William Tolbert, Jan. 17, Montgomery county. R. R. Feb. 3, 1826.
Silvester, Mary J. to Dr. John M. Davidson, Apr. 5, Mecklenburg county. R. R. My. 5, 1826.
Simonton, W. S. to Eliza M. Conner, Jly. 27, Lincoln county. R. R. Aug. 18, 1826.
Simpson, Mary to Ebbin Willis, Aug. 12, Beaufort. R. R. Sept. 1, 1826.
Simpson, Polly to Vincent Willis, Oct. 3, Rowan county. R. R. Oct. 6, 1826.
Skinner, Joshua to Elizabeth Blair, Feb. Edenton., R. R. Feb. 24, 1826.
Slade, Elizabeth to Mason L. Wiggins of Halifax county, Je. 1, Martin county. R. R. Je. 9, 1826.
Slater, Fielding to Alice Smith, Oct. 5, Rowan county. R. R. Nov. 3, 1826.
Sledge, Susan to Dr. W. Delony, Nav. 8, Warren county. R. R. Nov. 24, 1826.
Smith, Alex, to Nancy Hartman. Feb. 2, Rowan county. R. R. Feb. 17, 1826.
Smith, Alice to Fielding Slater, Oct. 5, Rowan county. R. R. Nov. 3, 1826.
Smith, D. L. of Tennessee to Catharine Parish, Jan., Warren county. R. R. Feb. 3, 1826.
Smith, Gideon B. of Raleigh to Elizabeth Bennett, Jan. 22, Baltimore. R. R. Feb. 3, 1826.

Smith, Henry O. of South Carolina to Temperance Waddill, Sept. 7, Moore county. R. R. Sept. 22, 1826.
Smith, James Dunn to Catharine Krider, Feb. 2, Rowan county. R. R. Feb. 17, 1826.
Smith, Jane to Lallerstedt Mallett of Bladen county, Aug. 2, Cumberland county. R. R. Aug. 4, 1826.
Smith, John to Rebecca Copes, Mar. Smithville. R. R. Mar. 17, 1826.
Smith, Mary to Jno. H. Goldston, Je. 15, Newbern. R. R. Je. 30, 1826.
Smith, Mrs. Rebecca to Rev. Thos. Worrell, Apr. 13, Granville county. R. R. My. 5, 1826.
Smith, Samuel to Mrs. Catharine Swink, Oct. 5, Rowan county . R. R. Oct. 31, 1826.
Smith, Rev. Zion to Sarah Page, Jan. 10, Wake county. R. R. Jan. 13, 1826.
Snow, Ann Tailor to Malcom M'Lean, Sept. 14, Fayetteville. R. R. Sept. 29, 1826.
Spearman, Penelope to Henry D. Machen, Dec., Newbern. R. R. Dec. 22, 1826.
Stanly, Elizabeth to E. Jones, Aug., Lenoir county. R. R. Sept. 15, 1826.
Steel, John to Nancy Woody, Dec., Orange county. R. R. Dec. 15, 1826.
Stevens, William to Sarah Boykin, Feb. 28, Sampson county. R. R. Mar. 17, 1826.
Stout, Narcissa of Randolph county to Charles Kinchclow of Tennessee, Mar. 5, Randolph county. R. R. Mar. 17, 1826.
Swain, David L. of Buncombe county to Eleanor H. White, Jan. 12, Raleigh. R. R. Jan. 20, 1826.
Swink, Mrs. Catharine to Samuel Smith, Oct. 5, Rowan county. R. R. Oct. 31, 1826.
Tally, Guilford to Martha Gardner, Jan. Warren county. R. R. Feb. 3, 1826.
Tate, Col. John B. of Burke county to Mary I. Webster of Maury county, Tenn. Jan. 17, R. R. Feb. 17, 1826.
Taylor, Catharine to Dougald M'Phail, Feb. 16, Cumberland county. R. R. Feb. 17, 1826.
Taylor, Caroline to William M'Knight, Nov. 30, Mecklenburg county. R. R. Dec. 15, 1826.
Taylor, Mrs. Elizabeth to L. H. M'Lean, Sept. 7, Halifax county. R. R. Sept. 22, 1826.
Taylor, Elizabeth to Short Kimball, Nov. 22, Warren county. R. R. Dec. 1, 1826.
Terrel, Sarah to Wm. Christian, Apr. 30, Montgomery county. R. R. Je. 9, 1826.
Terrence, Margaret to Wm. Wynans, Sept. 14, Mecklenburg county. R. R. Oct. 20, 1826.
Thorp, Eliza to Henry G. Cutler, Jly. 27, Northampton county. R. R. Aug. 4, 1826.
Thrift, Polly to James Parsons, Jr. Jly. 20, Guilford county. R. R. Aug. 18, 1826.
Tillett, Thomas to Mrs. Deborah Gray, Je. 6, Camden county. R. R. Jly. 7, 1826.

Tilman, Major Benjamin S. to Sarah G. M'Ilwaine, Je., Craven county. R. R. Jly. 7, 1826.
Tolbert, William to Rebecca Sill, Jan. 17, Montgomery county. R. R. Feb. 3, 1826.
Torrance, Sarah Ann to Edward G. Pasteur, My. Newbern. R. R. My. 5, 1826.
Toy, Dr. John D. to Penelope Boushall, Aug. Camden county. R. R. Sept. 1, 1826.
Trexler, Sally to Michael Davis, Aug. 31, Salisbury. R. R. Sept. 15, 1826.
Trotter, Ellen to Rev. James Weatherly, Je. 19, Beaufort county. R. R. Je. 30, 1826.
Trotter, William to Lavinia Williams, Aug. 30, Person county. R. R. Sept. 29, 1826.
Truit, John to Polly M'Master, Mar. 5, Randolph county. R. R. Mar. 17, 1826.
Tryon, Sarah Ann of Connecticut to Asa Hubbard of Wadesborough., Nov. R. R. Dec. 1, 1826.
Tucker, Sarah to John J. Kilpatrick of Greene county, Aug. 8, Lenoir county. R. R. Sept. 29, 1826.
Tunstall, Rutha Ann to John Mitchell, Mar. 9, Nash county. R. R. Mar. 31, 1826.
Turner, Gideon B. to Permelia T. Dodson, Mar. 9, Milton. R. R. Mar. 31, 1826.
Turner, Paul to Hannah Dancy, Aug. 24, Rowan county. R. R. Sept. 8, 1826.
Turrentine, Sally to Dr. Alfred Cook, Apr. 30, Rowan county. R. R. Je. 23, 1826.
Twiford, Edward W. to Sabria Colman, Aug. 17, Guilford county. R. R. Sept. 1, 1826.
Van Dyke, Lewis to Annie Rish, Aug. 8, Haywood county. R. R. Sept. 15, 1826.
Waddel, Haynes to Mary Fleming, Jan. 4, Wilmington. R. R. Jan. 27, 1826.
Waddell, Sarah to Dr. M. J. DeRossett of Wilmington, Jan. 22, Brunswick county. R. R. Sept. 22, 1826.
Waddill, Temperance to Henry O. Smith of South Carolina, Sept. 7, Moore county. R. R. Sept. 22, 1826.
Wallace, Reuben to Elizabeth Byrd, Jan., Lenoir county. R. R. Jan. 27, 1826.
Wallack, Peter to Catharine Shuford, Jan. 12, Lincoln county. R. R. Feb. 3, 1826.
Ward, Abigail to Edward Caraway, Aug. 15, Beaufort. R. R. Sept. 1, 1826.
Ward, Col. Eli. W. of Onslow county to Mrs. Eldah Shackelford, Aug. 22, Newbern. R. R. Aug. 25, 1826.
Waring, Henry Jr. of New York to Carolina Chapman, Je. 7, Newbern. R. R. Je. 30, 1826.
Warlick, Peter to Catharine Shuford, Jan. 12, Lincoln county. R. R. Feb. 17, 1826.
Watson, Alexander of Nashville to Jane A. Morton, Sept., New York. R. R. Sept. 29, 1826.

Watson, Elizabeth to Rev. Wm. H. Jordan, Feb. 9, Windsor. R. R. Feb. 24, 1826.
Watson, Joshua of Martin county to Alice B. Joyner, Martin county, Sept. 19. R. R. Sept. 29, 1826.
Watson, Sarah to Turner Carter, Aug. 6, Bertie county. R. R. Aug. 8, 1826.
Weatherly, Rev. James to Ellen Trotter, Je. 19, Beaufort county. R. R. Je. 30, 1826.
Weaver, E. to Mrs. Lovey Pendleton, Aug. 29, Lenoir county. R. R. Sept. 15, 1826.
Webb, Wm. S. to Mary E. Hall, Jan. Newbern. R. R. Feb. 3, 1826.
Webber, Elizabeth to Samuel C. Fisher of Newbern. Feb. 6. R. R. Feb. 17, 1826.
Webster, Mary I of Maury county, Tenn. to Col. John B. Tate of Burke county, Jan. 17. R. R. Feb. 17, 1826.
West, M. to Priscilla Bradley, Je., Halifax. R. R. Je. 9, 1826.
West, Lloyd to Edsey Gainey, Je., Fayetteville. R. R. Je. 30, 1826.
Weston, Parthena to Robert Creecy, Nov. 20, Edenton. R. R. Dec. 8, 1826.
Wethers, Mrs. Margaret to Nicholas Mikel, Aug. 17, Davidson county. R. R. Sept. 15, 1826.
Whitaker, John of Halifax to Penelope Marshall, Nov. 28, Edgecombe county. R. R. Dec. 15, 1826.
White, Eleanor H. to David L. Swain of Buncombe county, Jan. 12, Raleigh. R. R. Jan. 20, 1826.
White, Elizabeth to Allen Adams, Mar. 29, Wake county. R. R. Apr. 21, 1826.
Whitehead, Williamson to Janet Eccles, Jly. 31, Fayetteville. R. R. Aug. 4, 1826.
Wiggins, Mason L. of Halifax county to Elizabeth Slade, Je. 1, Martin county. R. R. Je. 9, 1826.
Wilburn, Capt. Joseph to Parthenia G. D. Saxton, Je. 22, Randolph county. R. R. Jly. 7, 1826.
Wiley, Rev. Philip Bruce to Claudia G. M. Hamilton Gregory, Nov. Elizabeth City. R. R. Nov. 10, 1826.
Wilkinson, John to Ann M'Kenzie, Jly. 20, Fayetteville. R. R. Jly. 21, 1826.
Williams, Benton to Bridget Powell, Nov. 26, Wake county. R. R. Dec. 1, 1826.
Williams, Elizabeth to Quinton Love, Aug. 24, Randolph county. R. R. Sept. 1, 1826.
Williams, Ferebe to John M'Alister of Bladen county, Nov. 8, Cumberland county. R. R. Nov. 17, 1826.
Williams, Lavinia to William Trotter, Aug. 30, Person county. R. R. Sept. 29, 1826.
Williams, Matilda, to Paschall Rouzee of Rowan county, Mar., Surry county. R. R. Apr. 14, 1826.
Williams, Susan of Surry county to Jas. R. Dodge of Lexington, Apr. 24, Surry county. R. R. Je. 9, 1826.
Williams, General William of Warren county to Delia H. Haywood, My. 9, Raleigh. R. R. My. 12, 1826.

Williamson, Susan A. to James H. Ruffin, Jan. 24, Person county. R. R. Feb. 17, 1826.
Willis, Vincent to Polly Simpson, Oct. 3, Rowan county. R. R. Oct. 6, 1826.
Wills, Elbin to Mary Simpson, Aug. 12, Beaufort. R. R. Sept. 1, 1826. 1826.
Wilson, David to Hannah Cobb, Aug. 17, Guilford county. R. R. Sept. 1,
Wilson, Davy A. to Dr. Middleton Dougherty, Aug. 18, Mecklenburg county. R. R. Sept. 1, 1826.
Witherspoon, Emeline to Lawson Lourance, Jan. 5, Lincoln county. R. R. Feb. 3, 1826.
Wiseman, John to Lucy Ann Reed, Oct. Davidson county. R. R. Oct. 6, 1826.
Woody, Nancy to John Steel, Dec., Orange county. R. R. Dec. 15, 1826.
Worrell, Rev. Thos. to Mrs. Rebecca Smith, Apr. 13, Granville county. R. R. My. 5, 1826.
Wynans, Wm. to Margaret Terrence, Sept. 14, Mecklenburg county. R. R. Oct. 20, 1826.
Yarbrough, Emily of Franklin county to Dr. James Glenn of Louisburg, Jan. 26. R. R. Jan. 27, 1826.
Yarbrough, Martha J. to Thomas J. Curtis of Franklin county, Jan. 11, Fayetteville. R. R. Jan. 13, 1826.
Yarborough, Mary to Richard Long, Dec., Salisbury. R. R. Dec. 8, 1826.
Yeomans, Wm. T. to Caroline J. Guthrie, Nov. 28, Washington, Beaufort county. R. R. Dec. 22, 1826.
Young, Caleb to Maria Freeman, Sept., Granville county. R. R. Sept. 15, 1826.
Young, Sarah to Joseph Cowan, Jr. Sept. 5, Rowan county. R. R. Sept. 22, 1826.
Young, Dr. W. P. of Rockingham to Ann W. Shelton, Sept. Guilford county. R. R. Oct. 6, 1826.
Zevely, Van Neman to Susan E. Peter, Aug. 20, Salem. R. R. Sept. 22, 1826.

1827

Adams, Harriet D. to Dr. John Malloy of Richmond county, Jan. 19, Adamsville, S. C. R. R. Jan. 30, 1827.
Adams, Jane to Gen. Richard D. S. McLean of Lincoln county, Apr. 17, York District, S. C. R. R. My. 8, 1827.
Alexander, Eliza to James Coffee, My. 26, Mecklenburg county. R. R. Je. 19, 1827.
Allemong, Ezra of Salisbury to Mary Teresa M'Donald, My. 27, Charleston, S. C. R. R. Je. 15, 1827.
Allen, Rev. Darius C. of Rhode Island to Eliza A. Slover, My., Newbern. R. R. My. 15, 1827.
Allen, Moses H. to Lucy W. Rhodes, Apr. 5, Wake county. R. R. Apr. 10, 1827.
Anderson, Elizabeth to John Richmond, Oct. 17, Caswell county. R. R. Nov. 6, 1827.
Anthony, Sally to Ludwick Sharp, Sept. 27, Orange county. R. R. Oct. 16, 1827.

Armstead, Eliza to Wm. Plummer of Franklin county, Je. 19, Bertie county. R. R. Jly. 6, 1827.
Armstrong, Miss to Charles Clendenin, Sept. 27, Orange county. R. R. Oct. 16, 1827.
Arrington, Richard to Mrs. Temperance Whitehead, My. 29, Nash county. R. R. Je. 5, 1827.
Avera, William to Nancy Hayes, Jan. 25, Wake county. R. R. Jan. 30, 1827.
Avery, Rev. John of Edenton to Ann Paine, Nov., Edenton. R. R. Dec. 4, 1827.
Baber, Mrs. Elizabeth to David Thally, Feb. 5, Wilmington. R. R. My. 1, 1827.
Badham, Wm. to Mary Britt, Oct. 11, Edenton. R. R. Nov. 6, 1827.
Bailey, Robert to Elizabeth Chauncey, Aug., Pasquotank county. R. R. Aug. 7, 1827.
Bartley, Henry to Maria E. W. Harris, Oct. 4, Northampton county. R. R. Oct. 19, 1827.
Bass, Turner to Mrs. Susan Dicken, Jan., Tarborough. R. R. Feb. 2, 1827.
Beal, Mary of Southampton county, Va. to Burwell Griffith, Je. 14. R. R. Je. 22, 1827.
Bedford, Dr. Robert to Nancy M. J. P. Turner of Raleigh, My. 22, Haywood county. R. R. Jly. 3, 1827.
Bell, Evelina, S. M. to Spyers Singleton Smith of Newbern, Je. 14, Hyde county. R. R. Je. 29, 1827.
Benbury, Richard W. to Martha Hoskins, Je. 26, Chowan county. R. R. Jly. 13, 1827.
Benson, Grace to Daniel F. Wheaton of Raleigh, Oct. 10, Greenville, S. C. R. R. Nov. 6, 1827.
Bigham, John to Nancy M'Dill of Mecklenburg county, Apr. 17, Chester District, S. C. R. R. My. 8, 1827.
Bingham, Mary S. to Rev. Thomas Lynch, My., Orange county. R. R. My. 8, 1827.
Bitting, Mary to Reuben D. Golding, Germantown, Stokes co., Aug. 5, R. R. Aug. 7, 1827.
Bittle, Ann to Dr. Henry Martin, Nov. 23, Wake Forest. R. R. Dec. 4, 1827.
Bland, Blany to Winifred S. Pope, Je. 14, Snowhill, Greene county. R. R. Je. 29, 1827.
Blount, Elizabeth Mutter to Harvey Blount of Washington, My. 31, Edenton. R. R. Je. 19, 1827.
Blount, Harvey of Washington to Elizabeth Mutter Blount, My. 31, Edenton.. R. R. Je. 19, 1827.
Blount, Mary to James Treadwell, Apr., Edenton. R. R. Apr. 24, 1827.
Blue, Margaret to Dugall Ray, Feb. 22, Bladen county. R. R. My. 1, 1827.
Blume, Benjamin H. of Northampton county to Mrs. Elizabeth Godwin, Apr. 5, Bertie county. R. R. Apr. 20, 1827.
Boatright, Jno. to Abigail Manson, Sept. 25, Mecklenburg county. R. R. Oct. 16, 1827.
Bond, Mary A. to John Washington of Kinston, Feb. 28, Raleigh. R. R. Mar. 2, 1827.

Boswell, Mrs. to William Cox, Apr. 24, Mecklenburg county. R. R. My. 15, 1827.
Boxwell, Wilmouth to Capt. William Dixon, Jan., Tarborough. R. R. Feb. 2, 1827.
Bradley, James to Nancy King, Jly. 25, Raleigh. R. R. Jly. 27, 1827.
Brazier, Mrs. Rebecca to John Woodall of Cumberland county, Jan. R. R. Feb. 9, 1827.
Brevard, Sarah to H. L. Sloan, Oct. 22, Iredell county. R. R. Nov. 6, 1827.
Briggs, Edmund to Priscilla Dobbins, Mar. 1, Rowan county. R. R. Mar. 20, 1827.
Brinkley, Capt. William to Elizabeth Moore, My. 1, Halifax county. R. R. Je. 1, 1827.
Britt, Mary to Wm. Badham, Oct. 11, Edenton. R. R. Nov. 6, 1827.
Brown, John E. to Elizabeth E. Carter, Feb. 24, Caswell county. R. R. My. 4, 1827.
Brown, John to Magdalen Troutman, Mar. 20, Rowan county. R. R. Apr. 3, 1827.
Brownrigg, Richard T. of Chowan county to Mary W. Hoskins of Edenton. R. R. Jly. 24, 1827.
Bryan, Sarah B. of Duplin county to Col. Joshua Moseley of Lenoir county, Je. 24, Duplin county. R. R. Jly. 13, 1827.
Bryant, Thos. to Ann Fry, Mar. 1, Moore county. R. R. Mar. 20, 1827.
Buie, Lydia to Daniel Smith, Feb. 29, Richmond county. R. R. My. 1, 1827.
Buie, Margaret D. to Tryam M'Farland of Richmond county, Aug. 14, Cumberland county. R. R. Aug. 28, 1827.
Bullock, Col. William of Chowan county to Lucy Ann King of Wake county, Feb. 9, Raleigh. R. R. Feb. 16, 1827.
Bunch, Margaret to Ebenezer Sampson, Apr., Raleigh. R. R. Apr. 20, 1827.
Burwell, Sarah T. to John S. Eaton, Aug. 15, Granville county. R. R. Aug. 28, 1827.
Bustion, William to Goff Ann Whitaker, Nov., Halifax. R. R. Nov. 16, 1827.
Butts, Elizabeth to Thomas Shuford, My. 31, Lincolnton. R. R. Je. 19, 1827.
Byrum, Robert of Petersburg, Va. to Caroline Ellis, Oct. 4, Northampton county. R. R. Oct. 19, 1827.
Cade, William to American W. Legrand, My. 3, Montgomery county. R. R. My. 8, 1827.
Caldwell, Catharine to Thomas W. Wilson of Wilkesborough, Oct. 23, Iredell county. R. R. Nov. 20, 1827.
Campbell, Fanny to Milas Dobbins, Aug. 23, Iredell county. R. R. Oct. 2, 1827.
Capps, Thomas to Rebecca Langford, Sept. 8, Warren county. R. R. Oct. 2, 1827.
Carleton, David of Fayetteville to Sarah P. Norcross, Oct., Boston. R. R. Oct. 9, 1827.
Carmichael, Janet to Archibald Ray, Mar., Cumberland county. R. R. Mar. 20, 1827.
Carr, Maj. Wm. of Columbia, Tenn. to Margaret M'Craig, Mar. 8, Orange county. R. R. Mar. 16, 1827.

Carrigan, William G. to Nancy M. Holt, My. 7, Orange county. R. R. My. 29, 1827.
Carson, Caroline R. to Sidney S. Erwin of Morganton, Apr. 10, Burke county. R. R. My. 1, 1827.
Carter, Elizabeth E. to John E. Brown, Feb. 24, Caswell county. R. R. My. 4, 1827.
Chalmers, Dr. John C. of Halifax county, Va. to Mary W. Henderson, Oct. 3, Milton. R. R. Oct. 16, 1827.
Chambers, John R. of Dinwiddie county, Va. to Rebecca D. Farrer, Nov. 21, Chatham county. R. R. Dec. 18, 1827.
Charlton, Thomas I to Sarah Leary, Mar. 27, Chowan county. R. R. Apr. 10, 1827
Chase, Margaret to Sam Knight, Feb., Pasquotank county. R. R. Mar. 2, 1827
Chauncey, Elizabeth to Robert Bailey, Aug., Pasquotank county. R. R. Mar. 2, 1827.
Cheshire, Thos. to Lydia Huffman, Mar., Davidson county. R. R. Mar. 20, 1827
Chitman, Harriet to Lieut. Thos. Cooper of Mecklenburg county, Oct., Lincoln county. R. R. Nov. 6, 1827.
Christopher, Elizabeth to John Compton, Nov., Orange county. R. R. Nov. 13, 1827.
Clay, Joseph W. of Milton to Elizabeth Virgina Hardey of Davidson county, Tenn., Apr. 25. R. R. Je. 1, 1827.
Clendenin, Charles to Miss Armstrong, Sept. 27, Orange county. R. R. Oct. 16, 1827.
Coffee, James to Eliza Alexander, My. 26, Mecklenburg county. R. R. Je. 19, 1827.
Cole, Carleton of Macon, Ga. to Susan U. Taylor of Hillsborough. Sept. 6, R. R. Sept. 18, 1827.
Coleman, Robert to Mary B. Taylor of Hillsborough, Oct., Macon, Ga. R. R. Nov. 6, 1827.
Colvin, William B. to Flora Shaw, Jly. 11, New Hanover county. R. R. Jly. 24, 1827.
Compton, John to Elizabeth Christopher, Nov., Orange county. R. R. Nov. 13, 1827.
Condy, Capt. Thomas H. to Mary Melissa Stevenson of Iredell county, My. 10. R. R. My. 29, 1827.
Conner, Lilly M. to Andrew Pierce of Cheraw, S. C., My., Lincoln county. R. R. My. 15, 1827.
Cooper, Lieut. Thos. of Mecklenburg county to Harriet Chitain, Oct., Lincoln county. R. R. Nov. 6, 1827.
Cooper, William to Sally Coupee, Apr. 12, Salisbury. R. R. My. 1, 1827.
Corbett, James L. to Susan Wallace, Je., Wilmington. R. R. Je. 5, 1827
Coston, George to Fanny Russell, Nov. 20, Wilmington. R. R. Dec. 18, 1827.
Coupee, Sally to William Cooper, Apr. 12, Salisbury. R. R. My. 1, 1827.
Cowan, Matilda C. to Jacob Tipps, Oct. 11, Iredell county. R. R. Nov. 20, 1827.
Cox, Mrs. Eliza Hope to Joseph Physioc, Feb. 25, Craven county. R. R. Mar. 27, 1827.
Cox, William to Mrs. Boswell, Apr. 24, Mecklenburg county. R. R. My. 15, 1827.

Craig, Margaret M. to Major Wm. Carr of Columbia, Tenn., Mar. 8, Orange county. R. R. Mar. 16, 1827.
Crawford, John B. of Raleigh to Louisa T. Harris, Jan. 18, Wake Forest. R. R. Jan. 26, 1827.
Crenshaw, Frances to George W. Thompson, Dec. 13, Wake Forest. R. R. Dec. 18, 1827.
Cross, Maj. Reddick of Hertford to Mrs. Sowerby of Northampton county. Mar. 15. R. R. Apr. 3, 1827.
Crump, Dr. Robert of Northampton county to Mildred Williamson, Oct. 2, Greenville, Va. R. R. Nov. 6, 1827.
Dandridge, Julianna Eleanor to Charles G. Richardson of Raleigh, Nov. 21, Richmond, Va. R. R. Dec. 4, 1827.
Davis, George to Mary Davis, Aug., Pasquotank county. R. R. Aug. 7, 1827.
Davis, Mary to George Davis, Aug., Pasquotank county R. R. Aug. 7, 1827.
Davis, Rachel to Louis Tomberean, My. 13, Raleigh. R. R. My. 15, 1827.
Davis, Rebecca to Rev. Daniel W. Kerr, Nov. 1, Wake county. R. R. Nov. 20, 1827.
DeBernier, Eleanor M. to Peter J. Mallett, Feb. 19, Charleston. R. R. My. 1, 1827.
Devereux, George Pollock of this State to Sarah Elizabeth Johnson of Stratford, Conn., My. 13, Stratford, Conn. R. R. Je. 6, 1827.
Dick, Hiram C. to Mary K. Stewart, Sept., Guilford county. R. R. Oct. 5, 1827.
Dicken, Mrs. Susan to Turner Bass, Jan., Tarborough. R. R. Feb. 2, 1827.
Dickens, Jos. to Charity Utly, Jan. 18, Chatham county. R. R. Feb. 9, 1827.
Dismukes, Nancy to Dr. Francis Williams of Surry county, Feb. 15, Rowan county. R. R. Mar. 13, 1827.
Dixon, Capt. William to Wilmouth Boxwell, Jan., Tarborough. R. R. Feb. 2, 1827.
Dobbins, Milas to Fanny Campbell, Aug. 23, Iredell county. R. R. Oct. 2, 1827.
Dobbins, Priscilla to Edmund Briggs, Mar. 1, Rowan county. R. R. Mar. 20, 1827.
Dougall, Wm. to Caroline J. McKay of Wilmington, Nov., R. R. Nov. 20, 1827.
Dubose, Sarah C. to Dr. Sterling Wheaton of Raleigh, Dec. 23, Camden, S. C. R. R. Jan. 19, 1827.
Dunevant, Jesse to Francis Overby, Oct. 25, Caswell county. R. R. Nov. 6, 1827.
Dunlap, Samuel C. of Rockingham to Miss Angelina Tatum, Oct., Guilford county. R. R. Oct. 19, 1827.
Eason, Harriet to Dr. Harrell B. Sessoms, Jly. 3, Bertie county. R .R. Jly. 24, 1827.
Eaton, John S. to Sarah T. Burwell, Aug. 15, Granville county. R. R. Aug. 28, 1827.
Elliott, Cynthia to John M'Kinnon of Fayetteville. Jly. 15, Randolph county. R. R. Jly. 24, 1827.

Ellis, Caroline to Robert Byrum of Petersburg, Va., Oct. 4, Northampton county R. R. Oct. 19, 1827.

Erwin, Sidney S. of Morganton to Caroline R. Carson, Apr. 10, Burke county. R. R. My. 1, 1827.

Evans, Thomas to Polly Mason, Aug. 23, Iredell county. R. R. Oct. 2, 1827.

Fairis, Joseph to Nancy Squires, Mar. 5, Mecklenburg county. R. R. Apr. 3, 1827.

Farrer, Rebecca D. to John R. Chambers of Dinwiddie county, Nov. 21, Chatham county. R. R. Dec. 18, 1827.

Fennen, Dixie C. to Ann P. Harwell, Dec. 1, Halifax. R. R. Dec. 4, 1827.

Fenner, Eliza of Raleigh to James Vaulx, Jan. 23, Tennessee. R. R. Mar. 6, 1827.

Fight, Moses to Mrs. Sophia Stars, Apr. 5, Rowan county. R. R. My. 1, 1827.

Fletcher, Sarah to Owen Hustin, Jan., Fayetteville. R. R. Jan. 30, 1827.

Fountain, Wm. of Guilford county to Esther Weatherly of Marlboro District, S. C., Apr. 1. R. R. Apr. 6, 1827.

Frances, Sarah to Thomas Webb, Jly. 5, Bertie county. R. R. Jly. 24, 1827.

Francis, Howell to Mrs. Nancy Hill, Apr. 20, Murfreesboro. R. R. My. 1, 1827.

Frazier, Nathan of Guilford county to Rebecca Swainey of Randolph county, My. 17, Randolph county. R. R. Je. 1, 1827.

French, G. R. of Rhode Island to Sarah Caroline French, Feb. 5, Wilmington. R. R. My. 1, 1827.

French, Sarah Caroline to G. R. French of Rhode Island, Feb. 5, Wilmington. R. R. My. 1, 1827.

Fry, Ann to Thos. Bryant, Mar. 1, Moore county. R. R. Mar. 20, 1827.

Fulgum, Sarah to Richard N. Ivey, Oct., Halifax county. R. R. Nov. 20, 1827.

Fuller, Barbara to Orren Tally, Oct. 18, Caswell county. R. R. Nov. 6, 1827.

Fuller, Thomas of Fayetteville to Catharine Raboteau, Mar. 7, Franklin county. R. R. Mar. 13, 1827.

Gaither, Sarah Ann to Col. William F. Kelly, Oct. 9, Rowan county. R. R. Oct. 23, 1827.

Gannon, Esther to Samuel Gilmore, Sept., Guilford county. R. R. Oct. 5, 1827.

Gholson, James H. of Brunswick county to Charlotte Louise Cary of Southampton county, Oct. 22. R. R. Dec. 4, 1827.

Gilmore, Samuel to Esther Gannon, Sept., Guilford county. R. R. Oct. 5, 1827.

Glover, John to Elizabeth Hill, Mar. 15, Rowan county. R. R. Apr. 3, 1827.

Godwin, Mrs. Elizabeth to H. Blume of Northampton county, Apr. 5, Bertie county. R. R. Apr. 20, 1827.

Golding, Reuben D. to Mary Bitting, Germantown, Stokes co., Aug. 5, R. R. Aug. 7, 1827.

Goode, Mary C. of Mecklenburg county to John Trumbull, Feb. 19, Bladen county. R. R. My. 1, 1827.

Goodrich, Celestia C. to William G. Webb, Oct. 12, Rockingham, Rockingham county. R. R. Oct. 23, 1827.
Green, Knight of Greene county to Elizabeth Lovick, Je. 20, Kinston. R. R. Je. 29, 1827.
Greeen, Susan of Warren county to James Kendrick of Mecklenburg county, Va. Sept. 6. R. R. Sept. 14, 1827.
Gregory, Isaac to Susan Harris, Feb., Pasquotank county. R. R. Mar. 2, 1827.
Gregory, Mackey to Mrs. Martha Gregory, Mar. 20, Chowan county. R. R. Apr. 3, 1827.
Gregory, Mrs. Martha to Mackey Gregory, Mar. 20, Chowan county. R. R. Apr. 3, 1827.
Griffith, Burwell of Hertford to Mary Beal of Southampton county, Va., Je. 14. R. R. Je. 22, 1827.
Grimes, Elley to Capt. G. Lanier, Feb. 13, Duplin county. R. R. Mar. 13, 1827.
Grist, Richard of Washington to Eliza H. Washington, My. 18, Kinston. R. R. Je. 29, 1827.
Hall, Eliza to Dr. Sheldon Lemmon, Nov. 6, Iredell county. R. R. Nov. 20, 1827.
Hamner, Rev. James G. of Fayetteville to Olivia Murray, New York, Sept. 18, New York. R. R. Sept. 28, 1827.
Hardey, Elizabeth Virginia of Davidson county, Tenn. to Joseph W. Clay of Milton, Apr. 25. R. R. Je. 1, 1827.
Harris, Louisa T. to John B. Crawford of Raleigh, Jan. 18, Wake Forest. R. R. Jan. 26, 1827.
Harris, Maria E. W. to Henry Bratley, Oct. 4, Northampton county. R. R. Oct. 19, 1827.
Harris, Susan to Isaac Gregory, Feb., Pasquotank county. R. R. Mar. 2, 1827.
Harvey, Mrs. Ann of Franklin county to Howell Webb of Raleigh. Franklin county. R. R. Dec. 18, 1827.
Harwell, Ann P. to Dixie C. Fennen, Dec. 1, Halifax. R. R. Dec. 4, 1827.
Hatch, Christopher A. to Mrs. Ann Jones, Je. 21, Onslow county. R. R. Jly. 13, 1827.
Hayes, Nancy to William Avera, Jan. 25, Wake county. R. R. Jan. 30, 1827.
Haywood William to Mrs. Elizabeth C. Norris, My. 14, Camden county. R. R. Je. 6, 1827.
Henderson, Mary W. to Dr. John C. Chalmers of Halifax county, Va., Oct. 3, Milton. R. R. Oct. 16, 1827.
Hileck, Michael, Jr. to Sally Josey, Mar. 6, Rowan county. R. R. Mar. 20, 1827.
Hill, Elizabeth to John Glover, Mar. 15, Rowan county. R. R. Apr. 3, 1827.
Hill, Mrs. Nancy to Howell Francis, Apr. 20, Murfreesboro. R. R. My. 1, 1827.
Holloman, Lydia to Bennett Ragan of Raleigh, Nov. 8, Wake county. R. R. Nov. 16, 1827.
Holt, Nancy M. to William G. Carrigan, My. 17, Orange county. R. R. My. 29, 1827.
Holthouser, Mary to Peter Mowery, Mar. 20, Rowan county. R. R. Apr. 3, 1827.

Horn, Millisset to Wade R. Thomas, Jan., Tarborough. R. R. Feb. 2, 1827.
Horton, Anthony W. to Isabella Jordan, My. 3, Fayetteville. R. R. My. 8, 1827.
Hoskins, Martha to Richard W. Benbury, Je. 26, Chowan county. R. R. Jly. 13, 1827.
Hoskins, Mary W. of Edenton to Richard T. Browning of Chowan county. Jly., Edenton. R. R. Jly. 24, 1827.
Howard, G. G. of Iredell county to Temperance C. Wilson of Hancock county, Ga., Feb. 27. R. R. Apr. 3, 1827.
Howard, Sarah S. to Giles M. Mallett, Je., Wilmington. R. R. Je. 5, 1827.
Huffman, Geo. to Margaret Summey, Apr. 22, Davidson county. R. R. My. 1, 1827.
Huffman, Jacob to Susan Shook, Sept. 20, Lincoln county. R. R. Oct. 23, 1827.
Huffman, Lydia to Thos. Cheshire, Mar., Davidson county. R. R. Mar. 20, 1827.
Hustin, Owen to Sarah Fletcher, Jan., Fayetteville. R. R. Jan. 30, 1827.
Hutson, Nancy to Bryson Moore, Sept. 27, Rowan county. R. R. Oct. 23, 1827.
Hutton, George W. to Susan Jordan, My. 3, Fayetteville. R. R. My. 8, 1827.
Ivey, Richard N. to Sarah Fulgum, Oct., Halifax county. R. R. Nov. 20, 1827.
Jeans, Sally W. to Jas. M'Nairy, Jr., My. 17, Guilford county. R. R. My. 18, 1827.
Jennings, Daniel to Lovey Sawyer, Aug., Pasquotank county. R. R. Aug. 7, 1827.
Johnson, James of Mecklenburg county to Nancy Torrence, Oct. 23, Iredell county. R. R. Nov. 20, 1827.
Johnson, Jas. of Mecklenburg county to Nancy Torrence of Iredell county, Oct. 23. R. R. Nov. 6, 1827.
Johnson, Sarah Elizabeth of Stratford, Conn. to George Pollock Devereaux of this State, My. 13, Stratford, Conn. R. R. Je. 6, 1827.
Jones, Mrs. Ann to Christopher A. Hatch, Je. 21, Onslow county. R. R. Jly. 13, 1827.
Jones, Joshua of Franklin county to Susan Sorsby of Nash county, My. 29, R. R. Je. 5, 1827.
Jones, Maria of Philadelphia to Edward L. Winslow, Mar. 28, Fayetteville. R. R. Apr. 3, 1827.
Jones, Mark to Nancy Neel, Feb. 4, Montgomery county. R. R. Mar. 2, 1827.
Jones, Mary B. of Wake county to Calvin Nicholson, Oct., Tennessee. R. R. Oct. 23, 1827.
Jones, Nancy to Col. Thomas King of Sampson county, Sept. 11, Wake county. R. R. Sept. 14, 1827.
Jones, Sarah Ann of Wilmington to David W. Stone, Aug. 15, Raleigh. R. R. Aug. 17, 1827.
Jones, Sarah R. to Smith Murphy of Alabama, Nov. 13, Wake county. R. R. Nov. 16, 1827.
Jones, Temperance to Col. Willis Whitaker, Nov. 27, Wake county. R. R. Dec. 11, 1827.

Jordan, Dillon, Jr. to Ann E. MacRacken, Feb., Fayetteville. R. R. Mar. 2, 1827.
Jordan, Isabella to Anthony W. Horton, My. 3, Fayetteville. R. R. My. 8, 1827.
Jordan, Susan to George W. Hutton, My. 3, Fayetteville. R. R. My. 8, 1827.
Josey, Sally to Hileck Michael, Jr., Mar. 6, Rowan county. R. R. Mar. 20, 1827.
Josey, Mrs. Martha to William Josey, Oct. 30. Northampton county. R. R. Nov. 20, 1827.
Josey, William to Mrs. Martha Josey, Oct. 30, Northampton county. R. R. Nov. 20, 1827.
Kelly, Col. William F. to Sarah Ann Gaither, Oct. 9, Rowan county. R. R. Oct. 23, 1827.
Kendrick, James of Mecklenburg county, Va. to Susan Green of Warren county, Sept. 6. R. R. Sept. 14, 1827.
Kennedy, Aaron A. to Jane Sloan, Nov. 13, Mecklenburg county. R. R. Dec. 18, 1827.
Kerr, Rev. Daniel W. to Rebecca Davis, Nov. 1, Wake county. R. R. Nov. 20, 1827.
King, Amanda D. to Rev. Henry N. Pharr of Mecklenburg county, Sept. 18, Iredell county. R. R. Oct. 5, 1827.
King, Lucy Ann of Wake county to Col. William Bullock of Chowan county, Feb. 9, Raleigh. R. R. Feb. 16, 1827.
King, Nancy to James Bradley, Jly. 25, Raleigh. R. R. Jly. 27, 1827.
King, Col. Thomas of Sampson county to Nancy Jones, Sept. 11, Wake county. R. R. Sept. 14, 1827.
Kingsbury, Russell to Mrs. Mary T. Osborn, Oct. 29, Halifax. R. R. Nov. 20, 1827.
Kirkman, Margaret P. to William Woodburn, Nov. 29, Guilford county. R. R. Dec. 18, 1827.
Knight, Sam to Margaret Chase, Feb., Pasquotank county. R. R. Mar. 2, 1827.
Lamb, Jacob to Sally Trueblood, My. 14, Pasquotank county. R. R. Je. 6, 1827.
Lane, Gilly to James Stout, Oct. 1, Randolph county. R. R. Oct. 26, 1827.
Langford, Rebecca to Thomas Capps, Sept. 8, Warren county. R. R. Oct. 2, 1827.
Lanier, Capt. G. to Elley Grimes, Feb. 13, Duplin county. R. R. Mar. 13, 1827.
Larkins, Lucy Jane to Richard Saunders, My. 24, New Hanover county. R. R. Je. 1, 1827.
Lassiter, Jesse to Sarah Wood, Je. 28, Lenoir county. R. R. Jly. 13, 1827.
Leary, Sarah to Thomas I. Carlton, Mar. 27, Chowan county. R. R. Apr. 10, 1827.
LeGrand, America W. to William Cade, My. 3, Montgomery county. R. R. My. 8, 1827.
Lemmon, Dr. Sheldon to Eliza Hall, Nov. 6, Iredell county. R. R. Nov. 20, 1827.
Leonard, Henry to Catharine M'Nair, Apr. 3, Richmond county. R. R. My. 1, 1827.
Lippard, Henry to Drucilla Turner, Mar. 1, Rowan county. R. R. Mar. 20, 1827.

Lloyd, Joseph R. of Tarborough to Maria A. Pugh of Bertie county, Jly. 19, Oxford. R. R. Aug. 3, 1827.
Locke, Esther to Dr. John Scott, Mar. 15, Rowan county. R. R. Apr. 3, 1827.
Lovick, Elizabeth to Knight Green of Greene county, Je. 20, Kinston. R. R. Je. 29, 1827.
Lynch, Rev. Thomas to Mary S. Bingham, My., Orange county. R. R. My 8, 1827.
Lyon, Delphia to James C. Whitaker, Oct. 16, Edgecombe county. R. R. Oct. 19, 1827.
M'Alister, James to Nancy Wynn, Mar. 22, Wake county. R. R. Mar. 27, 1827.
M'Cain, Mary to G. B. Willingham of Randolph county, Mar. 8, Guilford county. R. R. Mar. 16, 1827.
M'Connell, Tirza to Geo. H. Snow, Aug. 23, Iredell county. R. R. Oct. 2, 1827.
M'Cormick, Duncan, Jr. to Alla M'Nair, Jan. 12, Richmond county. R. R. Jan. 30, 1827.
M'Dill, Nancy of Mecklenburg county to John Bigham, Apr. 17, Chester District, S. C. R. R. My. 8, 1827.
M'Donald, Alex of South Carolina to Elizabeth M'Nair, Apr. 3, Richmond county. R. R. My. 1, 1827.
M'Donald, Mary Teresa to Ezra Allemong, My. 27, Charleston, S. C. R. R. Je. 15, 1827.
M'Farland, Tryan of Richmond county to Margaret D. Buie, Aug. 14, Cumberland county. R. R. Aug. 28, 1827.
M'Guire, Mary to Stephen Skinner, Aug. 4, Edenton. R. R. Aug. 10, 1827.
M'Kay, Caroline J. to Wm. Dougall, Nov., Wilmington. R. R. Nov. 20, 1827.
M'Kinnon John of Fayetteville to Cynthia Elliott, Jly. 15, Randolph county. R. R. Jly. 24, 1827.
M'Lain, Axah to David Wiley, Feb., Greensborough. R. R. Feb. 16, 1827.
M'Lean, Gen. Richard D. S. of Lincoln county to Jane Adams, Apr. 17, York District, S. C. R. R. My. 8, 1827.
M'Millan, Malcom to Sarah Ray, Apr. 26, Fayetteville. R. R. My. 1, 1827.
M'Nair, Alla to Duncan M'Cormick, Jr., Jan. 12, Richmond county. R. R. Jan. 30, 1827.
M'Nair, Capt. Archibald of Fayetteville to Jane M'Nair, My. 22, Richmond county. R. R. Je. 5, 1827.
M'Nair, Catharine to Henry Leonard, Apr. 3, Richmond county. R. R. My. 1, 1827.
M'Nair Elizabeth to Alex M'Donald of South Carolina, Apr. 3, Richmond county. R. R. My. 1, 1827.
M'Nair, Jane to Capt. Archibald M'Nair of Fayetteville, My. 22, Richmond county. R. R. Je. 5, 1827.
M'Nairy, Jas. Jr. to Sally W. Jeans, My. 17, Guilford county. R. R. My. 18, 1827.
M'Pherson, Flora Jane to William Ramsay, Feb. 29, Bladen county. R. R. My. 1, 1827.
M'Queen, Eliza to Joseph Palmer, Sept. 20, Chatham county. R. R. Oct. 16, 1827.

MacRacken, Ann E. to Dixon Jordan, Jr. Feb., Fayetteville. R. R. Mar. 2, 1827.
Mallett, Giles M. to Sarah S. Howard, Je., Wilmington. R. R. Je. 5, 1827.
Mallett, Peter J. of Fayetteville to Eleanor M. Debernier, Feb. 19, Charleston. R. R. My. 1, 1827.
Malloy, Dr. John of Richmond county to Harriet D. Adams, Jan. 19, Adamsville, S. C. R. R. Jan. 30, 1827.
Manson, Abigail to John Boatright, Sept. 25, Mecklenburg county. R. R. Oct. 16, 1827.
Martin, Dr. Henry to Ann Battle, Nov. 23, Wake Forest. R. R. Dec. 4, 1827.
Mason, Polly to Thomas Evans, Aug. 23, Iredell county. R. R. Oct. 2, 1827.
Massie, Sarah to Frank Stanly of Newbern, Nov., Alleghany county, Va. R. R. Nov. 16, 1827.
May, Louisa to Gen. Jesse Speight of Greene county, My. 3, Pitt county. R. R. My. 18, 1827.
Milam, Nathan to Elizabeth Fitz, Sept. 4, Warren county. R. R. Sept. 14, 1827.
Miller, Alexander to Elizabeth Stanly, Oct., Wilmington. R. R. Nov. 2, 1827.
Miller, Julia to John B. Miskell, Je. 19, Edenton. R. R. Aug. 10, 1827.
Miskell, John B. to Julia Miller, Je. 19, Edenton. R. R. Aug. 10, 1827.
Mitchell, William to Miss E. Newell, Oct. 26, Brunswick county. R. R. Nov. 20, 1827.
Montgomery, Maj. John to Mary B. Wylie, Jly. 17, Mecklenburg county. R. R. Aug. 10, 1827.
Morgan, Uriah to Mariam Munden, Feb., Pasquotank county. R. R. Mar. 2, 1827.
Moore, Bryson to Nancy Hutson, Sept. 27, Rowan county. R. R. Oct. 23, 1827.
Moore, Elizabeth to Thomas Riddick, Jly. 5, Pasquotank county. R. R. Jly. 17, 1827.
Moore, Elizabeth to Capt. William Brinkley, My. 1, Halifax county. R. R. Je. 1, 1827.
Moore, John to Mary Randolph, Apr. 19, Northampton county. R. R. My. 8, 1827.
Moore, Maniza P. to Wm. Turner, Apr., Wake county. R. R. Apr. 6, 1827.
Mosely, Col. Joshua of Lenoir county to Sarah B. Bryan of Duplin county, Je. 24, Duplin county. R. R. Jly. 13, 1827.
Moss, Jordan to Ann White, Feb. 28, Granville county. R. R. Mar. 9, 1827.
Mowery, Peter to Mary Holthouser, Mar. 20, Rowan county. R. R. Apr. 3, 1827.
Munden, Mariam to Uriah Morgan, Feb., Pasquotank county. R. R. Mar. 2, 1827.
Murphy, Smith of Alabama to Sarah R. Jones, Nov. 13, Wake county. R. R. Nov. 16, 1827.
Murray, Olivia of New York to Rev. James G. Hamner, New York. Sept. 18, New York. R. R. Sept. 28, 1827.

Musgrave, Lewis of Wayne county to Alice Speight of Greene county, My. 15. R. R. Je. 1, 1827.

Nash, Ann Eliza to Dr. Edmond Strudwich, Nov. 29, Hillsboro. R. R. Dec. 4, 1827.

Neagle, Dr. James R. C. of Lincoln county to Albertine Utzman, Oct. 23, Salisbury. R. R. Nov. 6, 1827.

Neel, Nancy to Mark Jones, Feb. 4, Montgomery county. R. R. Mar. 2, 1827.

Newell, Miss E. to William Mitchell, Oct. 26, Brunswick county. R. R. Nov. 20, 1827.

Newbouldo, Elizabeth to Chapen Saltonstall, Feb., Pasquotank county. R. R. Mar. 2, 1827.

Newton, Jesse to Elizabeth Quinn, Feb. 4, Duplin county. R. R. Mar. 13, 1827.

Nicholson, Calvin to Mary B. Jones of Wake county, Oct., Tennessee. R. R. Oct. 23, 1827.

Nicholson, Martha Ann Eliza Crawford Lewis to Maj. Jordan Walker, Dec. 5, Halifax county. R. R. Dec. 18, 1827.

Norcross, Sarah P. to David Carleton of Fayetteville, Oct., Boston. R. R. Oct. 9, 1827.

Norfleet, Mary of Bertie county to Dr. Richard Urquhart of Southampton, Va., Je. 19. R. R. Jly. 6, 1827.

Norris, Mrs. Elizabeth C. to William Haywood, My. 14, Camden county. R. R. Je. 6, 1827.

Osborn, Mrs. Mary T. to Russell Kingsbury, Oct. 29, Halifax county. R. R. Nov. 20, 1827.

Overby, Francis to Jesse Dunevant, Oct. 25, Caswell county. R. R. Nov. 6, 1827.

Paine, Ann to Rev. John Avery of Edenton, Nov. R. R. Dec. 4, 1827.

Paine, Elizabeth to Stephen Smith, Oct. 23, Caswell county. R. R. Nov. 6, 1827.

Palin, Reuben to Maria Ward, Aug., Pasquotank county. R. R. Aug. 7, 1827.

Palmer, Joseph to Eliza M'Queen, Sept. 20, Chatham county. R. R. Oct. 16, 1827.

Parker, Irena to Joseph Wyatt, Nov. 4, Rowan county. R. R. Nov. 20, 1827.

Pearson, Kesiah to Geo. D. Smith, Aug. 7, Rowan county. R. R. Aug. 21, 1827.

Peeples, Capt. Charles to Tirza Tatum, My. 15, Guilford county. R. R. My. 25, 1827.

Pender, Lucinda to Dr. Pleasanton S. Sugg, Jan., Tarborough. R. R. Feb. 2, 1827.

Perry, Mary E. of Franklin county to Dr. Leonard Henderson Seawell, Sept. 4, Raleigh. R. R. Sept. 7, 1827.

Pharr, Rev. Henry N. of Mecklenburg county to Amanda D. King, Sept. 18, Iredell county. R. R. Oct. 5, 1827.

Physioc, Joseph to Mrs. Elizabeth Hope Cox, Feb. 25, Craven county. R. R. Mar. 27, 1827.

Pierce, Andrew of Cheraw, S. C. to Lilly M. Conner, My., Lincoln county. R. R. My. 15, 1827.

Pitts, Rebecca of Nash county to John Tate of Bertie county, Je. 21. R. R. Jly. 27, 1827.
Plummer, Wm. of Franklin county to Eliza Armstead, Je. 19, Bertie county. R. R. Jly. 6, 1827.
Polk, Marshall T. of Tennessee to Laura T. Wilson, Nov. 1, Charlotte. R. R. Nov. 6, 1827.
Pope, Winifred S. to Blany Bland, Je. 14, Snowhill, Greene county. R. R. Je. 29, 1827.
Potter, Henry of Raleigh to Eleanor Putney of Wake county, Feb., South Carolina. R. R. Feb. 16, 1827.
Powers, Elizabeth H. to Bennett W. Stainmire of Raleigh, Nov. 13, Warrenton. R. R. Nov. 16, 1827.
Pugh, Maria A. of Bertie county to Joseph R. Lloyd of Tarboro, Jly. 19, Oxford. R. R. Aug. 3, 1827.
Putney, Eleanor of Wake county to Henry Potter of Raleigh, Feb., South Carolina. R. R. Feb. 16, 1827.
Quinn, Elizabeth to Jesse Newton, Feb. 4, Duplin county. R. R. Mar. 13, 1827.
Raboteau, Catharine to Thomas Fuller of Fayetteville, Mar. 7, Franklin county. R. R. Mar. 13, 1827.
Ragan, Bennett of Raleigh to Lycia Holloman, Nov. 8, Wake county. R. R. Nov. 16, 1827.
Rague, Thomas A. of Concord to Sarah Waddle, Nov. 13, Rowan county. R. R. Dec. 18, 1827.
Ramsey, William to Flora Jane M'Pherson, Feb. 29, Bladen county. R. R. My. 1, 1827.
Randolph, Mary to John Moore, Apr. 19, Northampton county. R. R. My. 8, 1827.
Raredon, Jesse C. of Cumberland county to Nancy P. Stephenson, My. 10, Wake county. R. R. My. 29, 1827.
Ray, Archibald to Janet Carmichael, Mar , Cumberland county. R. R. Mar. 20, 1827.
Ray, Dugall, to Margaret Blue, Feb. 22, Bladen county. R. R. My. 1, 1827.
Ray, Sarah to Malcolm M'Millan, Apr. 26, Fayetteville. R. R. My. 1, 1827.
Reed, Wilson to Catharine Whedbee, Mar. 18, Perquimons county. R. R. Apr. 10, 1827.
Rhodes, Lucy W. to Moses H. Allan, Apr. 5, Wake county. R. R. Apr. 10, 1827.
Richardson, Charles C. of Raleigh to Julianna Eleanor Dandridge, Nov. 21, Richmond, Va. R. R. Dec. 4, 1827.
Richmond, John to Elizabeth Anderson, Oct. 17, Caswell county. R. R. Nov. 6, 1827.
Ricks, Mary Ann of Chatham county to Henry Ward, Sept. 27, Raleigh. R. R. Oct. 2, 1827.
Riddick, Thomas to Elizabeth Moore, Jly. 5, Perquimons county. R. R. Jly. 17, 1827.
Roberts, Candiss to James Tyson of Carthage, Mar. 1, Moore county. R. R. Mar. 20, 1827.
Roberts, Eliza to Herring Waters of Lenoir county, Feb. 22, Duplin county. R. R. Mar. 27, 1827.

Robinson, Tempe to Capt. John Fogleman, Sept. 27, Orange county. R. R. Oct. 16, 1827.

Rogers, Catharine to Robert Short, Apr. 8, Halifax county. R. R. My. 8, 1827.

Rogers, Joseph to Hannah Short, Apr. 8, Halifax county. R. R. My. 8, 1827.

Russell, Fanny to George Coston, Nov. 20, Wilmington. R. R. Dec. 18, 1827.

Russell, Susan P. to James M. Wiggins, Dec. 13, Oxford. R. R. Jan. 2, 1827.

Russell, William C. of Tennessee to Elizabeth Thompson of Orange county, Feb. 12. R. R. My. 1, 1827.

Sadler, James of Lincoln county to Lucy Searcy, My. 3, Mecklenburg county. R. R. My. 15, 1827.

Saltonstall, Chaplin to Elizabeth Newboulds, Feb., Pasquotank county. R. R. Mar. 2, 1827.

Sampson, Ebenezer to Margaret Bunch, Apr., Raleigh. R. R. Apr. 20, 1827.

Saunders, Richard to Lucy Jane Larkins, My. 24, New Hanover county. R. R. Je. 1, 1827.

Sawyer, Chloe to Sterling Tisdale, Jly. 1, Camden county. R. R. Jly. 17, 1827.

Sawyer, Lovey to Daniel Jennings, Aug., Pasquotank county. R. R. Aug. 7, 1827.

Scott, Dr. John to Esther Locke, Mar. 15, Rowan county. R. R. Apr. 3,, 1827.

Searcy, Lucy to James Sadler of Lincoln county, My. 3, Mecklenburg county. R. R. My. 15, 1827.

Seawell, Dr. Leonard Henderson to Mary E. Perry of Franklin county. Sept. 4, Raleigh. R. R. Sept. 7, 1827.

Sessoms, Dr. Harrell B. to Harriet Eason, Jly. 3, Bertie county. R. R. Jly. 24, 1827.

Sharp, Ludwick to Sally Anthony, Sept. 27, Orange county. R. R. Oct. 16, 1827.

Shaw, Flora to William B. Colvin, Jly. 11, New Hanover county. R .R. Jly. 24, 1827.

Shook, Susan to Jacob Huffman, Sept. 20, Lincoln county. R. R. Oct. 23, 1827.

Short, Hannah to Joseph Rogers, Apr. 8, Halifax county. R. R. My. 8, 1827.

Short, Robert to Catharine Rogers, Apr. 8, Halifax county. R. R. My. 8, 1827.

Shuffield, Thos. to Sarah A. E. Beasley, Feb. 15, Duplin county. R. R. Mar. 13, 1827.

Shufford, Thomas to Elizabeth Butts, My. 31, Lincolnton. R. R. Je. 19, 1827.

Skinner, Stephen to Mary M'Guire, Aug. 4, Edenton. R. R. Aug. 10, 1827.

Sloan, H. L. to Sarah Brevard, Oct. 22, Iredell county. R. R. Nov. 6, 1827.

Sloan, Jane to Aaaron A. Kenndy, Nov. 13, Mecklenburg county. R. R. Dec. 18, 1827.

Slover, Eliza A. to Rev. Darius G. Allen, My., Newbern. R. R. My. 15, 1827.
Smith, Daniel to Lydia Buie, Feb. 29, Richmond county. R. R. My. 1, 1827.
Smith, Eldridge to Mrs. Ellen Smith, Feb. 7, Raleigh. R. R. Feb. 16, 1827.
Smith, Mrs. Ellen to Eldridge Smith, Feb. 7, Raleigh. R. R. Feb. 16, 1827.
Smith, Geo. D. to Kesiah Pearson, Aug. 7, Rowan county. R. R. Aug. 21, 1827.
Smith, Spyers Singleton of Newbern to Evelina S. M. Bell, Je. 14, Hyde county. R. R. Je. 29, 1827.
Smith, Stephen to Elizabeth Paine, Oct. 23, Caswell county. R. R. Nov. 6, 1827.
Snead, Daniel to Martha Webb, Jan. 14, Richmond county. R. R. Jan. 30, 1827.
Snow, Geo. H. to Tirza M'Connell, Aug. 23, Iredell county. R. R. Oct. 2, 1827.
Sorsby, Susan of Nash county to Joshua Jones of Franklin county, My. 29, R. R. Je. 5, 1827.
Sowersby, Mrs. of Northampton county to Maj. Reddick Cross of Hertford, Mar. 15. R. R. Apr. 3, 1827.
Speck, Daniel to Agnes Louisa Watt, Sept. 27, Iredell county. R. R. Oct. 16, 1827.
Speight, Alice of Greene county to Lewis Musgrave of Wayne county, My. 15. R. R. Je. 1, 1827.
Speight, Gen'l. Jesse of Greene county to Louisa May, My. 3, Pitt county. R. R. My. 18, 1827.
Spicer, Robert M. to Caroline P. Steel, Apr. 29, Fayetteville. R. R. My. 1, 1827.
Spiers, George to Elizabeth Wise of Murfreesborough, Mar. 15. R. R. Apr. 3, 1827.
Squires, Nancy to Joseph Faires, Mar. 5, Mecklenburg county. R. R. Apr. 3, 1827.
Stammire, Bennet H. of Raleigh to Elizabeth H. Powers, Nov. 13, Warrenton. R. R. Nov. 16, 1827.
Stanly, Elizabeth to Alexander Miller, Oct., Wilmington. R. R. Nov. 2, 1827.
Stanly, Frank of Newbern to Sarah Massie, Nov., Alleghany county, Va. R. R. Nov. 16, 1827.
Stars, Mrs. Sophia to Moses Fight, Apr. 5, Rowan county. R. R. My. 1, 1827.
Steel, Caroline P. to Robert M. Spicer, Apr. 29, Fayetteville. R. R. My. 1, 1827.
Stephenson, Nancy P. to Jesse C. Raredon of Cumberland county, My. 10, Wake county. R. R. My. 29, 1827.
Stevenson, Mary Melissa to Capt. Thomas H. Condy of Iredell county, My. 10. R. R. My. 29, 1827.
Stewart, Mary K. to Hiram C. Dick, Sept., Guilford county. R. R. Oct. 5, 1827.
Stone, David W. to Sarah Ann Jones of Wilmington, Aug. 15, Raleigh. R. R. Aug. 17, 1827.
Stout, James to Gilly Lane, Oct. 1, Randolph county. R. R. Oct. 26, 1827.

Strudwick, Dr. Edmond to Ann Eliza Nash, Nov. 29, Hillsboro. R. R. Dec. 4, 1827.
Sugg, Dr. Pleasanton S. to Lucinda Pender, Jan., Tarborough. R. R. Feb. 2, 1827.
Summey, Margaret to George Huffman, Apr. 22, Davidson county. R. R. My. 1, 1827.
Swainey, Rebecca of Randolph county to Nathan Frazier of Guilford county, My. 17, Randolph county. R. R. Je. 1, 1827.
Tally, Orren to Barbara N. Fuller, Oct. 18, Caswell county. R. R. Nov. 6, 1827.
Tate, John of Bertie county to Rebecca Pitts of Nash county, Je. 21. R. R. Jly. 27, 1827.
Tatum, Thirza to Capt. Charles Peebles, My. 15, Guilford county. R. R. My. 25, 1827.
Taylor, James to Mary G. Eaton, Aug. 16, Granville county. R. R. Aug. 28, 1827.
Taylor, Mary B. of Hillsborough to Robert Coleman, Oct., Macon, Ga. R. R. Nov. 6, 1827.
Taylor, Susan U. of Hillsborough to Carleton Cole of Macon, Ga., Sept. 6. R. R. Sept. 18, 1827.
Thally, David to Mrs. Elizabeth Baber, Feb. 5, Wilmington. R. R. My. 1, 1827.
Thomas, Wade R. to Milliscent Horn, Jan., Tarborough. R. R. Feb. 2, 1827.
Thompson, Elizabeth of Orange county to William C. Russell of Tennessee, Feb. 12. R. R. My. 1, 1827.
Thompson, George W. to Frances Crenshaw, Dec. 13, Wake Forest. R. R. Dec. 18, 1827.
Tipps, Jacob to Matilda C. Cowan, Oct. 11, Iredell county. R. R. Nov. 20, 1827.
Tisdale, Sterling to Chloe Sawyer, Jly. 1, Camden county. R. R. Jly. 17, 1827.
Tombereau, Louis to Rachel David, My. 13, Raleigh. R. R. My. 15, 1827.
Torrence, Nancy of Iredell county to Jas. Johnson of Mecklenburg county, Oct. 23. R. R. Nov. 6, 1827.
Treadwell, James to Mary Blount, Apr., Edenton. R. R. Apr. 24, 1827.
Troutman, Magdalen to John Brown, Mar. 20, Rowan county. R. R. Apr. 3, 1827.
Trueblood, Sally to Jacob Lamb, My. 14, Pasquotank county. R. R. Je. 6, 1827.
Turnbull, John to Mary C. Goode of Mecklenburg county, Va., Feb. 19, Bladen county. R. R. My. 1, 1827.
Turner, Drucilla to Henry Lippard, Mar. 1, Rowan county. R. R. Mar. 20, 1827.
Turner, Nancy M. J. P. of Raleigh to Dr. Robt. Bedford, My. 22, Haywood county. R. R. Jly. 3, 1827.
Turner, Wm. to Maniza P. Moore, Apr., Wake county. R. R. Apr. 6, 1827.
Tyson, James of Carthage to Candiss Roberts, Mar. 1, Moore county. R. R. Mar. 20, 1827.
Urquhart, Dr. Richard of Southampton, Va. to Mary Norfleet of Bertie county, Je. 19. R. R. Jly. 6, 1827.

Utly, Charity to Jos. Dickens, Jan. 18, Chatham county. R. R. Feb. 9, 1827.
Utzman, Albertine to Dr. James R. C. Neagle of Lincoln county, Oct. 23, Salisbury. R. R. Nov. 6, 1827.
Vaulz, James to Eliza Fenner of Raleigh, Jan. 23, Tennessee. R. R. Mar. 6, 1827.
Waddle, Sarah to Thomas A. Rague of Concord, Nov. 13, Rowan county. R. R. Dec. 18, 1827.
Walker, Maj. Jordan of Washington county to Martha Ann Eliza Crawford Lewis Nicholson, Dec. 5, Halifax county. R. R. Dec. 18, 1827.
Wallace, Susan to James I. Corbett, Je., Wilmington. R. R. Je. 5, 1827.
Ward, Henry to Mrs. Mary Ann Ricks of Chatham county. Sept. 27, Raleigh. R. R. Oct. 2, 1827.
Ward, Maria to Reuben Palin, Aug., Pasquotank county. R. R. Aug. 7, 1827.
Washington, Eliza H. to Richard Grist of Washington, My. 18, Kinston. R. R. Je. 29, 1827.
Washington, John of Kinston to Mary A. Bond, Feb. 28, Raleigh. R. R. Mar. 2, 1827.
Waters, Herring of Lenoir county to Eliza Roberts, Feb. 22, Duplin county. R. R. Mar. 27, 1827.
Watt, Agnes Louisa to Daniel Speck, Sept. 27, Iredell county. R. R. Oct. 16, 1827.
Weatherly, Esther of Marlboro District, S. C. to Wm. Fountain of Guilford county, Apr. 1. R. R. Apr. 6, 1827.
Webb, Howell of Raleigh to Mrs. Ann Harvey of Franklin county, Dec. 12, Franklin county. R. R. Dec. 18, 1827.
Webb, Martha to Daniel Snead, Jan. 14, Richmond county. R. R. Jan. 30, 1827.
Webb, Thomas to Sarah Frances, Jly. 5, Bertie county. R. R. Jly. 24, 1827.
Webb, William G. to Celestia C. Goodrich, Oct. 12, Rockingham, Richmond county. R. R. Oct. 23, 1827.
Wheaton, Daniel F. of Raleigh to Grace Benson, Oct. 19, Greenville, S. C. R. R. Nov. 6, 1827.
Wheaton, Dr. Sterling of Raleigh to Sarah C. Dubose, Dec. 23, Camden, S. C. R. R. Jan. 19, 1827.
Whedbee, Catharine to Wilson Reed, Mar. 18, Perquimons county. R. R. Apr. 10, 1827.
Whitaker, Goff Ann to William Bastion, Nov., Halifax. R. R. Nov. 16, 1827.
Whitaker, James C. to Delphia Lyon, Oct. 16, Edgecombe county. R. R. Oct. 19, 1827.
Whitaker, Col. Willis to Temperance Jones, Nov. 27, Wake county. R. R. Dec. 11, 1827.
White, Ann to Jordan Moss, Feb. 28, Granville county. R. R. Mar. 19, 1827.
Whitehead, Mrs. Temperance to Richard Arrington, My. 29, Nash county. R. R. Je. 5, 1827.
Wiggins, James M. to Susan P. Russell, Dec. 13, Oxford. R. R. Jan. 2, 1827.
Wiley, David to Axah M'Lain, Feb. 8, Greensborough. R. R. Feb. 16, 1827.

Williams, Dr. Francis of Surry county to Nancy Dismukes, Feb. 15, Rowan county. R. R. Mar. 13, 1827.
Williamson, Mildred to Dr. Robert Crump of Northampton county, Oct. 2, Greensville, Va. R. R. Nov. 6, 1827.
Willingham, G. B. of Randolph county to Mary M'Cain, Mar. 8, Guilford county. R. R. Mar. 16, 1827.
Wilson, Laura T. to Marshall T. Polk of Tennessee, Nov. 1, Charlotte. R. R. Nov. 6, 1827.
Wilson, Temperance C. of Hancock county, Ga. to G. G. Howard of Iredell county, Feb. 27. R. R. Apr. 3, 1827
Wilson, Thos. to Peggy Amick, Sept. 6, Randolph county. R. R. Sept. 14, 1827.
Wilson, Thomas W. of Wilkesborough to Catharine Caldwell, Oct. 23, Iredell county. R. R. Nov. 20, 1827.
Winslow, Edward L. to Marion Jones of Philadelphia. Mar. 28, Fayetteville. R. R. Apr. 3, 1827.
Wise, Elizabeth of Murfreesborough to George Spiers, Mar. 15. R. R. Apr. 3, 1827.
Wood, Deliah to Henry Wood, Nov. 23, Wake county. R. R. Dec. 11, 1827.
Wood, Henry to Deliah Wood, Nov. 23, Wake county. R. R. Dec. 11, 1827.
Wood, Sarah to Jesse Lassiter, Je. 28, Lenoir county. R. R. Jly. 13, 1827.
Woodall, John of Cumberland county to Mrs. Rebecca Brazier, Jan. R. R. Feb. 9, 1827.
Woodburn, William to Margaret P. Kirkman, Nov. 29, Guilford county. R. R. Dec. 18, 1827.
Wyatt, Joseph to Irena Parker, Nov. 4, Rowan county. R. R. Nov. 20, 1827.
Wylie, Mary B. to Maj. John Montgomery, Jly. 17, Mecklenburg county. R. R. Aug. 10, 1827.
Wynn, Nancy to James M'Alister, Mar. 22, Wake county. R. R. Mar. 27, 1827.

1828

Albritton, James, Jr. to Margaret Osmond, Dec. 11, Greene county. R. R. Jan. 8, 1828.
Alexander, Dr. Amzi to Mary Delia Harris, Oct. 30, Mecklenburg county. R. R. Nov. 25, 1828.
Allen, John to Miss Browning, Sept., Franklin county. R. R. Sept. 23, 1828.
Alston, Henrietta Green to Augusta H. Kenan, Je. 19, Georgia. R. R. Jly. 11, 1828.
Alexander, Dorcas Jane to Eli H. Lide of Darlington District, S. C., Dec. 4, Mecklenburg county. R. R. Jan. 14, 1828.
Anderson, William E. of Hillsborough to Elizabeth Burgwyn, Jan. 10, Guilford county. R. R. Jan. 22, 1828.
Area, Caroline E. to Geo. W. Spears, Oct. 7, Cabarrus county. R. R. Oct. 24, 1828.
Baker, Daniel B. to Mary Potter, Nov. 20, Smithville. R. R. Dec. 12, 1828.
Ballenger, Sarah Ann of Culpepper county, Va. to Thomas C. Frohock of Rowan county, Jan. 10, Sparta, Tenn. R. R. Feb. 12, 1828.
Banks, T. to Patsey Cone, Jan. 22, Edgecombe county. R. R. Feb. 8, 1828.
Barclay, Esther to John S. Raboteau, Jr. of Raleigh, Jly. 13, Cumberland county. R. R. Jly. 18, 1828.
Barr, John D. to Ann Overman, Sept., Greensborough. R. R. Oct. 3, 1828.
Barringer, Mary to Charles W. Harris, Jly. 1, Cabarrus county. R. R. Jly. 18, 1828.

Batts, Eliza to Wm. Gardner, Jan. 22, Edgecombe county. R. R. Feb. 8, 1828.
Bell, Mary to Cado Cherry, Nov. 16, Edgecombe county. R. R. Nov. 28, 1828.
Bennitt, Charles C. to Eveline A. Bennitt, Je. 29, Warren county. R. R. Aug. 15, 1828.
Bennitt, Eveline A. to Charles C. Bennitt, Je. 29, Warren county. R. R. Aug. 15, 1828.
Benson, Spencer to Nancy Rice, Mar. 27, Rowan county. R. R. Apr. 29, 1828.
Berry, Tresse D. to Elisha Woodward, Sr. Edgecombe county. R. R. Je. 10, 1828.
Blackburn, Hulit to Mrs. Bethany Flynt, Sept. 14, Stokes county. R. R. Oct. 14, 1828.
Blake, Rev. Bennet T. of Raleigh to Fetney I. Price, Feb. 21, Raleigh. R. R. Feb. 26, 1828.
Blakely, Thomas J. of Petersburg, Va. to Ann Stafford of Halifax, Oct. 13, Tarborough. R. R. Oct. 31, 1828.
Blanks, Susannah to Logustin P. Pool of Kentucky, Jan. 18, Granville county. R. R. Jan. 25, 1828.
Boddie, Louie to Bartholomew F. Moore, Dec. 2, Nash county. R. R. Dec. 12, 1828.
Boger, Sally to John Reinhardt, Sept. 25, Rowan county. R. R. Oct. 24, 1828.
Boon, Joseph G. to Harriet Latham, Sept. 25, Johnston county. R. R. Oct. 7, 1828.
Bost, William to Jacob Tarborough, Sept. 11, Lincoln county. R. R. Oct. 10, 1828.
Bouchier, James H. to Elizabeth Hammons, Macon county. My. 1, Franklin. R. R. Je. 6, 1828.
Bradley, Willie to Mrs. Lynch, Jan. 22, Edgecombe county. R. R. Feb. 8, 1828.
Branch, Mrs. Martha to Toby Lewis of Dumplintown, Jan., Halifax. R. R. Jan. 29, 1828.
Brevard, Mary M. to Richard T. Brumby of Columbia, S. C., My. Lincoln county. R. R. My. 13, 1828.
Brown, James to Rebecca Wilson, Jan. 10, Guilford county. R. R. Jan. 25, 1828.
Brown, Peter M. to Elizabeth Pool, Jan. 3, Salisbury. R. R. Jan. 14, 1828.
Browning, Miss to John Allen, Sept., Franklin county. R. R. Sept. 23, 1828.
Brownrigg, Mary Ann to Col. Hardy Cross of Virginia, Sept. 23, Chowan county. R. R. Oct. 10, 1828.
Brumby, Richard T. of Columbia, S. C. to Mary M. Brevard, My., Lincoln county. R. R. My. 13, 1828.
Bullock, Ann H. of Warren county to Nathaniel C. Bullock of Granville county, Jan. 24. R. R. Feb. 8, 1828.
Burgwin, Elizabeth to William E. Anderson of Hillsborough. Jan. 10, Guilford county. R. R. Jan. 22, 1828.
Burt, Harriet to Dr. Wm. Jones, Jan. 16, Granville county. R. R. Jan. 25, 1828.
Butt, Sarah to Malachi Russel of Elizabeth City, Aug., Norfolk. R. R. Aug. 29, 1828.

Bynum, John W. of Chatham county to Mrs. Daniel Gallent, Aug. 5, Mecklenlenburg county. R. R. Aug. 22, 1828.

Cade, Rebecca to David L. Evans, Dec. 4, Fayetteville. R. R. Dec. 5, 1828.

Callum, Mrs. Hannah to N. H. Harding, Dec. 3, Raleigh. R. R. Dec. 5, 1828.

Campbell, Elizabeth H. to Calvin J. Whitaker, My. 6, Warrenton. R. R. My. 9, 1828.

Carman, Wm. R. to Julia Carver, Apr. 16, Cumberland county. R. R. Apr. 25, 1828.

Carr, Dolly to Dr. Elijah Crosby, Feb. 14, Duplin county. R. R. Mar. 4, 1828.

Carraway, S. B. of Washington county to Harriet Wiggins, Jan. 10, Lenoir county. R. R. Jan. 25, 1828.

Carrell, Stephen to Nancy Glenn, Oct. 2, Orange county. R. R. Oct. 7, 1828.

Carver, Julia to Wm. R. Carman, Apr. 16, Cumberland county. R. R. Apr. 25, 1828.

Cathy, Esther to Robert Hannah, My. 2, Iredell county. R. R. Je. 17, 1828.

Chadwick, David W. of Carteret county to Charity Cratch, Mar. 16, Newbern. R. R. Mar. 21, 1828.

Cherry, Cado to Mary Bell, Nov. 16, Edgecombe county. R. R. Nov. 28, 1828.

Childs, George A. to Eliza Wilhite, My. 1, Raleigh. R. R. My. 6, 1828.

Chisholm, Whitson H. of Montgomery county to Martha Stanback, Feb. 26, Richmond county. R. R. Mar. 28, 1828.

Churchill, Charles of Connecticut to Miss Matilda Johnston, Sept. 11, Iredell county. R. R. Oct. 10, 1828.

Clancy, John D. to Laura A. Lindsay, Mar. 20, Greensborough. R. R. Mar. 25, 1828.

Clark, Louisa to Tho. Phillips, Je. 12, Orange county. R. R. Jly. 11, 1828.

Clement, Jesse A. to Melina Nail, Jan. 1, Salisbury. R. R. Jan. 14, 1828.

Cole, Lemuel to Anness Nichols, Jly. 3, Wake county. R. R. Jly. 22, 1828.

Collier, Maria to Charles M. Seawell of Fayetteville, My. 10, Decatur county, Ga. R. R. Je. 3, 1828.

Cone, Patsy to T. Banks, Jan. 22, Edgecombe county. R. R. Feb. 8, 1828.

Cook, Willie to Willy King, Sept. 26, Wake county. R. R. Sept. 30, 1828.

Cook, Miss Willoughby to G. W. Gary of Halifax, Je. 19, Southampton, Va. R. R. Jly. 11, 1828.

Courts, Daniel to Eliza A. Waugh, Apr. 3, Stokes county. R. R. Apr. 25, 1828.

Craig, Eliza to Seburn Lynch, Oct., Orange county. R. R. Oct. 14, 1828.

Crawford, Rebecca to Robert M. Knox, Je., Elizabeth City. R. R. Je. 13, 1828.

Creech, Eliza to Frederick M'Kay, Mar. 4, Greene county. R. R. Mar. 28, 1828.

Crosby, Dr. Elijah to Dolly Carr, Feb. 14, Duplin county. R. R. Mar. 4, 1828.

Cross, Col. Hardy of Virginia to Mary Ann Brownrigg, Sept. 23, Chowan county. R. R. Oct. 10, 1828.

Culpepper, John of this State to Mrs. Abigail Lansdale, Apr. 27, Montgomery county, Md. R. R. Je. 10, 1828.
Cumming, William H. of Greensboro to Lavinia Rose, Jly. 10, Roxboro. R. R. Jly. 11, 1828.
Cunningham, Rev. Paxton of Tennessee to Priscilla Eliza Davidson of Haywood county, Jan. 27. R. R. Feb. 26, 1828.
Currin, James to Margaret Smith, Dec. 27, Granville county. R. R. Jan. 25, 1828.
Curry, Cornelia to McDowell Woodside, My. 29, Mecklenburg county. R. R. Je. 17, 1828.
Daniel, Nathaniel C. of Granville county to Ann H. Bullock of Warren county, Jan. 24. R. R. Feb. 8, 1828.
Daniel, Walter K. of Halifax, Va. to Nancy P. Pool, Jan. 14, Granville county. R. R. Jan. 25, 1828.
Dannelly, Wm. C. to Ann Eliza Slade of Warrenton, Jan. 24, Macon, Ga. R. R. Feb. 8, 1828.
Davidson, Priscilla Eliza of Haywood county to Rev. Paxton Cunningham of Tennessee, Jan. 27. R. R. Feb. 26, 1828.
Dearing, Alex B. of Rockingham to Rutha M. Rogers, Stokes county, Nov. 13, Stokes county. R. R. Nov. 25, 1828.
Dellinger, Solomon of Lincoln county to Catharine Rendleman of Rowan county, My. 27. R. R. Je. 17, 1828.
Deloach, Martha to James Newland, Oct. 23, Raleigh. R. R. Oct. 28, 1828.
Dismukes, Dr. George W. to Mary S. Peguese of Anson county, My. 6, Wadesborough. R. R. My. 25, 1828.
Dixon, Martha B. of Duplin county to Lemuel D. Hatch of Newbern, Jan. 8, Duplin county. R. R. Jan. 25, 1828.
Dixon, Washington to Mary Ormond, Jan. 13, Greene county. R. R. Jan. 25, 1828.
Donaldson, Robert of New York to Susan Jane Gaston, Feb. 14, Newbern. R. R. Feb. 22, 1828.
Dotson, Mary Ann to Tubal Early Strange, Jan. 10, Greensborough. R. R. Jan. 22, 1828.
Douglass, Archibald of Fayetteville to Eliza F. Moore, My., Lumberton. R. R. Je. 3, 1828.
Dowdy, Elizabeth to James Smith, Mar., Camden county. R. R. Apr. 1, 1828.
Drake, Dr. John H. of Nash county to Mary Richard Williams of Pitt county, My. 27, Pitt county. R. R. Jly. 11, 1828.
Drake, Dr. N. J. of Nash county to Mrs. Eliza Thorne of Halifax county, Nov., Halifax county. R. R. Nov. 4, 1828.
Draughton, Drusilla to Burrill Dunn, Jan. 22, Edgecombe county. R. R. Feb. 8, 1828.
Dumas, Isham A. of Richmond county to Emeline Robinson, Mar. 5, Montgomery county. R. R. Mar. 25, 1828.
Dunn, Burrill to Drusilla Draughton, Jan. 22, Edgecombe county. R. R. Feb. 8, 1828.
Duplaine, Benoni C. of Raleigh to Susan Everly, Nov. 27, Philadelphia. R. R. Dec. 2, 1828.
Eaks, Emily to George W. Wilkinson, Jan. 16, Granville county. R. R. Jan. 25, 1828.

Eaton, Mary H. to Alex H. Falconer, Sept. 11, Warren county. R. R. Sept. 23, 1828.
Eaton, William of Warren county to Eliza L. Hickman, Jan. 1, King William county. R. R. Jan. 14, 1828.
Elliott, James to Mary Ann Relfe, Je., Elizabeth City. R. R. Je. 13, 1828.
Elliott, John to Eliza M. Smith, My., Iredell county. R. R. My. 13, 1828.
Ellis, Tabitha to Hartwell Reeves, Aug. 14, Raleigh. R. R. Aug. 19, 1828.
Evans, David L. to Rebecca Cado, Dec. 1, Fayetteville. R. R. Dec. 5, 1828.
Evans, Susan to William R. Smith of Halifax county. Jan. 22, Edgecombe county. R. R. Jan. 29, 1828.
Everly, Susan to Benoni C. Duplaine of Raleigh, Nov. 27, Philadelphia. R. R. Dec. 2, 1828.
Falconer, Alex H. to Mary H. Eaton, Sept. 11, Warren county. R. R. Sept. 23, 1828.
Farrar, Alex'r J. to Pamela S. Walton, Jan. 3, Granville county. R. R. Jan. 25, 1828.
Faulkner, Sarah D. to Dr. Henry L. Plummer, Je. 3, Warrenton. R. R. Je. 6, 1828.
Fenner, Mrs. Sarah of Franklin county to Henry N. Jasper of Washington, Beaufort county, Sept. 17. R. R. Oct. 14, 1828.
Ferguson, Mary E. to Henry L. Jones, Jly. 29, Fayetteville. R. R. Aug. 5, 1828.
Field, Fanny to Elijah Staley, Sept. 9, Randolph county. R. R. Oct. 3, 1828.
Finch, Miss E. M. to Thomas Godsey, My. 16, Iredell county. R. R. Je. 17, 1828.
Fisher, Mrs. Diana to Hon. Lemuel Sawyer, Nov., Brooklyn, N. Y. R. R. Nov. 25, 1828.
Flynt, Mrs. Bethany to Hulit Blackburn, Sept. 14, Stokes county. R. R. Oct. 14, 1828.
Forney, Fatima E. to Hugh A. Tate, Jan. 3, Burke county. R. R. Jan. 29, 1828.
Foscue, Sarah to Frederick Foy of Jones county, Aug. 27, Newbern. R. R. Aug. 29, 1828.
Foy, Frederick of Jones county to Sarah Foscue, Aug. 27, Newbern. R. R. Aug. 29, 1828.
Freshwater, Elizabeth to Redmon Infield, My., Wilmington. R. R. My. 13, 1828.
Franklin, Eliza to Edward Moore, Dec. 19, Granville county. R. R. Jan. 25, 1828.
Frohock, Thomas A. of Rowan county to Sarah Ann Ballenger of Culpepper county, Va., Jan. 10, Sparta, Tenn. R. R. Feb. 12, 1828.
Fuller, R. W. of Lumberton to Orra W. Powell, Feb. 19, Robeson county. R. R. Mar. 4, 1828.
Gallent, Mrs. Daniel to John W. Bynum of Chatham county, Aug. 5, Mecklenburg county. R. R. Aug. 22, 1828.
Gardner, Wm. to Eliza Batts, Jan. 22, Edgecombe county. R. R. Feb. 8, 1828.
Gary, G. W. of Halifax to Willoughby Cook, Je. 19, Southampton, Va. R. R. Jly. 11, 1828.
Gaston, Susan Jane to Robert Donaldson of New York, Feb. 14, Newbern. R. R. Feb. 22, 1828.

Gavin, Sarah Jane to Samuel Torrans, Mar. 20, Sampson county. R. R. Apr. 8, 1828.
Gee, Mrs. S. H. of Alabama to Mary T. Williams, Nov. Warren county. R. R. Nov. 28, 1828.
Gillespy, Alexander to Elizabeth Robinson, Feb. 7, Mecklenburg county. R. R. Mar. 4, 1828.
Gilmore, William S. of Greensboro to Catharine A. Gorrell, Mar. 13, Greene county. R. R. Mar. 28, 1828.
Glenn, Nancy to Stephen Carrell, Oct. 2, Orange county. R. R. Oct. 7, 1828.
Godsey, Thomas to Miss E. M. Finch, My. 16, Iredell county. R. R. Je. 17, 1828.
Gorrell, Catharine to William S. Gilmore of Greensboro, Mar. 13, Greene county. R. R. Mar. 28, 1828.
Gould, Eliza J. to Wm. D. Wood, Je. 17, Rowan county. R. R. Jly. 8, 1828.
Gowing, John to Margaret Stacy, Feb. 14, Newbern. R. R. Feb. 22, 1828.
Graves, Mary to Thos. W. Graves, Jly. 17, Caswell county. R. R. Aug. 5, 1828.
Graves, Thos. W. to Mary Graves, Jly. 17, Caswell county. R. R. Aug. 5, 1828.
Gregory, C. to Henrietta Henderson, Jan. 20, Onslow county. R. R. Feb. 8, 1828.
Gregory, Thomas L. B. to Mary Frances W. Pitman, Oct. 7, Halifax county. R. R. Oct. 31, 1828.
Green, John C. Jr. to Elizabeth Macon, Jan. 31, Warren county. R. R. Feb. 8, 1828.
Guffy, Henry to Elizabeth Walker, Sept. 30, Rowan county. R. R. Oct. 31, 1828.
Gunter, Henry to Harriet Josey, Jan., Halifax county. R. R. Jan. 22, 1828.
Hale, Edward J. to Sarah Jane Walker of Wilmington. My. 27, Fayetteville R. R. My. 30, 1828.
Hammons, Elizabeth of Macon county to James H. Bouchier, Je. 1, Franklin. R. R. Je. 6, 1828.
Hannah, Robert to Esther Cathy, My. 2, Iredell county. R. R. Je. 17, 1828.
Harding, N. H. to Mrs. Hannah Callum, Dec. 3, Raleigh. R. R. Dec. 5, 1828.
Hargrave, Jesse to Esther Lindsay, Sept. 14, Davidson county. R. R. Sept. 23, 1828.
Harnwell, Buckner to Rhoda Westmoreland, My. 2, Lincoln county. R. R. Je. 17, 1828.
Harrell, Sylvia to John Pender, Jan. 22, Edgecombe county. R. R. Feb. 8, 1828.
Hart, Catharine to George W. Whitfield, Feb., Johnson county. R. R. Feb. 29, 1828.
Harris, Charles W. to Mary Barringer, Jly. 1, Cabarrus county. R. R. Jly. 18, 1828.
Harris, Mary Delia to Dr. Amzi Alexander, Oct. 30, Mecklenburg county. R. R. Nov. 25, 1828.
Harriss, Richard to Rebecca S. Holmes, Je. 10, Brunswick county. R. R. Jly. 22, 1828.
Hatch, Lemuel D. of Newbern to Martha B. Dixon of Duplin county, Jan. 8, Duplin county. R. R. Jan. 25, 1828.
Haywood, Egbert of Davidson county to Sally Johnson of Warren county, Je. 8, Hardeman county, Tenn. R. R. Je. 17, 1828.

Henderson, Henrietta to C. Gregory, Jan. 20, Onslow county. R. R. Feb. 8, 1828.
Hendon, Louisa to John Seawell of Raleigh, My., Tennessee. R. R. My. 30, 1828.
Hendon, Dr. Wm. T. of Greene county to Maria T. Holliday, Dec., Newbern. R. R. Dec. 23, 1828.
Henry, James Edward to Ann Eliza Jones, Je. 25, Wilkes county. R. R. Jly. 22, 1828.
Hickman, Eliza L. to William Eaton of Warren county, Jan. 1, King William county. R. R. Jan. 14, 1828.
Hicks, Theresa A. T. of Franklin county to John M. Mason of Raleigh, Sept. 3, Franklin county. R. R. Sept. 9, 1828.
Hill, Samuel to Rebecca Hornaday, Apr., Orange county. R. R. Apr. 15, 1828.
Hillman, Laney to N. H. Thomas, Jan. 17, Halifax county. R. R. Jan. 29, 1828.
Hinton, Frederic A. of this State to Eliza Ann Howell of Philadelphia, Je. 10, Philadelphia. R. R. Je. 20, 1828.
Holliday, Maria T. to Dr. Wm. T. Hendon of Greene county, Dec., Newbern. R. R. Dec. 23, 1828.
Holmes, Rebecca S. to Richard Harriss, Je. 10, Brunswick county. R. R. Jly. 22, 1828.
Hooper, Eliza to John Hooper, Je. 17, Lincoln county. R. R. Jly. 11, 1828.
Hooper, John to Eliza Hooper, Je. 17, Lincoln county. R. R. Jly. 11, 1828.
Hopkins, Daniel to Mrs. Jenkins, Dec. 28, Edgecombe county. R. R. Jan. 22, 1828.
Hornaday, Rebecca to Samuel Hill, Apr., Orange county. R. R. Apr. 15, 1828.
Howell, Eliza Ann of Phila. to Frederic A. Hinton of this State, Je. 10, Philadelphia. R. R. Je. 20, 1828.
Houze, Thomas Y. to Frances Pickett, Sept. 25, Wadesborough. R. R. Oct. 14, 1828.
Hudler, Amos to Frances Tignor, Feb. 19, Newbern. R. R. Feb. 22, 1828.
Hughes, Dr. Isaac to Eliza Ann M'Lin, Dec., Newbern. R. R. Dec. 12, 1828.
Infield, Redmond to Elizabeth Freshwater, My., Wilmington. R. R. My. 13, 1828.
Ingalls, Capt. John to Ann Catharine Williams, Mar. 20, Newbern. R. R. Mar. 21, 1828.
Jackson, Micajah to Miss Temperance Ricks, Jan. 22, Edgecombe county. R. R. Feb. 8, 1828.
Jasper, Henry N. of Washington, Beaufort county to Mrs. Sarah Fenner of Franklin county, Sept. 17. R. R. Oct. 14, 1828.
Jenkins, Mrs. to Daniel Hopkins, Dec. 28, Edgecombe county. R. R. Jan. 22, 1828.
Johnson, John to Eliza Webb, Sept. 18, Rowan county. R. R. Oct. 14, 1828.
Johnston, Matilda to Charles Churchill of Connecticut, Sept. 11, Iredell county. R. R. Oct. 10, 1828.
Jones, Ann Eliza to James Edward Henry, Je. 25, Wilkes county. R. R. Jly. 22, 1828.

Jones, Henry L. to Mary E. Ferguson, Jly. 29, Fayetteville. R. R. Aug. 5, 1828.
Jones, Louisa to Ashley Saunders of Johnston county, Nov., Raleigh. R. R. Nov. 14, 1828.
Jones, Dr. Wm. to Harriet Burt, Jan. 16, Granville county. R. R. Jan. 25, 1828.
Josey, Harriet to Henry Gunter, Jan., Halifax county. R. R. Jan. 22, 1828.
Kenan, Augustus H. to Henrietta Green Alston, Je. 19, Georgia. R. R. Jly. 11, 1828.
Kerr, Whitfield of Statesville to Maria Louisa Wilson of Wilkesborough, Sept. 5, Wilkesborough. R. R. Sept. 23, 1828.
King, Willy to Willie Cook, Sept. 26, Wake county. R. R. Sept. 30, 1828.
Kirkman, Jane of Randolph county to William Stephenson of Guilford county, Nov. 6. R. R. Dec. 2, 1828.
Knox, Robert M. to Rebecca Crawford, Je., Elizabeth City. R. R. Je. 13, 1828.
Lamb, James to Ann Ozborne, Nov. 13, Randolph county. R. R. Dec. 2, 1828.
Landsdale, Mrs. Abigail to John Culpepper of this State, Apr. 27, Montgomery county, Md. R. R. Je. 10, 1828.
Latham, Harriet to Joseph G. Boon, Sept. 25, Johnston county. R. R. Oct. 7, 1828.
Lemay, Susannah F. to Nelson Philips of Hillsboro, Oct. 29, Lemay's X. Roads. R. R. Nov. 18, 1828.
Lemay, Thomas J. Jr. to Eliza Ann Sledge, My. 14, Franklin county. R. R. My. 20, 1828.
Leonard, Charity to Nathan Stanley of Guilford county, Nov. 6. R. R. Dec. 2, 1828.
Lewis, Emily A. to James Speed of Virginia, Dec. 24, Granville county. R. R. Jan. 25, 1828.
Lewis, Toby of Dumplintown to Mrs. Martha Branch, Jan., Halifax county. R. R. Jan. 29, 1828.
Lide, Eli H. of Darlington District, S. C. to Dorcas Jane Alexander, Dec. 4, Mecklenburg county. R. R. Jan. 14, 1828.
Lightfoot Caroline to James C. Mitchell, My. 2, Chatham county. R. R. Je. 3, 1828.
Lilly, Edmund F. of Montgomery county to Catharine Shaw, Apr., Cumberland county. R. R. Apr. 8, 1828.
Little, William of Stantonsburg to Temperance Speight, Mar. 27, Greene county. R. R. Apr. 11, 1828.
Lindsay, Laura A. to John D. Clancy, Mar. 20, Greensborough. R. R. Mar. 25, 1828.
Lindsay, Esther to Jesse Hargrave, Sept. 4, Davidson county. R. R. Sept. 23, 1828.
Lock, Henrietta R. M. to James West, Jan. 16, Granville county. R. R. Jan. 25, 1828.
Lynch, Lemuel of Hillsborough to Margaret Palmer of Orange county, Oct. 2. R. R. Oct. 7, 1828.
Lynch, Mrs. to Willie Bradley, Jan. 22, Edgecombe county. R. R. Feb. 8, 1828.

Lynch, Seburn to Eliza Craig, Oct., Orange county. R. R. Oct. 14, 1828.
M'Cay, Frederick to Eliza Creech, Mar. 4, Greene county. R. R. Mar. 28, 1828.
M'Collum, Mary to Joseph W. Marshall, Jan. 29, Hillsborough. R. R. Feb. 12, 1828.
M'Cullock, Mary to Jacob Propst, Apr. 1, Lincolnton. R. R. Apr. 29, 1828.
M'Cuiston, Sarah to William Unthank, Sept. 25, Guilford county. R. R. Sept. 26, 1828.
M'Lin, Eliza Ann to Dr. Isaac Hughes, Dec., Newbern. R. R. Dec. 12, 1828.
Macon, Elizabeth to John C. Green, Jr. Jan. 31, Warren county. R. R. Feb. 8, 1828.
Mahler, Peter to Susan Neal of Orange county, Jly., Tuscaloosa, Alabama. R. R. Jly. 22, 1828.
Manning, Adeline to Alexander Spence, Jan., Edenton. R. R. Jan. 22, 1828.
Marble, Jarvis to Harriet Robeson, Jan. 3, Guilford county. R. R. Jan. 22, 1828.
Mason, John M. of Raleigh to Theresa A. T. Hicks of Franklin county. Sept. 3, Franklin county. R. R. Sept. 9, 1828.
Marshall, Joseph W. of Milton to Mary M'Collum, Jan. 29, Hillsborough. R. R. Feb. 12, 1828.
Mayo, Frederick to Manisia Ganer Menetta Anders Sylvester Maivia Lewellen, Sherrard, Mar. 27, Edgecombe ocunty. R. R. Apr. 11, 1828.
Merrit, John to Susan Verell, Nov. 27, Beaufort. R. R. Dec. 12, 1828.
Mitchell, James C. to Caroline Lightfoot, My. 2, Chatham county. R. R. Je. 3, 1828.
Moore, Bartholomew to Louise Boddie, Dec. 2, Nash county. R. R. Dec. 12, 1828.
Moore, Edward to Eliza Franklin, Dec. 19, Granville county. R. R. Jan. 25, 1828.
Moore, Eliza F. to Archibald Douglass of Fayetteville. My., Lumberton. R. R. Je. 3, 1828.
Moore, Wesley to Ann Pitwood, Jan. 16, Granville county. R. R. Jan. 25, 1828.
Moss, Eliza B. to Dr. W. W. Turner, Dec. 11, Randolph county. R. R. Jan. 14, 1828.
Nail, Melinda to Jesse A. Clement, Jan. 1, Salisbury. R. R. Jan. 14, 1828.
Neal, Susan of Orange county to Peter Mahler, Jly., Tuscaloosa, Alabama. R. R. Jly. 22, 1828.
Newland, James to Martha Deloach, Oct. 23, Raleigh. R. R. Oct. 28, 1828.
Nicholas, Anness to Lemuel Cole, Jly. 3, Wake county. R. R. Jly. 22, 1828.
Norcom, Dr. John of Plymouth to Ann Eunice Walker, Dec. 17, Washington county. R. R. Jan. 25, 1828.
Norment, Rev. John H. to Mary Ann Spear, Jly. 17, Hillsboro. R. R. Jly. 22, 1828.
Ormond, Mary to Washington Dixon, Jan. 13, Greene county. R. R. Jan. 25, 1828.
Osmond, Margaret to James Albritton, Jr. Dec. 11, Greene county. R. R. Jan. 8, 1828.
Osborne, Ann to James Lamb, Nov. 13, Randolph county. R. R. Dec. 2, 1828.

Ozmount, Tho's to Abigail Parker, My. 10, Guilford county. R. R. Je. 3, 1828.
Palmer, Margaret of Orange county to Lemuel Lynch of Hillsborough, Oct. 2. R. R. Oct. 7, 1828.
Parker, Abigail to Tho's Ozmount, My. 10, Guilford county. R. R. Je. 3, 1828.
Patterson, Sarah M. to John C. Rhodes, Jan. 8, Orange county. R. R. Jan. 25, 1828.
Patton, James W. of Asheville to Jane Clarissa Walton, Jan. 24, Morganton. R. R. Feb. 26, 1828.
Pearce, Margaret to Rich'd B. Richards, Jan. 17, Halifax county. R. R. Jan. 29, 1828.
Peguese, Mary S. of Anson county to Dr. George W. Dismukes, Anson county, My. 6, Wadesborough. R. R. My. 25, 1828.
Pender, John to Sylvia Harrell, Jan. 22, Edgecombe county. R. R. Feb. 8, 1828.
Perkins, Elisha to Elizabeth Sherrill, Jan. 31, Lincoln county. R. R. Feb. 26, 1828.
Petway, Micajah to Elizabeth Skinner, Jan. 22, Edgecombe county. R. R. Feb. 8, 1828.
Philips, John to Mary Wilkins, Jan., Halifax county. R. R. Jan. 22, 1828.
Philips, Nelson of Hillsboro to Susannah F. Lemay, Oct. 29, Lemay's X. Roads. R. R. Nov. 18, 1828.
Phillips, Lucy T. of Wake county to Thomas M. D. Reed of Moore county, My. 13, Wake Forest. R. R. My. 16, 1828.
Phillips, Tho. to Louisa Clark, Je. 12, Orange county. R. R. Jly. 11, 1828.
Pickett, Eliza to Solomon Thompson, Feb., Orange county. R. R. Feb. 12, 1828.
Pickett, Frances to Thomas Y. Houze, Sept. 25, Wadesborough. R. R. Oct. 14, 1828.
Pitman, Mary Frances W. to Thomas L. B. Gregory, Oct. 7, Halifax county. R. R. Oct. 31, 1828.
Pitwood, Ann to Wesley Moore, Jan. 16, Granville county. R. R. Jan. 25, 1828.
Plummer, Dr. Henry L. to Sarah D. Faulkner, Je. 3, Warrenton. R. R. Je. 6, 1828.
Pool, Elizabeth to Peter M. Brown, Jan. 3, Salisbury. R. R. Jan. 14, 1828.
Pool, Logustin P. of Kentucky to Susannah Blanks, Jan. 18, Granville county. R. R. Jan. 25, 1828.
Pool, Nancy P. to Walter K. Daniel of Halifax, Va. Jan. 14, Granville county. R. R. Jan. 25, 1828.
Potter, Mary to Daniel B. Baker, Nov. 20, Smithville. R. R. Dec. 12, 1828.
Potter, Robert of Oxford to Isabella A. Taylor of Granville county, Apr. 9. R. R. Apr. 18, 1828.
Powell, Orra W. to R. W. Fuller of Lumberton, Feb. 19, Robeson county. R. R. Mar. 4, 1828.
Price, Fetney I. to Rev. Bennet T. Blake of Raleigh, Feb. 21, Raleigh. R. R. Feb. 26, 1828.
Propst, Jacob to Mary McCulloch, Apr. 1, Lincolnton. R. R. Apr. 29, 1828.
Raboteau, John S. Jr. of Raleigh to Esther Barclay, Jly. 13, Cumberland county. R. R. Jly. 18, 1828.

Read, Lydia M. to Joseph I. Simmons, Nov. 11, Halifax. R. R. Nov. 28, 1828.
Reed, Thomas M. D. of Moore county to Lucy T. Phillips of Wake county, My. 13, Wake Forest. R. R. My. 16, 1828.
Relfe, Mary Ann to James Elliott, Je., Elizabeth City. R. R. Je. 13, 1828.
Reeves, Hartwell to Tabitha Ellis, Aug. 14, Raleigh. R. R. Aug. 19, 1828.
Reinhardt, John to Sally Rogers, Sept. 25, Rowan county. R. R. Oct. 24, 1828.
Relay, Harriet to William C. Tucker, Je. 25, Raleigh. R. R. Je. 27, 1828.
Rendleman, Catharine of Rowan county to Solomon Dellinger of Lincoln county, My. 27. R. R. Je. 17, 1828.
Rhodes, John C. to Sarah M. Patterson, Jan. 8, Orange county. R. R. Jan. 25, 1828.
Rice, Nancy to Spencer Benson, Mar. 27, Rowan county. R. R. Apr. 29, 1828.
Richards, Rich'd B. to Margaret Pearce, Jan. 17, Halifax county. R. R. Jan. 29, 1828.
Ricks, Miss Temperance to Micajah Jackson, Jan. 22, Edgecombe county. R. R. Feb. 8, 1828.
Ridley, Mary to Thomas K. Speeler of Bertie county, My. 22, Granville county. R. R. Je. 3, 1828.
Roberson, Nancy to John Weeks, Jan. 8, Mecklenburg county. R. R. Jan. 29, 1828.
Robinson, Elizabeth to Alexander Gillespie, Feb. 7, Mecklenburg county. R. R. Mar. 4, 1828.
Robinson, Emeline to Isham A. Dumas of Richmond county, Mar. 5, Montgomery county. R. R. Mar. 25, 1828.
Rogers, Rutha M. of Stokes county to Alex B. Dearing of Rockingham. Nov. 13, Stokes county. R. R. Nov. 25, 1828.
Rose, Lavina to William H. Cumming of Greensboro, Jly. 10, Roxboro. R. R. Jly. 11, 1828.
Rothrock, Lydia to Charles Walk, Jan., Davidson county. R. R. Jan. 14, 1828.
Russel, Malachi of Elizabeth City to Sarah Butt, Aug., Norfolk. R. R. Aug. 29, 1828.
Russell, Susan to J. D. Young, Mar. 18, Newbern. R. R. Mar. 21, 1828.
Sanders, Ashley of Johnston county to Louisa Jones, Nov., Raleigh. R. R. Nov. 14, 1828.
Sawyer, Hon. Lemuel of this State to Mrs. Diana Fisher, Nov., Brooklyn, N. Y. R. R. Nov. 25, 1828.
Seawell, Charles M. of Fayetteville to Maria Collier, My. 10, Decatur county, Ga. R. R. Je. 3, 1828.
Seawell, John to Louisa Hendon of Raleigh, My., Tennessee. R. R. My. 30, 1828.
Shaw, Catharine to Edmund F. Lilly of Montgomery county, Apr., Cumberland county. R. R. Apr. 8, 1828.
Sherrard, Manisia Ganer Menetta Anders Sylvester Maivia Lewellen to Frederick Mayo, Mar. 27, Edgecombe county. R. R. Apr. 11, 1828.
Sherrill, Elizabeth to Elisha Perkins, Jan. 31, Lincoln county. R. R. Feb. 26, 1828.

Sherwood, Thomas A. to Mrs. Mark Taylor, Je., Elizabeth City. R. R. Je. 13, 1828.
Skinner, Elizabeth to Micajah Petway, Jan. 22, Edgecombe county. R. R. Feb. 8, 1828.
Slade, Ann Eliza of Warrenton to Wm. C. Dannelly, Jan. 24, Macon, Ga. R. R. Feb. 8, 1828.
Sledge, Eliza Ann to Thomas J. Lemay, Jr. My. 14, Franklin county. R. R. My. 20, 1828.
Smith, Edwin of Johnston county to Eliza A. Smith, Sept. 25, Wake county. R. R. Oct. 7, 1828.
Smith, Eliza A. to Edwin Smith of Johnston county, Sept. 25, Wake county. R. R. Oct. 7, 1828.
Smith, Eliza M. to John Elliott, My., Iredell county. R. R. My. 13, 1828.
Smith, James to Elizabeth Dowdy, Mar., Camden county. R. R. Apr. 1. 1828.
Smith, Margaret to James Currin, Dec. 27, Granville county. R. R. Jan. 25, 1828.
Smith, William R. of Halifax county to Susan Evans, Jan. 22, Edgecombe county. R. R. Jan. 29, 1828.
Spear, Capt. William A. of Anson county to Flora Wilkinson, My. 15, Robeson county. R. R. My. 27, 1828.
Spear, Mary Ann to Rev. John H. Norment, Jly. 17, Hillsboro. R. R. Jly. 22, 1828.
Spears, Geo. W. to Caroline E. Area, Oct. 7, Cabarrus county. R. R. Oct. 24, 1828.
Spied, James of Virginia to Emily A. Lewis, Dec. 24, Granville county. R. R. Jan. 25, 1828.
Speight, Temperance to William Little of Stantonsburg, Mar. 27, Greene county. R. R. Apr. 11, 1828.
Speller, Thomas K. of Bertie county to Mary Ridley, My. 22, Granville county. R. R. Je. 3, 1828.
Spence, Alexander to Adeline Manning, Jan., Edenton. R. R. Jan. 22, 1828.
Spruce, George to Mrs. Nancy Swain, Jan. 8, Guilford county. R. R. Jan. 22, 1828.
Stacy, Margaret to John Gowing, Feb. 14, Newbern. R. R. Feb. 22, 1828.
Stafford, Ann of Halifax to Thomas Blakely of Petersburg, Va. Oct. 13, Tarborough. R. R. Oct. 31, 1828.
Staley, Elijah to Fanny Field, Sept. 9, Randolph county. R. R. Oct. 3, 1828.
Standback, Martha to Whitson H. Chisholm of Montgomery county, Feb. 26, Richmond county. R. R. Mar. 28, 1828.
Stanley, Nathan to Charity Leonard of Guilford county, Nov. 6. R. R. Dec. 2, 1828.
Staton, Baker to Jeanette Young, Dec. 20, Edgecombe county. R. R. Jan. 22, 1828.
Stephenson, William of Guilford county to Jane Kirkman of Randolph county, Nov. 6. R. R. Dec. 2, 1828.
Strange, Tubal Early to Mary Ann Dotson, Jan. 10, Greensborough. R. R. Jan. 22, 1828.

Simmons, Joseph I. to Lydia M. Read, Nov. 11, Halifax. R. R. Nov. 28, 1828.
Swain, Mrs. Nancy to George Spruce, Jan. 8, Guilford county. R. R. Jan. 22, 1828.
Swaim, Nancy to Allen Swindle, Jan. 8, Randolph county. R. R. Jan. 25, 1828.
Swindle, Allen to Nancy Swaim, Jan. 8, Randolph county. R. R. Jan. 25, 1828.
Tarbaugh, Jacob to William Bost, Sept. 11, Lincoln county. R. R. Oct. 10, 1828.
Tate, Hugh A. to Fatima E. Forney, Jan. 3, Burke county. R. R. Jan. 29, 1828.
Taylor, Isabella of Granville county to Robert Potter of Oxford, Apr. 9. R. R. Apr. 18, 1828.
Taylor, Mrs. Mack to Thomas Sherwood, Je., Elizabeth City. R. R. Je. 13, 1828.
Tharp, Elizabeth to John Willis, Jly., Brunswick county. R. R. Jly. 11, 1828.
Thomas, N. H. to Laney Hillman, Jan. 17, Halifax county. R. R. Jan. 29, 1828.
Thompson, Solomon to Eliza Pickett, Feb., Orange county. R. R. Feb. 12, 1828.
Thorne, Mrs. Eliza of Halifax county to Dr. N. J. Drake of Nash county, Nov., Halifax county. R. R. Nov. 4, 1828.
Tignor, Frances to Amos Hudler, Feb. 19, Newbern. R. R. Feb. 22, 1828.
Torrans, Samuel to Sarah Jane Gavin, Mar. 20, Sampson county. R. R. Apr. 8, 1828.
Tucker, William C. to Harriet Relay, Je. 25, Raleigh. R. R. Je. 27, 1828.
Turner, Dr. W. W. T. to Eliza B. Moss, Jan. 11, Randolph county. R. R. Jan. 22, 1828.
Unthank, William to Sarah M'Cuiston, Sept. 25, Guilford county. R. R. Sept. 26, 1828.
Verell, Susan to John Merritt, Nov. 27, Beaufort. R. R. Dec. 12, 1828.
Walk, Charles to Lydia Rothrock, Jan., Davidson county. R. R. Jan. 14, 1828.
Walker, Ann Eunice to Dr. John Norcom of Plymouth, Dec. 17, Washington county. R. R. Jan. 25, 1828.
Walker, Elizabeth to Henry Guffy, Sept. 30, Rowan county. R. R. Oct. 31, 1828.
Walker, Sarah Jane of Wilmington to Edward J. Hale, My. 27, Fayetteville. R. R. My. 30, 1828.
Walton, Jane Clarissa to James W. Patton of Asheville, Jan. 24, Morganton. R. R. Feb. 26, 1828.
Walton, Pamelia S. to Alex'r F. Farrar, Jan. 3, Granville county. R. R. Jan. 25, 1828.
Waugh, Eliza A. to Daniel Courts, Apr. 3, Stokes county. R. R. Apr. 25, 1828.
Webb, Eliza to John Johnson, Sept. 18, Rowan county. R. R. Oct. 14, 1828.
Weeks, John to Nancy Roberson, Jan. 8, Mecklenburg county. R. R. Jan. 29, 1828.
West, James to Henrietta R. M. Lock, Jan. 16, Granville county. R. R. Jan. 25, 1828.

Westmoreland, Rhoda to Buckner Harnwell, My. 2, Lincoln county. R. R. Je. 17, 1828.
Whitaker, Calvin J. of Raleigh to Elizabeth H. Campbell, My. 6, Warrenton. R. R. My. 9, 1828.
Whitfield, George W. to Catharine Hart, Feb., Johnson county. R. R. Feb. 29, 1828.
Wiggins, Harriet to S. B. Carraway of Washington county, Jan. 10, Lenoir county. R. R. Jan. 25, 1828.
Wilhite, Eliza to George A. Childs, My. 1, Raleigh. R. R. My. 6, 1828.
Wilkerson, George W. to Emily Eaks, Jan. 16, Granville county. R. R. Jan. 25, 1828.
Wilkins, Mary to John Philips, Jan., Halifax county. R. R. Jan. 22, 1828.
Wilkinson, Flora to Capt. William A. Spear of Anson county, My. 15, Robeson county. R. R. My. 27, 1828.
Williams, Ann Catharine to Capt. John Ingalls, Mar. 20, Newbern. R. R. Mar. 21, 1828.
Williams, Mary Richard of Pitt county to Dr. John H. Drake of Nash county, My. 27, Pitt county. R. R. Jly. 11, 1828.
Williams, Mary T. to Mrs. S. H. Gee of Alabama, Nov., Warren county. R. R. Nov. 28, 1828.
Willis, John to Elizabeth Tharp, Jly., Brunswick county. R. R. Jly. 11, 1828.
Wilson, Maria Louisa of Wilkesborough to Whitfield Kerr of Statesville, Sept. 5. R. R. Sept. 23, 1828.
Wilson, Rebecca to James Wilson, Jan. 10, Guilford county. R. R. Jan. 25, 1828.
Wood, Wm. D. to Eliza J. Gould, Je. 17, Rowan county. R. R. Jly. 8, 1828.
Woodside, McDowell to Cornelia Curry, My. 29, Mecklenburg county. R. R. Je. 17, 1828.
Woodward, Elisha, Sr. to Tresse D. Berry, Je., Edgecombe county. R. R. Je. 10, 1828.
Young, J. D. to Susan Russell, Mar. 18, Newbern. R. R. Mar. 21, 1828.
Young, Jeanette to Baker Staton, Dec. 20, Edgecombe county. R. R. Jan. 22, 1828.

1829

Albea, Rensom to Hessey Robinson, Sept., Rowan county. R. R. Sept. 24, 1829.
Alexander, James to Mary M'Michael, Jan. 22, Guilford county. R. R. Jan. 30, 1829.
Alexander, Mrs. Mary to William Lucky, Dec. 18, Mecklenburg county. R. R. Jan. 9, 1829.
Alford, Jane to Samuel Rowan of South Carolina, Jan. 15, Robeson county. R. R. Jan. 23, 1829.
Allen, Darling of Anson county to Eliza Harrison, Dec. 22, Alleton, Montgomery county. R. R. Dec. 31, 1829.
Allen, Geo. to Mrs. Harriet Yancey of Raleigh, Jan. 15, Warren county. R. R. Jan. 23, 1829.
Allen, James V. to Eliza M. Johnson, My. 6, Halifax county. R. R. My. 29, 1829.

Alston, Col. Augustus of Sparta, Ga. to Miss M. H. Hawkins, Nov. 19, Warren county. R. R. Nov. 26, 1829.
Alston, Willis of Sparta to Elizabeth Sarah Howard of Greensborough, Ga. Dec. 18, Greensborough, Ga. R. R. Jan. 30, 1829.
Anderson, Joshua L. to Catharine Bradley, Dec. 25, Edgecombe county. R. R. Jan. 9, 1829.
Andrews, Alfred to Winifred Hyman, Mar. 12, Martin county. R. R. Mar. 27, 1829.
Andrews, John to Ellen Paschall, Jan. 22, Warren county. R. R. Feb. 13, 1829.
Apple, Eli to Mrs. Frances Rich, Je. 14, Orange county. R. R. Jly. 2, 1829.
Armfield, Lydia to John Bartlett, Sept., Guilford county. R. R. Sept. 17, 1829.
Attmore, George S. to Mary Taylor, Feb., Newbern. R. R. Feb. 20, 1829.
Austell, Rhody to John Pardue of Wilkes county, Jan. 15, Surry county. R. R. Feb. 13, 1829.
Bailey, Zebidie to Matilda Granberry, Jan. 1, Halifax county. R. R. Jan. 30, 1829.
Baker, Mary E. B. to Henry N. Howard, Feb. 24, Brunswick county. R. R. Mar. 20, 1829.
Banks, Adam G. of Wake county to Susan Leach of Johnston county, Je. 25, Johnston county. R. R. Jly. 2, 1829.
Banks, Thomas to Sarah Fletcher, Apr. 30, Perquimons county. R. R. My. 22, 1829.
Barnard, Caleb of Camden county to Polly Walker, Feb., Currituck county. R. R. Feb. 6, 1829.
Barnard, Margaret to Mr. Lemuel Cartwright, Feb., Camden county. R. R. Feb. 6, 1829.
Barnes, Lavinia D. to Whitmel Hill, Oct. 24, Halifax county. R. R. Dec. 3, 1829.
Barney, Geo. W. to Mary L. C. Haughton, Sept., Chowan county. R. R. Sept. 17, 1829.
Bartlett, John to Lydia Armfield, Sept., Guilford county. R. R. Sept. 17, 1829.
Battle, Catharine to Dr. John W. Lewis, Feb. 5, Edgecombe county. R. R. Feb. 20, 1829.
Bell, Felinda to John Smith of Newbern, Sept. 16, Hyde county. R. R. Oct. 1, 1829.
Bell, George to Martha Shakelford, Apr. 30, Onslow county. R. R. My. 29, 1829.
Bell, Lucretia to Barney Tisdale, Apr. 2, Elizabeth City. R. R. Apr. 17, 1829.
Bell, Mrs. Lucy to Henry Reeves of Northampton county, Jan. 22, Halifax county. R. R. Jan. 30, 1829.
Bell, Solomon of Carteret county to Betsy Ann Potter of Craven county, Mar. 26, Newbern. R. R. Apr. 10, 1829.
Bellamy, Dr. Edward C. to Ann B. Croom, Dec. 8, Lenoir county. R. R. Dec. 31, 1829.
Benbury, Mrs. Hannah to Col. Josiah M'Keel, Mar. 10, Chowan county. R. R. Mar. 27, 1829.
Berry, Elizabeth to Wm. Wilson. Feb., Camden county. R. R. Feb. 6, 1829.

Berry, Isaac to Matilda Sawyer, Mar. 26, Camden county. R. R. Apr. 17, 1829.
Bethel, Mary Ann to Samuel Moore of Caswell county, Feb., Rockingham. R. R. Feb. 27, 1829.
Bishop, Martha A. to Rev. Robert L. Caldwell of this State, Sept. 21, Prince Edward county, Va. R. R. Oct. 27, 1829.
Blanchard, Aletha of Duplin county to Thomas Torrans of Sampson county, Apr. 16. R. R. My. 1, 1829.
Blackwood, Mary to Jas. N. Strayhorn, Mar. 5, Orange county. R. R. Mar. 20, 1829.
Blount, Marietta to Col. Peter O. Picot, Dec. 3, Plymouth. R. R. Dec. 10, 1829.
Bond, Emily G. to David Lawrence of Tarboro, Oct., Greenville, Pitt county. R. R. Oct. 22, 1829.
Boon, Sarah of Johnston county to Christopher Christophers of Raleigh, Nov. 4, Johnston county. R. R. Nov. 12, 1829.
Borden, Benjamin of Carteret county to Margaret Hill, Feb. 19, Newbern. R. R. Feb. 27, 1829.
Borden, Mary Jane to Stephen Register, Oct. 1, Duplin county. R. R. Oct. 22, 1829.
Boswell, E. to William E. Hufham, Dec. 24, Pasquotank county. R. R. Jan. 9, 1829.
Bowdown, Elizabeth to Robert Smith of Franklin, Jan. 22, Warren county. R. R. Feb. 13, 1829.
Bozman, Mrs. Artimesia to William Jones of Perquimons county. Aug. 13, Gates county. R. R. Sept. 10, 1829.
Bradley, Catharine to Joshua Anderson, Dec. 25, Edgecombe county. R. R. Jan. 9, 1829.
Bradley, Mary G. to Edward H. Wingate, My. 7, Wilmington. R. R. My. 22, 1829.
Branch, William to Elizabeth Duncan, My. 14, Halifax county. R. R. My. 29, 1829.
Branson, Benjamin to Elvira Vestal, Sept., Chatham county. R. R. Oct. 1, 1829.
Bridges, Cilitha J. of Franklin county to John V. Crossland of Warrenton, Dec. 10, Franklin county. R. R. Dec. 24, 1829.
Bridges, Isaiah of Franklin county to Elizabeth Hutchins of Wake county, Nov. 17. R. R. Nov. 19, 1829.
Brinkley, Miles to Th. S. Stacey, Dec. 17, Perquimons county. R. R. Dec. 31, 1829.
Brockett, Mrs. Jane to Samuel Ferebee, Feb., Currituck county. R. R. Feb. 6, 1829.
Brown, Andrew to Mrs. James Minter, Jan. 22, Moore county. R. R. Jan. 30, 1829.
Brown, Sally to Michael Hileck, Nov. 12, Rowan county. R. R. Nov. 26, 1829.
Bruner, Edith to Daniel Gregory, Jan. 22, Rowan county. R. R. Feb. 13, 1829.
Bruner, Elizabeth to James Linn, Sept. 15, Rowan county. R. R. Nov. 5, 1829.

Bryan, Cynthia of Wilkes county to Benj. F. Petty of Alabama, Jan. 29. R. R. Feb. 27, 1829.
Bryan, Melton to Lucy Ann Lock, Oct. 8, New Hanover county. R. R. Oct. 22, 1829.
Bullock, Eliza to Walter A. Mangum of Orange county, Dec. 23, Franklin county. R. R. Dec. 31, 1829.
Bundy, William to Pherahee Murden, Jan. 22, Perquimons county. R. R. Feb. 20, 1829.
Burch, William F. to Charlotte St. George, Dec. 25, Wilmington. R. R. Jan. 9, 1829.
Burges, Mary to Adolph C. Eringhaus, Feb., Elizabeth city. R. R. Feb. 20, 1829.
Burgis, John M. to Mrs. Frances Underhill, Jan. 29, Halifax. R. R. Feb. 6, 1829.
Burgwyin, Margaret to Samuel I. Johnston, Sept. 30, Hillsboro. R. R. Oct. 1, 1829.
Burney, James of Columbus county to Sarah Coman, Je. 18, Raleigh. R. R. Je. 19, 1829.
Burr, Horace to Mary Jane Campbell, Nov., Wilmington. R. R. Nov. 12, 1829.
Burroughs, Thomas T. to Amelia H. Patterson, Jan. 29, Orange county. R. R. Feb. 13, 1829.
Buxton, Rev. Jarvis B. of Elizabeth City to Ann Cam of York county, Va. Oct. R. R. Nov. 5, 1829.
Byrum, Sally to James Hughs, My. 17, Bertie county. R. R. Je. 12, 1829.
Caldwell, Rev. Robert L. of this State to Martha A. Bishop, Sept. 21, Prince Edward county, Va. R. R. Oct. 29, 1829.
Callender, John R. to Anna H. Howard, Feb. 26, Wilmington. R. R. Mar. 20, 1829.
Cam, Ann of York county, Va. to Rev. Jarvis B. Buxton of Elizabeth City, Oct. R. R. Nov. 5, 1829.
Campbell, Mary Jane to Horace Burr, Nov., Wilmington. R. R. Nov. 12, 1829.
Carr, Lucilla to Thomas M. C. Prince of Chatham county, Sept., Edgecombe county. R. R. Sept. 4, 1829.
Carter, Isaac to Miss S. Hunt, Sept., Surry county. R. R. Sept. 24, 1828.
Carter, Sarah to Thomas Johnson of Iredell county. Jan., Surry county. R. R. Feb. 13, 1829.
Cartwright, Mrs. Lemuel to Margaret Barnard, Feb., Camden county. R. R. Feb. 6, 1829.
Cartwright, Mrs. Polly to David Williamson, Feb., Camden county. R. R. Feb. 6, 1829.
Castles, Margaret to Charles Ritchie, Jly. 16, Montgomery county. R. R. Aug. 20, 1829.
Cathart, James to Mary Kimble, Dec. 16, Charlotte. R. R. Jan. 9, 1829.
Causbee, Hance to Grace M. Cooper, Sept., Guilford county. R. R. Oct. 1, 1829.
Celly, John B. to Mary Rowan, Nov. 24, Rowan county. R. R. Dec. 10, 1829.
Chapman, James H. of Cumberland county to Ann Robinson, Feb., Bladen county. R. R. Feb. 13, 1829.

Cheairs, Ann E. to Philip D. Smith, Sept., Anson county. R. R. Sept. 17, 1829.
Chesher, Burch to Jane Headerson, My. 19, Mecklenburg county. R. R. Je. 5, 1829.
Christmas, John R. to Mary Thompson, Apr., Orange county. R. R. My. 1, 1829.
Christopher, Christophers of Raleigh to Sarah Boon of Johnston county, Nov. 4, Johnston county. R. R. Nov. 12, 1829.
Clark, Raney to Mathias Madren, Sept. 17, Pasquotank county. R. R. Oct. 8, 1829.
Clarke, William W. to Patsey Stevenson, Jan. 13, Newbern. R. R. Jan. 23, 1829.
Clay, Barbary to John Haase, Aug. 30, Lincoln county. R. R. Sept. 4, 1829.
Clingman, Alexander B. to Ann M. Clingman, Sept. 8, Surry county. R. R. Oct. 1, 1829.
Clingman, Ann M. to Alexander B. Clingman, Sept. 8, Surry county. R. R. Oct. 1, 1829.
Clitherall, Harriet Alexandrine to Major S. Spots of the U. S. Army, Oct. 14, Smithville, Brunswick county. R. R. Oct. 29, 1829.
Collier, Charles M. to Elizabeth Laws of Hampton, Va. Apr., Camden county. R. R. My. 1, 1829.
Collier, Elizabeth to John W. S. West, Feb. 12, Wayne county. R. R. Feb. 27, 1829.
Collins, Anthony to Sally Franklin, Sept., Surry county. R. R. Sept. 24, 1829.
Collins, Denis to Janette Griffith, Apr. 16, Wilmington. R. R. My. 1, 1829
Collins, Eveline to Eli Shuford, Je., Burke county. R. R. Jly. 2, 1829.
Collins, Mary M. to Matthew Page of Richmond, Va. Dec., Edenton. R. R. Dec. 31, 1829.
Coman, Sarah to James Burney of Columbus county. Je. 18, Raleigh. R. R. Je. 19, 1829.
Cooper, Grace M. to Hance Causbee, Sept., Guilford county. R. R. Oct. 1, 1829.
Copeland, Sarah to Alfred M. Gatlin, Dec., Perquimans county. R. R. Jan. 9, 1829.
Corbet, Margaret to S. Lewis, Dec. 24, Black River. R. R. Jan. 9, 1829.
Corsbie, John to Prudence S. Crose, Jan. 22, Guilford county. R. R. Jan. 30, 1829.
Cowan, James Jr. to Nancy Gillespie, Jan., Rowan county. R. R. Jan. 9, 1829.
Cowper, Eliza G. to Redmond R. Parker, Sept. 17, Murfreesboro. R. R. Oct. 1, 1829.
Craig, Charles to Mary A. Sneed, Dec. 18, Pasquotank county. R. R. Jan. 9, 1829.
Craig, Wm. to Nancy Weeks, Mar. 11, Wilmington. R. R. Mar. 27, 1829.
Cragin, Abner of Massachusetts to Martha Shepherd, Dec. 17, Elizabeth City. R. R. Dec. 31, 1829.
Crawford, Jane W. to James Leake, Feb., Rockingham county. R. R. Feb. 6, 1829.
Crawford, William D. to Christiana L. Mull, Jan. 20, Salisbury. R. R. Feb. 6, 1829.

Crawley, Harriet to Lemuel Johnston, Mar. 10, Johnston county. R. R. Mar. 20, 1829.
Creecy, Miss M. to Henry A. Skinner, Dec., Edenton. R. R. Dec. 10, 1829.
Cress, Absalom of Illinois to Catharine Fogleman, Sept. 9, Cabarrus county. R. R. Oct. 1, 1829.
Croom, Ann B. to Dr. Edward C. Bellamy, Dec. 8, Lenoir county. R. R. Dec. 31, 1829.
Croom, Richard to Winifred Whitfield, Apr. 9, Lenoir county. R. R. Apr. 17, 1829.
Crose, Prudence S. to John Corsbie, Jan. 22, Guilford county. R. R. Jan. 30, 1829.
Crossland, John V. of Warrenton to Cilitha J. Bridges of Franklin county, Dec. 10, Franklin county. R. R. Dec. 24, 1829.
Crowder, Isaac to Rachael Walton, Je., Wake county. R. R. Je. 5, 1829.
Cude, Ruhama to Marmaduke Thompson, Je. 16, Guilford county. R. R. Je. 26, 1829.
Curlin, Lydia to James Walker of Currituck county, Feb., Camden county. R. R. Feb. 6, 1829.
Daniel, Lewis to Pherebe Penny, Apr. 9, Wake county. R. R. My. 1, 1829.
Derossett, Dr. Armand J. Jr. to Eliza Jane Lord, My. 13, Wilmington. R. R. My. 29, 1829.
Deveng, Joseph G. to Catharine Hunt, Je., Rutherford county. R. R. Je. 12, 1829.
Dickerson, Nathaniel T. to Martha M'Tier, Dec., Rutherfordton. R. R. Jan. 9, 1829.
Dickson, Rachel to Samuel Sechler, Jly. 9, Rowan county. R. R. Aug. 6, 1829.
Dismukes, Mary J. to Reuben Pickett, Oct. 1, Anson county. R. R. Oct. 15, 1829.
Doak, Elizabeth to J. R. Paisley, Sept., Guilford county. R. R. Oct. 1, 1829.
Doby, Charlotte to Capt. Henry Hampton, Jan., Surry county. R. R. Feb. 13, 1829.
Dozier, Maria of Camden county to James Ferebee of Currituck county, Apr., Camden county. R. R. My. 1, 1829.
Dozier, Tully, Sr., to Tamozine Eustace, Dec., Camden county. R. R. Dec. 31, 1829.
Drake, Hartwell to Daniel Penery, Sept., Rowan county. R. R. Sept. 24, 1829.
Duke, Britton to Mary L. Purrington, My. 28, Scotland Neck. R. R.. Je. 26, 1829.
Duncan, Elizabeth to William Branch, My. 14, Halifax county. R. R. My. 29, 1829.
Dunn, Eliza Ann to Richard A. Wiggins of Madison county, Alabama. Sept. 17, Raleigh. R. R. Sept. 24, 1829.
Eason, Jane to Elijah Tuttle, My. 7, Germantown. R. R. My. 29, 1829.
Edmonds, Mary to Dr. G. A. Sykes, Sept., Northampton county. R. R. Sept. 17, 1829.
Edwards, Lucy A. to Mr. Palmer of Halifax, Va., Jly., Person county. R. R. Jly. 16, 1829.
Elmore, Nancy to Wm. Prior, My. 26, Halifax county. R. R. Je. 12, 1829.

Eliot, S. H. of York District, S. C. to Mary Smart, Oct. 8, Mecklenburg county. R. R. Nov. 12, 1829.
Ellerbee, Mary to Isaac H. Houze, Oct. 9, Wadesborough. R. R. Oct. 29, 1829.
Elliott, John to Mary Smith, Dec. 17, Cumberland county. R. R. Jan. 9, 1829.
Elliott, Joseph to Margaret White, Jan. 21, Perquimons county. R. R. Feb. 20, 1829.
Elliott, Polly to James Smith, Je., Beaufort county. R. R. Je. 12, 1829.
Erambert, Augustus, J. of Fayetteville to Martha Newberry, Apr. 14, Cumberland county. R. R. Apr. 17, 1829.
Eringhaus, Adolph C. to Mary Burges, Feb., Elizabeth City. R. R. Feb. 20, 1829.
Eure, Hillory to Mary Ann Minton, Oct. 8, New Hanover county. R. R. Oct. 29, 1829.
Eure, Mrs. Mary of Halifax county to Dr. Thomas W. Gregory of Northampton county, Oct. 24. R. R. Dec. 10, 1829.
Eustace, Tamozine to Tully Dozier, Sr. Dec., Camden county. R. R. Dec. 31, 1829.
Evason, Henry to Deborah Statia, Nov., Newbern. R. R. Nov. 12, 1829.
Farrish, Julia to Daniel M'Neill of Moore county, Oct. 1, Chatham county. R. R. Oct. 22, 1829.
Fenner, Juliana to David M'Knight, Nov., Jackson, Tenn. R. R. Nov. 12, 1829.
Ferebee, James of Currituck county to Maria Dozier of Camden county, Apr., Camden county. R. R. My. 1, 1829.
Ferebee, Samuel to Mrs. Jane Brockett, Feb., Currituck county. R. R. Feb. 6, 1829.
Ferebee, Thomas C. to Judith Mackey, Oct., Currituck county. R. R. Nov. 5, 1829.
Ferguson, Thomas of Newbern to Rebecca Wallace of Adams Creek, Jan. 1. R. R. Jan. 16, 1829.
Flemming, James to Mrs. Nancy Ann Pruet, Feb. 15, Lincoln county. R. R. Feb. 27, 1829.
Fletcher, Sarah to Thomas Banks, Apr. 30, Perquimans county. R. R. My. 22, 1829.
Fogleman, Catharine to Absalom Cress, Sept. 9, Cabarrus county. R. R. Oct. 1, 1829.
Forbes, Joshua of Camden county to Fanny Jennings, Dec., Pasquotank county. R. R. Jan. 9, 1829.
Fort, Lucy to William Roles, Jly. 23, Wake county. R. R. Aug. 6, 1829.
Fraley, Mrs. Betsey to John Grubb of Virginia, Jan. 25, Rowan county. R. R. Feb. 6, 1829.
Franklin, Mary C. of Surry county to Gabriel T. Moore of Stokes county, Sept. 24, Surry county. R. R. Oct. 22, 1829.
Franklin, Sally to Anthony Collins, Sept., Surry county. R. R. Sept. 24, 1829.
Frear, Henry to Mrs. Mary Johnston, Mar. 5, Halifax county. R. R. Mar. 20, 1829.
Freeland, Ann to James M'Causley, Nov., Orange county. R. R. Dec. 3, 1829.

Freeman, Rev. Josiah to Mrs. Mary Lord, Nov., Wilmington. R. R. Dec. 3, 1829.
Frohock, Mary of Rowan county to William C. Hazen, Nov., Tipton county, Tenn. R. R. Nov. 26, 1829.
Fulcher, Susan to Henry Haywood, Jly. 23, Williamston. R. R. Aug. 13, 1829.
Fuller, Lucretia to Jesse Peguin, Je. 16, Guilford county. R. R. Je. 26, 1829.
Gatlin, Alfred M. to Sarah Copeland, Dec., Perquimans county. R. R. Jan. 9, 1829.
Gee, Elizabeth H. to Wade West, Sept. 17, Halifax county. R. R. Oct. 1, 1829.
Gholson, Cary Ann to Thomas S. Gholson, My. 14, Washington. R. R. My. 22, 1829.
Gholson, Thomas S. of Brunswick, Va. to Cary Ann Gholson, My. 14, Washington. R. R. My. 22, 1829.
Gillespie, Nancy to James Cowan, Jan., Rowan county. R. R. Jan. 9, 1829.
Graham, Alexander of Charlotte to Mary Taylor, Jan. 29, Mecklenburg county. R. R. Feb. 27, 1829.
Granberry, Matilda to Zebidie Bailey, Jan. 1, Halifax county. R. R. Jan. 30, 1829.
Green, John to Sandal Lile, Jan. 27, Granville county. R. R. Jan. 30, 1829.
Gregory, Daniel to Mrs. Edith Bruner, Jan. 22, Rowan county. R. R. Feb. 13, 1829.
Gregory, Dr. Thomas W. of Northampton county to Mrs. Mary Eure of Halifax county, Oct. 24. R. R. Dec. 10, 1829.
Grice, Isaac C. to Martha Torrence, My., Sampson county. R. R. My. 22, 1829.
Grice, Susan B. to William Rogerson, My., Elizabeth City. R. R. My. 29, 1829.
Griffin, Lydia to Thomas Weeks, Jan. 22, Perquimans county. R. R. Feb. 20, 1829.
Griffin, Rebecca to John Small, Nov. 5, Cumberland county. R. R. Dec. 3, 1829.
Griffith, Jannette to Dennis Collins, Apr. 16, Wilmington. R. R. My. 1, 1829.
Grubb, John of Virginia to Mrs. Betsey Fraley, Jan. 25, Rowan county. R. R. Feb. 6, 1829.
Guess, Wm. W. to Frances Laws, Je. 11, Orange county. R. R. Jly. 2, 1829.
Gulley, William to Susan Hinds, Mar. 25, Duplin county. R. R. Apr. 10, 1829.
Gum, Dr. Allen to Minerva Henderson, Oct. 7, Caswell county. R. R. Oct. 29, 1829.
Haase, John to Barbary Clay, Aug. 30, Lincoln county. R. R. Sept. 4, 1829.
Hall, Rev'd James G. of Currituck county to Elizabeth Wood, Jly., Hertford, Perquimans county. R. R. Jly. 16, 1829.
Hall, John Jr. to Mary Hall, Dec. 8, Iredell county. R. R. Jan. 9, 1829.
Hall, Livia C. to Rev. William A. Hall, Dec. 8, Iredell county. R. R. Jan. 9, 1829.

Hall, Mary to John Hall, Jr. Dec. 3, Iredell county. R. R. Jan. 9, 1829.
Hall, Mildred F. to Maurice Waddell, Jan. 27, Brunswick county. R. R. Feb. 13, 1829.
Hall, Rev. William A. to Livia C. Hall, Dec. 8, Iredell county. R. R. Jan. 9, 1829.
Hall, Wm. L. to Sarah Watters, Feb. 12, Brunswick county. R. R. Feb. 27, 1829.
Hamilton, Euphemia to George S. M'Intosh of Savannah, Ga. My. 2, Granville county. R. R. My. 15, 1829.
Hampton, Capt. Henry G. to Charlotte Doby, Jan., Surry county. R. R. Feb. 13, 1829.
Handcock, Mary to James Wills of Edenton, Feb. 26, Newbern. R. R. Mar. 6, 1829.
Harrell, Winifred to Joseph Privet of Chowan county, May 21, Bertie county. R. R. Je. 12, 1829.
Harrison, Eliza to Darling Allen of Anson county, Dec. 22, Alleton, Montgomery county. R. R. Dec. 31, 1829.
Harrison, Rev. Wm. of Nova Scotia to Julia Merret of New Brunswick, Mar. 7, Murfreesboro. R. R. Mar. 27, 1829.
Harriss, Susan to Isaac Northrop, Sept., Wilmington. R. R. Sept. 17, 1829.
Hart, Adeline R. to Cyrus Simmons, Dec. 9, Statesville. R. R. Jan. 9, 1829.
Hartt, Mary J. N. to James B. Neely, Dec. 18, Mecklenburg county. R. R. Jan. 9, 1829.
Hartt, Thomas to Mary Thompson, My., Orange county. R. R. My. 29, 1829.
Hasell, Mrs. Eliza G. to Rev. Wm. S. Plummer, Je. 11, Hillsborough. R. R. Je. 19, 1829.
Haskett, Mrs. Mary to Henry Scott, Jan. 21, Perquimans county. R. R. Feb. 20, 1829.
Hatch, James of Jones county to Eliza Sears, Nov., Newbern. R. R. Nov. 12, 1829.
Hatrick, Samuel to Lucinda Wharton of Guilford county, Feb. 26. R. R. Mar. 6, 1829.
Haughton, Eliza to Robert R. Heath of Edenton, Feb. 9, Washington county. R. R. Feb. 27, 1829.
Haughton, Mary L. C. to Geo. W. Barney, Sept., Chowan county. R. R. Sept. 17, 1829.
Hauser, Henrietta Sophia to George F. Wilson, Je., Bethania. R. R. Jly. 2, 1829.
Hawkes, Rev. Francis L. to Olivia Hunt, Jan., New Haven. R. R. Jan. 16, 1829.
Hawkins, Miss M. H. to Col. Augustus Alston of Sparta, Ga. Nov. 19, Warren county. R. R. Nov. 26, 1829.
Hayne, Eliza W. to Col. William N. Parks, of Mecklenburg county, Apr. 2, Yorkville, S. C. R. R. My. 1, 1829.
Haywood, Henry to Susan Fulcher, Jly. 23, Williamston. R. R. Aug. 13, 1829.
Hazen, William C. to Mary Frohock of Rowan county, Nov., Tipton county, Tenn. R. R. Nov. 26, 1829.
Headerson, Jane to Burch Chester, My. 19, Mecklenburg county. R. R. Je. 5, 1829.

Heading, Sarah to David Patterson of Orange county, Mar. 5, Orange county. R. R. Mar. 20, 1829.
Heath, Robert R. of Edenton to Eliza Haughton, Feb. 9, Washington county. R. R. Feb. 27, 1829.
Henderson, Eliza to Jos. Pritchard, My. 31, Charlotte. R. R. Je. 19, 1829.
Henderson, Minerva to Dr. Allen Gunn, Oct. 7, Caswell county. R. R. Oct. 29, 1829.
Henley, Elias of Randolph county to Judith Mendenhall, Feb. 22, Guilford county. R. R. Mar. 6, 1829.
Henley, Susan to Joseph Merrett, Feb. 1, Halifax county. R. R. Feb. 13, 1829.
Herndon, Benjamin to Esther Smith, My. 17, Orange county. R. R. My. 29, 1829.
Hicks, Martha to John Huff, Je. 11, Stokes county. R. R. Jly. 2, 1829.
Hileck, Michael to Sally Brown, Nov. 12, Rowan county. R. R. Nov. 26, 1829.
Hill, Amanda A. to Dr. William M'Lean of Yorkville & Lincoln county, Apr. 2, York District, S. C. R. R. My. 1, 1829.
Hill, Margaret to Benjamin Borden of Carteret county, Feb. 19, Newbern. R. R. Feb. 27, 1829.
Hill, Whitmel to Lavinia D. Barnes, Oct. 24, Halifax county. R. R. Dec. 3, 1829.
Hinds, Susan to William Gulley, Mar. 25, Duplin county. R. R. Apr. 10, 1829.
Hodge, Capt. Arthur to Jane Perkins, My., Newbern. R. R. My. 15, 1829.
Hoffner, Margaret to Adam Powlass, Je. 11, Salisbury. R. R. Je. 26, 1829.
Hoke, Henry to Susan Hunsicker, Mar. 10, Lincoln county. R. R. Apr. 5, 1829.
Holley, Mary E. to Job Parker, Jly., Bertie county. R. R. Jly. 16, 1829.
Hollister, William to Jannett Taylor, Apr. 7, Newbern. R. R. Apr. 17, 1829.
Holmes, John to Caroline Wright, Dec. 17, Wilmington. R. R. Jan. 9, 1829.
Holtshauser, Jacob to Rachel Brown, Jan. 16, Rowan county. R. R. Feb. 13, 1829.
Hooker, Thomas to Nancy Jennings, Dec., Elizabeth City. R. R. Jan. 9, 1829.
Houze, Charlotte E. of Franklin county to Maj. James J. Thomas of Wadesboro, Dec. 3, Franklin county. R. R. Dec. 10, 1829.
Houze, Isaac H. to Mary Ellerbee, Oct. 9, Wadesborough. R. R. Oct. 29, 1829.
Howard, Anna H. to John R. Callender, Feb. 26, Wilmington. R. R. Mar. 20, 1829.
Howard, Elizabeth Sarah of Greensborough, Ga. to Willis Alston of Sparta, Dec. 18, Greensborough, Ga. R. R. Jan. 30, 1829.
Howard, Henry N. to Mary E. B. Baker, Feb. 24, Brunswick county. R. R. Mar. 20, 1829.
Huff, John to Martha Hicks, Je. 11, Stokes county. R. R. Jly. 2, 1829.
Hufham, William to E. Boswell, Dec. 24, Pasquotank county. R. R. Jan. 9, 1829.
Hughs, James to Sally Byrum, My. 17, Bertie county. R. R. Je. 12, 1829.

Hulin, William Jr. to Matilda Roberts, Dec. 23, Salisbury. R. R. Jan. 9, 1829.
Hunnings, Aquilla to Elizabeth B. Sawyer, My. 1, Elizabeth City. R. R. My. 29, 1829.
Humphreys, Nancy to Jacob Whittimore, Aug., Pasquotank county. R. R. Aug. 13, 1829.
Hunsicker, Susan to Henry Hoke, Mar. 10, Lincoln county. R. R. Apr. 5, 1829.
Hunt, Albert G. of Granville county to Louisa Rogers, Apr. 23, Wake county. R. R. My. 1, 1829.
Hunt, Catharine to Joseph G. Deveng, Je., Rutherford county. R. R. Je. 12, 1829.
Hunt, James to Diana Adelaide Martin, Jan., Wilkes county. R. R. Jan. 16, 1829.
Hunt, Olivia to Rev. Francis L. Hawkes, Jan., New Haven. R. R. Jan. 16, 1829.
Hunter, Reddick, to Narcissa Pullen, Mar. 5, Wake county. R. R. Mar. 6, 1829.
Hunter, Sarah E. A. to W. F. Riddick, Dec., Gates county. R. R. Dec. 31, 1829.
Hunter, Thos. B. to Emily Eliza Riddick, Feb. 5, Gates county. R. R. Feb. 20, 1829.
Hurt, Miss S. to Isaac Carter, Sept , Surry county. R. R. Sept. 24, 1829.
Hutchins, Elizabeth of Wake county to Isaiah Bridges of Franklin county, Nov. 17. R. R. Nov. 19, 1829.
Hyman, Winifred to Alfred Andrews, Mar. 12, Martin county. R. R. Mar. 27, 1829.
Ivey, Robert to Lucy L. Williams, Aug. 27, Halifax county. R. R. Sept. 10, 1829.
Jeffreys, George W. of Caswell county to Helen Jones, My. 27, Wake county. R. R. My. 29, 1829.
Jennings, Eleanor to John Pritchard, Dec. 17, Pasquotank county. R. R. Dec. 31, 1829.
Jennings, Mrs. Eliza to Joseph Lewis, Jan. 25, Mecklenburg county. R. R. Feb. 6, 1829.
Jennings, Fanny to Joshua Forbes of Camden county, Dec., Pasquotank county. R. R. Jan. 9, 1829.
Jennings, Nancy to Thomas Hooker, Dec., Elizabeth City. R. R. Jan. 9, 1829.
Jerkins, Jane to Emanual Whitfield, Sept., Washington. R. R. Sept. 17, 1829.
Jocelyn, Almerica to Frederick A. Moore, Sept. 17, New Hanover county. R. R. Oct. 1, 1829.
Johnson, Charles to Gilly Sisk, Jan., Surry county. R. R. Feb. 13, 1829.
Johnson, Eliza M. to Jane V. Allen, My. 6, Halifax county. R. R. My. 29, 1829.
Johnson, Frances M. to Capt. Wm. Malone, Sept. 3, Caswell county. R. R. Sept. 17, 1829.
Johnson, Thomas of Iredell county to Sarah Carter, Jan., Surry county. R. R. Feb. 13, 1829.

Johnston, Lemuel to Harriet Crawley, Mar. 10, Johnston county. R. R. Mar. 20, 1829.
Johnston, Mrs. Mary to Henry Frear, Mar. 5, Halifax county. R. R. Mar. 20, 1829.
Johnston, Samuel I. of Northampton county to Margaret Burgwin, Sept. 30, Hillsboro. R. R. Oct. 1, 1829.
Jones, Edward S. of Onslow county to Sarah Roberts, Mar. 26, Jones county. R. R. Apr. 10, 1829.
Jones, Helen to George W. Jeffreys of Caswell county, My. 27, Wake county. R. R. My. 29, 1829.
Jones, Indiana to Dr. Horace T. Royster of Williamsborough, Sept. 9, Granville county. R. R. Sept. 17, 1829.
Jones, John D. to Louisa Price, Apr. 8, Wilmington. R. R. My. 15, 1829.
Jones, William of Perquimans county to Mrs. Artimesia Bozman, Aug. 13, Gates county. R. R. Sept. 10, 1829.
Keller, Henry of Newman to Ann B. Stokes of Oglethorpe county, Mar. 1, Coweta, Ga. R. R. Mar. 27, 1829.
Kelly, Charles to Sally A. Pearce, Feb. 12, Swift Creek. R. R. Mar. 6, 1829.
Kern, David of Rowan county to Mary Ann Robards, Feb. 19, Granville county. R. R. Feb. 27, 1829.
Kewell, Mary to Benjamin Williams, Je., Tarborough. R. R. Je. 5, 1829.
Kilpatrick, Rufus to Eliza Young, Jan. 8, Rowan county. R. R. Jan. 23, 1829.
Kimble, Mary to James Cathcart, Dec. 16, Charlotte. R. R. Jan. 9, 1829.
King, Eliza Caroline to Alfred Williams, Feb. 24, Raleigh. R. R. Feb. 27, 1829.
Kirk, Franklin to Elizabeth O'Daniel, Oct. 8, Orange county. R. R. Oct. 29, 1829.
Kirkland, John U. of Hillsboro to Elizabeth A. Simpson, Feb. 19, Newbern. R. R. Feb. 27, 1829.
Kithcart, James to Mary Kimble, Dec. 16, Charlotte. R. R. Jan. 9, 1829.
Knight, Charles C. to Louisiana Lawrence, Dec. 22, Edgecombe county. R. R. Jan. 9, 1829.
Lamb, Charles J. H. to Sarah Sanderson, Jly. 28, Hyde county. R. R. Aug. 20, 1829.
Lammon, Elizabeth to Angus M'Donald, Jly., Robeson county. R. R. Jly. 30, 1829.
Langley, Cherry to Joshua Williams, My. 23, Edgecombe county. R. R. Jly. 2, 1829.
Larkins, James M. of New Hanover county to Miss S. E. Pearsall, Mar. 3, Duplin county. R. R. Mar. 27, 1829.
Lawrence, Catharine B. to Wm. Nickels, Jan. 29, Scotland Neck. R. R. Feb. 13, 1829.
Lawrence, David of Tarboro to Emily G. Bond, Oct., Greenville, Pitt county. R. R. Oct. 22, 1829.
Lawrence, Louisiana to Charles C. Knight, Dec. 22, Edgecombe county. R. R. Jan. 9, 1829.
Laws, Elizabeth of Hampton, Va. to Charles M. Collier, Apr., Camden county. R. R. My. 1, 1829.

Laws, Frances to Wm. W. Guess, Je. 11, Orange county. R. R. Jly. 2, 1829.
Leach, Susan of Johnston county to Adams G. Banks of Wake county, Je. 25, Johnston county. R. R. Jly. 2, 1829.
Leak, Eliza to Clement Marshall, Oct. 15, Rockingham, Richmond county. R. R. Oct. 22, 1829.
Leake, James to Jane W. Crawford, Feb., Rockingham, Richmond county. R. R. Feb. 6, 1829.
Leary, Tamer to Lieut. John Manning of U. S. Navy, Apr., Edenton. R. R. My. 1, 1829.
Ledwell, D. to Hannah Pool, Jan. 18, Rowan county. R. R. Feb. 6, 1829.
Legrand, Wm. C. to Jane Paul, Mar. 11, Anson county. R. R. Apr. 5, 1829.
Leigh, Eliza to John P. Perkins, Apr., Haywood county. R. R. Apr. 24, 1829.
Lemon, Eliza P. to Lewis Plum, Aug., Salem. R. R. Sept. 4, 1829.
Levy, George C. to Jane D. Savage, Dec. 24, Raleigh. R. R. Dec. 31, 1829.
Lewis, Dr. John W. to Catharine Battle, Feb. 5, Elgecombe county. R. R. Feb. 20, 1829.
Lewis, Joseph to Mrs. Eliza Jennings, Jan. 25, Mecklenburg county. R. R. Feb. 6, 1829.
Lewis, Priscilla to Uriah W. Skinner, My. 6, Halifax county. R. R. My. 29, 1829.
Lewis, S. to Margaret Ann Corbet, Dec. 24, Black River. R. R. Jan. 9, 1829.
Liles, Sandal to John Green, Jan. 27, Granville county. R. R. Jan. 30, 1829.
Liles, Elizabeth C. to Nelson P. Liles, Oct. 20, Anson county. R. R. Oct. 29, 1829.
Liles, Nelson P. to Elizabeth C. Liles, Oct. 20, Anson county. R. R. Oct. 29, 1829.
Lindsay, Mrs. Jane of Pasquotank county to Jonathan Lindsay of Currituck county, Jan. 8. R. R. Feb. 6, 1829.
Lindsay, Jonathan of Currituck county to Mrs. Jane Lindsay of Pasquotank county, Jan. 8. R. R. Feb. 6, 1829.
Lock, Lucy Ann to Melton Bryan, Oct. 8, New Hanover county. R. R. Oct. 22, 1829.
Long, William W. to Judith Oakes of Greensboro, Je., Rowan county. R. R. Je. 12, 1829.
Lord, Eliza Jane to Dr. Armand J. Derosett, My. 13, Wilmington. R. R. My. 29, 1829.
Lord, Mrs. Mary to Rev. Josiah Freeman, Nov., Wilmington. R. R. Dec. 3, 1829.
Lory, William F. to Mrs. Celia Mitchell, My., Pasquotank county. R. R. My. 22, 1829.
Lucky, William to Mrs. Mary Alexander, Dec. 18, Mecklenburg county. R. R. Jan. 9, 1829.
Luin, James to Elizabeth Bruner, Sept. 15, Rowan county. R. R. Nov. 5, 1829.
M'Aden, Dr. H. to Bartlett Yancey, Nov. 4, Caswell county. R. R. Nov. 12, 1829.

M"Cauley, James to Ann Freeland, Nov., Orange county. R. R. Dec. 3, 1829.

M'Clenahan, Dr. Spence to Sarah A. Taylor, My. 30, Chatham county. R. R. Je. 5, 1829.

M'Cullers, Martha M'Kinnia to Simon Smith, Sept., Wake county. R. R. Sept. 24, 1829.

M'Daniel, Starling to Margaret Moore, Aug., Montgomery county. R. R. Aug. 6, 1829.

M'Donald, Angus to Elizabeth Lammon, Jly., Robeson county. R. R. Jly. 30, 1829.

M'Duffie, Hon. George to Mary Rebecca Singleton, Sumter District, S. C. My. 27, Rutherford county. R. R. Je. 12, 1829.

M'Farland, Martha of New Hanover county to Geo. W. Pollock of Onslow county, Mar. 12, Topsail Sound. R. R. Mar. 27, 1829.

M'Guire, Penelope to Wm. S. Wills, Sept. 23, Gates county. R. R. Oct. 1, 1829.

M'Intosh, George S. of Savannah, Ga. to Euphemia A. Hamilton, My. 2, Granville county. R. R. My. 15, 1829.

M'Kay, Dr. John of Robeson county to Mary M'Neil, Feb. 24, Cumberland county. R. R. Feb. 27, 1829.

M'Keel, Col. Josiah to Mrs. Nannah Benbury, Mar. 10, Chowan county. R. R. Mar. 27, 1829.

M'Kethen, Sophia Ann to Th. D. Williams of Wilmington, Mar. 5, Brunswick county. R. R. Mar. 27, 1829.

M'Knight, David to Juliana Fenner, Nov., Jackson, Tenn. R. R. Nov. 12, 1829.

M'Lean, John C. to Rebecca Rankin, Mar. 19, Guilford county. R. R. Mar. 20, 1829.

M'Lean, Dr. William of Yorkville & Lincoln county to Amanda A. Hill, Apr. 2, York District, S. C. R. R. My. 1, 1829.

M'Lendon, James to Jane Thally, Apr. 7, Rocky Point. R. R. Apr. 24, 1829.

M'Leod, Jane of Iredell county to John M'Leod of Burke county, Feb. 15. R. R. Feb. 17, 1829.

M'Leod, John of Burke county to Jane M'Leod of Iredell county, Feb. 15. R. R. Feb. 17, 1829.

M'Michael, Mary to James Alexander, Jan. 22, Guilford county. R. R. Jan. 30, 1829.

M'Millan, Catharine to Neill Smith of Robeson county, Oct. 8, Laurel Hill, Richmond county. R. R. Oct. 15, 1829.

M'Neil, Mary to Dr. John M'Kay of Robeson county, Feb. 24, Cumberland county. R. R. Feb. 27, 1829.

M'Neill, Daniel of Moore county to Julia Farrish, Oct. 1, Chatham county. R. R. Oct. 22, 1829.

M'Ree, Lieut. Sam'l of the U. S. Army to Mary Wheaton, Wilmington, Apr. 9, Wilmington. R. R. Apr. 24, 1829.

M'Tier, Martha M. to Nathaniel T. Dickerson, Dec., Rutherfordton. R. R. Jan. 9, 1829.

Mackey, Judith to Thomas C. Ferebee, Oct., Currituck county. R. R. Nov. 5, 1829.

Madren, Mathias to Raney Clark, Sept. 17, Pasquotank county. R. R. Oct. 8, 1829.
Mainard, Edward to Delia Searls, Aug. 11, Raleigh. R. R. Aug. 13, 1829.
Malone, Capt. Wm. to Frances M. Johnson, Sept. 3, Caswell county. R. R. Sept. 17, 1829.
Mangum, Walter A. of Orange county to Eliza Bullock, Dec. 23, Franklin county. R. R. Dec. 31, 1829.
Manning, Lieut. John of U. S. Navy to Tamer Leary, Apr., Edenton. R. R. My. 1, 1829.
Marchant, Dr. Gideon C. to Mrs. Emily Trotman, Jan. 8, Camden county. R. R. Feb. 6, 1829.
Marshall, Catharine to Major Purdie Richardson of Brunswick county, Mar. 19, Anson county. R .R. Apr. 10, 1829.
Marshall, Clement to Eliza Leak, Oct. 15, Rockingham, Richmond county. R. R. Oct. 22, 1829.
Martin, Diana Adelaide to James Hunt, Jan., Wilkes county. R. R. Jan. 16, 1829.
Mathewson, Caroline to John Williams, Je., Tarborough. R. R. Je. 5, 1829.
Mendenhall, Judith to Elias Henley of Randolph county, Feb. 22, Guilford county. R. R. Mar. 6, 1829.
Merret, Joseph to Susan Henley, Feb. 1, Halifax county. R. R. Feb. 13, 1829.
Merrit, Julia of New Brunswick to Rev. Wm. Harrison of Novia Scotia, Mar. 7, Murfreesboro. R. R. Mar. 27, 1829.
Mickey, John S. to Gertrant E. Spach, Je. 11, Salem. R. R. Jly. 2, 1829.
Millikin, David J. to Antoinett E. Norfleet, My. 7, Halifax county. R. R. Jly. 9, 1829.
Minter, Mrs. James to Andrew Brown, Jan. 22, Moore county. R. R. Jan. 30, 1829.
Minton, Mary Ann to Hillory Eure, Oct. 8, New Hanover county. R. R. Oct. 29, 1829.
Mitchell, Mrs. Celia to William L. Lory, My., Pasquotank county. R. R. My. 22, 1829.
Mitchell, Mrs. Nancy to Capt. Willis Willcox, My. 26, Halifax county. R. R. Je. 12, 1829.
Mixon, Maria to Joseph Underhill, Dec., Chowan county. R. R. Dec. 10, 1829.
Moore, Frederick A. to Almerica Jocelyn, Sept. 17, New Hanover county. R. R. Oct. 1, 1829.
Moore, Gabriel T. of Stokes county to Mary C. Franklin of Surry county, Sept. 24, Surry county. R. R. Oct. 22, 1829.
Moore, Henry of Sampson county to Mary Smith of Lenoir county, Feb. 19, Duplin county. R. R. Mar. 6, 1829.
Moore, Margaret to Starling M'Daniel, Aug., Montgomery county. R. R. Aug. 6, 1829.
Moore, Samuel of Caswell county to Mary Ann Bethell, Feb., Rockingham. R. R. Feb. 27, 1829.
Morgan, Leartis to Julia Ann Tillery, Jan. 1, Halifax county. R. R. Jan. 30, 1829.

Morrison, Acenath to John Young, My. 14, Iredell county. R. R. Je. 5, 1829.
Mull, Christiana L. to William D. Crawford, Jan. 20, Salisbury. R. R. Feb. 6, 1829.
Murden, Pherahee to William Bundy, Jan. 22, Perquimans county. R. R. Feb. 20, 1829.
Murray, Julia Ann to Peter Trexler, My. 14, Iredell county. R. R. Je. 5, 1829.
Neely, James B. to Mary J. N. Hartt, Dec. 18, Mecklenburg county. R. R. Jan. 9, 1829.
Newberry, Martha to Augustus J. Erambert of Fayetteville, Apr. 14, Cumberland county. R. R. Apr. 17, 1829.
Nickels, Wm. to Catharine B. Lawrence, Jan. 29, Scotland Neck. R. R. Feb. 13, 1829.
Norfleets, Antoinett E. to David J. Millikin, My. 7, Halifax county. R. R. Jly. 9, 1829.
Norman, Rev. Simeon to Elizabeth Old, Jan. 22, Perquimans county. R. R. Feb. 17, 1829.
Norment, Thomas A. of Charlotte to Penelope K. Rowland, Jan. 28, Lumberton. R. R. Feb. 13, 1829.
Northrop, Isaac to Susan Harriss, Sept., Wilmington. R. R. Sept. 17, 1829.
Oakes, Judith of Greensboro to William W. Long, Je., Rowan county. R. R. Je. 12, 1829.
O'Daniel, Elizabeth to Franklin Kirk, Oct. 8, Orange county. R. R. Oct. 29, 1829.
Old, Elizabeth to Rev. Simeon Norman, Jan. 22, Perquimans county. R. R. Feb. 17, 1829.
Page, Matthew of Richmond, Va. to Mary M. Collins, Dec., Edenton. R. R. Dec. 31, 1829.
Paisley, J. R. to Elizabeth Doak, Sept., Guilford county. R. R. Oct. 1, 1829.
Palmer, Mr. of Halifax, Va. to Lucy A. Edwards, Jly., Person county. R. R. Jly. 16, 1829.
Pardue, John of Wilkes county to Rhody Anstill, Jan. 15, Surry county. R. R. Feb. 13, 1829.
Parker, Henry S. to Susan Pinkton, Je., Rowan county. R. R. Je. 12, 1829.
Parker, Job. to Mary E. Holley, Jly., Bertie county. R. R. Jly. 16, 1829.
Parker, Jno to Martha Tartt, Sept., Edgecombe county. R. R. Oct. 1, 1829.
Parker, Redmond R. to Eliza G. Cowper, Sept. 17, Murfreesboro. R. R. Oct. 1, 1829.
Parks, Col. William N. of Mecklenburg county to Eliza W. Hayne, Apr. 2, Yorkville, S. C. R. R. My. 1, 1829.
Paschall, Ellen to John Andrews, Jan. 22, Warren county. R. R. Feb. 13, 1829.
Patterson, Amelia H. to Thomas T. Burroughs, Jan. 29, Orange county. R. R. Feb. 13, 1829.
Patterson, David of Orange county to Sarah Heading, Mar. 5, Orange county. R. R. Mar. 20, 1829.
Paul, Jane to Wm. C. Legrand, Mar. 11, Anson county. R. R. Apr. 5, 1829.

Pearce, Sally A. to Charles Kelly, Feb. 12, Swift Creek. R. R. Mar. 6, 1829.
Pearce, Sally A. to Charles Kelly, Feb. 12, Swift Creek. R. R. Mar. 6, 1829.
Pearsall, Miss S. E. to James M. Larkins of New Hanover county, Mar. 3, Duplin county. R. R. Mar. 27, 1829.
Peguin, Jesse to Lucretia Fuller, Je. 16, Guilford county. R. R. Je. 26, 1829.
Peltier, Rosa to John M. Standin of Edenton, Jan. 25, Halifax. R. R. Feb. 6, 1829.
Penery, Daniel to Hartwell Drake, Sept., Rowan county. R. R. Sept. 24, 1829.
Pennington, Isaac to Abigail Sauls, Aug. 14, Wake county. R. R. Aug. 20, 1829.
Penny, Pherebe to Lewis Daniel, Apr. 9, Wake county. R. R. My. 1, 1829.
Perkins, Jane to Capt. Arthur Hodge, My., Newbern. R. R. My. 15, 1829.
Perkins, John P. to Eliza H. Leigh, Apr., Haywood county. R. R. Apr. 24, 1829.
Petty, Benj. F. of Alabama to Cynthia Bryan of Wilkes county. Jan. 29, R. R. Feb. 27, 1829.
Pickett, Reuben to Mary J. Dismukes, Oct. 1, Anson county. R. R. Oct. 15, 1829.
Picot, Col. Peter O. to Marietta Blount, Dec. 3, Plymouth. R. R. Dec. 10, 1829.
Pinkton, Susan to Henry S. Parker, Je., Rowan county. R. R. Je. 12, 1829.
Plum, Lewis to Eliza P. Lemon, Aug., Salem. R. R. Sept. 4, 1829.
Plummer, Rev. Wm. S. to Mrs. Eliza G. Hassell, Je. 11, Hillsborough. R. R. Je. 19, 1829.
Pollock, Geo. W. of Onslow county to Martha M'Farlane of New Hanover county, Mar. 12, Topsail Sound. R. R. Mar. 27, 1829.
Pool, Hannah to D. Ledwell, Jan. 18, Rowan county. R. R. Feb. 6, 1829.
Potter, Betsy Ann of Craven county to Solomon Bell of Carteret county, Mar. 26, Newbern. R. R. Apr. 10, 1829.
Powlass, Adam to Margaret Hoffner, Je. 11, Salisbury. R. R. Je. 26, 1829.
Price, Louisa to John D. Jones, Apr. 8, Wilmington. R. R. My. 15, 1829.
Prim, Elizabeth to Mr. Wells of Orange county, Sept., Randolph county. R. R. Sept. 17, 1829.
Prince, Thomas M. C. of Chatham county to Lucilla Carr, Sept., Edgecombe county. R. R. Sept. 4, 1829.
Prior, Wm. to Nancy Elmore, My. 26, Halifax county. R. R. Je. 12, 1829.
Pritchard, John to Eleanor Jennings, Dec. 17, Pasquotank county. R. R. Dec. 31, 1829.
Pritchard, Jos. to Eliza Henderson, My. 31, Charlotte. R. R. Je. 19, 1829.
Privet, Joseph of Chowan county to Winifred Harrell, My. 21, Bertie county. R. R. Je. 12, 1829.
Proby, Sarah to Henry Scott, My., Pasquotank county. R. R. My. 22, 1829.
Pruet, Mrs. Nancy Ann to James Fleming, Feb. 15, Lincoln county. R. R. Feb. 27, 1829.
Pullen, Narcissa to Reddick Hunter, Mar. 5, Wake county. R. R. Mar. 6, 1829.

Purrington, Mary L. to Britton Duke, My. 28, Scotland Neck. R. R. Je. 26, 1829.
Rankin, Rebecca to John C. M'Lean, Mar. 19, Guilford county. R. R. Mar. 20, 1829.
Reece, Mary to Hiram Spencer, Sept., Surry county. R. R. Sept. 24, 1829.
Reese, Agnes to Ezekiel R. Williams, Sept., Chatham county. R. R. Oct. 1, 1829.
Reeves, Henry of Northampton county to Mrs. Lucy Bell, Jan. 22, Halifax county. R. R. Jan. 30, 1829.
Register, Stephen to Mary Jane Borden, Oct. 1, Duplin county. R. R. Oct. 22, 1829.
Reinhardt, Col. Michael of Lincoln county to Maria Allen of Connecticut, Oct. 20, Lincolnton. R. R. Nov. 12, 1829.
Rhodes, Aquilla to Amelia White, Nov., Orange county. R. R. Dec. 3, 1829.
Rich, Mrs. Frances to Eli Apple, Je. 14, Orange county. R. R. Jly. 2, 1829.
Richardson, Major Purdie of Brunswick county to Catharine Marshall, Mar. 19, Anson county. R. R. Apr. 10, 1829.
Richardson, Sarah to Capt. Daniel Simpson, My., Elizabeth City. R. R. My. 22, 1829.
Riddick, Tho. B. to Emily Eliza Riddick, Feb. 5, Gates county. R. R. Feb. 20, 1829.
Riddick, W. F. to Sarah E. A. Hunter, Dec., Gates county. R. R. Dec. 31, 1829.
Ridley, John E. of Granville county to Amelia M. Toole of Franklin county, Sept. R. R. Sept. 24, 1829.
Ritchie, Charles to Margaret Castles, Jly. 16, Montgomery county. R. R. Aug. 20, 1829.
Robards, Mary Ann to David Kern of Rowan county, Feb. 19, Granville county. R. R. Feb. 27, 1829.
Roberts, Matilda to William Hulin, Jr. Dec. 23, Salisbury. R. R. Jan. 9, 1829.
Roberts, Sarah to Edward S. Jones of Onslow county. Mar. 26, Jones county. R. R. Apr. 10, 1829.
Robinson, Ann to James H. Chapman of Cumberland county, Feb., Bladen county. R. R. Feb. 13, 1829.
Robinson, Ann to James Wilson, Dec. 25, Masonboro Sound. R. R. Jan. 9, 1829.
Robinson, Hessey to Renson Albea, Sept., Rowan county. R. R. Sept. 24, 1829.
Rogers, Louisa to Albert G. Hunt of Granville county, Apr. 23, Wake county. R. R. My. 1, 1829.
Rogerson, William to Susan B. Grice, My., Elizabeth City. R. R. My. 29, 1829.
Roles, William to Lucy Fort, Jly. 23, Wake county. R. R. Aug. 6, 1829.
Rowan, Mary to John B. Celly, Nov. 24, Rowan county. R. R. Dec. 10, 1829.
Rowan, Samuel of South Carolina to Jane Alford, Jan. 15, Robeson county. R. R. Jan. 23, 1829.

Rowland, Penelope K. to Thomas A. Norment of Charlotte, Jan. 28, Lumberton. R. R. Feb. 13, 1829.
Royster, Dr. Horace T. of Williamsborough to Indiana Jones, Sept. 9, Granville county. R. R. Sept. 17, 1829.
St. George, Charlotte to William F. Burch, Dec. 25, Wilmington. R. R. Jan. 9, 1829.
Sanderson, Sarah to Charles J. H. Lamb, Jly. 28, Hyde county. R. R. Aug. 20, 1898.
Sauls, Abigail to Isaac Pennington, Aug. 14, Wake county. R. R. Aug. 20, 1829.
Savage, Jane D. to George C. Levy, Dec. 24, Raleigh. R. R. Dec. 31, 1829.
Sawyer, Frederick B. to Aquilla Hunnings, My. 10, Elizabeth City. R. R. My. 29, 1829.
Sawyer, John L. to Sarah Wright, Feb., Camden county. R. R. Feb. 6, 1829.
Sawyer, Matilda to Isaac Berry, Mar. 26, Camden county. R. R. Apr. 17, 1829.
Scott, Henry to Mrs. Mary Haskett, Jan. 21, Perquimans county. R. R. Feb. 20, 1829.
Scott, Henry to Sarah Proby, My., Pasquotank county. R. R. My. 22, 1829.
Scott, Sarah to Willis W. Wright, Apr. 2, Pasquotank county. R. R. Apr. 17, 1829.
Scott, William to Maria White, Feb. 15, Perquimans county. R. R. Feb. 20, 1829.
Searls, Delia to Edward Mainard, Aug. 11, Raleigh. R. R. Aug. 13, 1829.
Sears, Eliza to James Hatch of Jones county, Nov., Newbern. R. R. Nov. 12, 1829.
Sechler, Samuel to Rachel Dickson, Jly. 9, Rowan county. R. R. Aug. 6, 1829.
Sexton, Samuel to Susan Smith, Feb., Pasquotank county. R. R. Feb. 20, 1829.
Seymour, Capt. James M. of New York to Mary Caroline Vancleef, Nov. 11, Wilmington. R. R. Nov. 26, 1829.
Shackelford, Martha to George Bell, Apr. 30, Onslow county. R. R. My. 29, 1829.
Shaw, Catharine A. to David Shaw, Je. 18, Cumberland county. R. R. Jly. 2, 1829.
Shaw, David to Catharine A. Shaw, Je. 18, Cumberland county. R. R. Jly. 2, 1829.
Shepherd, Martha to Abner Cragin of Massachusetts, Dec. 17, Elizabeth City. R. R. Dec. 31, 1829.
Shuford, Eli to Eveline Collins, Je., Burke county. R. R. Jly. 2, 1829.
Simmons, Cyrus to Adeline R. Hart, Dec. 9, Statesville. R. R. Jan. 9, 1829.
Simpson, Capt. Daniel of Massachussetts to Sarah Richardson, My., Elizabeth City. R. R. My. 22, 1829.
Simpson, Elizabeth A. to John U. Kirkland of Hillsboro, Feb. 19, Newbern. R. R. Feb. 27, 1829.
Singleton, Mary Rebecca of Sumter District, S. C. to Hon. George M'Duffie of Rutherford county. R. R. Je. 12, 1829.
Sisk, Gilly to Charles Johnson, Jan., Surry county. R. R. Feb. 13, 1829.
Skinner, Henry A. to Miss M'Creecy, Dec., Edenton. R. R. Dec. 10, 1829.

Skinner, Uriah to Priscilla Lewis, My. 6, Halifax county. R. R. My. 29, 1829.
Small, John to Rebecca Griffin, Nov., Cumberland county. R. R. Dec. 3, 1829.
Smart, Mary to S. H. Elliott of York District, S. C. Oct. 8, Mecklenburg county. R. R. Nov. 12, 1829.
Smith, Esther to Benjamin Herndon, My. 17, Orange county. R. R. My. 29, 1829.
Smith, James to Polly Elliott, Je., Beaufort county. R. R. Je. 12, 1829.
Smith, John of Newbern to Felinda Bell, Sept. 16, Hyde county. R. R. Oct. 1, 1829.
Smith, Mary to John Elliott, Dec. 17, Cumberland county. R. R. Jan. 9, 1829.
Smith, Mary of Lenoir county to Henry Moore of Sampson county, Feb. 19, Duplin county. R. R. Mar. 6, 1829.
Smith, Neill of Robeson county to Catharine M'Millan, Oct. 8, Laurel Hill, Richmond county. R. R. Oct. 15, 1829.
Smith, Philip D. to Ann E. Cheairs, Sept., Anson county. R. R. Sept. 17, 1829.
Smith, Robt of Franklin county to Elizabeth Bowdown, Jan. 22, Warren county. R. R. Feb. 13, 1829.
Smith, Simon to Martha M'Kinna M'Cullers, Sept., Wake county. R. R. Sept. 24, 1829.
Smith, Susan to Samuel Sexton, Feb., Pasquotank county. R. R. Feb. 20, 1829.
Sneed, Mary A. to Charles Craig, Dec. 18, Pasquotank county. R. R. Jan. 9, 1829.
Spack, Gertraut E. to John S. Mickey, Je. 11, Salem. R. R. Jly. 2, 1829.
Spencer, Hiram to Mary Reece, Sept., Surry county. R. R. Sept. 24, 1829.
Spots, Major S. of U. S. Army to Harriet Alexandrine Clitherall, Oct. 14, Smithville, Brunswick county. R. R. Oct. 29, 1829.
Stacy, Th. S. to Mrs. Miles Brinkley, Dec. 17, Perquimans county. R. R. Dec. 31, 1829.
Standin, John M. of Edenton to Rosa Peltier, Jan. 25, Halifax. R. R. Feb. 6, 1829.
Stark, Oliver P. of Wilmington to Sarah Tillinghast, Oct. 8, Cumberland county. R. R. Oct. 15, 1829.
Statia, Deborah to Henry Evason, Nov., Newbern. R. R. Nov. 12, 1829.
Stevenson, Patsey to William W. Clarke, Jan. 13, Newbern. R. R. Jan. 23, 1829.
Stewart, Capt. David to Mary Watson, Jan. 15, Guilford county. R. R. Jan. 30, 1829.
Stokes, Ann B. of Oglethorpe county to Henry Keller of Newman, Ga. Mar. 1, Coweta county, Ga. R. R. Mar. 27, 1829.
Strayhorn, Jan. N. to Mary Blackwood, Mar. 5, Orange county. R. R. Mar. 20, 1829.
Sykes, Dr. G. A. to Mary Edmond, Sept., Northampton county. R. R. Sept. 17, 1829.
Tartt, Martha to Jno. Parker, Sept., Edgecombe county. R. R. Oct. 1, 1829.

Taylor, Jannett to William Hollister, Apr. 7, Newbern. R. R. Apr. 17, 1829.
Taylor, Mary to Alexander Graham of Charlotte, Jan. 29, Mecklenburg county. R. R. Feb. 27, 1829.
Taylor, Mary to George S. Attmore, Feb., Newbern. R. R. Feb. 20, 1829.
Taylor, Sarah A. to Dr. Spence M'Clenahan, My. 30, Chatham county. R. R. Je. 5, 1829.
Telfair, Margaret of Pitt county to Henry Toole of Tarborough, Oct. 20, Washington. R. R. Nov. 12, 1829.
Thally, Jane to James M'Lendon, Apr. 7, Rocky Point. R. R. Apr. 24, 1829.
Thomas, Maj. James J. of Wadesboro & Tennessee to Charlotte E. Houze of Franklin county, Dec. 3, Franklin county. R. R. Dec. 10, 1829.
Thompson, Marmaduke to Ruhama Cude, Je. 16, Guilford county. R. R. Je. 26, 1829.
Thompson, Mary to John R. Christmas, Apr., Orange county. R. R. My. 1, 1829.
Thompson, Mary to Thomas Hart, My., Orange county. R. R. My. 29, 1829.
Tillery, Julia Ann to Leartis Morgan, Jan. 1, Halifax county. R. R. Jan. 30, 1829.
Tillinghast, Sarah to Oliver P. Stark of Wilmington, Oct. 8, Cumberland county. R. R. Oct. 15, 1829.
Tisdale, Barney to Lucretia Bell, Apr. 2, Elizabeth City. R. R. Apr. 17, 1829.
Toole, Amelia M. of Franklin county to John E. Ridley of Granville county, Sept. R. R. Sept. 24, 1829.
Toole, Henry of Tarborough to Margaret Telfair of Pitt county, Oct. 20, Washington. R. R. Nov. 12, 1829.
Torrans, Thomas of Sampson county to Alitha Blanchard of Duplin county, Apr. 16. R. R. My. 1, 1829.
Torrence, Martha to Isaac C. Grice, My., Sampson county. R. R. My. 22, 1829.
Trexler, Peter to Julia Ann Murray, My. 14, Iredell county. R. R. Je. 5, 1829.
Trotman, Mrs. Emily to Dr. Gideon C. Marchant, Jan. 8, Camden county. R. R. Feb. 6, 1829.
Tuttle, Elijah to Jane Eason, My. 7, Germantown. R. R. My. 29, 1829.
Underhill, Mrs. Frances to John M. Burgis, Jan. 29, Halifax. R. R. Feb. 6, 1829.
Underhill, Joseph to Maria Mixon, Dec., Chowan county. R. R. Dec. 10, 1829.
Vancleef, Mary Caroline to Capt. James M. Seymour of New York, Nov. 11, Wilmington. R. R. Nov. 26, 1829.
Vestal, Elvira to Benjamin Bransom, Sept., Chatham county. R. R. Oct. 1, 1829.
Vines, Nancy to James Wilks, Oct. 29, Pitt county. R. R. Nov. 12, 1829.
Waddell, Maurice to Mildred F. Hall, Jan. 27, Brunswick county. R. R. Feb. 13, 1829.
Walker, James of Currituck county to Lydia Curlin, Feb., Camden county. R. R. Feb. 6, 1829.

Walker, Polly to Caleb Barnard of Camden county, Feb., Currituck county. R. R. Feb. 6, 1829.

Wallace, Rebecca of Adam's creek to Thomas Ferguson of Newbern, Jan. 1. R. R. Jan. 16, 1829.

Walton, Rachael to Isaac Crowder, Je., Wake county. R. R. Je. 5, 1829.

Watson, Mary to Capt. David Stewart, Jan. 15, Guilford county. R. R. Jan. 30, 1829.

Watters, Sarah to Wm. L. Hall, Feb. 12, Brunswick county. R. R. Feb. 27, 1829.

Waugh, Harrison M. to Mary M. Waugh, Jly. 9, Stokes county. R. R. Jly. 30, 1829.

Waugh, Mary to Harrison M. Waugh, Jly. 9, Stokes county. R. R. Jly. 30, 1829.

Weeks, Nancy to Wm. Craig, Mar. 11, Wilmington. R. R. Mar. 27, 1829.

Weeks, Thomas to Lydia Griffin, Jan. 22, Perquimans county. R. R. Feb. 20, 1829.

Wells, Mr. of Orange county to Elizabeth Prim, Sept., Randolph county. R. R. Sept. 17, 1829.

West, John W. S. of Lenoir county to Elizabeth Collier, Feb. 12, Wayne county. R. R. Feb. 27, 1829.

West, Wade to Elizabeth H. Gee, Sept. 17, Halifax county. R. R. Oct. 1, 1829.

Wharton, Lucinda of Guilford county to Samuel Hatrick, Feb. 26. R. R. Mar. 6, 1829.

Wheaton, Mary of Wilmington to Lieut. Sam'l M'Ree of the U. S. Army, Apr. 9, Wilmington. R. R. Apr. 24, 1829.

White, Amelia to Aquilla Rhodes, Nov., Orange county. R. R. Dec. 3, 1829.

White, Margaret to Joseph Elliott, Jan. 21, Perquimans county. R. R. Feb. 20, 1829.

White, Maria to William Scott, Feb. 14, Perquimans county. R. R. Feb. 20, 1829.

Whitfield, Emanuel to Jane Jerkins, Sept., Washington. R. R. Sept. 17, 1829.

Whitfield, Winifred to Richard Croom, Apr. 9, Lenoir county. R. R. Apr. 17, 1829.

Whittimore, Jacob to Nancy Humphreys, Aug., Pasquotank county. R. R. Aug. 13, 1829.

Wiggins, Richard A. of Madison county, Alabama to Eliza Ann Dunn, Sept. 17, Raleigh. R. R. Sept. 24, 1829.

Wilks, James to Nancy Vines, Oct. 29, Pitt county. R. R. Nov. 12, 1829.

Willcox, Capt. Willis to Mrs. Nancy Mitchell, My. 26, Halifax county. R. R. Je. 12, 1829.

Williams, Alfred to Eliza Caroline King, Feb. 24, Raleigh. R. R. Feb. 27, 1829.

Williams, Benjamin to Mary Kewell, Je., Tarborough. R. R. Je. 5, 1829.

Williams, Ezekiel R. to Agnes Reese, Sept., Chatham county. R. R. Oct. 1, 1829.

Williams, John to Caroline Mathewson, Je., Tarborough. R. R. Je. 5, 1829.

Williams, Joshua to Cherry Langley, My. 23, Edgecombe county. R. R. Jly. 2, 1829.
Williams, Lucy L. to Robert Ivey, Aug. 27, Halifax county. R. R. Sept. 10, 1829.
Williams, Th. D. of Wilmington to Sophia Ann M'Kethen, Mar. 5, Brunswick county. R. R. Mar. 27, 1829.
Williamson, David to Mrs. Polly Cartwright, Feb., Camden county. R. R. Feb. 6, 1829.
Wills, James of Edenton to Mary Handcock, Feb. 26, Newbern. R. R. Mar. 6, 1829.
Wills, Wm. S. to Penelope M'Guire, Sept. 23, Gates county. R. R. Oct. 1, 1829.
Wilson, George F. to Henrietta Sophia Hauser, Je., Bethania. R. R. Jly. 2, 1829.
Wilson, James to Ann Robinson, Dec. 25, Masonboro Sound. R. R. Jan. 9, 1829.
Wilson, Wm. to Elizabeth Berry, Feb., Camden county. R. R. Feb. 6, 1829.
Wingate, Edward H. to Mary G. Bradley, My. 7, Wilmington. R. R. My. 22, 1829.
Wood, Elizabeth to Rev'd. James G. Hall of Currituck county, Jly., Hertford, Perquimans county. R. R. Jly. 16, 1829.
Wright, Caroline to John Holmes, Dec. 17, Wilmington. R. R. Jan. 9, 1829.
Wright, Sarah to John L. Sawyer, Feb., Camden county. R. R. Feb. 6, 1829.
Wright, Willis W. of Virginia to Sarah Scott, Apr. 2, Pasquotank county. R. R. Apr. 17, 1829.
Yancey, Bartlett to Dr. H. M'Aden, Nov. 4, Caswell county. R. R. Nov. 12, 1829.
Yancey, Harriet of Raleigh to Geo. Allen, Jan. 15, Warren county. R. R. Jan. 23, 1829.
Young, Eliza to Rufus Kilpatrick, Jan. 8, Rowan county. R. R. Jan. 23, 1829.
Young, John to Acenath Morrison, My. 14, Iredell county. R. R. Je. 5, 1829.

1830

Adderton, Wm. to Amanda Hatch, Sept., Lexington. R. R. Sept. 9, 1830.
Alford, Susan to J. H. Hoffman, Dec. 5, Raleigh. R. R. Dec. 9, 1830.
Allen, Evelina to Jesse Johnston, Feb. 25, Halifax county. R. R. Apr. 8, 1830.
Allen, Jane to William J. Campbell, Mar. 18, Wilmington. R. R. Apr. 1, 1830.
Allen, Dr. John to Martha A. Whitted, Dec., Orange county. R. R. Dec. 9, 1830.
Allen, Col. Walter P. of Kinston to Mrs. S. Foy, My., Trenton, Jones county. R. R. My. 27, 1830.
Allison, Frances C. to Rev. Wm. G. H. Jones of Fayetteville, Apr., Petersburg. R. R. Apr. 29, 1830.

Allison, Robert G. of Iredell county to Harriet W. Chalmers, My. 30, Chapel Hill. R. R. My. 27, 1830.
Amis, Martha to Thomas Cheatham, Oxford. R. R. Nov. 11, 1830.
Anderson, Phoebe to Eaton Pullen, Dec., Halifax. R. R. Dec. 9, 1830.
Andrews, Otis of Beaufort county to Elizabeth Wheatley of Martin county. Feb. 11, Martin county. R. R. Mar. 11, 1830.
Armistead, Susan M. to Augustus Moore, Apr. 29, Edenton. R. R. My. 13, 1830.
Ashe, Elizabeth H. to Owen Holmes, Jan. 6, Wilmington. R. R. Jan. 21, 1830.
Austin, Martha of Tarborough to Rev. P. W. Dowd of Raleigh, Nov. R. R. Nov. 4, 1830.
Ayer, Gen. Henry W. to Sarah C. Salmon, Aug., Fayetteville. R. R. Sept. 2, 1830.
Bagley, Wm. of Perquimans county to Mary Newborn, My., Chowan county. R. R. My. 20, 1830.
Baldwin, Nathan to Melinda Hinshaw, Feb. 21, Guilford county. R. R. Mar. 11, 1830.
Banks, Thaddeus to Sarah Gregory, Sept., Pasquotank county. R. R. Oct. 7, 1830.
Banner, Martin to Mary Ogburn, Dec. 31, Stokes county. R. R. Feb. 4, 1830.
Barr, Jane Caroline to Col. John F. McCorkle, Nov., Rowan county. R. R. Mar. 11, 1830.
Barringer, Paul to Lovina Miller, Feb. 4, Rowan county. R. R. Mar. 11, 1830.
Barry, Richard to Miss Burns, Je. 15, Lincoln county. R. R. Jly. 15, 1830.
Battle, Amos J. to Margaret H. Parker, Jan. 7, Edgecombe county. R. R. Jan. 28, 1830.
Baxter, Ellen to John Hardin, Jan. 17, Rowan county. R. R. Mar. 11, 1830.
Beam, Louisa to Abraham Irvine, Apr., Rutherford county. R. R. Apr. 15, 1830.
Bedell, David H. of Burke county to Marina Wallace, Feb. 18, Iredell county. R. R. Mar. 11, 1830.
Bell, Emily to Thomas Cherry, Mar. 4, Tarborough. R. R. Mar. 25, 1830.
Bell, Mr. of Halifax, Va. to Martha Hughs, Feb. 17, Person county. R. R. Mar. 23, 1830.
Benford, John A. to Priscilla West, Dec., Halifax. R. R. Dec. 9, 1830.
Benson, Beauford to Julia Ann Blanchard, Apr. 8, Orange county. R. R. Apr. 29, 1830.
Berry, Dr. William A. to Ann Eliza Usher, Feb. 25, Wilmington. R. R. Apr. 8, 1830.
Bickering, William to Emma R. Peed, Nov., Washington, Beaufort county. R. R. Nov. 18, 1830.
Bidwell, Cyrus W. of Fayetteville to Harriet Gauze of Bladen county, My. 20, Bladen county. R. R. Je. 3, 1830.
Biggs, Joseph to Elizabeth Davis, Jly. 29, Robeson county. R. R. Aug. 12, 1830.
Blackwood, John to Polly M'Cauly, Apr. 13, Orange county. R. R. Apr. 29, 1830.
Blackwood, Margaret M. to John McCauley, Mar. 15, Orange county. R. R. Apr. 15, 1830.

Blanchard, Julia Ann to Beauford Benson, Apr. 8, Orange county. R. R. Apr. 29, 1830.
Blunt, Thomas D. to Mary R. Blunt of Southampton, Va. Jly. 21, Granville county. R. R. Aug. 19, 1830.
Bond, Eliza L. of Raleigh to Collins M. Clarke of Scotland Neck, Sept. 19, Kinston, Lenoir county. R. R. Oct. 28, 1830.
Bonner, Evan to Sophia D. Byhan, Je. 10, Salem. R. R. Je. 31, 1830.
Borden, Mary W. of Carteret county to Israel Sheldon of Hyde county, Feb. 25, Beaufort. R. R. Apr. 8, 1830.
Borden, Thomas R. of Beaufort to Miss A. Jones, Je. 28. R. R. Jly. 8, 1830.
Bost, Catharine to Charles Ludney, Sept., Cabarrus county. R. R. Sept. 9, 1830.
Bost, William to Elizabeth Lance, Apr., Cabarrus county. R. R. Apr. 29, 1830.
Bouchelle, J. E. to Mary E. Patton, Nov., Burke county. R. R. Nov. 4, 1830.
Boyd, Matilda S. to Joshua Davis, Aug. 12, Warren county. R. R. Aug. 26, 1830.
Boylan, William of Raleigh to Jane Elliott, Nov., Cumberland county. R. R. Nov. 18, 1830.
Branson, Sarah to Stephen Ward of Orange county, Feb. 25, Chatham county. R. R. Mar. 18, 1830.
Braxton, Hiram to Rachel Whitehead, Feb. 28, Chatham county. R. R. Mar. 18, 1830.
Brewster, Jacob H. to Ann Elixa Eagles, Mar. 16, New Hanover county. R. R. Apr. 1, 1830.
Brobson, Rev. Mr. to Hannah A. Cromartie, Je., Bladen county. R. R. Je. 10, 1830.
Brown, Edwin to Louisa Stansell, Mar., Pitt county. R. R. Mar. 23, 1830.
Brown, Mary of Washington, D. C. to John H. Wheeler of Hertford county, Apr. 19, Washington, D. C. R. R. Apr. 29, 1830.
Brown, William to Mary Vasseur, Sept., Halifax county. R. R. Sept. 23, 1830.
Bryan, John S. of Plymouth to Lucy D. Haywood, Feb. 21, Raleigh. R. R. Feb. 25, 1830.
Buffaloe, Bryant A. of Wake county to Adeline A. Cherry, Oct. 1, Martin county. R. R. Oct. 14, 1830.
Bunting, Minerva to Joseph Gibson, Feb. 2, Randolph county. R. R. Mar. 11, 1830.
Burnet, John W. of Columbia, S. C. to Mary E. Willis, Apr. Newbern. R. R. Apr. 29, 1830.
Burns, Miss to Richard Barry, Je. 15, Lincoln county. R. R. Jly. 15, 1830.
Byham, Sophia D. to Evan Bonner, Je. 10, Salem. R. R. Je. 31, 1830.
Campbell, Elizabeth to John C. Smith of Johnston county. Jan., Cumberland county. R. R. Jan. 21, 1830.
Campbell, William J. to Jane Allen, Mar. 18, Wilmington. R. R. Apr. 1, 1830.
Capehart, F. M. to Martha Cowper, Nov., Murfreesboro. R. R. Nov. 11, 1830.

Carlisle, Eliza Ann to Daniel Lovett, Feb. 14, Lenoir county. R. R. Mar. 11, 1830.
Carpenter, Peter to Sarah Setzer, Je., Lincoln county. R. R. Je. 10, 1830.
Carpenter, Susan to George F. Smith of Montgomery county, Je. 24, Anson county. R. R. Jly. 15, 1830.
Carson, Isabelle C. to John Lattimore, Je. 8, Rutherford county. R. R. Jly. 31, 1830.
Casey, Frederick to Margaret Sawyer, Jan., Elizabeth City. R. R. Jan. 31, 1830.
Chalmers, Dr. Chas. of Chapel Hill to Mary Williams M'Bryde of Moore county, Je., Moore county. R. R. Je. 10, 1830.
Chalmers, Harriet W. to Robert G. Allison, My. 20, Chapel Hill. R. R. My. 27, 1830.
Chalmers, Eleanor to Samuel Taylor, Feb. 4, Rowan county. R. R. Mar. 11, 1830.
Chambers, Maxwell to Catharine Troy, Jan., Salisbury. R. R. Jan. 28, 1830.
Chandler, Joel to Eliza Walker, Mar., Person county. R. R. Mar. 23, 1830.
Cheatham, Thomas to Martha Amis, Nov., Oxford. R. R. Nov. 11, 1830.
Cherry, Adeline A. to Bryant A. Buffaloe of Wake county, Oct. 1, Martin county. R. R. Oct. 14, 1830.
Cherry, Thomas to Emily Bell, Mar. 4, Tarborough. R. R. Mar. 25, 1830.
Chisholm, Mary of Lawrenceville to Ralph Gorrell of Greensboro, Nov. R. R. Dec. 2, 1830.
Clark, Benj. B. to Mary Ann Morehead, Dec. 14, Rutherford county. R. R. Feb. 4, 1830.
Clarke, Collins M. of Scotland Neck to Eliza L. Bond of Raleigh, Sept. 19, Kinston, Lenoir county. R. R. Oct. 28, 1830.
Commander, Mrs. Parthenia to Dr. James H. Williams, Je:, Pasquotank county. R. R. Jly. 31, 1830.
Cook, J. J. G. to Annabella Murchison of Fayetteville, Feb. 18, Cumberland county. R. R. Mar. 11, 1830.
Cook, Martha A. to George W. Gary, Nov., Halifax county. R. R. Nov. 11, 1830.
Cotner, Aaron to Charity Wells, Mar., Orange county. R. R. Mar. 18, 1830.
Cowper, Martha to F. M. Capehart, Nov., Murfreesboro. R. R. Nov. 11, 1830.
Cox, Presley T. of Giles county, Tenn. to Bethunia P. Smith, Nov. 24, Chatham county. R. R. Dec. 9, 1830.
Cox, Thomas to Mary Moffett, Sept., Randolph county. R. R. Oct. 7, 1830.
Coxe, Dr. D. Theodore of Philadelphia to Mary Halliday of Fayetteville, Mar. 11, Fayetteville. R. R. Mar. 18, 1830.
Cromartie, Hannah A. to Rev. Mr. Brobson, Je., Bladen county. R. R. Je. 10, 1830.
Cruthers, Emeline to Christopher Neal of Craven county, Nov., Beaufort county. R. R. Nov. 18, 1830.
Culpepper, Margaret to John M. King, Je., Elizabeth City. R. R. Jly. 31, 1830.
Currie, Sally to Aaron V. Lee, Aug. 19, Caswell county. R. R. Sept. 2, 1830.

Daniel, James to Jane Stuart, Aug. 19, Caswell county. R. R. Sept. 2, 1830.
Dashiell, Margaret to Jos. B. Hinton, of Beaufort county, Feb. 16, Raleigh. R. R. Feb. 18, 1830.
Daves, John F. to Elizabeth B. Graham, Jan., Newbern. R. R. Jan. 21, 1830.
Davis, Joshua to Matilda S. Boyd, Aug. 12, Warren county. R. R. Aug. 26, 1830.
Devereux, Frances A. to Rev. Leonidas Polk, My. 6, Raleigh. R. R. My. 13, 1830.
Dews, Eliza to William Robeson, Nov., Lincolnton. R. R. Nov. 4, 1830.
Dews, Martha to Rev. Stephen Frontis of Iredell county, Feb. 2, Lincolnton. R. R. Feb. 25, 1830.
Dickson, Mary Ann to Anderson Ferrill, Jan. 14, Orange county. R. R. Jan. 28, 1830.
Dobson, Martha J. to Charles E. Rcthe, Je., Davidson county. R. R. Je. 31, 1830.
Dockery, Dr. Henry to Ann M'Kay of Cheraw, S. C. Nov., Greenville, Pitt county. R. R. Nov. 18, 1830.
Dowd, Rev. P. W. of Raleigh to Martha Austin of Tarborough, Nov. R. R. 4, 1830.
Dry, Abraham to Polly Harkey, Apr., Cabarrus county. R. R. Apr. 15, 1830.
Duke, Wm. to S. Robards, Jan., Orange county. R. R. Jan. 21, 1830.
Dunbiddin, Jane to Robert J. Potts, Jan. 7, Wilmington. R. R. Jan. 21, 1830.
Dunval, William B. of Newbern to Eliza Murphy, Jan., Jones county. R. R. Jan. 28, 1830.
Eagles, Ann Eliza to Jacob H. Brewster, Mar. 16, New Hanover county. R. R. Apr. 1, 1830.
Eagles, Mrs. Caroline to Lieut. John H. Winder of U. S. Army, Nov. 10, Wilmington. R. R. Dec. 2, 1830.
Eaton, Nathaniel Macon of Warren county to Virginia Joanna Stith, Je. 22, Halifax. R. R. Je. 24, 1830.
Elliott, Exum to Eliza Pool, Feb. 18, Perquimans county. R. R. Mar. 11, 1830.
Elliott, Jane to William Boylan of Raleigh, Nov., Cumberland county. R. R. Nov. 18, 1830.
Ellis, Elizabeth to Giles Pearson, Mar. 11, Rowan county. R. R. Mar. 25, 1830.
Ellis, John S. to Fanny Moss, Oct. Granville county. R. R. Oct. 28, 1830.
Ellison, Henry A. to Caroline S. Telfair, Jan. 6, Washington. R. R. Jan. 21, 1830.
Ellyson, Zachariah to Mrs. Ceney Foster, Nov., Bertie county. R. R. Nov. 11, 1830.
Emry, Isaac to Elizabeth White, Dec. 14, Rutherford county. R. R. Feb. 4, 1830.
Eskridge, Rev. Vernon of Elizabeth City to Mary Ann M'Lin, Aug. 23, Newbern. R. R. Sept. 2, 1830.
Espy, Rev. Thomas of Iredell county to Mary Louisa Tate of Burke county, Apr. 21. R. R. My. 13, 1830.

Evans, Mary Ann to Dr. Samuel L. Southerland of Warrenton, Jan. 7, Edgecombe county. R. R. Jan. 28, 1830.
Falkner, Robert to Miss E. B. Wood, Dec., Person county. R. R. Dec. 9, 1830.
Fearing, Oliver to Sarah Ann Williams, Mar., Elizabeth City. R. R. Mar. 18, 1830.
Ferrill, Anderson to Mary Ann Dickson, Jan. 14, Orange county. R. R. Jan. 28, 1830.
Fisher, William to Miss M'Lure, Nov., Cabarrus county. R. R. Nov. 11, 1830.
Fort, Wm. of Wake county to Mrs. Elizabeth Whitfield of Johnson county, Dec. 20. R. R. Jan. 7, 1830.
Foster, Mrs. Ceney to Zachariah Ellyson, Nov., Bertie county. R. R. Nov. 11, 1830.
Foy, Mrs. S. to Col. Walter P. Allen of Kinston, My., Trenton, Jones county. R. R. My. 27, 1830.
Freeze, Lydia to Daniel Seaford, Sept., Rowan county. R. R. Sept. 9, 1830.
Freeze, Milly to Michael P. Shuping, Sept., Rowan county. R. R. Sept. 9, 1830.
Frontis, Rev. Stephen of Iredell county to Martha Dews, Feb. 2, Lincolnton. R. R. Feb. 25, 1830.
Fuller, John to Rebecca Mann, Jan. 26, Granville county. R. R. Feb. 4, 1830.
Gary, George W. to Martha A. Cook, Nov., Halifax county. R. R. Nov. 11, 1830.
Gauze, Harriet of Bladen county to Cyrus W. Bidwell of Fayetteville, My. 20, Bladen county. R. R. Je. 3, 1830.
Gibson, Joseph to Minerva Bunting, Feb. 2, Randolph county. R. R. Mar. 11, 1830.
Gibson, Margaret to Mathew B. Locke, Mar. 4, Rowan county. R. R. Mar. 18, 1830.
Gillespie, Margaret to Julius J. Reeves, Sept., Rowan county. R. R. Sept. 9, 1830.
Gilmer, Dr. James F. of Mecklenburg county to Sarah Harris, Apr., Cabarrus county. R. R. Apr. 15, 1830.
Glenn, Eliza A. of York District, S. C. to Whiten Stowe of Lincoln county, Mar. 8. R. R. My. 13, 1830.
Gooden, Joseph to Elmina Graham, My. 13, Rutherford county. R. R. Je. 3, 1830.
Gorrell, Ralph of Greensboro to Mary Chisholm of Lawrenceville, Nov. R. R. Dec. 2, 1830.
Graham, Archibald of Fayetteville to Ann M'Lean, Je., Cumberland county. R. R. Je. 10, 1830.
Graham, Elizabeth B. to John F. Daves, Jan., Newbern. R. R. Jan. 21, 1830.
Graham, Elmina to Joseph Gooden, My. 13, Rutherford county. R. R. Je. 3, 1830.
Gray, Mrs. Nancy to John Sowel, Dec., Moore county. R. R. Dec. 9, 1830.
Gregory, Rev. George N. of Washington to Jane W. Tyler, Aug. 24, Washington. R. R. Sept. 2, 1830.
Gregory, Sarah to Thaddeus Banks, Sept., Pasquotank county. R. R. Oct. 7, 1830.

Grimmer, Thomas to Nancy Whitehead, Aug. 10, Scotland Neck. R. R. Aug. 26, 1830.

Guffie, Rufus to Martha Ann Walton of Wake county, Sept. 29, Raleigh. R. R. Sept. 30, 1830.

Hall, Rob't to Martha Walker, Mar. 15, Orange county. R. R. Apr. 15, 1830.

Halliday, Margaret to John W. Sanford, Jly. 7, Fayetteville. R. R. Jly. 8, 1830.

Halliday, Mary of Fayetteville to Dr. D. Theodore Coxe of Philadelphia, Mar. 11, Fayetteville. R. R. Mar. 18, 1830.

Hamilin, Eliza J. to Benj. W. Williamson of Tennessee, Jan. 5, Halifax county. R. R. Jan. 21, 1830.

Hancock, Ann to Robert F. Pleasants, Jan., Hillsborough. R. R. Jan. 21, 1830.

Hardin, John to Ella Baxter, Jan. 17, Rowan county. R. R. Mar. 11, 1830.

Hardy, Harriet of Bertie county to Richard Wilder of Chowan county, Feb. 4, Bertie county. R. R. Mar. 11, 1830.

Harky, Elizabeth to John Utly, Nov., Cabarrus county. R. R. Nov. 11, 1830.

Harkey, Polly to Abraham Dry, Apr., Cabarrus county. R. R. Apr. 15, 1830.

Harrell, David to Mary D. Harrell, Aug. 15, Gates county. R. R. Oct. 7, 1830.

Harrell, Freeza to John H. Jones of Chowan county, Jly. 22, Bertie county. R. R. Aug. 19, 1830.

Harrell, Jesse to Tabitha Swanner, Dec., Martin county. R. R. Dec. 9, 1830.

Harrell, Mary D. to David Harrell, Aug. 15, Gates county. R. R. Oct. 7, 1830.

Harris, Miss to William Piper, Mar. 15, Orange county. R. R. Apr. 15, 1830.

Harris, Sarah to Dr. James F. Gilmer of Mecklenburg county, Apr., Cabarrus county. R. R. Apr. 15, 1830.

Harrison, Rebecca to Southern Higgs, Jan. 12, Granville county. R. R. Jan. 28, 1830.

Hart, Frances A. of Edgecombe county to James J. Hinton of Johnston county, Je. 17. R. R. Je. 31, 1830.

Hartman, Eliza to Capt. David Linn, Je. 24, Rowan county. R. R. Jly. 15, 1830.

Hatch, Amana to Wm. Adderton, Sept., Lexington. R. R. Sept. 9, 1830.

Hatch, Elizabeth to Dr. William Holland of Trenton, Jan., Lenoir county. R. R. Jan. 28, 1830.

Hatch, Hope, to Thomas W. C. Wingate, Jan., Jones county. R. R. Jan. 28, 1830.

Haywood, Lucy D. to John S. Bryan of Plymouth, Feb. 21, Raleigh. R. R. Feb. 25, 1830.

Henderson, William of Cabarrus county to Sarah C. Wilkinson, Apr., Salisbury. R. R. Apr. 15, 1830.

Henley, Mary Ann to Andrew Hunt, Feb. 17, Guilford county. R. R. Mar. 11, 1830.

Henly, Lucretia to Henry Hill, Mar. 5, Randolph county. R. R. Mar. 11, 1830.

Hester, John to Anne Lydia Reich, Je. 3, Salem. R. R. Jly. 31, 1830.
Hicks, George N. of Granville county to Mary Judge, Nov., Halifax county. R. R. Nov. 11, 1830.
Hicks, Lethe to D. P. Paschall, Oct., Granville county. R. R. Oct. 28, 1830.
Higgs, Southern to Rebecca Harrison, Jan. 12, Granville county. R. R. Jan. 28, 1830.
Hill, Dicey W. to Benjamin Patrick, Apr., Beaufort county. R. R. Apr. 15, 1830.
Hill, Mrs. Eliza K. to Peter Le Messurier, Dec. 7, Raleigh. R. R. Dec. 9, 1830.
Hill, Henry to Lucretia Henly, Mar. 5, Randolph county. R. R. Mar. 11, 1830.
Hill, Dr. John H. to Mary Ann B. Holmes, My. 9, Wilmington. R. R. My. 27, 1830.
Hill, Dr. William G. of Pittsborough to Adelaide Hunter, My. 18, Raleigh. R. R. My. 20, 1830.
Hinshaw, Melinda to Nathan Baldwin, Feb. 21, Guilford county. R. R. Mar. 11, 1830.
Hinton, James J. of Johnston county to Frances A. Hart of Edgecombe county, Je. 17. R. R. Je. 31, 1830.
Hinton, Jos. B. of Beaufort county to Margaret Dashiel, Feb. 16, Raleigh. R. R. Feb. 18, 1830.
Hoffman, J. H. to Susan Alford, Dec. 5, Raleigh. R. R. Dec. 9, 1830.
Hogg, Lydia to William R. D. Lindsley, Oct. 27, Hillsborough. R. R. Nov. 11, 1830.
Holland, Arnold to Pamelia Reid, My., Iredell county. R. R. My. 13, 1830.
Holland, Dr. William of Trenton to Elizabeth Hatch, Jan., Lenoir county. R. R. Jan. 28, 1830.
Holloway, Frances to Wm. King, Feb. 17, Person county. R. R. Mar. 23, 1830.
Holmes, Mary Ann B. to Dr. John H. Hill, My. 9, Wilmington. R. R. My. 27, 1830.
Holmes, Owen to Elizabeth H. Ashe, Jan. 6, Wilmington. R. R. Jan. 21, 1830.
Holshouser, Alexander to Sally Miller, Apr., Cabarrus county. R. R. Apr. 29, 1830.
Hooks, Eliza to Thos. Wright, Jr. Jan. 26, Duplin county. R. R. Feb. 4, 1830.
Hooks, Samuel D. to Sarah Eliza Wright, Jan. 28, Duplin county. R. R. Feb. 4, 1830.
Hooper, Frances G. to Wm. Weatherford, Feb. 4, Caswell county. R. R. Feb. 25, 1830.
Howard, Dorcas W. to Thomas W. Patrick, Apr., Washington, Beaufort county. R. R. Apr. 15, 1830.
Howard, Joseph to Mary Parham, Jan. 28, Granville county. R. R. Feb. 4, 1830.
Hoyl, Eli of Hoylesville to Cynthia S. Ramsour, Jan. 14, Lincolnton. R. R. Feb. 4, 1830.
Hubbard, Augustus to Frances Reader, Jan. 6, Raleigh. R. R. Jan. 14, 1830.

Hughs, Catharine to Ro. Yancey, Feb. 17, Person county. R. R. Mar. 23, 1830.
Hughs, Martha to Mr. Bell of Halifax, Va. Feb. 17, Person county. R. R. Mar. 23, 1830.
Hunt, Andrew to Mary Ann Henley, Feb. 17, Guilford county. R. R. Mar. 11, 1830.
Hunter, Adelaide to Dr. William G. Hill, My. 18, Raleigh. R. R. My. 20, 1830.
Hunter, Marina C. to John C. Savage, Je., Wilmington. R. R. Je. 10, 1830.
Husted, Hiram W. of Johnston county to Hariet A. Slocum, Jan. 3, Wayne county. R. R. Jan. 14, 1830.
Irvine, Abraham to Louisa Beam, Apr., Rutherford county. R. R. Apr. 15, 1830.
Jeffers, Nancy L. of Warren county to Chas D. Savage of Cumberland county, Feb. 17, Warren county. R. R. Apr. 1, 1830.
Johnson, Mary to Capt. Samuel Lowrie, Feb. 11, Mecklenburg county. R. R. Apr. 8, 1830.
Johnston, Henry to Emily Norfleet, Jan. 7, Edgecombe county. R. R. Jan. 28, 1830.
Johnston, Jesse to Evelina Allen, Feb. 25, Halifax county. R. R. Apr. 8, 1830.
Johnston, Miss R. M. W. to Archibald Smith of Raleigh, Aug., Augusta, Ga. R. R. Sept. 9, 1830.
Jones, Miss A. to Thomas R. Borden of Beaufort, Je. 28. R. R. Jly. 8, 1830.
Jones, Charlotte to Nelson Taylor of Martin county, Mar. 3, Scotland Neck. R. R. Mar. 25, 1830.
Jones, John H. of Chowan county to Freeza Harrell, Jly. 22, Bertie county. R. R. Aug. 19, 1830.
Jones, Rev. Wm. G. H. of Fayetteville to Frances C. Allison, Apr., Petersburg. R. R. Apr. 29, 1830.
Judge, Mary to George N. Hicks of Granville county, Nov., Halifax county. R. R. Nov. 11, 1830.
Kearney, Matilda to John B. Somervell, My. 19, Warren county. R. R. Je. 3, 1830.
Keaton, Sarah to Lewis Kornegay, Apr., Duplin county. R. R. Apr. 29, 1830.
Kellum, Jesse to Charity M'Michael, Jan. 28, Guilford county. R. R. Feb. 4, 1830.
Kelly, John to Mrs. James Thornton, Aug., Elizabeth City. R. R. Aug. 19, 1830.
Kesler, Samuel to Tabitha Miller, Sept., Iredell county. R. R. Sept. 9, 1830.
King, John M. to Margaret Culpepper, Je., Elizabeth City. R. R. Jly. 31, 1830.
King, Wm. to Frances Holloway, Feb. 17, Person county. R. R. Mar. 23, 1830.
Knox, John to Elizabeth M'Rum, Apr., Mecklenburg county. R. R. Apr. 15, 1830.
Knox, Margaret to William B. Wood, Apr. 1, Rowan county. R. R. Apr. 29, 1830.

Kornegay, Lewis to Sarah Keaton, Apr., Duplin county. R. R. Apr. 29, 1830.
Lance, Elizabeth to William Bost, Apr., Cabarrus county. R. R. Apr. 29, 1830.
Land, Benjamin to Ann W. Wilson, Apr., Currituck county. R. R. Apr. 22, 1830.
Lassiter, Mrs. Elizabeth to Rev. W. Reed of Perquimans county, Jly. 27, Gates county. R. R. Aug. 19, 1830.
Lattimore, John to Isabella C. Carson, Je. 8, Rutherford county. R. R. Jly. 31, 1830.
Lea, Aaron V. to Sally Currie, Aug. 19, Caswell county. R. R. Sept. 2, 1830.
Lees, David of Mecklenburg county to Nancy Wethers of York District, S. C. Mar. 8. R. R. My. 13, 1830.
Lewis, John of Gates county to Margaret A. Reid of Newbern, My., Somerton, Virginia. R. R. My. 27, 1830.
Lindsay, Harper to Martha Strange of Virginia, Nov., Greensborough. R. R. Nov. 25, 1830.
Lindsay, Mary to James T. Morehead of Rockingham county, My. 13, Greensborough. R. R. My. 27, 1830.
Lindsley, William R. D. to Lydia Hogg, Oct. 27, Hillsborough. R. R. Nov. 11, 1830.
Linn, Capt. David to Eliza Hartmen, Je. 24, Rowan county. R. R. Jly. 15, 1830.
Locke, Mathew B. to Margaret Gibson, Mar. 4, Rowan county. R. R. Mar. 18, 1830.
Long, Wm. L. to Mary Morrison, Dec. 29, Rutherford county. R. R. Feb. 4, 1830.
Loomis, Dr. Harris to Julia Mitchell, Apr., Newbern. R. R. Apr. 29, 1830.
Lovett, Daniel to Eliza Ann Carlisle, Feb. 14, Lenoir county. R. R. Mar. 11, 1830.
Lowrie, Capt. Samuel to Mary Johnson, Feb. 11, Mecklenburg county. R. R. Apr. 8, 1830.
Lowry, Benjamin to Ann Shaw, Je. 10, Pasquotank county. R. R. Jly. 31, 1830.
Ludney, Charles to Catharine Bost, Sept., Cabarrus county. R. R. Sept. 9, 1830.
M'Bryde, Mary Williams of Moore county to Dr. Chas. Chalmers of Chapel Hill, Je., Moore county. R. R. Je. 10, 1830.
M'Cauley, John to Margaret Blackwood, Mar. 15, Orange county. R. R. Apr. 15, 1830.
M'Cauley, Polly to John Blackwood, Apr. 13, Orange county. R. R. Apr. 29, 1830.
M'Colmon, Janet to Col. Thorogood Pate, Sept., Cumberland county. R. R. Oct. 7, 1830.
M'Corkle, Col. John F. to Jane Caroline Barr, Nov., Rowan county. R. R. Nov. 11, 1830.
M'Cullers, John of Johnston county to Jane Whitaker, Nov. 11, Wake county. R. R. Nov. 18, 1830.
M'Gehee, Amanda S. to William Terry of Danville, Va., Sept. 14. R. R. Sept. 23, 1830.

M'Graw, Calvin to Lovina Wagner, Apr., Cabarrus county. R. R. Apr. 15, 1830.
M'Kay, Ann of Cheraw, S. C. to Dr. Henry Dockery, Nov., Greenville, Pitt county. R. R. Nov. 18, 1830.
M'Lean Ann to Archibald Graham of Fayetteville, Je., Cumberland county. R. R. Je. 10, 1830.
M'Lin, Mary Ann to Rev. Vernon Eskeridge of Elizabeth City, Aug. 23, Newbern. R. R. Sept. 2, 1830.
M'Lure, Miss to William Fisher, Nov., Cabarrus county. R. R. Nov. 11, 1830.
M'Michael, Charity to Jesse Kellum, Jan. 28, Guilford county. R. R. Feb. 4, 1830.
M'Rae, Duncan G. to Ann S. Wingate, Mar. 11, Wilmington. R. R. Mar. 18, 1830.
M'Rum, Elizabeth to John Knox, Apr., Mecklenburg county. R. R. Apr. 15, 1830.
Mann, Rebecca to John Fuller, Jan. 26, Granville county. R. R. Feb. 4, 1830.
Marley, Jesse of Randolph county to Laura Mathews, Jan., Chatham county. R. R. Jan. 28, 1830.
Marlin, Margaret to James Tomason, Je. 10, Rowan county. R. R. Je. 31, 1830.
Martin, Mary Elizabeth to John S. Wood of Windsor, Jly., Hertford, Perquimans county. R. R. Jly. 15, 1830.
Mason, Sarah to Abraham Nash, Sept., Iredell county. R. R. Sept. 9, 1830.
Mathews, Laura to Jesse Marley of Randolph county, Jan., Chatham county. R. R. Jan. 28, 1830.
Mathias, Martha Ann to Jordan Simpson, My., Chowan county. R. R. My. 20, 1830.
Mayhew, Frankey to James Rankin, Sept., Iredell county. R. R. Sept. 9, 1830.
Messurer, Le Peter to Mrs. Eliza K. Hill, Dec. 7, Raleigh. R. R. Dec. 9, 1830.
Miller, Lovina to Paul Barringer, Feb. 4, Rowan county. R. R. Mar. 11, 1830.
Miller, Sally to Alexander Holshouser, Apr., Cabarrus county. R. R. Apr. 29, 1830.
Miller, Tabitha to Samuel Kesler, Sept., Iredell county. R. R. Sept. 9, 1830.
Moss, Fanny to John S. Ellis, Oct., Granville county. R. R. Oct. 28, 1830.
Mitchell, Elizabeth P. of Newbern to Isaac P. Partridge of Raleigh, Nov. 18, Newbern. R. R. Nov. 25, 1830.
Mitchell, Julia to Dr. Harris Loomis, Apr., Newbern. R. R. Apr. 29, 1830.
Moffett, Mary to Thomas Cox, Sept., Randolph county. R. R. Oct. 7, 1830.
Moody, Capt. Nathaniel to Elizabeth J. Null, Dec. 21, Stokes county. R. R. Feb. 4, 1830.
Moore, Augustus to Susan M. Armistead, Apr. 29, Edenton. R. R. My. 13, 1830.
Moore, Eliza to Joshua B. Oliver, New Hanover county, Apr., Jones county. R. R. Apr. 29, 1830.

Morehead, James T. of Rockingham county to Mary Lindsay, My. 13, Greensborough. R. R. My. 27, 1830.
Morehead, Mary Ann to Benj. B. Clark, Dec. 14, Rutherford county. R. R. Feb. 4, 1830.
Morris, Emma to Jacob Sessoms of Halifax county, Jly. 8, Martin county. R. R. Sept. 2, 1830.
Morrison, Mary to Wm. L. Long, Dec. 29, Rutherford county. R. R. Feb. 4, 1830.
Munn, John to Mary H. Salmon, Nov., Fayetteville. R. R. Nov. 18, 1830.
Murchison, Anabella of Fayetteville to J. G. Cook, Feb. 18, Cumberland county. R. R. Mar. 11, 1830.
Murphy, Eliza to William B. Duval of Newbern, Jan., Jones county. R. R. Jan. 28, 1830.
Murphy, Thomas R. to Rachel P. Watson, Aug., Fayetteville. R. R. Aug. 5, 1830.
Nash, Abraham to Sarah Mason, Sept., Iredell county. R. R. Sept. 9, 1830.
Neal, Christopher of Craven county to Emeline Cruthers, Nov., Beaufort county. R. R. Nov. 18, 1830.
Neel, Samuel J. to Louisa Ross, My. 6, Mecklenburg county. R. R. My. 27, 1830.
Nelson, Esther to Josephus Nelson, Feb. 24, Craven county. R. R. Apr. 8, 1830.
Nelson, Josephus to Esther Nelson, Feb. 24, Craven county. R. R. Apr. 8, 1830.
Newborn, Mary to Wm. Bagley of Perquimans county, My., Chowan county. R. R. My. 20, 1830.
Newby, Exum to Elizabeth Wilson, Apr., Pasquotank county. R. R. Apr. 22, 1830.
Newby, Samuel to Martha Ann Perry, Feb. 7, Perquimans county. R. R. Mar. 11, 1830.
Norfleet, Emily to Henry Johnston, Jan. 7, Edgecombe county. R. R. Jan. 28, 1830.
Norwood, Jane B. to Samuel W. Tillinghast of Fayetteville, Jly. 26, Hillsboro. R. R. Aug. 12, 1830.
Null, Elizabeth J. to Capt. Nathaniel Moody, Dec. 21, Stokes county. R. R. Feb. 4, 1830.
Nuttall, Isabella G. A. to Wm. O. Patton, Sept. 23, Granville county. R. R. Nov. 11, 1830.
Ogburn, Mary to Martin Banner, Dec. 31, Stokes county. R. R. Feb. 4, 1830.
Oliver, John of Jones county to Mrs. Penelope Simmons, Jan., Lenoir county. R. R. Jan. 28, 1830.
Oliver, Joshua B. of New Hanover county to Eliza Moore, Apr., Jones county. R. R. Apr. 29, 1830.
Parham, Mary to Joseph Howard, Jan. 28, Granville county. R. R. Feb. 4, 1830.
Parker, Margaret H. to Amos J. Battle, Jan. 7, Edgecombe county. R. R. Jan. 28, 1830.
Parker, Dr. Richard M. to Emeline Riddick, Jan., Gates county. R. R. Jan. 21, 1830.
Parker, Simon to Ann Smith, Apr. 6, Halifax. R. R. Apr. 22, 1830.

Parsons, Miss of Mansfield Nottinghamshire England to Rev. Benjamin Reichel of Salem, Apr. 12. R. R. Apr. 29, 1830.
Partridge, Isaac P. of Raleigh to Elizabeth P. Mitchell of Newbern, Nov. 18, Newbern. R. R. Nov. 25, 1830.
Paschall, D. P. to Lethe Hicks, Oct., Granville county. R. R. Oct. 28, 1830.
Pate, Col. Thorogood of Richmond county to Janet M'Colmon, Sept., Cumberland county. R. R. Oct. 7, 1830.
Patrick, Benjamin to Dicey W. Hill, Apr., Beaufort county. R. R. Apr. 15, 1830.
Patrick, Thomas W. to Dorcas W. Horward, Apr., Washington, Beaufort county. R. R. Apr. 15, 1830.
Patton, Mary E. to J. E. Bouchelle, Nov., Burke county. R. R. Nov. 4, 1830.
Patton, Wm. O. to Isabella G. A. Nuttall, Sept. 28, Granville county. R. R. Nov. 11, 1830.
Pearson, Giles to Elizabeth Ellis, Mar. 11, Rowan county. R. R. Mar. 25, 1830.
Peed, Emma R. to William Bickering, Nov., Washington, Beaufort county. R. R. Nov. 18, 1830.
Peeler, Henry to Sophia Trexler, Apr. 8, Rowan county. R. R. Apr. 29, 1830.
Perry, Martha Ann to Samuel Newby, Feb. 17, Perquimans county. R. R. Mar. 11, 1830.
Pike, Mrs. Susannah to Frederick Shoffner, Feb. 28, Orange county. R. R. Mar. 18, 1830.
Piper, William to Miss Harris, Mar. 15, Orange county. R. R. Apr. 15, 1830.
Plder, Elizabeth to Christopher Reinhardt, Sept., Burke county. R. R. Apr. 9, 1830.
Pleasants, Robert F. to Ann Hancock, Jan., Hillsborough. R. R. Jan. 21, 1830.
Poisson, John D. to Julia Toomer, Mar. 16, New Hanover county. R. R. Apr. 1, 1830.
Polk, Rev. Leonidas to Frances A. Devereux, My. 6, Raleigh. R. R. My. 13, 1830.
Pool, Eliza to Exum Elliott, Feb. 18, Perquimans county. R. R. Mar. 11, 1830.
Potts, Robert J. to Jane Dunbibbin, Jan. 7, Wilmington. R. R. Jan. 21, 1830.
Powell, Davis to Susan Powell, Aug. 17, Halifax county. R. R. Sept. 2, 1830.
Powell, Martha to William Webb, Oct. 21, Halifax county. R. R. Nov. 11, 1830.
Powell, Susan to Davis Powell, Aug. 17, Halifax county. R. R. Sept. 2, 1830.
Pullen, Eaton to Phoebe Anderson, Dec., Halifax. R. R. Dec. 9, 1830.
Puryear, Appling of Halifax county, Va. to Frances Wilkerson of Granville county, Mar. 4. R. R. Mar. 23, 1830.
Ramsour Cynthia S. to Eli Hoyle of Hoylesville, Jan. 14, Lincolnton. R. R. Feb. 4, 1830.

Rankin, James to Frankey Mayhew, Sept., Iredell county. R. R. Sept. 9, 1830.
Reed, Rev. W. of Perquimans county to Miss Elizabeth Lassiter, Jly. 27, Gates county. R. R. Aug. 19, 1830.
Reader, Frances to Augustus Hubbard, Jan. 6, Raleigh. R. R. Jan. 14, 1830.
Reeves, Julius J. to Margaret Gillespie, Sept., Rowan county. R. R. Sept. 9, 1830.
Reich, Lydia Anne to John Hisler, Je. 3, Salem. R. R. Jly. 31, 1830.
Reichel, Rev. Benjamin of Salem to Miss Parsons of Mansfield Nottinghanishire, England, Apr. 12. R. R. Apr. 29, 1830.
Reid, Margaret A. of Newbern to John Lewis of Gates county, My., Somerton, Virginia. R. R. My. 27, 1830.
Reid, Pamelia to Arnold Holland, My., Iredell county. R. R. My. 13, 1830.
Reinhardt, Christopher to Elizabeth Plder, Sept., Burke county. R. R. Sept. 9, 1830.
Riddick, Emeline to Dr. Richard M. Parker, Jan., Gates county. R. R. Jan. 21, 1830.
Ridley, Thomas D. to Mary R. Blunt of Southampton, Va., Jly. 21, Granville county. R. R. Aug. 19, 1830.
Robards, George of Orange county to Harriet Wells of Person county, Aug. 12. R. R. Sept. 2, 1830.
Robards, S. to Wm. Duke, Jan., Orange county. R. R. Jan. 21, 1830.
Robeson, William to Eliza Dews, Nov., Lincolnton. R. R. Nov. 4, 1830.
Robinson, Mrs. Hannah to Malcom Shaw, Dec., Cumberland county. R. R. Dec. 9, 1830.
Robwell, Robert, Jr. to Eliza Milam, Feb. 10, Warren county. R. R. Mar. 11, 1830.
Roseborough, Margaret to James J. Turner, Apr., Iredell county. R. R. Apr. 15, 1830.
Ross, Louisa to Samuel J. Neil, My. 6, Mecklenburg county. R. R. My. 27, 1830.
Rothe, Charles E. to Martha J. Dobson, Je., Davidson county. R. R. Je. 31, 1830.
Salmon, Mary H. to John Munn, Nov., Fayetteville. R. R. Nov. 18, 1830.
Salmon, Sarah C. to Gen. Henry W. Ayer, Aug., Fayetteville. R. R. Sept. 2, 1830.
Sandford, John W. to Margaret Halliday, Jly. 7, Fayetteville. R. R. Jly. 8, 1830.
Savage, Chas. D. of Cumberland county to Nancy L. Jeffers of Warren county, Feb. 17, Warren county. R. R. Apr. 1, 1830.
Savage, John C. to Marina C. Hunter, Je., Wilmington. R. R. Je. 10, 1830.
Sawyer, Margaret to Frederick Sawyer, Jan., Elizabeth City. R. R. Jan. 21, 1830.
Seaford, Daniel to Lydia Freeze, Sept., Rowan county. R. R. Sept. 9, 1830.
Sefford, Catharine to Daniel Stirewalt, Oct., Rowan county. R. R. Oct. 14, 1830.
Sessoms, Jacob of Halifax county to Emma Morriss, Jly. 8, Martin county. R. R. Sept. 2, 1830.
Setzer, Sarah to Peter Carpenter, Je., Lincoln county. R. R. Je. 10, 1830.

Sharborough, David to Mary Spaight of Gates county, Apr., Pasquotank county. R. R. Apr. 22, 1830.
Shaw, Ann to Benjamin Lowry, Je. 10, Pasquotank county. R. R. Je. 31, 1830.
Shaw, Malcom to Mrs. Hannah Robinson, Dec., Cumberland county. R. R. Dec. 9, 1830.
Sheldon, Israel of Hyde county to Mary W. Borden of Carteret county, Feb. 25, Beaufort. R. R. Apr. 8, 1330.
Shepperd, Hon. Augustine H. from this State to Martha Turner of Washington, D. C., Feb. 25, Washington. R. R. Mar. 11, 1830.
Sherly, Abgail of Norfolk to William Swaim, My., Greensborough. R. R. My. 13, 1830.
Sherrod, Capt. Wm. R. W. to Mary Taylor, Dec., Martin county. R. R. Dec. 9, 1830.
Shoffner, Frederick to Mrs. Susannah Pike, Feb. 28, Orange county. R. R. Mar. 18, 1830.
Shuping, Michael P. to Milly Freeze, Sept., Rowan county. R. R. Sept. 9, 1830.
Simmons, Mrs. Penelope to John Oliver of Jones county, Jan., Lenoir county. R. R. Jan. 28, 1830.
Simpson, Jordan to Martha Ann Mathias, My., Chowan county. R. R. My. 20, 1830.
Slade, Thos. of Martin county to Eliza R. Gordan of Norfolk, Oct. 28, Warren county. R. R. Nov. 11, 1830.
Slocum, Harriet A. to Hiram W. Husted, Jan. 3, Wayne county. R. R. Jan. 14, 1830.
Smith, Ann to Simon Parker, Apr. 6, Halifax county. R. R. Apr. 22, 1830.
Smith, Archibald of Raleigh to Miss R. M. W. Johnston, Aug., Augusta, Ga. R. R. Sept. 9, 1830.
Smith, Bethunia P. to Presley T. Cox of Giles county, Tenn., Nov. 24, Chatham county. R. R. Dec. 9, 1830.
Smith, George F. of Montgomery county to Susan Carpenter, Je. 24, Anson county. R. R. Jly. 15, 1830.
Smith, John C. of Johnston county to Elizabeth Campbell, Jan., Cumberland county. R. R. Jan. 21, 1830.
Smith, Meade A. to Elizabeth Williams, Nov., Oxford. R. R. Nov. 11, 1830.
Somervell, John B. to Matilda Kearney, My. 19, Warren county. R. R. Je. 3, 1830.
Southerland, Dr. Samuel L. of Warrenton to Mary Ann Evans, Jan. 7, Edgecombe county. R. R. Jan. 28, 1830.
Sowel, John to Mrs. Nancy Gray, Dec., Moore county. R. R. Dec. 9, 1830.
Spaight, Mary of Gates county to David Sharborough, Apr., Pasquotank county. R. R. Apr. 22, 1830.
Stansell, Louisa to Edwin Brown, Mar., Pitt county. R. R. Mar. 23, 1830.
Stirewalt, Daniel to Catharine Sefford, Oct., Rowan county. R. R. Oct. 14, 1830.
Stith, Virginia Joanna to Nathaniel Macon Eaton of Warren county, Je. 22, Halifax. R. R. Je. 24, 1830.
Stowe, Whiten of Lincoln county to Eliza A. Glenn of York District, S. C., Mar. 8. R. R. My. 13, 1830.

Strange, Martha of Virginia to Harper Lindsay, Nov., Greensboro. R. R. Nov. 25, 1830.

Stuart, Jane to James Daniel, Aug. 19, Caswell county. R. R. Sept. 2, 1830.

Stuart, Mary to William M. White, Sept. 13, Raleigh. R. R. Sept. 16, 1830.

Swaim, William to Abgail Sherly of Norfolk, Va., My., Greensborough. R. R. My. 13, 1830.

Swanner, Tabitha to Jesse Harrell, Dec., Martin county. R. R. Dec. 9, 1830.

Tate, Mary Louisa of Burke county to Rev. Thomas Espy of Iredell county, Apr. 21. R. R. My. 13, 1830.

Taylor, John C. of Granville county to Emily E. Tillinghast, Mar. 11, Fayetteville. R. R. Mar. 25, 1830.

Taylor, Mary to Capt. Wm. R. W. Sherrod, Dec., Martin county. R. R. Dec. 9, 1830.

Taylor, Nelson of Martin county to Charlotte Jones, Mar. 3, Scotland Neck. R. R. Mar. 25, 1830.

Taylor, Samuel of Charlotte to Eleanor Chambers, Feb. 4, Rowan county. R. R. Mar. 11, 1830.

Telfair, Caroline S. to Henry A. Ellison, Jan. 6, Washington. R. R. Jan. 21, 1830.

Terry, William L. of Danville, Va. to Amanda S. M'Gehee, Sept. 14, Person county. R. R. Sept. 23, 1830.

Thomas, Susan to James T. White, Oct. 3, Beaufort. R. R. Oct. 14, 1830.

Thomason, James to Margaret Marlin, Je. 10, Rowan county. R. R. Je. 31, 1830.

Thornton, Mrs. James to John Kelly, Aug., Elizabeth City. R. R. Aug. 19, 1830.

Tillinghast, Emily E. to John C. Taylor, Mar. 11, Fayetteville. R. R. Mar. 25, 1830.

Tillinghast, Samuel W. of Fayetteville to Jane B. Norwood, Jly. 26, Hillsboro. R. R. Aug. 12, 1830.

Toomer, Julia to John D. Poisson, Mar. 16, New Hanover county. R. R. Apr. 1, 1830.

Trexler, Sophia to Henry Peeler, Apr. 8, Rowan county. R. R. Apr. 29, 1830.

Troy, Catharine to Maxwell Chambers, Jan., Salisbury. R. R. Jan. 28, 1830.

Turner, James J. to Margaret Roseborough, Apr., Iredell county. R. R. Apr. 15, 1830.

Turner, Martha of Washington. D. C. to Hon. Augustine H. Shepperd from this State, Feb. 25, Washington, D. C. R. R. Mar. 11, 1830.

Tyler, Jane W. to Rev. George N. Gregory of Washington, Aug. 24, Washington. R. R. Sept. 2, 1830.

Utly, John to Elizabeth Harky, Nov., Cabarrus county. R. R. Nov. 11, 1830.

Vasseur, Mary to William Brown, Sept., Halifax county. R. R. Sept. 23, 1830.

Wagner, Lovina to Calvin M'Graw, Apr., Cabarrus county. R. R. Apr. 15, 1830.
Walker, Eliza to Joel Chandler, Mar., Person county. R. R. Mar. 23, 1830.
Walker, Martha to Robt. Hall, Mar. 15, Orange county. R. R. Apr. 15, 1830.
Wallace, Marina to David H. Bedell of Burke county, Feb. 18, Iredell county. R. R. Sept. 30, 1830.
Walton, Martha Ann of Wake county to Rufus Guffie, Sept. 29, Raleigh. R. R. Sept. 30, 1830.
Ward, Stephen of Orange county to Sarah Branson, Feb. 25, Chatham county. R. R. Mar. 18, 1830.
Watson, Rachel P. to Thomas R. Murphy, Aug., Fayetteville. R. R. Aug. 5, 1830.
Weatherford, Wm. to Frances G. Hooper, Feb. 4, Caswell county. R. R. Feb. 25, 1830.
Webb, William to Martha Powell, Oct. 21, Halifax county. R. R. Nov. 11, 1830.
Wells, Charity to Aaron Cotner, Mar., Orange county. R. R. Mar. 18, 1830.
Wells, Harriet of Person county to George Robards of Orange county, Aug. 12. R. R. Sept. 2, 1830.
West, Priscilla to John A. Benford, Dec., Halifax. R. R. Dec. 9, 1830.
Wethers, Nancy of York District, S. C. to David Lees of Mecklenburg county, Mar. 8. R. R. My. 13, 1830.
Wheatley, Martin of Martin county to Otis Andrews of Beaufort county. Feb. 11, Martin county. R. R. Mar. 11, 1830.
Wheeler, John W. of Hertford county to Mary Brown of Washington, D. C., Apr. 19, Washington, D. C. R. R. Apr. 29, 1830.
Whitaker, Jane to John M'Cullers of Johnston county, Nov. 11, Wake county. R. R. Nov. 18, 1830.
Whitaker, John K. to Harriet Whitaker, My. 26, Raleigh. R. R. My. 27, 1830.
White, Elizabeth to Isaac Emry, Dec. 14, Rutherford county. R. R. Feb. 4, 1830.
White, James T. to Susan Thomas, Oct. 3, Beaufort. R. R. Oct. 14, 1830.
White, William M. to Mary Stuart, Sept. 13, Raleigh. R. R. Sept. 16, 1830.
Whitehead, Nancy to Thomas Grimmer, Aug. 10, Scotland Neck. R. R. Aug. 26, 1830.
Whitehead, Rachel to Hiram Braxton, Feb. 28, Chatham county. R. R. Mar. 18, 1830.
Whitfield, Mrs. Elizabeth of Johnson county to Wm. Fort of Wake county, Dec. 20. R. R. Jan. 7, 1830.
Whitted, Martha A. to Dr. John Allen, Dec., Orange county. R. R. Dec. 9, 1830.
Wilder, Richard of Chowan county to Harriet Hardy of Bertie county, Feb. 4, Bertie county. R. R. Mar. 11, 1830.
Wilkerson, Frances of Granville county to Appling Puryear of Halifax county, Va. Mar. 4. R. R. Mar. 23, 1830.
Williams, Elizabeth to Meade A. Smith, Nov., Oxford. R. R. Nov. 11, 1830.
Williams, Dr. James H. to Mrs. Parthenia Commander, Je., Pasquotank county. R. R. Jly. 31, 1830.

Williams, Minerva B. of Person county to Dr. James E. Williamson, Sept. R. R. Sept. 30, 1830.
Williams, Sarah Ann to Oliver Fearing, Mar., Elizabeth City. R. R. Mar. 18, 1830.
Williamson, Benj. W. of Tennessee to Eliza J. Hamlin, Jan. 5, Halifax county. R. R. Jan. 21, 1830.
Williamson, Dr. James E. of Caswell county to Minerva B. Williams of Person county, Sept. R. R. Sept. 30, 1830.
Wilkinson, Sarah C. to William Henderson of Cabarrus county, Apr., Salisbury. R. R. Apr. 15, 1830.
Willis, Mary E. to John W. Burnet of Columbia, S. C. Apr., Newbern. R. R. Apr. 29, 1830.
Wilson, Ann W. to Benjamin Land, Apr., Currituck county. R. R. Apr. 22, 1830.
Wilson, Elizabeth to Exum Newby, Apr., Pasquotank county. R. R. Apr. 22, 1830.
Winder, Lieut. John H. of the U. S. Army to Mrs. Caroline Eagles, Nov. 10, Wilmington. R. R. Dec. 2, 1830.
Wingate, Ann S. to Duncan G. M'Rae, Mar. 11, Wilmington. R. R. Mar. 18, 1830.
Wingate, Thomas W. C. to Hope Hatch, Jan., Jones county. R. R. Jan. 28, 1830.
Wood, John S. of Windsor to Mary Elizabeth Martin, Jly., Hertford, Perquimans county. R. R. Jly. 15, 1830.
Wood, William B. to Margaret Knox, Apr. 1, Rowan county. R. R. Apr. 29, 1830.
Word, Miss E. B. to Robert Falkner, Dec., Person county. R. R. Dec. 9, 1830.
Wright, Sarah Eliza to Samuel D. Hooks, Jan. 28, Duplin county. R. R. Feb. 4, 1830.
Wright, Thos. Jr. to Eliza Hooks, Jan. 26, Duplin county. R. R. Feb. 4, 1830.
Yancey, Ro. to Catharine Hughs, Feb. 17, Person county. R. R. Mar. 23, 1830.

1831

Albertson, Benjamin of Elizabeth City to Louisa Moore of Rhode Island, Jly., Elizabeth City. R. R. Jly. 14, 1831.
Alexander, John M. of Mecklenburg county to Cynthia D. Williamson, My. 5, Mecklenburg county. R. R. Je. 9, 1831.
Alexander, Hon. Mark of Virginia to Sarah P. Turner of Warren county, Je. 1. R. R. Je. 16, 1831.
Allen, Emily of Lebanon, Tenn. to William E. Gorman, Jan. 2, Nashville, Tenn. R. R. Feb. 3, 1831.
Allison, Alexander S. J. to Frances D. Yarbrough, Jly. 14, Hillsborough. R. R. Aug. 4, 1831.
Alston, Arabella to Dr. Henry J. Macon, Je., Warren county. R. R. Je. 23, 1831.
Alston, Emily to William H. Harris, Feb., Halifax county. R. R. Mar. 3, 1831.

Alston, Sarah Y. to Dr. Alex Hamilton Taylor of Oxford, Dec. 18, Wake Forest. R. R. Jan. 6, 1831.
Amis, Junius of Northampton county to Celeste Hawkins, Oct. 29, Shocco Springs. R. R. Nov. 10, 1831.
Anderson, Rev. Philip of Washington to Susan J. Sparrow, Je., Newbern. R. R. Je. 9, 1831.
Anderson, William J. to Elizabeth Huske, Feb., Fayetteville. R. R. Feb. 14, 1831.
Anthony, Maj. Whitmel to Charity Barnes, Aug., Halifax county. R. R. Aug. 11, 1831.
Armistead, Emma to Alfred Temple, Oct., Chatham county. R. R. Nov. 3, 1831.
Armstrong, Thomas T. of this State to Mary Ann H. Jones of Giles county, Tenn., Jly. R. R. Jly. 21, 1831.
Arrington, Arthur of Nash county to Elizabeth Irwin, Dec., Edgecombe county. R. R. Jan. 13, 1831.
Arrington, Peter, Jr. to Sally Ann Burt, Je., Nash county. R. R. Jly. 7, 1831.
Atkinson, Rev. Irvine of Edenton to Mrs. Wm. C. Roberts, Aug., Edenton. R. R. Aug. 25, 1831.
Bailey, Miss S. A. to Miles A. Giles, Mar., Salisbury. R. R. Mar. 17, 1831.
Baker, Sarah to Robert M. M'Racker of Fayetteville, Dec., Brunswick county. R. R. Jan. 13, 1831.
Barnes, Charity to Maj. Whitmel Anthony, Aug., Halifax county. R. R. Aug. 11, 1831.
Beard, George to Mary E. Harrell, Dec., Washington. R. R. Jan. 13, 1831.
Beasley, Sylvanus to Martha A. Smith, My. 19, Wake county. R. R. My. 25, 1831.
Bethel, William W. of Rockingham county to Elizabeth A. Brown of Caswell county, Oct. R. R. Nov. 3, 1831.
Bevers, Mrs. Almond to Robert Perry, Je. 9, Raleigh. R. R. Je. 16, 1831.
Bilbry, James to Anne Walker, Jan., Edgecombe county. R. R. Jan. 13, 1831.
Black, Marietta to Dr. John Watters, Apr., New Hanover county. R. R. My. 5, 1831.
Blackman, Cullen A. of Wayne county to Evelina Virginia Boon, Sept. 28, Johnston county. R. R. Oct 13, 1831.
Blaney, Sarah D. S. of Smithville to John M'Rae of Wilmington, Dec. 23, Smithville. R. R. Jan. 13, 1831.
Blaney, William E. to Evelina Hoard, Oct. 20, Wilmington. R. R. Nov. 3, 1831.
Bledsoe, John R. to Miss H. Green, Je. 9, Waynesboro. R. R. Je. 23, 1831.
Blount, Lucy Olivia to Bryan Grimes of Pitt county, Je., Washington, Beaufort county. R. R. Je. 30, 1831.
Bond, Eliza M. to George Johnston, Sept., Hillsborough. R. R. Sept. 29, 1831.
Boon, Evelina Virginia to Cullen A. Blackman of Wayne county, Sept. 28, Johnston county. R. R. Oct. 13, 1831.
Bowen, Caroline E. to James F. Broadfoot of Cheraw, Je., Fayetteville. R. R. Je. 23, 1831.

Bradburn, Thomas of Mecklenburg county to Elizabeth Reid, Je., Lincoln county. R. R. Je. 9, 1831.

Brake, Nathaniel B. of Raleigh to Martha A. Hines of Nashville, Jly., Nashville. R. R. Aug. 11, 1831.

Branch, Rebecca B. of this State to Col. B. W. Williams of Tallehassee, Apr. 26, Washington, D. C. R. R. Apr. 28, 1831.

Brantly, Simeon L. of Chatham county to Sarah Ann Daniel, My. 18, Burke county, Ga. R. R. Je. 9, 1831.

Brasfield, Mary E. to William S. Ligon, Sept. 26, Wake county. R. R. Nov. 3, 1831.

Brasfield, Melissa to James Lynn, Je., Raleigh. R. R. Je. 9, 1831.

Breman, Levi of Gates county to Louisa Luter of Northampton county, Dec. 30, Northampton county. R. R. Jan. 20, 1831.

Brinkley, John to Mary L. Vines, Mar., Washington, Beaufort county. R. R. Mar. 17, 1831.

Broadfoot, James F. of Cheraw to Caroline E. Bowen, Je., Fayetteville. R. R. Je. 23, 1831.

Brothers, Susan to Ambrose M. Gardner, Jan., Pasquotank county. R. R. Jan. 20, 1831.

Brown, Elizabeth A. of Caswell county to William W. Bethel of Rockingham county, Oct. R. R. Nov. 3, 1831.

Brown, Eliza to Saltar Lloyd, Jly. 7, Bladen county. R. R. Jly. 21, 1831.

Bruce, George W. to Harriet Faucett, My. 5, Cabarrus county. R. R. Je. 9, 1831.

Bryan, J. W. to Ann Washington of Lenoir county, Feb., Newbern. R. R. Feb. 10, 1831.

Bryan, Wm. G. to Sarah Ann King, Dec. 22, Newbern. R. R. Jan. 13, 1831.

Bullard, James to Fanny Hearn, Oct., Chatham county. R. R. Nov. 3, 1831.

Buner, Miss F. to Daniel Sink, My., Iredell county. R. R. My. 25, 1831.

Burns, Henry to Rebecca Murphey, Aug. 2, Rockingham county. R. R. Aug. 25, 1831.

Burt, Sally Ann to Peter Arrington, Jr. Je., Nash county. R. R. Jly. 7, 1831.

Burton, Frances H. of Williamsborough, Granville county to Col. Samuel Dickens of Madison county, Tenn., Aug. 2. R. R. Aug. 25, 1831.

Campbell, Capt. John to Sarah Stevens, Oct., Fayetteville. R. R. Nov. 3, 1831.

Caraway, Eliza of Burke county to Benjamin Rector of Iredell county, Mar. 6, Burke county. R. R. Mar. 31, 1831.

Carson, Hon. Sam'l from this State to S. Catharine Wilson of Tennessee, My. 5, Surry county. R. R. Je. 9, 1831.

Cate, Usly to John G. Wisdom, Dec. 16, Person county. R. R. Jan. 13, 1831.

Chambers, Mrs. Harriet of Anson county to Hiram Jennings, Mar. 9, Wadesborough. R. R. Mar. 31, 1831.

Chander, Littebury to Panthea B. Royster, Feb., Granville county. R. R. Mar. 3, 1831.

Coart, Sarah C. to Rev. W. N. Hanks, Apr. 20, Newbern. R. R. Apr. 28, 1831.

Cocherman, Daniel to Lucinda Reece, Oct., Surry county. R. R. Oct. 13, 1831.
Cole, Stephen W. to Tabitha R. Ledbetter, Je., Richmond county. R. R. Je. 23, 1831.
Coleman, Laura to Lewis Krimminger, My. 5, Cabarrus county. R. R. Je. 9, 1831.
Collins, Frances to James G. Jones, Jly. 14, Halifax county. R. R. Jly. 28, 1831.
Corbin, Octavius N. to Sarah Jane Lillington, Dec. 24, Wilmington. R. R. Jan. 13, 1831.
Couch, Lucy H. to James M. Patterson, Jan. 27, Wake county. R. R. Feb. 24, 1831.
Cowan, Thomas to Margaret M. M'Milhenny, My., Wilmington. R. R. My. 25, 1831.
Crowell, Matilda to Dr. John A. Jelks, Dec., Halifax county. R. R. Jan. 13, 1831.
Crump, Joseph to Fanny Sturdivant, Oct., Chatham county. R. R. Nov. 3, 1831.
Daniel, Elizabeth Ann to Alexander Q. Grissom of Granville county, Jan. 24, Wake county. R. R. Feb. 3, 1831.
Daniel, George C. of Halifax to Lavinia C. Hardee, Mar., Northampton county. R. R. Mar. 31, 1831.
Daniel, Sarah Ann to Simeon L. Brantly of Chatham county, My. 18, Burke county, Ga. R. R. Je. 9, 1831.
Darden, Theodosia to Rev. Henry Swinson of Duplin county, My. 11, Greene county. R. R. Je. 9, 1831.
Darden, William A. to Eliza Holliday, My. 12, Greene county. R. R. Je. 9, 1831.
Deloach, Elizabeth A. J. to Archer Tench, Jly. 28, Raleigh. R. R. Aug 4, 1831.
Dickens, Col. Samuel of Madison county, Tenn. to Frances H. Burton of Williamsborough, Granville county, Aug. 2. R. R. Aug. 25, 1831.
Dunbibin, Junis C. to Mrs. Elizabeth Perrin, Apr. 21, Wilmington. R. R. My. 5, 1831.
Eppes, Mary Eliza to Michael Ferrall, Oct. 31, Halifax. R. R. Nov. 10, 1831.
Eure, Rebecca to Orestes K. Smallwood, Jan., Halifax county. R. R. Jan. 13, 1831.
Faucett, Harriet to George W. Bruce, My. 5, Cabarrus county. R. R. Je. 9, 1831.
Ferrall, Michael to Mary Eliza Eppes, Oct. 31, Halifax. R. R. Nov. 10, 1831.
Fesperinan, Tena to John Holtsoner, Oct., Rowan county. R. R. Oct. 13, 1831.
Fewell, Richard R. to Mary B. Odeneal, Aug. 31, Rockingham county. R. R. Sept. 8, 1831.
Forrest, George D. E. to Ann Gillett, Feb., Newbern. R. R. Mar. 3, 1831.
Gardner, Ambrose M. to Susan Brothers, Jan., Pasquotank county. R. R. Jan. 20, 1831.
Gaston, Alexander Francis to Eliza Jones, Mar., Newbern. R. R. Mar. 24, 1831.

Giles, Milo A. to Miss S. A. Bailey, Mar., Salisbury. R. R. Mar. 17, 1831.
Gillett, Ann to George D. E. Forest, Feb., Newbern. R. R. Mar. 3, 1831.
Gilliam, Eliza of Oxford to W. P. Wright of Fayetteville, Apr. 21, Oxford. R. R. Apr. 28, 1831.
Gilliam, Henry of Gates county to Elizabeth Wood, Dec., Perquimans county. R. R. Jan. 13, 1831.
Glasgow, Mary Ann to Lewis S. Whitfield of Lenoir county, Oct., Greene county. R. R. Oct. 13, 1831.
Goclet, John B. of Washington county to Jane Smith, Dec., Edenton. R. R. Jan. 13, 1831.
Goneke, Celestia of Raleigh to Whitmel Tunstall, Aug. 24, Danville, Va. R. R. Sept. 21, 1831.
Gordon, Johnson of Person county to Caroline Hardie of Raleigh, Je., Orange county. R. R. Jly. 7, 1831.
Gorman, William E. of Raleigh to Emily Allen of Lebanon, Tennessee, Jan. 2, Nashville, Tenn. R. R. Feb. 3, 1831.
Green, Capt. Farnifold of U. S. Navy to Laura Pearson, Jly., Newbern. R. R. Aug. 4, 1831.
Green, Miss H. to John R. Bledsoe, Je. 9, Waynesboro. R. R. Je. 23, 1831.
Green, William A. of Franklin county to Ann L. Smith, Feb. 10, Wake Forest. R. R. Feb. 17, 1831.
Grier, Susan N. of Mecklenburg county to Rev. Arch'd White of Baltimore, Apr. 19, Mecklenburg county. R. R. My. 5, 1831.
Grimes, Bryan of Pitt county to Lucy Olivia Blount, Je., Washington, Beaufort county. R. R. Je. 30, 1831.
Grissom, Alexander Q. of Granville county to Elizabeth Ann Daniel, Jan. 24, Wake county. R. R. Feb. 3, 1831.
Hamner, Rev. James G. of Maryland and Fayetteville to Jane M'Elderry, Dec., New York. R. R. Jan. 13, 1831.
Hancock, Sarah to John M. Jones of Edenton, Jly., Newbern. R. R. Jly. 14, 1831.
Handcock, James to Elizabeth Stevenson, Feb., Newbern. R. R. Feb. 10, 1831.
Hardee, Lavinia C. to George C. Daniel of Halifax, Mar., Northampton county. R. R. Mar. 31, 1831.
Hardie, Caroline of Raleigh to Johnson Gordon of Person county, Je., Orange county. R. R. Jly. 7, 1831.
Harrell, Mary E. to George Beard, Dec., Washington. R. R. Jan. 13, 1831.
Harris, Rowena to Geo. R. Reese, Jly. 21, Northampton county. R. R. Aug. 4, 1831.
Harris, William H. to Emily Alston, Feb., Halifax county. R. R. Mar. 3, 1831.
Harrison, John R. to Mary Harris, My. 17, Raleigh. R. R. My. 19, 1831.
Hawkins, Celeste to Junius Amis of Northampton county, Oct. 29, Shocco Springs. R. R. Nov. 10, 1831.
Hawkins, Thomas H. to Martha Reed, My., Edgecombe county. R. R. My. 25, 1831.
Hawks, Rev. W. N. to Sarah C. Coart, Apr. 20, Newbern. R. R. Apr. 28, 1831.
Hearn, Fanny to James Bullard, Oct., Chatham county. R. R. Nov. 3, 1831.

Hed, Josiah Q. of Tennessee to Dorcas Sherrell, Jly., Lincoln county. R. R. Jly. 21, 1831.
Hill, Eliza Ann to William A. Wright, Dec. 29, Wilmington. R. R. Jan. 13, 1831.
Hill, William R. to Sarah Ann Simmons, Jan. 12, Raleigh. R. R. Jan. 20, 1831.
Hines, Martha A. of Nashville to Nathaniel B. Brake of Raleigh, Jly., Nashville. R. R. Aug. 11, 1831.
Hobson, Samuel A. to Ann Morehead, My., Rockingham. R. R. My. 25, 1831.
Holliday, Eliza to William A. Darden, My. 12, Greene county. R. R. Je. 9, 1831.
Holtstouser, John to Tena Fesperinan, Oct., Rowan county. R. R. Oct. 13, 1831.
Howard, Alexis to Susan Slade, Jly. 27, Caldwell county, Je. R. R. Aug. 25, 1831.
Howard, Louisa to Edward W. Montford of Onslow county, Je., Jones county. R. R. Je. 23, 1831.
Hoyl, Abel to Nancy H. V. Moorman, Je., Lincolnton. R. R. Je. 23, 1831.
Hundley, W. A. to Miss E. A. Lewis, Aug., Warren county. R. R. Aug. 11, 1831.
Hutchins, Merritt to Elizabeth Stevens, Jan. 4, Wake county. R. R. Jan. 6, 1831.
Irwin, Elizabeth to Arthur Arrington of Nash county, Dec., Edgecombe county. R. R. Jan. 13, 1831.
Jacobs, Gen. Jonathan H. to Mrs. James Fletcher, Mar., Perquimans county. R. R. Mar. 17, 1831.
Jelks, Dr. John A. to Matilda Crowell, Dec., Halifax county. R. R. Jan. 13, 1831.
Jennings, Hiram to Mrs. Harriet Chambers of Anson county, Mar. 9, Wadesborough. R. R. Mar. 31, 1831.
Jerkins, Alonza T. to Sarah M'Ilwain, Jly., Craven county. R. R. Jly. 14, 1831.
Joiner, Worthy to Hardie Johnson, My., Duplin county. R. R. My. 25, 1831.
Jones, Buckner to Frances White, Dec. 22, Newbern. R. R. Jan. 13, 1831.
Jones, Francis Ann of this State to Daniel S. M'Cauley, U. S. Consul for the Regency of Tripoli in Barbary, Oct. 24, Phila. R. R. Nov. 10, 1831.
Jones, Eliza to Alexander Francis Gaston, Mar., Newbern. R. R. Mar. 24, 1831.
Jones, Frederic J. to Hannah A. Shine, Jly., Newbern. R. R. Jly. 21, 1831.
Jones, James G. to Frances Collins, Jly. 14, Halifax county. R. R. Jly. 28, 1831.
Jones, John to Elizabeth Sloan, Je., Hillsborough. R. R. Je. 16, 1831.
Jones, John M. of Edenton to Sarah Hancock, Jly., Newbern. R. R. Jly. 14, 1831.
Jones, Mary Ann H. of Giles county, Tenn. to Thomas T. Armstrong of this State, Jly. R. R. Jly. 21, 1831.
Jones, Dr. Walter G. to Evelina Pickett, Dec. 8, Wadesboro. R. R. Jan. 13, 1831.
Johnson, Hardie to Worthy Joiner, My., Duplin county. R. R. My. 25, 1831.

Johnston, George M. to Eliza M. Bond, Sept., Hillsborough. R. R. Sept. 29, 1831.
Johnson, Margaret B. to James G. Rowe, Apr. 27, Charleston, S. C. R. R. My. 5, 1831.
Johnston, Willie W. to Sarah Miller, Apr. 22, Raleigh. R. R. My. 25, 1831.
Kerr, Martha W. of Richmond, Va. to Dr. James F. Martin of Mocksville, My. 5, Surry county. R. R. Je. 9, 1831.
King, Sarah Ann to Wm. G. Bryan, Dec. 22, Newbern. R. R. Jan. 13, 1831.
Kittrall, Daniel to Nancy Witherington, Dec. 22, Newbern. R. R. Jan. 13, 1831.
Krimminger, Lewis to Laura Coleman, My. 5, Cabarrus county. R. R. Je. 9, 1831.
Lavender, Benjamin A. to Helen Leroy, Mar., Washington, Beaufort county. R. R. Mar. 17, 1831.
Lawrence, Josephus D. M. of Northampton county to Elizabeth R. Powell, Jan. 6, Halifax county. R. R. Jan. 20, 1831.
Leck, Joel to Sylvester Pope, Jan. 6, Halifax county. R. R. Jan. 20, 1831.
Ledbetter, Tabitha R. to Col. Stephen W. Cole, Je., Richmond county. R. R. Je. 23, 1831.
Ligon, William S. to Mary E. Brasfield, Sept. 26, Wake county. R. R. Nov. 3, 1831.
Leroy, Helen to Benjamin A. Lavender, Mar., Washington, Beaufort county. R. R. Mar. 17, 1831.
Lewis, Miss E. A. to W. A. Hundley, Aug., Warren county. R. R. Aug. 11, 1831.
Lillington, Sarah Jane to Octavius N. Corbin, Dec. 24, Wilmington. R. R. Jan. 13, 1831.
Lloyd, Saltar to Eliza Brown, Jly. 7, Bladen county. R. R. Jly. 21, 1831.
Luter, Louisa of Northampton county to Levi Breman of Gates county, Dec. 30, Northampton county. R. R. Jan. 20, 1831.
Lynn, James to Melissa Brasfield, Je., Raleigh. R. R. Je. 9, 1831.
Macon, Dr. Henry J. to Arabella Alston, Je., Warren county. R. R. Je. 23, 1831.
M'Cauley, Daniel S., U. S. Consul for the Regency of Tripoli in Barbary to Francis Ann Jones of this State, Oct. 24, Philadelphia. R. R. Nov. 10, 1831.
M'Caw, William H. of Yorkville, S. C. to Elizabeth Slaughter, Feb., Salisbury. R. R. Feb. 24, 1831.
M'Elderry, Jane to Rev. James G. Hamner of Maryland and Fayetteville, Dec., New York. R. R. Jan. 13, 1831.
M'Ilhenny Margaret to Thomas Cowan, My., Wilmington. R. R. My. 25, 1831.
M'Ilwain, Sarah to Alonza T. Jerkins, Jly., Craven county. R. R. Jly. 14, 1831.
M'Knight, Eleanor M. of Fayette county, Tenn. to David L. Sherrill of Lincoln county, Oct., Iredell county. R. R. Oct. 20, 1831.
M'Nair, Mary Ann to Capt. John C. Smith, Mar. 31, Richmond county. R. R. Apr. 21, 1831.
M'Pherson, Nancy to Greenbury Sutton, Mar., Elizabeth City. R. R. Mar. 24, 1831.

M'Racken, Robert M. of Fayetteville to Sarah Baker, Dec., Brunswick county. R. R. Jan. 13, 1831.
M'Rae, John of Wilmington to Sarah D. S. Blaney of Smithville, Dec. 23, Smithville. R. R. Jan. 13, 1831.
Miller, Sarah to Willie W. Johnston, Apr. 22, Raleigh. R. R. My. 25, 1831.
Mitchenor, John to Miss E. Nance, Feb., Wake county. R. R. Mar. 17, 1831.
Montford, Edward W. of Onslow county to Louisa Howard, Je., Jones county. R. R. Je. 23, 1831.
Moore, Henry of Chatham county to Kezia Whitfield of Lenoir county, Jly. 6, Lenoir county. R. R. Jly. 14, 1831.
Moore, Louisa of Rhode Island to Benjamin Albertson of Elizabeth City, Jly., Elizabeth City. R. R. Jly. 14, 1831.
Moore, Mrs. Sampson to Zachariah Trice, My. 16, Orange county. R. R. Je. 9, 1831.
Morehead, Ann to Samuel A. Hobson, My., Rockingham. R. R. My. 25, 1831.
Murphey, Rebecca to Henry Burns, Aug. 2, Rockingham county. R. R. Aug. 25, 1831.
Martin, Dr. James F. of Mocksville to Martha Kerr of Richmond, Va., My. 5, Surry county. R. R. Je. 9, 1831.
Moorman, Nancy H. V. to Abel Hoyl, Je., Lincolnton. R. R. Je. 23, 1831.
Morrison, Washington of Charlotte to Rosannah Patton, Sept., Asheville. R. R. Sept. 29, 1831.
Myers, Louis R. to Harriet E. B. Worthington of Pitt county, Jly., Washington. R. R. Jly. 14, 1831.
Nance, Miss E. to John Mitchenor, Feb., Wake county. R. R. Mar. 17, 1831.
O'Cain, John to Maniza Phillpot, Jan., Martin county. R. R. Jan. 13, 1831.
Odeneal, Mary B. to Richard R. Fewell, Aug. 31, Raleigh. R. R. Sept. 8, 1831.
Patton, Rosannah to Washington Morrison of Charlotte, Sept., Asheville. R. R. Sept. 29, 1831.
Patterson, James M. to Lucy H. Couch, Jan. 27, Wake county. R. R. Feb. 24, 1831.
Pearson, Laura to Capt. Farnifold Green of U. S. Navy, Jly., Newbern. R. R. Aug. 4, 1831.
Perrin, Elizabeth to Junius C. Dunbibin, Apr. 21, Wilmington. R. R. My. 5, 1831.
Perry, A. J. of Hertford county to Julia Ann Powell, Jan. 6, Halifax county. R. R. Jan. 20, 1831.
Perry, David B. of Williamston to Mrs. Mary Williams, Mar., Washington, Beaufort county. R. R. Mar. 17, 1831.
Perry, Robert of Raleigh to Mrs. Almond Bevers, Je. 9, Raleigh. R. R. Je. 16, 1831.
Phillpot, Maniza to John O'Cain, Jan., Martin county. R. R. Jan. 13, 1831.
Pickett, Evelina to Dr. Walter G. Jones, Dec. 8, Wadesboro. R. R. Jan. 13, 1831.
Pittman, Caroline G. to Elisha Pittman, Dec., Halifax county. R. R. Jan. 13, 1831.

Pittman, Elisha to Caroline G. Pittman, Dec., Halifax county. R. R. Jan. 13, 1831.

Pool, Joseph H. of Elizabeth City to Ann E. Proctor of Camden county, Sept. 15. R. R. Oct. 20, 1831.

Pope, Sylvester to Joel Leck, Jan. 6, Halifax county. R. R. Jan. 20, 1831.

Powell, Elizabeth R. to Josephus D. M. Lawrence of Northampton county, Jan. 6, Halifax county. R. R. Jan. 20, 1831.

Powell, Julia Ann to A. J. Perry of Hertford county, Jan. 6, Halifax county. R. R. Jan. 20, 1831.

Powell, Sophia to John B. Turner, Sept. 28, Johnston county. R. R. Oct. 13, 1831.

Price, Needham of Wake county to Nancy Saunders of Johnston county, Jan. R. R. Jan. 13, 1831.

Prichett, Nancy to James H. Quails, Jan. 6, Halifax county. R. R. Jan. 20, 1831.

Proctor, Ann E. of Camden county to Joseph H. Pool of Elizabeth City, Sept. 15. R. R. Oct. 20, 1831.

Pugh, William W. of Louisiana to William A. Thompson of Bertie county, Aug. 10. R. R. Sept. 1, 1831.

Pulliam, Martha Ann to Walter J. Ramsay, Je. 2, Raleigh. R. R. Jly. 7, 1831.

Quails, James H. to Nancy J. Prichett, Jan. 6, Halifax county. R. R. Jan. 20, 1831.

Ramsay, Walter J. to Martha Ann Pulliam, Je. 2, Raleigh. R. R. Jly. 7, 1831.

Rankin, Rev. Jesse of Orange county to Ann D. Salmon, Je., Fayetteville. R. R. Je. 30, 1831.

Rector, Benjamin of Iredell county to Eliza Caraway of Burke county, Mar. 6, Burke county. R. R. Mar. 31, 1831.

Reece, Lucinda to Daniel Cochernan, Oct., Surry county. R. R. Oct. 13, 1831.

Reed, Martha to Thomas H. Hawkins, My., Edgecombe county. R. R. My. 25, 1831.

Reese, Geo. R. to Rowena Harris, Jly. 21, Northampton county. R. R. Aug. 4, 1831.

Reid, Elizabeth to Thomas Bradburn of Mecklenburg county, Je., Lincoln county. R. R. Je. 9, 1831.

Roberts, Mrs. Wm. C. to Rev. Irvine Atkinson of Edenton, Aug., Edenton. R. R. Aug. 25, 1831.

Ross, Margaret to Benj. J. Spruill, Dec., Edgecombe county. R. R. Jan. 13, 1831.

Rowe, Harriet Herrinan to Dennis Watson, Apr., Craven county. R. R. My. 5, 1831.

Rowe, James G. of Onslow county to Margaret B. Johnson, Apr. 27, Charleston, S. C. R. R. My. 5, 1831.

Royster, Panthea B. to Littlebury Chandler, Feb., Granville county. R. R. Mar. 3, 1831.

Rudisil, Dr. James of Mecklenburg county to Amanda Alexander, Aug., Lincoln county. R. R. Aug. 11, 1831.

Russell, Susan of Washington, Beaufort county to Dr. Fountain Watson of Wythe county, Va., Je., Salem. R. R. Je. 9, 1831.

Salmon, Ann D. to Rev. Jesse Rankin of Orange county, Je., Fayetteville. R. R. Je. 30, 1831.
Sanderson, Mrs. Thomas to Rev. John A. Shaw of Newport, R. I. Mar., Currituck county. R. R. Mar. 24, 1831.
Sanders, Nancy of Johnston county to Needham Price of Wake county, Jan. R. R. Jan. 13, 1831.
Shaw, Rev. John A. of Newport, R. I. to Mrs. Thomas Sanderson, Mar., Currituck county. R. R. Mar. 24, 1831.
Sherrell, David L. of Lincoln county to Eleanor M. M'Knight of Fayette county, Tenn., Oct., Iredell county. R. R. Oct. 20, 1831.
Sherrell, Dorcas to Josiah Q. Hed of Tennessee, Jly., Lincoln county. R. R. Jly. 21, 1831.
Shine, Hannah A. to Frederic A. Jones, Jly., Newbern. R. R. Jly. 21, 1831.
Simmons, Sarah Ann to William R. Hill, Jan. 12, Raleigh. R. R. Jan. 20, 1831.
Sink, Daniel to Miss F. Buner, My., Iredell county. R. R. My. 25, 1831.
Slade, Susan to Alexis Howard, Jly. 27, Caldwell county. R. R. Aug. 25, 1831.
Slaughter, Elizabeth to William H. M'Caw of Yorkville, S. C., Feb., Salisbury. R. R. Feb. 24, 1831.
Sloan, Elizabeth to John Jones, Je., Hillsborough. R. R. Je. 16, 1831.
Smallwood, Orestes K. to Rebecca Eure, Jan., Halifax county. R. R. Jan. 13, 1831.
Smith, Ann L. to William A. Green of Franklin county, Feb. 10, Wake Forest. R. R. Feb. 17, 1831.
Smith, Jane to John B. Goclet of Washington, Dec., Edenton. R. R. Jan. 13, 1831.
Smith, Capt. John C. to Mary Ann M'Nair, Mar. 31, Richmond county. R. R. Apr. 21, 1831.
Smith, Martha to Sylvanus Beasley, My. 19, Wake county. R. R. My. 25, 1831.
Smith, Mary W. of Granville county to Thomas C. Williams of Warren county, Oct. 18, Granville county. R. R. Oct. 27, 1831.
Sparrow, Susan J. to Rev. Philip Anderson of Washington, Je., Newbern. R. R. Je. 9, 1831.
Spears, Dr. A. to Margaret E. Williams, Oct. 18, New Hanover county. R. R. Nov. 3, 1831.
Spruill, Benj. J. to Margaret Ross, Dec., Edgecombe county. R. R. Jan. 13, 1831.
Stevens, Elizabeth to Merritt Hutchins, Jan. 4, Wake county. R. R. Jan. 6, 1831.
Stevens, Sarah to Capt. John Campbell, Oct., Fayetteville. R. R. Nov. 3, 1831.
Stevenson, Elizabeth to James Handcock, Feb., Newbern. R. R. Feb. 10, 1831.
Stevenson, Martin, Jr. to Mary Taylor, Jly. 26, Newbern. R. R. Jly. 28, 1831.
Strudwick, Martha of Hillsborough to Col. Elisha Young of Tuscaloosa, Ala., Jan., Tuscaloosa, Ala. R. R. Jan. 27, 1831.
Strudwick, William F. to Elizabeth Webb, Je., Hillsborough. R. R. Je. 16, 1831.

Sturdivant, Fanny to Joseph Crump, Oct., Chatham county. R. R. Nov. 3, 1831.
Sutton, Greenbury to Nancy M'Pherson, Mar., Elizabeth City. R. R. Mar. 24, 1831.
Swinson, Rev. Henry of Duplin county to Theodosia Darden, My. 11, Greene county. R. R. Je. 9, 1831.
Taylor, Dr. Alex Hamilton of Oxford to Sarah Y. Alston, Dec. 18, Wake Forest. R. R. Jan. 6, 1831.
Taylor, Mary to Martin Stevenson, Jr., Jly. 26, Newbern. R. R. Jly. 28, 1831.
Temple, Alfred to Emma Armistead, Oct., Chatham county. R. R. Nov. 3, 1831.
Tench, Archer to Elizabeth A. J. Deloach, Jly. 28, Raleigh. R. R. Aug. 4, 1831.
Thompson, William A. of Bertie county to William W. Pugh of Louisiana, Aug. 10. R. R. Sept. 1, 1831.
Torreans, Catharine to Wright Williams of Elizabeth City, Dec. 22, Newbern. R. R. Jan. 13, 1831.
Trice, Zachariah to Mrs. Sampson Moore, My. 16, Orange county. R. R. Je. 9, 1831.
Tunstall, Whitmel to Celestia Goneke of Raleigh, Aug. 24, Danville, Va. R. R. Sept. 1, 1831.
Turner, John B. to Sophia Powell, Sept. 28, Johnston county. R. R. Oct. 13, 1831.
Turner, Sarah P. of Warren county to Hon. Mark Alexander of Virginia, Je. 1. R. R. Je. 16, 1831.
Vines, Mary to John Brinkley, Mar., Washington, Beaufort county. R. R. Mar. 17, 1831.
Waller, Anne to James Bilbry, Jan., Edgecombe county. R. R. Jan. 13, 1831.
Washington, Ann of Lenoir county to J. W. Bryan, Feb., Newbern. R. R. Feb. 10, 1831.
Watson, Dennis to Harriet Herrimon Rowe, Apr., Craven county. R. R. My. 5, 1831.
Watson, Dr. Fountain of Wythe county, Va. to Susan Russell of Washington, Beaufort county, Je., Salem. R. R. Je. 9, 1831.
Watters, Dr. John to Marietta Black, Apr., New Hanover county. R. R. My. 5, 1831.
Webb, Elizabeth to William F. Strudwick, Je., Hillsborough. R. R. Je. 16, 1831.
White, Rev. Arch'd of Baltimore to Susan N. Grier of Mecklenburg county, Apr. 19, Mecklenburg county. R. R. My. 5, 1831.
White, Frances to Buckner Jones, Dec. 22, Newbern. R. R. Jan. 13, 1831.
Whitfield, Kezia of Lenoir county to Henry Moore of Chatham county, Jly. 6, Lenoir county. R. R. Jly. 14, 1831.
Whitfield, Lewis S. of Lenoir county to Mary Ann Glasgow, Oct., Greene county. R. R. Oct. 13, 1831.
Williams, Col. B. W. of Tallahassee to Rebecca B. Branch of this State, Apr. 26, Washington, D. C. R. R. Apr. 28, 1831.
Williams, Margaret E. to Dr. A. Spears, Oct. 18, New Hanover county. R. R. Nov. 3, 1831.

Williams, Mrs. Mary to David B. Perry, Mar., Washington, Beaufort county. R. R. Mar. 17, 1831.
Williams, Thomas C. of Warren county to Mary W. Smith of Granville county, Oct. 18, Granville county. R. R. Oct. 27, 1831.
Williams, Wright of Elizabeth City to Catharine Torrans, Dec. 22, Newbern. R. R. Jan. 13, 1831.
Williamson, Cynthia to John M. Alexander of Mecklenburg county, My. 5, Mecklenburg county. R. R. Je. 9, 1831.
Wilson, S. Catherine of Tennessee to Hon. Sam'l Carson of this State, My. 5, Surry county. R. R. Je. 9, 1831.
Wisdom, John G. to Usly Cate, Dec. 16, Person county. R. R. Jan. 13, 1831.
Witherington, Nancy to Daniel Kittral, Dec. 22, Newbern. R. R. Jan. 13, 1831.
Wood, Elizabeth to Henry Gilliam of Gates county, Dec., Perquimans county. R. R. Jan. 13, 1831.
Worthington, Harriet E. B. of Pitt county to Louis R. Myers, Jly., Washington. R. R. Jly. 14, 1831.
Wright, W. P. of Fayetteville to Eliza Gilliam, Apr. 21, Oxford. R. R. Apr. 28, 1831.
Wright, William A. to Eliza Ann Hill, Dec. 29, Wilmington. R. R. Jan. 13, 1831.
Yarbrough, Frances D. to Alexander S. J. Allison, Jly. 14, Hillsborough. R. R. Aug. 4, 1831.
Young, Col. Elisha of Tuscaloosa, Ala. to Martha Strudwick of Hillsborough, Jan., Tuscaloosa, Ala. R. R. Jan. 27, 1831.

1832

Anderson, Joseph J. to Susan E. Overstreet, Nov. 15, Halifax county. R. R. Nov. 30, 1832.
Black, Ann to John Davis of Granville county, Nov., Fayetteville. R. R. Nov. 15, 1832.
Britton, Ellen to Lewis W. Thompson, Nov., Bertie county. R. R. Dec. 7, 1832.
Brogdon, Nathan to Cuzziah Hood, Nov., Wayne county. R. R. Nov. 15 1832.
Davis, John of Granville county to Ann Black, Nov., Fayetteville. R. R. Nov. 15, 1832.
Dicken, Ephraim of Edgecombe county to Charlotte Whitehead, Nov. 6, Edgecombe county. R. R. Nov. 23, 1832.
Graham, Hamilton of Newbern to Minerva Little, Dec. 13, Littleton, Warren county. R. R. Dec. 21, 1832.
Harrell, John to Eliza J. M. Harvey, Nov. 8, Halifax county. R. R. Nov. 23, 1832.
Harris, Charles J. of Cabarrus county to Jane Lenora Springs, Nov., Mecklenburg county. R. R. Nov. 15, 1832.
Harvey, Mrs. Eliza J. M. to John Harrell, Nov. 8, Halifax county. R. R. Nov. 23, 1832.
Holman, Wilson to Elizabeth Turner, Nov., Anson county. R. R. Nov. 15, 1832.

Hood, Cuzziah to Nathan Brogdon, Nov., Wayne county. R. R. Nov. 15, 1832.

Horne, Lawrence to Elizabeth Mercer, Nov. 6, Edgecombe county. R. R. Nov. 23, 1832.

Hunt, Elizabeth T. to E. Towns of Norfolk, Nov. 8, Granville county. R. R. Nov. 30, 1832.

Lands, Augustus to Frances O'Brien, Nov. 15, Granville county. R. R. Nov. 30, 1832.

Little, Minerva to Hamilton Graham of Newbern, Dec. 13, Littleton, Warren county. R. R. Dec. 21, 1832.

Martin, Elizabeth to Henry Swan, Nov., Wilkes county. R. R. Nov. 15, 1832.

Mercer, Elizabeth to Lawrence Horne, Nov. 6, Edgecombe county. R. R. Nov. 23, 1832.

Moore, Maurice to Sarah Ann Watts, Nov. 1, Williamston, Martin county. R. R. Nov. 23, 1832.

Nunnally, Mary to Peyton T. Stublefield of Rockingham, Nov., Caswell county. R. R. Nov. 15, 1832.

O'Brien, Frances to Augustus Lands, Nov. 15, Granville county. R. R. Nov. 30, 1832.

Overstreet, Susan E. to Joseph J. Anderson, Nov. 15, Halifax county. R. R. Nov. 30, 1832.

Raboteau, Eleanor to Wm. Waddill, Jr., Nov., Fayetteville. R. R. Nov. 30, 1832.

Rayner, Miss L. to George E. Thomas, Nov., Bertie county. R. R. Dec. 7, 1832.

Springs, Jane Lenora to Charles J. Harris of Cabarrus county, Nov., Mecklenburg county. R. R. Nov. 15, 1832.

Stublefield, Peyton T. of Rockingham to Mary Nunnally, Nov., Caswell county. R. R. Nov. 15, 1832.

Swan, Henry to Elizabeth Martin, Nov., Wilkes county. R. R. Nov. 15, 1832.

Thomas, George E. to Miss L. Rayner, Nov., Bertie county. R. R. Dec. 7, 1832.

Thompson, Lewis W. to Ellen Britton, Nov., Bertie county. R. R. Dec. 7, 1832.

Towns, E. of Norfolk to Elizabeth T. Hunt, Nov. 8, Granville county. R. R. Nov. 30, 1832.

Turner, Elizabeth to Wilson Holman, Nov., Anson county. R. R. Nov. 15, 1832.

Watts, Sarah Ann to Maurice Moore, Nov. 1, Williamston, Martin county. R. R. Nov. 23, 1832.

Waddill, Wm. Jr. to Eleanor Raboteau, Nov., Fayetteville. R. R. Nov. 30, 1832.

Whitehead, Charlotte to Ephraim Dicken of Edgecombe county, Nov. 6, Edgecombe county. R. R. Nov. 23, 1832.

1833

Abernethy, William A. to Barbara Reinhardt, Apr. 2, Lincoln county. R. R. Apr. 9, 1833.

Adcock, Frances to John H. Liles, Jr. of Anson county, Feb. 19, Anson county. R. R. Mar. 12, 1833.
Alford, Sophia to Zachariah Drake, Feb., Robeson county. R. R. Mar. 5, 1833.
Alston, Joseph J. of Tennessee to Louisa D. Thomas, Je., Louisburg. R. R. Jly. 9, 1833.
Ambrose, Ann Maria to Robert W. James of Wilmington, Apr. 3, Onslow county. R. R. Apr. 16, 1833.
Andrews, William J. of Edgecombe to Virginia Hawkins, My. 8, Franklin county. R. R. My. 28, 1833.
Arrington, Mary to Thomas R. Wiggins, Apr. 11, Nash county. R. R. Apr. 30, 1833.
Bagge, Rebecca to Rev. Henry A. Shultz, Apr. 16, Salem. R. R. Apr. 30, 1833.
Bailey, Capt. Anson to Elizabeth Barksdale, Jly., Fayetteville. R. R. Jly. 23, 1833.
Baine, Sarah to William G. Townsend of Cabarrus county, Oct. 31, Mecklenburg county. R. R. Dec. 3, 1833.
Baine, William T. of Pittsborough to Martha Ann Hill of Wake county, Sept. 4, Raleigh. R. R. Sept. 10, 1833.
Baker, Laura to Rev. Joseph Saunders, Mar. 25, Martin county. R. R. My. 21, 1833.
Baldwin, H. J. of South Carolina to Lucy Ann Daniel, Jan. 15, Ashborough, Randolph county. R. R. Feb. 1, 1833.
Barksdale, Elizabeth to Capt. Anson Bailey, Jly., Fayetteville. R. R. Jly. 23, 1833.
Barringer, Paul B. to Mary P. Carson, Apr. 4, Concord. R. R. Apr. 30, 1833.
Bell, Lucinda to William S. Mhoon, Sept. 18, Raleigh. R. R. Sept. 24, 1833.
Berryman, Mary to Richard Cole, Mar. 7, Moore county. R. R. Mar. 26, 1833.
Bizzell, William H. to Mary Fort, Apr., Wayne county. R. R. Apr. 23, 1833.
Blake, Mary S. to George C. McNeill, Dec. 27, Fayetteville. R. R. Jan. 18, 1833.
Blue, Malcom to Isabella M. Patterson, Oct., Moore county. R. R. Nov. 5, 1833.
Bradley, Rev. Jacky to Susan Russell of Fayetteville, Mar. 7, Robeson county. R. R. Mar. 26, 1833.
Branch, Sarah to James Hunter, Jly. 16, Enfield, Halifax county. R. R. Jly. 30, 1833.
Bridges, Mrs. Jane B. to Elisha Harrison, Mar. 28, Johnston couunty. R. R. Apr. 2, 1833.
Brinkley, John A. to Jane Parrish, Dec. 5, Granville county. R. R. Jan. 18, 1833.
Brooke, Anna Matilda of Montgomery county, Pa. to Bernard Dupry of Raleigh, Oct. 29, Phila. R. R. Nov. 12, 1833.
Brown, Asa A. of Wilmington to Lucy Brown, Dec. 19, Bladen county. R. R. Jan. 11, 1833.

Brown, Geo. W. to Harriet B. Long of Salisbury, My. 21. R. R. Jly. 9, 1833.
Brown, Lucy to Asa A. Brown of Wilmington, Dec. 19, Bladen county. R. R. Jan. 11, 1833.
Bryan, Mary to Thomas Mayo, Feb. 19, Edgecombe county. R. R. Mar. 12, 1833.
Bryan, John to Mary L. Ellison, Apr. 4, Craven county. R. R. Apr. 9, 1833.
Bryant, Mrs. Priscilla to James Ethergain, Aug. 22, Scotland Neck, Halifax county. R. R. Sept. 10, 1833.
Buffaloe, William of Raleigh to Margaret Farrow, Oct. 1, Hyde county. R. R. Oct. 15, 1833.
Bunting, Samuel to Eliza Moore, Feb., Sampson county. R. R. Mar. 12, 1833.
Burch, Oliver L. of Raleigh to Cornelia R. Lewis, Oct. 31, Chapel Hill. R. R. Nov. 5, 1833.
Burnett, Caroline to Ebenezer Hyman, Jan. 15, Martin county. R. R. Feb. 1, 1833.
Burton, Frances A. M. to Michael Hoke of Lincolnton, Apr. 8, Beatties Ford, Lincoln county. R. R. My. 21, 1833.
Caison, Cannon of Fayetteville to Harriet Jessop, Apr. 10, Bladen county. R. R. My. 21, 1833.
Calhoun, A. C. to Eugenia Chappell, Jan. 3, Cumberland county. R. R. Jan. 25, 1833.
Callender, Mrs. Anna to Mr. Vansycle of Newbern, Jan. 3, New Hanover county. R. R. Jan. 25, 1833.
Cameron, Paul C. to Ann Ruffin, Dec. 20, Orange county. R. R. Jan. 4, 1833.
Cameron, Dr. Thomas N. to Isabella Wilkins, Dec., Fayetteville. R. R. Dec. 24, 1833.
Campbell, Frances of Brunswick county to Hugh Y. Waddell, Apr. 23, Clarendon. R. R. Je. 4, 1833.
Candler, George W. to Rachel E. Moore, Je., Buncombe county. R. R. Je. 18, 1833.
Capeheart, George W. to Susan R. Martin, Nov., Winton. R. R. Dec. 3, 1833.
Caroline, Mary Bird of Orange county to Jordan Hill of Raleigh, Oct. 24, Greensboro, Alabama. R. R. Nov. 5, 1833.
Carson, Mary P. to Paul B. Barringer, Apr. 4, Concord. R. R. Apr. 30, 1833.
Carson, Ruth Matilda to Wm. B. Hawkins, Jly. 7, Burke county. R. R. Jly. 23, 1833.
Carter, Louisa Jane of Chatham county to Hiram Hadley of Indiana, Apr. 21, Chatham county. R. R. Je. 4, 1833.
Chambers, Wm. to Nancy Thompson, Feb. 16, Orange county. R. R. Mar. 19, 1833.
Chapman, Isabella C. to Arthur Lewis of Wilmington, Oct., Cumberland county. R. R. Nov. 12, 1833.
Chappell, Eugenia to A. A. Calhoun, Jan. 3, Cumberland county. R. R. Jan. 25, 1833.

Cherry, Elizabeth to Thomas Howell of Martin county, Feb. 3, Pitt county. R. R. Feb. 26, 1833.
Cherry, Merina to Robert Rew, Dec. 27, Washington, Beaufort county. R. R. Jan. 25, 1833.
Chipley, Juliana St. Clair to Dr. Elisha Stedman of Pittsborough, Apr., Kentucky. R. R. Apr. 16, 1833.
Christman, Thomas F. to Grizzy Ann Hill, Jly. 16, Wake county. R. R. Jly. 23, 1833.
Clark, Frances H. of Scotland Neck to Andrew B. White of Pennsylvania, Apr. 11, Scotland Neck. R. R. Apr. 30, 1833.
Clark, Laura P. to John W. Cotten, Dec., Tarborough. R. R. Jan. 4, 1833.
Clark, Louisa to Archibald Forbes, Jan. 21, Greenville, Pitt county. R. R. Feb. 1, 1833.
Clark, Margaret to Lewis Thompson, Jan. 22, Bertie county. R. R. Feb. 1, 1833.
Clark, Maria to James Parks, Mar. 7, Hillsborough. R. R. Mar. 19, 1833.
Clark; Dr. A. A. to Margaret J. Nicholson, Mar. 18, Bladen county. R. R. My. 7, 1833.
Cofied, Sarah of Bertie county to Wm. E. L. Parrish, Feb., Cumberland county. R. R. Mar. 5, 1833.
Cole, Richard to Mary Berryman. Mar. 7, Moore county. R. R. Mar. 26, 1833.
Collins, Major William F. of Nash county to Apphia S. Williams, Dec. 18, Chatham county. R. R. Dec. 24, 1833.
Cotten, John W. to Laura P. Clark, Dec., Tarborough. R. R. Jan. 4, 1833.
Cousins, Wm. A. of Virginia to Matilda Duty, Dec. 5, Granville county. R. R. Jan. 18, 1833.
Craig, Laura S. to Dr. John H. Treadwell, Sept., Montgomery county. R. R. Oct. 1, 1833.
Crawford, Thomas R. of Beaufort county to Susan Fonville, Mar., Craven county. R. R. Mar. 12, 1833.
Crenshaw, Mary Ann to John M. Fleming, Mar. 12, Wake Forest. R. R. Mar. 19, 1833.
Cutlar, Ann E. to Thomas F. Davis, My. 20, Wilmington. R. R. Je. 4, 1833.
Daniel, Lucy Ann to H. J. Baldwin of South Carolina, Jan. 15, Ashborough, Randolph county. R. R. Feb. 1, 1833.
Davis, Thomas F. to Ann E. Cutlar, My. 20, Wilmington. R. R. Je. 4, 1833.
Deberry, Wilson to Elizabeth Wall, Aug., Montgomery county. R. R. Aug. 20, 1833.
Deloach, Louisa W. to William W Taylor, Feb. 14, Raleigh. R. R. Feb. 22, 1833.
Dennis, Rev. James to Caroline Helm, Sept. 24, Smithfield. R. R. Oct. 1, 1833.
Dinkins, Lucinda to Lewis G. Slaughter of Salisbury, My. 20, Mecklenburg county. R. R. Jly. 9, 1833.
Dodd, James to Eliza M. Evans of Fayetteville, Feb. 21, Cumberland county. R. R. Mar. 12, 1833.
Dodson, Lucy M. to Jacob Ramsour of Lincolnton, Oct. 3, Milton. R. R. Oct. 15, 1833.

Donaldson, Amanda Malvina to John Winslow of Fayetteville, Oct. 2, Wake county. R. R. Oct. 15, 1833.
Donoho, Wm. C. to Nancy Miles, Mar. 21, Caswell county. R. R. Apr. 2, 1833.
Dossey, Margaret P. of Society Hill, S. C. to John B. Williams of Windsor, Oct. 15. R. R. Nov. 12, 1833.
Drake, Zachariah to Sophia Alford, Feb., Robeson county. R. R. Mar. 5, 1833.
Dupuy, Bernard of Raleigh to Anna Matilda Brooke of Montgomery county, Pa., Oct. 29, Philadelphia. R. R. Nov. 12, 1833.
Duty, Matilda to Wm. A. Cousins of Virginia, Dec. 5, Granville county. R. R. Jan. 18, 1833.
Edwards, Winifred to Joseph M. M'Kinney, Apr. 2, Greene county. R. R. Apr. 16, 1833.
Ellison, Mary L. to John Bryan, Apr. 4, Craven county. R. R. Apr. 16, 1833.
Ethergain, James to Mrs. Priscilla Bryant, Aug. 22, Scotland Neck, Halifax county. R. R. Sept. 10, 1833.
Evans, Eliza to James Dodd of Fayetteville, Feb. 21, Cumberland county. R. R. Mar. 12, 1833.
Faison, Eliza Ann to Patrick Murphy, Je., Sampson county. R. R. Je. 18, 1833.
Faison, Jas. of Sampson county to Elizabeth Lane, Oct. 15, Wayne county. R. R. Oct. 29, 1833.
Farrow, Margaret to William Buffaloe of Raleigh, Oct. 1, Hyde county. R. R. Oct. 15, 1833.
Finley, Caroline Ellen to James Harper of Burke county, Sept., Augusta county, Va. R. R. Sept. 24, 1833.
Fleming, John M. to Mary Ann Crenshaw, Mar. 12, Wake Forest. R. R. Mar. 19, 1833.
Fonville, Susan to Thomas R. Crawford of Beaufort county, Mar., Craven county. R. R. Mar. 12, 1833.
Forbes, Archibald to Louisa Ann Clark, Jan. 21, Greenville, Pitt county. R. R. Feb. 1, 1833.
Fort, Mary to William H. Bizzell, Apr., Wayne county. R. R. Apr. 23, 1833.
Foster, Wililam H. of Louisburg to Ann Eliza Taylor, Jly., Franklin county. R. R. Jly. 30, 1833.
Foster, William of Louisburg to Mary Ellen Wiatt, Aug. 29, Raleigh. R. R. Sept. 3, 1833.
Freeman, Edith of Robeson county to Thomas L. Todd of South Carolina, Apr. 4, Lumberton. R. R. My. 21, 1833.
Freeman, Capt. Richard P. to Sarah L. J. Worley, Sept., Bertie county. R. R. Sept. 24, 1833.
Gant, Joshua R. to Ann W. Reeves, Sept., Orange county. R. R. Sept. 24, 1833.
Garland, Hannah S. to David Ryan, Jly., Bertie county. R. R. Jly. 30, 1833.
Garrett, Dr. Richard W. to Mary T. Lea, My., Chatham county. R. R. My. 28, 1833.

Gauze, John Peter to Hannah Jane Green, Feb. 21, Brunswick county. R. R. Mar. 5, 1833.
Gibson, James to Janet Newberry, Sept., Fayetteville. R. R. Oct. 1, 1833.
Goodloe, Attelia of this State to Richard C. Williams of Dresden, Dec. 31, Fayette county, Tenn. R. R. Mar. 12, 1833.
Goodloe, Robert C. to Mary Ann Harper, Dec. 18, Franklin county. R. R. Jan. 18, 1833.
Goodwin, Maria L. to Benson F. Jones, Oct. 1, Raleigh. R. R. Oct. 8, 1833.
Guy, Wm. H. to Susan M'Cullers, Sept. 24, Smithfield. R. R. Oct. 1, 1833.
Graves, Mary of Caswell county to James Mebane of Orange county, Feb., Caswell county. R. R. Feb. 22, 1833.
Green, Hannah Jane to Peter John Gauze, Feb. 21, Brunswick county. R. R. Mar. 5, 1833.
Hackney, Candace Hinton to Albert G. Hinton, Aug., Chatham county. R. R. Aug. 13, 1833.
Hadley, Hiram of Indiana to Louisa Jane Carter of Chatham county, Apr. 21, Chatham county. R. R. Je. 4, 1833.
Hall, Sarah to Richard H. Smith, Dec. 4, Warrenton. R. R. Dec. 17, 1833.
Harper, James of Burke county to Caroline Ellen Finley, Sept., Augusta county, Va. R. R. Sept. 24, 1833.
Harper, Mary Ann to Robert C. Goodloe, Dec. 18, Franklin county. R. R. Jan. 18, 1833.
Harrison, Elisha to Mrs. Jane B. Bridges, Mar. 28, Johnston county. R. R. Apr. 2, 1833.
Hatch, Caroline E. to Henry G. Smith of Lenoir county, Jan. 21, Fayette county, Tenn. R. R. Apr. 9, 1833.
Hauser, William to Ann Susanna Shultz, Dec. 26, Salem. R. R. Jan. 18, 1833.
Hawkins, Virginia to William J. Andrews of Edgecombe county, My. 8, Franklin county. R. R. My. 28, 1833.
Hawkins, Wm. B. to Ruth Matilda Carson, Jly. 7, Burke county. R. R. Jly. 23, 1833.
Hayes, John L. to Margaret M. Smith, Nov. 7, Charlotte. R. R. Dec. 3, 1833.
Hearn, Mary R. to Danford Richards, Feb. 3, Tarborough. R. R. Feb. 26, 1833.
Herring, Rachel to William M. Miller of Duplin county, Mar. 5, Lenoir county. R. R. Mar. 12, 1833.
Helm, Caroline to Rev. James Dennis, Sept. 24, Smithfield. R. R. Oct. 1, 1833.
Heyer, Harriet to Rev. Henry A. Rowland of Fayetteville, Sept., New York. R. R. Sept. 10, 1833.
Hill, Grizzy Ann to Thomas F. Christman, Jly. 16, Wake county. R. R. Jly. 23, 1833.
Hill, Jordan of Raleigh to Miss Caroline Mary Bird of Orange county, Oct. 24, Greensboro, Alabama. R. R. Nov. 5, 1833.
Hill, Martha Ann of Wake county to William T. Bain of Pittsborough, Sept. 4, Raleigh. R. R. Sept. 10, 1833.
Hill, Winifred B. to Rev. William Norwood, Apr. 11, Scotland Neck. R. R. Apr. 23, 1833.

Hinton, Albert G. to Candace Hinton Hackney, Aug., Chatham county. R. R. Aug. 13, 1833.
Hoke, Michael of Lincolnton to Frances A. M. Burton, Apr. 8, Beatties Ford, Lincoln county. R. R. My. 21, 1833.
Holderby, George H. to Delilah Morehead, Sept., Rockingham county. R. R. Sept. 24, 1833.
Holmes, Mary to Capt. Alexander M'Neill, Aug. 15, Cumberland county. R. R. Sept. 3, 1833.
Holt, John R. to Catherine Trolinger, Aug. 23, Orange county. R. R. Sept. 10, 1833.
Horne, John R. of Edgecombe county to Eliza Jane Burt, Oct. 24, Nash county. R. R. Nov. 12, 1833.
House, Sarah Willis to Col. Archibald S. M'Neill of Cumberland county, Feb., Haywood, Chatham county. R. R. Mar. 5, 1833.
Howard, Eliza S. to William N. Peden, Oct. 30, New Hanover county. R. R. Nov. 19, 1833.
Howell, Thomas of Martin county to Elizabeth Cherry, Feb. 3, Pitt county. R. R. Feb. 26, 1833.
Hunter, James to Sarah Branch, Jly. 16, Enfield, Halifax county. R. R. Jly. 30, 1833.
Hunter, Mildred to Benjamin Williams of Chatham county, Apr. 23, Wake county. R. R. Je. 4, 1833.
Hughes, Matthew to Penelope Perry, Nov., Bertie county. R. R. Dec. 3, 1833.
Huie, Robt of Salisbury to Mary Partee, Sept. 26, Rowan county. R. R. Oct. 15, 1833.
Hyman, Ebenezer to Caroline Burnett, Jan. 15, Martin county. R. R. Feb. 1, 1833.
Jacocks, Mary Caroline to James V. Reed, Jly. 23, Perquimans county. R. R. Aug. 13, 1833.
James, Robert W. of Wilmington to Ann Maria Ambrose, Apr. 3, Onslow county. R. R. Apr. 16, 1833.
Jeffreys, William O. to Mary M'Gary, Sept., Fayetteville. R. R. Oct. 1, 1833.
Jessop, Harriet to Cannon Caison of Fayetteville, Apr. 10, Bladen county. R. R. My. 21, 1833.
Johnson, C. S. to Sibella Murchison, Apr. 10, Cumberland county. R. R. My. 14, 1833.
Jones, Ann Elizabeth to Henry W. Montague, My., Wake county. R. R. My. 28, 1833.
Jones, Benson F. of Oxford to Maria L. Goodwin, Oct. 1, Raleigh. R. R. Oct. 8, 1833.
Jones, Susan J. to P. R. Stringfield, Sept., New Hanover county. R. R. Sept. 24, 1833.
Jones, Thomas to Evelina Taylor, Dec., Martin county. R. R. Jan. 4, 1833.
Kendall, Miss to Thomas Randle, Jan. 3, Montgomery county. R. R. Jan. 25, 1833.
Kennedy, Capt. Josiah of Moore county to Ann Eliza M'Neill, Aug., Tennessee. R. R. Aug. 20, 1833.
Kidd, Nabby to George M'Neill, Aug., Fayetteville. R. R. Aug. 13, 1833.

Lane, Elizabeth to Jas. Faison of Sampson county, Oct. 15, Wayne county. R. R. Oct. 29, 1833.
Lawrence, Dr. Josiah of Tarboro to Mary Eliza Toole, Feb. 20, Greenville. R. R. Mar. 12, 1833.
Lea, Mary T. to Dr. Richard W. Garrett, My., Chatham county. R. R. My. 28, 1833.
Lea, Thomas L. to Ann Wright, Apr. 18, Caswell county. R. R. My. 7, 1833.
Leach, James T. to Elizabeth W. Saunders, Jly. 21, Johnston county. R. R. Jly. 30, 1833.
Leak, F. T. of Rockingham to Harriet Harris Marsh of Northampton, Mass., Apr. 16, Rockingham. R. R. My. 28, 1833.
Lewis, Arthur of Wilmington to Isabella C. Chapman, Oct., Cumberland county. R. R. Nov. 12, 1833.
Lewis, Cornelia R. to Oliver L. Burch of Raleigh, Oct. 31, Chapel Hill. R. R. Nov. 5, 1833.
Liles, John H. Jr. to Frances Adcock of Anson county, Feb. 19, Anson county. R. R. Mar. 12, 1833.
Lilly, David C. of Montgomery county to Eliza Spencer, Jly., Anson county. R. R. Jly. 23, 1833.
Lindsay, Nancy Lavinia to Milton H. Saunders, Jly. 30, Guilford county. R. R. Aug. 20, 1833.
Long, Harriet B. of Salisbury to Geo W. Brown, My. 21, Jly. 9, 1833.
Love, Jane to Dr. Osborne Sugg, Je. 4, Wake county. R. R. Je. 11, 1833.
Lumpkin, Elizabeth to Geo. Winburn, Dec. 7, Granville county. R. R. Feb. 18, 1833.
Lumsden, F. A. of Raleigh to Mrs. Clara W. Powell, Apr., Wilmington. R. R. Apr. 23, 1833.
Lynum, Alice to Thomas Reynolds, Dec., Raleigh. R. R. Dec. 31, 1833.
M'Coy, Emeline of Bladen county to William Nash Whitted, Sept. 7, Hillsborough. R. R. Sept. 24, 1833.
M'Crane, Isabella to Malcom M. M'Kay, Apr. 14, Cumberland county. R. R. My. 28, 1833.
M'Gary, Mary to William O. Jeffreys, Sept., Fayetteville. R. R. Oct. 1, 1833.
M'Cullers, Susan to Wm. H. Guy, Sept., Smithfield. R. R. Oct. 1, 1833.
M'Kay, Malcolm M. to Isabella M'Crane, Apr. 14, Cumberland county. R. R. My. 28, 1833.
M'Kinney, Joseph M. to Winifred Edwards, Apr. 2, Greene county. R. R. Apr. 16, 1833.
M'Laughlin, Benjamin L. of South Carolina to Eliza M'Lean, Jly., Richmond county. R. R. Jly. 30, 1833.
M'Lean, Major Alexander D. to Catharine M'Lean, Jan. 3, Cumberland county. R. R. Jan. 25, 1833.
M'Lean, Catharine to Major Alexander M'Lean, Jan. 3, Cumberland county. R. R. Jan. 25, 1833.
M'Lean, Eliza to Benjamin L. M'Laughlin of South Carolina, Jly., Richmond county. R. R. Jly. 30, 1833.
M'Neill, Ann Eliza to Capt. Josiah Kennedy of Moore county, Aug., Tennessee. R. R. Aug. 20, 1833.
M'Neill, Capt. Alexander to Mary Holmes, Aug. 15, Cumberland county. R. R. Sept. 3, 1833.

M'Neill, Col. Archibald S. of Cumberland county to Sarah Willis House, Feb., Haywood, Chatham county. R. R. Mar. 5, 1833.

M'Neill, George C. to Mary S. Blake, Dec. 27, Fayetteville. R. R. Jan. 18, 1833.

M'Neill, George to Nabby Kidd, Aug., Fayetteville. R. R. Aug. 13, 1833.

M'Rae, John to Catharine Ann Smith, Nov. 7, Cumberland county. R. R. Nov. 19, 1833.

Mahoney, James of Cheraw, S. C. to Helen P. Richardson of Bladen county, Dec. 27, Fayetteville. R. R. Jan. 18, 1833.

Mask, Fanny of Richmond county to Elijah Whealington of Alabama, Apr. 21, Richmond county. R. R. My. 7, 1833.

Marsh, Harriet Harris of Northampton, Mass to F. T. Leake of Rockingham, Apr. 16. R. R. My. 28, 1833.

Martin, Emily A. to James Waddill of Wadesborough, Sept. 26, Anson county. R. R. Oct. 15, 1833.

Martin, Susan R. to George W. Capeheart, Nov., Winton. R. R. Dec. 3, 1833.

Martin, William of Granville county to Sarah Yeargin, Feb. 5, Wake county. R. R. Feb. 15, 1833.

Mayo, Thomas to Mary Bryan, Feb. 19, Edgecombe county. R. R. Mar. 12, 1833.

Mebane, James of Orange county to Mary Graves of Caswell county, Feb., Caswell county. R. R. Feb. 22, 1833.

Mendenhall, Rhoda to Messer A. Vestal of Jamestown, Feb., Guilford county. R. R. Mar. 5, 1833.

Meredith, Elizabeth to Calvin Peacock, Jan. 3, Montgomery county. R. R. Jan. 25, 1833.

Mhoon, William S. to Lucinda A. Bell, Sept. 18, Raleigh. R. R. Sept. 24, 1833.

Miles, Nancy to Wm. C. Donoho, Mar. 21, Caswell county. R. R. Apr. 2, 1833.

Miller, Thomas of Burke county to Mary Ann Robards, Granville county, Jan. R. R. Jan. 18, 1833.

Miller, William M. of Duplin county to Rachel Herring, Mar. 5, Lenoir county. R. R. Mar. 12, 1833.

Mitchell, Jane of Newbern to Jones Watson, Sept. 10, Chapel Hill. R. R. Sept. 24, 1833.

Montague, Henry to Ann Elizabeth Jones, My., Wake county. R. R. My. 28, 1833.

Moore, Alfred to Cresy Van, Jan. 8, Greenville, Pitt county. R. R. Feb. 1, 1833.

Moore, Cornelia G. to Junius P. Moore, Je. 3, Person county. R. R. Jly. 9, 1833.

Moore, Rachel E. to George W. Candler, Je., Buncombe county. R. R. Je. 18, 1833.

Moore, Junius P. to Cornelia G. Moore, Je. 3, Person county. R. R. Jly. 9, 1833.

Morehead, Delilah to George H. Holderby, Sept., Rockingham county. R. R. Sept. 24, 1833.

Murchison, Sibella to C. S. Johnson, Apr. 10, Cumberland county. R. R. My. 14, 1833.

Murphey, Alexander A. to Eliza G. Womack, Apr. 16, Haywood county. R. R. Apr. 30, 1833.
Murphy, Patrick to Eliza Ann Faison, Je., Sampson county. R. R. Je. 18, 1833.
Newberry, Janet to James Gibson, Sept., Fayetteville. R. R. Oct. 1, 1833.
Newsom, James D. of Wake county to Miss Perry, Mar., Franklin county. R. R. Mar. 19, 1833.
Nicholson, Margaret J. to Dr. A. A. Clarke, Mar. 18, Bladen county. R. R. My. 7, 1833.
Norwood, Rev. William to Winifred B. Hill, Apr. 11, Scotland Neck. R. R. Apr. 23, 1833.
Parish, Jane to John A. Brinkley, Dec. 5, Granville county. R. R. Jan. 18, 1833.
Parks, James to Maria Clark, Mar. 7, Hillsborough. R. R. Mar. 19, 1833.
Parrish, Wm. E. L. to Sarah Cofield of Bertie county, Feb., Cumberland county. R. R. Mar. 5, 1833.
Partee, Mary to Robt. Huie of Salisbury, Sept. 26, Rowan county. R. R. Oct. 15, 1833.
Patterson, Isabella M. to Malcolm Blue, Oct., Moore county. R. R. Nov. 5, 1833.
Peacock, Calvin to Elizabeth Meredith, Jan. 3, Montgomery county. R. R. Jan. 25, 1833.
Peden, William N. to Eliza S. Howard, Oct. 30, New Hanover county. R. R. Nov. 19, 1833.
Perry, Miss to James D. Newsom of Wake county, Mar., Franklin county. R. R. Mar. 19, 1833.
Perry, Penelope to Matthew Hughes, Nov., Bertie county. R. R. Dec. 3, 1833.
Potter, Olivia to John M. Stedman, Nov. 7, Fayetteville. R. R. Nov. 19, 1833.
Powell, Mrs. Clara W. to F. A. Lumsden of Raleigh, Apr., Wilmington. R. R. Apr. 23, 1833.
Pucket, Eli to Ann W. Swain, Apr., Iredell county. R. R. Apr. 23, 1833.
Purcell, Malcolm to Clarky Sophia Drake, Feb., Robeson county. R. R. Mar. 5, 1833.
Ramsour, Jacob of Lincolnton to Lucy M. Dodson, Oct. 3, Milton. R. R. Oct. 15, 1833.
Randle, Thomas to Miss Kendall, Jan. 3, Montgomery county. R. R. Jan. 25, 1833.
Reed, James V. to Mary Caroline Jacobs, Jly. 23, Perquimans county. R. R. Aug. 13, 1833.
Reeves, Ann W. to Joshua R. Gant, Sept., Orange county. R. R. Sept. 24, 1833.
Reinhardt, Barbara to William A. Abernethy, Apr. 2, Lincoln county. R. R. Apr. 9, 1833.
Rew, Robert to Merna Cherry, Dec. 27, Washington, Beaufort county. R. R. Jan. 25, 1833.
Reynolds, Thomas to Alice Lynum, Dec., Raleigh. R. R. Dec. 31, 1831.
Richards, Danford to Mary R. Hearn, Feb. 3, Tarborough. R. R. Feb. 26, 1833.

Richardson, Helen P. of Bladen county to James Mahoney, Cheraw, S. C., Dec. 27, Fayetteville. R. R. Jan. 18, 1833.
Riley, Hannah to Daniel Thompson, Feb. 14, Orange county. R. R. Mar. 19, 1833.
Robards, Mary Ann to Thomas Miller of Burke county, Jan., Granville county. R. R. Jan. 18, 1833.
Rowland, Rev. Henry A. of Fayetteville to Harriet Heyer, Sept., New York. R. R. Sept. 10, 1833.
Ruffin, Ann to Paul C. Cameron, Dec. 20, Orange county. R. R. Jan. 4, 1833.
Russell, Susan of Fayetteville to Rev. Jacky Bradley, Mar. 7, Robeson county. R. R. Mar. 26, 1833.
Ryan, David to Hannah S. Garland, Jly., Bertie county. R. R. Jly. 30, 1833.
Sanders, Elizabeth W. to James T. Leach, Jly. 21, Johnston county. R. R. Jly. 30, 1833.
Saunders, Rev. Joseph to Laura Baker, Mar. 25, Martin county. R. R. My. 21, 1833.
Saunders, Milton H. to Nancy Lavinia Lindsay, Jly. 30, Guilford county. R. R. Aug. 20, 1833.
Seawell, Henrietta of Fayetteville to Col. James H. Smith of Palmyra, Halifax county, Nov. 6, Fayetteville. R. R. Nov. 19, 1833.
Sherrill, Adam of Lincoln county to Ann Thompson, Apr., Iredell county. R. R. Apr. 23, 1833.
Shultz, Ann Susanna to William Hauser, Dec. 26, Salem. R. R. Jan. 18, 1833.
Shultz, Rev. Henry A. to Rebecca Bagge, Apr. 16, Salem. R. R. Apr. 30, 1833.
Slaughter, Lewis G. of Salisbury to Lucinda Dinkins, My. 20, Mecklenburg county. R. R. Jly. 9, 1833.
Slocum, John C. of Wayne county to Rachel Rebecca Wright, Feb. 28, Duplin county. R. R. Mar. 12, 1833.
Smith, Catharine Ann to John M'Rae, Nov. 7, Cumberland county. R. R. Nov. 19, 1833.
Smith, Henry G. of Lenoir county to Caroline E. Hatch, Jan. 21, Fayette county, Tenn. R. R. Apr. 9, 1833.
Smith, Col. James H. of Palmyra, Halifax county to Henrietta Seawell of Fayetteville, Nov. 6, Fayetteville. R. R. Nov. 19, 1833.
Smith, Joseph H. of Rockingham county to Susan Swain, Feb. 7, Guilford county. R. R. Mar. 5, 1833.
Smith, Margaret M. to John L. Hayes, Nov. 7, Charlotte. R. R. Dec. 3, 1833.
Smith, Richard H. of Scotland Neck to Sarah Hall, Dec. 4, Warrenton. R. R. Dec. 17, 1833.
Spencer, Eliza to David C. Lilly of Montgomery county, Jly., Anson county. R. R. Jly. 23, 1833.
Stedman, Dr. Elisha B. of Pittsborough to Juliana St. Clair Chipley, Apr., Kentucky. R. R. Apr. 16, 1833.
Stedman, John M. to Olivia Potter, Nov. 7, Fayetteville. R. R. Nov. 19, 1833.

Stringfield, P. R. to Susan J. Jones, Sept., New Hanover county. R. R. Sept. 24, 1833.
Sugg, John to Rebecca Love, My. 7, Wake county. R. R. My. 14, 1833.
Sugg, Dr. Osborne to Jane Love, Je. 4, Wake county. R. R. Je. 11, 1833.
Swain, Ann W. to Eli Pucket, Apr., Iredell county. R. R. Apr. 23, 1833.
Swain, Susan to Joseph H. Smith of Rockingham county, Feb. 7, Guilford county. R. R. Mar. 5, 1833.
Taylor, Ann Eliza to William H. Foster of Louisburg, Jly., Franklin county. R. R. Jly. 30, 1833.
Taylor, Evelina to Thomas Jones, Dec., Martin county. R. R. Jan. 4, 1833.
Taylor, William W. to Louisa W. Deloach, Feb. 14, Raleigh. R. R. Feb. 22, 1833.
Thompson, Ann to Adam Sherrill of Lincoln county, Apr., Iredell county. R. R. Apr. 23, 1833.
Thompson, Daniel to Hannah Riley, Feb. 14, Orange county. R. R. Mar. 19, 1833.
Thompson, Lewis to Margaret W. Clark, Jan. 22, Bertie county. R. R. Feb. 1, 1833.
Thompson, Nancy to Wm. Chambers, Feb. 16, Orange county. R. R. Mar. 19, 1833.
Todd, Thomas L. of South Carolina to Edith Freeman of Robeson county, Apr. 4, Lumberton. R. R. My. 21, 1833.
Toole, Mary Eliza to Dr. Josiah Lawrence of Tarboro, Feb. 20, Greenville. R. R. Mar. 12, 1833.
Torrence, Margaret to Benj. F. Young of Iredell county, Apr., Mecklenburg county. R. R. Apr. 30, 1833.
Townsend, William G. of Cabarrus county to Sarah Baine, Oct. 31, Mecklenburg county. R. R. Dec. 3, 1833.
Treadwell, Dr. John H. to Laura S. Craig, Sept., Montgomery county. R. R. Oct. 1, 1833.
Trolinger, Catharine to John R. Holt, Aug. 23, Orange county. R. R. Sept. 10, 1833.
Tucker, Horace P. to Mary Ann Williams, Aug. 28, Raleigh. R. R. Sept. 3, 1833.
Van, Cresy to Alfred Moore, Jan. 3, Greenville, Pitt county. R. R. Feb. 1, 1833.
Vansycle, Mr. of Newbern to Mrs. Anna Callender, Jan. 3, New Hanover county. R. R. Jan. 25, 1833.
Vestal, Messer A. to Rhoda Mendenhall of Jamestown, Feb., Guilford county. R. R. Mar. 5, 1833.
Waddell, Hugh Y. to Frances Campbell of Brunswick county, Apr. 23, Clarendon. R. R. Je. 4, 1833.
Waddill, James of Wadesborough to Emily A. Martin, Sept. 26, Anson county. R. R. Oct. 15, 1833.
Wall, Elizabeth to Wilson Deberry, Aug., Montgomery county. R. R. Aug. 20, 1833.
Waples, Nathaniel to Maria E. Mumford, Apr. 23, Lumberton. R. R. My. 21, 1833.
Watson, Jones to Jane Mitchell of Newbern, Sept. 10, Chapel Hill. R. R. Sept. 24, 1833.

Whealington, Elijah of Alabama to Fanny Mask of Richmond county, Apr. 21, Richmond county. R. R. My. 7, 1833.
White, Andrew B. of Pennsylvania to Frances H. Clark of Scotland Neck, Apr. 11, Scotland Neck. R. R. Apr. 30, 1833.
Whitted, William Nash to Emeline M'Coy of Bladen county, Sept. 7, Hillsborough. R. R. Sept. 24, 1833.
Wiatt, Mary Ellen to William Foster of Louisburg, Aug. 29, Raleigh. R. R. Sept. 3, 1833.
Wiggins, Thomas R. to Mary Arrington, Apr. 11, Nash county. R. R. Apr. 30, 1833.
Wilkings, Isabella to Dr. Thomas N. Cameron, Dec., Fayetteville. R. R. Dec. 24, 1833.
Williams, Apphic S. to Major William F. Collins of Nash county, Dec. 18, Chatham county. R. R. Dec. 24, 1833.
Williams, Benjamin of Chatham county to Mildred Hunter, Apr. 23, Wake county. R. R. Je. 4, 1833.
Williams, John B. of Windsor to Margaret P. Dossey of Society Hill, S. C., Oct. 15. R. R. Nov. 12, 1833.
Williams, Mary Ann to Horace P. Tucker, Aug. 28, Raleigh. R. R. Sept. 3, 1833.
Williams, Richard C. of Dresden to Attelia Goodloe of this State, Dec. 31, Fayette county, Tenn. R. R. Mar. 12, 1833.
Winburn, Geo. to Elizabeth Lumpkin, Dec. 7, Granville county. R. R. Feb. 18, 1833.
Winslow, John of Fayetteville to Amanda Malvina Donaldson, Oct. 2, Wake county. R. R. Oct. 15, 1833.
Womack, Eliza G. to Alexander A. Murphey, Apr. 16, Haywood county. R. R. Apr. 30, 1833.
Worley, Sarah L. J. to Capt. Richard P. Freeman, Sept., Bertie county. R. R. Sept. 24, 1833.
Wright, Ann to Thomas L. Lea, Apr. 18, Caswell county. R. R. My. 7, 1833.
Wright, Rachel Rebecca to John C. Slocum of Wayne county, Feb. 28, Duplin county. R. R. Mar. 12, 1833.
Yeargin, Sarah to William Martin of Granville county, Feb. 5, Wake county. R. R. Feb. 15, 1833.
Young, Benj. F. of Iredell county to Margaret Torrence, Apr., Mecklenburg county. R. R. Apr. 30, 1833.

1834

Alexander, Rachel to Wilson Montgomery, Je., Mecklenburg county. R. R. Je. 17, 1834.
Alexandria, Cazenove of Alexandria to Hon. William B. Shepard of this State, Oct., Alexandria. R. R. Oct. 21, 1834.
Allen, John to Sally Hutcheson, My. 1, Orange county. R. R. My. 13, 1834.
Allen, Sarah P. to Capt. John S. Oglesby, Oct., Milton. R. R. Oct. 28, 1834.
Alspaugh, Rev. Henry to Emily Clifton, Aug. 21, Fayetteville. R. R. Aug. 26, 1834.
Alston, Grissy to James Thomas, Je. 19, Wake county. R. R. Jly. 1, 1834.
Alston, Samuel to Adeline W. Perry, Apr. 1, Wake county. R. R. Apr. 15, 1834.

Ashe, John Baptiste of Fayetteville to Eliza Hay of Fayetteville, Dec. 24, Brownsville, Haywood county, Tenn. R. R. Mar. 18, 1834.
Ashley, Mary to James D. Royster, Feb. 13, Raleigh. R. R. Feb. 18, 1834.
Atkins, Henry of Orange county to Flora M'Neill, Jan., Cumberland county. R. R. Jan. 7, 1834.
Atkins, Hutchins to Mrs. Caroline Edwards of Wake county, Je., Raleigh. R. R. Jly. 1, 1834.
Ayres, William of Danville, Va. to Julia A. Henderson of Caswell county, Oct. 15. R. R. Oct. 28, 1834.
Barnum, Dr. Richard K. to Mrs. Newton Wood, Oct. 28, Wake county. R. R. Nov. 11, 1834.
Battle, Arabella of Rocky Mount to Joseph J. Dilliard of Raleigh, My. 27, Chatham county. R. R. Je. 3, 1834.
Bebee, Eliza to Maj. John M. Strong, Dec., Fayetteville. R. R. Dec. 9, 1834.
Bellemy, Samuel Crowell M. D. of Nash county to Elizabeth Jane Croom, Jly., Lenoir county. R. R. Jly. 15, 1834.
Benbury, Lavinia to Robert T. Paine, Apr., Chowan county. R. R. Je. 10, 1834.
Bently, Mary Thomas to Romulus Lawrence Moore of Raleigh, Sept. 4, Montgomery county, Md. R. R. Sept. 16, 1834.
Birth, William W. to Elizabeth Taylor, My., Washington, D. C. R. R. My. 13, 1834.
Bishop, Amanda A. H. to William W. Brickell, Apr. 29, Halifax county. R. R. My. 13, 1834.
Bishop, Rev. P. E. of York District, S. C. to Adeline M'Knight, Oct., Iredell county. R. R. Oct. 28, 1834.
Black, Mary Jane to Barnett Williams, Apr., Fayetteville. R. R. Apr. 29, 1834.
Blacknall, Margaret J. to Thomas M. Pierce of Halifax, Jly., Louisburg. R. R. Jly. 15, 1834.
Blacknall, Sarah B. to Tryon Yancey, Sept., Oxford. R. R. Sept. 30, 1834.
Blick, Robert of Petersburg, Va. to Ann Eliza Clifton, Aug. 10, Wake county. R. R. Aug. 12, 1834.
Blodget, Susan Fidelia to Benjamin Brantly of this State, Je. 26, Augusta, Ga. R. R. Jly. 15, 1834.
Blount, Mrs. Frances of Hillsborough to William Hill, Apr. 6, Raleigh. R. R. Apr. 8, 1834.
Blount, Mrs. Sarah L. to Gavin Hogg, Apr. 2, Raleigh. R. R. Apr. 8, 1834.
Blum, Martha to John Griffin, Oct., Stokes county. R. R. Oct. 21, 1834.
Boggan, Norfleet D. to Jane G. Hammond, Aug. 21, Wadesborough. R. R. Sept. 9, 1834.
Boyd, Lucy Nelson of Edgecombe county to Dr. John W. Potts of Tarboro, Nov. 4, Boydton, Va. R. R. Nov. 18, 1834.
Boyd, Mary of Mecklenburg, Va. to Thomas P. Hawkins of Louisburg, Nov. 4, Boydton, Va. R. R. Nov. 18, 1834.
Brandie, Samuel S. to Adaline Perry, Nov., Louisburg. R. R. Nov. 11, 1834.
Brantly, Benjamin of this State to Susan Fidelia Blodget, Je. 26, Augusta, Ga. R. R. Jly. 15, 1834.
Brickell, William W. to Amanda A. H. Bishop, Apr. 29, Halifax county. R. R. My. 13, 1834.
Bridgers, James O. to Harriet Jane Moore of Lumberton, Dec., Brunswick county. R. R. Dec. 9, 1834.

Briggs, Sarah to Irby Sanders, Apr. 14, Person county. R. R. Je. 10, 1834.
Bright, Ellen to Samuel Gordon, Sept., Pasquotank county. R. R. Sept. 30, 1834.
Brock, James N. to Mary M. Maxwell, Oct., Rowan county. R. R. Oct. 28, 1834.
Brooks, William C. to Fear Fearing of Philadelphia, Dec., Elizabeth City. R. R. Dec. 9, 1834.
Brown, Jeremiah M. to Margaret Fraley, Feb., Salisbury. R. R. Feb. 4, 1834.
Bryan, Mrs. Mary E. to Peleg Pearce, Nov., Fayetteville. R. R. Nov. 4, 1834.
Buffalow, John of Raleigh to Elizabeth M'Leod, My., Cumberland county. R. R. Je. 3, 1834.
Buie, Mary Ann to Alex'r Watson of Robeson county, Apr., Cumberland county. R. R. Apr. 29, 1834.
Burges, Midshipman, U. S. N. William H. to Eugenia Fenner, Oct. 15, Franklin county. R. R. Oct. 21, 1834.
Burt, Harriet Amando to Dr. James Phillips of Edgecombe county, Apr. 25, Hilliardton, Nash county. R. R. My. 13, 1834.
Burgin, Gen. Alney to Salina Whitson, Oct., Burke county. R. R. Oct. 28, 1834.
Burwell, John S. of Lynesville to Sally E. Hayes of Warren county, Nov. 5, Warren county. R. R. Nov. 11, 1834.
Buxton, Rev. Jarvis B. of Fayetteville to Mrs. Harriet H. Jennings, Apr. 3, Wadesboro. R. R. Apr. 15, 1834.
Byram, Mary Ann to Henry Shell, Nov., Mecklenburg county. R. R. Nov. 11, 1834.
Cameron, Flora to Capt. Neill Shaw, Apr., Cumberland county. R. R. Apr. 22, 1834.
Campbell, Rev. D. A. to Margaret Kerr, Apr. 10, New Hanover county. R. R. Apr. 29, 1834.
Campbell, Marsden to Catharine Moore, Dec., Brunswick county. R. R. Dec. 9, 1834.
Campbell, Marsden, Jr. of Brunswick county to Mary B. Greene, Je. 5, Wilmington. R. R. Jly. 1, 1834.
Campbell, Polly M. to John M. Vawter of Stokes county, Oct., Surry county. R. R. Oct. 21, 1834.
Cannon, Mary E. to William Dallas Haywood, Oct. 22, Raleigh. R. R. Oct. 28, 1934.
Cannon, Mrs. Robert to Samuel B. Spruill of Northampton county, Feb. 8, Raleigh. R. R. Feb. 11, 1834.
Carter, Elbert to Lucinda Spivey, My. 4, Wake county. R. R. My. 6, 1834.
Chipley, Mary Eloisa to Dr. John S. Richardson of Fayetteville, Apr., Lexington, Ky. R. R. Apr. 8, 1834.
Christophers, John J. to Elizabeth Haylander, Sept. 2, Raleigh. R. R. Sept. 9, 1834.
Clark, Barnes G. to Rebecca C. Dupree, Nov., Northampton county. R. R. Nov. 18, 1834.
Clark, Susan to Harvey Hughes, Sept., Orange county. R. R. Sept. 16, 1834.

Clark, William to Dilley Wilson, Jly. 22, Chatham county. R. R. Aug. 12, 1834.
Clements, Peyton C. to Angeline Rencher, Aug. 23, Wake county. R. R. Sept. 9, 1834.
Clerk, Thomas to Creasy Reavis, Oct. 23, Wake county. R. R. Oct. 28, 1834.
Clifton, Ann Eliza to Robert Blick of Petersburg, Va., Aug. 10, Wake county. R. R. Aug. 12, 1834.
Clifton, Emily to Rev. Henry Alspaugh, Aug. 21, Fayetteville. R. R. Aug. 26, 1834.
Cobb, Fanny to Archibald S. M'Millan, Oct., Robeson county. R. R. Oct. 21, 1834.
Coits, John C. of Cheraw, S. C. to Ellen P. North of New London, Conn., Je. 11, Chapel Hill. R. R. Jly. 1, 1834.
Cotton, Emily to William R. Dickson, Oct., Scotland Neck. R. R. Oct. 28, 1834.
Cornell, William to Mary Gaddy, Jan., Fayetteville. R. R. Jan. 7, 1834.
Coston, Hugh T. of Wilmington to Tabitha E. Hawes, Aug. 7, Bladen county. R. R. Aug. 26, 1834.
Cowan, Thomas to Mary Ashe London, Dec., Wilmington. R. R. Dec. 30, 1834.
Creekman, Nancy to Alexander H. Russell, Oct. 29, Newbern. R. R. Nov. 11, 1834.
Croom, Elizabeth Jane to Samuel Crowell Bellemy, M. D. of Nash county, Jly., Lenoir county. R. R. Jly. 15, 1834.
Curran, Martha to Capt. Samuel B. Meacham, Apr. 27, Oxford. R. R. Je. 10, 1834.
Debnam, Thomas R. to Priscilla Macon, Apr. 14, Franklin county. R. R. Je. 10, 1834.
Dennis, John to Eliza Jones, Oct., Chowan county. R. R. Oct. 28, 1834.
Dickson, William R. to Emily Cotton, Oct., Scotland Neck. R. R. Oct. 28, 1834.
Dilliard, Joseph J. of Raleigh to Arabella Battle of Rocky Mount, My. 27, Chatham county. R. R. Je. 3, 1834.
Dixon, Elizabeth to Joab Kemp of Chatham county, Oct. 9, Chatham county. R. R. Nov. 11, 1834.
Donaldson, Frances E. to James Huske of Fayetteville, Oct. 23, Wake Forest. R. R. Oct. 28, 1834.
Donoho, Mrs. Mary A. to Martin P. Huntington, Oct., Milton. R. R. Oct. 21, 1834.
Drennan, Ann of Wilson county, Tennessee to Major John C. Hampton of Surry county, Apr. 24, Franklin, Tenn. R. R. My. 20, 1834.
Dugger, Daniel of Petersburg, Va. to Mary E. Green, Mar. 20, Warrenton. R. R. Apr. 1, 1834.
Duke, Narcissa to John Stanford, Oct., Chowan county. R. R. Oct. 28, 1834.
Dupree, Rebecca C. to Barnes G. Clark, Nov., Northampton county. R. R. Nov. 18, 1834.
Durham, Nathaniel G. of Caswell county to Mary Rose of Person county, Oct. 23, Caswell county. R R. Nov. 4, 1834.

Edwards, Mrs. Caroline of Wake county to Hutchins Atkins, Je., Raleigh. R. R. Jly. 1, 1834.

Elliott, Elisha to Mrs. Parthena Fleetwood, Oct., Chowan county. R. R. Oct. 28, 1834.

Eppes, Martha M. to F. S. Marshall, Nov. 4, Halifax. R. R. Nov. 18, 1834.

Etheredge, Penelope to Malachi Russel, Sept., Elizabeth City. R. R. Sept. 23, 1834.

Fearing, Fear of Philadelphia to William C. Brooks, Dec., Elizabeth City. R. R. Dec. 9, 1834.

Fenner, Eugenia to Midshipman U. S. N. William H. Burges, Oct. 15, Franklin county. R. R. Oct. 21, 1834.

Flanagan, Mary to James T. Morris, Je. 3, Wilmington. R. R. Jly. 1, 1834.

Fleetwood, Mrs. Parthena to Elisha Elliott, Oct., Chowan county. R. R. Oct. 28, 1834.

Forbes, John M. to Susan Shannonhouse, Dec., Elizabeth City. R. R. Dec. 9, 1834.

Foxhall, Mary to Wilson Sessums, Sept., Edgecombe county. R. R. Sept. 16, 1834.

Fraley, Margaret to Jeremiah M. Brown, Feb., Salisbury. R. R. Feb. 4, 1834.

Gaddy, Mary to William Cornell, Jan., Fayetteville. R. R. Jan. 7, 1834.

Gordon, Samuel to Ellen Bright, Sept., Pasquotank county. R. R. Sept. 30, 1834.

Gorman, Thomas M. to Elizabeth A. Miller, Jly. 16, Raleigh. R. R. Jly. 22, 1834.

Greene, Mary B. to Marsden Campbell, Jr. of Brunswick county, Je. 5, Wilmington. R. R. Jly. 1, 1834.

Green, Mary E. to Daniel Dugger of Petersburg, Va., Mar. 20, Warrenton. R. R. Apr. 1, 1834.

Griffin, John to Martha Blum, Oct., Stokes county. R. R. Oct. 21, 1834.

Hall, Albert G. of Wilmington to Rebecca Haywood, Dec. 23, Raleigh. R. R. Dec. 30, 1834.

Hamilton, John to Rebecca Bryant, Aug. 19, New Hanover county. R. R. Sept. 23, 1834.

Hammond, Jane G. to Norfleet D. Boggan, Aug. 21, Wadesborough. R. R. Sept. 9, 1834.

Hampton, Ellen J. to Wm. Murphey, Jan. 9, Salisbury. R. R. Jan. 28, 1834.

Hampton, Major John C. of Surry county to Ann Drennan of Wilson county, Tennessee, Apr. 24, Franklin, Tennessee. R. R. My. 20, 1834.

Hanks, Benjamin F. to Miss H. Wallace, Aug. 11, Newbern. R. R. Aug. 12, 1834.

Hannah, Isabella to Henry Linsey, Sept., Orange county. R. R. Sept. 16, 1834.

Hanrahan, Joseph R. of Washington, Beaufort county to Ann H. Singleton, Nov. 11, Newbern. R. R. Dec. 30, 1834.

Harding, Greenberry P. of Surry county to Rebecca Miller of Stokes county, Oct., Surry county. R. R. Oct. 21, 1834.

Harrison, Frances S. of Anson county to M. M. Misenhimer, Apr. 10, Cabarrus county. R. R. My. 13, 1834.

Hawes, Tabitha E. to Hugh T. Coston of Wilmington, Aug. 7, Bladen county. R. R. Aug. 26, 1834.
Hawkins, Thomas P. of Louisburg to Mary Boyd of Mecklenburg, Va., Nov. 4, Boydton, Va. R. R. Nov. 18, 1834.
Hay, Eliza of Fayetteville to John Baptiste Ashe, Dec. 24, Brownsville, Haywood county, Tenn. R. R. Mar. 18, 1834.
Hayes, Sally E. of Warren county to John S. Burwell of Lynesville, Nov. 5, Warren county. R. R. Nov. 11, 1834.
Haylander, Elizabeth to John J. Christophers, Sept. 2, Raleigh. R. R. Sept. 9, 1834.
Haywood, Rebecca to Albert G. Hall of Wilmington, Dec. 23, Raleigh. R. R. Dec. 30, 1834.
Haywood, William Dallas to Mary E. Cannon, Oct. 22, Raleigh. R. R. Oct. 28, 1834.
Henderson, Julia A. of Caswell county to William Ayres of Danville, Va., Oct. 15. R. R. Oct. 28, 1834.
Henderson, Margaret to Pearsall Thompson, Nov. 29, Mecklenburg county. R. R. Dec. 9, 1834.
Hester, Martha J. of Franklin county to Duncan C. Winston, Oct. 9. R. R. Nov. 4, 1834.
High, Calvin M. of Alabama to Lavina Sarah Jeter of Raleigh, Aug. 21, Raleigh. R. R. Aug. 26, 1834.
Hill, William to Mrs. Frances Blount of Hillsborough, Apr. 6, Raleigh. R. R. Apr. 8, 1834.
Hilyard, Mary Q. to Nelson H. Munger of Yorkville, S. C., Jly., Chapel Hill. R. R. Jly. 15, 1834.
Hines, Benjamin to Sarah P. Holder, Mar. 18, Milton. R. R. Apr. 8, 1834.
Hines, Peter E. to Sarah Maenair, Feb., Tarboro. R. R. Feb. 25, 1834.
Hines, Richard H. of Edgecombe county to Caroline Snead, Nov. 11, Newbern. R. R. Dec. 30, 1834.
Hodges, Mary to Cary W. West, Jly., Caswell county. R. R. Jly. 8, 1834.
Hogan, Louisa A. of Randolph county to Dr. William R. Holt of Lexington, Nov. 11. R. R. Dec. 9, 1834.
Hogg, Gavin to Mrs. Sarah L. Blount, Apr. 2, Raleigh. R. R. Apr. 8, 1834.
Hoke, Marcus L. of Lincolnton to Hannah E. Smith, Jly., Asheville, Buncombe county. R. R. Jly. 8, 1834.
Holder, Sarah P. to Benjamin Hines, Mar. 18, Milton. R. R. Apr. 8, 1834.
Holderby, Maj. Anderson B. of Rockingham county to Martha Smith, Jly., Pittyslvania, Va. R. R. Jly. 3, 1834.
Holloway, Susan to Allen Nichols, Jly. 15, Wake county. R. R. Jly. 22, 1834.
Holt, Dr. William R. of Lexington to Louisa A. Hogan of Randolph county, Nov. 11. R. R. Dec. 9, 1834.
Holton, T. J. to Rachel R. Jones, Jly., Charlotte. R. R. Jly. 8, 1834.
Howard, Laban to Jane E. Lewis, Jly., Newbern. R. R. Jly. 15, 1834.
Hughes, Harvey to Susan Clark, Sept., Orange county. R. R. Sept. 16, 1834.
Hunter, Ann to F. Smith, Feb. 13, Raleigh. R. R. Feb. 18, 1834.
Huntington, Martin P. to Mrs. Mary A. Donoho, Oct., Milton. R. R. Oct. 21, 1834.

Huske, James of Fayetteville to Frances E. Donaldson, Oct. 23, Wake Forest. R. R. Oct. 28, 1834.
Hutcheson, Sally to John Allen, My. 1, Orange county. R. R. My. 13, 1834.
Jelks, Louisa of Halifax county to Dr. G. Sills, Nov. 13, Nash county. R. R. Dec. 2, 1834.
Jennings, Harriet H. to Rev. Jarvis B. Buxton of Fayetteville, Apr. 3, Wadesboro. R. R. Apr. 15, 1834.
Jeter, Eliza Ann to John A. Minniece of Smithfield, Aug. 21, Raleigh. R. R. Aug. 26, 1834.
Jeter, Lavinia Sarah of Raleigh to Calvin M. High of Alabama, Aug. 21, Raleigh. R. R. Aug. 26, 1834.
Johnson, Susan to James Puttick, Sept. 11, Raleigh. R. R. Sept. 16, 1834.
Johnson, Thomas J. to Ann Maria Walton, Je. 5, Raleigh. R. R. Je. 10, 1834.
Jones, Eliza to John Dennis, Oct., Chowan county. R. R. Oct. 28, 1834.
Jones, John H. to Rebecca Winstead, Apr. 15, Person county. R. R. Je. 10, 1834.
Jones, Rachel R. to T. J. Holton, Jly., Charlotte. R. R. Jly. 8, 1834.
Kemp, Joab to Elizabeth Dixon of Chatham county, Oct. 9, Orange county. R. R. Nov. 11, 1834.
Kerr, Margaret to Rev. D. A. Campbell, Apr. 10, New Hanover county. R. R. Apr. 29, 1834.
Latta, John C. to Priscilla Eldridge Shaw of Fayetteville, Dec., Fayetteville. R. R. Dec. 9, 1834.
Lazarus, Angeline to Charles Moses of South Carolina, Dec., Wilmington. R. R. Dec. 9, 1834.
Lea, Dr. Willis of Leasburg, Caswell county to Sarah Pugh Wilson of Pittsylvania county, Va., My. 1. R. R. My. 13, 1834.
Lewis, Jane E. to Laban Howard, Jly., Newbern. R. R. Jly. 15, 1834.
Lewis, Merriwether of Milton to Pherabe Seawell, Feb. 6, Raleigh. R. R. Feb. 11, 1834.
Lindsay, Elizabeth of Currituck county to Wilson Reed of Perquimans county, Oct., Currituck county. R. R. Oct. 7, 1834.
Linsey, Henry to Isabella Hannah, Sept., Orange county. R. R. Sept. 16, 1834.
Little, Margaret to Wm. G. Taylor, Jly., Newbern. R. R. Jly. 15, 1834.
London, Mary Ashe to Thomas Cowan, Dec., Wilmington. R. R. Dec. 30, 1834.
Lovick, George P. to Mrs. Phoebe Pearce, Jly. 17, Caswell county. R. R. Aug. 12, 1834.
Lunsford, Elizabeth to Maj. Allen Yancey, Oct. 23, Caswell county. R. R. Nov. 4, 1834.
M'Allister, Lovedy to Alfred A. M'Kethen, Jan., Cumberland county. R. R. Jan. 7, 1834.
M'Cain, J. W. to Milly Starns, Apr. 3, Mecklenburg county. R. R. My. 13, 1834.
M'Callian, Martha to Col. Jehu Ward, Apr. 8, Orange county. R. R. Je. 10, 1834.
M'Clelland, John N. to Martha Parks, Je., Wilkes county. R. R. Je. 17, 1834.

M'Cullars, John to Aley Ann Warren, My. 29, Wake county. R. R. Je. 10, 1834.
M'Gehee, Albert G. of Alabama to Ann V. Payne, Nov., Caswell county. R. R. Nov. 4, 1834.
M'Gougan, John to Margaret M'Nair, Apr. 24, Robeson county. R. R. My. 13, 1834.
M'Intosh, Catherine to Angus Wilkinson of Robeson county, Mar. 27, Richmond county. R. R. Apr. 15, 1834.
M'Intosh, Daniel to Margaret Shaw, Apr., Moore county. R. R. Apr. 8, 1834.
M'Iver, Rev. Alexander of Clinton to Raphael Miller, Jan., Duplin county. R. R. Jan. 7, 1834.
M'Kee, Mary to Dr. James Stitt, Nov. 4, Mecklenburg county. R. R. Dec. 2, 1834.
M'Kee, Nancy to Wm. T. Stitt, Nov. 4, Mecklenburg county. R. R. Dec. 2, 1834.
M'Kethen, Alfred A. to Lovedy M'Allister, Jan., Cumberland county. R. R. Jan. 7, 1834.
M'Knight, Adeline to Rev. P. E. Bishop of York District, S. C., Oct., Iredell county. R. R. Oct. 28, 1834.
M'Leod, Elizabeth to John Buffalow of Raleigh, My., Cumberland county. R. R. Je. 3, 1834.
M'Millan, Archibald S. to Fanny Cobb, Oct., Robeson county. R. R. Oct. 21, 1834.
M'Murray, Mary to Charles Mason, Apr. 17, Person county. R. R. My. 13, 1834.
M'Nair, Margaret to John M'Gougan, Apr. 24, Robeson county. R. R. My. 13, 1834.
M'Neill, Flora to Henry Atkins of Orange county, Jan., Cumberland county. R.R. Jan. 7, 1834.
M'Queen, Dr. Edmond of Lumberton to Susan A. Moore of Lumberton, Mar. 28, Marion, S. C. R. R. Apr. 22, 1834.
Maclin, Joseph J. of Franklin county to Susan Martin of Granville county, Sept. R. R. Sept. 30, 1834.
Macon, Priscilla to Thomas R. Debnam, Apr. 14, Franklin county. R. R. Je. 10, 1834.
Maenair, Sarah to Peter E. Hines, Feb., Tarboro. R. R. Feb. 25, 1834.
Maneyfee, Dr. Benjamin S. to Elizabeth M'Craw, Oct. 10, Surry county. R. R. Nov. 4, 1834.
Marshall, F. S. to Martha M. Eppes, Nov. 4, Halifax. R. R. Nov. 18, 1834.
Martin, Susan of Granville county to Joseph J. Maclin of Franklin county, Sept. R. R. Sept. 30, 1834.
Martin, Susan B. to Frederick B. Shepard, Nov. 16, Elizabeth City. R. R. Dec. 2, 1834.
Mason, Charles to Mary M'Murray, Apr. 17, Person county. R. R. My. 13, 1834.
Maxwell, Mary M. to James N. Brock, Oct., Rowan county. R. R. Oct. 28, 1834.
Meacham, Capt. Samuel B. to Martha Curran, Apr. 27, Oxford. R. R. Je. 10, 1834.

Middleton, Sarah to Wm. Middleton, Oct., Chowan county. R. R. Oct. 28, 1834.
Middleton, Wm. to Sarah Middleton, Oct., Chowan county. R. R. Oct. 28, 1834.
Miller, Elizabeth A. to Thomas M. Gorman, Jly. 16, Raleigh. R. R. Jly. 22, 1834.
Miller, Raphael to Rev. Alexander M'Iver of Clinton, Jan., Duplin county. R. R. Jan. 7, 1834.
Miller, Rebecca of Stokes county to Greenberry P. Harding of Surry county, Oct., Surry county. R. R. Oct. 21, 1834.
Miller, Richard to Mary Ann Shaw, Apr., Duplin county. R. R. Apr. 22, 1834.
Minniece, John A. of Smithfield to Eliza Ann Jeter, Aug. 21, Raleigh. R. R. Aug. 26, 1834.
Misenhimer, M. M. to Frances S. Harrison of Anson county, Apr. 10, Cabarrus county. R. R. My. 13, 1834.
Montgomery, Wilson to Rachel Alexander, Je., Mecklenburg county. R. R. Je. 17, 1834.
Moore, Alex'r H. to Eleanor Prince, Mar. 25, Chatham county. R. R. Apr. 1, 1834.
Moore, Catharine to Marsden Campbell, Dec., Brunswick county. R. R. Dec. 9, 1834.
Moore, Elizabeth M. to Major Joseph J. Ward, Mar. 19, Franklin county. R. R. Apr. 1, 1834.
Moore, Elizabeth P. to Dr. William Rodes, Apr. 15, Orange county. R. R. My. 13, 1834.
Moore, Harriet Jane of Lumberton to James O. Bridgers, Dec., Brunswick county. R. R. Dec. 9, 1834.
Moore, Hester to Ann Eliza Whitfield, Nov. 5, Granville county. R. R. Dec. 2, 1834.
Moore, Romulus Lawrence of Raleigh to Mary Thomas Bently, Sept. 4, Montgomery county, Maryland. R. R. Sept. 16, 1834.
Moore, Susan A. of Lumberton to Dr. Edmond M'Queen of Lumberton, Mar. 28, Marion, S. C.. R. R. Apr. 22, 1834.
Morris, James T. to Mary Flanagan, Je. 3, Wilmington. R. R. Jly. 1, 1834.
Moses, Charles of South Carolina to Angeline Lazarus, Dec., Wilmington. R. R. Dec. 9, 1834.
Munger, Nelson H. of Yorkville, S. C. to Mary Q. Hilyard, Jly., Chapel Hill. R. R. Jly. 15, 1834.
Murphy, Wm. to Ellen J. Hampton, Jan. 9, Salisbury. R. R. Jan. 28, 1834.
Nelson, Susan F. T. to James G. Stanly, Jr. of U. S. Navy, Oct. 29, Newbern. R. R. Nov. 11, 1834.
Nichols, Allen to Susan Holloway, Jly. 15, Wake county. R. R. Jly. 22, 1834.
Nichols, Mrs. John to Grandison Philpot, Dec., Wake county. R. R. Dec. 30, 1834.
Nichols, Rachel to Randolph Pendergrass of Virginia, Je. 19, Wake county. R. R. Jly. 1, 1834.
Nixon, John to Sarah Sutton, Nov. 13, Edenton. R. R. Dec. 2, 1834.
Nixon, John to Sarah Sutton, Dec., Durants Neck, Perquimans county. R. R. Dec. 9, 1834.

North, Ellen P. of New London, Connecticut to John C. Coits of Cheraw, South Carolina, Je. 11, Chapel Hill. R. R. Jly. 1, 1834.
Oglesby, Capt. John S. to Sarah P. Allen, Oct., Milton. R. R. Oct. 28, 1834.
Orr, Amanda to John Stitt, Nov. 4, Mecklenburg county. R. R. Dec. 2, 1834.
Paine, Robert T. to Lavinia Benbury, Apr., Chowan county. R. R. Je. 10, 1834.
Parks, Martha to John N. M'Clelland, Je., Wilkes county. R. R. Je. 17, 1834.
Patton, Julia A. to Joseph H. Wilson of Charlotte, Sept. 24, Asheville, Buncombe county. R. R. Oct. 14, 1834.
Payne, Ann V. to Albert G. M'Gehee of Alabama, Nov., Caswell county. R. R. Nov. 4, 1834.
Pearce, Peleg to Mrs. Mary E. Bryan, Nov., Fayetteville. R. R. Nov. 4, 1834.
Pearce, Mrs. Phoebe to George P. Lovick, Jly. 17, Caswell, Lenoir county. R. R. Aug. 12, 1834.
Pearsall, Robert C. to Jane Sophronia Tate, Mar. 18, Morganton. R. R. Apr. 8, 1834.
Peck, Willis of Yorkville, S. C. & Raleigh to Anna E. Zimmerman, Nov. 12, Lincolnton. R. R. Dec. 2, 1834.
Pendergrass, Randolph of Virginia to Rachel Nichols, Je. 19, Wake county. R. R. Jly. 1, 1834.
Perry, Adeline W. to Samuel Alston, Apr. 1, Wake county. R. R. Apr. 15, 1834.
Perry, Adaline to Samuel S. Brandie, Nov., Louisburg. R. R. Nov. 11, 1834.
Philpott, Grandison of Granville county to Mrs. John Nichols, Dec., Wake county. R. R. Dec. 30, 1834.
Philips, Dr. James of Edgecombe county to Harriet Amanda Burt, Apr. 23, Hilliardton, Nash county. R. R. My. 13, 1834.
Pierce, Thomas M. of Halifax to Margaret J. Blacknall, Jly., Louisburg. R. R. Jly. 15, 1834.
Pippen, Catharine E. to Harman Ward, Jan. 9, Edgecombe county. R. R. Jan. 28, 1834.
Potts, Dr. John W. of Tarboro to Lucy Nelson Boyd, Edgecombe county, Nov. 4, Boydton, Va. R. R. Nov. 18, 1834.
Prince, Eleanor to Alex'r H. Moore, Mar. 25, Chatham county. R. R. Apr. 1, 1834.
Puttick, James to Susan Johnson, Sept. 11, Raleigh. R. R. Sept. 16, 1834.
Rainy, Betsy to Rev. Henry Speck, Mar. 5, Orange county. R. R. Apr. 1, 1834.
Reavis, Creasy to Thomas Clerk, Oct. 23, Wake county. R. R. Oct. 28, 1834.
Reavis, John to Eleanor Thomas of Raleigh, Oct. 21, Wake county. R. R. Oct. 28, 1834.
Reed, Wilson of Perquimans county to Elizabeth Lindsay of Currituck county, Oct., Currituck county. R. R. Oct. 7, 1834.
Rencher, Angeline to Peyton C. Clements, Aug. 23, Wake county. R. R. Sept. 9, 1834.

Richardson, Dr. John S. of Fayetteville to Mary Eloisa Chipley, Apr., Lexington, Ky. R. R. Apr. 8, 1834.
Robley, Providence to James Watson, Je., Rowan county. R. R. Je. 17, 1834.
Rodes, Dr. William to Elizabeth P. Moore, Apr. 15, Orange county. R. R. My. 13, 1834.
Rose, Mary of Person county to Nathaniel G. Durham of Caswell county, Oct. 23, Caswell county. R. R. Nov. 4, 1834.
Royster, James D. to Mary Ashley, Feb. 13, Raleigh. R. R. Feb. 18, 1834.
Russell, Alexander H. to Nancy Creekman, Oct. 29, Newbern. R. R. Nov. 11, 1834.
Russell, Malachi to Penelope Etheridge, Sept., Elizabeth City. R. R. Sept. 23, 1834.
Sanders, Irby to Sarah Briggs, Apr. 14, Person county. R. R. Je. 10, 1834.
Scales, Eliza to Joseph Twitchel, Jly., Rockingham county. R. R. Jly. 15, 1834.
Seawell, Pherabee to Merriwether Lewis, of Milton, Feb. 6, Raleigh. R. R. Feb. 11, 1834.
Sessums, Wilson to Mary Foxhall, Sept., Edgecombe county. R. R. Sept. 16, 1834.
Shannonhouse, Susan to John M. Forbes, Dec., Elizabeth City. R. R. Dec 9, 1834.
Shaw, Mary Ann to Richard Miller, Apr., Duplin county. R. R. Apr. 22, 1834.
Shaw, Capt. Neill to Flora Cameron, Apr., Cumberland county. R. R. Apr. 22, 1834.
Shaw, Priscilla Eldridge of Fayetteville to John C. Latta, Dec., Fayetteville. R. R. Dec. 9, 1834.
Shell, Henry to Mary Ann Byram, Nov., Mecklenburg county. R. R. Nov. 11, 1834.
Shepard, Frederick B. to Susan B. Martin, Nov. 16, Elizabeth City. R. R. Dec. 2, 1834.
Shepard, Hon. William B. of this State to Charlotte Cazenove of Alexandria, Oct., Alexandria. R. R. Oct. 21, 1834.
Shuford, Jacob R. of Asheville to Mary E. Smith, Jly., Asheville, Buncombe county. R. R. Jly. 8, 1834.
Sills, Dr. G. to Louisa Jelks of Halifax county, Nov. 13, Nash county. R. R. Dec. 2, 1834.
Singleton, Ann H. to Joseph R. Hanrahan of Washington, Beaufort county, Nov. 11, Newbern. R. R. Dec. 30, 1834.
Smith, F. to Ann Hunter, Feb. 13, Raleigh. R. R. Feb. 18, 1834.
Smith, Hannah E. to Marcus L. Hoke of Lincolnton, Jly., Asheville, Buncombe county. R. R. Jly. 8, 1834.
Smith, Martha to Maj. Anderson Holderby of Rockingham county, Jly., Pittsylvania, Va. R. R. Jly. 8, 1834.
Smith, Mary E. to Jacob R. Shuford of Asheville, Jly., Asheville, Buncombe county. R. R. Jly. 8, 1834.
Speck, Rev. Henry to Betsy Rainy, Mar. 5, Orange county. R. R. Apr. 1, 1834.
Spivey, Lucinda to Elbert Carter, My. 4, Wake county. R. R. My. 6. 1834.

Spruill, Samuel B. of Northampton county to Mrs. Robert Cannon, Feb. 8, Raleigh. R. R. Feb. 11, 1834.
Stanford, John to Narcissa Duke, Oct., Chowan county. R. R. Oct. 28, 1834.
Stanly, James G. Jr. of U. S. Navy to Susan F. T. Nelson, Oct. 29, Newbern. R. R. Nov. 11, 1834.
Stitt, Dr. James to Mary M'Kee, Nov. 4, Mecklenburg county. R. R. Dec. 2, 1834.
Stitt, John to Ann Orr, Nov. 4, Mecklenburg county. R. R. Dec. 2, 1834.
Stitt, Wm. T. to Nancy M'Kee, Nov. 4, Mecklenburg county. R. R. Dec. 2, 1834.
Starns, Milly to J. W. M'Cain, Apr. 3, Mecklenburg county. R. R. My. 13, 1834.
Strong, Maj. John M. to Eliza Bebee, Dec., Fayetteville. R. R. Dec. 9, 1834.
Sutton, Sarah to John Nixon, Nov. 13, Edenton. R. R. Dec. 2, 1834.
Tate, Jane Sophronia to Robert C. Pearsall, Mar. 18, Morganton. R. R. Apr. 8, 1834.
Taylor, Elizabeth to William W. Birth, My., Washington, D. C. R. R. My. 13, 1834.
Taylor, Wm. G. to Margaret Little, Jly., Newbern. R. R. Jly. 15, 1834.
Thomas, Eleanor of Raleigh to John Reavis, Oct. 21, Wake county. R. R. Oct. 28, 1834.
Thomas, Harriet to Jeremiah Watkins, Jan., Montgomery county. R. R. Jan. 7, 1834.
Thomas, James to Grissy Alston, Je. 19, Wake county. R. R. Jly. 1, 1834.
Thompson, Pearsall to Margaret Henderson, Nov. 20, Mecklenburg county. R. R. Dec. 9, 1834.
Toomer, Mary I. to Warren Winslow, Jan. 15, Fayetteville. R. R. Jan. 21, 1834.
Twitchel, Joseph to Eliza Scales, Jly., Rockingham county. R. R. Jly. 15, 1834.
Vawter, John M. of Stokes county to Polly M. Campbell, Oct., Surry county. R. R. Oc. 21, 1834.
Wallace, Miss H. to Benjamin F. Hanks, Aug. 11, Newbern. R. R. Aug. 12, 1834.
Walton, Ann Maria to Thomas J. Johnson, Je. 5, Raleigh. R. R. Je. 10, 1834.
Ward, Harman to Catharine E. Pippin, Jan. 9, Edgecombe county. R. R. Jan. 28, 1834.
Ward, Col. Jehu to Martha M'Callian, Apr. 8, Orange county. R. R. Je. 10, 1834.
Ward, Major Joseph J. to Elizabeth M. Moore, Mar. 19, Franklin county. R. R. Apr. 1, 1834.
Ware, Lucy S. of Edgefield District, S. C. to Nathaniel Whitlow of Augusta, Ga. & this State, Jan. 2. R. R. Jan. 28, 1834.
Warren, Aley Ann to John M'Cullars, My. 29, Wake county. R. R. Je. 10, 1834.
Watkins, Jeremiah to Harriet Thomas, Jan., Montgomery county. R. R. Jan. 7, 1834.

Watson, Alex'r of Robeson county to Mary Ann Buie, Apr., Cumberland county. R. R. Apr. 29, 1834.
Watson, James to Providence Robley, Je., Rowan county. R. R. Je. 17, 1834.
West, Cary W. to Mary Hodges, Jly., Caswell county. R. R. Jly. 8, 1834.
Whitaker, Joseph A. of Wake county to Rebecca P. Yarbrough, Feb. 20, Franklin county. R. R. Feb. 25, 1834.
Whitfield, Eliza Ann to Hester Moore, Nov. 5, Granville county. R. R. Dec. 2, 1834.
Whitfield, Gaius of Alabama to Mary Ann B. Whitfield, Jly. 15, Lenoir county. R. R. Jly. 22, 1834.
Whitfield, Mary Ann B. to Gaius Whitfield of Alabama, Jly. 15, Lenoir county. R. R. Jly. 22, 1834.
Whitlow, Nathaniel H. of Augusta, Ga. and this State to Lucy S. Ware of Edgefield District, S. C. Jan. 2. R. R. Jan. 28, 1834.
Whitson, Salina to Gen'l Alney Burgin, Oct., Burke county. R. R. Oct. 28, 1834.
Wilkinson, Angus of Robeson county to Catherine M'Intosh, Mar. 27, Richmond county. R. R. Apr. 15, 1834.
Williams, Barnett to Mary Jane Black, Apr., Fayetteville. R. R. Apr. 29, 1834.
Wilson, Dilley to William Clark, Jly. 22, Chatham county. R. R. Aug. 12, 1834.
Wilson, Joseph H. of Charlotte to Julia A. Patton, Sept. 24, Asheville, Buncombe county. R. R. Oct. 14, 1834.
Wilson, Sarah Pugh of Pittsylvania county, Va. to Dr. Willis Lea of Leasburg, Caswell county, My. 1. R. R. My. 13, 1834.
Winslow, Warren to Mary I. Toomer, Jan. 15, Fayetteville. R. R. Jan. 21, 1834.
Winstead, Rebecca to John H. Jones, Apr. 15, Person county. R. R. Je. 10, 1834.
Winston, Duncan C. to Martha J. Hester of Franklin county, Oct. 9. R. R. Nov. 4, 1834.
Wood, Mrs. Newton to Dr. Richard K. Barnum, Oct. 28, Wake county. R. R. Nov. 11, 1834.
Yancey, Maj. Allen to Elizabeth Lunsford, Oct. 23, Caswell county. R. R. Nov. 4, 1834.
Yancy, Tryon to Sarah B. Blacknall, Sept., Oxford. R. R. Sept. 30, 1834.
Yarbrough, Rebecca to Joseph A. Whitaker of Wake county, Feb. 20, Franklin county. R. R. Feb. 25, 1834.
Zimmerman, Anna E. to Willis Peck of Yorkville, S. C. & Raleigh, Nov. 12, Lincolnton. R. R. Dec. 2, 1834.

1835

Abernathy, Miles W. to Ann Hoke, Je. 18, Lincolnton. R. R. Jly. 14, 1835.
Alexander, Dr. Andrew A. to Angelina Davis, Sept. 20, Mecklenburg county. R. R. Nov. 10, 1835.
Allen, Miranda C. to John A. Carter, Sept. 8, Iredell county. R. R. Sept. 29, 1835.
Amis, Thomas to Sarah Davis, Dec. 22, Warrenton. R. R. Jan. 20, 1835.

Armistead, William A. M. D. to Sophia Capehart, Mar., Bertie county. R. R. Mar. 17, 1835.
Armonie, Capt. Samuel D. to Mrs. Ellen Carter, Sept. 29, Newbern. R. R. Oct. 13, 1835.
Armstrong, Thomas J. to Martha Ann Wilson, Oct. 5, New Hanover county. R. R. Oct. 20, 1835.
Arnet, Mary to Abner Powell, Jly., Germantown, Stokes county. R. R. Jly. 14, 1835.
Arnold, Susan M. to Council R. Wright of Duplin county, Feb., Fayetteville. R. R. Feb. 10, 1835.
Atkins, Lucinda P. to John Burroughs, Aug., Orange county. R. R. Aug. 18, 1835.
Atkins, William to Jane D. Ballard, Aug., Orange county. R. R. Aug. 18, 1835.
Bailey, Frances to Reuben Trainum, Oct., Person county. R. R. Oct. 13, 1835.
Baker, Dorcas to J. R. Gardner, Aug. 20, Charlotte. R. R. Sept. 8, 1835.
Baker, Mary to Joseph Rigan, Feb., Robeson county. R. R. Feb. 10, 1835.
Ballard, Jane D. to William Atkins, Aug., Orange county. R. R. Aug. 18, 1835.
Ballew, John S. of Burke county to Mary Warlick, Sept. 20, Lincoln county. R. R. Oct. 27, 1835.
Baskett, Robert to Mary Bowdon, Sept. 10, Warren county. R. R. Oct. 6, 1835.
Battle, John A. M. to Frances E. K. Clitherall, Aug., Elizabeth City. R. R. Aug. 4, 1835.
Barringer, Daniel M. of Cabarrus county to Ann Mathison, Oct. 12, Moore county. R. R. Nov. 3, 1835.
Beasley, Jane to John B. Tinney, Je. 11, Raleigh. R. R. Je. 16, 1835.
Beaton, Peggy to Wm. D. Bryan, Aug. 13, Edgecombe county. R. R. Sept. 8, 1835.
Belden, Robert C. to Elizabeth H. Walker, My. 21, Fayetteville. R. R. My. 26, 1835.
Belew, Elizabeth to Hampton Lindsay, Aug. 25, Anson county. R. R. Sept. 29, 1835.
Belden, Sarah J. to James Hart, My., Fayetteville. R. R. Je. 2, 1835.
Biggie, Archibald to Nancy Love, Sept. 24, Caswell county. R. R. Oct. 13, 1835.
Blackwood, Margaret to Capt. Wm. Cook, Sept. 20, Mecklenburg county. R. R. Nov. 10, 1835.
Blount, Caroline H. to Wm. H. Washington of Wayne county Aug. 12, Newbern. R. R. Aug. 25, 1835.
Blount, Rebecca to John B. Campbell, My. 17, Lumberton. R. R. Je. 2, 1835.
Blount, Gen. Wm. A. of Washington, Beaufort county to Ann B. Littlejohn of Edenton, Feb. R. R. Feb. 17, 1835.
Blue, Barbara E. to H. J. Reid, Aug. 8, Cumberland county. R. R. Aug. 25, 1835.
Bodie, Lucy to B. F. Moore, My. 28, Nash county. R. R. Je. 2, 1835.
Boswell, Dempsey to Nancy Patterson, Sept. 30, Montgomery county. R. R. Oct. 20, 1835.

Borretz, Elizabeth to Edward H. Satterfield of Alexandria, Louisiana, Aug. 25, Edenton. R. R. Sept. 15, 1835.
Bowdon, Mary to Robert Baskett, Sept. 10, Warren county. R. R. Oct. 6, 1835.
Bowling, Lucy of Iredell county to Benjamin Horton of Alabama, Sept. 11, Iredell county. R. R. Nov. 10, 1835.
Boyett, Mary J. of Gates county to John S. Roberts of Gatesville, Dec. 30, Gates county. R. R. Jan. 6, 1835.
Branson, Mrs. Abner to Isaac W. Grice, Je., Sampson county. R. R. Je. 23, 1835.
Brodie, John of Franklin county to Harriet H. Ligon, Sept. 15, Wake Forest. R. R. Sept. 22, 1835.
Brooks, Ann Amanda to Dr. William Withers, Je. 28, Stokes county. R. R. Jly. 14, 1835.
Brothers, Margaret to ·C. C. Mason, Oct. 8, Mecklenburg county. R. R. Nov. 3, 1835.
Brower, Lucinda to Capt. Alfred Staly, Feb. 12, Anson county. R. R. Mar. 10, 1835.
Brown, Charles to Omer Moser, Jly. 16, Mecklenburg county. R. R. Aug. 18, 1835.
Brown, Charles to Sarah B. Foote, Dec., Warren county. R. R. Jan. 20, 1835.
Brown, Jesse to Lavinia M. M'Pheeters, Nov. 2, Raleigh. R. R. Nov. 10, 1835.
Brown, Peter of Charlotte to Martha Gay, Feb., Salisbury. R. R. Mar. 3, 1835.
Brugman, Mrs. Mary A. to Andrew H. Richardson, Aug. 13, Newbern. R. R. Aug. 25, 1835.
Bryan, Wm. D. to Peggy Beaton, Aug. 13, Edgecombe county. R. R. Sept. 8, 1835.
Bucker, Sophia to Levi Rhodes, Jly. 31, Davidson county. R. R. Aug. 18, 1835.
Burges, Nancy to James F. Fulford, Jly. 4, Carteret county. R. R. Aug. 4, 1835.
Burroughs, John to Lucinda P. Atkins, Aug., Orange county. R. R. Aug. 18, 1835.
Burt, Maguire of Caswell county to Mary Ann Campbell, Jly. 21, Orange county. R. R. Aug. 4, 1835.
Burton, Maj. Robert A. to Elizabeth Kearny Hilliard, Mar. 18, Halifax county. R. R. Apr. 14, 1835.
Butler, W. G. to Elizabeth Hooker, Aug. 25, Anson county. R. R. Sept. 29, 1835.
Butler, Zilphia to Samuel Hooker, Aug. 25, Anson county. R. R. Sept. 29, 1835.
Byers, Margaret to Dr. George W. Stinson of Lancaster District, S. C., Apr., Iredell county. R. R. Apr. 14, 1835.
Bynum, Hon. Jesse A. of Halifax District to Maria Funston of Virginia, Mar. 19, Washington, D. C. R. R. Mar. 31, 1835.
Bynum, Nancy to Abner Wilkinson, Aug. 16, Edgecombe county. R. R. Sept. 8, 1835.

Calloway, Dr. James to Mary Louisa Carmichael, Je. 25, Wilkesborough. R. R. Jly. 14, 1835.
Cameron, Anna M. to Alexander M. Kirkland, Feb. 29, Hillsborough. R. R. Mar. 10, 1835.
Campbell, John B. to Rebecca Blount, My. 17, Lumberton. R. R. Je. 2, 1835.
Campbell, Mary Ann to Maguire Burt of Caswell county, Jly. 21, Orange county. R. R. Aug. 4, 1835.
Campbell, Sarah of Cumberland county to Ransom Saunders of Johnston county, Je. 30, Cumberland county. R. R. Jly. 21, 1835.
Campbell, Williamson H. of Iredell county to Jemina Mabry of Wilkes county, Sept. 1, Iredell county. R. R. Nov. 10, 1835.
Capehart, Sophia to William A. Armistead, M. D. Mar., Bertie county. R. R. Mar. 17, 1835.
Carmichael, Mary Louisa to Dr. James Calloway, Je. 25, Wilkesborough. R. R. Jly. 14, 1835.
Carpenter, Mr. of Fayetteville to Emmeline Dilliard, Apr. 21, Raleigh. R. R. Apr. 28, 1835.
Carpenter, Sarah Elizabeth of Wake county to Willie Whitley of Johnson county, Sept. 24. R. R. Oct. 20, 1835.
Carraway, Lavinia J. to Dr. Samuel Masters, My. 7, Newbern. R. R. My. 26, 1835.
Carson, T. C. of Rutherford to Miss M. A. M'Bee, Oct. 6, Lincolnton. R. R. Oct. 27, 1835.
Carter, Mrs. Ellen to Capt. Samuel D. Armonie, Sept. 29, Newbern. R. R. Oct. 13, 1835.
Carter, John A. to Miranda C. Albea, Sept. 8, Iredell county. R. R. Sept. 29, 1835.
Caudle, E. to Thomas Good, Feb., Stokes county. R. R. Mar. 3, 1835.
Clarke, Isaac W. to Delia Thomerson, Oct. 15, Chatham county. R. R. Nov. 17, 1835.
Clark, James to Nancy Crutchfield, Aug., Chatham county. R. R. Sept. 1, 1835.
Clarke, Henry S. of Beaufort county to Alvaney M. Staton of Pitt county, My., Greenville, Pitt county. R. R. Je. 2, 1835.
Cliffard, Ahira to Rosanna Hall, Feb., Rowan county. R. R. Mar. 3, 1835.
Clifford, Rachael to James White, Feb., Rowan county. R. R. Mar. 3, 1835.
Clitherall, Frances E. K. to John A. M. Battle, Aug., Elizabeth City. R. R. Aug. 4, 1835.
Coggins, Sally to Aaron Mobly, Aug., Chatham county. R. R. Sept. 1, 1835.
Colbart, Nancy of Iredell county to John Gray of Rowan county, Oct. 8, Iredell county. R. R. Nov. 3, 1835.
Coleman, Col. Daniel to Maria N. Mahan, Apr. 3, Concord, Cabarrus county. R. R. Apr. 14, 1835.
Collier, Tabitha C. to Henry Y. Overcast, Jly. 14, Cabarrus county. R. R. Aug. 18, 1835.
Comer, Harriet to Dr. Sidney X. Johnson, Sept. 15, Lincoln county. R. R. Oct. 13, 1835.

Cook, Capt. Wm. to Margaret Blackwood, Sept. 20, Mecklenburg county. R. R. Nov. 10, 1835.

Cooper, Charles A. to Rebecca P. Shultz, Sept. 29, Salem. R. R. Nov. 10, 1835.

Cotton, Jane to Exum Lewis, Jr. Sept. 29, Edgecombe county. R. R. Oct. 13, 1835.

Cousins, Sarah Varnick of Orange county, New York to Rev. Wm. H. Morrison of Cabarrus county, Jly. 30, Charlotte. R. R. Aug. 18, 1835.

Coward, Nancy to Col. William Dixon, Oct., Green county. R. R. Nov. 3, 1835.

Coward, Samuel H. to Lucretia Edwards, Oct., Lenoir county. R. R. Nov. 3, 1835.

Craige, Robert Newton to Mary Howard, Mar. 19, Salisbury. R. R. Apr. 7, 1835.

Craige, Samuel to Elizabeth Howard, Oct. 20, Rowan county. R. R. Nov. 3, 1835.

Creecy, Mary to Henry C. Walker of Norfolk, Va. Aug., Hertford, Perquimans county. R. R. Sept. 1, 1835.

Crook, Dr. A. B. of Greenville, S. C. to Sarah Hoke, Je., Lincolnton. R. R. Je. 23, 1835.

Crump, Lucinda J. of Chatham county to Richerson Faucett of Haywood county, Dec. 3. R. R. Dec. 29, 1835.

Crutchfield, Nancy to James Clark, Aug., Chatham county. R. R. Sept. 1, 1835.

Crutchfield, Patsey to Matthias M. Johnson, Aug., Chatham county. R. R. Sept. 1, 1835.

Curtis, Mrs. Elizabeth to Edmund B. Skinner, Jly. 16, Perquimans county. R. R. Aug. 4, 1835.

Danforth R. to Ellen Humphreys, Sept. 16, Greensborough, Guilford county. R. R. Oct. 6, 1835.

Davis, Angelina to Dr. Andrew A. Alexander, Sept. 20, Mecklenburg county. R. R. Nov. 10, 1835.

Davis, Eliza to Dr. Louis J. Poison, Mar., Wilmington. R. R. Mar. 10, 1835.

Davis, Sarah to Thomas Amis, Dec. 22, Warrenton. R. R. Jan. 20, 1835.

Dickson, Lucy J. to Dr. David Russel of Vernon, Alabama, Oct. 8, Duplin county. R. R. Oct. 20, 1835.

Dilliard, Emmeline to Mr. Carpenter of Fayetteville, Apr. 21, Raleigh. R. R. Apr. 28, 1835.

Dinkins, Emily to Dr. Samuel B. Watson, Sept. 8, Charlotte. R. R. Sept. 29, 1835.

Dixon, Col. William to Nancy Coward, Oct., Greene county. R. R. Nov. 3, 1835.

Door, John N. of Germany to Mary Gregory of Lumberton, Jly. 7, Lumberton. R. R. Jly. 21, 1835.

Douthitt, George to Nancy Springle, Sept. 14, Davidson county. R. R. Nov. 10, 1835.

Dowel, Elizabeth to Joseph Privett, Sept. 15, Iredell county. R. R. Nov. 10, 1835.

Drake, Lewis S. to Elizabeth Ivey, Oct. 5, Halifax county. R. R. Nov. 3, 1835.

Eagle, Caroline to Thomas Lewis, Aug. 20, Rowan county. R. R. Sept. 8, 1835.
Eaton, Benjamin to E. Tatum, Feb., Rowan county. R. R. Mar. 3, 1835.
Eaton, Elizabeth Kemp Macon of Warren county to Eaton G. Field of Boydton, Feb., Warrenton. R. R. Feb. 10, 1835.
Edwards, Lucretia to Samuel H. Coward, Oct., Lenoir county. R. R. Nov. 3, 1835.
Elliott, Elizabeth Donoho to Dr. J. Williams of Cabarrus county, Dec., Rutherford county. R. R. Dec. 29, 1835.
Erwin, William C. to Martha M. Walton, Je. 18, Morganton. R. R. Je. 30, 1835.
Evans, Robert to Temperance Jordan, Aug. 20, Edenton. R. R. Sept. 8, 1835.
Fagan, Emma to William G. Frazier, Aug. 13, Plymouth. R. R. Sept. 1, 1835.
Faggart, Matthias to Eleanor Scott, Jly. 17. R. R. Aug. 18, 1835.
Farley, Abner to Ann Owen, Sept. 22, Caswell county. R. R. Oct. 13, 1835.
Faucett, David A. to Mary A. Patterson, Sept. 3, Orange county. R. R. Oct. 6, 1835.
Faucett, Richerson of Haywood county to Lucinda J. Crump of Chatham county, Dec. 3. R. R. Dec. 29, 1835.
Fenner, Col. John M. of Madison county, Tenn. & Raleigh to Miriam Williams, Apr. 15, Henry county Tennessee. R. R. My. 26, 1835.
Ferguson, Ann of Chapel Hill to Robert J. Halliday of Fayetteville, My. 14, Chapel Hill. R. R. My. 19, 1835.
Field, Eaton G. of Boydton to Elizabeth Kemp Macon Eaton of Warren county, Feb., Warrenton. R. R. Feb. 10, 1835.
Flauner, Bennet to Susan A. Green, Feb., Newbern. R. R. Mar. 3, 1835.
Fleming, Maj. Samuel to H. Ann Eliza Greenlee, Oct. 13, Burke county. R. R. Nov. 17, 1835.
Folsome, Derius of Charlotte to Mary Hampton, Sept. 3, Cabarrus county. R. R. Sept. 29, 1835.
Foote, Sarah B. to Charles Brown, Dec., Warren county. R. R. Jan. 20, 1835.
Frank, Joseph A. to Barbary Upright, Oct. 8, Rowan county. R. R. Oct. 27, 1835.
Frank, Peter to Peggy Ricard, Jly., Lexington, Davidson county. R. R. Jly. 14, 1835.
Frazier, William G. to Emma Fagan, Aug. 13, Plymouth. R. R. Sept. 1, 1835.
Fulford, James W. to Nancy Burges, Jly. 4, Carteret county. R. R. Aug. 4, 1835.
Fulford, Capt. Samuel to Elizabeth Gaskill of Portsmouth, Carteret county, Aug. 24, Pamptico Lighthouse. R. R. Sept. 15, 1835.
Fuller, Akey of York District, S. C. to Margaret Whiteside, Sept. 23, Mecklenburg county. R. R. Oct. 20, 1835.
Funsten, Maria of Virginia to Hon. Jesse A. Bynum of Halifax District, Mar. 19, Washington, D. C. R. R. Mar. 31, 1835.
Gale, Enoch R. of Elizabeth City to Elizabeth Lockhart of Virginia, Jly. 15. R. R. Aug. 4, 1835.

Gardner, J. R. to Dorcas Baker, Aug. 20, Charlotte. R. R. Sept. 8, 1835.
Gaskill, Elizabeth of Portsmouth, Carteret county to Capt. Samuel Fulford, Aug. 24, Pamptico Lighthouse. R. R. Sept. 15, 1835.
Gatlin, Sarah to Turner Reavis of Smithfield, Jan. 20, Kinston. R. R. Jan. 27, 1835.
Gay, Martha to Peter Brown of Charlotte, Feb., Salisbury. R. R. Mar. 3, 1835.
Gillespie, Dr. D. to Lucy Jane Pearsall, Feb., Duplin county. R. R. Feb. 17, 1835.
Gillis, Mary to David Roe, Oct. 5, Montgomery county. R. R. Oct. 27, 1835.
Gillis, Mary to David Rough, Oct. 6, Montgomery county. R. R. Nov. 3, 1835.
Goneke, John F. of Raleigh to Lucy Ann Houghton, Jly. 19, Madison Springs, Georgia. R. R. Aug. 4, 1835.
Good, Thomas to E. Caudle, Feb., Stokes county. R. R. Mar. 3, 1835.
Gorham, Emily to Henry C. Jordan, My., Greenville, Pitt county. R. R. Je. 2, 1835.
Gray, John of Rowan county to Nancy Colbart of Iredell county, Oct. 8, Iredell county. R. R. Nov. 3, 1835.
Green, Richard of Raleigh to Julia J. Sneed, Sept., Oxford. R. R. Sept. 8, 1835.
Green, Susan A. to Bennet Flauner, Feb., Newbern. R. R. Mar. 3, 1835.
Green, Susan B. to Nathaniel Waples, Aug., Newbern. R. R. Sept. 1, 1835.
Greene, John to Rebecca Jane Mitchell, Apr., Franklin county. R. R. Apr. 14, 1835.
Greenlee, H. Ann Eliza to Maj. Samuel Fleming, Oct. 13, Burke county. R. R. Nov. 17, 1835.
Gregory, Mary of Lumberton to John N. Door of Germany, Jly. 7, Lumberton. R. R. Jly. 21, 1835.
Grice, Isaac W. to Mrs. Abner Branson, Je., Sampson county. R. R. Je. 23, 1835.
Grubbs, James of Milton to Ann Louisa Gunter of Pittyslvania, Va. Oct. 6. R. R. Oct. 20, 1835.
Gunn, James to Frances A. Henderson, My., Caswell county. R. R. Je. 2, 1835.
Gunn, Wm. P. of Caswell county to Sarah M'Cain, Jly., High Rock. R. R. Jly. 14, 1835.
Gunter, Ann Louisa of Pittyslvania, Va. to James Grubbs of Milton, Oct. 6. R. R. Oct. 20, 1835.
Haden, Franklin W. to Irena Miller, Je. 14, Davidson county. R. R. Jly. 14, 1835.
Haile, Elijah to Emeline Jackson, Oct., Halifax county. R. R. Nov. 3, 1835.
Hails, Mary Eliza A. to John M. Reeves, Aug. 13, Bladen county. R. R. Sept. 8, 1835.
Hair, Daniel to Miss Tanner, Sept. 22, Iredell county. R. R. Oct. 20, 1835.
Hall, Rosanna to Ahira Cliffard, Feb., Rowan county. R. R. Mar. 3, 1835.
Halliday, Robert J. of Fayetteville to Ann Ferguson of Chapel Hill, My. 14, Chapel Hill. R. R. My. 19, 1835.

Hampton, Mary to Derius Folsome of Charlotte, Sept. 3, Cabarrus county. R. R. Sept. 29, 1835.
Hannigan, James to Sarah A. Stewart, Feb., Mecklenburg county. R. R. Mar. 3, 1835.
Harrison, Martha to Nathaniel R. Tunstall, Jan., Franklin county. R. R. Jan. 6, 1835.
Harrison, William A. of Wake county to Mary M'Kee, Mar. 3, Raleigh. R. R. Mar. 10, 1835.
Hart, James to Sarah J. Belden, My., Fayetteville. R. R. Je. 2, 1835.
Hart, John of Mecklenburg county to Mrs. Violet W. Lindsay, Apr., Lincoln county. R. R. Apr. 14, 1835.
Hartsfield, Capt. Wesley to Candace Smith, Mar. 19, Wake Forest. R. R. Mar. 24, 1835.
Harvey, Julia M. to Alexander H. Stanly, Feb., Newbern. R. R. Mar. 3, 1835.
Hawks, Rev. Cicero S. to Ann Jones, Jan. 19, Newbern. R. R. Mar. 3, 1835.
Head, Cynthia to Benjamin Noles, Sept. 8, Iredell county. R. R. Sept. 29, 1835.
Hearn, Sarah to Charles J. Nelson, Oct. 29, Newbern. R. R. Nov. 17, 1835.
Henderson, Frances A. to James Gunn, My., Caswell county. R. R. Je. 2, 1835.
Henderson, George W. of Lincolnton to Amanda Malvina Moore, Sept. 22, Spartanburg District, S. C. R. R. Oct. 20, 1835.
Hensby, Calvin to Susan Martin, Aug., Rockingham county. R. R. Aug. 25, 1835.
High, Mary C. of Wake county to William P. Taylor of Chatham county, Feb. 11, Wake county. R. R. Feb. 24, 1835.
Hill, Daniel to Susan Irwin Toole of Edgecombe county, Dec. 5, Franklin county. R. R. Dec. 29, 1835.
Hill, E. Ann to John Skinner of Chowan county, Apr. 28, Louisburg. R. R. My. 26, 1835.
Hill, Ellen G. to Jos. J. Somerville of Granville county, Jly. 28, Louisburg. R. R. Aug. 4, 1835.
Hill, William to Susan Shields, My., Caswell county. R. R. Je. 2, 1835.
Hiliard, Elizabeth Kearny to Maj. Robert A. Burton, Mar. 18, Halifax county. R. R. Apr. 14, 1835.
Hillyard, Elijah of Nash county to Rebecca Ann Powell, Nov. 24, Wake county. R. R. Dec. 8, 1835.
Hoell, Capt. Welcome to Lucinda Price, Oct. 22, Washington, Beaufort county. R. R. Nov. 17, 1835.
Hoke, Ann to Miles W. Abernathy, Je. 18, Lincolnton. R. R. Jly. 14, 1835.
Hoke, Sarah to Dr. A. B. Crook of Greenville, S. C., Je., Lincolnton. R. R. Je. 23, 1835.
Hooker, Elizabeth to W. G. Butler, Aug. 25, Anson county. R. R. Sept. 29, 1835.
Hooker, Samuel to Zilphia Butler, Aug. 25, Anson county. R. R. Sept. 29, 1835.
Horn, Whitmel of Florida to Mary F. Telfair, Jan., Washington. R. R. Jan. 6, 1835.
Horton, Benjamin of Alabama to Lucy Bowling of Iredell county, Sept. 11, Iredell county. R. R. Nov. 10, 1835.

Houghton, Lucy Ann to John F. Goneke of Raleigh, Jly. 19, Madison Springs, Georgia. R. R. Aug. 4, 1835.
Howard, Elizabeth W. to Samuel Craige, Oct. 20, Rowan county. R. R. Nov. 3, 1835.
Howard, Mary to Robert Newton Craige, Mar. 19, Salisbury. R. R. Apr. 7, 1835.
Humphreys, Ellen to R. Danforth, Sept. 16, Greensborough, Guilford county. R. R. Oct. 6, 1835.
Hurley, Joshua to Susan Jenkins, Sept., Montgomery county. R. R. Sept. 29, 1835.
Ivey, Elizabeth to Lewis S. Drake, Oct. 5, Halifax county. R. R. Nov. 3, 1835.
Jackson, Emeline to Elijah Haile, Oct., Halifax county. R. R. Nov. 3, 1835.
Jeane, Mrs. Nancy to James M'Nairy, Sr., Jly. 30, White Plains, Guilford county. R. R. Aug. 18, 1835.
Jenkins, Lavinia to Wm. Jenkins, Jly. 13, Montgomery county. R. R. Sept. 8, 1835.
Jenkins, Susan to Joshua Hurley, Sept., Montgomery county. R. R. Sept. 29, 1835.
Jenkins, Wm. to Lavinia Jenkins, Jly. 13, Montgomery county. R. R. Sept. 8, 1835.
Johnson, Matthias M. to Patsey Crutchfield, Aug., Chatham county. R. R. Sept. 1, 1835.
Johnson, Dr. Sidney X. to Harriet Comer, Sept. 15, Lincoln county. R. R. Oct. 13, 1835.
Joice, Patsey to William Wren, Oct. 1, Newbern. R. R. Oct. 13, 1835.
Joiner, Mary of Pitt county to Hugh H. Parker of Greene county, Aug. 19, Pitt county. R. R. Sept. 8, 1835.
Jones, Ann to Rev. Cicero S. Hawks, Jan. 19, Newbern. R. R. Mar. 3, 1835.
Jones, Calvin of Pulaski, Tennessee to Mildred Williamson, Oct., Person county. R. R. Oct. 27, 1835.
Jones, John H. of Raleigh to Charity W. Smith of Cumberland county, Dec., Wake county. R. R. Dec. 8, 1835.
Jordan, Henry C. to Emily Gorham, My., Greenville, Pitt county. R. R. Je. 2, 1835.
Jordan, Temperance to Robert Evans, Aug. 20, Edenton. R. R. Sept. 8, 1835.
Kendall, Wm. P. of Wadesborough to Eliza Randle, Oct. 7, Montgomery county. R. R. Oct. 20, 1835.
Kerr, Major James to Frances M'Neal, Oct. 8, Caswell county. R. R. Oct. 20, 1835.
Kimball, Edward of Oxford to Mary Lawson, Jly. 13, Person county. R. R. Aug. 4, 1835.
King, Susan of Lawrence county to Tignal Jones of Morgan county (both formerly of Wake county) Je. 28, Alabama. R. R. Jly. 7, 1835.
Kirk, Richard of Davidson county to Patience Parks, Oct. 8, Rowan county. R. R. Oct. 27, 1835.
Kirkland, Alexander M. to Anna M. Cameron, Feb. 29, Hillsborough. R. R. Mar. 10, 1835.

Langhorne, Rev. Geo. W. of the Va. Conference to Elizabeth W. Moore, Jan. 29, Chatham county. R. R. Feb. 24, 1835.
Lawson, Mary to Edward Kimball of Oxford, Jly. 13, Person county. R. R. Aug. 4, 1835.
Lentz, Christiana to Alex M. Miller, Oct. 15, Rowan county. R. R. Oct. 27, 1835.
Lewis, Caroline to William J. Lougee, Apr. 22, Raleigh. R. R. Apr. 28, 1835.
Lewis, Eliza to John W. Pierce of Fayetteville, My. 20, Franklin county. R. R. My. 26, 1835.
Lewis, Exum, Jr. to Jane Cotton, Sept. 29, Edgecombe county. R. R. Oct. 13, 1835.
Lewis, Thomas to Carolina Eagle, Aug. 20, Rowan county. R. R. Sept. 8, 1835.
Ligon, Harriet H. to John Brodie of Franklin county, Sept. 15, Wake Forest. R. R. Sept. 22, 1835.
Lindsay, Hampton to Elizabeth Belew, Aug. 25, Anson county. R. R. Sept. 29, 1835.
Lindsay, Mrs. Violet W. to John Hart of Mecklenburg county, Apr., Lincoln county. R. R. Apr. 14, 1835.
Lippitt, Jeremiah to Eliza M. S. Moore, Jly., Wilmington. R. R. Jly. 21, 1835.
Little, Sarah B. of Wilmington to Edward Lee Winslow of Fayetteville, My. 9, Oxford. R. R. My. 19, 1835.
Littlejohn, Ann B. of Edenton to Gen. Wm. A. Blount of Washington, Beaufort county, Feb. R. R. Feb. 17, 1835.
Lockhart, Elizabeth of Virginia to Enoch R. Gale of Elizabeth City, Jly. 15. R. R. Aug. 4, 1835.
Loftin, Cornelius to Louisa Noah, Jly. 24, Davidson county. R. R. Aug. 18, 1835.
London, Frances to Lallerstedt, Mallett of Bladen county, Je., Wilmington. R. R. Je. 23, 1835.
Lougee, William J. to Caroline Lewis, Apr. 22, Raleigh. R. R. Apr. 28, 1835.
Love, Nancy to Archibald Biggie, Sept. 24, Caswell county. R. R. Oct. 13, 1835.
Lovell, Thomas B. to Eliza Wolff, Aug. 16, Stokes county. R. R. Sept. 8, 1835.
Mabry, Jemina of Wilkes county to Williamson H. Campbell of Iredell county, Sept. 1, Iredell county. R. R. Nov. 10, 1835.
M'Bee, Miss M. A. to T. C. Carson of Rutherford, Oct. 6, Lincolnton. R. R. Oct. 27, 1935.
M'Cain, Sarah to Wm. P. Gunn of Caswell county, Jly., High Rock. R. R. Jly. 14, 1835.
M'Daniel, Mrs. Ann to Joseph Sommers, Sept. 17, Newbern. R. R. Oct. 13, 1835.
M'Evoy, Mary to John A. Stanfield of Oxford, Je., Murfreesboro. R. R. Je. 23, 1835.
M'Iver, Daniel of Wadesborough to Mary Scott, Jly. 29, Anson county. R. R. Sept. 15, 1835.
M'Kay, Col. Archibald to Catharine B. M'Nair, Oct. 29, Robeson county. R. R. Nov. 17, 1835.
M'Kee, Mary to William A. Harrison of Wake county, Mar. 3, Raleigh. R. R. Mar. 10, 1835.

M'Kenzie, Margaret to John M'Rorie of Lexington, Sept., Rowan county. R. R. Sept. 29, 1835.

M'Lauren, Col. John C. of Richmond county to Margaret M'Neill, Nov., Robeson county. R. R. Nov. 3, 1835.

M'Millan, John H. of Fayetteville to Mary Ann Shepperd, Feb., St. Louis, Mo. R. R. Feb. 17, 1835.

M'Nair, Catharine B. to Col. Archibald M'Kay, Oct. 29, Robeson county. R. R. Nov. 17, 1835.

M'Nairy, James Sr. to Mrs. Nancy Jeane, Jly. 30, White Plains, Guilford county. R. R. Aug. 18, 1835.

M'Naspie, Jane of Raleigh to Charles H. Williams, My. 13, Pittsborough. R. R. My. 26, 1835.

M'Neal, Frances to Major James Kerr, Oct. 8, Caswell county. R. R. Oct. 20, 1835.

M'Neill, Margaret to Col. John C. M'Lauren of Richmond county, Nov., Robeson county. R. R. Nov. 3, 1835.

M'Pheeters, Lavinia M. to Jesse Brown, Nov. 2, Raleigh. R. R. Nov. 10, 1835.

M'Rorie, John of Lexington to Margaret M'Kenzie, Sept., Rowan county. R. R. Sept. 29, 1835.

Mahan, Maria N. to Col. Daniel Coleman, Apr. 3, Concord, Cabarrus county. R. R. Apr. 14, 1835.

Mallett, Lallenstedt of Bladen county to Frances London, Je., Wilmington. R. R. Je. 23, 1835.

Mauney, Elizabeth V. to Benjamin Perry, Nov., Beaufort, Carteret county. R. R. Nov. 10, 1835.

Mason, C. C. to Margaret Brothers, Oct. 8, Mecklenburg county. R. R. Nov. 3, 1835.

Mason, Eli to Salina S. Reid, Sept. 7, Iredell county. R. R. Oct. 27, 1835.

Masters, Dr. Samuel of Washington to Lavinia J. Carraway, My. 7, Newbern. R. R. My. 26, 1835.

Mathison, Ann to Daniel M. Barringer of Cabarrus county, Oct. 12, Moore county. R. R. Nov. 3, 1835.

Mebane, Alexander to Elizabeth Paul, Jly. 14, Orange county. R. R. Aug. 4, 1835.

Miller, Alex M. to Christiana Lentz, Oct. 15, Rowan county. R. R. Oct. 27, 1835.

Miller, Irena to Franklin W. Haden, Je. 14, Davidson county. R. R. Jly. 14, 1835.

Mitchell, Jane to John Greene, Apr., Franklin county. R. R. Apr. 14, 1835.

Mobly, Aaron to Sally Coggins, Aug., Chatham county. R. R. Sept. 1, 1835.

Montgomery, John to Eliza Nichols, Oct. 1, Mecklenburg county. R. R. Oct. 20, 1835.

Moore, Amanda Malvina to George W. Henderson of Lincolnton, Sept. 22, Spartanburg District, S. C. R. R. Oct. 20, 1835.

Moore, Amanda of Yorkville to Leroy Springs of Charlotte, Oct. 15, Yorkville, South Carolina. R. R. Nov. 3, 1835.

Moore, B. F. to Lucy Bodie, My. 28, Nash county. R. R. Je. 2, 1835.

Moore, Eliza M. S. to Jeremiah Lippitt, Jly., Wilmington. R. R. Jly. 21, 1835.
Moore, Elizabeth W. to Rev. Geo. W. Langhorne of the Virginia Conference, Jan. 29, Chatham county. R. R. Feb. 24, 1835.
Moore, Master Thompson to Caroline Westbrook, Sept. 7, Caswell county. R. R. Sept. 29, 1835.
Mordecai, Augustus of Raleigh to Rosina U. Young, Mar. 5, Richmond, Va. R. R. Mar. 10, 1835.
Moring, Alfred to Elizabeth M. O'Kelley, Feb. 17, Chatham county. R. R. Feb. 24, 1835.
Morris, James E. to Mary Thompson, Aug., Newbern. R. R. Sept. 1, 1835.
Morris, Capt. Joseph C. of Rhode Island to Ann Eliza Vaughan, Oct. 13, Elizabeth City. R. R. Nov. 3, 1835.
Morrison, Rev. Wm. H. of Cabarrus county to Sarah Varick Cousins of Orange county, New York, Jly. 30, Charlotte. R. R. Aug. 18, 1835.
Moser, Omer to Charles Brown, Jly. 16, Mecklenburg county. R. R. Aug. 18, 1835.
Moye, Col. Macon to Emily Saunders, Jly. 15, Pitt county. R. R. Aug. 4, 1835.
Nelson, Charles J. to Sarah Hearn, Oct. 29, Newbern. R. R. Nov. 17, 1835.
Newby, Thomas of Perquimans county to Margaret White of Pasquotank county, Jly. 30. R. R. Aug. 18, 1835.
Nichols, Eliza to John Montgomery, Oct. 1, Mecklenburg county. R. R. Oct. 20, 1835.
Noah, Louisa to Cornelius Lofton, Jly. 24, Davidson county. R. R. Aug. 18, 1835.
Noles, Benjamin to Cynthia Head, Sept. 8, Iredell county. R. R. Sept. 29, 1835.
Nunnally, Capt. Archibald to Caroline Spence, Sept. 16, Milton. R. R. Oct. 6, 1835.
O'Kelley, Elizabeth M. to Alfred Morning, Feb. 17, Chatham county. R. R. Feb. 24, 1835.
Oliver, Thomas M. of Raleigh to Frances M. Stewart, Jan., Newbern. R. R. Jan. 27, 1835.
Overcast, Henry Y. to Tabitha C. Collier, Jly. 14, Cabarrus county. R. R. Aug. 18, 1835.
Owen, Ann to Abner Farley, Sept. 22, Caswell county. R. R. Oct. 13, 1835.
Owen, James of Tipton county, Tennessee to Ellen Wiseman, Sept. 10, Davidson county. R. R. Oct. 27, 1835.
Parker, Mrs. Ann to Ralph Smedley, Jly. 14, Raleigh. R. R. Jly. 21, 1835.
Parker, Hugh H. of Greene county to Mary Joiner of Pitt county, Aug. 19, Pitt county. R. R. Sept. 8, 1835.
Parks, Patience to Richard Kirk of Davidson, Oct. 8, Rowan county. R. R. Oct. 27, 1835.
Patterson, Mary A. to David A. Faucett, Sept. 3, Orange county. R. R. Oct. 6, 1835.
Patterson, Nancy to Dempsey Boswell, Sept. 30, Montgomery county. R. R. Oct. 20, 1835.
Paul, Elizabeth to Alexander Mebane, Jly. 14, Orange county. R. R. Aug. 4, 1835.

Pearsall, Lucy Jane to Dr. D. Gillespie, Feb., Duplin county. R. R. Feb. 17, 1835.
Peebles, Lucy to Edward Pierce, Sept. 20, Nash county. R. R. Nov. 10, 1835.
Pemberton, James D. to Charlotte J. Stanback, Feb., Richmond county. R. R. Feb. 17, 1835.
Perry, Benjamin to Elizabeth V. Mauney, Nov., Beaufort, Carteret county. R. R. Nov. 10, 1835.
Pettus, Miss H. M. A. of Mecklenburg county to Thomas Rozzell of Lincoln county, Nov. 1. R. R. Nov. 3, 1835.
Pierce, Edward to Lucy Peebles, Sept. 20, Nash county. R. R. Nov. 10, 1835.
Pierce, John W. of Fayetteville to Eliza Lewis, My. 20, Franklin county. R. R. My. 26, 1835.
Pitts, Henry to Mrs. Nancy Wright, Oct., Halifax county. R. R. Nov. 3, 1835.
Poison, Dr. Louis J. to Eliza Davis, Mar., Wilmington. R. R. Mar. 10, 1835.
Porter, Lucia Chaucey to John Weddell of Louisiana & Wilmington, Aug. 25, Alexandria. R. R. Sept. 15, 1835.
Powell, Abner to Mary Arnet, Jly., Germantown, Stokes county. R. R. Jly. 14, 1835.
Powell, Rebecca Ann to Elijah Hillyard of Nash county, Nov. 24, Wake county. R. R. Dec. 8, 1835.
Prather, Sidney to Catharine Roney, Sept. 17, Orange county. R. R. Sept. 29, 1835.
Price, Lucinda to Capt. Welcome Hoell, Oct. 22, Washington, Beaufort county. R. R. Nov. 17, 1835.
Privett, Joseph to Elizabeth Dowel, Sept. 15, Iredell county. R. R. Nov. 10, 1835.
Privett, Susannah of Iredell county to Benjamin Tilman of Tennessee, Sept. 1, Iredell county. R. R. Nov. 10, 1835.
Randle, Eliza to Wm. P. Kendall of Wadesborough, Oct. 7, Montgomery county. R. R. Oct. 20, 1835.
Reavis, Turner of Smithfield to Sarah Gatlin, Jan. 20, Kinston. R. R. Jan. 27, 1835.
Reeves, John M. to Mary Eliza A. Hails, Aug. 13, Bladen county. R. R. Sept. 8, 1835.
Reddick, Richard to Ann Wells, Je., Raleigh. R. R. Je. 9, 1835.
Reich, Maria Louisa to John U. Vogler of Lincolnton, Je. 25, Salem. R. R. Jly. 14, 1835.
Reid, H. J. to Barbara E. Blue, Aug. 8, Cumberland county. R. R. Aug. 25, 1835.
Reid, Salina S. to Eli Mason, Sept. 7, Iredell county. R. R. Oct. 27, 1835.
Rhodes, Levi to Sophia Bucker, Jly. 31, Davidson county. R. R. Aug. 18, 1835.
Ricard, Peggy to Peter Frank, Jly., Lexington, Davidson county. R. R. Jly. 14, 1835.
Richardson, Andrew H. to Mrs. Mary A. Brugman, Aug. 13, Newbern. R. R. Aug. 25, 1835.
Rigan, Joseph to Mary Baker, Feb., Robeson county. R. R. Feb. 10, 1835.

Robards, William H. of this State to Susan A. Watkins, Dec., Goochland, Va. R. R. Jan. 20, 1835.
Roberts, John S. of Gatesville to Mary J. Boyett, Gates county, Dec. 30, Gates county. R. R. Jan. 6, 1835.
Roe, David to Mary Gillis, Oct. 5, Montgomery county. R. R. Oct. 27, 1835.
Rough, David to Mary Gillis, Oct. 6, Montgomery county. R. R. Nov. 3, 1835.
Roles, Olivia to Thomas J. Terrell, Sept. 17, Rolesville. R. R. Sept. 22, 1835.
Roney, Catharine to Sidney Prather, Sept. 17, Orange county. R. R. Sept. 29, 1835.
Roseman, Mrs. Sarah of Rowan county to James Young of Cabarrus county, Aug. 27, Rowan county. R. R. Sept. 8, 1835.
Rowland, Isaac to Eleanor Smith, Jly. 18. R. R. Aug. 18, 1835.
Rozzell, Thomas of Lincoln county to Miss H. M. A. Pettus of Mecklenburg county, Nov. 1. R. R. Nov. 3, 1835.
Russell, Dr. David of Vernon, Alabama to Lucy J. Dickson, Oct. 8, Duplin county. R. R. Oct. 20, 1835.
Sandus, Lorenzo to Alsey Roach, Aug., Rockingham county. R. R. Aug. 25, 1835.
Satterfield, Edward H. of Alexandria, Louisiana to Elizabeth Borretz, Aug. 25, Edenton. R. R. Sept. 15, 1835.
Saunders, Emily to Col Macon Moye, Jly. 15, Pitt county. R. R. Aug. 4, 1835.
Saunders, Ransome of Johnston county to Sarah Campbell of Cumberland county, Je. 30, Cumberland county. R. R. Jly. 21, 1835.
Scott, Eleanor to Mathias Faggart, Jly. 17. R. R. Aug. 18, 1835.
Scott, Mary to Daniel M'Iver of Wadesborough, Jly. 29, Anson county. R. R. Sept. 15, 1835.
Shaver, Margaret to Sidney Spears, Feb., Salisbury. R. R. Feb. 17, 1835.
Sheatly, Mrs. Susan P. to Rice C. Spears of Virginia, Feb., Morganton. R. R. Feb. 17, 1835.
Shepperd, Mary Ann to John H. M'Millan of Fayetteville, Feb., St. Louis, Mo. R. R. Feb. 17, 1835.
Shultz, Rebecca P. to Charles A. Cooper, Sept. 29, Salem. R. R. Nov. 10, 1835.
Skinner, Edmund B. to Mrs. Elizabeth Curtis, Jly. 16, Perquimans county. R. R. Aug. 4, 1835.
Skinner, John of Chowan county to E. Ann Hill, Apr. 28, Louisburg. R. R. My. 26, 1835.
Smedley, Ralph to Mrs. Ann Parker, Jly. 14, Raleigh. R. R. Jly. 21, 1835.
Smith, Candace to Capt. Wesley Hartsfield, Mar. 19, Wake Forest. R. R. Mar. 24, 1835.
Smith, Charity W. of Cumberland county to John H. Jones of Raleigh, Dec., Wake county. R. R. Dec. 8, 1835.
Smith, Eleanor to Isaac Rowland, Jly. 18. R. R. Aug. 18, 1835.
Smith, Franklin to Isabella Torrence, Sept. 10, Mecklenburg county. R. R. Sept. 29, 1835.
Smith, Joseph to Eliza Townsend. Oct. 15, Robeson county. R. R. Nov. 17, 1835.

Smith, Louisa to Anthony A. Willis, Jly. 3, Carteret county. R. R. Aug. 4, 1835.
Sneed, Julia J. to Richard Green of Raleigh, Sept., Oxford. R. R. Sept. 8, 1835.
Somerville, Jos. J. of Granville county to Ellen G. Hill, Jly. 28, Louisburg. R. R. Aug, 4, 1835.
Sommers, Joseph to Mrs. Ann M'Daniel, Sept. 17, Newbern. R. R. Oct. 13, 1835.
Southerland, Solon to Mary E. Jordan, Dec. 23, Granville county. R. R. Jan. 20, 1835.
Sparrow, Stephen D. to Eliza Ann Spencer, Aug., Hyde county. R. R. Sept. 1, 1835.
Spears, Rice C. of Virginia to Mrs. Susan P. Sheatly, Feb., Morganton, R. R. Feb. 17, 1835.
Spears, Sidney to Margaret Shaver, Feb., Salisbury. R. R. Feb. 17, 1835.
Spence, Caroline to Capt. Archibald Nunnally, Sept. 16, Milton. R. R. Oct. 6. 1835.
Spencer, Eliza Ann to Stephen D. Sparrow, Aug., Hyde county. R. R. Sept. 1, 1835.
Springle, Nancy to George Douthitt, Sept. 14, Davidson county. R. R. Nov. 10, 1835.
Springs, Leroy of Charlotte to Amandah Moore of Yorkville, Oct. 15, Yorkville, South Carolina. R. R. Nov. 3, 1835.
Staly, Capt. Alfred to Lucinda Brower, Feb. 12, Anson county. R. R. Mar. 10, 1835.
Stanback, Charlotte J. to James D. Pemberton, Feb., Richmond county. R. R. Feb. 17, 1835.
Stanly, Alexander H. to Julia M. Harvey, Feb., Newbern. R. R. Mar. 3, 1835.
Stanfield, John A. of Oxford to Mary M'Elvoy, Je., Murfreesboro. R. R. Je. 23, 1835.
Staton, Alvaney M. of Pitt county to Henry S. Clarke of Beaufort county, My., Greenville, Pitt county. R. R. Je. 2, 1835.
Stewart, Frances M. to Thomas M. Oliver of Raleigh, Jan., Newbern. R. R. Jan. 27, 1835.
Stewart, Sarah A. to James Hannigan, Feb., Mecklenburg county. R. R. Mar. 3, 1835.
Stinson, Dr. George W. of Lancaster District, South Carolina to Margaret Byers, Apr., Iredell county. R. R. Apr. 14, 1835.
Stone, Mary to Henry White, Aug. 27, Pasquotank county. R. R. Sept. 15, 1835.
Tanner, Miss to Daniel Hair, Sept. 22, Iredell county. R. R. Oct. 20, 1835.
Tatum, E. to Benjamin Eaton, Feb., Rowan county. R. R. Mar. 3, 1835.
Taylor, William P. of Chatham county to Mary C. High of Wake county, Feb. 11, Wake county. R. R. Feb. 24, 1835.
Telfair, Mary F. to Whitmel Horn of Florida, Jan., Washington. R. R. Jan. 6, 1835.
Terrill, Thomas J. to Olivia Roles, Sept. 17, Rolesville. R. R. Sept. 22, 1835.
Thigpen, Elizabeth to Richard Warren of Pitt county, Oct. 8, Edgecombe county. R. R. Nov. 3, 1835.

Thomerson, Delia to Isaac W. Clarke, Oct. 15, Chatham county. R. R. Nov. 17, 1835.
Thompson, Mary to James E. Morris, Aug., Newbern. R. R. Sept. 1, 1835.
Thorp, John of Nash county to Virginia Wood, My. 28, Louisburg. R. R. Je. 23, 1835.
Tilman, Benjamin of Tennessee to Susannah Privett of Iredell county, Sept. 1, Iredell county. R. R. Nov. 10, 1835.
Tinney, John B. to Jane Beasley, Je. 11, Raleigh. R. R. Je. 16, 1835.
Toole, Susan Irwin of Edgecombe county to Daniel Hill, Dec. 5, Franklin county. R. R. Dec. 29, 1835.
Torrence, Isabella to Franklin Smith, Sept. 10, Mecklenburg county. R. R. Sept. 29, 1835.
Townsend, Eliza to Joseph Smith, Nov., Robeson county. R. R. Nov. 3, 1835.
Trainum, Jeffrey to Sarah Baily, Oct., Person county. R. R. Oct. 13, 1835.
Trainum, Reuben to Frances Bailey, Oct., Person county. R. R. Oct. 13, 1835.
Tunstall, Nathaniel R. to Martha Harrison, Jan., Franklin county. R. R. Jan. 6, 1835.
Upright, Barbary to Joseph A. Frank, Oct. 8, Rowan county. R. R. Oct. 27, 1835.
Vaughan, Ann Eliza to Capt. Joseph C. Morris of Rhode Island, Oct. 13, Elizabeth City. R. R. Nov. 3, 1835.
Vogler, John U. of Lincolnton to Maria Louisa Reich, Je. 25, Salem. R. R. Jly. 14, 1835.
Waddell, John of Louisiana & Wilmington to Lucia Chauncey Porter, Aug. 25, Alexandria. R. R. Sept. 15, 1835.
Walker, Eliza H. to Robert C. Belden, My. 21, Fayetteville. R. R. My. 26, 1835.
Walker, Henry C. of Norfolk, Va. to Mary Creecy, Aug., Hertford, Perquimans county. R. R. Aug. 1, 1835.
Walton, Martha M. to William C. Erwin, Je. 18, Morganton. R. R. Je. 30, 1835.
Waples, Nathaniel to Susan B. Green, Aug., Newbern. R. R. Sept. 1, 1835.
Warlick, Mary to John S. Ballew of Burke county, Sept. 20, Lincoln county. R. R. Oct. 27, 1835.
Warren, Richard of Pitt county to Elizabeth Thigpen, Oct. 8, Edgecombe county. R. R. Nov. 3, 1835.
Washington, Wm. H. of Wayne county to Caroline H. Blount, Aug. 12, Newbern. R. R. Aug. 25, 1835.
Watkins, Susan A. to William H. Robards of this State, Dec., Goochland, Va. R. R. Jan. 20, 1835.
Watson, Dr. Samuel B. to Emily Dinkins, Sept. 8, Charlotte. R. R. Sept. 29, 1835.
Wells, Anne to Richard Reddick, Je., Raleigh. R. R. Je. 9, 1835.
Westbrook, Caroline to Master Thompson Moore, Sept. 7, Caswell county. R. R. Sept. 29, 1835.
Whitaker, Ann Maria to Wm. H. Wills, My. 13, Halifax county. R. R. Je. 2, 1835.
White, Henry to Mary Stone, Aug. 27, Pasquotank county. R. R. Sept. 15, 1835.

White, James to Rachael Clifford, Feb., Rowan county. R. R. Mar. 3, 1835.
White, Margaret of Pasquotank county to Thomas Newby of Perquimans county, Jly. 30, 1835. R. R. Aug. 18, 1835.
Whiteside, Margaret to Akey Fuller of York District, South Carolina, Sept. 23, Mecklenburg county. R. R. Oct. 20, 1835.
Whitley, Willie of Johnson county to Sarah Elizabeth Carpenter of Wake county, Sept. 24. R. R. Oct. 20, 1835.
Wilkinson, Abner to Nancy Bynum, Aug. 16, Edgecombe county. R. R. Sept. 8, 1835.
Williams, Charles H. to Jane M'Naspie of Raleigh, My. 13, Pittsborough. R. R. My. 26, 1835.
Williams, Dr. J. of Cabarrus county to Elizabeth Donoho Elliott, Dec., Rutherford county. R. R. Dec. 29, 1835.
Williams, Miriam to Col. John M. Fenner of Madison county Tennessee & Raleigh, Apr. 15, Henry county. R. R. My. 26, 1835.
Williamson, Mildred to Calvin Jones of Pulaski, Tennessee, Oct., Person county. R. R. Oct. 27, 1835.
Wills, Anthony A. to Louisa Smith, Jly. 3, Carteret county. R. R. Aug. 4, 1835.
Wills, Wm. H. to Ann Maria Whitaker, My. 13, Halifax county. R. R. Je. 2, 1835.
Wilson, Martha Ann to Thomas J. Armstrong, Oct. 5, New Hanover county. R. R. Oct. 20, 1835.
Winslow, Edward Lee of Fayetteville to Sarah B. Little of Wilmington, My. 9, Oxford. R. R. My. 19, 1835.
Wiseman, Ellen to James Owen of Tipton county, Tennessee, Sept. 10, Davidson county. R. R. Oct. 27, 1835.
Wiseman, Mary D. to Rich'd B. Womack, Jly. 8, Davidson county. R. R. Aug. 4, 1835.
Withers, Dr. William to Ann Amanda Brooks, Je. 28, Stokes county. R. R. Jly. 14, 1835.
Wolff, Eliza to Thomas B. Lovell, Aug. 16, Stokes county. R. R. Sept. 8, 1835.
Womack, Rich'd B. to Mary W. Wiseman, Jly. 8, Davidson county. R. R. Aug. 4, 1835.
Wood, Virginia to John Thorp of Nash county, My. 28, Louisburg. R. R. Je. 23, 1835.
Wren, William to Patsey Joice, Oct. 1, Newbern. R. R. Oct. 13, 1835.
Wright, Council R. of Duplin county to Susan M. Arnold, Feb., Fayetteville. R. R. Feb. 10, 1835.
Wright, Mrs. Nancy to Henry Pitts, Oct., Halifax county. R. R. Nov. 3, 1835.
Young, James of Cabarrus county to Mrs. Sarah Roseman of Rowan county, Aug. 27, Rowan county. R. R. Sept. 8, 1835.
Young, Rosina U. to Augustus Mordecai of Raleigh, Mar. 5, Richmond, Va. R. R. Mar. 10, 1835.

1836

Alexander, Allen of Lincolnton to Adelaide Graham, My. 26, Rowan county. R. R. Je. 28, 1836.

Alexander, Isaac F. of Rutherford county to Judith C. M'Kenzie of Greenville District, S. C., Jan. 2. R. R. Mar. 1, 1836.
Alexander, James of Cabarrus county to Mary Allen of Mecklenburg county, Feb. 18. R. R. Mar. 8, 1836.
Alexander, Margaret D. to John M'Query, Jan. 2, Mecklenburg county. R. R. Mar. 1, 1836.
Allegood, Milly to William C. Allegood, Apr., Beaufort county. R. R. Apr. 26, 1836.
Allegood, William C. to Milly Allegood, Apr., Beaufort county. R. R. Apr. 26, 1836.
Allen, Mary of Mecklenburg county to James Alexander of Cabarrus county, Feb. 18. R. R. Mar. 8, 1836.
Allen, Reynold to Jane Kennon, My. 18, Wake county. R. R. My. 24, 1836.
Alford, Willie to Clarissa Fullmore, Oct., Robeson county. R. R. Nov. 8, 1836.
Alston, Ariella of Halifax county to James B. Hawkins of Warren county, Jan. 16, Butterwood. R. R. Feb. 2, 1836.
Anderson, Albert G. of Caswell county to Mary Thatch of Perquimans county, Jan. 7. R. R. Jan. 26, 1836.
Anderson, Rev. Wm. of Virginia Conference to Paulina Ann Kezee of Caswell county, Mar. 15. R. R. Apr. 19, 1836.
Andrez, Col. Samuel H. to Mrs. William Jones, Je., Bladen county. R. R. Je. 28, 1836.
Archer, Wm. of Jamaica to Caroline Crandall, Feb. 20, Wilmington. R. R. Mar. 8, 1836.
Arnold, Elizabeth to Ransom Ridge, Oct. 11, Randolph county. R. R. Nov. 8, 1836.
Ashe, William S. to Sarah Ann Green, Jan. 6, Wilmington. R. R. Jan. 26, 1836.
Austil, Major to Mary Moore, Oct. 16, Surry county. R. R. Nov. 22, 1836.
Austin, Catharine E. of Washington, Beaufort county to George W. Kelly of Massachusetts, Oct., Portsmouth, this State. R. R. Nov. 8, 1836.
Autry, Rev. Dr. S. of this State to Emily R. Brown, Oct., Madison county, Alabama. R. R. Nov. 8, 1836.
Badger, George E. to Mrs. Delia Williams, Apr. 16, Raleigh. R. R. Apr. 19, 1836.
Bailey, Celina to Thomas Jenkins, Je. 20, Raleigh. R. R. Jly. 12, 1836.
Bain, John to Louisa C. Benton, Jan. 7, Hillsborough. R. R. Jan. 26, 1836.
Ballantine, Rosa to Maj. Wm. E. Crump, My., Jackson, Northampton county. R. R. My. 31, 1836.
Barber, Martha Ann to T. S. Chambers, Dec. 31, Rowan county. R. R. Jan. 26, 1836.
Barnett, Ann to Joseph M. Stanfield of Person county, Je., Milton. R. R. Je. 7, 1836.
Barringer, Elizabeth to Edwin Harris, Aug. 9, Cabarrus county. R. R. Aug. 23, 1836.
Barry, Jona A. to Mary Steadman Owen, My. 16, Wilmington. R. R. My. 31, 1836.
Beatty, Henry B. of Cumberland county to Jane Morisey, My. 4, Sampson county. R. R. My. 24, 1836.
Beaver, Daniel to Leah Catchy, Apr., Rowan county. R. R. Apr. 19, 1836.

Bell, Margaret to Lawrence H. Hearn, My., Tarboro. R. R. My. 31, 1836.
Belt, John P. to Mary A. Bradford of Connecticut, Apr., Iredell county. R. R. Apr. 19, 1836.
Benton, Louisa C. to John Bain, Jan. 7, Hillsborough. R. R. Jan. 26, 1836.
Bethel, Agnes G. of Rockingham to Dr. Thomas Torian of Halifax, Va., Je. 29. R. R. Jly. 12, 1836.
Biles, Alex of Salisbury to Hannah J. Kingsberry, Sept. 22, Lancaster, S. C. R. R. Oct. 18, 1836.
Bird, Horace of Watertown to Fanny Fish of Salem, My., Salem. R. R. My. 31, 1836.
Blair, J. to Abigail M'Crara, Aug. 25, Burke county. R. R. Sept. 27, 1836.
Blake, Capt. Isham of Fayetteville to Mary F. Hall of Brunswick county, Oct. 26. R. R. Nov. 8, 1836.
Bland, Olivia E. to Joseph Littlejohn of Oxford, Apr. 20, Vicksburg, Mississippi. R. R. Je. 28, 1836.
Blue, Nancy A. of Cumberland county to Ephriam Singletary of Bladen county, Jan. 24, Fayetteville. R. R. Feb. 2, 1836.
Billes, Rev. Edwin A. of Salisbury to Harriet A. Pailer of Charleston, S. C., Mar. 6, Charleston. R. R. Mar. 29, 1836.
Bond, Henry F. to Sarah Clark, My. 3, Scotland Neck, Halifax county. R. R. My. 17, 1836.
Borland, Dr. Euclid to Elizabeth R. Moore, My. 12, Murfreesborough. R. R. My. 31, 1836.
Bowers, Mrs. Sarah to Thomas Twine of Gates county, Oct., Portsmouth, Va. R. R. Nov. 1, 1836.
Bracewell, Rooda to William Hayles, My., Edgecombe county. R. R. My. 31, 1836.
Bradford, Mary A. of Connecticut to John P. Belt, Apr., Iredell county. R. R. Apr. 19, 1836.
Brassfield, Caroline to William H. Whitaker, Jan. 14, Wake county. R. R. Jan. 26, 1836.
Bridges, Elisha to Betsey Jones, Dec. 22, Lincoln county. R. R. Jan. 5, 1836.
Brinson, James M'C. to Sarah Mitchell, Dec. 20, Newbern. R. R. Jan. 5, 1836.
Brown, Emily R. to Rev. Dr. A. Autry of this State, Oct., Madison county, Alabama. R. R. Nov. 8, 1836.
Brown, Peyton H. of Louisburg to Sarah Turner of Warren county, My., Warren county. R. R. My. 17, 1836.
Brown, R. F. of Wilmington to Mrs. Caroline A. Nelson, My., Fayetteville. R. R. My. 31, 1836.
Brown, Wm. R. of Martin county to Ellen Hyman of Edgecombe county, Dec. 7. R. R. Feb. 2, 1836.
Buchanan, Wm. James to Mary Ann Murphey, Jan. 24, Fayetteville. R. R. Feb. 2, 1836.
Burch, Jesse to Eliza Pass, Jan. 18, Person county. R. R. Mar. 1, 1836.
Butler, Mary to Alexander Puryear, Dec. 22, Granville county. R. R. Jan. 5, 1836.
Butt, Elizabeth to Henry Picard, Feb. 18, Elizabeth City. R. R. Mar. 8, 1836.
Byrum, Jacob to Leah Byrum, Je., Edenton. R. R. Je. 7, 1836.
Byrum, Leah to Jacob Byrum, Je., Edenton. R. R. Je. 7, 1836.

Cabarrus, Mary to Thomas H. Keane of La Grange, Jly., Shelby county, Ga. R. R. Jly. 19, 1836.
Cage, J. Douglas to Sophia A. Wright of Salisbury, Dec., La Grange, Tenn. R. R. Dec. 27, 1836.
Cameron, John D. to Jane Smith, Jan. 4, Richmond county. R. R. Mar. 1, 1836.
Campbell, Evelina B. to John Keer, Jr., Jan. 23, Yanceyville, Caswell county. R. R. Feb. 2, 1836.
Carroll, John B. of New York to Henrietta B. Smith, Jan. 10, Newbern. R. R. Jan. 12, 1836.
Carson, Alfred to Myra Correll, Aug. 30, Iredell county. R. R. Sept. 27, 1836.
Carson, R. C. of Concord to Harriet Wilson, Dec. 8, Mecklenburg county. R. R. Jan. 5, 1836.
Carstaphen, Sarah to Thos. Pender of Plymouth, Dec. 10, Edgecombe county. R. R. Jan. 26, 1836.
Carter, Chloe to Frederick Whitehurst, Je. 13, Pasquotank county. R. R. Je. 28, 1836.
Carter, Mrs. Cornelia A. to John M. Daniel, Jly. 28, Milton. R. R. Aug. 2, 1836.
Catchy, Leah to Daniel Beaver, Apr., Rowan county. R. R. Apr. 19, 1836.
Chambers, T. S. to Martha Ann Barber, Dec. 31, Rowan county. R. R. Jan. 26, 1836.
Chance, Sarah to Joseph Smith, Apr. 2, Richmond county. R. R. Apr. 26, 1836.
Cheek, Caroline to James Twitty, My., Warren county. R. R. My. 31, 1836.
Cheney, Mary Y. of Warrenton to H. Greely of New York, Jly. 4, Warrenton. R. R. Aug. 2, 1836.
Chumbley, Larkin to Elizabeth Montgomery, Jan. 23, Milton. R. R. Feb. 2, 1836.
Chum, Adelia Arinda to John J. Humphreys of Talladega, Alabama, Dec. 19. R. R. Jan. 5, 1836.
Chunn, Alfred of Asheville to Margaret M'Kesson of Morganton, Dec. 17, Lincoln county. R. R. Jan. 5, 1836.
Clancy, Elizabeth B. to Charles N. B. Evans, Jr., Je., Hillsborough. R. R. Je. 7, 1836.
Clark, Sarah to Henry F. Bond. My. 3, Scotland Neck, Halifax county. R. R. My. 17, 1836.
Clark, Mrs. Susannah to Jesse Durham, Aug. 22, Orange county. R. R. Jly. 19, 1836.
Clarke, Susan to Newton Crawford, Sept. 6, Iredell county. R. R. Sept. 27, 1836.
Clayland, Mrs. Sarah to Nathaniel Taylor of Mocksville, Jan. 20, Forks of the Yadkin. R. R. Feb. 2, 1836.
Clemens, Mary to Ephraim D. Harris, Je. 2, Surry county. R. R. Je. 28, 1836.
Cobb, Amelia to Charles B. Frances, Feb. 16, Bertie county. R. R. Mar. 15, 1836.
Cobb, Gray E. of Robeson county, to Sarah Graham, Apr., Richmond county. R. R. Apr. 19, 1836.
Coleman, Charles of Halifax county, Va. to Sarah A. Eaton, Mar. 3, Granville county. R. R. Mar. 29, 1836.
Cook, Caroline to Capt. James Wilson, Jan. 28, Mecklenburg county. R. R. Mar. 1, 1836.
Cook, Martha of Northampton county to Edw'd Murphy, Apr. 2, Murfreesboro. R. R. Apr. 26, 1836.
Correll, Cynthia to James Nolley, My., Salisbury. R. R. My. 17, 1836.

Correll, Myra to Alfred Carson, Aug. 30, Iredell county. R. R. Sept. 27, 1836.
Cotton, Emily to Jos. Crump, Oct., Chatham county. R. R. Oct. 11, 1836.
Cowan, John to Mary G. Robison, Dec. 31, Rowan county. R. R. Jan. 26, 1836.
Cowan, Martha M. to Dr. Benj. I. Hicks of Oxford, Mar. 29, Warren county, Mississippi. R. R. Je. 28, 1836.
Craig, John to Malinda Miner, Apr. 7, Wentworth, Rockingham county. R. R. Apr. 26, 1836.
Craige, Burton of Salisbury to Eliza P. Erwin, Sept. 15, Burke county. R. R. Sept. 27, 1836.
Crandall, Caroline to Wm. Archer of Jamaica, Feb. 20, Wilmington. R. R. Mar. 8, 1836.
Crawford, Newton to Susan Clarke, Sept. 6, Iredell county. R. R. Sept. 27, 1836.
Creecy, Charles of Chowan county to Edith Goodman of Gates county, Mar. 22, Gates county. R. R. Apr. 26, 1836.
Crump, Jos. to Emily Cotton, Oct., Chatham county. R. R. Oct. 11, 1836.
Crump, Lucinda J. to Richardson Faucett, Dec. 3, Chatham county. R. R. Jan. 5, 1836.
Crump, Maj. Wm. E. to Rosa Ballatine, My., Jackson, Northampton county. R. R. My. 31, 1836.
Culverhouse, Hugh to Rebecca Wood, Jan. 22, Salisbury. R. R. Feb. 2, 1836.
Currie, Lauchlin of Alabama to Sarah M'Donald, Dec. 4, Richmond county. R. R. Jan. 5, 1836.
Currie, Sarah to Alexander Graham, Oct. 13, Moore county. R. R. Nov. 1, 1836.
Curry, Margaret to Moses A. White, Jan. 15, Salisbury. R. R. Feb. 2, 1836.
Dancy, Delha to Angesilaus S. Foreman of Virginia, Nov., Tarboro. R. R. Nov. 22, 1836.
Daniel, John M. to Mrs. Cornelia A. Carter, Jly. 28, Milton. R. R. Aug. 2, 1836.
Daniel, Joseph J. to Margaret Neville, Sept. 14, Halifax county. R. R. Oct. 4, 1836.
Davis, Susan to J. D. Liles of Tindallsville, Anson county, Je. 2, South Carolina. R. R. Je. 28, 1836.
Decoin, Robert L. of New Orleans, La to Jane R. Righton, Oct., Chowan county. R. R. Nov. 1, 1836.
Devereux, Elizabeth P. to Thomas F. Jones of Perquimans county, Jly. 29, Raleigh. R. R. Aug. 2, 1836.
Dey, Joseph of Norfolk to Elizabeth Robertson, Sept., Currituck county. R. R. Oct. 11, 1836.
Dryden, Louisa of Virginia to Enock R. Gale, Je. 30, Elizabeth City. R. R. Jly. 19, 1836.
Dudley, Christopher, Jr. to Agnes B. Hattridge, My. 10, Wilmington. R. R. My. 31, 1836.
Dunn, Wm. V. to Elizabeth M'Quay, Feb. 2, Charlotte. R. R. Mar. 1, 1836.
Duren, Sarah to James Rorie, Feb, Anson county. R. R. Mar. 8, 1836.
Durham, Martha to John P. Rainey, Dec. 5, Caswell county. R. R. Feb. 2, 1836.

Durham, Jesse to Mrs. Susanna Clark, Aug. 22, Orange county. R. R. Jly. 19, 1836.
Eaton, Elizabeth W. to Dr. Edward W. Faulcon, Nov. 14, Warren county. R. R. Nov. 22, 1836.
Eaton, Sarah A. to Charles Coleman of Halifax county, Va., Mar. 3, Granville county. R. R. Mar. 29, 1836.
Elliott, Elizabeth D. to Dr. J. Williams of Cabarrus county, Jan., Rutherford county. R. R. Jan. 5, 1836.
Ellis, Mrs. A. to Nathaniel M. Terrill of Tarboro, Sept., Washington, Beaufort county. R. R. Oct. 11, 1836.
Ellison, Wm. J. I. to Frances Hyman, Jan. 6, Williamston, Martin county. R. R. Jan. 26, 1836.
Erwin, Eliza P. to Burton Craig of Salisbury, Sept. 15, Burke county. R. R. Sept. 27, 1836.
Erwin, Elizabeth to Eli M. Stewart, Dec. 19, Rowan county. R. R. Jan. 5, 1836.
Estes, Sophia to H. P. Grenell, Aug. 20, Burke county. R. R. Sept. 27, 1836.
Evans, Charles N. B. Jr. to Elizabeth B. Clancy, Je., Hillsborough. R. R. Je. 7, 1836.
Evans, Thomas of Chowan county to Mrs. Jacob Goodwin, Nov., Perquimans county. R. R. Nov. 22, 1836.
Faucett, John R. to Catharine S. Freeland, Jan. 22, Orange county. R. R. Feb. 2, 1836.
Faucett, Richardson to Lucinda J. Crump, Dec. 3, Chatham county. R. R. Jan. 5, 1836.
Faulcon, Dr. Edward W. to Elizabeth W. Eaton, Nov. 14, Warren county. R. R. Nov. 22, 1836.
Fidler, Joseph to Polly Shellhorn, Apr. 14, Stokes county. R. R. Apr. 26, 1836.
Finle, Augustus of Milton to Ann Edwards Williamson of Caswell county, Je. 9. R. R. Je. 21, 1836.
Fish, Fanny of Salem to Horace Bird of Watertown, My., Salem. R. R. My. 31, 1836.
Fisher, Isaac to Ann Webb, Sept. 4, Burke county. R. R. Sept. 27, 1836.
Fisher, Thomas to Caroline W. Gay, Dec. 23, Halifax county. R. R. Jan. 26, 1836.
Flauner, Mary E. to William H. Mayhew of Washington, Beaufort county, Dec. 25, Newbern. R. R. Jan. 12, 1836.
Fleming, Charlotte I. to Rev. William M. Green, Dec. 23, Pittsborough. R. R. Jan. 5, 1836.
Flow, James to Mary E. M'Neely, Apr. 12, Mecklenburg county. R. R. My. 10, 1836.
Foreman, Agesilaus S. of Virginia to Delha Dancy, Nov., Tarboro. R. R. Nov. 22, 1836.
Foreman, John L. of Pitt county to Martha E. Hoskins, Feb. 26, Chowan county. R. R. Mar. 15, 1836.
Forester, Smith of Charleston, S. C. to Addison C. Hinton of Wake county, Oct. 4, Washington, D. C. R. R. Oct. 18, 1836.
Fort, William, Jr. to Amy Ann Myatt, Je. 8, Wake county. R. R. Je. 28, 1836.

Fraley, Benjamin of Salisbury to Jane P. Wallace of Cabarrus county, Oct. 23, Cabarrus county. R. R. Nov. 8, 1836.
Frances, Charles B. to Amelia Cobb, Feb. 16, Bertie county. R. R. Mar. 15, 1836.
Freeland, Catharine S. to John R. Faucett, Jan. 22, Orange county. R. R. Feb. 2, 1836.
Freeman, John of Montgomery county to Maria Moss of Salisbury, Jan. 20, Salisbury. R. R. Feb. 2, 1836.
Fullmore, Clarissa to Willie Alford, Oct., Robeson county. R. R. Nov. 8, 1836.
Gale, Enock R. to Louisa Dryden of Virginia, Je. 30, Elizabeth City. R. R. Jly. 19, 1836.
Gay, Caroline W. to Thomas Fisher, Dec. 23, Halifax county. R. R. Jan. 26, 1836.
Gheen, Warren to Sarah Winders, Feb. 13, Rowan county. R. R. Mar. 1, 1836.
Gibson, Hetty P. to Jesse P. Wiseman of Davidson county, Oct. 28, Rowan county. R. R. Nov. 8, 1836.
Giles, William B. to Almeria Reston of Wilmington, Je. 22, Bladen county. R. R. Je. 28, 1836.
Gilleland, Henderson to Lavinia Jones, Dec. 30, Lincoln county. R. R. Jan. 5, 1836.
Gillespie, Capt. James of Rowan county to Jane Ramsey of Rutherford county & Pennsylvania, Jan. 29, Rutherfordton. R. R. Mar. 1, 1836.
Goodman, Edith of Gates county to Charles Creecy of Chowan county, Mar. 22, Gates county. R. R. Apr. 26, 1836.
Goodwin, Mrs. Jacob to Thomas Evans of Chowan county, Nov., Perquimans county. R. R. Nov. 22, 1836.
Graham, Adelaide to Allen Alexander of Lincolnton, Rowan county, My. 26, Rowan county. R. R. Je. 28, 1836.
Graham, Alexander to Sarah Currie, Oct. 13, Moore county. R. R. Nov. 1, 1836.
Graham, Sarah to Gray E. Cobb of Robeson county, Apr., Richmond county. R. R. Apr. 19, 1836.
Graham, William A. of Hillsboro to Susan Washington, Je. 8, Newbern. R. R. Je. 21, 1836.
Graves, Ann S. to Solomon Graves of Newton county, Ga., My. 22, Yanceyville, Caswell county. R. R. Je. 7, 1836.
Graves, Elizabeth to Col. William Lea, Je. 20, Yanceyville. R. R. Jly. 12, 1836.
Graves, Henry Lee of Yanceyville to Rebecca Williams Graves, Feb. 3, Caswell county. R. R. Mar. 1, 1836.
Graves, Maj. John H. of Yanceyville to Julia Ann Hill of Chatham county, Je. 14, Orange county. R. R. Je. 28, 1836.
Graves, Rebecca Williams to Henry Lee Graves of Yanceyville, Feb. 3, Caswell county. R. R. Mar. 1, 1836.
Graves, Solomon of Newton county, Ga. to Ann S. Graves, My. 22, Yanceyville, Caswell county. R. R. Je. 7, 1836.
Gray, E. D. to Sarah E. Weathers, Sept., Mecklenburg county. R. R. Oct. 11, 1836.

Greely, H. of New York to Mary Y. Cheney of Warrenton, Jly. 5, Warrenton. R. R. Jly. 19, 1836.
Green, Howel to Catharine M'Duffie, Dec., Richmond county. R. R. Jan. 5, 1836.
Green, Sarah Ann to William S. Ashe, Jan. 6, Wilmington. R. R. Jan. 26, 1836.
Green, Rev. William M. to Charlotte I. Fleming, Dec. 23, Pittsborough. R. R. Jan. 5, 1836.
Grenell, H. P. to Sophia Estes, Aug. 20, Burke county. R. R. Sept. 27, 1836.
Hall, Mary F. of Brunswick county to Capt. Asham Blake of Fayetteville, Oct. 26. R. R. Nov. 8, 1836.
Hamilton, Wm. R. of Petersburg, Va. to Mary Turner, Mar. 1, Granville county. R. R. Mar. 29, 1836.
Hampton, Joseph W. to Sarah Stirewalt of Cabarrus county, Mar. 13, Lexington. R. R. Mar. 29, 1836.
Harbert, Margaretta to Rev. James O. Stedman of Fayetteville, Nov., Philadelphia. R. R. Nov. 22, 1836.
Hardin, Lauriston B. of Raleigh to Anna M. H. Hooe of Alexandria, Jan. 16, Alexandria. R. R. Mar. 1, 1836.
Harris, Edwin to Elizabeth Barringer, Aug. 9, Cabarrus county. R. R. Aug. 23, 1836.
Harris, Ephraim D. to Mary Clemons, Je. 2, Surry county. R. R. Je. 28, 1836.
Harris, Mary to John Ragland, Feb. 13, Granville county. R. R. Mar. 1, 1836.
Harrison, Andrew W. of Caswell county to Matilda H. Sharp of Manchester, Va., Oct., Caswell county. R. R. Oct. 25, 1836.
Harvey, Elizabeth B. to Rev. Wm. W. Williams, Aug. 9, Palmyra, Martin county. R. R. Aug. 23, 1836.
Hatch, Mary to Albert G. Anderson of Caswell county, Jan., Perquimans county. R. R. Feb. 2, 1836.
Hattridge, Agnes B. to Christopher Dudley, Jr., My. 10, Wilmington. R. R. My. 31, 1836.
Hawkins, Frank to Ann Carolina Read, Jan. 3, Halifax county. R. R. Mar. 1, 1836.
Hawkins, James B. of Warren county to Ariella Alston of Halifax county, Jan. 16, Butterwood. R. R. Feb. 2, 1836.
Hayles, William to Rhoda Bracewell, My., Edgecombe county. R. R. My. 31, 1836.
Hearn, Lawrence H. to Margaret Bell, My., Tarboro. R. R. My. 31, 1836.
Henderson, Jane C. to Dr. Luco Mitchell, Dec. 24, Salisbury. R. R. Jan. 5, 1836.
Henderson, Priscilla to Dr. Willie Jones of Milton, My. 5, Caswell county. R. R. My. 17, 1836.
Herndon, S. J. to Isaac Kirk, Jan 8, Salem. R. R. Mar. 1, 1836.
Hicks, Dr. Benj. I. of Oxford to Martha M. Cowan, Mar. 29, Warren county, Mississippi. R. R. Je. 28, 1836.
High, Eliza C. to Joseph L. Moring, Jan. 3, Wake county. R. R. Mar. 1, 1836.

Hill, Julia Ann of Chatham county to Maj. John H. Graves of Yanceyville, Je. 14, Orange county. R. R. Je. 28, 1836.
Hill, Thomas of New Hanover county to Eliza Y. Toomer, Apr. 21, Fayetteville. R. R. Apr. 26, 1836.
Hill, Thos. B. of Halifax county to Maria Simpson of Newbern, Sept. 15, Hillsboro. R. R. Sept. 27, 1836.
Hilliard, Martha to Utley Benton, Jly. 14, Chapel Hill. R. R. Jly. 19, 1836.
Hines, Peter E. of Edgecombe county to Mary May, Feb. 18, Pitt county. R. R. Mar. 8, 1836.
Hinton, Addison C. of Wake county to Annie Smith Forster of Charleston, S. C., Oct. 4, Washington, D. C. R. R. Oct. 18, 1835.
Hinton, Caroline of New York to Dr. Thomas P. Hinton, Feb. 4, Pasquotank county. R. R. Mar. 15, 1836.
Hinton, Dr. Thomas P. to Caroline Hinton of New York, Feb. 4, Pasquotank county. R. R. Mar. 15, 1836.
Hodge, Mrs. Nancy of Rowan county to John Pealer of Montgomery county, Apr. R. R. Apr. 19, 1836.
Holbrooks, Wm. of Cabarrus county to Elizabeth Stezer of Rowan county, Apr. 12, Mecklenburg county. R. R. My. 10, 1836.
Hooe, Anna M. H.. of Alexandria to Lauriston B. Hardin of Raleigh, Jan. 16, Alexandria. R. R. Mar. 1, 1836.
Hooper, George of Alabiania to Caroline Mallet, Oct. 7, Fayetteville. R. R. Oct. 25, 1836.
Hoskins, Martha E. to John L. Foreman of Pitt county, Feb. 26, Chowan county. R. R. Mar. 15, 1836.
Howell, Josiah, Jr. to Winifred Perry, Dec. 31, Bertie county. R. R. Jan. 26, 1836.
Howell, James to Jane Witherton, Jan., Bertie county. R. R. Jan. 26, 1836.
Howerton, Frances J. to Thomas L. White of Milton, Je. 16, Halifax county, Va. R. R. Je, 28, 1836.
Humphreys, John J. of Talladega, Alabama to Adelia Armida Chum, Dec. 19, Asheville. R. R. Jan. 5, 1836.
Huske, Joanna to Dr. Benjamin Robinson, My., Fayetteville. R. R. My. 31, 1836.
Hutcheson, Elizabeth to Manliff Ozment, Jan. 21, Guilford county. R. R. Mar. 1, 1836.
Hyman, Ellen of Edgecombe county to Wm. R. Brown of Martin county, Dec. 7. R. R. Feb. 2, 1836.
Hyman, Frances to Wm. J. I. Ellison, Jan. 6, Williamston, Martin county. R. R. Jan. 26, 1836.
Ingram, Wesley M. of Anson county to Rachel Mason of Richmond county, Dec. 17, Richmond county. R. R. Jan. 5, 1836.
Ingram, Wincey P. to John C. Wadsworth of Cheraw, Feb. 25, Anson county. R. R. Mar. 8, 1836.
Iredell, Annie to Cadwaller Jones of Hillsboro, Jan. 5, Raleigh. R. R. Jan. 12, 1836.
Irvine, Isaac J. to Esther M. Ray of Rutherford county, Je. 2, Rutherford county. R. R. Je. 28, 1836.
Jacocks, Charles of Bertie county to Martha A. Mullen, Dec., Elizabeth City. R. R. Dec. 27, 1836.

James, Sarah Julia to Andrew M'Intyre of Kenansville, Jan. 4, Wilmington. R. R. Mar. 1, 1836.
Jenkins, Thomas to Celina Bailey, Je. 20, Raleigh. R. R. Jly. 12, 1836.
Johnston, Delia to John W. Prout, Dec. 18, Raleigh. R. R. Dec. 20, 1836.
Johnston, Mary to Winslow M'Ree, Feb. 18, Mecklenburg county. R. R. Mar. 8, 1836.
Jones, Betsey to Elisha Bridges, Dec. 22, Lincoln county. R. R. Jan. 5, 1836.
Jones, Cadwaller of Hillsboro to Annie Iredell, Jan. 5, Raleigh. R. R. Jan. 12, 1836.
Jones, Eli A. of Caswell county to Ann L. Vanhook of Person county, Je. 16, Person county. R. R. Jly. 12, 1836.
Jones, Lavinia to Henderson Gilleland, Dec. 30, Lincoln county. R. R. Jan. 5, 1836.
Jones, Louisa to Hon. A. Rencher of Salisbury, Sept. 27, Pittsboro, Chatham county. R. R. Oct. 18, 1836.
Jones, Thomas F. of Perquimans county to Elizabeth P. Devereux, Jly. 29, Raleigh. R. R. Aug. 2, 1836.
Jones, Mrs. William to Col. Samuel H. Andrez, Je., Bladen county. R. R. Je. 28, 1836.
Jones, Dr. Willie of Milton to Priscilla Henderson, My. 5, Caswell county. R. R. My. 17, 1836.
Johnson, Nancy of Wake county to Lisbon Williams, Sept. 22, Raleigh. R. R. Sept. 27, 1836.
Jordan, Amanda Malvina to Geo Sanders of Washington, Mar. 10, Pitt county. R. R. Mar. 29, 1836.
Justice, Mrs. Ann L. to James Morrow, Jly., Orange county. R. R. Jly. 26, 1836.
Keane, Thomas H. of La Grange to Mary Cabarrus of Shelby county, Ga., Jly. R. R. Jly. 19, 1836.
Kelly, George W. of Massachusetts to Catharine E. Austin of Washington, Beaufort county, Oct., Portsmouth, N. C. R. R. Nov. 8, 1836.
Kelly, Dr. James A. to Margaret Patterson, Feb., Moore county. R. R. Feb. 2, 1836.
Keer, John Jr. to Evelina B. Campbell, Jan. 23, Yanceyville, Caswell county. R. R. Feb. 2, 1836.
Kelson, Joanna of Spartanburg District, S. C. to Rev. William C. Rankin of Rutherford county, Sept. 29. R. R. Oct. 25, 1836.
Kennon, Jane to Reynold Allen, My. 18, Wake county. R. R. My. 24, 1836.
Kezee, Paulina Ann of Caswell county to Rev. Wm. Anderson of Virginia Conference, Mar. 15. R. R. Apr. 19, 1836.
Kingsberry, Hannah J. to Alex Biles of Salisbury, Sept. 22, Lancaster, S. C. R. R. Oct. 18, 1836.
Kingsbury, Eliza of New York to Joseph James Ridley, Oct. 24, Oxford. R. R. Nov. 1, 1836.
Kirk, Isaac to S. J. Herndon, Jan. 8, Salem. R. R. Mar. 1, 1836.
Laboyteaux, Wm. to Sally Thompson, Je. 13, Elizabeth City. R. R. Je. 28, 1836.
Lasseter, Mrs. Harriet to Mungo T. Ponton, Dec. 8, Halifax county. R. R. Jan. 5, 1836.

Lawrence, Joshua L. to Harriet Mayo, Oct., Edgecombe county. R. R. Oct. 11, 1836.

Lawrence, Maria to Haywood Parker of this State, Apr., Greensboro, Alabama. R. R. My. 2, 1836.

Lea, Col. William to Elizabeth Graves, Je. 20, Yanceyville. R. R. Jly. 12, 1836.

Lee, Sidney of Caswell county to Frances Torian, Apr. 20, Halifax county, Va. R. R. My. 3, 1836.

Lee, Susan Virginia of Norfolk to Wm. S. Wright of Chowan county, Sept. 22, Norfolk. R. R. Oct. 4, 1836.

Lenoir, Laura L. C. to Joseph C. Norwood of Hillsboro, Je. 14, Fort Defiance, Wilkes county. R. R. Je. 28, 1836.

Liles, J. D. of Tindallsville, Anson county to Susan Davis, Je., South Carolina. R. R. Je. 28, 1836.

Lindsay, Amanda to James N. Ross, Feb., Guilford county. R. R. Apr. 19, 1836.

Littlejohn, Joseph of Oxford to Olivia E. Bland, Apr. 20, Vicksburg, Mississippi. R. R. Je. 28, 1836.

Lyon, Benton T. to Penelope C. Pittman, My., Edgecombe county. R. R. My. 31, 1836.

M'Allister, Rachel to Samuel Whitaker, Mar. 14, Wake county. R. R. My. 2, 1836.

M'Collum, Margaret J. to George W. Reeves of Somerville, Tenn., Sept. 8, Hillsborough. R. R. Sept. 27, 1836.

M'Combs, Joseph to Miss M. Parks, Apr. 12, Mecklenburg county. R. R. My. 10, 1836.

M'Crara, Abigail to J. Blair, Aug. 25, Burke county. R. R. Sept. 27, 1836.

M'Donald, Sarah to Lauchlin, Currie of Alabama, Dec. 4, Richmond county. R. R. Jan. 5, 1836.

M'Duffie, Catharine to Hovel Green, Dec., Richmond county. R. R. Jan. 5, 1836.

M'Intyre, Andrew of Kenansville to Sarah Julia James, Jan. 4, Wilmington. R. R. Mar. 1, 1836.

M'Kenzie, Judith C. of Greenville District, S. C. to Isaac Alexander of Rutherford county, Jan. 2. R. R. Mar. 1, 1836.

M'Kesson, Margaret of Morganton to Alfred Chum of Asheville, Dec. 17, Lincoln county. R. R. Jan. 5, 1836.

M'Lean, Flora to John M'Lean, Mar. 10, Robeson county. R. R. Mar. 29, 1836.

M'Lean, Capt. Henry to Sophia Weeks, Feb., Fayetteville. R. R. Feb. 2, 1836.

M'Lean, John to Flora M'Lean, Mar. 10, Robeson county. R. R. Mar. 29, 1836.

M'Millan, William to Ann M'Neill, Oct., Cumberland county. R. R. Nov. 8, 1836.

M'Neely, Mary E. to James Flow, Apr. 12, Mecklenburg county. R. R. My. 10, 1836.

M'Neill, Ann to William M'Millan, Oct., Cumberland county. R. R. Nov. 8 1836.

M'Quay, Elizabeth to Wm. V. Dunn, Feb. 2, Charlotte. R. R. Mar. 1, 1836.

M'Query, John to Margaret D. Alexander, Jan. 2, Mecklenburg county. R. R. Mar. 1, 1836.
M'Ree, Winslow to Mary Johnston, Feb. 18, Mecklenburg county. R. R. Mar. 8, 1836.
Mallett, Caroline to George Hooper of Alabama, Oct. 7, Fayetteville. R. R. Oct. 25, 1836.
Marsh, William M. to Nancy E. Oden, Apr. 19, Beaufort county. R. R. My. 10, 1836.
Marshall, Capt. Henry of Surry county to Maria Vance of Stokes county, Apr. 14, Stokes county. R. R. Apr. 26, 1836.
Mason, Rachel of Richmond county to Wesley M. Ingram of Anson county, Dec. 17, Richmond county. R. R. Jan. 5, 1836.
Maxwell, James to Virginia M. Nunnery, Apr., Warrenton. R. R. My. 10, 1836.
May, Mary to Peter E. Hines, Feb. 18, Pitt county. R. R. Mar. 8, 1836.
Mayhew, William H. of Washington, Beaufort county to Mary E. Flauner, Dec. 25, Newbern. R. R. Jan. 12, 1836.
Mayo, Harriet to Joshua L. Lawrence, Oct., Edgecombe county. R. R. Oct. 11, 1836.
Mervy, Joseph of Cheraw, S. C. to Jane Potter, Feb. 11, Fayetteville. R. R. Mar. 1, 1836.
Miller, Mrs. Rhoda to Drury Parker, Jan. 11, Rowan county. R. R. Mar. 1, 1836.
Miner, Malinda to John Craig, Apr. 7, Wentworth, Rockingham county. R. R. Apr. 26, 1836.
Mitchell, Dr. Lucco to Jane C. Henderson, Dec. 24, Salisbury. R. R. Jan. 5, 1836.
Mitchell, Sarah to James M. C. Brinson, Dec. 20, Newbern. R. R. Jan. 5, 1836.
Montgomery, Elizabeth to Larkin Chumbley, Jan. 23, Milton. R. R. Feb. 2, 1836.
Moore, Alexander to Elizabeth White, Sept. 1, Burke county. R. R. Sept. 27, 1836.
Moore, Elizabeth R. to Dr. Euclid Borland, My. 12, Murfreesborough. R. R. My. 31, 1836.
Moore, Mary to Major Austill, Oct. 16, Surry county. R. R. Nov. 22, 1836.
Morgan, Sarah Ann to Jesse Watkins, Jan. 4, Richmond county. R. R. Jan. 26, 1836.
Moring, Joseph L. to Eliza C. High, Jan. 3, Wake county. R. R. Mar. 1, 1836.
Morisey, Jane to Henry B. Beatty of Cumberland county, My. 4, Sampson county. R. R. My. 24, 1836.
Morris, Davidson of Princess Ann county, Va. to Sarah Jones of Currituck county, Currituck county, Apr. R. R. Apr. 19, 1836.
Morris, Sarah Ann to James Phelps, Feb. 18, Beaufort, Carteret county. R. R. Mar. 8, 1836.
Morrow, James to Mrs. Ann L. Justice, Jly., Orange county. R. R. Jly. 26, 1836.
Moss, Maria of Salisbury to John Freeman of Montgomery county, Jan. 20, Salisbury. R. R. Feb. 2, 1836.

Mullen, Martha A. to Charles Jacocks of Bertie county, Dec., Elizabeth City. R. R. Dec. 27, 1836.
Murphey, David of Sampson county to Emeline P. Whitaker of Raleigh, Mar. 3, Raleigh. R. R. Mar. 8, 1836.
Murphey, Mary Ann to Wm. James Buchanan, Jan. 24, Fayetteville. R. R. Feb. 2, 1836.
Murphy, Charles to Caroline Russum, Dec. 27, Guilford county. R. R. Mar. 1, 1836.
Murphy, Edw'd to Martha Cook of Northampton county, Apr. 2, Murfreesboro. R. R. Apr. 26, 1836.
Myatt, Amy Ann to William Fort, Jr., Je. 8, Wake county. R. R. Je. 28, 1836.
Nelson, Mrs. Caroline A. to R. F. Brown of Wilmington, My., Fayetteville. R. R. My. 31, 1836.
Neville, Margaret to Joseph J. Daniel, Sept. 14, Halifax county. R. R. Oct. 4, 1836.
Nolley, James to Cynthia Correll, My., Salisbury. R. R. My. 17, 1836.
Norfleet, John H. to Susan M. Verrell, Je. 6, Person county. R. R. Jly. 19, 1836.
Norfleet, John M. to Susan M. Verrell, Je. 9, Person county. R. R. Jly. 12, 1836.
Norwood, Joseph C. of Hillsboro to Laura L. C. Lenoir, Je. 14, Fort Defiance, Wilkes county. R. R. Je. 28, 1836.
Nunnery, Virginia M. to James Maxwell, Apr., Warrenton. R. R. My. 10, 1836.
Oden, Nancy E. to William M. Marsh, Apr. 19, Beaufort county. R. R. My. 10, 1836.
Ogden, George to Mrs. Arcadia Ormond, Aug. 4, Washington, Beaufort county. R. R. Aug. 23, 1836.
Ormond, Mrs. Arcadia to George Ogden, Aug. 4, Washington, Beaufort county. R. R. Aug. 23, 1836.
Orrel, Lorenzo D. to Miss E. Spence, Aug. 11, Guilford county. R. R. Sept. 13, 1836.
Owen, Mary Steadman to Jona A. Barry, My. 16, Wilmington. R. R. My. 31, 1836.
Owen, William H. to Mary Pendergast, Apr., Chapel Hill. R. R. My. 3, 1836.
Owens, Samuel to Jane Winders, Feb. 13, Rowan county. R. R. Mar. 1, 1836.
Ozment, Manliff to Elizabeth Hutchson, Jan. 21, Guilford county. R. R. Mar. 1, 1836.
Pace, John to Louisa Sledge, Oct. 7, Fayetteville. R. R. Oct. 25, 1836.
Page, Elizabeth J. to Joseph Thaxton of Halifax, Va., Apr. 29, Person county. R. R. My. 10, 1836.
Page, Malvina to Stimson H. Whitaker, Jan., Wake county. R. R. Jan. 12, 1836.
Paisley, Sarah Jane to Robert M. Sloan, Aug. 25, Guilford county. R. R. Sept. 13, 1836.
Palmer, Martha to Joshua Ricks, Jan. 21, Guilford county. R. R. Mar. 1, 1836.

Panky, Stephen, Jr. to Rachel Williams, Dec. 4, Richmond county. R. R. Jan. 5, 1836.

Parker, Drury to Mrs. Rhoda Miller, Jan. 11, Rowan county. R. R. Mar. 1, 1836.

Parker, Haywood of this State to Maria Lawrence, Apr., Greensboro, Alabama. R. R. My. 2, 1836.

Parker, Lydia to Capt. Matthew Pierce of Halifax county, Dec. 22, Nansemond county, Va. R. R. Jan. 26, 1836.

Parks, Miss M. to Joseph M'Combs, Apr. 12, Mecklenburg county. R. R. My. 10, 1836.

Pass, Eliza to Jesse Burch, Jan. 18, Person county. R. R. Mar. 1, 1836.

Patterson, Margaret to Dr. James A. Kelly, Feb., Moore county. R. R. Feb. 2, 1836.

Patton, Ann Eliza to Robert F. Parnell of Halifax, My., Philadelphia. R. R. My. 31, 1836.

Payne, Elizabeth to J. Stokes, Oct. 12, Caswell county. R. R. Oct. 25, 1836.

Pealer, John of Montgomery county to Mrs. Nancy Hodge of Rowan county, Apr. R. R. Apr. 19, 1836.

Peebles, Eliza to Henry S. Williams of Tennessee, Dec. 13, Northampton county. R. R. Dec. 20, 1836.

Peel, John to Elizabeth Witherton, Jan. 6, Bertie county. R. R. Jan. 26, 1836.

Pender, Solomon of Mississippi to Margaret Rhodes, My. 31, Bertie county. R. R. Je. 31, 1836.

Pender, Thos. of Plymouth to Sarah Carstaphen, Dec. 10, Edgecombe county. R. R. Jan. 26, 1836.

Pendergrast, Mary to William H. Owen, Apr., Apr. Chapel Hill. R. R. My. 3, 1836.

Perry, Jackson of Raleigh to Jane Williams, Apr. 14, Charlotte. R. R. Apr. 26, 1836.

Perry, Lucy W. to Wm. H. Williams of Warren county, Je. 15, Franklin county. R. R. Je. 28, 1836.

Perry, Winifred to Josiah Howell, Jr., Dec. 31, Bertie county. R. R. Jan. 26, 1836.

Phelps, James W. to Sarah Ann Morris, Feb. 18, Beaufort, Carteret county. R. R. Mar. 8, 1836.

Picard, Henry to Elizabeth Butt, Feb. 18, Elizabeth City. R. R. Mar. 8, 1836.

Pierce, Capt. Matthew of Halifax county to Lydia Parker, Dec. 22, Nansemond county, Va. R. R. Jan. 26, 1836.

Pinckston, Nancy to Burrel Roberts, Feb. 4, Rowan county. R. R. Mar. 1, 1836.

Pinkston, Mary to Alex Shupping, Mar., Rowan county. R. R. Apr. 19, 1836.

Pittman, Penelope C. to Benton T. Lyon, My., Edgecombe county. R. R. My. 31, 1836.

Plummer, John to Eliza Wharton, Oct. 20, Davidson county. R. R. Nov. 8, 1836.

Polk, Mrs. Laura to Dr. William Tait of Morganton, Sept. 27, Charlotte. R. R. Oct. 11, 1836.

Ponton, Mungo T. to Mrs. Harriet Lasseter, Dec. 8, Halifax county. R. R. Jan. 5, 1836.
Pool, Lewis of Wake county to Catharine Shaw, Je. 16, Raleigh. R. R. Je. 21, 1836.
Potter, Jane to Joseph Mervy of Cheraw, S. C., Feb. 11, Fayetteville. R. R. Mar. 1, 1836.
Prout, John W. to Delia Johnston, Dec. 18, Raleigh. R. R. Jan. 5, 1836.
Purnell, Robert F. of Halifax to Ann Eliza Patton, My., Philadelphia. R. R. My. 31, 1836.
Puryear, Alexander to Mary Butler, Dec. 22, Granville county. R. R. Jan. 5, 1836.
Ragland, John to Mary Harris, Feb. 13, Granville county. R. R. Mar. 1, 1836.
Rainey, John P. to Martha Durham, Dec. 5, Caswell county. R. R. Feb. 2, 1836.
Rainey, John W. of Salisbury to Margaret V. Wilkerson, Oct. 20, Cabarrus county. R. R. Nov. 8, 1836.
Rainor, Mary to Stephen O. Sutton, Feb. 10, Sampson county. R. R. Mar. 1, 1836.
Ramsay, Joseph of Plymouth to Margaret Burcher, Je., Elizabeth City. R. R. Je. 28, 1836.
Ramsey, Jane of Rutherford county & Pennsylvania to Capt. James Gillespie of Rowan county, Jan. 28, Rutherfordton. R. R. Mar. 1, 1836.
Rankin, Rev. William C. of Rutherford county to Joanna Kelso of Spartanburg District, S. C., Sept. 29. R. R. Oct. 25, 1836.
Ray, Esther M. to Isaac J. Irvine of Rutherford county, Je. 2, Rutherford county. R. R. Je. 28, 1836.
Read, Ann Carolina to Frank Hawkins, Jan. 3, Halifax county. R. R. Mar. 1, 1836.
Reeves, George W. of Somerville, Tenn. to Margaret J. M'Collum, Sept. 8, Hillsborough. R. R. Sept. 27, 1836.
Relf, Margaret to Henry Skinner, Apr. 7, Camden county. R. R. Apr. 26, 1836.
Rencher, Hon. A. of Salisbury to Louisa Jones, Sept. 27, Pittsboro, Chatham county. R. R. Oct. 18, 1836.
Reston, Almeria to William B. Giles of Wilmington, Je. 22, Bladen county. R. R. Je. 28, 1836.
Rhodes, Margaret to Solomon Pender of Mississippi, My. 31, Bertie county. R. R. Je. 31, 1836.
Ricks, Joshua to Martha Palmer, Jan. 21, Guilford county. R. R. Mar. 1, 1836.
Ridenhour, Sophia to James A. Scott, Apr., Cabarrus county. R. R. Apr. 26, 1836.
Ridge, Ransom to Elizabeth Arnold, Oct. 11, Randolph county. R. R. Nov. 8, 1836.
Ridley, Joseph James to Eliza Kingsbury of New York, Oct. 24, Oxford. R. R. Nov. 1, 1836.
Righton, Jane R. to Robert L. Decoin of New Orleans, La., Oct., Chowan county. R. R. Nov. 1, 1836.

Roberts, Burrel to Nancy Pinckston, Feb. 4, Rowan county. R. R. Mar. 1, 1836.
Roberts, Elizabeth to Joseph Dey of Norfolk, Sept., Currituck county. R. R. Oct. 11, 1836.
Robeson, Grisey to Thomas A. Waitt, Jly., Wake county. R. R. Je. 28, 1836.
Robinson, Dr. Benjamin W. to Joanna Huske, My., Fayetteville. R. R. My. 31, 1836.
Robison, Mary G. to John Cowan, Dec. 31, Rowan county. R. R. Jan. 26, 1836.
Rorie, James to Sarah Duren, Feb 19, Anson county. R. R. Mar. 8, 1836.
Ross, James N. to Amanda Lindsay, Feb., Guilford county. R. R. Apr. 19, 1836.
Roulhac, J. G. B. of Bertie county to Catharine Ruffin, Nov. 24, Orange county. R. R. Dec. 13, 1836.
Rudd, Lucinda of Milton to N. B. Thomas, Jan. 29, Person county. R. R. Mar. 1, 1836.
Rude, Angelina P. to George W. Williamson, Apr. 12, Mecklenburg county. R. R. My. 10, 1836.
Ruffin, Catharine to J. G. Roulhac of Bertie county, Nov. 24, Orange county. R. R. Dec. 13, 1836.
Russell, Elizabeth to Marmaduke Savage, Sept. 15, Halifax. R. R. Oct. 4, 1836.
Russell, Mrs. Frances M. to George B. Tunstall, Nov. 15, Franklin county. R. R. Nov. 22, 1836.
Russum, Caroline to Charles Murphy, Dec. 27, Guilford county. R. R. Mar. 1, 1836.
Sanders, Geo. of Washington to Amanda Malvina Jordan, Mar. 10, Pitt county. R. R. Mar. 29, 1836.
Savage, Marmaduke to Elizabeth Russell, Sept. 15, Halifax. R. R. Oct. 4, 1836.
Scott, James A. to Sophie Ridenhour, Apr., Cabarrus county. R. R. Apr. 26, 1836.
Scott, Dr. William D. to Margaret Rankin, Je. 30, Guilford county. R. R. Jly. 19, 1836.
Setzer, Elizabeth of Rowan county to William Holbrooks of Cabarrus county, Mar. 29, Rowan county. R. R. Apr. 19, 1836.
Sharp, Matilda of Manchester, Va. to Andrew W. Harrison, Oct. 4, Caswell county. R. R. Nov. 1, 1836.
Shaw, Catharine to Lewis Pool of Wake county, Je. 16, Raleigh. R. R. Je. 21, 1836.
Shaw, Henry M. to Mary K. Trotman, Apr. 2, Camden county. R. R. Apr. 26, 1836.
Shellhorn, Polly to Joseph Fidler, Apr. 14, Stokes county. R. R. Apr. 26, 1836.
Sherwood, Nancy to Henry Yates, Aug. 11, Guilford county. R. R. Sept. 13, 1836.
Shield, S. D. to Mary S. Snow, Jan. 3, Halifax county. R. R. Mar. 1, 1836.
Shultz, Theodore to Dr. F. H. Shuman, Oct. 14, Salem. R. R. Nov. 1, 1836.
Shuman, Dr. F. H. to Theodora Shultz, Oct. 14, Salem. R. R. Nov. 1, 1836.

Shupping, Alex to Mary Pinkston, Mar., Rowan county. R. R. Apr. 19, 1836.
Simpson, Maria of Newbern to Thos. B. Hill of Halifax county, Sept. 15, Hillsboro. R. R. Sept. 27, 1836.
Singletary, Ephraim of Bladen county to Nancy A. Blue of Cumberland county, Fayetteville, Jan. 24. R. R. Feb. 2, 1836.
Singleton, Robert of Edenton to Mrs. Margaret Ann Vannayse of New York, Apr. 2. R. R. Apr. 26, 1836.
Skinner, Henry to Margaret Reef, Apr. 7, Camden county. R. R. Apr. 26, 1836.
Sledge, Louisa to John Pace, Oct. 7, Fayetteville. R. R. Oct. 25, 1836.
Sloan, Robert M. to Sarah Jane Paisley, Aug. 25, Guilford county. R. R. Sept. 13, 1836.
Smith, Henrietta B. to John B. Carroll of New York, Jan. 10, Newbern. R. R. Jan. 12, 1836.
Smith, Jane to John D. Cameron, Jan. 4, Richmond county. R. R. Mar. 1, 1836.
Smith, Joseph to Sarah Chance, Apr. 2, Richmond county. R. R. Apr. 26,
Smith, Mary to Samuel W. Williams, Sept. 15, Wake county. R. R. Oct. 4, 1836.
Snow, Mary S. to S. D. Shield, Jan. 3, Halifax county. R. R. Mar. 1, 1836.
Somerville, Catharine to William John Taylor, U. S. Navy, Aug. 4, Warrenton. R. R. Aug. 16, 1836.
Spence, Miss E. to Lorenzo D. Orrel, Aug. 11, Guilford county. R. R. Sept. 13, 1836.
Stamps, Minton of Madison, Rockingham county to Martha P. Stetson, Je. 14, Stokes county. R. R. Je. 28, 1836.
Stanfield, Joseph M. to Ann Barnett of Person county, Je., Milton. R. R. Je. 7, 1836.
Stedman, Rev. James O. of Fayetteville to Margaretta Harbert, Nov., Philadelphia. R. R. Nov. 22, 1836.
Stetson, Martha P. to Minton Stamps of Madison, Rockingham county, Je. 14, Stokes county. R. R. Je. 28, 1836.
Stewart, Eli M. to Elizabeth Erwin, Dec. 19, Rowan county. R. R. Jan. 5, 1836.
Stirewalt, Sarah of Cabarrus county to Joseph W. Hampton, Mar. 13, Lexington. R. R. Mar. 29, 1836.
Stokes, J. to Elizabeth Payne, Oct. 12, Caswell county. R. R. Oct. 25, 1836.
Stokes, Joel to Elizabeth C. Payne, Oct. 12, Caswell county. R. R. Nov. 1, 1836.
Stuart, Daniel to Mary M'Callum, Mar. 3, Robeson county. R. R. Mar. 29, 1836.
Sugg, George W. of Lincoln county to Margaret Roder of Mecklenburg county, Jly. R. R. Jly. 26, 1836.
Sutton, Stephen O. to Mary Rainor, Feb. 10, Sampson county. R. R. Mar. 1, 1836.
Swann, Eveline to John F. Zimmerman, Jan. 27, Waughton, Stokes county. R. R. Feb. 2, 1836.
Tait, Dr. William of Morganton to Mrs. Laura Polk, Sept. 27, Charlotte. R. R. Oct. 11, 1836.

Taylor, Drury S. to Lucy L. Taylor of Granville county, Dec. 26, Tipton county, Tenn. R. R. Mar. 29, 1836.
Taylor, Lucy L. of Granville county to Drury S. Taylor, Dec. 26, Tipton county, Tenn. R. R. Mar. 29, 1836.
Taylor, Nathaniel of Mocksville to Mrs. Sarah Clayland, Jan. 20, Forks of the Yadkin. R. R. Feb. 2, 1836.
Terrill, Nathaniel M. of Tarboro to Mrs. Eliza A. Ellis, Sept., Washington, Beaufort county. R. R. Oct. 11, 1836.
Thatch, Mary of Perquimans county to Albert G. Anderson of Caswell county, Jan. 7. R. R. Jan. 26, 1836.
Thaxton, Joseph of Halifax, Va. to Elizabeth J. Page, Apr. 29, Person county. R. R. My. 10, 1836.
Thomas, N. B. to Lucinda Rudd of Milton, Jan. 29, Person county. R. R. Mar. 1, 1836.
Thompson, Sally to Wm. Laboyteaux, Je. 13, Elizabeth City. R. R. Je. 28, 1836.
Toomer, Eliza Y. to Thomas Hill of New Hanover county, Apr. 21, Fayetteville. R. R. Apr. 26, 1836.
Torian, Frances to Sidney S. Lee of Caswell county, Apr. 20, Halifax county. R. R. My. 3, 1836.
Torian, Dr. Thomas of Halifax, Va. to Agness G. Bethel of Rockingham, Je. 29. R. R. Jly. 12, 1836.
Trotman, Mary K. to Henry M. Shaw, Apr. 2, Camden county. R. R. Apr. 26, 1836.
Tunstall, George B. to Mrs. Frances M. Russell, Nov. 15, Franklin county. R. R. Nov. 22, 1836.
Turner, Mary to Wm. R. Hamilton of Petersburg, Va., Mar. 1, Granville county. R. R. Mar. 29, 1836.
Turner, Sarah of Warren county to Peyton H. Brown of Louisburg, My., Warren county. R. R. My. 17, 1836.
Turner, William to Christiana Walton, Je. 22, Wake county. R. R. Je. 28, 1836.
Twine, Thomas of Gates county to Mrs. Sarah Bowers, Oct., Portsmouth, Va. R. R. Nov. 1, 1836.
Twitty, James to Caroline Cheek, My., Warren county. R. R. My. 31, 1836.
Utley, Benton to Martha Hilliard, Jly. 14, Chapel Hill. R. R. Jly. 19, 1836.
Utley, Caroline to Henderson Utley, Sept. 8, Wake county. R. R. Oct. 4, 1836.
Utley, Henderson to Caroline Utley, Sept. 8, Wake county. R. R. Oct. 4, 1836.
Vance, Maria of Stokes county to Capt. Henry Marshall of Surry county, Apr. 14, Stokes county. R. R. Apr. 26, 1836.
Vanhook, Ann L. of Person county to Eli A. Jones of Caswell county, Je. 16, Caswell county. R. R. Jly. 12, 1836.
Vannayse, Mrs. Margaret Ann of New York to Robert Singleton of Edenton, Apr. 2. R. R. Apr. 26, 1836.
Verrell, Susan M. to John H. Norfleet, Je. 6, Person county. R. R. Jly. 19, 1836.
Wadsworth, John C. of Cheraw to Wincey P. Ingram, Feb. 25, Anson county. R. R. Mar. 8, 1836.

Waitt, Thomas A. to Grisey Robeson, Jly., Wake county. R. R. Je. 28, 1836.
Wallace, Jane P. of Cabarrus county to Benjamin Fraley of Salisbury, Oct. 23, Cabarrus county. R. R. Nov. 8, 1836.
Walton, Christiana to William Turner, Je. 22, Wake county. R. R. Je. 28, 1836.
Washington, Susan to William A. Graham of Hillsboro, Je. 8, Newbern. R. R. Je. 21, 1836.
Watkins, Jesse to Sarah Ann Morgan, Jan. 4, Richmond county. R. R. Jan. 26, 1836.
Weathers, Sarah E. to E. D. Gray, Sept., Mecklenburg county. R. R. Oct. 11, 1836.
Webb, Ann to Isaac Fisher, Sept. 4, Burke county. R. R. Sept. 27, 1836.
Weeks, Sophia to Capt. Henry M'Lean, Feb., Fayetteville. R. R. Feb. 2, 1836.
Wharton, Eliza to John Plummer, Oct. 20, Davidson county. R. R. Nov. 8, 1836.
Whitaker, Emeline of Raleigh to David Murphey of Sampson county, Mar. 3, Raleigh. R. R. Mar. 8, 1836.
Whitaker, Samuel, Jr. to Rachel M'Allister, Mar. 14, Wake county. R. R. My. 2, 1836.
Whitaker, Stimson H. to Malvina Page, Jan., Wake county. R. R. Jan. 12, 1836.
Whitaker, William H. to Caroline Brassfield, Jan. 14, Wake county. R. R. Jan. 26, 1836.
White, Elizabeth to Alexander Moore, Sept. 1, Burke county. R. R. Sept. 27, 1836.
White, Moses A. to Margaret Curry, Jan. 15, Salisbury. R. R. Feb. 2, 1836.
White, Thomas L. of Milton to Frances J. Howerton, Je. 16, Halifax county, Va. R. R. Je. 28, 1836.
Whitehurst, Frederick to Chloe Carter, Je. 13, Pasquotank county. R. R. Je. 28, 1836.
Wilkerson, Margaret V. to John W. Rainey of Salisbury, Oct. 20, Cabarrus county. R. R. Nov. 8, 1836.
Williams, Mrs. Delia to George E. Badger, Apr. 16, Raleigh. R. R. Apr. 19, 1836.
Williams, Henry S. of Tennessee to Eliza Peebles, Dec. 13, Northampton county. R. R. Dec. 20, 1836.
Williams, Dr. J. of Cabarrus county to Elizabeth D. Elliott, Jan., Rutherford county. R. R. Jan. 5, 1836.
Williams, Jane to Jackson Perry of Raleigh, Apr. 14, Charlotte. R. R. Apr. 26, 1836.
Williams, John Taylor, U. S. Navy to Catharine Somerville, Aug. 4, Warrenton. R. R. Aug. 16, 1836.
Williams, Lisbon to Nancy Johnson of Wake county, Sept. 22, Raleigh. R. R. Sept. 27, 1836.
Williams, Rachel to Stephen Panky, Jr., Dec. 4, Richmond county. R. R. Jan. 5, 1836.
Williams, Samuel W. to Mary Smith, Sept. 15, Wake county. R. R. Oct. 4, 1836.

Williams, Wm. H. of Warren county to Lucy W. Perry, Je. 15, Franklin county. R. R. Je. 28, 1836.
Williams, Rev. Wm. W. to Elizabeth B. Harvey, Aug. 9, Palmyra, Martin county. R. R. Aug. 23, 1836.
Williamson, Ann Edwards of Caswell county to Augustus Finle of Milton, Je. 9. R. R. Je. 21, 1836.
Williamson, George W. to Angelina P. Rude, Apr. 12, Mecklenburg county. R. R. My. 10, 1836.
Willis, Oscar of Burke county to Sarah Ann Willis, Oct. 20, Halifax. R. R. Nov. 1, 1836.
Willis, Sarah Ann to Oscar Willis of Burke county, Oct. 20, Halifax. R. R. Nov. 1, 1836.
Wilson, Harriet to R. C. Carson of Concord, Dec. 8, Mecklenburg county. R. R. Jan. 5, 1836.
Wilson, Capt. James to Caroline Cook, Jan. 28, Mecklenburg county. R. R. Mar. 1, 1836.
Winders, Jane to Samuel Owens, Feb. 13, Rowan county. R. R. Mar. 1, 1836.
Winders, Sarah to Warren Gheen, Feb. 13, Rowan county. R. R. Mar. 1, 1836.
Wiseman, Jesse P. of Davidson county to Hetty P. Gibson, Oct. 28, Rowan county. R. R. Nov. 8, 1836.
Witherton, Elizabeth to John Peel, Jan. 6, Bertie county. R. R. Jan. 26, 1836.
Witherton, Jane to James Howell, Jan., Bertie county. R. R. Jan. 26, 1836.
Wood, Rebecca to Hugh Culverhouse, Jan. 22, Salisbury. R. R. Feb. 2, 1836.
Wright, Sophia A. of Salisbury to Cage J. Douglass, Dec., La Grange, Tenn. R. R. Dec. 27, 1836.
Yates, Henry to Nancy Sherwood, Aug. 11, Guilford county. R. R. Sept. 13, 1836.
Zimmerman, John F. to Eveline Swann, Jan. 27, Waughtown, Stokes county. R. R. Feb. 2, 1836.

1837

Abernathy, Agnes B. to Albert A. Oglesby, Nov., Lincoln county. R. R. Nov. 6, 1837.
Abernathy, Susan to Alfred Hoke, Oct., Lincoln county. R. R. Oct. 23, 1837.
Abernathy, William to Leak Robinson, Jan. 26, Lincoln county. R. R. Feb. 21, 1837.
Adams, Margaret Ann to M. Smithwick, Je., Pitt county. R. R. Je. 6, 1837.
Adams, Margaret J. to Angus Malloy, Jan., Stewartsville, Richmond county. R. R. Jan. 31, 1837.
Adams, Samuel F. to Frances Reid, Oct., Rockingham county. R. R. Oct. 30, 1837.
Adams, William P. of Rockingham to Mrs. Nancy E. Overby, Oct., Person county. R. R. Oct. 30, 1836.
Alexander, Abram R. to Sarah E. Hudson, Oct., Cabarrus county. R. R. Oct. 30, 1837.

Alexander, Mrs. Elizabeth of Richmond, Va. to Col. Girard Alexander of Campbell county, Va., Mar., Edenton. R. R. Mar. 28, 1837.
Alexander, Col. Girard of Campbell county, Va. to Elizabeth Alexander of Richmond, Va., Mar., Edenton. R. R. Mar. 28, 1837.
Allen, Henry to Sarah Rogers, Oct. 24, Wake county. R. R. Oct. 30, 1837.
Allen, Richard to Mrs. John Flurnoy, Apr., Anson county. R. R. My. 9, 1837.
Allen, Stephen W. to Nancy A. Rea, Jan. 31, Mecklenburg county. R. R. Feb. 21, 1837.
Allison, Ann L. to Charles Overman of Greensboro, Apr., Charlotte. R. R. Apr. 25, 1837.
Anders, Hannah J. to William S. Johnson, Oct., Bladen county. R. R. Oct. 23, 1837.
Andrews, Elizabeth to Patrick M'Gowan, Feb. 25, Raleigh. R. R. Feb. 28, 1837.
Andrews, Emeline to Andrew Baggerly, Nov., Irdell county. R. R. Nov. 27, 1837.
Andrews, Jeremiah to Euphemia May, Aug. 31, Guilford county. R. R. Sept. 18, 1837.
Andrews, Jesse of Montgomery county to Letitia Brower, Sept., Randolph county. R. R. Sept. 25, 1837.
Applewhite, Elizabeth to W. Cox, Aug. 29, Wayne county. R. R. Sept. 4, 1837.
Armfield, E. D. of Mocksville to Elizabeth Belt, Dec., Irdell county. R. R. Dec. 18, 1837.
Ashe, Thomas of Fayetteville to Rosa A. Hill, Nov. 21, Pittsborough. R. R. Nov. 27, 1837.
Atkinson, Ruth to James T. Quartermus, Je., Greenville. R. R. Je. 6, 1837.
Autry, Matthew to Margaret Ann Phares of Bladen county, Nov., Cumberland county. R. R. Nov. 20, 1837.
Aycock, Martha A. of Wake Forest to Micajah Medley, Nov., Wake county. R. R. Nov. 6, 1837.
Aydlotte, Nancy to Thomas M'Makin, Apr., Greensboro. R. R. My. 9, 1837.
Backus, Salmon S. to Caroline Burgevin, Nov., Newbern. R. R. Nov. 6, 1837.
Baggerly, Andrew to Emeline Andrews, Nov., Iredell county. R. R. Nov. 27, 1837.
Baggerly, Elizabeth to John Furchase, Je., Iredell county. R. R. Je. 6, 1837.
Bailey, Francis C. to Michael N. Fisher, Oct., Craven county. R. R. Oct. 9, 1837.
Bain, Jane H. to Andrew Jones, Aug. 10, Mecklenburg county. R. R. Aug. 28, 1837.
Baker, Eliza J. W. to Rev. James Pervis of Greensboro, Oct., Salisbury. R. R. Oct. 16, 1837.
Baker, Elizabeth to Nathan Chaffin, Mar., Davie county. R. R. Apr. 4, 1837.
Baker, Simmons, Jr. to Elizabeth Hawkins of Raleigh, Dec., Warren county. R. R. Dec. 4, 1837.
Ballard, William to Elizabeth M'Corkle, Nov., Lincoln county. R. R. Nov. 6, 1837.

Banks, John of Wilmington to Louisa Shailor Whittenbury of Hartford, Conn., Jan., Cumberland county. R. R. Jan. 31, 1837.
Banner, Lewis B. to Nancy Flippin, Dec., Stokes county. R. R. Dec. 18, 1837.
Barefield, James to Elizabeth Carpenter, Mar., Rutherford county. R. R. Apr. 18, 1837.
Baxter, Elizabeth to Amos Harrill, Apr., Rutherford county. R. R. Apr. 18, 1837.
Beam, John to Elizabeth Bridgers, Apr., Rutherford county. R. R. Apr. 18, 1837.
Beasley, Fielding to Mary M'Leod, Feb. 12, Raleigh. R. R. Feb. 14, 1837.
Beason, Elizabeth to Joseph M'Cullock of Guilford county, Jly., Randolph county. R. R. Jly. 17, 1837.
Bell, Mary Eliza of Newbern to John H. Garner, Oct., Gainesville, Ga. R. R. Oct. 9, 1837.
Belt, Elizabeth to E. D. Armfield of Mocksville, Dec., Iredell county. R. R. Dec. 18, 1837.
Belt, Mary C. to John A. Roseborough of Rowan county, Dec., Iredell county. R. R. Dec. 18, 1837.
Benbury, Richard of Chowan county to Mary Leigh, Dec., Perquimans county. R. R. Dec. 4, 1837.
Bendinfield, Martha to Wesley Hill, Dec., Wake county. R. R. Dec. 4, 1837.
Bennett, Mary to William Flynt, Jly. 20, Stokes county. R. R. Aug. 7, 1837.
Beverly, Daniel G. to Miss M'Cloud, Jan. 12, Anson county. R. R. Jan. 31, 1837.
Biddle, Sam'l S. of Craven county to Mary B. Williams, Nov., Beaufort county. R. R. Nov. 13, 1837.
Blackwell, John of Granville county to Mary Ann Webb of Person county, Aug. 22. R. R. Sept. 18, 1837.
Blake, Rev. Bennet T. to Mrs. S. Miles, Feb. 17, Wake county. R. R. Feb. 28, 1837.
Blake, Sarah F. to Peter P. Cox, Nov., Anson county. R. R. Nov. 13, 1837.
Blaney, Susan Jane to John Oliver of Carteret county, Nov., Newbern. R. R. Nov. 6, 1837.
Blount, Joe E. to Mrs. Margaret Ann Lawton, Je., Washington, Beaufort county. R. R. Je. 13, 1837.
Blount, Mary E. of Edenton to Nathan Perkins of Pasquotank county, Dec., Perquimans county. R. R. Dec. 18, 1837.
Bogey, Penelope to John H. Richardson, Feb. 1, Craven county. R. R. Feb. 21, 1837.
Bond, James of Rockingham to Sarah Coleman, Mar., Cabarrus county. R. R. Mar. 21, 1837.
Bond, Samuel T. to Sarah F. Skinner, Jan. 5, Edenton. R. R. Jan. 31, 1837.
Bonner, Jane A. to James Newbould, Aug. 22, Edenton, Pasquotank county. R. R. Aug. 28, 1837.
Bowden, Mrs. Mildred to John H. Wilkins, Oct., Rutherford county. R. R. Oct. 9, 1837.
Bragg, Sidney Ann to George W. Taylor, Mar., Washington, Beaufort county. R. R. Mar. 7, 1837.
Bray, Emily to Joseph Page, My., Randolph county. R. R. My. 9, 1837.

Brewer, Elizabeth to Enoch Cooper, Nov., Davidson county. R. R. Nov. 27, 1837.
Bridges, Elizabeth to John Beam, Apr., Rutherford county. R. R. Apr. 18, 1837.
Bringle, Phebe to Daniel Leonard, Je. 25, Lexington, Davidson county. R. R. Jly. 17, 1837.
Brunkard, William to Jane England, Dec. 27, Raleigh. R. R. Jan. 10, 1837.
Brison, George R. to Harriet Clark, Oct., Lincoln county. R. R. Oct. 9, 1837.
Brock, Nathaniel to Clarissa Smith, Nov., Davie county. R. R. Nov. 20, 1837.
Brooks, Samuel to Penelope Swindell, Jly., Hyde county. R. R. Aug. 7, 1837.
Brown, Andrew to Rosina Williams, Apr., Rowan county. R. R. Apr. 18, 1837.
Brown, Emma to Isham Peterson, Aug. 24, Wilmington. R. R. Sept. 4, 1837.
Brower, Letitia to Jesse Andrews of Montgomery county, Sept., Randolph county. R. R. Sept. 25, 1837.
Bryan, Ann P. to Henry Roberts of Wayne county, Aug. 8, Jericho, Wayne county. R. R. Aug. 28, 1837.
Bunting, Dr. Thomas of Sampson county to Elizabeth Holmes, Mar., Wilmington. R. R. Mar. 28, 1837.
Burch, James to Demarius Moody, Nov., Rutherford county. R. R. Nov. 13, 1837.
Burgevin, Caroline to Salmon S. Backus, Nov., Newbern. R. R. Nov. 6, 1837.
Butler, Sarah E. to Maj. Robert M' D. Tate, Oct., Burke county. R. R. Oct. 16, 1837.
Byers, Mrs. Ann C. of Iredell county to David Parks of Charlotte, Jly. 11, Iredell county. R. R. Jly. 31, 1837.
Bynum, John G. of Rutherfordton to Mary M'Dowell, Dec., Burke county. R. R. Dec. 18, 1837.
Bynum, Margaret Ann to Tyre Glenn, Nov., Stokes county. R. R. Nov. 27, 1837.
Calder, Flora to Joseph A. Frazier, Apr., Mecklenburg county. R. R. My. 9, 1837.
Calder, Margaret to Robert G. Robison, Apr., Mecklenburg county. R. R. My. 9, 1837.
Caldwell, Eliza B. to James C. Frazier, Nov., Cabarrus county. R. R. Nov. 20, 1837.
Cameron, Dr. William to Emma Moore, Dec. 8, Hillsborough. R. R. Dec. 18, 1837.
Campbell, Eliza C. of Fayetteville to Joseph Seawell, Je. 24, Mobile, Alabama. R. R. Jly. 17, 1837.
Cannon, Henry J. of Raleigh to Sarah S. Peebles of Northampton county, Jan. 23, Northampton county. R. R. Feb. 28, 1837.
Cannon, Sarah of Caswell county to William Mangum of Thornsville, Jan. 14, Granville county. R. R. Feb. 14, 1837.
Carmon, Joshua of Fayetteville to Mrs. Ann Tyson, Nov., Moore county. R. R. Nov. 20, 1837.

Carpenter, Elizabeth to James Barfield, Mar., Rutherford county. R. R. Apr. 18, 1837.
Carrington, Amelia to William Walker, Feb., Orange county. R. R. Feb. 14, 1837.
Carter,, Eliza to Absalom Scales, Oct., Stokes county. R. R. Oct. 30, 1837.
Carter, Nancy to Capt. Samuel Smoot, Nov., Davie county. R. R. Nov. 20, 1837.
Carter, Rowland of Montgomery county to Mrs. Unice Cowan, Salisbury. R. R. Oct. 30, 1837.
Chaffin, Nathan to Elizabeth Baker, Mar., Davie county. R. R. Apr. 4, 1837.
Chambers, Eleanor J. to Hugh A. Crawford, Jly. 27, Meltonsville. R. R. Aug. 7, 1837.
Chitty, Trougot to Frederic Reede, Jly. 25, Salem. R. R. Aug. 7, 1837.
Christianberry, William P. to Mary Magary, Je., Mecklenburg county. R. R. Je. 13, 1837.
Clancy, Sarah to Levi W. Young of Alabama, Mar. 17, Hillsborough. R. R. Mar. 28, 1837.
Clark, Harriet E. to George R. Brison, Oct., Lincoln county. R. R. Oct. 9, 1837.
Clark, Henry J. B. of Washington, Beaufort county to Matilda D. Clark, Oct., Newbern. R. R. Oct. 9, 1837.
Clark, W. R. to Charlotte A. M'Culloch, Oct. 12, Lincolnton. R. R. Oct. 30, 1837.
Claybrooks, Richard to Esther Dent, Dec. 6, Davie county. R. R. Dec. 23, 1837.
Clingman, Francis P. to Apphia Rose of Stokes county, Apr., Morgan county, Alabama. R. R. My. 9, 1837.
Cloud, Mary Ann to Alexander Woodson of Rockingham, Mar., Stokes county. R. R. Mar. 21, 1837.
Coleman, Sarah to James Bond of Rockingham, Mar., Cabarrus county. R. R. Mar. 21, 1837.
Connor, Hardy C. to Eliza Perry, Oct., Trenton, Jones county. R. R. Oct. 9, 1837.
Conrad, Amanda S. to Henry A. Lemly of Salisbury, Jan., Stokes county. R. R. Jan. 3, 1837.
Cook, Milanda of this State to Mr. Tomlison, Jly. 27, Madison county, Tennessee. R. R. Aug. 28, 1837.
Cooper, Enoch to Elizabeth Brewer, Nov., Davidson county. R. R. Nov. 27, 1837.
Cordan, William C. to Nancy Satchwell, Je., Pitt county. R. R. Je. 6, 1837.
Cotten, Franklin of Rowan county to Sarah Current, Mar., Iredell county. R. R. Mar. 28, 1837.
Cowan, Mrs. Unice to Rowland Carter of Montgomery county. Oct., Salisbury. R. R. Oct. 30, 1837.
Coward, Cynthia to William Wilson, Nov., Rutherford county. R. R. Nov. 27, 1837.
Cox, Peter to Sarah F. Blake, Nov., Rutherford county. R. R. Nov. 27, 1837.
Cox, W. to Elizabeth Applewhite, Aug. 29, Wayne county. R. R. Sept. 4, 1837.

Cozart, Hiram W. to Rachel Phillips, Je. 25, Rowan county. R. R. Jly. 17, 1837.
Crawford, Elisha to Elizabeth Night, Oct., Rockingham. R. R. Oct. 9, 1837.
Crawford, Hugh A. to Eleanor J. Chambers, Jly. 27, Meltonsville. R. R. Aug. 7, 1837.
Crosby, Ann Maria to Henry M. Johnson, Aug. 20, Fayetttville. R. R. Oct. 2, 1837.
Crow, Israel to Elmira Neel, Apr., Montgomery county. R. R. Apr. 18, 1837.
Crowder, Pherebee to Holland Jewel, Feb. 1, Wake county. R. R. Feb. 14, 1837.
Crump, Alexander of Montgomery county to Wincy Gholson of Randolph county, Sept., Randolph county. R. R. Oct. 7, 1837.
Current, Sarah to Franklin Cotten of Rowan county, Mar., Iredell county. R. R. Mar. 28, 1837.
Currier, James to Julian Mitchell, Mar. 2, Caswell county. R. R. Mar. 21, 1837.
Davis, Archibald H. of Franklin to Cornelia C. Kearney, Nov., Warren county. R. R. Nov. 13, 1837.
Davis, Charles W. to Nancy Mendenhall, Je. 17, Guilford county. R. R. Jly. 17, 1837.
Davis, Mary to Rev. William Harper of Chatham county, Oct., Moore county. R. R. Oct. 9, 1837.
Davis, Robert to Rhody Turnage, Jly., Wayne county. R. R. Aug. 7, 1837.
Dayley, Mary to Thomas Sifford, Nov., Rutherford county. R. R. Nov. 13, 1837.
Dempsey, William D. of Virginia to Sarah Ann Harbin, Mar., Iredell county. R. R. Mar. 28, 1837.
Dent, Esther to Richard Claybrooks, Dec. 6, Davie county. R. R. Dec. 23, 1837.
Denton, William of Rutherford county to Ann Flowers of Lincoln county, Nov., Lincoln county. R. R. Nov. 27, 1837.
Devany, Samuel to Charity Staley, Dec., Guilford county. R. R. Dec. 18, 1837.
Devereux, Frances to Henry Watkins Miller, Je. 15, Raleigh. R. R. Je. 19, 1837.
Dewey, Charles to Juliana Haylander, Jan. 5, Raleigh. R. R. Jan. 10, 1837.
Dilworth, Junius to Eliza Jane Lockhart, Je., Hillsborough. R. R. Jly. 17, 1837.
Dobbins, Elizabeth to William Tomlison, Mar., Iredell county. R. R. Mar. 28, 1837.
Dota, William H. of Onslow county to Martha Caroline Lane, Sept., Wilmington. R. R. Oct. 2, 1837.
Downing, Narcissa to James Harrison, Sept., Washington county. R. R. Oct. 2, 1837.
Drake, Louisa of Jackson to James W. Newsom, Je. 27. R. R. Jly. 10, 1837.
Dudley, Christian C. to Alfred Martin, Oct., Wilmington. R. R. Oct. 23, 1837.
Duhadway, Amanda C. to James H. Myrover of Fayetteville, Apr., Charleston. R. R. Apr. 25, 1837.

Dunn, Lucy M. to Henry Seawell of Raleigh, Jan. 24, Wake Forest. R. R. Jan. 31, 1837.
Dyer, Sally to William Woodward, Apr., Chapel Hill. R. R. Apr. 25, 1837.
Eagle, Catharine Ann to Simeon Lents, Mar., Rowan county. R. R. Apr. 4, 1837.
Earneheart, Silas to Caroline Goodman, Apr., Rowan county. R. R. My. 2, 1837.
Edmonston, Wm. D. of Snow Hill to Julia A. Pipkin of Wayne county, Aug. 10. R. R. Aug. 28, 1837.
Elliott, Elizabeth to Richard Smith, Sept., Edenton. R. R. Oct. 2, 1837.
Elliott, Lavinia to Joseph Spence, Dec., Perquimans county. R. R. Dec. 4, 1837.
Elliott, Sarah Ann to James W. Hathaway, Nov., Chowan county. R. R. Nov. 13, 1837.
Ennis, John to Rebecca Gargis, Nov., Halifax county. R. R. Nov. 27, 1837.
England, Jane to William Brunkard, Dec. 27, Raleigh. R. R. Jan. 10, 1837.
Farrow, Ann G. of Washington, Beaufort county to David G. Patton of Edinburgh, Scotland, Aug. 1, Washington, Beaufort county. R. R. Aug. 14, 1837.
Feinster, William R. to Eliza P. S. Morrison, Nov., Iredell county. R. R. Nov. 27, 1837.
Furchase, John to Elizabeth Beggarly, Je., Iredell county. R. R. Je. 6, 1837.
Fisher, John to Elizabeth Hallman, Oct. 17, Lincoln county. R. R. Oct. 30, 1837.
Fisher, Joseph of Rowan county to Barbara Nuseman, Oct., Cabarrus county. R. R. Oct. 23, 1837.
Fisher, Michael N. to Francis C. Bailey, Oct., Craven county. R. R. Oct. 9, 1837.
Fitchel, Jeremiah to Eliza White, Nov., Iredell county. R. R. Nov. 27, 1837.
Fite, Barbara Ann to Asa Presley, Feb. 5, Mecklenburg county. R. R. Feb. 21, 1837.
Fitzgerald, Pleasant of Milton to Lucinda Jane Stimson of Pittsylvania county, Va., Feb. 14. R. R. Feb. 28, 1837.
Fletcher, Jane to Stephen Skinner, Nov., Chowan county. R. R. Nov. 27, 1837.
Flippin, Nancy to Lewis B. Banner, Dec., Stokes county. R. R. Dec. 18, 1837.
Flowers, Ann of Lincoln county to William Denton of Rutherford county, Nov., Lincoln county. R. R. Nov. 27, 1837.
Flurnoy, Mrs. John to Richard Allen, Apr., Anson county. R. R. My. 9, 1837.
Flynt, William to Mary Bennett, Jly. 20, Stokes county. R. R. Aug. 7, 1837.
Foard, Robert W. to Marie Emeline Partee, Feb. 5, Rowan county. R. R. Feb. 21, 1837.
Foreman, Mrs. Elizabeth to Edmund B. Freeman of Raleigh, Nov. 14, Pitt county. R. R. Nov. 20, 1837.
Foscue, Christiana to James Hancock of Newbern, Oct., Jones county. R. R. Oct. 16, 1837.

Foster, Dorcas H. to Dr. John M. Happoldt, Mar., Mecklenburg county. R. R. Mar. 21, 1837.
Foster, Mary to Capt. Jacob Leavitt of Duxbury, Mass., Mar., Pasquotank county. R. R. Mar. 21, 1837.
Fowler, Nathaniel to Lavinia Garrison, My., New Hanover county. R. R. Je. 6, 1837.
Frazier, James to Mary Purnell, Je. 6, Halifax. R. R. Je. 19, 1837.
Frazier, James C. to Eliza B. Caldwell, Nov., Cabarrus county. R. R. Nov. 20, 1837.
Frazier, Joseph A. to Flora Calder, Apr., Mecklenburg county. R. R. My. 9, 1837.
Fraley, Alexander G. to Mary Smoot, Mar., Davie county. R. R. Mar. 28, 1837.
Freeman, Edmund B. of Raleigh to Mrs. Elizabeth Foreman, Nov. 14, Pitt county. R. R. Nov. 20, 1837.
Freeze, Jacob to Sarah Leazor, Apr., Rowan county. R. R. My. 2, 1837.
Freeze, Thomas to Alvina Lipe, Mar., Rowan county. R. R. Apr. 4, 1837.
Fry, Jonathan of Surry county to Rachel M'Lelland, Oct., Iredell county. R. R. Oct. 30, 1837.
Futrall, Thomas A. of Greene county to Mrs. Julia Ann Marsh, Jan. 10, Chatham county. R. R. Jan. 31, 1837.
Gamble, John to Rebecca Parker, My. 11, Wake county. R. R. My. 16, 1837.
Gantt, Nancy M. to Thomas Williams, Nov., Rutherford county. R. R. Nov. 20, 1837.
Gargis, Rebecca to John Ennis, Nov., Halifax county. R. R. Nov. 27, 1837.
Garner, John H. to Mary Eliza Bell of Newbern, Oct., Gainesville, Ga. R. R. Oct. 9, 1837.
Garrison, Lavinia to Nathaniel Fowler, My., New Hanover county. R. R. Je. 6, 1837.
Gary, Amarantha to William C. Palmer of Orange county, Apr., Marion, Alabama. R. R. My. 2, 1837.
Gatlin, Mary M. to Franklin Knox, Je., Kinston, Lenoir county. R. R. Je. 13, 1837.
Gee, David to Mrs. Mary E. Jones, Jan., Fayetteville. R. R. Jan. 3, 1837.
Gettys, Margaret to John Price, Mar., Rutherford. R. R. Mar. 21, 1837.
Gholson, Wincy of Randolph county to Alexander Crump of Montgomery county, Sept., Randolph county. R. R. Oct. 9, 1837.
Giles, Mrs. Sarah to Col. Edward Yarbrough, Jan., Salisbury. R. R. Jan. 10, 1837.
Gill, Winifred to William Smithwick, Nov., Bertie county. R. R. Nov. 13, 1837.
Glenn, Tyre to Margaret Ann Bynum, Nov., Stokes county. R. R. Nov. 27, 1837.
Goneke, Sarah E. of Covington, Ga. to Barzillai Graves, of Caswell county, Jly. 6, Covington, Georgia. R. R. Aug. 21, 1837.
Goodman, Caroline to Silas Earneheart, Apr., Rowan county. R. R. My. 2, 1837.
Gordon, Dr. Benjamin to Maria Louisa Jones, Nov., Hertford. R. R. Nov. 27, 1837.

Gordon, Edward S. of Camden county to Penelope Lowry, Mar., Pasquotank county. R. R. Mar. 7, 1837.
Graham, John of Moore county to Arena Parson, Apr., Montgomery county. R. R. My. 9, 1837.
Graves, Ann to Howe Mebane of Bertie county, Feb. 9, Yanceyville. R. R. Feb. 28, 1837.
Graham, Mary Ann of Lincoln county to James H. Orr of Charlotte, Jly. 11. R. R. Jly. 24, 1837.
Graves, Barzillai of Caswell county to Sarah E. Goneke of Covington, Ga., Jly. 6, Covington, Ga. R. R. Aug. 21, 1837.
Graves, Maria Louisa to Rev. Thomas U. Wilkes of Georgia, Nov., Caswell county. R. R. Nov. 13, 1837.
Gray, Mrs. Nancy to Joseph Manning, Je., Pitt county. R. R. Je. 6, 1837.
Green, William H. of Bertie county to Cynthia Powell, Nov., Hertford county. R. R. Dec. 4, 1837.
Gregory, Frederick to Mary F. Mixon, Nov., Chowan county. R. R. Nov. 13, 1837.
Grimes, Catharine to William Walton, Je. 25, Rowan county. R. R. Jly. 17, 1837.
Haddock, Nancy to Major Timblick, My., Guilford county. R. R. Je. 6, 1837.
Hagadon, David to Isabella Mitchell, Jan., Halifax. R. R. Jan. 31, 1837.
Hall, John H. to Mrs. Mary Snively, Nov. 16, Fayetteville. R. R. Nov. 20, 1837.
Hall, Lucinda of Montgomery county to Jacob Miller, My., Randolph county. R. R. My. 16, 1837.
Hallman, Elizabeth to John Fisher, Oct. 17, Lincoln county. R. R. Oct. 30, 1837.
Hamilton, Elizabeth to Andrew Yount, Nov., Lincoln county. R. R. Nov. 27, 1837.
Hancock, James of Newbern to Christiana Foscus, Oct., Jones county. R. R. Oct. 16, 1837.
Happoldt, Dr. John M. to Dorcas H. Foster, Mar., Mecklenburg county. R. R. Mar. 21, 1837.
Harbin, Sarah Ann to William D. Dempsey of Virginia, Mar., Iredell county. R. R. Mar. 28, 1837.
Hardcastle, George to Nancy Harrison, Oct., Edenton. R. R. Oct. 9, 1837.
Hare, James to Christiana M'Rae, Jan. 8, Wadesboro. R. R. Jan. 31, 1837.
Hargrave, John L. of Davidson county to Caroline C. S. Parker, Mar., Tarboro. R. R. Mar. 7, 1837.
Harper, Rev. William of Chatham county to Mary Davis, Oct., Moore county. R. R. Oct. 9, 1837.
Harrill, Amos to Elizabeth Baxter, Apr., Rutherford county. R. R. Apr. 18, 1837.
Harrington, William D. to Lydia Margaret M'Neill, Dec., Moore county. R. R. Dec. 4, 1837.
Harris, Alpheus to Pamela E. Howard, My., Surry county. R. R. My. 16, 1837.
Harris, Temperance to John Lockhart of Greensborough, Alabama, Jly. 27, Orange county. R. R. Aug. 14, 1837.

Harrison, James to Narcissa Downing, Sept., Washington county. R. R. Oct. 2, 1837.
Harrison, Nancy to George Hardcastle, Oct., Edenton. R. R. Oct. 9, 1837.
Harry, Capt. John H. of Texas to Sarah F. M'Culloch, Dec. 6, R. R. Dec. 23, 1837.
Hart, Temperance to William F. C. Smith, Mar., Orange county. R. R. Mar. 28, 1837.
Hathaway, Burton W. to Mary B. Roberts, Mar., Edenton. R. R. Mar. 21, 1837.
Hathaway, James W. to Sarah Ann Elliott, Nov., Chowan county. R. R. Nov. 13, 1837.
Hawes, Francis to Susan Williams, Jly. 25, Wilmington. R. R. Aug. 7, 1837.
Hawkins, Elizabeth of Raleigh to Simmons Baker, Jr., Dec., Warren county. R. R. Dec. 4, 1837.
Haylander, Juliana to Charles Dewey, Jan. 5, Raleigh. R. R. Jan. 10, 1837.
Head, Isham to Sarah M'Guire, Oct., Rutherfordton. R. R. Oct. 16, 1837.
Henderson, Ludolphus of Caswell county to Elizabeth C. Parker of Orange county, My. 3, Orange county. R. R. My. 16, 1837.
Hickman, Agnes Ellett of Warrenton to N. H. Washington, Mar. 8, Warrenton. R. R. Mar. 21, 1837.
Hill, Kemp of Franklin county to Eliza Ligon, Sept. 19, Wake Forest. R. R. Sept. 25, 1837.
Hill, Rosa A. to Thomas Ashe of Fayetteville, Nov. 21, Pittsborough. R. R. Nov. 27, 1837.
Hill, Wesley to Martha Bendinfield, Dec., Wake county. R. R. Dec. 4, 1837.
Hines, Bryan of Erie Alabama to Elmina Hoyle, Sept. 12, Hoylesville. R. R. Sept. 25, 1837.
Hinson, Margaret Jane to Augustus C. Rose of Oneida, N. Y., Dec., Anson county. R. R. Dec. 4, 1837.
Hoke, Alfred to Susan Abernathy, Oct., Lincoln county. R. R. Oct. 23, 1837.
Holderby, Robert W. to Mary Ann Jones, Nov., Wentworth, Rockingham county. R. R. Nov. 27, 1837.
Holland, Mary Ann to Henry B. Lazenby, Nov., Iredell county. R. R. Nov. 27, 1837.
Holland, William M. to Margaret Reed, Oct., Lincoln county. R. R. Oct. 16, 1837.
Holmes, Elizabeth to Dr. Thomas Bunting of Sampson county, Mar., Wilmington. R. R. Mar. 28, 1837.
Holmes, Nicholas to Nancy Ann Moore, Mar., Orange county. R. R. Mar. 28, 1837.
Holt, Adam to Miss A. N. Smith, Jan., Halifax. R. R. Jan. 31, 1837.
Hooks, Rev. Curtis of Wayne county to Ann W. Lovick, Oct., Kinston, Lenoir county. R. R. Oct. 9, 1837.
Hoskins, Thomas S. of Raleigh to Harriet W. Wilson, Aug. 22, Perquimans county. R. R. Aug. 28, 1837.
Houston, George, Jr. to Mary Jane Montgomery of Washington, D. C., Jly. 19, Washington, D. C. R. R. Jly. 24, 1837.
Howard, Pamela E. to Alpheus Harris, My., Surry county. R. R. My. 16, 1837.

Hoyle, Elinina to Bryan Himes of Erie, Alabama, Sept. 12, Hoylesville. R. R. Sept. 25, 1837.
Hudson, Margaret to William S. Reeves, Oct., Cabarrus county. R. R. Oct. 30, 1837.
Hudson, Sarah E. to Abraham R. Alexander, Oct., Cabarrus county. R. R. Oct. 30, 1837.
Huggins, Margaret to Dr. James M. Moore, Je., Iredell county. R. R. Je. 6, 1837.
Hunter, Isaac to Louisa Riddick, Dec., Gates county. R. R. Dec. 18, 1837.
Hurt, John H. to Mary Jane Woodruff, Oct., Surry county. R. R. Oct. 16, 1837.
Hyder, Harriet to Abel Robards, Oct., Rutherford county. R. R. Oct. 23, 1837.
Irwin, Edwin Jones of Burke county to Ann E. Phifer, Dec. 6, Cabarrus county. R. R. Dec. 18, 1837.
Irwin, Elizabeth to David R. Killough, Oct. 30, Cabarrus county. R. R. Nov. 20, 1837.
Jackson, Morland to Mary Jane B. Ray, Mar., Orange county. R. R. Mar. 28, 1837.
Jackson, William H. of Orange county to Ruth J. Pillow, Je. 13, Giles county, Tenn. R. R. Aug. 21, 1837.
James, Francis A. to Mary Ann Todd, Apr., Salisbury. R. R. My. 9, 1837.
James, Francis A. to Capt. Robert Tays, Nov., Iredell county. R. R. Nov. 27, 1837.
Jarrot, Edward D. of Fayetteville to Mary Love of Rockingham, Richmond county, Jan., Cheraw, S. C. R. R. Jan. 31, 1837.
Jenkins, Salina R. to John D. Rankin, Sept. 12, Lincoln county. R. R. Sept. 25, 1837.
Jewel, Holland to Pherebee Crowder, Feb. 1, Wake county. R. R. Feb. 14, 1837.
Johnson, Dr. Charles E. of Edenton to Emily Skinner, Nov., Chowan county. R. R. Nov. 13, 1837.
Johnson, Henry M. to Ann Maria J. Crosby, Aug. 20, Fayetteville. R. R. Oct. 2, 1837.
Johnson, John M. of Cumberland county to Margaret Monroe, Je. 22, Moore county. R. R. Jly. 17, 1837.
Johnson, Juliana of Warren county to Thomas L. Jump of Raleigh, Feb. 7, Washington, D. C. R. R. Feb. 14, 1837.
Johnson, William to Betsey Vaughan, Mar. 20, Wake Forest. R. R. Apr. 25, 1837.
Johnson, William S. to Hannah J. Anders, Oct., Bladen county. R. R. Oct. 23, 1837.
Johnston, Fisher to Fanny Pearson, Je., Orange county. R. R. Je. 13, 1837.
Jolly, Frances T. to John N. Roper, Je. 8, Warrenton. R. R. Je. 19, 1837.
Jones, Andrew to Jane H. Bain, Aug. 10, Mecklenburg county. R. R. Aug. 28, 1837.
Jones, Elizabeth Ann to Henry Porter of Raleigh, Jan. R. R. Jan. 3, 1837.
Jones, Kimbrough to Mary W. Warren, Sept. 19, Wake county. R. R. Sept. 25, 1837.
Jones, Lydia D. to Presley P. Perry of Franklin, Nov. 29, Wake county. R. R. Dec. 4, 1837.
Jones, Maria Louisa to Dr. Benjamin Gordon, Nov., Hertford. R. R. Nov. 27, 1837.

Jones, Mary Ann to Robert W. Holderby, Nov., Wentworth, Rockingham county. R. R. Nov. 27, 1837.
Jones, Mrs. Mary E. to David Gee, Jan., Fayetteville. R. R. Jan. 3, 1837.
Jones, Sarah E. to Col. Wm. Jones of Mississippi and South Carolina, Oct. 19, Fort Defiance, Wilkes county. R. R. Nov. 6, 1837.
Jones, Col. Wm. of Mississippi & South Carolina to Sarah E. Jones, Oct. 19, Fort Defiance, Wilkes county. R. R. Nov. 6, 1837.
Jump, Thomas L. of Raleigh to Juliana Lee Johnson of Warren county, Feb. 7, Washington, D. C. R. R. Feb. 14, 1837.
Kearnes, Larkin to Mary Lassiter, Je., Randolph county. R. R. Je. 13, 1837.
Kearnes, Silas to Sarah Lassiter, Je., Randolph county. R. R. Je. 13, 1837.
Kearney, Cornelia C. to Archibald H. Davis of Franklin, Nov., Warren county. R. R. Nov. 13, 1837.
Kelly, Elizabeth to William W. Marcum, Je., Wake county. R. R. Je. 13, 1837.
Kelly, Philip O. of Lincoln county to Mary Ann White of Iredell county, Jan. 29, Iredell county. R. R. Feb. 14, 1837.
Killough, David R. to Elizabeth Irwin, Oct. 30, Cabarrus county. R. R. Nov. 20, 1837.
King, Emeline to Robert J. Merritt, Nov., Halifax county. R. R. Nov. 27, 1837.
King, Henrietta C. of Raleigh to George H. Sears of Newbern, My. 16, Linden, Alabama. R. R. Je. 6, 1837.
Kingsbury, Russell of Oxford to Lucy R. Pickett, Nov., Elizabeth City. R. R. Nov. 27, 1837.
Kinley, John to Anna Smith, Jly. 2, Guilford county. R. R. Jly. 17, 1837.
Knox, Franklin to Mary M. Gatlin, Je., Kinston, Lenoir county. R. R. Je. 13, 1837.
Krider, Mary Letitia to Rev. James E. Morrison, Nov., Rowan county. R. R. Nov. 27, 1837.
Lane, Ann Maria to William S. Mitchell of Mississippi, Sept., Wilmington. R. R. Oct. 2, 1837.
Lane, Martha Caroline to William H. Dota of Onslow county, Sept., Wilmington. R. R. Oct. 2, 1837.
Laughlin, Alfred to Zuritha Jane Perry of Franklin county, My. R. R. My. 16, 1837.
Langley, Sarah to Samuel Owens, Nov., Beaufort county. R. R. Nov. 20, 1837.
Lassiter, Mary to Larkin Kearnes, Je., Randolph county. R. R. Je. 13, 1837.
Lassiter, Sarah to Silas Kearnes, Je., Randolph county. R. R. Je. 13, 1837.
Lawton, Mrs. Margaret Ann to Jos. E. Blount, Je., Washington, Beaufort county. R. R. Je. 13, 1837.
Lazenby, Henry B. to Mary Ann Holland, Nov., Iredell county. R. R. Nov. 27, 1837.
Leavitt, Capt. Jacob of Duxbury Massachussetts to Mary Foster, Mar., Perquimans county. R. R. Mar. 21, 1837.
Leazor, Sarah to Jacob Freeze, Apr., Rowan county. R. R. My. 2, 1837.
Ledbetter, Sarah to Augustine Williams, Jly. 16, Lincoln county. R. R. Aug. 7, 1837.

Lee, Green H. to Irena Walker, Oct., Davidson county. R. R. Oct. 9, 1837.
Leeper, Matthew to Peggy Mariner, Oct., Lincoln county. R. R. Oct. 9, 1837.
Leigh, Mary to Richard Benbury of Chowan county, Dec., Perquimans county. R. R. Dec. 4, 1837.
Lemly, Henry A. of Salisbury to Amanda S. Conrad, Jan., Stokes county. R. R. Jan. 3, 1837.
Lents, Simeon to Catharine Ann Eagle, Mar., Rowan county. R. R. Apr. 4, 1837.
Leonard, Daniel to Phebe Bringle, Je. 25, Lexington, Davidson county. R. R. Jly. 17, 1837.
Lethco, Jacob to Lucy P. Waddell, Je., Randolph county. R. R. Je. 13, 1837.
Lipe, Alvina to Thomas Freeze, Mar., Rowan county. R. R. Apr. 4, 1837.
Ligon, Eliza to Kemp Hill of Franklin county, Sept. 19, Wake Forest. R. R. Sept. 25, 1837.
Lindsay, Elizabeth T. to Joshua T. Smith, Oct., Rockingham. R. R. Oct. 23, 1837.
Linebarger, Mary to Joseph Rankin, Lincoln county. R. R. Nov. 27, 1837.
Lockhart, Eliza Jane to Junius Dilworth, Je., Hillsborough R. R. Jly. 17, 1837.
Lockhart, John of Greensborough, Alabama to Temperance Harris, Jly. 27, Orange county. R. R. Aug. 14, 1837.
Love, Mary of Rockingham, Richmond county to Edward D. Jarrot of Fayetteville, Jan., Cheraw, S. C. R. R. Jan. 31, 1837.
Love, Mary to Benjamin H. Smith, Nov., Halifax county. R. R. Nov. 27, 1837.
Lovick, Ann W. to Rev. Curtis Hooks of Wayne county, Oct., Kinston, Lenoir county. R. R. Oct. 9, 1837.
Lovick, Sarah M. to Dr. Charles C. Wilson, Aug. 24, Newbern. R. R. Sept. 4, 1837.
Lowrie, Middy Lee to Buckner Ray, Nov., Wake county. R. R. Nov. 20, 1837.
Lowry, Penelope to Edward S. Gordon of Camden county, Mar., Pasquotank county. R. R. Mar. 7, 1837.
Luin, Rebecca to Edmund Sain, Mar., Davie county. R. R. Apr. 4, 1837.
Lucas, William A. to Harriet Williams, Je. 14, Raleigh. R. R. Je. 19, 1837.
Lunn, Capt. John to Sarah Taylor, Mar., Davie county. R. R. Apr. 4, 1837.
Lyles, Harriet to Andrew M'Dowell of Spartanburg District, S. C., Oct., Rutherford county. R. R. Oct. 23, 1837.
M'Arthur, Catharine to James Monroe, Nov., Bladen county. R. R. Nov. 13, 1837.
M'Bryde, Malcom to Mrs. Mary M'Neill, Nov. 2, Robeson county. R. R. Nov. 13, 1837.
M'Callum, Margaret to Duncan M'Nair, Jan., Robeson county. R. R. Jan. 3, 1837.
M'Cloud, Miss to Daniel G. Beverly, Jan. 12, Anson county. R. R. Jan. 31, 1837.
M'Corkle, Elizabeth to William Ballard, Nov., Lincoln county. R. R. Nov. 6, 1837.
M'Culloch, Charlotte A. to W. R. Clark, Oct. 12, Lincolnton. R. R. Oct. 30, 1837.

M'Culloch, Joseph of Guilford county to Elizabeth Beason, Jly., Randolph county. R. R. Jly. 17, 1837.
M'Culloch, Sarah F. to Capt. John H. Harry of Texas, Dec. 6. R. R. Dec. 23, 1837.
M'Cutchan, Rev. J. S. to Elizabeth T. Salmon of Fayetteville, Oct., Oxford. R. R. Oct. 16, 1837.
M'Dowell, Andrew of Spartanburg District, S. C. to Harriet Lyles, Oct., Rutherford county. R. R. Oct. 23, 1837.
M'Dowell, Mary to John B. Bynum of Rutherfordton, Dec., Burke county. R. R. Dec. 18, 1837.
M'Gowan, Patrick to Elizabeth Andrews, Feb. 25, Raleigh. R. R. Feb. 28, 1837.
M'Guire, Sarah to Isham Head, Oct., Rutherfordton. R. R. Oct. 16, 1837.
M'Intire, Harriet N. to Alexander Purcell, Feb., Robeson county. R. R. Feb. 21, 1837.
M'Intyre, Mrs. Margaret E. to Edward Pitman of Mecklenburg county, Dec., New Hanover county. R. R. Dec. 4, 1837.
M'Kay, Peter to Sealy Stewart, Feb., Robeson county. R. R. Feb. 21, 1837.
M'Kinnon, Ann to Neil M'Neil, Apr., Moore county. R. R. Apr. 18, 1837.
M'Kimmon, James to Amelia Poumairat of Baltimore, Oct. 26, Raleigh. R. R. Oct. 30, 1837.
M'Lelland, Rachel to Jonathan Fry of Surry county, Oct., Iredell county. R. R. Oct. 30, 1837.
M'Leod, Mary to Fielding Beaseley, Feb. 12, Raleigh. R. R. Feb. 14, 1837.
M'Makin, Thomas to Nancy Aydlotte, Apr., Greensboro. R. R. My. 9, 1837.
M'Murray, Eleanor to Newton Wharton, Sept. 26, Guilford county. R. R. Oct. 16, 1837.
M'Murray, Mary D. to Albert Rankin, Sept. 26, Guilford county. R. R. Oct. 16, 1837.
M'Nair, Duncan to Margaret M'Callum, Jan., Robeson county. R. R. Jan. 3, 1837.
M'Neely, Maria to T. Melmoth Young of Statesville, Dec., Mocksville. R. R. Dec. 18, 1837.
M'Neil, Neil to Ann M'Kinnon, Apr., Moore county. R. R. Apr. 18, 1837.
M'Neill, Lydia Margaret to William D. Harrington, Dec., Moore county. R. R. Dec. 4, 1837.
M'Neill, Margaret to Capt. Roderick M'Rae, Sept. 7, of Wilmington, Cumberland county. R. R. Oct. 9, 1837.
M'Neill, Mrs. Mary to Malcom M'Bryde, Nov. 2, Robeson county. R. R. Nov. 13, 1837.
M'Rae, Christiana to James Hare, Jan. 8, Wadesboro. R. R. Jan. 31, 1837.
M'Rae, Capt. Roderick of Wilmington to Margaret M'Neill, Sept. 7, Cumberland county. R. R. Oct. 9, 1837.
Magary, Mary to William P. Christianberry, Je., Mecklenburg county. R. R. Je. 13, 1837.
Malloy, Angus to Margaret J. Adams, Jan., Stewartsville, Richmond county. R. R. Jan. 31, 1837.
Malone, Capt. Lewis to Margaret Richmond, Mar., Caswell county. R. R. Mar. 28, 1837.
Mangum, William of Thornsville to Sarah Cannoon of Caswell county, Jan. 14, Granville county. R. R. Feb. 14, 1837.
Manning, Joseph to Mrs. Nanncy Gray, Je., Pitt county. R. R. Je. 6, 1837.

Marcum, William W. to Elizabeth Kelly, Je., Wake county. R. R. Je. 13, 1837.
Mariner, Peggy to Matthew Leeper, Oct., Lincoln county. R. R. Oct. 9, 1837.
Marsh, Mrs. Julia Ann to Thomas A. Futrall of Greene county, Jan. 10, Chatham county. R. R. Jan. 31, 1837.
Marshall, Eleazer to Mary Willson, Nov., Iredell county. R. R. Nov. 27, 1837.
Martin, Alfred to Christian C. Dudley, Oct., Wilmington. R. R. Oct. 23, 1837.
Matthews, Capt. Thomas P. to Winifred W. Nicholson, Mar. 7, Halifax county. R. R. Mar. 21, 1837.
May, D. to Charlotte Rawls of Franklin county, Mar., Wake county. R. R. Mar. 28, 1837.
May, Euphemia to Jeremiah Andrews, Aug. 31, Guilford county. R. R. Sept. 18, 1837.
Mayo, Martha E. to Arthur Mooring, Martin county, Sept. R. R. Sept. 25, 1837.
Meador, John R. to Magdalene D. Guerant, Mar., Rockingham. R. R. Mar. 28, 1837.
Mebane, Giles of Orange county to Mary C. Yancey, Mar. 8, Milton. R. R. Mar. 21, 1837.
Mebane, Howe of Bertie county to Ann Graves, Feb. 9, Yanceyville. R. R. Feb. 28, 1837.
Medley, Micajah to Martha A. Aycock of Wake Forest, Nov., Wake county. R. R. Nov. 6, 1837.
Mendenhall, Nancy to Charles W. Davis, Je. 17, Guilford county. R. R. Jly. 17, 1837.
Merritt, Robert J. to Emeline King, Nov., Halifax county. R. R. Nov. 27, 1837.
Miles, Mrs. S. to Rev. Bennet T. Blake, Feb. 17, Wake county. R. R. Feb. 28, 1837.
Miller, Henry Watkins to Frances Devereux, Je. 15, Raleigh. R. R. Je. 19, 1837.
Miller, Jacob to Lucinda Hall of Montgomery county, My., Randolph county. R. R. My. 16, 1837.
Mitchell, William S. of Mississippi to Ann Maria Lane, Sept., Wilmington. R. R. Oct. 2, 1837.
Mitchell, Isabella to David Hagadon, Jan., Halifax. R. R. Jan. 31, 1837.
Mitchell, Julian to James Currier, Mar. 2, Caswell county. R. R. Mar. 21, 1837.
Mixon, Mary F. to Frederick Gregory, Nov., Chowan county. R. R. Nov. 13, 1837.
Monroe, James to Catharine M'Arthur, Nov., Bladen county. R. R. Nov. 13, 1837.
Monroe, Margaret to John M. Johnson of Cumberland county, Je. 22, Moore county. R. R. Jly. 17, 1837.
Montferran, Francis to Ann Perry, Apr., Fayetteville. R. R. Apr. 18, 1837.
Montgomery, Mary Jane of Washington, D. C. to George Houston, Jr., Jly. 19, Washington, D. C. R. R. Jly. 24, 1837.

Montgomery, Susan D. to John Tally of Cabarrus county, Dec., Mecklenburg county. R. R. Dec. 18, 1837.
Moody, Albran, W. of Rockingham to Ann Williams, Apr., Richmond county. R. R. Apr. 18, 1837.
Moody, Demarius to James Burch, Nov., Rutherford county. R. R. Nov. 13, 1837.
Moore, Emma to Dr. William Cameron, Dec. 8, Hillsborough. R. R. Dec. 18, 1837.
Moore, Dr. James M. to Margaret Huggins, Je., Iredell county. R. R. Je. 6, 1837.
Moore, Nancy Ann to Nicholas Holmes, Mar., Orange county. R. R. Mar. 28, 1837.
Moore, Samuel of Pitt county to Mary Ann Williford, Mar., Edgecombe county. R. R. Mar. 21, 1837.
Mooring, Arthur to Martha E. Mayo, Sept., Martin county. R. R. Sept. 25, 1837.
Morrison, Eliza P. S. to William R. Feinster, Nov., Iredell county. R. R. Nov. 27, 1837.
Morrison, Rev. James E. to Mary Letitia Krider, Nov., Rowan county. R. R. Nov. 27, 1837.
Myers, Anne to Wm. H. Sturdevant of Wadesboro, Jan. 10, Wadesboro. R. R. Jan. 31, 1837.
Myrover, James H. of Fayetteville to Amanda C. Duhadway, Apr., Charlotte, S. C. R. R. Apr. 25, 1837.
Neel, Elmira to Israel Crow, Apr., Montgomery county. R. R. Apr. 18, 1837.
Newbould, James to Jane A. Bonner, Aug. 22, Edenton, Pasquotank county. R. R. Aug. 28, 1837.
Newsom, James W. to Louisa Drake of Jackson, Je. 27. R. R. Jly. 10, 1837.
Newsome, Mary B. of Halifax to William W. Winbourne of Verna, Mississippi, Sept. 28. R. R. Oct. 16, 1837.
Nicholson, Winifred W. to Capt. Thomas P. Matthews, Mar. 7, Halifax county. R. R. Mar. 21, 1837.
Night, Elizabeth to Elisha Cranford, Oct., Rockingham. R. R. Oct. 9, 1837.
Noe, John of Carteret county to Susan Willis of Newbern, Jan. 13, Newbern. Jan. 31, 1837.
Nuseman, Barbara to Joseph Fisher of Rowan county, Oct., Cabarrus county. R. R. Oct. 23, 1837.
Oglesby, Albert A. to Agnes B. Abernathy, Nov., Lincoln county. R. R. Nov. 6, 1837.
Oliver, John of Carteret county to Susan Jane Blaney, Nov., Newbern. R. R. Nov. 6, 1837.
Overby, Mrs. Nancy E. to William B. Adams of Rockingham, Oct., Person county. R. R. Oct. 30, 1837.
Orr, James H. of Charlotte to Mary Ann Graham of Lincoln county, Jly. 11. R. R. Jly. 24, 1837.
Outlaw, David to Mrs. Emily Ryan, Je., Bertie county. R. R. Je. 19, 1837.
Overman, Charles of Greensboro to Ann L. Allison, Apr., Charlotte. R. R. Apr. 25, 1837.
Oweno, Samuel to Sarah Langley, Nov., Beaufort county. R. R. Nov. 20, 1837.

Page, Joseph to Emily Bray, My., Randolph county. R. R. My. 9, 1837.
Pain, Mary to William Taylor, Mar., Rutherford county. R. R. Mar. 21, 1837.
Palmer, William C. of Orange county to Amarentha Gary, Apr., Marion, Alabama. R. R. My. 2, 1837.
Parker, Caroline C. S. to John L. Hargrave of Davidson county, Mar., Tarboro. R. R. Mar. 7, 1837.
Parker, Edward C. to Mrs. Celia Price, Oct., Tarborough. R. R. Oct. 9, 1837.
Parker, Elizabeth C. of Orange county to Ludolphus Henderson of Caswell county, My. 3, Orange county. R. R. My. 16, 1837.
Parker, Rebecca to John Gamble, My. 11, Wake county. R. R. My. 16, 1837.
Parks, David of Charlotte to Mrs. Ann C. Byers of Iredell county, Jly. 11, Iredell county. R. R. Jly. 31, 1837.
Parks, Mary to Matthias Ward, Mar., Rowan county. R. R. Mar. 28, 1837.
Parson, Arena to John Graham of Moore county, Apr., Montgomery county. R. R. My. 9, 1837.
Parson, William to Ruth Sexton, Oct., Jefferson, Ashe county. R. R. Oct. 30, 1837.
Partin, Maria Emeline to Robert W. Foard, Feb. 5, Rowan county. R. R. Feb. 21, 1837.
Parten, Mr. to Susan Powell, Nov., Wake county. R. R. Nov. 6, 1837.
Paton, David of Edinburg Scotland to Ann G. Farrow of Washington, Beaufort county, Aug. 10, Washington, Beaufort county. R. R. Aug. 14, 1837.
Pearce, Elizabeth to Alexander B. Summers, of New York, Oct. 5, Fayetteville. R. R. Oct. 9, 1837.
Pearson, Fanny to Fisher Johnston, Je., Orange county. R. R. Je. 13, 1837.
Peebles, Sarah S. of Northampton county to Henry J. Cannon of Raleigh, Jan. 23, Northampton county. R. R. Feb. 28, 1837.
Perkins, Nathan of Pasquotank county to Mary E. Blount of Edenton, Dec., Perquimans county. R. R. Dec. 18, 1837.
Perry, Ann to Francis Montferran, Apr, Fayetteville. R. R. Apr. 18, 1837.
Perry, Eliza to Hardy O. Conner, Oct., Trenton, Jones county. R. R. Oct. 9, 1837.
Perry, Zuretha Jane of Franklin county to Alfred Laughlin, My R. R. My. 16, 1837.
Perry, Presley P. of Franklin to Lydia D. Jones, Nov. 29, Wake county. R. R. Dec. 4, 1837.
Pervis, Rev. James of Greensboro to Eliza J. W. Baker, Oct., Salisbury. R. R. Oct. 16, 1837.
Peterson, Isham to Emma Brown, Aug. 24, Wilmington. R. R. Sept. 4, 1837.
Phares, Margaret Ann of Bladen county to Matthew Autry, Nov., Cumberland county. R. R. Nov. 20, 1837.
Phifer, Ann E. to Edwin Jones Irwin of Burke county, Dec. 6, Cabarrus county. R. R. Dec. 18, 1837.
Philips, Rachel to Hiram W. Cozart, Je. 25, Rowan county. R. R. Jly. 17, 1837.

Pickett, Lucy R. to Russell Kingsbury of Oxford, Nov., Elizabeth City. R. R. Nov. 27, 1837.
Pillow, Ruth J. to William H. Jackson, Je. 13, Giles county, Tenn. R. R. Aug. 21, 1837.
Timblick, Major to Nancy Haddock, My., Guilford county. R. R. Je. 6, 1837.
Pipkin, Julia A. of Wayne county to Wm. D. Edmonston, Aug. 10. R. R. Aug. 28, 1837.
Pitman, Edward of Mecklenburg county to Mrs. Margaret E. M'Intyre, Dec., New Hanover county. R. R. Dec. 4, 1837.
Ponsonby, Mrs. Elizabeth to Capt. Daniel Verser of Pittsylvania, Va., Oct., Milton. R. R. Oct. 16, 1837.
Pool, Theophilus of Johnston county to Rebecca Taylor, Sept., Raleigh. R. R. Sept. 18, 1837.
Porter, Henry of Raleigh to Elizabeth Ann Jones, Jan. R. R. Jan. 3, 1837.
Poumairat, Amelia of Baltimore to James M'Kimmon, Oct. 26, Raleigh. R. R. Oct. 30, 1837.
Powell, Cynthia to William H. Green of Bertie county, Nov., Hertford county. R. R. Dec. 4, 1837.
Powell, Mary to Rev. Rufus Wiley, Sept., Wake county. R. R. Sept. 25, 1837.
Powell, Susan to Mr. Parten, Nov., Wake county. R. R. Nov. 6, 1837.
Presley, Asa to Barbara Ann Fite, Feb. 5, Mecklenburg county. R. R. Feb. 21, 1837.
Price, Mrs. Celia to Edward C. Parker, Sept., Tarboro. R. R. Sept. 25, 1837.
Price, John to Margaret Gettys, Mar., Rutherford. R. R. Mar. 21, 1837.
Proctor, Mrs. Mary to Thos Simons, Dec., Edenton. R. R. Dec. 18, 1837.
Purcell, Alexander to Harriet N. M'Intire, Feb., Robeson county. R. R. Feb. 21, 1837.
Purdie, Helen Jane to Dr. Human H. Robinson, Jan., Elizabethtown, Bladen county. R. R. Jan. 3, 1837.
Purnell, Mary to James Frazier, Je. 6, Halifax. R. R. Je. 19, 1837.
Quartermus, James T. to Ruth Atkinson, Je., Greenville. R. R. Je. 6, 1837.
Ralston, Samuel to Sarah Ann Jordan, Je., Pitt county. R. R. Je. 6, 1837.
Randolph, Tighton to Caroline Whiteman, Jan., Chowan county. R. R. Jan. 31, 1837.
Rankin, Albert to Mary D. M'Murray, Sept. 26, Guilford county. R. R. Oct. 16, 1837.
Rankin, John D. to Salina R. Jenkins, Sept. 12, Lincoln county. R. R. Sept. 25, 1837.
Rankin, Joseph to Mary Linebarger, Nov., Lincoln county. R. R. Nov. 27, 1837.
Raven, Abraham, N. B. to Elizabeth Carraway, Nov., Newbern. R. R. Nov. 27, 1837.
Rawls, Charlotte of Franklin county to D. May, Mar., Wake county. R. R. Mar. 28, 1837.
Ray, Buckner to Middy Lee Lowrie, Nov., Wake county. R. R. Nov. 20, 1837.
Ray, Mary Jane B. to Morland Jackson, Mar., Orange county. R. R. Mar. 28, 1837.

Rea, Nancy A. to Stephen W. Allen, Jan. 31, Mecklenburg county. R. R. Feb. 21, 1837.
Reed, Margaret to William M. Holland, Oct., Lincoln county. R. R. Oct. 16, 1837.
Reede, Frederica to Trougot Chitty, Jly. 25, Salem. R. R. Aug. 7, 1837.
Reeves, William S. to Margaret Hudson, Oct., Cabarrus county. R. R. Oct. 30, 1837.
Reid, Frances to Samuel F. Adams, Oct., Rockingham county. R. R. Oct. 30, 1837.
Reinhardt, Lawson to Susan Shuford, Sept., Lincoln county. R. R. Oct. 2, 1837.
Richardson, John H. to Penelope Bogey, Feb. 1, Craven county. R. R. Feb. 21, 1837.
Richmond, Margaret to Capt. Lewis Malone, Mar., Caswell county. R. R. Mar. 28, 1837.
Riddick, Louisa to Isaac Hunter, Dec., Gates county. R. R. Dec. 18, 1837.
Roake, Eli C. to Martha R. Rye, Apr. 13, Davie county. R. R. My. 2, 1837.
Robards, Abel to Harriet Hyder, Oct., Rutherford county. R. R. Oct. 23, 1837.
Roberts, Henry to Ann P. Bryan of Wayne county, Aug. 8, Jericho, Wayne county. R. R. Aug. 28, 1837.
Roberts, Mary B. to Burton W. Hathaway, Mar., Edenton. R. R. Mar. 21, 1837.
Robinson, Caroline to Thomas Stewart, Nov., Lincoln county. R. R. Nov. 27, 1837.
Robinson, Dr. Human H. to Helen Jane Purdie, Jan., Elizabethtown, Bladen county. R. R. Jan. 3, 1837.
Robinson, Leah to William Abernathy, Jan. 26, Lincoln county. R. R. Feb. 21, 1837.
Robison, Robert G. to Margaret Calder, Apr., Mecklenburg county. R. R. My. 9, 1837.
Rogers, Sarah to Henry Allen, Oct. 24, Wake county. R. R. Oct. 30, 1837.
Roper, John N. to Frances T. Jolly, Je. 8, Warrenton. R. R. Je. 19, 1837.
Rose, Augustus C. of Oneida county, N. Y. to Margaret Jane Hindon, Dec., Anson county. R. R. Dec. 4, 1837.
Rose, Apphia of Stokes county to Frances P. Clingman, Apr., Morgan county, Alabama. R. R. My. 9, 1837.
Roseborough, John A. to Mary C. Belt of Rowan county, Dec., Iredell county. R. R. Dec. 18, 1837.
Ross, Frances of Mecklenburg county to Benjamin Trott of Salisbury, Je., Lancasterville, S. C. R. R. Je .13, 1837.
Royster, Irena to John Steele, Nov., Raleigh. R. R. Nov. 13, 1837.
Russell, Susan Jane to William H. Russell, Nov., Newbern. R. R. Nov. 6, 1837.
Russell, William H. to Susan Jane Russell, Nov., Newbern. R. R. Nov. 6, 1837.
Ryan, Mrs. Emily to David Outlaw, Je., Bertie county. R. R. Je. 19, 1837.
Rye, Martha R. to Eli C. Roake, Apr. 13, Davie county. R. R. My. 2, 1837.
Sain, Edmund to Rebecca Linn, Mar., Davie county. R. R. Apr. 4, 1837.
Salmon, Elizabeth T. of Fayetteville to Rev. J. S. M'Cutcheon, Oct., Oxford. R. R. Oct. 16, 1837.

Satchwell, Nancy to William C. Cordan, Je., Pitt county. R. R. Je. 6, 1837.
Saunier, Pierre to Harriet L. Williams, Oct., Charlotte. R. R. Oct. 9, 1837.
Sawyer, Sarah to Jesse Trueblood, Mar., Pasquotank county. R. R. Mar. 21, 1837.
Scales, Absalom to Eliza Carter, Oct., Stokes county. R. R. Oct. 30, 1837.
Scott, Thomas to Mary Thom, Aug. 31, Guilford county. R. R. Sept. 18, 1837.
Sears, George H. of Newbern to Henrietta C. King of Raleigh, My. 18, Linden, Alabama. R. R. Je. 6, 1837.
Seats, Abner to Rosanna Skyles, Oct., Rowan county. R. R. Oct. 30, 1837.
Seawell, Henry of Raleigh to Lucy M. Dunn, Jan. 24, Wake Forest. R. R. Jan. 31, 1837.
Seawell, Joseph to Eliza C. Campbell of Fayetteville, Je. 24, Mobile, Alabama. R. R. Jly. 17, 1837.
Sexton, Ruth to William Parsons, Oct., Jefferson, Ashe county. R. R. Oct. 30, 1837.
Shuford, Susan to Lawson Reinhardt, Sept., Lincoln county. R. R. Oct. 2, 1837.
Sifford, Thomas to Mary Dayley, Nov., Rutherford county. R. R. Nov. 13, 1837.
Simons, Thomas to Mrs. Mary Proctor, Dec., Edenton. R. R. Dec. 18, 1837.
Sink, Mary to Peter Sink, Oct., Davidson county. R. R. Oct. 30, 1837.
Sink, Peter, to Mary Sink, Oct., Davidson county. R. R. Oct. 30, 1837.
Skeen, Nathaniel to Mary Snider, Apr., Davidson county. R. R. Apr. 18, 1837.
Skinner, Emily to Dr. Charles E. Johnson of Edenton, Nov., Chowan county. R. R. Nov. 13, 1837.
Skinner, Sarah F. to Samuel T. Bond, Jan. 5, Edenton. R. R. Jan. 31, 1837.
Skinner, Stephen to Jane Fletcher, Nov., Chowan county. R. R. Nov. 27, 1837.
Skyles, Rosanna to Abner Seats, Oct., Rowan county. R. R. Oct. 30, 1837.
Smith, Miss A. N. to Adam Holt, Jan., Halifax. R. R. Jan. 31, 1837.
Smith, Anna to John Kinley, Jly. 2, Guilford county. R. R. Jly. 17, 1837.
Smith, Benjamin H. to Mary Love, Nov., Halifax county. R. R. Nov. 27, 1837.
Smith, Clarissa to Nathaniel Brock, Nov., Davie county. R. R. Nov. 20, 1837.
Smith, Joshua T. to Elizabeth T. Lindsay, Oct., Rockingham. R. R. Oct. 23, 1837.
Smith, Richard to Elizabeth Elliott, Sept., Edenton. R. R. Oct. 2, 1837.
Smith, William F. C. to Temperance Hart, Mar., Orange county. R. R. Mar. 28, 1837.
Smithwick, M. to Margaret Ann Adams, Je., Pitt county. R. R. Je. 6, 1837.
Smithwick, William to Winifred Gill, Nov., Bertie county. R. R. Nov. 13, 1837.
Smoot, Mary to Alexander G. Fraley, Mar., Davie county. R. R. Mar. 28, 1837.
Smoot, Capt. Samuel to Nancy Carter, Nov., Davie county. R. R. Nov. 20, 1837.

Snider, Mary to Nathaniel Skeen, Apr., Davidson county. R. R. Apr. 18, 1837.
Snively, Mrs. to John H. Hall, Nov. 16, Fayetteville. R. R. Nov. 20, 1837.
Southall, James to Sarah Wheeler, Je., Hertford. R. R. Je. 19, 1837.
Spence, Joseph to Lavinia Elliott, Dec., Perquimans county. R. R. Dec. 4, 1837.
Spencer, William S. of Morganton to Eliza Ann Tate, Oct., Burke county. R. R. Oct. 16, 1837.
Staley, Charity to Samuel Devany, Dec., Guilford county. R. R. Dec. 18, 1837.
Steele, John to Irena Royster, Nov. 8, Raleigh. R. R. Nov. 13, 1837.
Stevens, Henry to Nancy Walton, Feb. 1, Wake county. R. R. Feb. 14, 1837.
Stewart, Sealy to Peter M'Kay, Feb., Robeson county. R. R. Feb. 21, 1837.
Stewart, Thomas to Caroline Robinson, Nov., Lincoln county. R. R. Nov. 27, 1837.
Stimson, Lucinda Jane of Pittsylvania county, Va., to Pleasant Fitzgerald of Milton, Feb. 14. R. R. Feb. 28, 1837.
Stockton, William F. to Mary Wilson, Apr. 27, Stokes county. R. R. My. 16, 1837.
Stokes, Dudley G. of Caswell county to Frances Bethell of Rockingham county, Feb. 9. R. R. Feb. 28, 1837.
Sturdevant, Wm. H. of Wadesboro to Anne Myers, Jan. 10, Wadesboro. R. R. Jan. 31, 1837.
Summers, Alexander B. of New York to Elizabeth L. Pearce, Oct. 5, Fayetteville. R. R. Oct. 9, 1837.
Summers, Belinda to John T. Tomlinson, Je., Iredell county. R. R. Je. 6, 1837.
Summers, Thomas F. to Casandra Tomlinson, Oct., Iredell county. R. R. Oct. 30, 1837.
Swindell, Penelope to Samuel Brooks, Jly., Hyde county. R. R. Aug. 7, 1837.
Swink, Mary to Tobias Wise, Mar., Rowan county. R. R. Apr. 4, 1837.
Tally, John of Cabarrus county to Susan D. Montgomery, Dec., Mecklenburg county. R. R. Dec. 18, 1837.
Tate, Eliza Ann to William S. Spencer of Morganton, Oct., Burke county. R. R. Oct. 16, 1837.
Tate, Maj. Robert McD. to Sarah E. Butler, Oct., Burke county. R. R. Oct. 16, 1837.
Taylor, George W. to Sidney Ann Bragg, Mar., Washington, Beaufort county. R. R. Mar. 7, 1837.
Taylor, Rebecca to Theophilus Pool of Johnston county, Sept., Raleigh. R. R. Sept. 18, 1837.
Taylor, Sarah to Capt. John Lunn, Mar., Davie county. R. R. Apr. 4, 1837.
Taylor, William to Mary Pain, Mar., Rutherford county. R. R. Mar. 21, 1837.
Tays, Capt. Robert to Frances A. James, Nov., Iredell county. R. R. Nov. 27, 1837.
Teague, William to Elizabeth Watts, Oct., Iredell county. R. R. Oct. 30, 1837.

Thom, Mary to Thomas Scott, Aug. 31, Guilford county. R. R. Sept. 18, 1837.
Todd, Mary Ann to Francis A. James, Apr., Salisbury. R. R. My. 9, 1837.
Tomlinson, Casandra to Thomas F. Summers, Oct., Iredell county. R. R. Oct. 30, 1837.
Tomlinson, John T. to Belinda Summers, Je., Iredell county. R. R. Je. 6, 1837.
Tomlinson, Mr. to Milanda Cook of this State, Jly. 27, Madison county, Tenn. R. R. Aug. 28, 1837.
Tomlinson, William to Elizabeth Dobbins, Mar., Iredell county. R. R. Mar. 28, 1837.
Trott, Benjamin of Salisbury to Frances Ross of Mecklenburg county, Je., Lancasterville, S. C. R. R. Je. 13, 1837.
Trueblood, Jesse to Sarah Sawyer, Mar., Pasquotank county. R. R. Mar. 21, 1837.
Turnage, Rhody to Robert Davis, Jly., Wayne county. R. R. Aug. 7, 1837.
Twitty, Jane E. to William A. Williams, Nov., Warren county. R. R. Nov. 13, 1837.
Tyson, Mrs. Ann to Joshua Carmon of Fayetteville, Nov., Moore county. R. R. Nov. 20, 1837.
Vaughan, Betsey to William Johnson, Mar. 20, Wake Forest. R. R. Apr. 25, 1837.
Verser, Capt. Daniel of Pittsylvania, Va. to Mrs. Elizabeth Ponsonby, Oct., Milton. R. R. Oct. 16, 1837.
Waddill, Lucy P. to Jacob Letho, Je., Randolph county. R. R. Je. 13, 1837.
Walker, Irena to Green H. Lee, Oct., Davidson county. R. R. Oct. 9, 1837.
Walker, William to Amelia Carrington, Feb., Orange county. R. R. Feb. 14, 1837.
Walton, Nancy to Henry Stevens, Feb. 1, Wake county. R. R. Feb. 14, 1837.
Walton, William to Catharine Grimes, Je. 25, Rowan county. R. R. Jly. 17, 1837.
Ward, Matthias to Mary Parks, Mar., Rowan county. R. R. Mar. 28, 1837.
Warren, Mary W. to Kimbrough Jones, Sept. 19, Wake county. R. R. Sept. 25, 1837.
Washington, N. H. of Virginia to Agnes Ellet Hickman of Warrenton, Mar. 8, Warrenton. R. R. Mar. 21, 1837.
Watt, Lenora to James M. Williamson of Person county, Oct., Rockingham county. R. R. Oct. 9, 1837.
Watts, Elizabeth to William Teague, Oct., Iredell county. R. R. Oct. 30, 1837.
Weaver, Conrod to Nancy Weston, Sept., Lincoln county. R. R. Oct. 2, 1837.
Webb, Mary Ann of Person county to John Blackwell of Granville county, Aug. 22. R. R. Sept. 18, 1837.
Weston, Nancy to Conrod Weaver, Sept., Lincoln county. R. R. Oct. 2, 1837.
Wharton, Newton to Eleanor M'Murry, Sept. 26, Guilford county. R. R. Oct. 16, 1837.
Wheeler, Sarah to James Southall, Je., Hertford. R. R. Je. 19, 1837.

White, Eliza to Jeremiah Fitchel, Nov., Iredell county. R. R. Nov. 27, 1837.
White, Mary Ann of Iredell county to Philip O. Kelly of Lincoln county, Jan. 29, Iredell county. R. R. Feb. 14, 1837.
Whiteman, Caroline to Randolph Tighten, Jan., Chowan county. R. R. Jan. 31, 1837.
Whittenburg, Louisa Shailor of Hartford, Conn. to John Banks of Wilmington, Jan., Cumberland county. R. R. Jan. 31, 1837.
Wiley, Rev. Rufus to Mary Powell, Sept., Wake county. R. R. Sept. 25, 1837.
Wilkes, Rev. Thomas U. of Georgia to Maria Louisa Graves, Nov., Caswell county. R. R. Nov. 13, 1837.
Williams, Ann to Albran W. Moody of Rockingham, Apr., Richmond county. R. R. Apr. 18, 1837.
Williams, Augustine to Sarah Ledbetter, Jly. 16, Lincoln county. R. R. Aug. 7, 1837.
Williams, Harriet L. to Pierre Saunier, Oct., Charlotte. R. R. Oct. 9, 1837.
Wilkins, John H. to Mrs. Mildred Bowden, Oct., Rutherford county. R. R. Oct. 9, 1837.
Williams, Mary B. to Sam'l S. Biddle of Craven county, Nov., Beaufort county. R. R. Nov. 13, 1837.
Williams, Rosina to Andrew Brown, Apr., Rowan county. R. R. Apr. 18, 1837.
Williams, Susan to Francis Hawes, Jly. 25, Wilmington. R. R. Aug. 7, 1837.
Williams, Thomas to Nancy M. Gantt, Nov., Rutherford county. R. R. Nov. 20, 1837.
Williams, William A. to Jane E. Twitty, Nov., Warren county. R. R. Nov. 13, 1837.
Williamson, James M. of Person county to Lenora Watt, Oct., Rockingham county. R. R. Oct. 9, 1837.
Williford, Mary Ann to Samuel Moore of Pitt county, Mar., ·Edgecombe county. R. R. Mar. 21, 1837.
Willis, Susan of Newbern to John Noe of Carteret county, Jan. 12, Newbern. R. R. Jan. 31, 1837.
Wilson, Dr. Charles C. to Sarah M. Lovick, Aug. 24, Newbern. R. R. Sept. 4, 1837.
Wilson, Harriet W. to Thomas S. Hoskins, Aug. 22, Perquimans county. R. R. Aug. 28, 1937.
Wilson, Mary to Eleazer Marshall, Nov., Iredell county. R. R. Nov. 27, 1837.
Wilson, Mary to William F. Stockton, Apr. 27, Stokes county. R. R. My. 16, 1837.
Wilson, William to Cynthia Coward, Nov., Rutherford county. R. R. Nov. 27, 1837.
Winbourne, William W. of Verna Mississippi to Mary B. Newsom of Halifax, Sept. 28. R. R. Oct. 16, 1837.
Wise, Tobias to Mary Swink, Mar., Rowan county. R. R. Apr. 4, 1837.
Woodruff, Mary Jane to John H. Hurt, Oct., Surry county. R. R. Oct. 16, 1837.

Woodson, Alexander of Rockingham to Mary Ann Cloud, Mar., Stokes county. R. R. Mar. 21, 1837.
Woodward, William to Sally Dyer, Apr., Chapel Hill. R. R. Apr. 25, 1837.
Wright, Catharine A. to William Wright, Jr., Oct. 10, Duplin county. R. R. Oct. 23, 1837.
Wright, William, Jr., to Catharine A. Wright, Oct. 10, Duplin county. R. R. Oct. 23, 1837.
Yancey, Mary C. to Giles Mebane of Orange county, Mar. 8, Milton. R. R. Mar. 21, 1837.
Yarbrough, Col. Edward to Mrs. Sarah Giles, Jan., Salisbury. R. R. Jan. 10, 1837.
Young, Levi W. of Alabama to Sarah Clancy, Mar. 17, Hillsborough. R. R. Mar. 28, 1837.
Young, T. Melmoth of Statesville to Maria M'Neely, Dec., Mocksville. R. R. Dec. 18, 1837.
Yount, Andrew to Elizabeth Hamilton, Nov., Lincoln county. R. R. Nov. 27, 1837.

1838

Baldwin, John R. to Mary Craig, Oct., Orange county. R. R. Nov. 5, 1838.
Boon, Julia Ann to Dr. Alexander F. Telfair, Nov. 18, Johnston county. R. R. Nov. 26, 1838.
Bost, Elizabeth to William Wallace, Oct., Rowan county. R. R. Nov. 5, 1838.
Boykin, Edwin to Jane E. Jones, Nov. 6, Johnston county. R. R. Nov. 19, 1838.
Cannady, Angeline to Jackson Estes, Oct. 17, Wake county. R. R. Nov. 5, 1838.
Chadwick, James to Jane Nicholson, Nov. 8, Raleigh. R. R. Nov. 12, 1838.
Cockerall, R. W. of Nash county to Wheaton Williams, Dec., Greensboro, Alabama. R. R. Dec. 31, 1838.
Craig, Mary to John R. Baldwin, Oct., Orange county. R. R. Nov. 5, 1838.
Crenshaw, Martha J. to Michael W. Thompson, Nov. 15, Wake Forest. R. R. Nov. 19, 1838.
Deale, Eli to Eliza Rudisill, Nov., Lincoln county. R. R. Nov. 19, 1838.
Estes, Jackson to Angeline Cannady, Oct. 17, Wake county. R. R. Nov. 5, 1838.
Fort, Thomas to Celia Ann Selby, Oct. 31, Raleigh. R. R. Nov. 5, 1838.
Garey, Rebecca Ridley of Northampton county to Wm. G. Mebane, Dec. 12, Hertford county. R. R. Dec. 31, 1838.
Hamlet, Martha to John Allen, Nov., Person county. R. R. Nov. 12, 1838.
Hart, Nancy to Thomas Pratt, Oct., Orange county. R. R. Nov. 5, 1838.
Holland, Franklin H. to Mary Ann Quin, Nov., Lincoln county. R. R. Nov. 19, 1838.
Holt, Michael W. to Ann Webb, Nov., Hillsboro. R. R. Nov. 19, 1838.
Jones, Jane E. to Edwin Boykin, Nov. 6, Johnston county. R. R. Nov. 19, 1838.
Jones, Priscilla D. to John White of Warrenton, Nov. 28, Warren county. R. R. Dec. 3, 1838.
King, Dr. Wm. R. to Temperance W. Tunstall, Nov. 28, Franklin county. R. R. Dec. 24, 1838.

Lea, William Eason to Bedy H. White, Oct. 27, Raleigh. R. R. Nov. 5, 1838.
M'Bane, H. to Sarah Ann Parker, Nov. 24, Raleigh. R. R. Nov. 26, 1838.
M'Daniel, Martha of Macon county to Col. Isaac Wilkerson, Oct. 21, Yancey county. R. R. Dec. 24, 1838.
Mebane, Wm. G. to Rebecca Ridley Garey of Northampton county, Dec. 12, Hertford county. R. R. Dec. 31, 1838.
Nicholson, Jane to James Chadwick, Nov. 8, Raleigh. R. R. Nov. 12, 1838.
Parker, Sarah Ann to H. M'Bane, Nov. 24, Raleigh. R. R. Nov. 26, 1838.
Perkins, Martha S. to Franklin D. Reinhart, Nov., Lincoln county. R. R. Nov. 19, 1838.
Pleasants, Susan to John Roseman, Nov. 10, Raleigh. R. R. Nov. 12, 1838.
Pratt, Thomas G. to Nancy Hart, Oct., Orange county. R. R. Nov. 5, 1838.
Quin, Mary Ann to Franklin H. Holland, Nov., Lincoln county. R. R. Nov. 19, 1838.
Ray, Henry C. to Mrs. Cynthia Baily, Mar., Wake county. R. R. Mar. 18, 1838.
Reinhardt, Franklin D. to Martha S. Perkins, Nov., Lincoln county. R. R. Nov. 19, 1838.
Roseman, John to Susan Pleasants, Nov. 10, Raleigh. R. R. Nov. 12, 1838.
Rudisill, Eliza to Eli Deale, Nov., Lincoln county. R. R. Nov. 19, 1838.
Sechler, Rosina to Henry Sloop, Oct., Rowan county. R. R. Nov. 5, 1838.
Selby, Celia Ann to Thomas Fort, Oct. 31, Raleigh. R. R. Nov. 5, 1838.
Sloop, Henry to Rosina Sechler, Oct., Rowan county. R. R. Nov. 5, 1838.
Sully, Ellen of Philadelphia to Col. John H. Wheeler of Charlotte, Nov. 8, Philadelphia. R. R. Nov. 12, 1838.
Telfair, Dr. Alexander F. to Julia Ann Boon, Nov. 18, Johnston county. R. R. Nov. 26, 1838.
Thompson, Michael W. to Martha Crenshaw, Nov. 15, Wake Forest. R. R. Nov. 19, 1838.
Tunstall, Temperance W. to Dr. Wm. R. King, Nov. 28, Franklin county. R. R. Dec. 24, 1838.
Wallace, William to Elizabeth Bost, Oct., Rowan county. R. R. Nov. 5, 1838.
Webb, Ann to Dr. Michael Holt, Nov., Hillsboro. R. R. Nov. 19, 1838.
White, Bedy H. to William Eason Lea, Oct. 27, Raleigh. R. R. Nov. 5, 1838.
White, John of Warrenton to Priscilla D. Jones, Nov. 28, Warren county. R. R. Dec. 3, 1838.
Wheeler, Col. John H. of Charlotte to Ellen Sully of Philadelphia, Nov. 8, Philadelphia. R. R. Nov. 12, 1838.
Wilkerson, Col. Isaac to Martha M'Daniel of Macon county, Oct. 21, Yancey county. R. R. Dec. 24, 1838.
Williams, Wheaton to R. W. Cockerall of Nash county, Dec., Greensboro, Alabama. R. R. Dec. 31, 1838.

1839

Adams, Frances of Richland District, S. C. to George Washington Lowe of Washington, D. C., Feb. 12. R. R. Mar. 4, 1839.
Agle, Sophia to Jesse Hodge, Dec., Rowan county. R. R. Dec. 7, 1839.

Allen, Elizabeth of Charleston, S. C. to Rev. Thomas W. Campbell, Sept., Salisbury. R. R. Sept. 21, 1839.

Allen, John to Martha Hamlet, Nov., Person county. R. R. Nov. 12, 1839.

Allen, Martha of Halifax county to Maj. Micajah T. J. Alston of Mississippi, Nov. 11. R. R. Dec. 7, 1839.

Allred, Mary to Mathias D. Pray, Aug., Randolph county. R. R. Aug. 31, 1839.

Almon, John W. to Eliza Covington, Apr., Richmond county. R. R. Apr. 13, 1839.

Alston, Maj. Micajah T. J. of Mississippi to Martha Allen of Halifax county, Nov. 11. R. R. Dec. 7, 1839.

Anderson, Albert G. of Hillsborough to Jane Thatch, Jly., Perquimans county. R. R. Jly. 20, 1839.

Anderson, Mary May to Edwin T. Yancey of Warrenton, Dec., La Grange, Tenn. R. R. Dec. 14, 1839.

Andrew, Martha to Matthew Ward, Mar., Randolph county. R. R. Mar. 23, 1839.

Armstrong, Frances to William Morrow, Jr., Feb. 14, Orange county. R. R. Mar. 30, 1839.

Austin, Catharine E. to Wm. Martin Crenshaw of Wake Forest, Feb. 12, Tarboro. R. R. Mar. 18, 1839.

Bailey, Mrs. Cynthia to Henry C. Ray, Mar., Wake county. R. R. Mar. 18, 1839.

Barbee, Sidney M. to Frances Hardie, My. 8, Raleigh. R. R. My. 11, 1839.

Bassarere, John to Dorcas H. Carraway, Aug., Newbern. R. R. Aug. 17, 1839.

Baucom, John to Fanny Jordan, Jan., Wake county. R. R. Jan. 21, 1839.

Bell, Agnes, H. to Thomas Sanford of Wilmington, Nov. 7, Cumberland county. R. R. Nov. 9, 1839.

Bell, William C. to Alida Moore Maria Manney, Jan., Beaufort. R. R. Feb. 4, 1839.

Benners, Sarah F. of Craven county to James H. Norwood of Hillsboro, Apr. 3, Franklin county. R. R. Apr. 20, 1839.

Boles, Mastin to Eliza M'Kenzie, Dec., Montgomery county. R. R. Dec. 7, 1839.

Bostian, Jacob to Sarah Rainer, Jly., Salisbury. R. R. Jly. 6, 1839.

Bower, Col. George of Jefferson to America Rosseau of Wilkes county, Dec., Wilkes county. R. R. Dec. 14, 1839.

Boylan, Priscilla P. of Raleigh to Judge William T. Brown of Nashville, Mar., Tennessee. R. R. Apr. 6, 1839.

Bragg, Dr. John of Petersburg, Va. to Maria Hill, Apr. 24, Raleigh. R. R. Apr. 27, 1839.

Brazzel, Rebecca to Jesse Rawlings, Aug., Halifax. R. R. Aug. 17, 1839.

Brown, Salina F. to Nathan B. Walker, Je. 24, Louisburg. R. R. Je. 29, 1839.

Brown, Judge William T. of Nashville to Mrs. Priscilla P. Boylan of Raleigh, Mar., Tennessee. R. R. Apr. 6, 1839.

Brummel, Lucy to Rev. Thomas Jones of this State, Aug., Davidson county. R. R. Sept. 7, 1839.

Busbee, Elizabeth W. to Henry H. Harris, Dec. 19, Wake county. R. R. Dec. 21, 1839.

Bynum, Hon. Jesse A. of Halifax to Mrs. Emeline Ray of Rapids, La., Je. 28. R. R. Jly. 6, 1839.
Bynum, Mark to Mary Clegg, Feb. 18, Chatham county. R. R. Mar. 23, 1839.
Caldwell, David F. to Mrs. Matthew Troy, Aug., Salisbury. R. R. Aug. 17, 1839.
Calvin, N. M'Adoo to Isabella M'Connell, Mar., Guilford county. R. R. Mar. 23, 1839.
Cameron, Susan to John A. Moore, Je., Newbern. R. R. Je. 15, 1839.
Campbell, Henrietta C. to Murphy V. Jones of Alabama, Mar., Cumberland county. R. R. Mar. 30, 1839.
Campbell, Rev. Thos. W. to Elizabeth Allen of Charleston, S. C., Sept., Salisbury. R. R. Sept. 21, 1839.
Carrol, Henry W. of York District, S. C. to Lavinia Weathers, Sept., Lincoln county. R. R. Sept. 14, 1839.
Carter, John T. of Petersburg, Va. to Susan J. Thompson of Wake county, Aug. 11, Wake county. R. R. Aug. 17, 1839.
Cason, Sidney to William Jarman, Dec., Anson county. R. R. Dec. 7, 1839.
Cauble, Margaret to Moses Trexler, Aug., Rowan county. R. R. Sept., 7, 1839.
Charles, George W. to Frances D. Gregory, Feb., Elizabeth City. R. R. Feb. 11, 1839.
Clegg, Mary to Mark Bynum, Feb. 18, Chatham county. R. R. Mar. 23, 1839.
Coal, Dennis to Lucinda Knipper, Apr. 9, Wake county. R. R. My. 4, 1839.
Coleman, Mrs. Lucy Ann of this State to Henry W. Conner of Lincoln District, Mar. 9, Washington, D. C. R. R. Mar. 23, 1839.
Collins, Eliza Ann to William Edwards, Feb. 14, Orange county. R. R. Mar. 30, 1839.
Conner, Henry W. of Lincoln District to rMs. Lucy Ann Coleman of this State, Mar. 9, Washington, D. C. R. R. Mar. 23, 1839.
Connor, Maria to Frederick Linebarger, Sept., Lincoln county. R. R. Sept. 14, 1839.
Covington, Eliza to John W. Almon, Apr., Richmond county. R. R. Apr. 13, 1839.
Cox, James W. of Lenoir county to Sally Sherard of Wayne county, Mar. 12. R. R. Mar. 23, 1839.
Cozart, Charles to Sarah Lyrely, Dec., Rowan county. R. R. Dec. 14, 1839.
Craven, Emeline A. to Samuel J. Finch, Jly. 25, Randolph county. R. R. Aug. 17, 1839.
Crenshaw, Wm. Martin of Wake Forest to Catharine E. Austin, Feb. 12, Tarboro. R. R. Mar. 18, 1839.
Davis, Jane to Duncan Smith, Apr., Richmond county. R. R. Apr. 13, 1839.
Davis, Peter R. Jr. to Catharine N. White, Nov. 6, Warren county. R. R. Nov. 23, 1839.
Dawson, Miss to Mr. Ellison, Aug., Randolph county. R. R. Aug. 31, 1839.
Deberry, Ann to C. W. Wooley of Lawrenceville, Dec., Montgomery county. R. R. Dec. 14, 1839.
Dejarnatt, Capt. Wm. C. to Huldah Roberts, Dec., Surry county. R. R. Dec. 7, 1839.

Dickinson, Jeanette D. to Edward E. Hall, Sept., Newbern. R. R. Sept. 28, 1839.
Dixon, Elizabeth to John R. Lawrence, Aug., Rowan county. R. R. Aug. 31, 1839.
Dobbin, Anness C. to John W. Huske, Jan., Fayetteville. R. R. Jan. 21, 1839.
Drake, Dr. John C. of Nashville to Mary Ann Flewellen of Monroe county, Ga., Apr. 3, Monroe county, Ga. R. R. Apr. 20, 1839.
Dunbar, Sophia to Capt. Richard J. Wade of this State, Mar., New York, N. Y. R. R. Mar. 30, 1839.
Earp, Grizzy to Bryan Jordan, Jan., Wake county. R. R. Jan. 21, 1839.
Edwards, Sylvester to Miss M. Rhodes, Jly. 4, Wake county. R. R. Jly. 13, 1839.
Edwards, William to Eliza Ann Collins, Feb. 14, Orange county. R. R. Mar. 30, 1839.
Ellison, Mr. to Miss Dawson, Aug., Randolph county. R. R. Aug. 31, 1839.
Ferrell, Ann to Francis P. Haywood of Raleigh, Sept. 10, Florida. R. R. Sept. 28, 1839.
Ferrell, Elizabeth to Willie Loyd, Sept., Wake county. R. R. Oct. 5, 1839.
Finch, Samuel J. to Emeline A. Craven, Jly. 25, Randolph county. R. R. Aug. 17, 1839.
Flewellen, Mary Ann of Monroe county, Georgia to Dr. John C. Drake of Nashville, Apr. 3, Monroe county, Ga. R. R. Apr. 20, 1839.
Forney, Susan to Richard V. Michaux, Aug., Burke county. R. R. Aug. 17, 1839.
Frederick, Elizabeth J. to Charles Henry of New Hanover county, Apr., Sampson county. R. R. Apr. 6, 1839.
Fuller, Achrebolinda to William B. Roberts, Apr. 9, Wake county. R. R. My. 4, 1839.
Gee, John to Sarah Holloway, Nov. 14, Wake county. R. R. Dec. 7, 1839.
Gillaspie, D. A. to Matilda F. Webster, Aug., Guilford county. R. R. Sept. 7, 1839..
Gilmer, James to Nancy Ann Smith, Apr., Guilford county. R. R. Apr. 6, 1839.
Gilmore, William to Rachael Williams, Jan., Fayetteville. R. R. Jan. 21, 1839.
Gordon, Eliza M. to William M. Walker, Sept. 11, Granville county. R. R. Sept. 21, 1839.
Goskins, Rob. to Mrs. Catharine E. Kelly, My. 1, Washington, Beaufort county. R. R. My. 11, 1839.
Grant, Edmund, to Celia Richardson, Je., Newbern. R. R. Je. 15, 1839.
Grant, James of Raleigh to Eliza Hubbard of Massachusetts, Feb., Chicago, Ill. R. R. Feb. 25, 1839.
Gray, Thomas to Miss E. Locke, Aug., Davie county. R. R. Aug. 17, 1839.
Gray, Thomas to Mary Ann Treadwell, Jan., Sampson county. R. R. Jan. 21, 1839.
Gregory, Frances D. to George W. Charles, Feb., Elizabeth City. R. R. Feb. 11, 1839.
Grice, Mrs. Susan R. of Sampson county to William Watson, Jan., Fayetteville. R. R. Jan. 21, 1839.

Gwyn, James of Wilkesboro to Mary A. Lenoir, Jly., Fort Defiance, Wilkes county. R. R. Jly. 6, 1839.
Hall, Edward E. to Jeanette D. Dickinson, Sept., Newbern. R. R. Sept. 28, 1839.
Hall, Elizabeth to Wilson Veach, Aug., Davie county. R. R. Aug. 1?, 1839.
Hamblin, Mary to Alfred E. Outz, Apr. 25, Wake county. R. R. My. 11, 1839.
Hanrahan, Mrs. Ann to Daniel Y. Shine, Aug., Newbern. R. R. Aug. 17, 1839.
Hardie, Frances to Sidney M. Barbee, My. 8, Raleigh. R. R. My. 11, 1839.
Harrell, Dr. J. to Mary Lockwood, Feb., Elizabeth City. R. R. Feb. 11, 1839.
Harrell, Melinda to Daniel Mills, Sept., Lincolnton. R. R. Sept. 21, 1839.
Harris, Mary to Richard Phillips of West Tennessee, Jly. 29, Wake Forest. R. R. Sept. 7, 1839.
Harris, Henry H. to Elizabeth W. Busbee, Dec. 19, Wake county. R. R. Dec. 21, 1839.
Harrison, William K. to Martha Verser, Nov., Caswell county. R. R. Nov. 23, 1839.
Haughton, Mary to Isaac Rhew, Feb. 14, Orange county. R. R. Mar. 30, 1839.
Hayes, Elizabeth L. to Charles L. Torrence of Salisbury, Apr., Lincoln county. R. R. Apr. 13, 1839.
Haywood, Francis P. of Raleigh to Ann Ferrell, Sept. 10, Florida. R. R. Sept. 28, 1839.
Henderson, David Wallace of Rockingham county to Martha Ann Irvine, Je., Person county. R. R. Je. 22, 1839.
Henderson, Margaret E. to Wm. T. Outlaw, Apr. 25, Raleigh. R. R. Apr. 27, 1839.
Hendricks, Rebecca to Emsby M'Masters, Aug., Randolph county. R. R. Aug. 31, 1839.
Henry, Charles of New Hanover county to Elizabeth J. Frederick, Apr., Sampson county. R. R. Apr. 6, 1839.
Hester, Elizabeth Ann to Wm. H. Lyon, Jan. 31, Granville county. R. R. Feb. 18, 1839.
Hicks, Thomas to Henrietta Norwood, Mar., Wake county. R. R. Mar. 18, 1839.
Hill, Dr. B. J. of Duplin county to Mrs. Ann Maria Ward, Jly., Wayne county. R. R. Jly. 20, 1839.
Hill, Christopher D. to Elizabeth C. Williams, Sept., Duplin county. R. R. Sept. 28, 1839.
Hill, Maria to Dr. John Bragg of Petersburg, Va., Apr. 24, Raleigh. R. R. Apr. 27, 1839.
Hinton, Delia to John D. Powell of Wake Forest, Apr. 30, Wake county. R. R. Je. 8, 1839.
Hobart, Mary Elizabeth of Hingham, Mass. to William Stringer, Nov. 30, Raleigh. R. R. Dec. 7, 1839.
Hodge, Jesse to Sophia Agle, Dec., Rowan county. R. R. Dec. 7, 1839.
Holloway, Sarah to John Gee, Nov. 14, Wake county. R. R. Dec. 7, 1839.
Hopkins, Solomon of Pennsylvania to Esther Ann M'Gee, Mar., Greensboro. R. R. Mar. 23, 1839.

Hord, Martha P. to Joseph M'Entire, Mar., Lincoln county. R. R. Mar. 30, 1839.
Hord, Richard T to Margaret Thompson of Rutherford, Mar., Lincoln county. R. R. Mar. 30, 1839.
Howard, James W. of Jones county to Sarah A. G. Williams, Nov., Beaufort county. R. R. Nov. 23, 1839.
Hubbard, Eliza of Massachusetts to James Grant of Raleigh, Feb., Chicago, Ill. R. R. Feb. 25, 1839.
Hunter, Jane to Rev. Wm. S. Johnson of Raleigh, Oct. 3, Wake county. R. R. Oct. 12, 1839.
Huske, John W. to Anness C. Dobbin, Jan., Fayetteville. R. R. Jan. 21, 1839.
Irvine, Martha Ann to David Wallace Henderson of Rockingham county, Je., Person county. R. R. Je. 22, 1839.
Jackson, John A. to Matilda Sexton, Sept., Wake county. R. R. Oct. 5, 1839.
Jarmon, William to Sidney Cason, Dec., Anson county. R. R. Dec. 7, 1839.
Jenkins, Lucy Ann to William Meacham, Jr., Apr., Richmond county. R. R. Apr. 13, 1839.
Johnson, Rev. Wm. S. of Raleigh to Jane Hunter, Oct. 3, Wake county. R. R. Oct. 12, 1839.
Jones, Alexander S. of Mecklenburg county, Va. to Lucinda J. Littlejohn of Oxford, Apr. 3, Granville county. R. R. Apr. 13, 1839.
Jones, Isaac C. to Miss M. Yeargam, Aug., Randolph county. R. R. Aug. 31, 1839.
Jones, Mary Eliza to J. B. Somervell, Feb., Warren county. R. R. Mar. 4, 1839.
Jones, Murphy V. of Alabama to Henrietta C. Campbell, Mar., Cumberland county. R. R. Mar. 30, 1839.
Jones, Rev. Thomas of this State to Lucy Brummel, Aug., Davidson county. R. R. Sept. 7, 1839.
Jeffreys, Isabella M. to C. V. Lanier of Danville, Jan., Caswell county. R. R. Feb. 4, 1839.
Jordan, Bryan to Grizzy Earp, Jan., Wake county. R. R. Jan. 21, 1839.
Jordan, Fanny to John Baucom, Jan., Wake county. R. R. Jan. 21, 1839.
Kelly, Catharine E. to Rob Goskins, My. 1, Washington, Beaufort county. R. R. My. 11, 1839.
Killian, Francis J. to Marcus H. Rudisill, Sept., Lincoln county. R. R. Sept. 14, 1839.
King, Martha to Etheldred Thomas, Nov. 14, Wake county. R. R. Dec. 7, 1839.
King, Susan Ann to James J. Sledge, Feb., Warren county. R. R. Mar. 4, 1839.
Kinney, Mary A. to Rev. Harvey Stanly of Raleigh, Aug., Elizabeth City. R. R. Aug. 31, 1839.
Knight, Nathaniel to Mary J. M'Rae, Nov., Lawrenceville, Montgomery county. R. R. Nov. 9, 1839.
Knipper, Lucinda to Dennis Coal, Apr. 9, Wake county. R. R. My. 4, 1839.
Kyle, Eleanor of Raleigh to Col. Walter Leake Otey, Aug. 1, Raleigh. R. R. Aug. 3, 1839.
Leach, Mary to John M'Arthur, Mar., Robeson county. R. R. Mar. 30, 1839.

Leach, Col. John to Mary Ann M'Neill, Mar., Robeson county. R. R. Mar. 23, 1839.
Lanier, C. V. of Danville, Va. to Isabella M. Jeffreys, Jan., Caswell county. R. R. Feb. 4, 1839.
Lawrence, John R. to Elizabeth Dixon, Aug., Rowan county. R. R. Aug. 31, 1839.
Legrand, Hampton to Martha Whitaker of Halifax, Jly., Richmond county. R. R. Jly. 20, 1839.
Lenoir, Mary A. to James Gwyn of Wilksboro, Jly., Fort Defiance, Wilkes county. R. R. Jly. 6, 1839.
Linebarger, Frederick to Maria Connor, Sept., Lincoln county. R. R. Sept. 14, 1839.
Littlejohn, John Lucinda J. of Oxford to Alexander S. Jones of Mecklenburg county, Va., Apr. 3, Granville county. R. R. Apr. 13, 1839.
Locke, Miss E. to Thomas Gray, Aug., Davie county. R. R. Aug. 17, 1839.
Lockwood, Mrs. Mary to Dr. J. Harrell, Feb., Elizabeth City. R. R. Feb. 11, 1839.
Lowe, George Washington of Washington, D. C. to Frances Adams of Richland District, S. C., Feb. 12. R. R. Mar. 4, 1839.
Loyd, Joseph to Mary Seawel, Sept., Granville county. R. R. Oct. 5, 1839.
Loyd, Willie to Elizabeth Ferrell, Sept., Wake county. R. R. Oct. 5, 1839.
Lumsden, Martha to Neill M'Pherson, My., Fayetteville. R. R. My. 4, 1839.
Lyon, Wm. H. to Elizabeth Ann Hester, Jan. 31, Granville county. R. R. Feb. 18, 1839.
Lyrely, Sarah to Charles Cozart, Dec., Rowan county. R. R. Dec. 14, 1839.
Lytle, Dr. James H. to Jane H. Reinhardt, Dec., Lincolnton. R. R. Dec. 7, 1839.
M'Adoo, Calvin N. to Isabella M'Connel, Mar., Guilford county. R. R. Mar. 23, 1839.
M'Alister, Alexander to Janet M'Lean, Je., Cumberland county. R. R. Je. 29, 1839.
M'Arthur, John to Mary Leach, Mar., Robeson county. R. R. Mar. 30, 1839.
M'Connell, Isabella to Calvin M'Adoo, Mar., Guilford county. R. R. Mar. 23, 1839.
M'Craw, Paulina to Darius Rawley of Rockingham, Jan., Surry county. R. R. Jan. 21, 1839.
M'Entire, Joseph to Martha P. Hord, Mar., Lincoln county. R. R. Mar. 30, 1839.
M'Gee, Esther Ann to Solomon Hopkins of Pennsylvania, Mar., Greensboro. R. R. Mar. 23, 1839.
M'Kenzie, Eliza to Mastin Boles, Dec., Montgomery county. R. R. Dec. 7, 1839.
M'Kinnon, Murdock to Catharine M'Leod, Apr., Richmond county. R. R. Apr. 13, 1839.
M'Lean, Janet to Alexander M'Alister, Je., Cumberland county. R. R. Je. 29, 1839.
M'Lean, David to Jane S. Paisley, Aug., Guilford county. R. R. Sept. 7, 1839.
M'Leod, Catharine to Murdock M'Kinnon, Apr., Richmond county. R. R. Apr. 13, 1839.
M'Mahan, Jomes to Nelly Wilson, Apr., Yancey county. R. R. Apr. 6, 1839.

M'Masters, Emsby to Rebecca Hendricks, Aug., Randolph county. R. R. Aug. 31, 1839.

M'Neill, Mary Ann to Col. John Leach, Mar., Robeson county. R. R. Mar. 23, 1839.

M'Pherson, Neill to Martha Lumsden, My., Fayetteville. R. R. My. 4, 1839.

M'Rae, Hugh of Anson county to Flora M'Rae, Dec., Richmond county. R. R. Dec. 7, 1839.

M'Rae, Flora to Hugh M'Rae of Anson county, Dec., Richmond county. R. R. Dec. 7, 1839.

M'Rae, Mary J. to Nathaniel Knight, Nov., Lawrenceville, Montgomery county. R. R. Nov. 9, 1839.

M'Wilson, Jane to Theophilus Stimpson of Statesville, Dec., Rowan county. R. R. Dec. 7, 1839.

Manney, Alida Maria to William S. Bell, Jan., Beaufort. R. R. Feb. 4, 1839.

Meacham, William, Jr. to Lucy Ann Jenkins, Apr., Richmond county. R. R. Apr. 13, 1839.

Mebane, James, Jr. of Yanceyville to Susan A. Turner, Jly., Hillsborough. R. R. Jly. 20, 1839.

Michaux, Martha to Benton Tatum, Apr., Guilford county. R. R. Apr. 6, 1839.

Michaux, Richard V. to Susan Forney, Aug., Burke county. R. R. Aug. 17, 1839.

Miller, Jane to Harrison Taylor, Nov., Orange county. R. R. Nov. 23, 1839.

Mills, Daniel to Melinda Harrill, Sept., Lincolnton. R. R. Sept. 21, 1839.

Moore, John A. to Susan Cameron, Je., Newbern. R. R. Je. 15, 1839.

Morrow, William, Jr. to Frances Armstrong, Feb. 14, Orange county. R. R. Mar. 30, 1839.

Mundy, John W. to Anne M. C. Stedman of Raleigh, Dec. 27, Benton, Alabama. R. R. Jan. 21, 1839.

Murdock, Sarah to William Simonton, Mar., Iredell county. R. R. Mar. 23, 1839.

Nicholson, Thomas W. to Martha E. Thorn, Aug., Halifax. R. R. Aug. 17, 1836.

Norwood, Henrietta to Thomas Hicks, Mar., Wake county. R. R. Mar. 18, 1839.

Norwood, James H. of Hillsboro to Sarah F. Benners of Craven county, Apr. 3, Franklin county. R. R. Apr. 20, 1839.

Otey, Col. Walter Leake to Eleanor Kyle of Raleigh, Aug. 1, Raleigh. R. R. Aug. 3, 1839.

Outlaw, Wm. T. to Margaret E. Henderson, Apr. 25, Raleigh. R. R. Apr. 27, 1839.

Outz, Alfred to Mary Hamblin, Apr. 25, Wake county. R. R. My. 11, 1839.

Page, Madison to Grizzy Ann Page, Apr. 25, Wake county. R. R. Apr. 27, 1839.

Paisley, Jane S. to David M'Lean, Aug., Guilford county. R. R. Sept. 7, 1839.

Parnell, Thomas Jefferson to Dorothy Williamson, Dec., Lawrenceville. R. R. Dec. 7, 1839.

Pattilo, Mary Jane to Samuel R. Smith of Tennessee, Dec. 4, Warrenton. R. R. Dec. 14, 1839.

Pearce, Filman to Eliza Swink, Aug., Salisbury. R. R. Sept. 7, 1839.
Peden, Maj. William W. of Wilkes county to May Taylor Williams, Apr., Surry county. R. R. Apr. 13, 1839.
Penny, Susan to Clement Smith, Mar., Wake county. R. R. Mar. 18, 1839.
Phifer, John of Cabarrus county to Elizabeth C. Ramsour, Je., Lincoln county. R. R. Je. 22, 1839.
Phillips, Richard of West Tennessee to Mary Harris, Jly. 29, Wake Forest. R. R. Sept. 7, 1839.
Pinkly, Mary to James White, Aug., Davie county. R. R. Aug. 17, 1839.
Pittman, Penelope to Rhesa S. Williams of Columbus, Je., Cumberland county. R. R. Je. 29, 1839.
Powell, John D. of Wake Forest to Delia Hinton, Apr. 30, Wake county. R. R. Je. 8, 1839.
Pray, Mathias D. to Mary Allred, Aug., Randolph county. R. R. Aug. 31, 1839.
Ramer, Sarah to Jacob Bostian, Jly., Salisbury. R. R. Jly. 6, 1839.
Ramsour, Elizabeth C. to John Phifer of Cabarrus county. R. R. Je. 22, 1839.
Rawley, Darius of Rockingham to Paulina M'Craw, Jan., Surry county. R. R. Jan. 21, 1839.
Rawlings, Jesse to Rebecca Brazzel, Aug., Halifax. R. R. Aug. 17, 1839.
Ray, Mrs. Emeline of Rapid, La. to Hon. Fesse A. Bynum of Halifax, Je. 28. R. R. Jly. 6, 1839.
Reinhardt, Jane H. to Dr. James H. Lytle, Dec., Lincolnton. R. R. Dec. 7, 1839
Rhew, Isaac to Mary Haughton, Feb. 14, Orange county. R. R. Mar. 30, 1839
Rhodes, Miss M. to Sylvester Edwards, Jly. 4, Wake county. R. R. Jly. 13, 1839
Richardson, Celia to Edmund Grant, Je., Newbern. R. R. Je. 15, 1839
Riley, Mary to Christian Whitsell, Feb. 14, Orange county. R. R. Mar. 30, 1839
Robards, Col. Horace L. of Oxford to Elizabeth Jane Watkins, Nov. 13, Goochland county, Va. R. R. Nov. 23, 1839
Roberts, Huldah to Capt. Wm. C. Dejarnatt, Dec., Surry county. R. R. Dec. 7, 1839
Roberts, William B. to Achrebolinda Fuller, Apr. 9, Wake county. R. R. My. 4, 1839
Rosseau, America of Wilkes county to Col. George Bower of Jefferson, Dec., Wilkes county. R. R. Dec. 14, 1839
Rudisill, Marcus H. to Francis J. Killian, Sept., Lincoln county. R. R. Sept. 14, 1839
Rush, Miles I. of Montgomery county to Elizabeth Smith, Dec., Richmond county. R. R. Dec. 7, 1839
Sanford, Thomas of Wilmington to Agnes H. Bell, Nov. 7, Cumberland county. R. R. Nov. 9, 1839
Sater, Manasseh to Emily Shipp, Sept. 12, Wake county. R. R. Sept. 21, 1839
Saunders, John of Davidson to Abigail Stafford, Aug., Stokes county. R. R. Aug. 17, 1839
Seawel, Mary to Joseph Loyd, Sept., Granville county. R. R. Oct. 5, 1839

Sexton, Matilda to John A. Jackson, Sept., Wake county. R. R. Oct. 5, 1839

Sherard, Sally Ann of Wayne county to James W. Cox of Lenoir county, Mar. 12. R. R. Mar. 23, 1839

Shine, Daniel Y. to Mrs. Ann Hanrahan, Aug., Newbern. R. R. Aug. 17, 1839

Shipp, Emily to Manasseh Sater, Sept. 12, Wake county. R. R. Sept. 21, 1839

Simonton, William to Sarah Murdock, Mar., Iredell county. R. R. Mar. 23, 1839

Skeen, Mathew to Delinda Wood, Jly. 18, Randolph county. R. R. Jly. 27, 1839

Sledge, James J. to Susan Ann King, Feb., Warren county. R. R. Mar. 4, 1839

Smith, Duncan to Jane David, Apr., Richmond county. R. R. Apr. 13, 1839

Smith, Elizabeth to Miles I. Rush of Montgomery county, Dec., Richmond county. R. R. Dec. 7, 1839

Smith, Nancy Ann to James Gilmer, Apr., Guilford county. R. R. Apr. 6, 1839

Smith, Samuel R. of Tennessee to Mary Jane Pattilo, Dec. 4, Warrenton. R. R. Dec. 14, 1839

Smith, Clement to Susan Penny, Mar., Wake county. R. R. Mar. 18, 1839

Somervell, J. B. to Mary Eliza Jones, Feb., Warren county. R. R. Mar. 4, 1839

Sorrell, Nancy to Abel Upchurch, Nov. 1, Wake county. R. R. Dec. 7, 1839

Stafford, Abigail to John Saunders of Davidson, Aug., Stokes county. R. R. Aug. 17, 1839

Stanly, Rev. Harvey of Raleigh to Mary A. Kinney, Aug., Elizabeth City. R. R. Aug. 31, 1839

Stedman, Anne, M. C. of Raleigh to John W. Mundy, Dec. 27, Benton, Lowndes county, Alabama. R. R. Jan. 21, 1839

Stevens, Benjamin to Mrs. Karon Thompson, Apr. 19, Johnston county. R. R. Apr. 27, 1839

Stimpson, Theophilus of Statesville to Jane M'Wilson, Dec., Rowan county. R. R. Dec. 7, 1839

Stringer, William to Mary Elizabeth Hobart of Hingham, Mass. Nov. 30, Raleigh. R. R. Dec. 7, 1839

Stringfellow, Harriet M. to Rev. D. McNeill Turner of Fayetteville, Oct., Chester District, S. C. R. R. Oct. 12, 1839

Swink, Eliza to Filman Pearce, Aug., Salisbury. R. R. Sept. 7, 1839

Tatum, Benton to Martha Michaux, Apr., Guilford county. R. R. Apr. 6, 1839

Taylor, Harrison to Jane Miller, Nov., Orange county. R. R. Nov. 23, 1839

Thatch, Jane to Albert G. Anderson of Hillsborough, Jly., Perquimans county. R. R. Jly. 20, 1839

Thomas, Etheldred to Martha King, Nov. 14, Wake county. R. R. Dec. 7, 1839

Thompson, Mrs. Karon to Benjamin Stevens, Apr. 19, Johnston county. R. R. Apr. 27, 1839

Thompson, Margaret to Richard T. Hord of Rutherford, Mar., Lincoln county. R. R. Mar. 30, 1839

Thompson, Susan J. of Wake county to John T. Carter of Petersburg, Va., Aug. 11, Wake county. R. R. Aug. 17, 1839
Thorn, Martha E. to Thomas W. Nicholson, Aug., Halifax. R. R. Aug. 17, 1839
Torrence, Charles L. of Salisbury to Elizabeth L. Hayes, Apr., Lincoln county. R. R. Apr. 13, 1839
Treadwell, Mary Ann to Thomas Gray, Jan., Sampson county. R. R. Jan. 21, 1839
Trexler, Moses to Margaret Cauble, Aug., Rowan county. R. R. Sept. 7, 1839
Troy, Mrs. Mathew to David F. Caldwell, Aug., Salisbury. R. R. Aug. 17, 1839
Turner, Rev. D. M'Neill of Fayetteville to Harriet M. Stringfellow, Oct., Chester District, S. C. R. R. Oct. 12, 1839
Turner, Susan A. to James Mebane, Jr. of Yanceyville, Jly., Hillsborough. R. R. Jly. 20, 1839
Upchurch, Abel to Nancy Sorrell, Nov. 1, Wake county. R. R. Dec. 7, 1839
Vanhook, Elizabeth L. to Wm. R. Webb of Bertie county, Nov., Leesburg, Caswell county. R. R. Dec. 7, 1839
Veach, Wilson to Elizabeth Hall, Aug., Davie county. R. R. Aug. 17, 1839
Verser, Martha to William K. Harrison, Nov., Caswell county. R. R. Nov. 23, 1839
Wade, Capt. Richard J. of this State to Sophia Dunbar, Mar., New York City, N. Y. R. R. Mar. 30, 1839
Walker, Nathan B. to Salina F. Brown, Je. 24, Louisburg. R. R. Je. 29, 1839
Walker, William M. to Eliza M. Gordon, Sept. 11, Granville county. R. R. Sept. 21, 1839
Wallace, Samuel to Mary Ann Hunter, Aug., Newbern. R. R. Aug. 17, 1839
Ward, Mrs. Ann Maria to Dr. B. J. Hill of Duplin county, Jly., Wayne county. R. R. Jly. 20, 1839
Ward, George to Nancy Winston, Apr. 9, Granville county. R. R. My. 4, 1839
Ward, Matthew to Martha Andrew, Mar., Randolph county. R. R. Mar. 23, 1839
Watkins, Elizabeth Jane to Col. Horace L. Robards of Oxford, Nov. 13, Goochland county, Va. R. R. Nov. 23, 1839
Watson, William R. to Mrs. Susan R. Grice of Sampson county, Jan., Fayetteville. R. R. Jan. 21, 1839
Weathers, Lavinia to Henry W. Carrol of York District, S. C., Sept., Lincoln county. R. R. Sept. 14, 1839
Webb, Wm. R. of Bertie county to Elizabeth L. Vanhook, Nov., Leesburg, Caswell county. R. R. Dec. 7, 1839
Webster, Matilda F. to D. A. Gillaspie, Aug., Guilford county. R. R. Sept. 7, 1839
Whitaker, Martha to Hampton Legrand of Halifax, Jly., Richmond county. R. R. Jly. 20, 1839
White, Catharine M. to Peter R. Davis, Jr., Nov. 6, Warren county. R. R. Nov. 23, 1839
White, James to Mary Pinkly, Aug., Davie county. R. R. Aug. 17, 1839

Whitsell, Christian to Mary Riley, Feb. 14, Orange county. R. R. Mar. 30, 1839
Williams, Elizabeth C. to Christopher D. Hill, Sept., Duplin county. R. R. Sept. 28, 1839
Williams, Mary Taylor to Maj. William W. Peden of Wilkes county, Apr., Surry county. R. R. Apr. 13, 1839
Williams, Rachael to William Gilmore, Jan., Fayetteville. R. R. Jan. 21, 1839
Williams, Rhesa S. of Columbus to Penelope Pittman, Je., Cumberland county. R. R. Je. 29, 1839
Williams, Sarah A. G. to James W. Howard of Jones county, Nov., Beaufort county. R. R. Nov. 23, 1839
Williamson, Dorothy to Thomas Jefferson Parnell, Dec., Lawrenceville. R. R. Dec. 7, 1839
Winston, Nancy to George Ward, My., Granville county. R. R. My. 4, 1839
Wilson, Nelly to James M'Mahan, Apr., Yancey county. R. R. Apr. 6, 1839
Wood, Delinda to Mathew Skeen, Jly. 18, Randolph county. R. R. Jly. 27, 1839
Wooley, C. W. of Lawrenceville to Ann Deberry, Dec., Montgomery county. R. R. Dec. 14, 1839
Yancey, Edwin T. of Warrenton to Mary May Anderson, Dec., La Grange, Tenn. R. R. Dec. 14, 1839

1840

Alston, Joseph to Deceimus Palmer, Jan., Chatham county. R. R. Jan. 24, 1840
Andrews, Elizabeth to Walter Robinson, Oct., Montgomery county. R. R. Oct. 27, 1840
Andrews, Mary Lucy to Wesley S. Blake, Dec. 22, Raleigh. R. R. Dec. 29, 1840
Archer, Rev. Philmer to Mary S. Compton, Nov. 5, Franklin county. R. R. Nov. 17, 1840
Arey, Phoebe to Tobias Brown, Nov., Rowan county. R. R. Nov. 17, 1840
Armstrong, William to Emily Hawkins, Nov. 25, Washington, Beaufort county. R. R. Dec. 8, 1840
Atwaters, Jehial of Orange county to Martha Warren, Dec. 10, Wake county. R. R. Dec. 22, 1840
Avent, Sarah to Obadiah Farrar, Mar. 19, Chatham county. R. R. Mar. 27, 1840
Bacon, Calvin to Martha Woods, Jan. 9, Orange county. R. R. Jan. 28, 1840
Bailey, Nancy B. to Robert B. Watt, Dec., Rockingham. R. R. Dec. 11, 1840
Baker, John C. of Richmond county to Susan Council, Dec. 4, Bladen county. R. R. Jan. 3, 1840
Baker, Rev. Richard of Florida to Mary E. Horne of Newbern, My. 20, Newbern. R. R. Je. 2, 1840
Ballard, Amelia B. to Robert M. Horah, Mar., Salisbury. R. R. Apr. 3, 1840
Ballard, Lott of Onslow county & Sumpter county, Alabama to Margaret Ann M'Intosh, Nov., Noxubee county, Mississippi. R. R. Nov. 24, 1840

Barclay, Matilda Walburgh to Pollock T. Burgwyn of this State, Mar., New York. R. R. Mar. 10, 1840
Barlow, Mickins to Labon Ferrell, My. 21, Wake county. R. R. My. 29, 1840
Barnes, Nancy to Burgess Thomason, Feb., Davidson county. R. R. Feb. 4, 1840
Barr, Wm. of Rowan county to Mrs. Dorcas Shelton, Jan., Iredell county. R. R. Jan. 14, 1840
Beachem, A. M. to Mrs. Mary Orman, Mar., Beaufort county. R. R. Mar. 31, 1840
Beckwich, Margaret Ann of Raleigh to Rev. Edwin Geer of Wadesborough, Dec. 2, Raleigh. R. R. Dec. 4, 1840
Benton, Capt. Burwell F. to Susan A. Watson, Oct. 11, Anson county. R. R. Nov. 17, 1840
Bethel, Major William D. of Rockingham to Mary M. Jeffreys, Dec. 1, Person county. R. R. Dec. 22, 1840
Blackwood, Nathaniel H. of Raleigh to Mary E. Jones of Johnston county, Feb., Guilford county. R. R. Feb. 18, 1840
Blake, Wesley S. to Mary Lucy Andrews, Dec. 22, Raleigh. R. R. Dec. 29, 1840
Blocker, John C. of Fayetteville to Julia Ann Bradley, Jan., Tarboro. R. R. Jan. 24, 1840
Blount, Mary E. J. to Littlejohn Topping, Nov., Lenoir county. R. R. Dec. 8, 1840
Bond, William to Elizabeth Caffee, Dec., Washington. R. R. Jan. 1, 1840
Bonner, Charles W. to Caroline D. Redditt, Nov. 25, Washington, Beaufort county. R. R. Dec. 8, 1840
Bonner, Mary Eliza to Benjamin Franklin Havens, Dec., Washington. R. R. Jan. 1, 1840
Braddy, Julia Ann to John C. Blocker of Fayetteville, Jan., Tarboro. R. R. Jan. 24, 1840
Brandon, Mrs. Elmira to J. D. Lumsden, Aug. 20, Lincoln county. R. R. Sept. 1, 1840
Brandon, Elizabeth P. to Thomas A. Freeland, Nov., Iredell county. R. R. Nov. 17, 1840
Brandon, Elvira to Rev. James H. Hall, Jan., Rowan county. R. R. Jan. 3, 1840
Bridges, Young of Johnston county to Isabella Evans, Apr. 23, Hillsboro. R. R. My. 5, 1840
Brooks, William T. of Chatham county to Emily Fort, Dec. 19, Wake county. R. R. Jan. 1, 1840
Brown, Capt. Allen to Letitia Clark, Jan., Orange county. R. R. Jan. 28, 1840
Brown, Mrs. Elizabeth C. to George H. Lirely, Apr., Rowan county. R. R. Apr. 21, 1840
Brown, Tobias to Phoebe Arey, Nov., Rowan county. R. R. Nov. 17, 1840
Bruce, Mary of Northampton county to James Upton of Halifax county. R. R. Jan. 21, 1840
Buie, Anabella M. D. to Neill M'Neill, Apr., Robeson county. R. R. Apr. 21, 1840
Bullock, Eliza to John W. Carr, Jan., Chapel Hill. R. R. Jan. 14, 1840

Bullock, Joshua K. to Emily Vines, Nov. 19, Pitt county. R. R. Nov. 27, 1840
Burgwyn, Julia of Newbern to Rev. Cameron F. M'Rae, Dec. 29, Raleigh. R. R. Jan. 1, 1840
Burgwyn, T. Pollock of this State to Ann Matilda Walburgh Barclay, Mar., New York. R. R. Mar. 10, 1840
Buxton, Mary Frances to Thomas S. Lutterlok, Sept., Fayetteville. R. R. Sept. 2, 1840
Caffee, Elizabeth to William Bond, Dec., Washington. R. R. Jan. 1, 1840
Caldwell, Dr. E. to Elizabeth Motz of Raleigh, Aug. 19, Lincoln county. R. R. Sept. 4, 1840
Campbell, A. D. of Alabama to Flora A. M'Arn, Nov., Richmond county. R. R. Dec. 4, 1840
Capps, Sarah Ann of Mecklenburg county to Robert N. Peoples, Jan., Cabarrus county. R. R. Jan. 14, 1840
Carnes, Col. James A. to Elizabeth M. Jones of Wilmington, Nov. 29, Somerville, Tennessee. R. R. Dec. 8, 1840
Carr, John W. to Eliza Bullock, Jan., Chapel Hill. R. R. Jan. 14, 1840
Carrell, James to Lucinda King, Feb., Raleigh. R. R. Feb. 18, 1840
Carson, Rev. Robert J. of N. C. Conference to Mrs. Mary L. G. Williams, Apr., Martin county. R. R. Apr. 7, 1840
Casper, Adam to Sophia Peeler, Feb., Rowan county. R. R. Feb. 4, 1840
Cates, Elizabeth to Henderson Taylor, Apr., Orange county. R. R. My. 5, 1840
Clark, David T. to Frances M. Goodloe, Aug. 20, Orange county. R. R. Sept. 1, 1840
Clark, Letitia to Capt. Allen Brown, Jan., Orange county. R. R. Jan. 28, 1840
Clendenin, Catharine to William Turner, Dec., Orange county. R. R. Dec. 8, 1840
Compton, Mary S. to Rev. Philmer Archer, Nov. 5, Franklin county. R. R. Nov. 17, 1840
Cook, Calvin to Miss E. Williams, Feb., Montgomery county. R. R. Feb. 28, 1840
Coon, Anderson to Sarah Jones, Feb., Davie county. R. R. Feb. 4, 1840
Cooper, Martha to Yancy Glenn, Je., Wake county. R. R. Je. 26, 1840
Cooper, Theophilus to Jennet N. Moran, Feb., Halifax. R. R. Feb. 4, 1840
Cooper, Mrs. William, Oct., Rowan county. R. R. Oct. 20, 1840
Correl, Sophia R. to David Linn, Feb., Rowan county. R. R. Feb. 25, 1840
Corriker, Sarah to John Erwin, Jan. 9, Salisbury. R. R. Jan. 24, 1840
Council, Susan to John C. Baker of Richmond county, Dec. 4, Bladen county. R. R. Jan. 3, 1840
Cox, Susan to Nicanor Murray, Jan., Wilmington. R. R. Jan. 28, 1840
Cowan, Charlotte to Joel H. Jenkins, Nov. 5, Salisbury. R. R. Nov. 17, 1840
Cowan, James L. to Mary Eliza Vail, Nov. 5, Salisbury. R. R. Nov. 17, 1840
Cozens, Martha C. to Dr. Lee A. Moore, Mar., Lincoln county. R. R. Mar. 17, 1840
Crabtree, Eliza to John Hunter, Jan. 16, Orange county. R. R. Jan. 28, 1840

Crabtree, Henry to Louisa Crabtree, Jan., Hillsboro. R. R. Jan. 28, 1840
Crabtree, Louisa to Henry Crabtree, Jan., Hillsboro. R. R. Jan. 28, 1840
Crabtree, Moses to Mahala Latta, Sept. 24, Orange county. R. R. Oct. 9, 1840
Creason, Sopha to Richard Julian, Mar., Rowan county. R. R. Mar. 17, 1840
Crouch, Sarah J. to John Webb, Apr., Montgomery county. R. R. Apr. 10, 1840
Crudup, Caroline to Shepard Lee of Anson county, Feb., Montgomery county. R. R. Feb. 4, 1840
Culbreth, Blackman to Jane Owen, Apr., Sampson county. R. R. Apr. 21, 1840
Currell, William to Nancy Draper, Jan., Washington county. R. R. Jan. 3, 1840
Currie, Margaret to Joseph Tate, Jan. 16, Orange county. R. R. Jan. 28, 1840
Davis, Anne W. of New Hanover county to Thos. C. Miller of Wilmington, Jly. 14, Pittsboro. R. R. Aug. 4, 1840
Davis, Caroline to Anthony A. Person, Dec. 18, Franklin county. R. R. Jan. 1, 1840
Darr, Catherine to Joseph Hederick, Oct., Davidson county. R. R. Oct. 20, 1840
Dewesse, Caroline to Ephraim Martin, Jan., Mecklenburg county. R. R. Jan. 21, 1840
Dodson, Francis of Milton to Col. Andrew Motz, Oct., Milton. R. R. Oct. 23, 1840
Doggat, George T. to Eliza C. Wharton, Jan., Guilford county. R. R. Jan. 24, 1840
Dolby, Mrs. Jane M. to Jeremiah C. Perkins, Apr., Washington, Beaufort county. R. R. Apr. 7, 1840
Donnell, Edmund to Margaret Hamilton, Oct., Rutherfordton. R. R. Oct. 23, 1840
Donnell, Mary to Hon. Charles Shepard, Apr. 1, Newbern. R. R. Apr. 7, 1840
Dortch, Celeste to Capt. David M'Daniel of Raleigh, Jan. 22, Nash county. R. R. Feb. 18, 1840
Dove, Ann E. of Washington to Lieut Wm. Lee Young, U.S.M. of Cabarrus county, Aug. 11, Washington, D. C. R. R. Sept. 4, 1840
Dowty, Lodowick, Jr. to Joanna Warren, Mar., Beaufort. R. R. Mar. 31, 1840
Dowty, Lodowick, Sr. to Mrs. Letitia Willie, Beaufort county. R. R. Mar. 31, 1840
Dozier, Martha L. to George A. Williams of Elizabeth City, Jan., Currituck county. R. R. Jan. 17, 1840
Duskin, Mary A. to David D. Paul, Dec. 23, Orange county. R. R. Jan. 14, 1840
Draper, Nancy to William Currell, Jan., Washington county. R. R. Jan. 3, 1840
Dula, Susan A. of Wilkes county to Benjamin S. Martin of Burke county, Oct. 20, Wilkes county. R. R. Nov. 3, 1840

Dunlap, Gen. Richard of Texas to Mary Louisa Winn, My. 25, Newbern. R. R. Je. 2, 1840

Dunham, Samuel to Eliza Ann Spicer, Jan., Wilmington. R. R. Jan. 14, 1840

Dunn, Laura W. to Geo. C. Smith of Rolesville, Jan., Wake county. R. R. Jan. 10, 1840

Elliot, Temperance to William Pritchet, Feb., Greensboro. R. R. Feb. 21, 1840

Elliott, William of Guilford county to Margaret Jenkins, Feb., Richmond county. R. R. Feb. 21, 1840

Ellis, Mrs. Julia to Jones Spencer, Jan., Hyde county. R. R. Jan. 3, 1840

Eppes, Sarah C. to William D. Griffen, Mar., Granville county. R. R. Mar. 10, 1840

Erwin, Mrs. Esther N. to Capt. Thomas R. Shuford, Oct., Rutherford county. R. R. Oct. 23, 1840

Erwin, John to Sarah Corriker, Jan. 9, Salisbury. R. R. Jan. 24, 1840

Evans, Isabella to Young Bridges of Johnston county, Apr. 23, Hillsboro. R. R. My. 5, 1840

Evans, Joseph to Jane Miller Gause, Nov. 11, Fayetteville. R. R. Nov. 17, 1840

Farrar, Obadiah to Sarah Avent, Mar. 9, Chatham county. R. R. Mar. 27, 1840

Faucett, Geo. A. to Nancy A. Faucett, Dec., Orange county. R. R. Dec. 8, 1840

Faucett, Lucinda to Joseph J. Woodrow of Philadelphia, Hillsborough, Jan. R. R. Jan. 14, 1840

Faucett, Nancy A. to Geo. A. Faucett, Dec., Orange county. R. R. Dec. 8, 1840

Faust, Jacob to Lavinia Sommers, Mar., Guilford county. R. R. Mar. 27, 1840

Fenner, Mary M. to Mungo P. Purnell, Je., Halifax. R. R. Je. 12, 1840

Ferrand, Mary N. of Salisbury to Archibald Henderson, Dec. 14, Salisbury. R. R. Dec. 22, 1840

Ferrell, Labou to Mickins Barlow, My. 21, Wake county. R. R. My. 29, 1840

Fluranoy, Harriet M. to Rodin Staton, Oct. 11, Anson county. R. R. Nov. 17, 1840

Folger, Andrew J. to Surmira Perry, Mar., Stokes county. R. R. Mar. 6, 1840

Fort, Emily to William T. Brooks of Chatham county, Dec. 19, Wake county. R. R. Jan. 1, 1840

Foster, Willis to Susannah Littlejohn, Feb., Rutherford county. R. R. Feb. 4, 1840

Fraley, Ann Maria to Obadiah Woodson, Dec. 15, Salisbury. R. R. Dec. 22, 1840

Frank, Elizabeth to Casper Hedrick, Oct., Davidson county. R. R. Oct. 20, 1840

Freeland, Thomas A. to Elizabeth P. Brandon, Nov., Iredell county. R. R. Nov. 17, 1840

Foscue, John E. to Caroline Foy, Jones county, Oct., Newbern. R. R. Oct. 23, 1840

Foy, Caroline to John E. Foscue, Jones county, Oct., Newbern. R. R. Oct. 23, 1840
Foy, Charles H. of Jones county to Elizabeth Smith, Oct., Newbern. R. R. Oct. 23, 1840
Freeze, Penelope to William Gillan, Aug. 20, Cabarrus county. R. R. Sept. 4, 1840
Fulford, Joseph to Sarah F. Hyman, My. 20, Newbern. R. R. Je. 2, 1840
Gant, Hon. W. W. of Texas to Mrs. H. E. Hoke of Asheville, Je. 18, Burke county. R. R. Jly. 3, 1840
Gattis, Jane to Abel Maddy, Jan., Orange county. R. R. Jan. 14, 1840
Gattis, Rebecca to William B. Thompson of Indiana, Jan., Orange county. R. R. Jan. 17, 1840
Gause, Jane Miller to Joseph Evans, Nov. 11, Fayetteville. R. R. Nov. 17, 1840
Geer, Rev. Edwin of Wadesborough to Margaret Ann Beckwick of Raleigh, Dec. 2, Raleigh. R. R. Dec. 4, 1840
Ghillespie, Joseph to Obediance Smith, Feb., Mecklenburg county. R. R. Feb. 21, 1840
Gholson, Ann to Dr. John G. Hanner, Oct., Chatham county. R. R. Oct. 20, 1840
Gillan, William to Penelope Freeze, Aug. 20, Cabarrus county. R. R. Sept. 4, 1840
Gillespie, Archibald of Rowan county to Drucilla S. Gray, Feb., Mecklenburg county. R. R. Feb. 4, 1840
Gilmer, Dorcas N. to Dr. Francis M. Ross, Jan., Charlotte. R. R. Jan. 14, 1840
Giohan, Wm. of Dallas county, Alabama to Margaret A. Stedman of Raleigh, Mar. 12, Benton, Alabama. R. R. Apr. 10, 1840
Glenn, Yancy to Martha Cooper, Je., Wake county. R. R. Je. 26, 1840
Goodloe, Frances M. to David T. Clark, Aug. 20, Orange county. R. R. Sept. 22, 1840
Goodnight, Margaret E. to William H. Williford, Oct., Cabarrus county. R. R. Oct. 20, 1840
Gorman, Martha Spears of Raleigh to Edward E. Harris of Petersburg, Va., Sept. 30, Raleigh. R. R. Oct. 2, 1840
Gray, Drucilla S. to Archibald Gillespie of Rowan county, Feb., Mecklenburg county. R. R. Feb. 4, 1840
Gray, James H. to Margaret Hill, Mar., Mecklenburg county. R. R. Mar. 31, 1840
Gray, Joseph to Dorcas Shields, Jan., Mecklenburg county. R. R. Jan. 14, 1840
Greenwood, Abner B. of Clarksville, Va. to Sarah Jones of Franklin county, Feb. 25, Franklin county. R. R. Mar. 3, 1840
Greenwood, Reddith to Sarah Philips, Feb., Surry county. R. R. Feb. 4, 1840
Griffen, William D. to Sarah C. Eppes, Mar., Granville county. R. R. Mar. 10, 1840
Griffin, Bryan to Martha Rowland, Oct. 30, Anson county. R. R. Nov. 17, 1840
Griggs, Lydia to William Moore, Jan., Anson county. R. R. Jan. 24, 1840

Grist, Mrs. Eliza H. of Newbern to Dr. Reuben Knox of St. Louis, Missouri, Jly. 21, Hillsborough. R. R. Jly. 28, 1840

Guest, Eleanora Nelson to Samuel M. Semmes, My. 14, Washington, D. C. R. R. My. 22, 1840

Guion, Haywood of Lincolnton to Carolina R. Moore, Jan. 30, Orange county. R. R. Feb. 7, 1840

Gun, Huldah to Daniel Melchor, Feb., Cabarrus county. R. R. Feb. 25, 1840

Hall, Rev. James R. to Elvira Brandon, Jan., Rowan county. R. R. Jan. 3, 1840

Hamilton, Margaret to Edmund Donnell, Oct., Rutherfordton. R. R. Oct. 23, 1840

Hanner, Dr. John G. to Ann Gholson, Oct., Chatham county. R. R. Oct. 20, 1840

Harrington, James of Anson county to Jincey Henry, Feb., Richmond county. R. R. Feb. 21, 1840

Harris, Edward E. of Petersburg, Va. to Martha Spears Gorman of Raleigh, Sept. 30, Raleigh. R. R. Oct. 2, 1840

Hatch, Edmund H. to Louisa M. Larsque, Nov., Trenton, Jones county. R. R. Nov. 6, 1840

Havens, Benjamin Franklin to Mary Eliza Bonner, Dec., Washington. R. R. Jan. 1, 1840

Hawkins, Emily to William Armstrong, Nov. 24, Washington, Beaufort county. R. R. Dec. 8, 1840

Hedrick, Casper to Elizabeth Frank, Oct., Davidson county. R. R. Oct. 20, 1840

Hedrick, Joseph to Catharine Darr, Oct., Davidson county. R. R. Oct. 20, 1840

Henderson, Ann Isabella to James T. Houston of Cabarrus county, Mar., Mecklenburg county. R. R. Mar. 17, 1840

Henderson, Archibald to Mary N. Ferrand of Salisbury, Dec. 14, Salisbury. R. R. Dec. 22, 1840

Hendricks, Louisa to William S. Stoker, Feb., Davie county. R. R. Feb. 4, 1840

Henly, Martha to Capt. Duncan K. Ruch, Jan., Randolph county. R. R. Jan. 7, 1840

Henry, Jincey to James Harrington of Anson county, Feb., Richmond county. R. R. Feb. 21, 1840

Hepburn, Dr. Jas. C. of Milton, Pennsylvania to Clarissa Maria Lette, Nov., Fayetteville. R. R. Nov. 6, 1840

High, Rebecca to James Mariot, Oct. 20, Raleigh. R. R. Oct. 23, 1840

Hill, Elizabeth to Henry Miller, Oct., Rowan county. R. R. Oct. 20, 1840

Hill, Margaret H. to James H. Gray, Mar., Mecklenburg county. R. R. Mar. 31, 1840

Hill, Mary to Joseph King, Aug. 5, Stokes county. R. R. Aug. 18, 1840

Hilliard, Sarah of Nash county to Col. George W. Polk of Raleigh, Nov. 24, Franklin, Tenn. R. R. Dec. 22, 1840

Hodges, Mary to Abraham Reddick, Apr., Gates county. R. R. Apr. 10, 1840

Hoke, Mrs. H. E. of Asheville to Hon. W. W. Gant of Texas, Je. 18. R. R. Jly. 3, 1840

Hopkins, Thomas of Rockingham to Mary Smith, Feb., Guilford county. R. R. Feb. 21, 1840
Horah, Robert M. to Amelia B. Ballard, Mar., Salisbury. R. R. Apr. 3, 1840
Horne, Mary E. of Newbern to Rev. Richard Baker of Florida, My. 20, Newbern. R. R. Je. 2, 1840
Horne, Dr. W. H. to Mary E. Porter, Nov., Snow Hill, Green county. R. R. Dec. 4, 1840
Horner, Julia of Orange county to George Robin of Granville county, Sept. 29, Orange county. R. R. Oct. 9, 1840
Houston, James T. of Cabarrus county to Ann Isabella Henderson, Mar., Mecklenburg county. R. R. Mar. 17, 1840
Howard, William M. to Sarah Taliaferro, My., Surry county. R. R. My. 15, 1840
Hunter, Jacob to Sarah Jane Robertson, Mar. 3, Wake Forest. R. R. Mar. 6, 1840
Hunter, John to Eliza Crabtree, Jan. 16, Orange county. R. R. Jan. 28, 1840
Hyman, Sarah F. to Joseph Fulford, My. 20, Newbern. R. R. Je. 2, 1840
Jamcism, Rev. James to Susan W. Jordan, Mar. 3, Roxboro. R. R. Mar. 17, 1840
Jeffreys, Mary M. to Major William D. Bethel of Rockingham, Dec. 1, Person county. R. R. Dec. 22, 1840
Jenkins, Joel H. to Charlotte Cowan, Nov. 5, Salisbury. R. R. Nov. 17, 1840
Jenkins, Margaret to William Elliott of Guilford county, Feb., Richmond county. R. R. Feb. 21, 1840
Jenkins, Nancy A. to Alexander Rankin, Apr., Lincoln county. R. R. Apr. 14, 1840
Johnston, Dr. George R. to Sarah M'Culloch, My. 7, Rowan county. R. R. My. 19, 1840
Jones, Elizabeth M. of Wilmington to Col. James A. Carnes, Nov. 29, Somerville, Tennessee. R. R. Dec. 8, 1840
Jones, Esther of Guilford county and Philadelphia to Phineas Nixon of Randolph county, Jan., New Garden. R. R. Jan. 24, 1840
Jones, Mary E. of Johnston county to Nathaniel H. Blackwood of Raleigh, Feb., Guilford county. R. R. Feb. 18, 1840
Jones, Sarah to Anderson Coon, Feb., Davie county. R. R. Feb. 4, 1840
Jones, Sarah of Franklin county to Abner B. Greenwood of Clarksville, Va., Feb. 25, Franklin county. R. R. Mar. 3, 1840
Jones, Thos. C. to Mary Murray, Feb. 11, Raleigh. R. R. Feb. 14, 1840
Jordan, Susan W. to Rev. James Jamcison, Mar. 3, Roxboro. R. R. Mar. 17, 1840
Jordan, Thomas to Sarah Wilkerson, Apr., Orange county. R. R. Apr. 7, 1840
Josey, Mary Ann to Jacob Fetzer, Apr., Rowan county. R. R. Apr. 21, 1840
Julian, Richard to Sophia Creason, Mar., Rowan county. R. R. Mar. 17, 1840
Kendall, Ann to James L. Ross of Lincoln county, Nov., Davidson county. R. R. Nov. 3, 1840

King, Joseph to Mary Hill, Aug. 5, Stokes county. R. R. Aug. 18, 1840
King, Lucinda to James Carrell, Feb., Raleigh. R. R. Feb. 18, 1840
Knox, Dr. Reuben of St. Louis, Mo. to Mrs. Eliza H. Grist of Newbern, Jly. 21, Hillsborough. R. R. Jly. 28, 1840
Laroque, Louisa M. to Edmund H. Hatch, Nov., Trenton, Jones county. R. R. Nov. 6, 1840
Latta, Mahala to Moses Crabtree, Sept. 24, Orange county. R. R. Oct. 9, 1840
Leak, Hannah to Edmund J. Lilly of Fayetteville, Jan., Rockingham, Richmond county. R. R. Jan. 24, 1840
Leak, William C. to Ann P. Steel, Apr., Rockingham, Richmond county. R. R. Apr. 28, 1840
Lee Shepard of Anson county to Carolina Crudup, Feb., Montgomery county. R. R. Feb. 4, 1840
Leete, Clarissa Maria to Dr. James C. Hepburn of Milton, Pennsylvania, Nov., Fayetteville. R. R. Nov. 6, 1840
Lemly, Mary Elizabeth to John I. Shaver, Jan., Salisbury. R. R. Jan. 24, 1840
Lentz, Rosa Maria to Mathias Misenheimer, Mar., Rowan county. R. R. Mar. 17, 1840
Levy, Henry to Catharine F. Nicholson, Je. 3, Raleigh. R. R. Je. 5, 1840
Lewis, Emma to Rev. John F. Speight, Sept. 29, Mount Prospect, Edgecombe county. R. R. Oct. 20, 1840
Lewis, James C. to Sarah H. Nisbit, Apr., Iredell county. R. R. Apr. 21, 1840
Lilly, Edmund J. of Fayetteville to Hannah Leak, Jan., Rockingham, Richmond county. R. R. Jan. 24, 1840
Lindsay, Jane E. to W. J. M'Connel, Apr., Guilford county. R. R. Apr. 10, 1840
Linebarger, Epsey W. to John S. Robinson, Nov., Lincoln county. R. R. Nov. 10, 1840
Linebarger, Hosea to Susan Sherrill, Nov., Lincoln county. R. R. Nov. 10, 1840
Linn, David to Sophia R. Correl, Feb., Rowan county. R. R. Feb. 25, 1840
Linn, Margaret to John M. Ritchie, Apr., Rowan county. R. R. Apr. 21, 1840
Lirely, George H. to Mrs. Elizabeth C. Brown, Apr., Rowan county. R. R. Apr. 21, 1840
Lisk, William G. to Elizabeth Mills, Oct., Montgomery county. R. R. Oct. 27, 1840
Littlejohn, Susannah to Willis Foster, Feb., Rutherford county. R. R. Feb. 4, 1840
Long, Ferryman to Eliza Frances Cook, Feb., Granville county. R. R. Feb. 7, 1840
Loudon, Eliza Ann to Lieut. Wm. Henry Wright, U.S.A., Nov., Wilmington. R. R. Dec. 1, 1840
Lucas, Jesse B. to Elizabeth Satchwell, Feb., Beaufort county. R. R. Feb. 4, 1840
Lumsden, J. D. to Mrs. Elmira Brandon, Aug. 20, Lincoln county. R. R. Sept. 1, 1840
Lumsden, William to Malinda Spivy, Jan. 30, Raleigh. R. R. Feb. 4, 1840

Lutterloh, Sophia M. to Maj. James M. Palmer of Hillsboro, Jan. 21, Chatham county. R. R. Jan. 28, 1840

Lutterloh, Thomas S. to Mary Frances Buxton, Sept., Fayetteville. R. R. Sept. 22, 1840

M'Alphin, Catharine A. to Joseph S. Totten of Natchez, Mississippi, Sept. 24, Yanceyville. R. R. Oct. 9, 1840

M'Arn, Flora A. to A. D. Campbell of Alabama, Nov., Richmond county. R. R. Dec. 4, 1840

M'Cain, Mrs. George W. to Martin Rush, Feb., Montgomery county. R. R. Feb. 28, 1840

M'Cay, James P. to Barbary M'Intosh, Apr., Iredell county. R. R. Apr. 21, 1840

M'Clintock, William to Sarah Weatherly, Jan., Guilford county. R. R. Jan. 3, 1840

M'Connel, W. J. to Jane E. Lindsay, Apr., Guilford county. R. R. Apr. 10, 1840

M'Coy, Ann to James M. Russell, Oct., Newbern. R. R. Oct. 23, 1840

M'Cullock, Sarah to Dr. George R. Johnston, My. 7, Rowan county. R. R. My. 19, 1840

M'Daniel, Capt. David of Raleigh to Celeste Dortch, Jan. 22, Nash county. R. R. Feb. 18, 1840

M'Dowell, Eliza G. of Burke county to N. W. Woodfin of Asheville, Je. 16, Burke county. R. R. Jly. 3, 1840

M'Gilvary, James to Eliza Tyson, Mar., Moore county. R. R. Mar. 10, 1840

M'Ginnis, Eliza to Robert Query, Jan., Mecklenburg county. R. R. Jan. 14, 1840

M'Intosh, Barbary to James P. M'Cay, Apr., Iredell county. R. R. Apr. 21, 1840

M'Intosh, Margaret Ann to Lott Ballard of Onslow county & Sumpter county, Alabama, Nov., Noxubee county, Mississippi. R. R. Nov. 24, 1840

M'Lean, Mary Jane to John R. Thom, Jan., Guilford county. R. R. Jan. 17, 1840

M'Neill, Archibald to Nancy M'Neill, Mar., Robeson county. R. R. Mar. 6, 1840

M'Neill, Nancy to Archibald M'Neill, Mar., Robeson county. R. R. Mar. 6, 1840

M'Neill, Neill to Annabella M. D. Buie, Apr., Robeson county. R. R. Apr. 21, 1840

M'Pheeters, Margaret Ann to John Wilson of Milton, Jan. 29, Raleigh. R. R. Jan. 31, 1840

M'Pherson, Daniel to Mary Ann Monroe, Mar., Robeson county. R. R. Mar. 6, 1840

M'Pherson, Elizabeth to Albert G. Proctor, Apr., Camden county. R. R. Apr. 7, 1840

M'Rae, Rev. Cameron F. to Julia Burgwyn of Newbern, Dec. 29, Raleigh. R. R. Jan. 1, 1840

Maddy, Abel to Jane Gattis, Jan., Orange county. R. R. Jan. 14, 1840

Mariot, James to Rebecca High, Oct. 20, Raleigh. R. R. Oct. 23, 1840

Martin, Benjamin S. of Burke county to Susan A. Dula of Wilkes county, Oct. 20, Wilkes county. R. R. Nov. 3, 1840

Martin, Ephraim to Caroline Dewesse, Jan., Mecklenburg county. R. R. Jan. 21, 1840

Matthews, Philadelphia H. to James C. Smith, Nov., Fayetteville. R. R. Dec. 4, 1840

Mebane, Francis of Orange county to Fenner M. Walker of Greensborough, Sept. 22, Orange county. R. R. Oct. 9, 1840

Meekins, Capt. Benjamin to Mrs. Ann M. Morton, Jan., Washington, Beaufort county. R. R. Jan. 17, 1840

Melchor, Daniel to Huldah Gunn, Feb., Cabarrus county. R. R. Feb. 25, 1840

Meredith, Laura to Richard T. Rea, Aug. 8, Wake county. R. R. Aug. 11, 1840

Meredith, Rebecca to Walter Terry, My. 1, Wadesborough. R. R. My. 15, 1840

Miller, Henry to Elizabeth Hill, Oct, Rowan county. R. R. Oct. 20, 1840

Miller, Thos. C. of Wilmington to Anne W. Davis of New Hanover county, Jly. 14, Pittsboro. R. R. Aug. 4, 1840

Mills, Elizabeth to William G. Lisk, Oct., Montgomery county. R. R. Oct. 27, 1840

Misenheimer, Mathias to Rosa Maria Lentz, Mar., Rowan county. R. R. Mar. 17, 1840

Monroe, Mary Ann to Daniel M'Pherson, Mar., Robeson county. R. R. Mar. 6, 1840

Moore, Caroline R. to Haywood Guion of Lincolnton, Jan. 30, Orange county. R. R. Feb. 7, 1840

Moore, Dr. Lee A. to Martha C. Cozens, Mar., Lincoln county. R. R. Mar. 17, 1840

Moore, William to Lydia Griggs, Jan., Anson county. R. R. Jan. 24, 1840

Moran, Jennet N. to Theophilus Cooper, Feb., Halifax. R. R. Feb. 4, 1840

Morton, Mrs. Ann M. to Capt. Benjamin Meeks, Jan., Washington, Beaufort county. R. R. Jan. 17, 1840

Moseley, James to Nancy Sales, Feb., Surry county. R. R. Feb. 4, 1840

Motz, Col. Andrew to Frances Dodson of Milton. R. R. Oct. 23, 1840

Motz, Elizabeth to Dr. E. Caldwell of Raleigh, Aug. 19, Lincoln county. R. R. Sept. 4, 1840

Murray, Mary to Thos. C. Jones, Feb. 11, Raleigh. R. R. Feb. 14, 1840

Murray, Necanor to Mrs. Susan Cox, Jan., Wilmington. R. R. Jan. 28, 1840

Murray, William Jr. to Elizabeth O. K. Reeves, Jan., Orange county. R. R. Jan. 28, 1840

Palmer, Maj. James M. of Hillsboro to Sophia M. Lutterlok, Jan. 21, Chatham county. R. R. Jan. 28, 1840

Nicholson, Daniel B. to Jane Nicholson, Mar., Richmond county. R. R. Mar. 10, 1840

Nicholson, Jane to Daniel B. Nicholson, Mar., Richmond county. R. R. Mar. 10, 1840

Nisbit, Sarah H. to James C. Lewis, Apr., Iredell county. R. R. Apr. 21, 1840

Nixon, Phineas of Randolph county to Esther Jones of Guilford county and Philadelphia, Jan., New Garden. R. R. Jan. 24, 1840

Orman, Mrs. Mary to A. M. Beachem, Mar., Beaufort county. R. R. Mar. 31, 1840

Overman, Moses to Susan Wilcox, Feb., Pasquotank county. R. R. Feb. 4, 1840
Owen, Jane to Blackman Culbreth, Apr., Sampson county. R. R. Apr. 21, 1840
Page, James of Randolph county to Martha Shamburger, Feb., Moore county. R. R. Feb. 21, 1840
Paisley, James to Elizabeth J. Scott, Sept. 3, Guilford county. R. R. Sept. 15, 1840
Paul, David D. to Mary A. Duskin, Dec. 23, Orange county. R. R. Jan. 14, 1840
Payne, Charles to Catharine Sherwood, Jan., Randolph county. R. R. Jan. 7, 1840
Peeler, Noah to Linda Pool, Nov., Rowan county. R. R. Nov. 17, 1840
Peeler, Sophia to Adam Casper, Feb., Rowan county. R. R. Feb. 4, 1840
Peoples, Robert N. to Sarah Ann Capps of Mecklenburg county, Jan., Cabarrus county. R. R. Jan. 14, 1840
Perkins, Jeremiah C. to Mrs. Jane M. Dolby, Apr., Washington, Beaufort county. R. R. Apr. 7, 1840
Person, Anthony A. to Caroline Davis, Dec. 18, Franklin county. R. R. Jan. 1, 1840
Perry, Surmira to Andrew J. Folger, Mar., Stokes county. R. R. Mar. 6, 1840
Pervines, James E. to Isabella Rogers, Mar., Cabarrus county. R. R. Mar. 17, 1840
Philips, Sarah to Reddith Greenwood, Feb., Surry county. R. R. Feb. 4, 1840
Pickett, Martha Jane of Duplin county to Allen W. Thompson of New York, My. 7, Fayetteville. R. R. My. 19, 1840
Pittman, Allen A. to Malvina Whitaker of Halifax county, Mar., LaFayette, Mississippi. R. R. Apr. 3, 1840
Polk, Col. George W. of Raleigh to Sarah Hilliard of Nash county, Nov. 24, Franklin, Tenn. R. R. Dec. 22, 1840
Pool, Linda to Noah Peeler, Nov., Rowan county. R. R. Nov. 17, 1840
Pritchet, William to Temperance Elliot, Feb., Greensboro. R. R. Feb. 21, 1840
Proctor, Albert G. to Elizabeth M'Pherson, Apr., Camden county. R. R. Apr. 7, 1840
Purnell, Mungo P. to Mary M. Fenner, Je., Halifax. R. R. Je. 12, 1840
Query, Robert to Eliza M'Ginnis, Jan., Mecklenburg county. R. R. Jan. 14, 1840
Ramsour, Geo. S. to Elizabeth M. Warlick, Jan., Lincoln county. R. R. Jan. 3, 1840
Rankin, Catharine to T. Woodburn, Oct., Rutherfordton. R. R. Oct. 23, 1840
Rea, Richard T. to Lura Meredith, Aug. 8, Wake county. R. R. Aug. 11, 1840
Redditt, Carolina D. to Charles W. Bonner, Nov. 25, Washington, Beaufort county. R. R. Dec. 8, 1840
Reed, Caroline to John N. Sharp, Feb., Mecklenburg county. R. R. Feb. 21, 1840

Reeves, Elizabeth O. K. to William Murray, Jan. 14, Orange county. R. R. Jan. 28, 1840

Ritchie, John to Margaret Linn, Apr., Rowan county. R. R. Apr. 21, 1840

Rankin, Alexander to Nancy A. Jenkins, Apr., Lincoln county. R. R. Apr. 14, 1840

Reddick, Abraham to Mary Hodges, Apr., Gates county. R. R. Apr. 10, 1840

Riley, Samuel to Ann Watson, Feb., Orange county. R. R. Mar. 3, 1840

Roberson, Margaret to Bourbon Smith of Raleigh, Feb., Warrenton. R. R. Feb. 18, 1840

Robertson, Jane to Jacob Hunter, Mar. 3, Wake Forest. R. R. Mar. 6, 1840

Robinson, Elizabeth to Jacob Stirewalt, Je., Cabarrus county. R. R. Je. 12, 1840

Robinson, John S. to Epsey W. Linebarger, Nov., Lincoln county. R. R. Nov. 10, 1840

Robinson, W. to Elizabeth Stacy, Feb., Montgomery county. R. R. Feb. 28, 1840

Robinson, Walter to Elizabeth Andrews, Oct., Montgomery county. R. R. Oct. 27, 1840

Rogers, Isabella to James E. Pervins, Mar., Cabarrus county. R. R. Mar. 17, 1840

Rolin, George of Granville county to Julia Horner of Orange county, Sept. 29, Orange county. R. R. Oct. 9, 1840

Ross, James L. of Lincoln county to Ann Kendall, Nov., Davidson county. R. R. Nov. 3, 1840

Ross, Dr. Francis M. to Dorcas N. Gilmer, Jan., Charlotte. R. R. Jan. 14, 1840

Rowland, Martha to Bryan Griffin, Oct. 30, Anson county. R. R. Nov. 17, 1840

Royster, Adaline to William C. Upchurch, Dec. 16, Raleigh. R. R. Dec. 22, 1840

Ruffin, Mary H. to Samuel G. Williams, Aug. 4, Franklin county. R. R. Aug. 11, 1840

Rush, Capt. Duncan K. to Martha Henly, Jan., Randolph county. R. R. Jan. 7, 1840

Rush, Martin to Mrs. George W. M'Cain, Feb., Montgomery county. R. R. Feb. 28, 1840

Russell, James M. to Ann M'Coy, Oct., Newbern. R. R. Oct. 23, 1840

Sales, Nancy to James Mosely, Feb., Surry county. R. R. Feb. 4, 1840

Satchwell, Elizabeth to Jesse B. Lucas, Feb., Beaufort county. R. R. Feb. 4, 1840

Scott, Elizabeth J. to James Paisley, Sept. 3, Guilford county. R. R. Sept. 15, 1840

Semmes, Samuel M. of Cumberland, Md. to Eleanora Nelson Guest, My. 14, Washington, D. C. R. R. My. 22, 1840

Setzer, Jacob to Mary Ann Josey, Apr., Rowan county. R. R. Apr. 21, 1840

Shamburger, Martha to James Page of Randolph county, Feb., Moore county. R. R. Feb. 21, 1840

Shankle, Priscilla to Robert Snuggs, Jan., Montgomery county. R. R. Jan. 3, 1840

Sharp, John M. to Caroline Reed, Feb., Mecklenburg county. R. R. Feb. 21, 1840
Shaver, John I. to Mary Elizabeth Lemly, Jan., Salisbury. R. R. Jan. 24, 1840
Shelton, Mrs. Dorcas to Wm. Barr of Rowan county, Jan., Iredell county. R. R. Jan. 14, 1840
Shepard, Hon. Charles to Mary Donnell, Apr. 1, Newbern. R. R. Apr. 7, 1840
Sherrill, Susan to Hosea Linebarger, Nov., Lincoln county. R. R. Nov. 10, 1840
Sherwood, Catharine to Charles Payne, Jan., Randolph county. R. R. Jan. 7, 1840
Shields, Dorcas to Joseph Gray, Jan., Mecklenburg county. R. R. Jan. 14, 1840
Shinn, Ann C. to Samuel Smith, Feb., Iredell county. R. R. Feb. 25, 1840
Shuford, Capt. Thomas R. to Mrs. Esther N. Erwin, Oct., Rutherford county. R. R. Oct. 23, 1840
Skinner, Penelope D. to Thomas D. Warren of Virginia, Mar. 12, Edenton. R. R. Mar. 27, 1840
Simmons, Elizabeth Jane of Jones county to William J. Ward of Onslow county, Feb. R. R. Feb. 21, 1840
Smith, Bourbon of Raleigh to Margaret Roberson, Feb., Warrenton. R. R. Feb. 18, 1840
Smith, Elizabeth to Charles H. Foy of Jones county, Oct., Newbern. R. R. Oct. 23, 1840
Smith, Geo. C. of Rolesville to Laura W. Dunn, Jan., Wake county. R. R. Jan. 10, 1840
Smith, James to Mrs. Margaret Wallace, Jan., Mecklenburg county. R. R. Jan. 14, 1840
Smith, James C. to Philadelphia H. Matthews, Nov., Fayetteville. R. R. Dec. 4, 1840
Smith, Mary to Thomas Hopkins of Rockingham, Feb., Guilford county. R. R. Feb. 21, 1840
Smith, Obedience to Joseph Ghillespie, Feb., Mecklenburg county. R. R. Feb. 21, 1840
Smith, Samuel to Ann C. Shinn, Feb., Iredell county. R. R. Feb. 25, 1840
Snellings, William to Frances Warren, Feb. 4, Wake county. R. R. Feb. 7, 1840
Snuggs, Robert to Priscilla Shankle, Jan., Montgomery county. R. R. Jan. 3, 1840
Sommers, Lavinia to Jacob Faust, Mar., Guilford county. R. R. Mar. 27, 1840
Southerland, Mrs. Mary to Dr. Willie White of Pitt county, Dec. 23, Orange county. R. R. Jan. 14, 1840
Speight, Rev. John F. to Emma Lewis, Sept. 29, Mount Prospect, Edgecombe county. R. R. Oct. 20, 1840
Spencer, Jones to Mrs. Julia Ellis, Jan., Hyde county. R. R. Jan. 3, 1840
Spicer, Eliza Ann to Samuel Dunham, Jan., Wilmington. R. R. Jan. 14, 1840
Spivy, Malinda to William Lumsden, Jan. 30, Raleigh. R. R. Feb. 4, 1840

Stacy, Elizabeth to W. Robinson, Feb., Montgomery county. R. R. Feb. 28, 1840

Staton, Rodin to Harriet M. Fluranoy, Oct. 11, Anson county. R. R. Nov. 17, 1840

Stedman, Margaret A. of Raleigh to Wm. Giohan of Dallas county, Alabama, Mar. 12, Benton, Alabama. R. R. Apr. 10, 1840

Steel, Ann P. to William C. Leak, Apr., Rockingham, Richmond county. R. R. Apr. 28, 1840

Stirewalt, Jacob, Jr. to Elizabeth Robinson, Je., Cabarrus county. R. R. Je. 12, 1840

Stoker, William S. to Louisa Hendricks, Feb., Davie county. R. R. Feb. 4, 1840

Story, Lemuel to Frances Webb, Oct., Montgomery county. R. R. Oct. 27, 1840

Summerow, Peter to Elmira L. Ramsour, Mar. 19, Lincolnton. R. R. Mar. 27, 1840

Tate, Joseph to Margaret Currie, Jan. 16, Orange county. R. R. Jan. 28, 1840

Taylor, Henderson to Elizabeth Cates, Apr., Orange county. R. R. My. 5, 1840

Taylor, Martha H. of Louisburg, Franklin county to William W. Ward of Haywood county, Apr. 9. R. R. My. 5, 1840

Taliaferro, Sarah to William M. Howard, My., Surry county. R. R. My. 15, 1840

Terry, Walter to Rebecca Meredith, My. 1, Wadesborough. R. R. My. 15, 1840

Torrence, Edwin B. to Isabella Wells, Jan., Rutherford county. R. R. Jan. 31, 1840

Thom, John R. to Mary Jane M'Lean, Jan., Guilford county. R. R. Jan. 17, 1840

Thomason, Burgess to Nancy Barnes, Feb., Davidson county. R. R. Feb. 4, 1840

Thompson, Allen W. of New York to Martha Jane Pickett of Duplin county, My. 7, Fayetteville. R. R. My. 19, 1840

Thompson, William B. of Indiana to Rebecca Gattis, Jan., Orange county. R. R. Jan. 17, 1840

Topping, Littlejohn to Mary E. J. Blount, Nov., Lenoir county. R. R. Dec. 8, 1840

Totten, Joseph S. of Natchez, Mississippi to Catharine A. M'Alphin, Sept. 24, Yanceyville. R. R. Oct. 9, 1840

Turner, William to Catharine Clendenin, Dec., Orange county. R. R. Dec. 8, 1840

Tyson, Eliza to James M'Gilvary, Mar., Moore county. R. R. Mar. 10, 1840

Upton, James of Halifax county to Mary Bruce of Northampton county, Jan. 6. R. R. Jan. 21, 1840

Upchurch, William C. to Adaline Royster, Dec. 16, Raleigh. R. R. Dec. 22, 1840

Vail, Mary Eliza to James L. Cowan, Nov. 5, Salisbury. R. R. Nov. 17, 1840

Vines, Emily to Joshua K. Bullock, Nov. 19, Pitt county. R. R. Nov. 27, 1840

Walker, Fatima of Randolph county to Joseph A. Worth of Asheborough, Aug. 20, Davidson county. R. R. Sept. 4, 1840
Walker, Fenner M. of Greensborough to Francis Mebane of Orange county, Sept. 22, Orange county. R. R. Oct. 9, 1840
Wallace, Mrs. Margaret to James Smith, Jan., Mecklenburg county. R. R. Jan. 14, 1840
Ward, William J. of Onslow county to Elizabeth Jane Simmons of Jones county, Feb. R. R. Feb. 21, 1840
Ward, William W. of Haywood county to Martha H. Taylor of Louisburg, Franklin county, Apr. 9. R. R. My. 5, 1840
Warlick, Elizabeth M. to Geo. S. Ramsour, Jan., Lincoln county. R. R. Jan. 3, 1840
Warren, Frances to William Snellings, Feb. 4, Wake county. R. R. Feb. 7, 1840
Warren, Joanna to Lodowick Dowty, Jr., Mar., Beaufort. R. R. Mar. 31, 1840
Warren, Martha to Jehial Atwaters of Orange county, Dec. 10, Wake county. R. R. Dec. 22, 1840
Warren, Thomas D. of Virginia to Penelope D. Skinner, Mar. 12, Edenton. R. R. Mar. 27, 1840
Watson, Ann to Samuel Riley, Feb., Orange county. R. R. Mar. 3, 1840
Watson, Susan A. to Capt. Burwell F. Benton, Oct. 11, Anson county. R. R. Nov. 17, 1840
Watt, Robert B. to Nancy B. Bailey, Dec., Rockingham. R. R. Dec. 11, 1840
Weatherly, Sarah to William M'Clintock, Jan., Guilford county. R. R. Jan. 3, 1840
Webb, Frances to Lemuel Story, Oct., Montgomery county. R. R. Oct. 27, 1840
Webb, John to Sarah J. Crouch, Apr., Montgomery county. R. R. Apr. 10, 1840
Wells, Isabella to Edwin B. Torrence, Jan., Rutherford county. R. R. Jan. 31, 1840
Whitaker, Malvina to Allen A. Pittman of Halifax county, Mar., La Fayette county, Mississippi. R. R. Apr. 3, 1840
White, Dr. Willie of Pitt county to Mrs. Mary Southerland, Dec. 23, Orange county. R. R. Jan. 14, 1840
Wilcox, Susan to Moses Overman, Feb., Pasquotank county. R. R. Feb. 4, 1840
Wilkerson, Sarah to Thomas Jordan, Apr., Orange county. R. R. Apr. 7, 1840
Wilkinson, David to Lucy A. M. Williford, Oct., Rowan county. R. R. Oct. 20, 1840
Williams, Miss E. to Calvin Cook, Feb., Montgomery county. R. R. Feb. 28, 1840
Williams, George A. of Elizabeth City to Martha L. Dozier, Jan., Currituck county. R. R. Jan. 17, 1840
Williams, Mary L. G. to Rev. Robert J. Carson of N. C. Conference, Apr., Martin county. R. R. Apr. 7, 1840
Williams, Samuel G. to Mary H. Ruffin, Aug. 4, Franklin county. R. R. Aug. 11, 1840

Willie, Mrs. Letitia to Lodowick Dowty, Sr., Beaufort county. R. R. Mar. 31, 1840
Williford, Lucy A. M. to David Wilkinson, Oct., Rowan county. R. R. Oct. 20, 1840
Williford, William H. to Margaret E. Goodnight, Oct., Cabarrus county. R. R. Oct. 20, 1840
Wilson, John of Milton to Margaret Ann M'Pheeters, Jan. 29, Raleigh. R. R. Jan. 31, 1840
Winn, Mary Louisa to Gen. Richard Dunlap of Texas, My. 25, Newbern. R. R. Je. 2, 1840
Woodburn, T. to Catharine Rankin, Oct., Rutherfordton. R. R. Oct. 23, 1840
Wodfin, N. W. of Asheville to Eliza G. M'Dowell of Burke county, Je. 16, Burke county. R. R. Jly. 3, 1840
Woodrow, Joseph J. of Philadelphia to Lucinda Faucett, Hillsborough, Jan. R. R. Jan. 14, 1840
Woods, Martha to Calvin Bacon, Jan. 9, Orange county. R. R. Jan. 28, 1840
Woodson, Obadiah to Ann Maria Fraley, Dec. 15, Salisbury. R. R. Dec. 22, 1840
Worth, Joseph A. of Asheborough to Fatima Walker of Randolph county, Aug. 20, Davidson county. R. R. Sept. 4, 1840
Wright, Joshua G. of Rockingham county to Mary Jones of Person county, Je. 17. R. R. Jly. 3, 1840
Wright, Lieut. Wm. Henry, U.S.M. to Eliza Ann London, Nov., Wilmington. R. R. Dec. 1, 1840
Young, Lieut. Wm. Lee, U.S.M. of Cabarrus county to Ann E. Dove of Washington, Aug. 11, Washington, D. C. R. R. Sept. 4, 1840

1841

Adams, Howell to Mary E. Moran, Jan., Halifax. R. R. Jan. 8, 1841
Adams, Mary Eliza to Dr. Julius S. Bracken of Orange county, Mar., Greensboro. R. R. Mar. 19, 1841
Alexander, Allen M. to Rhoda M. Davis, My., Randolph county. R. R. My. 21, 1841
Alexander, Amanda to William K. Reid, Jan., Mecklenburg county. R. R. Jan. 22, 1841
Allen, Fielding to Gilly Drum, My., Iredell county. R. R. My. 21, 1841
Allen, Mary Caroline to Dr. Avery M. Powell of Caldwell county, Oct. 13, Iredell county. R. R. Oct. 29, 1841
Allston, Charity to James L. Wortham, Oct., Granville county. R. R. Oct. 19, 1841
Alsobrook, Jane to Benjamin C. Cooke of Granville county, Dec., Hillsboro. R. R. Dec. 17, 1841
Alspaugh, Emmanuel to Nancy Jane Douthit, Dec., Surry county. R. R. Dec. 25, 1841
Anderson, Margaret J. to Hugh B. Guthrie, Jly. 29, Chatham county. R. R. Sept. 17, 1841
Anderson, Wm. W. to Jane Capps, Apr., Mecklenburg county. R. R. Apr. 27, 1841

Andrews, William N. to Maria Taylor, Jly. 1, Raleigh. R. R. Jly. 6, 1841
Angel, Anderson to Margaret E. Mills, My., Stokes county. R. R. My. 25, 1841
Arney, John to Ann Catharine Mosteller, Apr., Lincoln county. R. R. Apr. 27, 1841
Ashe, Susan Hay to David Hay Grove of Tennessee, Nov., Wilmington. R. R. Nov. 16, 1841
Ashley, Louisa to James W. Walton, Feb. 23, Raleigh. R. R. Feb. 26, 1841
Bailey, Lucy to Wyatt Mangum, Dec. 16, Wake county. R. R. Dec. 25, 1841
Baily, Mary to Wm. Gordon, Mar., Washington, Beaufort county. R. R. Mar. 16, 1841
Baker, Elizabeth to William H. Dudley of Wilmington, Nov. 10, Raleigh. R. R. Nov. 12, 1841
Baker, Julia I. to James Henry Gautier, Feb., Washington, Beaufort county. R. R. Feb. 23, 1841
Bain, David to Rachel G. Robison, My., Mecklenburg county. R. R. Je. 1, 1841
Baker, Emily to Dr. A. S. Hall, Je., Halifax county. R. R. Je. 29, 1841
Baker, Nancy to Henry Blum, Nov., Salem. R. R. Nov. 16, 1841
Barber, Samuel R. of Tennessee to Mrs. Elizabeth H. Ruth, Jan. 4, Raleigh. R. R. Feb. 2, 1841
Barclift, John H. to Penelope Waff, Aug., Edenton. R. R. Aug. 10, 1841
Barnhardt, George H. to Mary Ann Hellick, Aug. 5, Rowan county. R. R. Sept. 3, 1841
Barnhart, Mary to Martin Harky, Jan., Cabarrus county. R. R. Jan. 29, 1841
Barrier, Ann to Joseph Walk, Nov., Davidson county. R. R. Nov. 23, 1841
Barrow, Dr. William to Eliza R. Calvert, Oct., Jackson, Northampton county. R. R. Oct. 12, 1841
Barry, Henry A. to Nancy L. Taylor of Chapel Hill, Je., Raleigh, West Tennessee. R. R. Je. 29, 1841
Barry, Dr. Wm. A. F. to Frances A. Taylor of Chapel Hill, Je., Raleigh, West Tennessee. R. R. Je. 29, 1841
Beard, A. S. of Davidson county to Martha Huison, Oct., Anson county. R. R. Oct. 29, 1841
Beaty, Cynthia to Andrew Rodden, Je., Mecklenburg county. R. R. Je. 15, 1841
Belvin, Biddy to John Thompson, Dec. 2, Wake county. R. R. Dec. 25, 1841
Benbury, Richard W. of Edenton to Sarah Riddick, Je., Gates county. R. R. Je. 22, 1841
Benbury, Sarah A. to Dr. Richard E. Weston, Aug., Woodville, Perquimans county. R. R. Aug. 3, 1841
Bennett, Ann J. to Dr. Benjamin Ingram, Jan., Anson county. R. R. Jan. 29, 1841
Bennet, Dr. Wm. H. of Anson county to Elizabeth Bulls of Wake county, Aug. 12, Smithfield, Johnston county. R. R. Aug. 13, 1841
Bentel, Edwin to Lucinda Shaub, Dec., Salem. R. R. Dec. 25, 1841
Bentley, William F. of Greensborough, Alabama to Sarah Dupre of Raleigh, Sept. 9, Wake county. R. R. Sept. 14, 1841
Biles, Hudson to Mary Pennington, My., Stanly county. R. R. My. 7, 1841

Biles, James to Martha Steele, Apr., Salisbury. R. R. My. 7, 1841
Biles, Tabitha to Truxton Kirk, My., Stanly county. R. R. My. 7, 1841
Bishop, Susan Elizabeth to Henry D. Gilbert, Nov., Wilmington. R. R. Nov. 23, 1841
Bitting, Walter R. to Susan Hampton, Nov., Stokes county. R. R. Nov. 16, 1841
Bivens, Sarah to Joseph Harris, Apr., Lincoln county. R. R. Apr. 16, 1841
Bizzell, Mary to John Hinson, Feb. 7, Wayne county. R. R. Feb. 26, 1841
Black, Henry of Orange county to Eliza Grey of Greene county & Maine, Mar., New York City. R. R. Mar. 23, 1841
Blackburn, Austin to Caroline Midferd, My., Halifax. R. R. My. 21, 1841
Blackstock, Priscilla A. to John W. Wells, My., Buncombe county. R. R. My. 14, 1841
Blackwelder, Wilson to Leak Cruse, My., Cabarrus county. R. R. My. 25, 1841
Blakely, Udney Maria of this State to Rt. Hon. Baron Von Bretton, My. 19, St. Croix, W. I. R. R. Je. 22, 1841
Blatchford, Mrs. Gorthenia to Levin B. Long of Bath, Sept., Washington, Beaufort county. R. R. Sept. 21, 1841
Blickensdierfer, Jacob of Ohio to Louisa Kramsh of Salem, Jly. 20, Bethlehem, Pa. R. R. Aug. 17, 1841
Blount, Capt. Joseph E. of Washington, Beaufort county to Mary E. Smithwick, Aug. 12, Jamestown, Martin county. R. R. Aug. 24, 1841
Blum, Henry to Nancy Baker, Salem. R. R. Nov. 16, 1841
Boddie, Van R. of Nash county to Caroline Perry, Apr. 14, Nash county. R. R. Apr. 23, 1841
Boggan, Eliza to Willis J. Willoughby, Je., Anson county. R. R. Je. 18, 1841
Bost, Jemima M. to William L. Mehaffy, Aug. 18, Lincoln county. R. R. Sept. 3, 1841
Boyce, Elam B. to Sarah Ann Hunter, Oct., Mecklenburg county. R. R. Oct. 19, 1841
Boylan, Irena to Richard P. Finch, Dec. 15, Wake county. R. R. Dec. 17, 1841
Bracken, Dr. Julius S. of Orange county to Mary Eliza Adams, Mar., Greensboro. R. R. Mar. 19, 1841
Brannock, Eliza Ann to Sidney Smith of Alabama, My., Guilford county. R. R. My. 14, 1841
Brant, John Frederick to Lavima Matilda Brazier, Dec., Greensboro. R. R. Jan. 1, 1841
Brazier, Lavima Matilda to John Frederick Brant, Dec., Greensboro. R. R. Jan. 1, 1841
Bretton, Rt. Hon. Baron Von to Udney Maria Blakely of this State, My. 19, St. Croix, W. I. R. R. Je. 22, 1841
Brickell, William, Sr. to Mrs. Nancy Watson, Nov., Halifax county. R. R. Nov. 9, 1841
Bridgers, Susan to Geraldus Shurley, Jan., Edgecombe county. R. R. Jan. 29, 1841
Briggs, Ann to Hugh M'Lean, Jr., Oct., Richmond. R. R. Oct. 29, 1841
Brinn, Reading to Mary Wilkinson, Je., Beaufort. R. R. Je. 15, 1841

Brooks, Jane Elizabeth to Benjah Swindell, Sept., Washington, Beaufort county. R. R. Sept. 3, 1841
Brooks, Dr. William M. to Virginia Ward, Dec., Milton. R. R. Dec. 17, 1841
Brothers, William R. to Christian Small, Mar., Gates county. R. R. Mar. 30, 1841
Brown, Harris A. to Mary Smithdeal, Apr., Rowan county. R. R. Apr. 16, 1841
Brown, John D. of Fayetteville to Louisa Pool, Aug., Salisbury. R. R. Aug. 10, 1841
Browning, Benjamin to Sophia Dickens, Jan., Halifax. R. R. Jan. 8, 1841
Bryan, Dr. Jesse G. to Fanny M. Havens, My., Washington, Beaufort county. R. R. My. 4, 1841
Buffaloe, Samantha Ann to John A. Wicker, Oct. 19, Wake county. R. R. Oct. 22, 1841
Bulls, Elizabeth of Wake county to Dr. Wm. H. Bennet of Anson county, Aug. 12, Smithfield, Johnston county. R. R. Aug. 13, 1841
Burke, Harman H. of Chatham county to Mrs. Louisiana Knight, My., Edgecombe county. R. R. My. 28, 1841
Burton, Elizabeth to Eli Hoyle, Oct. 6, Beatty's Ford. R. R. Oct. 19, 1841
Caldwell, Tod R. of Burke county to Minerva Cain, Dec. 16, Hillsboro. R. R. Jan. 1, 1841
Cain, Minerva to Tod R. Caldwell, Dec. 16, Hillsboro. R. R. Jan. 1, 1841
Cain, Samuel to Mary Jarrott, Nov., Fayetteville. R. R. Nov. 16, 1841
Calvert, Eliza R. to Dr. William Barrow, Oct., Jackson, Northampton county. R. R. Oct. 12, 1841
Campbell, Alexander to Lucy Smith, Sept., Iredell county. R. R. Sept. 14, 1841
Campbell, Robert of St. Louis, Mo. to Virginia Kyle, Feb. 25, Raleigh. R. R. Mar. 2, 1841
Capps, Jane to Wm. W. Anderson, Apr., Mecklenburg county. R. R. Apr. 27, 1841
Caraway, Francis to John W. Grist, Apr. 13, Newbern. R. R. My. 4, 1841
Carliles, Sparkman to Sarah Wiggins, My., Halifax. R. R. My. 21, 1841
Carpenter, Elizabeth to Samuel Carpenter, Apr., Lincoln county. R. R. Apr. 16, 1841
Carpenter, Samuel to Elizabeth Carpenter, Apr., Lincoln county. R. R. Apr. 16, 1841
Cates, Eliza to Washington King, Dec., Orange county. R. R. Dec. 31, 1841
Cherry, Martha to Joshua L. Lyon, My., Edgecombe county. R. R. My. 28, 1841
Clark, Harriet to Samuel J. Gribble, Jan., Charlotte. R. R. Jan. 22, 1841
Clark, William W. to Hannah Jarvis, Jly., Newbern. R. R. Jly. 16, 1841
Clemmons, Sarah I. to Samuel A. Dalton, Jly., Clemonsville, Davidson county. R. R. Jly. 16, 1841
Clouss, William to Mary Miller, Nov., Davidson county. R. R. Nov. 23, 1841
Clutts, Caleb to Elizabeth Moose, My., Rowan county. R. R. My. 11, 1841
Coleman, Dr. George C. of La Fayette, Georgia to Ellen M. Douglas of Danville, Va., Jan., Rutherfordton. R. R. Jan. 29, 1841

Collier, John J. of Alabama to Ann Nelson Hughes of Raleigh, Dec. 7, Wake county. R. R. Dec. 10, 1841
Collins, Elizabeth to George W. White, Mar., Cumberland county. R. R. Mar. 26, 1841
Compton, Rev. George C. to Edney G. Pierce, Oct., Williamston. R. R. Oct. 26, 1841
Congleton, Georgia Ann to Capt. Asa J. Duran, Oct., Washington, Beaufort county. R. R. Oct. 26, 1841
Connor, Malinda to Peter Little, Aug., Lincoln county. R. R. Aug. 10, 1841
Conrad, Joseph to Elizabeth Nicholson, Nov., Davidson county. R. R. Nov. 9, 1841
Cook, James of Franklin county to Jane Ann Kingsbury of New Hartford, Connecticut, Aug. 4, Louisburg. R. R. Aug. 10, 1841
Cooke, Benjamin C. of Granville county to Jane Alsobrook, Dec., Hillsboro. R. R. Dec. 17, 1841
Cooper, Dr. Lewis to Catharine Yarbrough, Oct. 19, Franklin county. R. R. Oct. 22, 1841
Cowan, Thomas to Margaret Young, Aug. 5, Rowan county. R. R. Sept. 3, 1841
Crenshaw, Gen. Daniel S. of Forestville, Wake county to Signora M. Martin of Franklin county, Jan. 10, Franklin county. R. R. Je. 15, 1841
Cruse, Leah to Wilson Blackwelder, My, Cabarrus county. R. R. My. 25, 1841
Curry, Sarah to Michael Sink, Nov., Davidson county. R. R. Nov. 23, 1841
Dailey, J. F. to Jane M. Kibler, Aug. 18, Lincoln county. R. R. Sept. 3, 1841
Dalton, Samuel A. to Sarah I. Clemmons, Jly., Clemonsville, Davidson county. R. R. Jly. 16, 1841
Daniel, Mary Eliza to Dr. W. T. Skelton, Nov., Halifax county. R. R. Nov. 9, 1841
Davis, Nelson to Francis Laffoon, Dec. 16, Wake county. R. R. Dec. 25, 1841
Davis, Robert to Russia Ann Nettle, Jan., Edgecomb county. R. R. Jan. 29, 1841
Davis, Rhoda M. to Allen M. Alexander, My., Randolph county. R. R. My. 21, 1841
Deford, Louisa to Henry Picard, Mar., Elizabeth City. R. R. Mar. 30, 1841
Denny, John R. to Elizabeth M'Lean, Dec., Greensboro. R. R. Dec. 31, 1841
Dewesse, Margaret to James Reed, Jan., Mecklenburg county. R. R. Jan. 22, 1841
Dickens, Sophia to Benjamin Browning, Jan., Halifax. R. R. Jan. 8, 1841
Dismukes, Dr. R. T. to Martha Jane Ramsay, Jan., Iredell county. R. R. Jan. 29, 1841
Dobbins, Margaret C. to James L. Nesbit, Sept., Iredell county. R. R. Sept. 14, 1841
Douglas, Ellen M. of Danville, Va. to Dr. George C. Coleman of La Fayette, Georgia, Jan., Rutherfordton. R. R. Jan. 29, 1841
Douthit, Nancy Jane to Emmanuel Alspaugh, Dec., Surry county. R. R. Dec. 25, 1841
Drum, Gilly to Fielding Allen, My., Iredell county. R. R. Nov. 21, 1841

Dudley, William H. of Wilmington to Elizabeth Baker, Nov. 10, Raleigh.
R. R. Nov. 12, 1841
Dunn, Lucy B. to Capt. William Simmons, Feb. 11, Wake Forest. R. R.
Feb. 19, 1841
Dunn, Lucy D. to John S. Moring, Dec. 2, Wake county. R. R. Dec. 7, 1841
DuPre, Sarah of Raleigh to William F. Bentley of Greensborough, Alabama,
Sept. 9, Wake county. R. R. Sept. 14, 1841
Duran, Capt. Asa J. to Georgia Ann Congleton, Oct., Washington, Beaufort
county. R. R. Oct. 26, 1841
Eacles, Harrison to Christina Mock, Mar., Davidson county. R. R. Mar. 26,
1841
Eborn, Mary Ann to Lewis Satterthwaite, Jan., Beaufort county. R. R.
Jan. 15, 1841
Ehringhaus, Amelia M. G. to Carl Hendricks of New York, Mar., Elizabeth
City. R. R. Mar. 23, 1841
Ellis, Sally Ann to Reuben Manning, Mar., Washington, Beaufort county.
R. R. Mar. 16, 1841
English, Robert to Priscilla Picket, Dec., Guilford county. R. R. Dec. 31,
1841
Epps, Nancy to Thomas L. Lofflin, Jly., Davidson county. R. R. Jly. 2, 1841
Estes, Col. Triplett T. of Petersburg to Mrs. Elizabeth Jones of Granville
county, Jly. R. R. Jly. 2, 1841
Eure, Maria to William Lowe, Aug., Halifax. R. R. Aug. 3, 1841
Faison, Benjamin, Jr., to Dorcas Massey, My. 27, Rolesville. R. R. Je. 4,
1841
Fariss, Clarissa to T. E. Patton of Buncombe county, Mar., Lafayette,
Georgia. R. R. Mar. 16, 1841
Feimster, Jerusha C. to William F. Morrison, Je., Iredell county. R. R.
Je. 15, 1841
Felton, Ann Eliza to Rev. Edward Wadsworth, Je. 15, Raleigh. R. R.
Je. 18, 1841
Fennell, Charles N. to Catharine J. Hargis, Je. 27, Fayetteville. R. R.
Jly. 2, 1841
Fentress, Jemima to Laban Swaim, Mar., Randolph county. R. R. Mar. 16,
1841
Field, Dr. George W. of Mecklenburg county, Virginia to Francis Blount
Littlejohn, Feb. 24, Oxford. R. R. Mar. 16, 1841
Finch, Richard P. to Irena Boylan, Dec. 15, Wake county. R. R. Dec. 17,
1841
Finlator, Robert to Sarah Ann Lumsden of Raleigh, My. 11, Fayetteville.
R. R. My. 18, 1841
Flack, William Ann to John K. M'Guire of Fayetteville, My., Charleston,
South Carolina. R. R. My. 14, 1841
Fleetwood, Mary N. to William Morris, Je., Perquimans county. R. R.
Je. 25, 1841
Flemings, Jesse A. of Edgecombe county to Ann Pittman, Nov., Halifax
county. R. R. Nov. 9, 1841
Floyd, John M. of Dekalb, Mississippi to Annie Jane Smith, Dec., Columbus
county. R. R. Dec. 17, 1841
Forney, Mary L. to Wm. P. Reinhardt, My., Burke county. R. R. My. 21,
1841

Foster, David C. to Abigail Graham, My., Rowan county. R. R. My. 11, 1841
Fox, John of Charleston, South Carolina to Sarah A. Watts, Oct., Fayetteville. R. R. Oct. 29, 1841
Fowler, Henry to Nancy Mabry, My., Williamsborough, Granville county R. R. My. 21, 1841
Gaither, Henrietta to John Taylor, Mar., Mocksville. R. R. Mar. 5, 1841
Gardiner, John C. of Franklinton to Mary Ann Hill, My., Petersburg, Virginia. R. R. Je. 4, 1841
Gardner, Charlotte D. to James C. Perry, Nov. 9, Wilmington. R. R. Nov. 23, 1841
Gardner, Mary Maria to Wm. H. Huntley, Anson county, Dec., Guilford county. R. R. Dec. 31, 1841
Gardner, William to Penelope N. Hill, My. 6, Randolph county. R. R. My. 21, 1841
Gautier, James Henry to Julia I. Baker, Feb., Washington, Beaufort county. R. R. Feb. 23, 1841
Gibbs, Seth, Jr. to Frances Luten, Jly., Middleton, Hyde county. R. R. Jly. 27, 1841
Gilbert, Henry D. to Susan Elizabeth Bishop, Nov., Wilmington. R. R. Nov. 23, 1841
Gill, Eliza T. to Joseph J. Little, Nov. 24, Franklin county. R. R. Jan. 5, 1841
Glass, Richard C. to Margaret G. Keer, Aug., Orange county. R. R. Aug. 3, 1841
Godwin, Richard W. of Franklinton to Sarah S. Perry, Nov. 16, Franklin county. R. R. Jan. 5, 1841
Goodwin, Elizabeth of Chatham county to John E. Nettles of Haywood county, Apr., Chatham county. R. R. Apr. 20, 1841
Gordon, Wm. to Mary Baily, Mar., Washington, Beaufort county. R. R. Mar. 16, 1841
Graham, Abigail to David C. Foster, My., Rowan county. R. R. My. 11, 1841
Graham, Richard to Sophia Lyerly, My., Rowan county. R. R. My. 11, 1841
Gray, Frances to Hinton Utley, Apr. 15, Raleigh. R. R. Apr. 20, 1841
Gray, Robert of Randolph county to Mary M. Wiley, Feb., Guilford county. R. R. Feb. 2, 1841
Gribble, Samuel J. to Harriet Clark, Jan., Charlotte. R. R. Jan. 22, 1841
Green, Angelina Ziegenfuss of Raleigh to John J. Upchurch of Henderson, Granville county, Je. 1, Raleigh. R. R. Je. 4, 1841
Green, Mrs. Hannah to Dr. Chr. Zimmerman of Columbia, South Carolina, Jly., Rockingham, Richmond county. R. R. Jly. 2, 1841
Green, Isabella to Wm. S. Smith, Dec., Granville county. R. R. Dec. 17, 1841
Green, Mary to James Simmons, Je., Montgomery county. R. R. Je. 18, 1841
Grey, Eliza of Greene county & Maine to Henry Black of Orange county, Mar., New York City. R. R. Mar. 23, 1841
Grist, John W. to Mary Francis Caraway, Apr. 13, Newbern. R. R. My. 4, 1841

Grove, David Hay of Tennessee to Susan Hay Ashe, Nov., Wilmington. R. R. Nov. 16, 1841
Guthrie, Hugh B. to Margaret J. Anderson, Jly. 29, Chatham county R. R. Sept. 17, 1841
Haden, D. F. to Susan Shuman, Apr., Salisbury. R. R. Apr. 27, 1841
Hadley, Charlotte to Alexander Webb, Jan., Richmond county. R. R. Jan. 22, 1841
Hagen, Francis F. of Nazareth, Pennsylvania to Clara C. Reichel, Jly. 6, Salem. R. R. Jly. 16, 1841
Hall, Dr. A. S. to Emily Baker, Je., Halifax county. R. R. Je. 29, 1841
Hall, Caroline Z. to Clinton Dewit Wilson, Jan., Rowan county. R. R. Jan. 29, 1841
Hall, Everard of Raleigh to Maria L. Hunter, Sept. 8, Springhill, Wake county. R. R. Sept. 3, 1841
Hall, Wm. to Martha Mabry, Jan., Halifax. R. R. Jan. 8, 1841
Hampton, Susan to Walter R. Bitting, Nov., Stokes county. R. R. Nov. 16, 1841
Hanner, Roddy E. to Nancy E. Rankin, Mar., Guilford county. R. R. Apr 2, 1841
Hare, Moses D. to Mrs. Elizabeth Moore, Je., Edenton. R. R. Je. 29, 1841
Hargis, Catharine J. to Charles N. Fennell, Je. 27, Fayetteville. R. R. Jly. 2, 1841
Hargrave, Franklin of Lexington to Mary W. Parker, Mar., Tarboro. R. R. Mar. 5, 1841
Harky, Martin to Mary Barnhart, Jan., Cabarrus county. R. R. Jan. 29, 1841
Harper, Ann R. to Oscar D. Lipscombe, Mar., Weldon. R. R. Mar. 26, 1841
Haughton, Mary S. to John W. Roberts, Aug., Edenton. R. R. Aug. 10, 1841
Harris, Joseph to Sarah L. Bivens, Apr., Lincoln county. R. R. Apr. 16, 1841
Harris, Lucy A. to William A. Harris, Sept. 8, Granville county. R. R. Sept. 17, 1841
Harris, William A. to Lucy A. Harris, Sept. 8, Granville county. R. R. Sept. 17, 1841
Harrison, Margaret Jane to David Maxwell, Je., Mecklenburg county. R. R. Je. 25, 1841
Harvell, Sarah to Samuel Taylor, Oct., Milton. R. R. Oct. 26, 1841
Hasten, Peter of Stokes county to Nancy Hedgecock, Nov., Davidson county. R. R. Nov. 9, 1841
Hastings, William to Lucy Ann M'Cullers, Jan. 19, Smithfield. R. R. Jan. 26, 1841
Havens, Fanny M. to Dr. Jesse G. Bryan, My., Washington, Beaufort county. R. R. My. 4, 1841
Hawkins, Eleanor to John Meekins, Je., Beaufort. R. R. Je. 15, 1841
Hawkins, Elizabeth to Jesse Herrington, Jan., Washington, Beaufort county. R. R. Jan. 15, 1841
Heathcock, James to Mary Ann Leiz, Jly., Rowan county. R. R. Jly. 2, 1841
Hedgecock, Nancy to Peter Hasten of Stokes county, Nov., Davidson county. R. R. Nov. 9, 1841

Heflin, Lucy A. to Dr. James Russel, Feb., Granville county. R. R. Feb. 5, 1841

Hester, William B. of Louisburg to Elizabeth M. Yarbrough, Jan. 5, Franklin county. R. R. Jan. 12, 1841

Hellen, Hannah to Thomas C. Wallace, Jly., Beaufort, Carteret county. R. R. Jly. 16, 1841

Hellick, Mary Ann to George H. Barnhardt, Aug. 5, Rowan county. R. R. Sept. 3, 1841

Henricks, Carl of New York to Amelia M. G. Ehringhaus, Mar., Elizabeth City. R. R. Mar. 23, 1841

Herbst, Ann Aurelia to Henry Edward Reich, Dec., Salem. R. R. Dec. 25, 1841

Herrington, Jesse to Elizabeth Hawkins, Jan., Washington, Beaufort county. R. R. Jan. 15, 1841

Hicks, Mrs. Mary to Jesse P. Wiseman, My., Rowan county. R. R. My. 7, 1841

Highsmith, Lewis B. of New Hanover county to Sarah A. Melvin, Mar., Sampson county. R. R. Mar. 26, 1841

Highsmith, William of New Hanover county to Elizabeth Melvin, Mar., Sampson county. R. R. Mar. 26, 1841

Hill, Ann to Elihu Mendenhall, Jly., Randolph county. R. R. Jly. 2, 1841

Hill, Mary Ann to John C. Gardiner of Franklinton, My., Petersburgh, Virginia. R. R. Je. 4, 1841

Hill, Margaret L. to Wentworth W. Pierce of Portsmouth, Va., Je., Duplin county. R. R. Je. 25, 1841

Hill, Mary to Henry Morgan, Nov., Rowan county. R. R. Nov. 9, 1841

Hill, Penelope N. to William Gardner, My. 6, Randolph county. R. R. My. 21, 1841

Hinkle, Andrew to Mrs. Mary Sport, Jly., Davie county. R. R. Jly. 2, 1841

Hinsdale, Samuel J. of Buffalo, New York to Elizabeth C. Wetmore, Sept. 2, Fayetteville. R. R. Sept. 10, 1841

Hinsdale, Sarah to William R. Lovin, Mar., Cumberland county. R. R. Mar. 26, 1841

Hinson, John to Mary Bizzell, Feb. 7, Wayne county. R. R. Feb. 26, 1841

Holden, W. W. to Ann Augusta Young, Nov. 3, Raleigh. R. R. Nov. 5, 1841

Holder, Nancy to Nelson Holder, Mar., Stokes county. R. R. Mar. 16, 1841

Holder, Nelson to Nancy Holder, Mar., Stokes county. R. R. Mar. 16, 1841

Holmes, Theophilus H. of U. S. Army to Laura Wetmore, Je. 5, Fayetteville. R. R. Je. 11, 1841

Hoover, Elizabeth of Ashborough to Maj. Thomas M. Moore of Person county, Jan. 13. R. R. Feb. 9, 1841

Hopkins, Mary to Martin P. Wright, Sept., Rockingham. R. R. Sept. 3, 1841

Horton, Mary Ann to Peter H. Knight, Jan. 14, Raleigh. R. R. Jan. 26, 1841

Howell, Charlotte W. to Allen Newsom, Oct., Stanly county. R. R. Oct. 15, 1841

Howell, William Ely to Martha Jane Vaughan, Oct., Scotland Neck, Halifax county. R. R. Oct. 8, 1841

Hoyle, Eli to Elizabeth Burton, Oct. 6, Beatty's Ford. R. R. Oct. 19, 1841

Hughes, Ann Nelson of Raleigh to John J. Collier of Alabama, Dec. 7, Wake county. R. R. Dec. 10, 1841
Huison, Martha to A. S. Beard of Davidson county, Oct., Anson county. R. R. Oct. 29, 1841
Hudson, Richard to Sarah Parnell, Jly., Mocksville. R. R. Jly. 16, 1841
Hunt, Edward to Ellen Vass, Oct., Granville county. R. R. Oct. 19, 1841
Hunter, Arimesia Maria to Joseph Mullen of Pasquotank county, Mar., Gates county. R. R. Mar. 30, 1841
Hunter, Maria L. to Everard Hall of Raleigh, Sept. 8, Springhill, Wake county. R. R. Sept. 3, 1841
Hunter, Martha to Johnson Olive, Dec. 23, Wake county. R. R. Dec. 31, 1841
Hunter, Sarah Ann to Elam B. Boyce, Oct., Mecklenburg county. R. R. Oct. 19, 1841
Hunter, William B. to Elizabeth M. Yarbrough, Jan. 5, Franklin county. R. R. Jan. 22, 1841
Huntley, Wm. H. of Anson county to Mary Maria Gardner, Dec., Guilford county. R. R. Dec. 31, 1841
Hyman, Sarah to Jesse J. Smith, Je., Beaufort. R. R. Je. 15, 1841
Ingram, Dr. Benjamin to Ann J. Bennett, Jan., Anson county. R. R. Jan. 29, 1841
Jackson, A. of Franklin county to Elizabeth Watters of Lenoir county, My. 25, Kinston. R. R. Je. 1, 1841
Jarrott, Mary to Samuel Cain, Nov., Fayetteville. R. R. Nov. 16, 1841
Jarvis, Hannah to William W. Clark, Jly., Newbern. R. R. Jly. 16, 1841
Jeffreys, Ann E. to Dr. Jas. W. M'Cain of Rockingham county, Dec., Person county. R. R. Dec. 25, 1841
Jennings, Dr. Wm. P. to Mary E. King, Jly., Wadesborough. R. R. Jly. 6, 1841
Jiggetts, Mary Ann to Edwin Whitehead, My., Halifax. R. R. My. 21, 1841
Jones, Charity Hellen to William A. Whitfield, Dec. 1, Wake county. R. R. Dec. 3, 1841
Jones, Mrs. Elizabeth of Granville county to Col. Triplett T. Estes of Petersburg, Jly. R. R. Jly. 2, 1841
Jones, Seth to Hawkins Lowry, Dec. 8, Wake county. R. R. Dec. 25, 1841
Jones, Rev. Wm. M. Green Johnston of Chapel Hill to Mary A. Stewart, Oct., Raleigh. R. R. Nov. 5, 1841
Joyner, Dr. Noah of Greenville to Emily A. Williams, My., Pitt county. R. R. My. 21, 1841
Keer, Margaret G. to Richard C. Glass, Aug., Orange county. R. R. Aug. 3, 1841
Kerr, Jane L. to Daniel B. P. Moorman, Feb., Lincolnton. R. R. Feb. 2, 1841
Ketcham, Alonzo R. to Sarah Hinsdale, Mar., Cumberland county. R. R. Mar. 26, 1841
Kelly, Polly to Neill M'Nair of Richmond county, Nov., Robeson county. R. R. Nov. 23, 1841
Kibler, Jane M. to J. F. Dailey, Aug. 18, Lincoln county. R. R. Sept. 3, 1841
King, Francis to Mary Ann Murrell, Nov. 4, Wake county. R. R. Nov. 12, 1841

King, Mary E. to Dr. Wm. P. Jennings, Jly., Wadesborough. R. R. Jly. 6, 1841
King, Washington to Eliza Cates, Dec., Orange county. R. R. Dec. 31, 1841
Kingsbury, Jane Ann of New Hartford, Connecticut to James Cook of Franklin county, Aug. 4, Louisburg. R. R. Aug. 10, 1841
Kinney, Silas to Hannah Myers, Nov., Davidson county. R. R. Nov. 23, 1841
Kirk, Truxton to Tabitha Biles, My., Stanly county. R. R. My. 7, 1841
Klutts, Charles to Christiana Walton, Apr., Rowan county. R. R. Apr. 16, 1841
Knight, Mrs. Louisiana to Harman H. Burke of Chatham county, My., Edgecomb county. R. R. My. 28, 1841
Knight, Peter H. to Mary Ann Horton, Jan. 14, Raleigh. R. R. Jan. 26, 1841
Kramsh, Louisa of Salem to Jacob Blickensdoerfer of Ohio, Jly. 20, Bethlehem, Pennsylvania. R. R. Aug. 17, 1841
Kyle, Virginia to Robert Campbell of St. Louis, Missouri, Feb. 25, Raleigh. R. R. Mar. 2, 1841
Laffoon, Francis to Nelson Davis, Dec. 16, Wake county. R. R. Dec. 25, 1841
Lane, Dr. Wm. B. to Frances M'Cain, Apr., Asheboro. R. R. Apr. 23, 1841
Lanier, Mary to Robert M. Wall, Feb. 11, Anson county. R. R. Feb. 26, 1841
Laton, Mary to Littlebury Privitt, Jan., Franklin county. R. R. Jan. 19, 1841
Leak, Hannah Pickett to Robert Leake Steele, My., Rockingham, Richmond county. R. R. My. 25, 1841
Ledbetter, Eliza D. to Thomas H. Tomlinson, Jan., Montgomery county. R. R. Jan. 29, 1841
Leiz, Mary Ann to James Heathcock, Jly., Rowan county. R. R. Jly. 2, 1841
Lewis, Louisa G. to Dr. Wm. Webb of Northampton county, Jly., Lawrenceville, Brunswick county, Virginia. R. R. Jly. 23, 1841
Lingle, John to Margaret Peeler, Mar., Rowan county. R. R. Mar. 30, 1841
Lipscomb, Oscar D. to Ann R. Harper, Mar., Weldon. R. R. Mar. 26, 1841
Little, Joseph J. of Alabama to Eliza T. Gill, Nov. 24, Franklin county. R. R. Jan. 5, 1841
Little, Peter to Malinda Connor, Aug., Lincoln county. R. R. Aug. 10, 1841
Littlejohn, Francis Blount to Dr. George W. Field of Mecklenburg county, Va., Feb. 24, Oxford. R. R. Mar. 16, 1841
Lofflin, Thomas L. to Nancy Epps, Jly., Davidson county. R. R. Jly. 2, 1841
Long, Levin B. of Bath to Mrs. Gorthenia Blatchford, Sept., Washington, Beaufort county. R. R. Sept. 21, 1841
Lovin, William R. to Sarah Hinsdale, Mar., Cumberland county. R. R. Mar. 26, 1841
Love, William to Maria Eure, Aug., Halifax. R. R. Aug. 3, 1841
Lowry, Hawkins to Seth Jones, Dec. 8, Wake county. R. R. Dec. 25, 1841
Lumsden, Sarah Ann to Robert Finlator of Raleigh, My. 11, Fayetteville. R. R. My. 18, 1841
Luten, Frances to Seth Gibbs, Jr., Jly., Middleton, Hyde county. R. R. Jly. 27, 1841

Lyerly, Sophia to Richard Graham, My., Rowan county. R. R. My. 11, 1841
Lyon, Joshua L. to Martha Cherry, My., Edgecomb county. R. R. My. 28, 1841
Mabry, Martha to Wm. Hall, Jan., Halifax. R. R. Jan. 8, 1841
Mabry, Nancy to Henry Fowler, My., Williamsborough, Granville county. R. R. My. 21, 1841
Mallett, Charles Beatty to Margaret Wright, Nov. 17, Fayetteville. R. R., Nov. 23, 1841
Mallett, Dr. William of Fayetteville to Caroline DeBernier Walker, Oct., Hillsboro. R. R. Nov. 2, 1841
M'Cain, Frances to Dr. Wm. B. Lane, Apr., Asheboro. R. R. Apr. 23, 1841
M'Cain, Dr. Jas. W. of Rockingham county to Ann E. Jeffreys, Dec., Person county. R. R. Dec. 25, 1841
M'Combs, Matilda to Charles Wilson, My., Mecklenburg county. R. R. Je. 1, 1841
M'Cullers, Lucy Ann to William Hastings, Jan. 19, Smithfield. R. R. Jan. 26, 1841
M'Cullock, Margaret C. to James A. G. Potts, Jan., Mecklenburg county. R. R. Jan. 22, 1841
M'Donald, Daniel to Catharine Phillips, Dec., Moore county. R. R. Dec. 17, 1841
M'Elroy, William J. of Salem to Rachel Oaks, Aug. 10, Davie county. R. R. Aug. 17, 1841
M'Guire, John K. of Fayetteville to William Ann Flack, My., Charleston, South Carolina. R. R. My. 14, 1841
M'Kay, Jane to John Pendergrass, My., Iredell county. R. R. My. 21, 1841
M'Kee, David to Lucy Ann Woods, Dec., Orange county. R. R. Dec. 31, 1841
M'Kenzie, Daniel of Moore county to Flora Martin, Jan., Richmond county. R. R. Jan. 22, 1841
M'Kenzie, John W. of Danville, Virginia to Martha Walters, Mar., Caswell county. R. R. Apr. 2, 1841
M'Lain, Henry to Isabella C. White, My., Iredell county. R. R. My. 21, 1841
M'Laughlin, John of Fayetteville to Effy Jane Munroe, Nov., Cumberland county. R. R. Nov. 23, 1841
M'Lean, Augustus to Catharine L. Schenck, Feb., Lincolnton. R. R. Feb. 19, 1841
M'Lean, Elizabeth to John R. Denny, Dec., Greensboro. R. R. Dec. 31, 1841
M'Lean, Hugh, Jr. to Ann Briggs, Oct., Richmond. R. R. Oct. 29, 1841
M'Nair, Neill of Richmond county to Polly Kelly, Nov. 1, Robeson county. R. R. Nov. 23, 1841
M'Rae, Ann to Alexander Stewart of Moore county, Oct., Richmond county. R. R. Oct. 15, 1841
Mangum, Wyatt to Lucy Bailey, Dec. 16, Wake county. R. R. Dec. 25, 1841
Manning, Reuben to Sally Ann Ellis, Mar., Washington, Beaufort county. R. R. Mar. 16, 1841
Martin, Flora to Daniel M'Kenzie of Moore county, Jan., Richmond county. R. R. Jan. 22, 1841
Martin, Signora M. of Franklin county to Gen. Daniel S. Crenshaw of Forestville, Je. 10, Franklin county. R. R. Je. 15, 1841

Massey, Caroline of Petersburg, Virginia to T. C. Williams of Weldon, Nov. 7, Petersburg, Va. R. R. Nov. 16, 1841
Massey, Dorcas to Benjamin Faison, Jr., My. 27, Rolesville. R. R. Je. 4, 1841
Maxwell, David to Margaret Jane Harrison, Je., Mecklenburg county. R. R. Je. 25, 1841
Mebane, Lemuel of Orange county to Caroline Yancey, Nov., Caswell county. R. R. Nov. 9, 1841
Mehaffy, William L. to Jemima M. Bost, Aug. 18, Lincoln county. R. R. Sept. 3, 1841
Melvin, Elizabeth to William Highsmith of New Hanover county, Mar., Sampson county. R. R. Mar. 26, 1841
Melvin, Sarah A. to Lewis B. Highsmith of New Hanover county, Mar., Sampson county. R. R. Mar. 26, 1841
Meekins, John to Eleanor Hawkins, Je., Beaufort. R. R. Je. 15, 1841
Mendenhall, Elihu to Ann Hill, Jly., Randolph county. R. R. Jly. 2, 1841
Midferd, Caroline to Austin Blackburn, My., Halifax. R. R. My. 21, 1841
Miller, Mary to William Clouss, Nov., Davidson county. R. R. Nov. 23, 1841
Mills, Margaret E. to Anderson Angel, My., Stokes county. R. R. My. 25, 1841
Minan, America to Andrew Swisgood, Nov., Davidson county. R. R. Nov. 23, 1841
Minor, Levin to Priscilla Walker, Mar., Rockingham. R. R. Mar. 26, 1841
Mock, Christina to Harrison Eacles, Mar., Davidson county. R. R. Mar. 26, 1841
Moran, Mary E. to Howell Adams, Jan., Halifax. R. R. Jan. 8, 1841
Morgan, Ann to John Wolfenden, Je., Beaufort county. R. R. Je. 29, 1841
Morgan, Henry to Mary Hill, Nov., Rowan county. R. R. Nov. 9, 1841
Moose, Elizabeth to Caleb Clutts, My., Rowan county. R. R. My. 11, 1841
Moore, Mrs. Elizabeth to Moses D. Hare, Je., Edenton. R. R. Je. 29, 1841
Moore, Jane Amanda to James P. White, Jly., Iredell county. R. R. Jly. 16, 1841
Moore, Louisa B. of Mississippi to Samuel J. Proctor of Camdonia, Mar., Elizabeth City. R. R. Mar. 16, 1841
Moore, Maj. Thomas M. of Person county to Elizabeth Hoover of Ashborough, Jan. 13. R. R. Feb. 9, 1841
Moorman, Daniel B. P. to Jane L. Kerr, Feb., Lincolnton. R. R. Feb. 2, 1841
Moring, John S. to Lucy D. Dunn, Dec. 2, Wake county. R. R. Dec. 7, 1841
Morris, William to Mary N. Fleetwood, Je., Perquimans county. R. R. Je. 25, 1841
Morrison, William F. to Jerusha C. Feinster, Je., Iredell county. R. R. Je. 15, 1841
Mosteller, Ann Catharine to John Arney, Apr., Lincoln county. R. R. Apr. 27, 1841
Mullen, Joseph of Pasquotank county to Arimesia Maria Hunter, Mar., Gates county. R. R. Mar. 30, 1841
Munroe, Effy Jane to John M'Laughlin of Fayetteville, Nov., Cumberland county. R. R. Nov. 23, 1841

Murrell, Harriet to Stephen L. Tucker of Raleigh, Mar. 25, Wake Forest. R. R. Mar. 30, 1841
Murrell, Mary Ann to Francis King, Nov. 4, Wake county. R. R. Nov. 12, 1841
Myers, Hannah to Silas Kinney, Nov., Davidson county. R. R. Nov. 23, 1841
Nesbit, James L. to Margaret C. Dobbins, Sept., Iredell county. R. R. Sept. 14, 1841
Nettle, Russia Ann to Robert Davis, Edgecomb county. R. R. Jan. 29, 1841
Nettles, John E. of Haywood county to Elizabeth Goodwin of Chatham county, Apr., Chatham county. R. R. Apr. 20, 1841
Newman, Rachel to Ammial G. Swain, Dec., Guilford county. R. R. Dec. 31, 1841
Newsom, Allen to Charlotte W. Howell, Oct., Stanly county. R. R. Oct. 15, 1841
Nichols, Harriet H. to William F. Strayhorn, Dec., Hillsborough. R. R. Dec. 31, 1841
Nicholson, Elizabeth to Joseph Conrad, Nov, Davidson county R. R. Nov. 9, 1841
Norfleet, John W. to Susan Pittman, Jan., Halifax. R. R. Jan. 8, 1841
Oakes, Rachel to William J. M'Elroy, Aug. 10, Davie county. R. R. Aug. 17, 1841
Oldham, William H. of Memphis, Tennessee to Elizabeth Robeson, Nov., Bladen county. R. R. Nov. 16, 1841
Olive, Johnson to Martha Hunter, Dec. 23, Wake county. R. R. Dec. 31, 1841
Owens, Peter to Delah C. Brown, Oct., Salisbury. R. R. Oct. 26, 1841
Overcash, Tobias to Coaby Yost, Mar., Rowan county. R. R. Mar. 30, 1841
Patrick, Martha W. to Thomas B. Windfield, My., Beaufort county. R. R. My. 4, 1841
Parker, Lucy P. to Dr. John H. Young of Granville county, Jan. 19, Orange county. R. R. Feb. 2, 1841
Parker, Mary W. to Franklin Hargrave of Lexington, Mar., Tarboro. R. R. Mar. 5, 1841
Parks, Mrs. Catharine to Moses Peeler, My., Rowan county. R. R. My. 25, 1841
Parnell, Sarah to Richard Hudson, Jly., Mocksville. R. R. Jly. 16, 1841
Parsley, Eliza of Raleigh to William Walton of Rutherford county, My. 18, Forestville. R. R. Je. 1, 1841
Patterson, Martha I. to Benjamin Rogers, Jr. of Wake county, Je., Orange county. R. R. Je. 29, 1841
Patton, Mrs. Nancy to William Ross, Je., Mecklenburg county. R. R. Je. 15, 1841
Patton, T. E. of Buncombe county to Clarissa Fariss, Mar., Lafayette, Georgia. R. R. Mar. 16, 1841
Pearce, Harriet to Ambrose Upchurch, Jan. 7, Franklin county. R. R. Jan. 19, 1841
Pearsall, William D. of Duplin county to Sarah Whitaker of Raleigh, Jan. 22, Raleigh. R. R. Jan. 29, 1841
Peed, Josephus to Julia Roe, Sept., Beaufort, Washington county. R. R. Sept. 3, 1841

Peed, Mary Jane to Absalom T. Roe, Sept., Beaufort, Washington county. R. R. Sept. 3, 1841

Peede, John S. to Olivia Ann Redditt, Jan., Beaufort county. R. R. Jan. 15, 1841

Peeler, Margaret to John Lingle, Mar., Rowan county. R. R. Mar. 30, 1841

Peeler, Moses to Mrs. Catharine Parks, My., Rowan county. R. R. My. 25, 1841

Pendergrass, John to Jane M'Kay, My., Iredell county. R. R. My. 21, 1841

Pennington, Mary to Hudson Biles, My., Stanly county. R. R. My. 7, 1841

Perry, Caroline to Van R. Boddie of Nash county, Apr. 14, Nash county. R. R. Apr. 23, 1841

Perry, James C. to Charlotte D. Gardner, Nov. 9, Wilmington. R. R. Nov. 23, 1841

Perry, Sarah S. to Richard W. Godwin, Nov. 16, Franklin county. R. R. Jan. 5, 1841

Phillips, Catharine to Daniel M'Donald, Dec., Moore county. R. R. Dec. 17, 1841

Picard, Henry to Louisa Deford, Mar., Elizabeth City. R. R. Mar. 30, 1841

Picket, Priscilla to Robert English, Dec., Guilford county. R. R. Dec. 31, 1841

Pierce, Edney G. to Rev. George C. Compton, Oct., Williamston. R. R. Oct. 26, 1841

Pierce, Wentworth W. of Portsmouth, Virginia to Margaret L. Hill, Je., Duplin county. R. R. Je. 25, 1841

Pittman, Ann to Jesse A. Flemings of Edgecombe county, Nov., Halifax county. R. R. Nov. 9, 1841

Pittman, Susan to John W. Norfleet, Jan., Halifax. R. R. Jan. 8, 1841

Pool, Louisa to John D. Brown of Fayetteville, Aug., Salisbury. R. R. Aug. 10, 1841

Pope, Elijah to Felicia N. Rawls, Nov., Halifax county. R. R. Nov. 16, 1841

Pope, Marcellus to Dorothy Whitehead, My., Halifax. R. R. My. 21, 1841

Potts, James A. G. to Margaret C. M'Culloch, Jan., Mecklenburg county. R. R. Jan. 22, 1841

Powell, Dr. Avery M. of Caldwell county to Mary Caroline Allen, Oct. 13, Iredell county. R. R. Oct. 29, 1841

Privitt, Littlebury to Mary Laton, Jan., Franklin county. R. R. Jan. 19, 1841

Proctor, Samuel J. of Camdonia to Louisa B. Moore of Mississippi, Mar., Elizabeth City. R. R. Mar. 16, 1841

Ramsay, Martha Jane to Dr. R. T. Dismukes, Jan., Iredell county. R. R. Jan. 29, 1841

Rankin, Nancy E. to Roddy E. Hanner, Mar., Guilford county. R. R. Apr. 2, 1841

Rawls, Felicia N. to Elijah Pope, Nov., Halifax county. R. R. Nov. 16, 1841

Redditt, Olivia Ann to John S. Peede, Jan., Beaufort county. R. R. Jan. 15, 1841

Reed, James to Margaret Dewesse, Jan., Mecklenburg county. R. R. Jan. 22, 1841

Reich, Amelia to C. H. Winkler, Apr., Salem. R. R. Apr. 27, 1841

Reich, Henry Edward to Ann Aurelia Herbst, Dec., Salem. R. R. Dec. 25, 1841

Reichel, Clara C. to Francis F. Hagen, Jly. 6, Salem. R. R. Jly. 16, 1841
Reid, William K. to Amanda Alexander, Jan., Mecklenburg county. R. R. Jan. 22, 1841
Reinhardt, Wm. P. to Mary L. Forney, My., Burke county. R. R. My. 21, 1841
Rencher, Daniel of Alabama to Catharine J. Warren, Mar., Wake Forest. R. R. Mar. 26, 1841
Riddick, Sarah to Richard W. Benbury of Edenton, Je., Gates county. R. R. Je. 22, 1841
Robards, Jane to Sampson Royster of Shelby county, Tennessee, Dec., Granville county. R. R. Dec. 17, 1841
Roberts, John W. to Mary S. Haughton, Aug., Edenton. R. R. Aug. 10, 1841
Robeson, Elizabeth to William H. Oldham of Memphis, Tennessee, Nov., Bladen county. R. R. Nov. 16, 1841
Robinson, Miss A. M. to Samuel M'Clary Robinson, Aug., Lincoln county. R. R. Aug. 10, 1841
Robinson, Samuel M'Clary to Miss A. M. Ann Robinson, Aug., Lincoln county. R. R. Aug. 10, 1841
Robison, Rachel G. to David Bain, My., Mecklenburg county. R. R. Je. 1, 1841
Rodden, Andrew to Cynthia Beaty, Je., Mecklenburg county. R. R. Je. 15, 1841
Roe, Alsalom T. to Mary Jane Peed, Sept., Beaufort, Washington county. R. R. Sept. 3, 1841
Roe, Julia to Josephus Peed, Sept., Beaufort, Washington county. R. R. Sept. 3, 1841
Rogers, Benjamin, Jr. of Wake county to Martha I. Patterson, Je., Orange county. R. R. Je. 29, 1841
Ross, James of Davidson county to Charlotte Vernon, Apr., Salisbury. R. R. Apr. 27, 1841
Ross, William to Mrs. Nancy Patton, Je., Mecklenburg county. R. R. Je. 15, 1841
Royster, Sampson of Shelby county, Tennessee to Jane Robards, Dec., Granville county. R. R. Dec. 17, 1841
Russell, Dr. James to Lucy A. Heflin, Feb., Granville county. R. R. Feb. 5, 1841
Ruth, Elizabeth H. to Samuel R. Barber of Tennessee, Jan. 4, Raleigh. R. R. Feb. 2, 1841
Sapp, Maria to Cyrus Weisner, Apr., Stokes county. R. R. Apr. 27, 1841
Satchwell, Benjamin E. to Harriet A. Winfield, Jly., Beaufort. R. R. Jly. 27, 1841
Satterthwaite, Lewis to Mary Ann Eborn, Jan., Beaufort county. R. R. Jan. 15, 1841
Schenck, Catharine L. to Augustus M'Lean, Feb., Lincolnton. R. R. Feb. 19, 1841
Shaub, Lucinda to Edwin Bentel, Dec., Salem. R. R. Dec. 25, 1841
Shaw, J. Q. of Orange county to Pheriby Williams, Aug., Somerville, Tennessee. R. R. Aug. 24, 1841
Shoff, Crissy to Alexander Trantham, Nov., Davidson county. R. R. Nov. 23, 1841

Shuman, Susan to D. F. Haden, Apr., Salisbury. R. R. Apr. 27, 1841
Shurley, Geraldus to Susan Bridgers, Jan., Edgecombe county. R. R. Jan. 29, 1841
Simmons, James to Mary Green, Je., Montgomery county. R. R. Je. 18, 1841
Simmons, Capt. William H. to Lucy B. Dunn, Feb. 11, Wake Forest. R. R. Feb. 19, 1841
Sink, Michael to Sarah Curry, Nov., Davidson county. R. R. Nov. 23, 1841
Skelton, Dr. W. T. to Mary Eliza Daniel, Nov., Halifax county. R. R. Nov. 9, 1841
Small, Christian to William R. Brothers, Mar., Gates county. R. R. Mar. 30, 1841
Smith, Annie Jane to John M. Floyd of Dekalb, Mississippi, Dec., Columbus county. R. R. Dec. 17, 1841
Smith, Jesse J. to Sarah Hyman, Je., Beaufort. R. R. Je. 15, 1841
Smith, Lucy to Alexander Campbell, Sept., Iredell county. R. R. Sept. 14, 1841
Smith, Sarah I. to George Willis of Fredericksburg, Virginia, Oct., Milton. R. R. Oct. 26, 1841
Smith, Sidney of Alabama to Eliza Ann Brannock, My., Guilford county. R. R. My. 14, 1841
Smith, Wm. S. to Isabella Green, Dec., Granville county. R. R. Dec. 17, 1841
Smithdeal, Mary to Harris A. Brown, Apr., Rowan county. R. R. Apr. 16, 1841
Smithwick, Mary E. to Capt. Joseph E. Blount of Washington, Beaufort county, Aug. 12, Jamestown, Martin county. R. R. Aug. 24, 1841
Snider, Miss A. to James Thayer, Mar., Randolph county. R. R. Mar. 30, 1841
Snyder, Ann to James Thayre, Feb., Randolph county. R. R. Feb. 26, 1841
Sport, Mrs. Mary to Andrew Hinkle, Jly., Davie county. R. R. Jly. 2, 1841
Stanly, James G. of Craven county to Elizabeth Wilkins, Sept., Newbern. R. R. Sept. 24, 1841
Steele, Martha to James Biles, Apr., Salisbury. R. R. My. 7, 1841
Steele, Robert Leake to Hannah Pickett Leak, My., Rockingham county. R. R. My. 25, 1841
Stewart, Alexander of Moore county to Ann M'Rae, Oct., Richmond county. R. R. Oct. 15, 1841
Stewart, Mary A. to Rev. Wm. M. Green Johnston Jones of Chapel Hill, Oct., Raleigh. R. R. Nov. 5, 1841
Strayhorn, William F. to Harriet H. Nichols, Dec., Hillsborough. R. R. Dec. 31, 1841
Stuart, Hannah M. to S. W. Whiting, My. 19, Raleigh. R. R. My. 21, 1841
Styers, James to Clarissa Verner, Mar., Stokes county. R. R. Mar. 16, 1841
Swaim, Leban to Jemima Fentress, Mar., Randolph county. R. R. Mar. 16, 1841
Swain, Ammial G. to Rachel Newman, Dec., Guilford county. R. R. Dec. 31, 1841
Swan, Dr. John of Pittsborough to Frances Waddell of Chatham county, Sept., Hillsboro. R. R. Sept. 28, 1841

Swindell, Benajah to Jane Elizabeth Brooks, Sept., Washington, Beaufort county. R. R. Sept. 3, 1841
Swisgood, Andrew to America Minan, Nov., Davidson county. R. R. Nov. 23, 1841
Sykes, Emilie to John Workman, Oct., Orange county. R. R. Oct. 12, 1841
Tarpley, Nancy M. to Joseph J. Trollinger, Jr., Jly. 15, Orange county. R. R. Jly. 23, 1841
Taylor, Frances A. to Dr. Wm. A. F. Barry of Chapel Hill, Je., Raleigh, West Tennessee. R. R. Je. 29, 1841
Taylor, John to Henrietta Gaither, Mar., Mocksville. R. R. Mar. 5, 1841
Taylor, Maria to William N. Andrews, Jly. 1, Raleigh. R. R. Jly. 6, 1841
Taylor, Nancy L. to Henry A. Barry of Chapel Hill, Je., Raleigh, West Tennessee. R. R. Je. 29, 1841
Taylor, Samuel to Sarah Harvell, Oct., Milton. R. R. Oct. 26, 1841
Thayer, James to Miss A. Snider, Mar., Randolph county. R. R. Mar. 30, 1841
Thayre, James to Ann Snyder, Feb., Randolph county. R. R. Feb. 26, 1841
Thomason, William to Mrs. John Trott, Jan., Rowan county. R. R. Jan. 29, 1841
Thompson, John to Biddy Belvin, Dec. 2, Wake county. R. R. Dec. 25, 1841
Tillett, Rev. John to Elizabeth Wyche, Oct., Granville county. R. R. Oct. 19, 1841
Todd, Sophia R. to W. W. Todd, Apr., Charlotte. R. R. Apr. 27, 1841
Todd, W. W. to Sophia R. Todd, Apr., Charlotte. R. R. Apr. 27, 1841
Tomlinson, Thomas H. to Eliza D. Ledbetter, Jan., Montgomery county. R. R. Jan. 29, 1841
Trantham, Alexander to Crissy Shoff, Nov., Davidson county. R. R. Nov. 23, 1841
Trexler, Anna to Henry A. Walton, Mar., Rowan county. R. R. Mar. 30, 1841
Trollinger, Joseph J., Jr. to Nancy M. Tarpley, Jly. 15, Orange county. R. R. Jly. 23, 1841
Trott, Mrs. John to William Thomason, Jan., Rowan county. R. R. Jan. 29, 1841
Tucker, Stephen L. of Raleigh to Harriet Murrell, Mar. 25, Wake Forest. R. R. Mar. 30, 1841
Upchurch, Ambrose to Harriet Pearce, Jan. 7, Franklin county. R. R. Jan. 19, 1841
Upchurch, John J. of Henderson, Granville county to Angelina Ziegenfuss Green of Raleigh, Je. 1, Raleigh. R. R. Je. 4, 1841
Utley, Hinton to Frances Gray, Apr. 15, Raleigh. R. R. Apr. 20, 1841
Vass, Ellen to Edward Hunt, Oct., Granville county. R. R. Oct. 19, 1841
Vaughan, Martha Jane to William Ely Howell, Oct., Scotland Neck, Halifax county. R. R. Oct. 8, 1841
Verner, Clarissa to James Styers, Mar., Stokes county. R. R. Mar. 16, 1841
Vernon, Charlotte to James Ross of Davidson county, Apr., Salisbury. R. R. Apr. 27, 1841
Waddell, Frances of Chatham county to Dr. John Swan of Pittsborough, Sept., Hillsboro. R. R. Sept. 28, 1841

Wadsworth, Rev. Edward to Ann Eliza Felton, Je. 15, Raleigh. R. R. Je. 18, 1841

Waff, Penelope to John H. Barclift, Aug., Edenton. R. R. Aug. 10, 1841

Wallace, Thomas C. to Hannah Hellen, Jly., Beaufort, Carteret county. R. R. Jly. 16, 1841

Walk, Joseph to Ann Barrier, Nov., Davidson county. R. R. Nov. 23, 1841

Walker, Caroline DeBernier to Dr. William Mallett of Fayetteville, Oct., Hillsboro. R. R. Nov. 2, 1841

Walker, Priscilla to Levon Minor, Mar., Rockingham. R. R. Mar. 26, 1841

Wall, Robert M. to Mary Lanier, Feb. 11, Anson county. R. R. Feb. 26, 1841

Walton, Christiana to Charles Klutts, Apr., Rowan county. R. R. Apr. 16, 1841

Walton, Henry A. to Anna Trexler, Mar., Rowan county. R. R. Mar. 30, 1841

Walton, James W. to Louisa Ashley, Feb. 23, Raleigh. R. R. Feb. 26, 1841

Walton, William of Rutherford county to Eliza Parsley of Raleigh, My. 18, Forestville. R. R. Je. 1, 1841

Ward, Virginia to Dr. William M. Brooks, Dec., Milton. R. R. Dec. 17, 1841

Warren, Catharine J. to Daniel Rencher of Alabama, Mar., Wake Forest. R. R. Mar. 26, 1841

Watson, Mrs. Nancy to William Brickell, Sr., Nov., Halifax county. R. R. Nov. 9, 1841

Watters, Elizabeth of Lenoir county to A. Jackson of Franklin county, My. 25, Kinston. R. R. Je. 1, 1841

Walters, Martha to John W. M'Kenzie of Danville, Va., Mar., Caswell county. R. R. Apr. 2, 1841

Walton, George S. to Mary E. Walton, Jan., Rowan county. R. R. Jan. 29, 1841

Walton, Mary E. to George S. Walton, Jan., Rowan county. R. R. Jan. 29, 1841

Watts, Sarah A. to John Fox of Charleston, S. C., Oct., Fayetteville. R. R. Oct. 29, 1841

Webb, Alexander to Charlotte Hadley, Jan., Richmond county. R. R. Jan. 22, 1841

Weisner, Cyrus to Maria Sapp, Apr., Stokes county. R. R. Apr. 27, 1841

Wells, John W. to Priscilla A. Blackstock, My., Buncombe county. R. R. My. 14, 1841

Weston, Dr. Richard E. to Sarah A. Benbury, Aug., Woodville, Perquimans county. R. R. Aug. 3, 1841

Wetmore, Elizabeth C. to Samuel J. Hinsdale, Sept. 2, Fayetteville. R. R. Sept. 10, 1841

Wetmore, Laura to Theophilus H. Holmes of U. S. Army, Je. 5, Fayetteville. R. R. Je. 11, 1841

Whitaker, Sarah of Raleigh to William D. Pearsall of Duplin county, Jan. 22, Raleigh. R. R. Jan. 29, 1841

White, George W. to Elizabeth Collins, Mar., Cumberland county. R. R. Mar. 26, 1841

White, Isabella C. to Henry M'Lain, My., Iredell county. R. R. My. 21, 1841

White, James P. to Jane Amanda Moore, Jly., Iredell county. R. R. Jly. 16, 1841
Whitfield, William A. to Charity Hellen Jones, Dec. 1, Wake county. R. R. Dec. 3, 1841
Whitehead, Dorothy to Marcellus Pope, My., Halifax. R. R. My. 21, 1841
Whitehead, Edwin to Mary Ann Jiggetts, My., Halifax. R. R. My. 21, 1841
Whiting, S. W. to Hannah M. Stuart, My. 19, Raleigh. R. R. My. 21, 1841
Whitley, Eliza to Nathaniel Wright, Je., Beaufort county. R. R. Je. 29, 1841
Wicker, John A. to Samantha Ann Buffaloe, Oct. 19, Wake county. R. R. Oct. 22, 1841
Wiggins, Sarah to Sparkman Carlisles, My., Halifax. R. R. My. 21, 1841
Wiley, Mary M. to Robert Gray of Randolph county, Feb., Guilford county. R. R. Feb. 2, 1841
Wilkins, Elizabeth to James G. Stanly of Craven county, Sept., Newbern. R. R. Sept. 24, 1841
Wilkins, Dr. Wm. Webb of Northampton county to Louisa G. Lewis, Jly., Lawrenceville, Brunswick, Virginia. R. R. Jly. 23, 1841
Wilkinson, Mary to Reading Brinn, Je., Beaufort. R. R. Je. 15, 1841
Williams, Emily A. to Dr. Noah Joyner of Greenville, My., Pitt county. R. R. My. 21, 1841
Williams, Pheriby to J. Q. Shaw of Orange county, Aug., Somerville, Tennessee. R. R. Aug. 24, 1841
Willis, George to Sarah I. Smith of Fredericksburg, Virginia, Oct., Milton. R. R. Oct. 26, 1841
Williams, T. C. of Weldon to Caroline Massey of Petersburg, Virginia, Nov. 7, Petersburg, Va. R. R. Nov. 16, 1841
Willoughby, Willis J. to Eliza Boggan, Je., Anson county. R. R. Je. 18, 1841
Windfield, Thomas B. to Martha W. Patrick, My., Beaufort county. R. R. My. 4, 1841
Winfield, Harriet A. to Benjamin E. Satchwell, Jly., Beaufort. R. R. Jly. 27, 1841
Winkler, C. H. to Amelia Reich, Apr., Salem. R. R. Apr. 27, 1841
Wilson, Charles to Matilda M'Combs, My., Mecklenburg county. R. R. Je. 1, 1841
Wilson, Dewit Clinton to Caroline Z. Hall, Jan., Rowan county. R. R. Jan. 29, 1841
Wiseman, Jesse P. to Mrs. Mary Hicks, My., Rowan county. R. R. My. 7, 1841
Wolfenden, John to Ann Morgan, Je., Beaufort county. R. R. Je. 29, 1841
Woods, Lucy Ann to David M'Kee, Dec., Orange county. R. R. Dec. 31, 1841
Workman, Henry N. to Temperance Workman, Oct., Orange county. R. R. Oct. 12, 1841
Workman, John to Emilie Sykes, Oct., Orange county. R. R. Oct. 12, 1841
Workman, Temperance to Henry N. Workman, Oct., Orange county. R. R. Oct. 12, 1841
Wortham, James L. to Charity Allston, Oct., Granville county. R. R. Oct. 19, 1841

Wright, Margaret to Charles Beatty Mallett, Nov. 17, Fayetteville. R. R. Nov. 23, 1841
Wright, Martin P. to Mary Hopkins, Sept., Rockingham. R. R. Sept. 3, 1841
Wright, Nathaniel to Eliza Whitley, Je., Beaufort county. R. R. Je. 29, 1841
Wyche, Elizabeth to Rev. John Tillett, Oct., Granville county. R. R. Oct. 19, 1841
Yancey, Caroline to Lemuel Mebane of Orange county, Nov., Caswell county. R. R. Nov. 9, 1841
Yarbrough, Catharine to Dr. Lewis Cooper, Oct. 19, Franklin county. R. R. Oct. 22, 1841
Yarbrough, Elizabeth M. to William B. Hester, Jan. 5, Franklin county. R. R. Jan. 12, 1841
Yost, Cosby to Tobias Overcash, Mar., Rowan county. R. R. Mar. 30, 1841
Young, Ann Augusta to W. W. Holden, Nov. 3, Raleigh. R. R. Nov. 5, 1841
Young, Dr. John H. of Granville county to Lucy P. Parker, Jan. 19, Orange county. R. R. Feb. 2, 1841
Young, Margaret to Thomas Cowan, Aug. 5, Rowan county. R. R. Sept. 3, 1841
Zimmerman, Dr. Chr. of Columbia, South Carolina to Hannah Green, Jly., Rockingham, Richmond county. R. R. Jly. 2, 1841

1842

Adams, Henderson to Mrs. Dobson, Aug., Davidson county. R. R. Aug. 30, 1842
Albright, George to Barbary Holt, Feb., Orange county. R. R. Feb. 15, 1842
Alexander, George of Mecklenburg county to Sarah P. Harris, Feb., Cabarrus county. R. R. Feb. 8, 1842
Alexander, Sophronia to Calvin Patton, Feb., Buncombe county. R. R. Mar. 1, 1842
Allen, Julia E. to Thomas Richardson, Apr., Newbern. R. R. Apr. 29, 1842
Allen, Samuel of Granville county to Louisa Jones, Jan. 22, Franklinton. R. R. Feb. 11, 1842
Allison, Robert W. of Concord to Sarah Ann Phifer, Je., Cabarrus county. R. R. Je. 14, 1842
Ambrose, Miss H. E. to Lewis C. Henderson, Jan., Onslow county. R. R. Jan. 21, 1842
Anderson, William S. to Francis Caroline Radcliffe of Charleston, South Carolina, Jly., Wilmington. R. R. Jly. 15, 1842
Arendell, Louisa P. to Rev. William Closs, Sept. 1, Louisburg, Franklin county. R. R. Sept. 23, 1842
Armfield, Jonathan of Greensboro to Sarah Jane Brown, Je., Rowan county. R. R. Je. 17, 1842
Atkins, Elizabeth F. to Obadiah Page, Mar., Wake county. R. R. Mar. 22, 1842
Atkins, Martha J. to Pleasant Trice, Apr. 26, Orange county. R. R. My. 6, 1842
Atkinson, Delany to George M'Millan, Jan., Fayetteville. R. R. Feb. 4, 1842

Atwater, Martha to Manley Strowd, Aug., Orange county. R. R. Aug. 23, 1842
Austin, A. A. to Martha Joyner, Mar., Halifax. R. R. Mar. 15, 1842
Avent, Harriet to Calvin Bray, Mar., Chatham county. R. R. Mar. 18, 1842
Bagge, Antoinetta L. to Samuel E. Brietz, Apr., Salem. R. R. Apr. 8, 1842
Bailey, William H. of Hertford county to Maria Pate, Apr., Richmond county. R. R. Apr. 26, 1842
Baker, Joseph to Eliza Couch, Feb., Hillsboro. R. R. Feb. 15, 1842
Baker, Julia Imogene of Norfolk to James H. Gautier, Jan., Washington, Beaufort county. R. R. Feb. 1, 1842
Baker, Wm. H. to Martha A. Stephens, Feb., Mecklenburg county. R. R. Feb. 22, 1842
Ball, Alfred L. of Milton to Cynthia C. Hill of Raleigh, My. 31, Raleigh. R. R. Je. 3, 1842
Barr, Margaret Amanda to Dr. Robert S. Smart, Feb., Rowan county. R. R. Mar. 1, 1842
Barringer, Jane C. to Gen. W. C. Means, Jan., Cabarrus county. R. R. Jan. 11, 1842
Battle, Susan to Dr. William H. McKee, Mar. 8, Raleigh. R. R. Mar. 11, 1842
Beatty, Hayes W. to Eliza Robinson, My. 12, Fayetteville. R. R. My. 13, 1842
Benbow, Paris of Fayetteville to Mary Kennedy, Je. 9, Wayne county. R. R. Je. 24, 1842
Benson, William S. to Penelope Jones, Oct., Bath, Beaufort county. R. R. Nov. 1, 1842
Berry, Benjamin W. of Wilmington to Miss A. E. Williams of New Hanover county, Oct. 13. R. R. Oct. 28, 1842
Berry, Betsey Hill to John Gammell, Jan., Wilmington. R. R. Jan. 25, 1842
Berry, Mary to James Sitton, Feb., Henderson county. R. R. Feb. 11, 1842
Berry W. to Miss A. E. Williams, Oct., New Hanover county. R. R. Oct. 25, 1842
Bethune, Alexander of Charlotte to Catharine M'Gilvary, Jan., Fayetteville. R. R. Jan. 21, 1842
Bevers, Jane to Major Reuben Flemming, Feb. 24, Wake county. R. R. Mar. 1, 1842
Bishop, H. to Sarah Ann Sholer, My., Wilmington. R. R. My. 20, 1842
Black, Narcissa to John R. Weddington of Cabarrus county, Sept., Mecklenburg county. R. R. Sept. 23, 1842
Blum, Mary A. to David Kelly of Surry county, Oct., Stokes county. R. R. Nov. 1, 1842
Blunt, Sarah J. P. of Greenville county, Virginia to Henry Peebles of Northampton county. R. R. Mar. 8, 1842
Boger, Catharine to Miles Mowry, Feb., Salisbury. R. R. Feb. 18, 1842
Bondurant, Anna M. to James H. Curtis of Fayetteville, Feb., Linden, Alabama. R. R. Feb. 22, 1842
Boon, Margaret Ann to Hector M'Millan, Oct., Fayetteville. R. R. Oct. 25, 1842
Bostick, Frances Ann to Jno. T. McColl, Jly., Richmond county. R. R. Jly. 12, 1842

Boyd, Nancy to Jackson Poe, Dec., Chatham county. R. R. Dec. 9, 1842
Bozzel, Mary L. to Samuel F. Kerr, Feb., Mecklenburg county. R. R. Feb. 22, 1842
Bradley, Ann to Alonzo J. Wills, Jan., Newbern. R. R. Feb. 4, 1842
Branch, Joseph to Jane Marshall, Feb., Halifax county. R. R. Feb. 8, 1842
Branch, Margaret to Mr. Partin, Feb., Halifax county. R. R. Feb. 8, 1842
Bray, Calvin to Harriet Avent, Mar., Chatham county. R. R. Mar. 18, 1842
Brietz, Samuel E. to Antoinetta L. Bagge, Apr., Salem. R. R. Apr. 8, 1842
Briggs, Ann E. to Charles C. Nelson of Newbern, Apr. 25, Raleigh. R. R. Apr. 26, 1842
Broadfoot, William G. to Frances Wetmore, Feb., Fayetteville. R. R. Feb. 8, 1842
Brooks, Clarissa to John Tyler, Jan., Washington, Beaufort county. R. R. Jan. 11, 1842
Brown, Charles P. to Priscilla W. Crenshaw, Jly., Stokes county. R. R. Jly. 22, 1842
Brown, Jacob to Eliza J. Rothrock, Apr. 7, Davidson county. R. R. My. 3, 1842
Brown, Martha M. to John Stuart, Mar. 17, Wake county. R. R. Mar. 25, 1842
Brown, Mary A. to William Dixon, Jr. of Green county, Jan., Greenville, Pitt county. R. R. Jan. 11, 1842
Brown, Sarah Jane to Jonathan Armfield of Greensboro, Je., Rowan county. R. R. Je. 17, 1842
Brown, Susan A. to Maj. R. G. Rankin of Wilmington, My., Smithville, Brunswick county. R. R. My. 20, 1842
Brown, Sylvester to Hannah Roundtree, Je., Pitt county. R. R. Je. 10, 1842
Burgin, Alney of Burke county to Drucilla Whitson, Feb., Buncombe county. R. R. Mar. 1, 1842
Byrne, Thos. H. to Mary P. Walker, Jly., Fayetteville. R. R. Jly. 22, 1842
Burton, Rev. Robert O. to Elizabeth H. Joyner, Apr., Halifax county. R. R. Apr. 8, 1842
Cain, P. H. to Susan W. Cheshire, Jan., Davie county. R. R. Feb. 1, 1842
Caldwell, Jos. P. of Statesville to Amanda M'Culloch, Oct., Rowan county. R. R. Nov. 1, 1842
Cameron, Walter A. of Hillsboro to Elizabeth P. Walker, Mar., Petersburg. R. R. Mar. 15, 1842
Campbell, Jane Isabella to Angus Munn, Feb., Cumberland county. R. R. Feb. 22, 1842
Cannon, Sarah L. to Atlas J. Peebles, Dec. 15, Jackson. R. R. Jan. 4, 1842
Capehart, Amelia of Murfreesboro to John Kimberly of New York City, Jly. 14, Murfreesboro. R. R. Jly. 29, 1842
Capel, Neomy to Andrew J. Thomas, Jan., Anson county. R. R. Jan. 21, 1842
Capps, Thomas to Martha Smith, My., Lincoln county. R. R. My. 24, 1842
Carmalt, Julia H. to Leonard H. Royster of Raleigh, Sept., Washington, Beaufort county. R. R. Sept. 6, 1842
Carmichael, Levin to Susan Newman, Feb., Hillsboro. R. R. Feb. 8, 1842
Carpenter, Willis to Ulcey Jones, Jly. 20, Wake county. R. R. Aug. 2, 1842
Carter, Joseph to Sarah Ann Charlotte, Jan., Newbern. R. R. Feb. 4, 1842

Carter, Mary to John Hendricks, Feb., Davie county. R. R. Feb. 18, 1842
Casey, Margaret to George Washington Rose of Charleston, South Carolina, Jly. 22, Fayetteville. R. R. Aug. 5, 1842
Charlotte, Sarah Ann to Joseph Carter, Jan., Newbern. R. R. Feb. 4, 1842
Cheshire, Sarah Frances to Joseph B. Webb, Jr. of Hillsboro, Mar., Edenton. R. R. Mar. 11, 1842
Cheshire, Susan W. to P. H. Cain, Jan., Davie county. R. R. Feb. 1, 1842
Christy, John H. to Ann Aurelia Roberts, Aug., Buncombe county. R. R. Sept. 6, 1842
Clark, John Newton to Theresa Tinnin, Mar., Orange county. R. R. Mar. 15, 1842
Clark, Julia to Edgar Cuthbert, Apr., Newbern. R. R. Apr. 29, 1842
Clarke, Warner to Eliza Williamson, Je. 8, Salisbury. R. R. Je. 17, 1842
Clifton, H. B. of Sampson county to Mary Whitfield, Apr., Duplin county. R. R. Apr. 19, 1842
Clifton, Nancy S. to John H. Whitfield of Duplin county, Jan., Sampson county. R. R. Jan. 21, 1842
Cline, Elizabeth S. to Joshua B. Hudson, Feb., Cabarrus county. R. R. Feb. 8, 1842
Clodfelter, George A. to Isabella R. Gray, Feb., Iredell county. R. R. Feb. 8, 1842
Closs, Rev. William to Louisa P. Arendell, Sept. 1, Louisburg, Franklin county. R. R. Sept. 23, 1842
Coart, Mary Elizabeth to William Dunn, Apr., Newbern. R. R. Apr. 8, 1842
Coatney, Martha to Edward Vick, Jr., Jly., Anson county. R. R. Jly. 29, 1842
Cobia, Mrs. Louisa of Charleston, South Carolina & Wilmington to John I. Roberts of Chapel Hill, Sept. 20, Chapel Hill. R. R. Sept. 27, 1842
Cochran, Robert, Jr. to Marinda Virginia Weisiger, Apr., Fayetteville. R. R. Apr. 19, 1842
Cole, Georgia to Mary Ann Long, Aug., Rockingham, Richmond county. R. R. Aug. 23, 1842
Coleman, Dr. R. to Catharine Scott both of this State, My., Tallahatchie, Mississippi. R. R. Je. 3, 1842
Collier, Major John W. of Wayne county to Caroline Oliver, Jan., Newbern. R. R. Jan. 18, 1842
Couch, Eliza to Joseph Baker, Feb., Hillsboro. R. R. Feb. 15, 1842
Couch, Susan to Harris Kirkman, Oct., Greensboro. R. R. Oct. 18, 1842
Crawford, Eliza Ann to Samuel Terry of Richmond county, Mar., Rockingham. R. R. Mar. 18, 1842
Crenshaw, Priscilla W. to Charles P. Brown, Jly., Stokes county. R. R. Jly. 22, 1842
Cromartie, Mary C. to John M. Fennell of New Hanover county, Apr., Bladen county. R. R. Apr. 26, 1842
Crudup, Martha to Joshua Perry of Franklin, My. 11, Granville county. R. R. My. 17, 1842
Cry, Catharine to James M. Godfrey, Jly., Mecklenburg county. R. R. Aug. 2, 1842
Curtis, James H. of Fayetteville to Anna M. Bondurant, Feb., Linden, Alabama. R. R. Feb. 22, 1842

Cuthbert, Edgar to Julia Clark, Apr., Newbern. R. R. Apr. 29, 1842
Davis, James to Elizabeth Ann O'Briant, Oct., Warren county. R. R. Oct. 18, 1842
Davis, Mary Susan to A. B. M'Caleb of Wilmington, Jan., Duplin county. R. R. Jan. 21, 1842
Devereux, John, Jr. to Margaret Mordecai, My. 25, Wake county. R. R. My. 27, 1842
Dillehay, John of Macon county, Alabama to Jane Sledge, Aug. 10, Halifax county. R. R. Aug. 26, 1842
Dinkins, A. D. of Mississippi to Cynthia D. Springs, Jly., Mecklenburg county. R. R. Aug. 2, 1842
Dixon, George W. to Mrs. Catharine Gibson, Nov., Newbern. R. R. Nov. 22, 1842
Dixon, William, Jr., of Greene county to Mary A. Brown, Jan., Greenville, Pitt county. R. R. Jan. 11, 1842
Dobson, Mrs. to Henderson Adams, Aug., Davidson county. R. R. Aug. 30, 1842
Duckett, Mary Matilda to John A. Patton of Georgia, Aug., Buncombe county. R. R. Sept. 6, 1842
Dudley, Eliza Ann to Thomas R. Purnell, My., Wilmington. R. R. My. 20, 1842
Dumas, Franklin of Richmond county to Jane Wall, Sept., Stanly county. R. R. Sept. 9, 1842
Dunn, William to Mary Elizabeth Coart, Apr., Newbern. R. R. Apr. 8, 1842
Eagle, Margaret to William Holbrooks, Feb., Rowan county. R. R. Feb. 18, 1842
Earnheart, Margaret to John Waggoner of Cabarrus county, Feb., Rowan county. R. R. Feb. 18, 1842
Edwards, Emily of Chatham county to Jeremiah Walker, Apr. 5, Guilford county. R. R. Apr. 29, 1842
Edwards, Frances to Robert Woody, Jan., Chatham county. R. R. Feb. 4, 1842
Elliott, Eleanor to Peter Thurston, Jan., Greensboro. R. R. Feb. 4, 1842
Evans, William to Jane Winfield, Jan., Beaufort. R. R. Jan. 21, 1842
Everest, Rev. Charles W. of Connecticut to Sarah Louisa Mallett, My. 31, Fayetteville. R. R. Je. 3, 1842
Faires, Margaret A. to C. A. Hoover, Jly., Mecklenburg county. R. R. Aug. 2, 1842
Fennell, John M. of New Hanover county to Mary C. Cromartie, Apr., Bladen county. R. R. Apr. 26, 1842
Field, Charlotte to William W. Warren, Jan., Guilford county. R. R. Feb. 4, 1842
Finn, Mrs. Eliza C. to Irwin Battle, Jan., Mecklenburg county. R. R. Jan. 11, 1842
Flack, Saunders to Susan Webb, Feb., Guilford county. R. R. Feb. 11, 1842
Flemming, Major Reuben to Jane Bevers, Feb. 24, Wake county. R. R. Mar. 1, 1842
Flintiff, William to Rebecca Hogan, Aug., Orange county. R. R. Aug. 23, 1842

Foard, Carolina to Hezekiah Turner of Rowan county, Feb., Davie county. R. R. Feb. 8, 1842
Forest, Roland to Jane A. Moss, Oct., Stanly county. R. R. Oct. 21, 1842
Forlaw, Susan J. to Capt. Wm. Sabiston, Je., Beaufort, Carteret county. R. R. Je. 10, 1842
Foust, Jane to Edwin M. Holt, Feb., Orange county. R. R. Feb. 15, 1842
Franklin, Columbus C. to Anna A. Gwyn, Jan. 12, Cedar Hill, Jonesville. R. R. Feb. 4, 1842
Frazier, Richard to Mary Jane Watson, Dec., Chatham county. R. R. Dec. 9, 1842
Galbraith, Charlotte of Duplin, Ireland & Raleigh to Henry Dana Ward of New York, My., Fairfax county, Virginia. R. R. Je. 3, 1842
Gamble, Ellen to J. B. Walton, Jan., Fayetteville. R. R. Feb. 4, 1842
Gammell, John to Betsey Hill Berry, Jan., Wilmington. R. R. Jan. 25, 1842
Gardner, Bryan to Caroline Nelson, Sept., Newbern. R. R. Sept. 30, 1842
Gardner, Mary Maria to William H. Huntley of Anson county, Jan., Guilford county. R. R. Jan. 21, 1842
Gardner, Samuel W. to Lucy Stacy, Aug., Montgomery county. R. R. Aug. 5, 1842
Garner, Malinda to Samuel Hughes, Aug., Davie county. R. R. Aug. 30, 1842
Gaston, Eliza of this State to George W. Graham of Washington, Nov. 15, Georgetown, District of Columbia. R. R. Nov. 22, 1842
Gautier, James H. to Julia Imogene Baker of Norfolk, Jan., Washington, Beaufort county. R. R. Feb. 1, 1842
Gibson, Mrs. Catharine to George W. Dixon, Nov., Newbern. R. R. Nov. 22, 1842
Gill, John to Sarah Hicks, Mar. 23, Wake county. R. R. Mar. 25, 1842
Godfrey, James M. to Catharine Cry, Jly., Mecklenburg county. R. R. Aug. 2, 1842
Goodnight, Mrs. Margaret C. to John A. Overcast of Rowan county, Feb., Cabarrus county. R. R. Feb. 8, 1842
Goodwin, Ann to James Harrell of Gates county, Feb., Chowan county. R. R. Feb. 8, 1842
Graham, George W. of Washington to Eliza Gaston of this State, Nov. 15, Georgetown, District of Columbia. R. R. Nov. 22, 1842
Graham, James to Helen Justice, Aug., Orange county. R. R. Aug. 23, 1842
Gray, Elizabeth H. to Robert Moffitt both formerly of Raleigh, Mar. 22, Belleville, Illinois. R. R. My. 27, 1842
Gray, Isabella R. to George A. Clodfelter, Feb., Iredell county. R. R. Feb. 8, 1842
Green, Cecelia Susan to Moses Haywood, Dec., Montgomery county. R. R. Dec. 9, 1842
Green, Rosa to Thomas King, Oct, Halifax county. R. R. Oct. 25, 1842
Gregory, David to Rina Williams, Dec., Fayetteville. R. R. Dec. 9, 1842
Gwyn, Anna A. to Columbus C. Franklin, Jan. 12, Cedar Hill, Jonesville. R. R. Feb. 4, 1842
Hacket, Eliza L. to Nathan D. Hunt of Jonesville, Jan. 11, Mulberry Hill, Wilkes county. R. R. Feb. 1, 1842
Hall, Jane to Alfred Hester, Feb., Macon county. R. R. Mar. 1, 1842

Hampton, Robert to William Holland of Sampson county, Feb., Davidson county. R. R. Mar. 1, 1842

Hampton, Susan to William Holland of Salem, Feb., Davidson county. R. R. Feb. 25, 1842

Hardison, Susan B. to John G. Whitecar, Jan., Plymouth, Washington county. R. R. Jan. 21, 1842

Hardy, Mary Eleanor to Starky B. Sharp of Hertford county, Nov., Woodville, Bertie county. R. R. Nov. 29, 1842

Harrell, James of Gates county to Ann Goodwin, Feb., Chowan county. R. R. Feb. 8, 1842

Harris, Rev. A. F. to Margaret Louisa Lambeth, Feb., Davidson county. R. R. Feb. 25, 1842

Harris, Fletcher to Martha Sledge, Oct., Granville county. R. R. Oct. 18, 1842

Harris, Sarah P. to George Alexander of Mecklenburg county, Feb., Cabarrus county. R. R. Feb. 8, 1842

Hastings, James to Mary Reeves, Feb., Orange county. R. R. Feb. 15, 1842

Hatch, Franklin to Jane Poe, Dec., Chatham county. R. R. Dec. 9, 1842

Haywood, Moses to Cecelia Susan Green, Dec., Montgomery county. R. R. Dec. 9, 1842

Henderson, Lewis C. to Miss H. E. Ambrose, Jan., Onslow county. R. R. Jan. 21, 1842

Hendricks, John to Mary Carter, Feb., Davie county. R. R. Feb. 18, 1842

Herring, Mrs. Nancy to William Henry Warren, Oct., Sampson county. R. R. Oct. 25, 1842

Hester, Alfred to Jane Hall, Feb., Macon county. R. R. Mar. 1, 1842

Hewlett, A. V. W. to Jane Whitenbury, Jan., Wilmington. R. R. Jan. 25, 1842

Hicks, Lucy to Capt. James Overby, Sept., Granville county. R. R. Sept. 23, 1842

Hicks, Priscilla M. to Dr. Wm. M. Mason, Jan. 15, Buncombe county. R. R. Feb. 1, 1842

Hicks, Sarah to John Gill, Mar. 23, Wake county. R. R. Mar. 25, 1842

Higginbotham, Mrs. Mary C. to Col. James White of Cabarrus county, My., Charlotte. R. R. My. 24, 1842

Hill, Cynthia C. of Raleigh to Alfred L. Ball of Milton, My. 31, Raleigh. R. R. Je. 3, 1842

Hill, Dr. Nicholas to Nancy Jones, Dec., Granville county. R. R. Dec. 9, 1842

Hines, Peter of Edgecombe county to Emma J. Snow, Mar. 22, Raleigh. R. R. Mar. 25, 1842

Hinton, Mary B. to John L. Prichard of Danville, Georgia, Sept. 1, Wake county. R. R. Sept. 6, 1842

Hogan, Rebecca to William Flintiff, Aug., Orange county. R. R. Aug. 23, 1842

Holbrooks, William to Margaret Eagle, Feb., Rowan county. R. R. Feb. 18, 1842

Holden, Attelia W. to John F. Lyons of Granville county, My. 11, Orange county. R. R. My. 24, 1842

Holland, William of Salem to Susan Hampton, Feb., Davidson county.
R. R. Feb. 25, 1842

Holland, William of Sampson county to Robert Hampton, Feb., Davidson county. R. R. Mar. 1, 1842

Holt, Barbary to George Albright, Feb., Orange county. R. R. Feb. 15, 1842

Holt, Edwin M. to Jane Foust, Feb., Orange county. R. R. Feb. 15, 1842

Holt, John of Orange county to Sarah Jane Mebane of Guilford county, Je. 16, Guilford county. R. R. Je. 28, 1842

Hoover, C. A. to Margaret A. Faires, Jly., Mecklenburg county. R. R. Aug. 2, 1842

Hoppers, Adam P. to Esther M. Lusk, Feb., Buncombe county. R. R. Mar. 1, 1842

Horton, Mrs. U. C. of Augusta, Georgia to Henry L. Myrover, Apr., Fayetteville. R. R. Apr. 26, 1842

Howard, Julius to Aide Sykes, Feb., Orange county. R. R. Feb. 8, 1842

Hudson, Joshua B. to Elizabeth S. Cline, Feb., Cabarrus county. R. R. Feb. 8, 1842

Hudson, William to Pamela Winchester, Feb., Mecklenburg county. R. R. Feb. 22, 1842

Huggins, Elizabeth to R. C. Slagle, Feb., Macon county. R. R. Mar. 1, 1842

Hughes, Samuel to Malinda Garner, Aug., Davie county. R. R. Aug. 30, 1842

Hunt, Nathan, D. of Jonesville to Eliza L. Hacket, Jan. 11, Mulberry Hill, Wilkes county. R. R. Feb. 1, 1842

Hunter, Editha Duleena to James Wallace, Mar., Mecklenburg county. R. R. Mar. 15, 1842

Hunter, Edward R. of this State to Carmi Ann Watts, Sept., Portsmouth, Virginia. R. R. Sept. 27, 1842

Huntley, William H. of Anson county to Mary Maria Gardner, Jan., Guilford county. R. R. Jan. 21, 1842

Hutchinson, John to Martha Shute, Jan., Newbern. R. R. Jan. 18, 1842

Ingles, Eliza to Jefferson Parker, Jan., Davie county. R. R. Feb. 1, 1842

Ingram, John to Jane Stokes, Feb., Rowan county. R. R. Feb. 18, 1842

Iredell, Penelope J. to Griffith J. M'Ree of Wilmington, Oct. 20, Raleigh. R. R. Oct. 25, 1842

Irwin, Battle to Mrs. Eliza C. Finn, Jan., Mecklenburg county. R. R. Jan. 11, 1842

Israel, Mary Lancaster to Dr. James R. Washington of Kinston, Lenoir county, Je., Philadelphia. R. R. Je. 10, 1842

Israel, Nelson of Cherokee county to Indiana Lane, Feb., Buncombe county. R. R. Feb. 11, 1842

Israel, Capt. P. to Sarah E. Wolf, Jan. 15, Buncombe county. R. R. Feb. 1, 1842

Jacobs, Lavinia to Washington Thomason, Oct., Rowan county. R. R. Oct. 21, 1842

Jacobs, Mary to Drewry Smith, Oct., Salisbury. R. R. Nov. 1, 1842

Jarrel, Mary to James Stuart, Oct., Richmond county. R. R. Oct. 28, 1842

Jewett, Caroline M. to Rev. John R. M'Intosh, Jly., Robeson county. R. R. Jly. 12, 1842

Johnson, Harriet to W. T. Shipp, Feb., Lincoln county. R. R. Feb. 22, 1842

Jones, Amelia Ann to William W. Whitaker, Dec., Wake county. R. R. Dec. 30, 1842

Jones, Henry J. to Rachel E. Wilson, Jan. 15, Buncombe county. R. R. Feb. 1, 1842

Jones, Louisa to Samuel Allen of Granville county, Jan. 22, Franklinton. R. R. Feb. 11, 1842

Jones, Louisa E. of Wake county to Dr. Jacob G. Walker of Leasburg, Caswell county. R. R. Jly. 15, 1842

Jones, Nancy to Dr. Nicholas Hill, Dec., Granville county. R. R. Dec. 9, 1842

Jones, Penelope to William S. Benson, Oct., Bath, Beaufort county. R. R. Nov. 1, 1842

Jones, Ulcey to Willis Carpenter, Jly. 20, Wake county. R. R. Aug. 2, 1842

Jones, Rev. William M. of the N. C. Conference to Eliza Ann Page, Sept. 27, Wake county. R. R. Oct. 7, 1842

Joyner, Elizabeth H. to Rev. Robert O. Burton, Apr., Halifax county. R. R. Apr. 8, 1842

Joyner, Martha to A. A. Austin, Mar., Halifax. R. R. Mar. 15, 1842

Justice, Helen to James Graham, Aug., Orange county. R. R. Aug. 23, 1842

Kelly, David of Surry county to Mary A. Blum, Oct., Stokes county. R. R. Nov. 1, 1842

Kennedy, Mary to Paris Benbow of Fayetteville, Je. 9, Wayne county. R. R. Je. 24, 1842

Kerr, Eliza to John Patterson of Iredell county, Feb., Mecklenburg county. R. R. Feb. 22, 1842

Kerr, Samuel F. to Mary L. Bozzel, Feb., Mecklenburg county. R. R. Feb. 22, 1842

Kimberly, John of New York City to Caroline Amelia Capehart of Murfreesboro, Jly. 14, Murfreesboro. R. R. Jly. 29, 1842

Kinchen, Roycraft to Nancy Thomasson, Oct., Wake county. R. R. Oct. 7, 1842

King, Thomas to Rosa Green, Oct., Halifax county. R. R. Oct. 25, 1842

Kingsbury, Henrietta W. to Wm. C. Love, Aug., Salisbury. R. R. Aug. 30, 1842

Kirkman, Harris to Susan Couch, Oct., Greensboro. R. R. Oct. 18, 1842

Kissler, Rev. Paul of this State to Mary Wingard of Lexington, South Carolina, Jan., South Carolina. R. R. Jan. 21, 1842

Lambeth, Amanda Malvina to John Shoup, Feb., Davidson county. R. R. Feb. 25, 1842

Lambeth, Margaret Louisa to Rev. A. F. Harris, Feb., Davidson county. R. R. Feb. 25, 1842

Lane, Indiana to Nelson Israel of Cherokee county, Feb., Buncombe county. R. R. Feb. 11, 1842

Leak, Mary Jane to Thomas Steele, Jan., Rockingham, Richmond county. R. R. Jan. 21, 1842

Lewis, Mildred to Louis Thorp, Oct., Oxford. R. R. Nov. 1, 1842

Liles, Caroline to John D. Williams, Oct., Anson county. R. R. Oct. 7, 1842

Lillington, J. A. to Elizabeth Kerr Williams of Wake county, Aug. 9, Surry county. R. R. Aug. 19, 1842
Lloyd, K. to Elizabeth M'Dowell, Jan. 5, Wake county. R. R. Jan. 11, 1842
Locke, William to Augusta Wheeler, New York, Apr. 30, Salisbury. R. R. My. 3, 1842
Long, Mary Ann to Georgie Cole, Aug., Rockingham, Richmond county. R. R. Aug. 23, 1842
Love, Wm. C. to Henrietta W. Kingsbury, Aug., Salisbury. R. R. Aug. 30, 1842
Lusk, Esther M. to Adam P. Hoppers, Feb., Buncombe county. R. R. Mar. 1, 1842
Lynch, Dr. John of Cheraw, South Carolina to Eliza Ellen Macnamara, Sept. 8, Armfield, Rowan county. R. R. Sept. 23, 1842
Lyons, John F. of Granville county to Attelia W. Holden, My. 11, Orange county. R. R. My. 24, 1842
M'Caleb, A. B. of Wilmington to Mary Susan Davis, Jan., Duplin county. R. R. Jan. 21, 1842
M'Coll, Jno. T. to Frances Ann Bostick, Jly., Richmond county. R. R. Jly. 12, 1842
M'Connell, Robert K. to Elizabeth Ross, Feb., Cabarrus county. R. R. Feb. 8, 1842
M'Cullock, Amanda to Jos. P. Caldwell, of Statesville, Oct., Rowan county. R. R. Nov. 1, 1842
M'Daniel, Caroline to Davis Oldham, Mar., Chatham county. R. R. Mar. 18, 1842
M'Dowell, Elizabeth to K. Lloyd, Jan. 5, Wake county. R. R. Jan. 11, 1842
M'Dowell, John of Bladen county to Miss Randle, Aug., Stanly county. R. R. Aug. 30, 1842
M'Gilvery, Catharine to Alexander Bethune, Jan., Fayetteville. R. R. Jan. 21, 1842
M'Intosh, Rev. John R. to Caroline M. Jewett, Jly., Robeson county. R. R. Jly. 12, 1842
M'Kee, Dr. William H. to Susan Battle, Mar. 8, Raleigh. R. R. Mar. 11, 1842
M'Laurin, John to Effy Stalker, Jan., Richmond county. R. R. Feb. 4, 1842
M'Lendon, John G. of Cheraw, South Carolina to Elizabeth M'Leod, Jly., Anson county. R. R. Jly. 29, 1842
M'Leod, Elizabeth to John G. M'Lendon of Cheraw, South Carolina, Jly., Anson county. R. R. Jly. 29, 1842
M'Millan, George to Delany Atkinson, Jan., Fayetteville. R. R. Feb. 4, 1842
M'Millan, Hector to Margaret Ann Boon, Oct., Fayetteville. R. R. Oct. 25, 1842
M'Namara, Eliza Ellen to Dr. John Lynch of Cheraw, South Carolina, Sept. 8, Armfield, Rowan county. R. R. Sept. 23, 1842
M'Pheeters, James G. of Raleigh to Susan Thorowgood of Norfolk, Mar. 3, Petersburg. R. R. Mar. 11, 1842
M'Ree, Griffith J. of Wilmington to Penelope J. Iredell, Oct. 20, Raleigh. R. R. Oct. 25, 1842

Mallett, Sarah Louisa to Rev. Charles W. Everest of Connecticut, My. 31, Fayetteville. R. R. Je. 3, 1842

Manning, Thomas to Rhoda White, Aug., Guilford county. R. R. Aug. 30, 1842

Marsh, Elizabeth Ann to Maj. James F. Rives, Feb., Chatham county. R. R. Feb. 22, 1842

Marsh, James F. to Mary W. Troy, Feb., Randolph county. R. R. Feb. 22, 1842

Marshall, Jane to Joseph Branch, Feb., Halifax county. R. R. Feb. 8, 1842

Mason, John to Elizabeth Morgan, Jan., Davie county. R. R. Feb. 1, 1842

Mason, Dr. Wm. M. to Priscilla M. Hicks, Jan. 15, Buncombe county. R. R. Feb. 1, 1842

Means, Gen. W. C. to Jane C. Barringer, Jan., Cabarrus county. R. R. Jan. 11, 1842

Mebane, Sarah Jane of Guilford county to John Holt of Orange county, Je. 16, Guilford county. R. R. Je. 28, 1842

Mendenhall, Charles to Rachel Veach, Aug., Guilford county. R. R. Aug. 30, 1842

Mendenhall, Dr. George M. of Westville, Mississippi to Elizabeth J. Thomas, Apr., Anson county. R. R. My. 12, 1842

Mendenhall, Mordecai of Guilford county to Lydia Pugh of Chatham county, Jan., Randolph county. R. R. Jan. 21, 1842

Minor, B. B. of Richmond, Virginia to Virginia M. Otey, My. 26, Columbia, Tennessee. R. R. Je. 17, 1842

Moffit, Robert to Elizabeth H. Gray both formerly of Raleigh, Mar. 22, Belleville, Illinois. R. R. My. 27, 1842

Monroe, Dr. Hugh A. of Unionsville, South Carolina to Lucy Gillespie Wright, Apr., Bladen county. R. R. My. 13, 1842

Moore, Mrs. Mary to James W. Osborne, Apr., Charlotte. R. R. Apr. 19, 1842

Moore, William of Fayetteville to Serreptha Ann Ritter, Jan., Moore county. R. R. Jan. 21, 1842

Mordecai, Margaret to John Devereux, Jr., Wake county. R. R. My. 27, 1842

Morgan, Elizabeth to John Mason, Jan., Davie county. R. R. Feb. 1, 1842

Morrison, Alexander to Sally F. Shaw, Jan., Cumberland county. R. R. Jan. 21, 1842

Moss, Jane A. to Roland Forest, Oct., Stanly county. R. R. Oct. 21, 1842

Mowry, Miles to Catharine Boger, Feb., Salisbury. R. R. Feb. 18, 1842

Munn, Angus to Jane Campbell, Feb., Cumberland county. R. R. Feb. 22, 1842

Murray, Mordacy B. to Robert G. Terrell, Sept. 20, Raleigh. R. R. Sept. 23, 1842

Murrell, Martha M. of Wake county to Richard Whiting, Jly., Tuscaloosa, Alabama. R. R. Jly. 12, 1842

Myrover, Henry L. to Mrs. U. C. Horton of Augusta, Georgia, Apr., Fayetteville. R. R. Apr. 26, 1842

Nash, Frederick K. to Margaret Potter, Feb. 16, Fayetteville. R. R. Feb. 22, 1842

Neel, Emily to George F. Oehler, Jan., Cabarrus county. R. R. Jan. 21, 1842

Nelms, J. P. to Miss S. J. Parsons, Je., Anson county. R. R. Je. 24, 1842
Nelson, Charles C. of Newbern to Ann E. Briggs, Apr. 25, Raleigh. R. R. Apr. 26, 1842
Nelson, Tho. Edward to Mrs. Mary Ann Whitely, Dec. 15, Pitt county. R. R. Jan. 14, 1842
Newlin, Oliver to Sarah Ellen Puryear, Aug., Orange county. R. R. Aug. 23, 1842
Newman, Susan to Levin Carmichael, Feb., Hillsboro. R. R. Feb. 8, 1842
O'Briant, Elizabeth Ann to James Davis, Oct., Warren county. R. R. Oct. 18, 1842
O'Daniel, Adeline to Jackson Stone, My., Chatham county. R. R. My. 24, 1842
Oehler, George F. to Emily Neel, Jan., Cabarrus county. R. R. Jan. 21, 1842
Oldham, Davis to Caroline M'Daniel, Mar., Chatham county. R. R. Mar. 18, 1842
Oliver, Caroline to Major John W. Collier of Wayne county, Jan., Newbern. R. R. Jan. 18, 1842
Osborne, James W. to Mrs. Mary Ann Moore, Apr., Charlotte. R. R. Apr. 19, 1842
Otey, Virginia M. to B. B. Minor of Richmond, Virginia, My. 26, Columbia, Tennessee. R. R. Je. 17, 1842
Overby, Capt. James to Lucy Hicks, Sept., Granville county. R. R. Sept. 23, 1842
Overcast, John A. of Rowan county to Mrs.. Margaret C. Goodnight, Feb., Cabarrus county. R. R. Feb. 8, 1842
Overman, William to Mary E. Slater, Oct., Davidson county. R. R. Oct. 7, 1842
Page, Eliza Ann to Rev. William M. Jordan of N. C. Conference, Sept. 27, Wake county. R. R. Oct. 7, 1842
Page, Obadiah to Elizabeth F. Atkins, Mar., Wake county. R. R. Mar. 22, 1842
Pahel, John to Mary Sloop, Feb., Rowan county. R. R. Feb. 18, 1842
Parker, Jefferson to Eliza Ingles, Jan., Davie county. R. R. Feb. 1, 1842
Parsons, Miss S. J. to J. P. Nelms, Je., Anson county. R. R. Je. 24, 1842
Partin, Mr. to Margaret Branch, Feb., Halifax county. R. R. Feb. 8, 1842
Pate, Maria to William H. Bailey of Hertford county, Apr., Richmond county. R. R. Apr. 26, 1842
Patterson, John of Iredell county to Eliza Kerr, Feb., Mecklenburg county. R. R. Feb. 22, 1842
Patton, Calvin to Sophronia Alexander, Feb., Buncombe county. R. R. Mar. 1, 1842
Patton, John A. of Georgia to Mary Matilda Duckett, Aug., Buncombe county. R. R. Sept. 6, 1842
Peebles, Atlas J. to Sarah L. Cannon, Dec. 15, Jackson. R. R. Jan. 4, 1842
Peebles, Henry of Northampton county to Sarah J. P. Blunt of Greenville county, Virginia. R. R. Mar. 8, 1842.
Perry, Joshua of Franklin to Martha Crudup, My. 11, Granville county. R. R. My. 17, 1842
Person, Anthony A. to Elizabeth M. Terrell, Dec., Franklin county. R. R. Dec. 30, 1842

Phifer, Sarah Ann to Robert W. Allison of Concord, Je., Cabarrus county. R. R. Je. 14, 1842

Poe, Jackson to Nancy Boyd, Dec., Chatham county. R. R. Dec. 9, 1842

Poe, Jane to Franklin Hatch, Dec., Chatham county. R. R. Dec. 9, 1842

Polk, Susan to Hon. Kenneth Rayner of Washington, District of Columbia, Jly. 12, Raleigh. R. R. Jly. 15, 1842

Pool, Jane to Aaron Wright, Oct., Montgomery county. R. R. Oct. 28, 1842

Potter, Margaret to Frederick K. Nash, Feb. 16, Fayetteville. R. R. Feb. 22, 1842

Prichard, John L. of Danville, Georgia to Mary B. Hinton, Sept. 1, Wake county. R. R. Sept. 6, 1842

Pugh, Lydia of Chatham county to Mordecai Mendenhall of Guilford county, Jan., Randolph county. R. R. Jan. 21, 1842.

Purnell, Thomas R. to Eliza Ann Dudley, My., Wilmington. R. R. My. 20, 1842

Puryear, Sarah Ellen to Oliver Newlin, Aug., Orange county. R. R. Aug. 23, 1842

Radcliffe, Francis Caroline of Charleston, South Carolina to William S. Anderson, Jly., Wilmington. R. R. Jly. 15, 1842

Randle, Miss to John M'Dowell of Bladen county, Aug., Stanly county. R. R. Aug. 30, 1842

Rankin, Adam M. to Louisa M. Kerr, Jly., Guilford county. R. R. Aug. 2, 1842

Rankin, Maj. R. G. of Wilmington to Susan A. Brown, My., Smithville, Brunswick county. R. R. My. 20, 1842

Ray, Henry M. of Cabarrus county to Martha A. Sumpter, Jan., Iredell county. R. R. Jan. 21, 1842

Rayner, Hon. Kenneth of Washington, District of Columbia to Susan Polk, Jly. 12, Raleigh. R. R. Jly. 15, 1842

Reeves, Mary to James Hastings, Feb., Orange county. R. R. Feb. 15, 1842

Ribelin, Asa to Susan C. Walton, Apr. 7, Davidson county. R. R. My. 3, 1842

Richardson, Thomas to Julia E. Allen, Apr., Newbern. R. R. Apr. 29, 1842

Ridley, Mrs. Mary to John C. Taylor, Sept., Granville county. R. R. Sept. 13, 1842

Ritter, Serreptha Ann to William Moore of Fayetteville, Jan., Moore county. R. R. Jan. 21, 1842

Rives, Maj. James F. to Elizabeth Ann Marsh, Feb., Chatham county. R. R. Feb. 22, 1842

Roberts, Ann Aurelia to John H. Christy, Aug., Buncombe conty. R. R. Sept. 6, 1842

Roberts, John I. of Chapel Hill to Mrs. Lonisa Cobea of Charleston, South Carolina & Wilmington, Sept. 20, Chapel Hill. R. R. Sept. 30, 1842

Robinson, Eliza to Hayes W. Beatty, My. 12, Fayetteville. R. R. My. 13, 1842

Roney, Henry to Elizabeth Tarpley, Aug., Orange county. R. R. Aug. 23, 1842

Rose, George Washington of Charleston, South Carolina to Margaret Casey, Jly. 22, Fayetteville. R. R. Aug. 5, 1842
Ross, Elizabeth to Robert K. M'Counell, Feb., Cabarrus county. R. R. Feb. 8, 1842
Rothrock, Eliza J. to Jacob Brown, Apr. 7, Davidson county. R. R. My. 3, 1842
Roundtree, Hannah to Sylvester Brown, Je., Pitt county. R. R. Je. 10, 1842
Royster, Leonard H. of Raleigh to Julia H. Carmalt, Sept., Washington, Beaufort county. R. R. Sept. 6, 1842
Russell, Daniel L. to Caroline E. Sanders, Jan., Onslow county. R. R. Jan. 21, 1842
Russel, Charles to Mrs. Jane Skinner of Edenton, Aug., Portsmouth. R. R. Aug. 16, 1842
Sabiston, Capt. Wm. to Susan J. Forlaw, Je., Beaufort, Carteret county. R. R. Je. 10, 1842
Safret, Sarah to John Yost, Feb., Rowan county. R. R. Feb. 18, 1842
Sanders, Caroline E. to Daniel L. Russel, Jan., Onslow county. R. R. Jan. 21, 1842
Scott, Catharine to Dr. R. Coleman both of this State, My., Tallahatchie, Mississippi. R. R. Je. 3, 1842
Sharp, Starky B. of Hertford county to Mary Eleanor Hardy, Nov., Woodville, Bertie county. R. R. Nov. 29, 1842
Shaw, Sally F. to Alexander Morrison, Jan., Cumberland county. R. R. Jan. 21, 1842
Shipp, W. T. to Harriet Johnson, Feb., Lincoln county. R. R. Feb. 22, 1842
Sholer, Sarah Ann to H. Bishop, My., Wilmington. R. R. My. 20, 1842
Shoup, John to Amanda Malvina Lambeth, Feb., Davidson county. R. R. Feb. 25, 1842
Shute, Martha to John Hutchison, Jan., Newbern. R. R. Jan. 18, 1842
Sitton, James to Mary Berry, Feb., Henderson county. R. R. Feb. 11, 1842
Skinner, Mrs. Jane of Edenton to Charles Russell, Aug., Portsmouth. R. R. Aug. 16, 1842
Slagle, R. C. to Elizabeth Huggins, Feb., Macon county. R. R. Mar. 1, 1842
Slater, Mary E. to William Overman, Oct., Davidson county. R. R. Oct. 7, 1842
Sledge, Jane to John Dillehay of Macon county, Alabama, Aug. 10, Halifax county. R. R. Aug. 26, 1842
Sledge, Martha to Fletcher Harris, Oct., Granville county. R. R. Oct. 18, 1842
Sloop, Mary to John Pahel, Feb., Rowan county. R. R. Feb. 18, 1842
Smart, Dr. Robert S. to Margaret Amanda Barr, Feb., Rowan county. R. R. Mar. 1, 1842.
Smith, Drewry to Mary Jacobs, Oct., Salisbury. R. R. Nov. 1, 1842
Smith, Martha to Thomas Capps, My., Lincoln county. R. R. My. 24, 1842
Snow, Emma J. to Peter Hines of Edgecombe county, Mar. 22, Raleigh. R. R. Mar. 25, 1842
Springs, Cynthia D. to A. D. Dinkins of Mississippi, Jly., Mecklenburg county. R. R. Aug. 2, 1842

Springs, Margaret A. to Dr. John Withers of York District, South Carolina, Jly., Mecklenburg county. R. R. Aug. 2, 1842

Stacy, Lucy to Samuel W. Gardner, Aug., Montgomery county. R. R. Aug. 5, 1842

Stalker, Effy to John M'Laurin, Jan., Richmond county. R. R. Feb. 4, 1842

Steele, Thomas to Mary Jane Leak, Jan., Rockingham, Richmond county. R. R. Jan. 21, 1842

Stephens, Martha A. to Wm. H. Baker, Feb., Mecklenburg county. R. R. Feb. 22, 1842

Stewart, James to Mary Jarrel, Oct., Richmond county. R. R. Oct. 28, 1842

Stokes, Jane to John Ingram, Feb., Rowan county. R. R. Feb. 18, 1842

Stone, Jackson to Adeline O'Daniel, My, Chatham county. R. R. My. 24, 1842

Strowd, Manley to Martha Atwater, Aug., Orange county. R .R. Aug. 23, 1842

Stuart, John to Martha M. Brown, Mar. 17, Wake county. R. R. Mar. 25, 1842

Sumpter, Martha A. to Henry M. Ray of Cabarrus county, Jan., Iredell county. R. R. Jan. 21, 1842

Swaim, Mrs. Abiah to Lyndon Swaim of Greensborough, Nov. 3, Greensboro. R. R. Nov. 8, 1842

Swaim, Lyndon of Greensborough to Mrs. Abiah Swaim, Nov. 3, Greensboro. R. R. Nov. 8, 1842

Sykes, Aide to Julius Howard, Feb., Orange county. R. R. Feb. 8, 1842

Tapp, William to Mary Thompson, My., Chatham county. R. R. My. 24, 1842

Tarpley, Elizabeth to Henry Roney, Aug., Orange county. R. R. Aug. 23, 1842

Taylor, John C. to Mrs. Mary Ridley, Sept., Granville county. R. R. Sept. 13, 1842

Terrell, Elizabeth M. to Anthony A. Person, Dec., Franklin county. R. R. Dec. 30, 1842.

Terrell, P. D. of Wake county to Mildred Wheless, Feb. 8, Nash county. R. R. Feb. 18, 1842

Terrell, Robert G. to Mordacy B. Murray, Sept. 20, Raleigh. R. R. Sept. 23, 1842

Terry, Samuel of Richmond county to Eliza Ann Crawford, Mar., Rockingham. R. R. Mar. 18, 1842

Thomas, Andrew J. to Neomy Capel, Jan., Anson county. R. R. Jan. 21, 1842

Thomas, Elizabeth J. to Dr. George M. Mendenhall, of Westville, Mississippi, Apr., Anson county. R. R. My. 12, 1842

Thomason, Washington to Lavinia Jacobs, Oct., Rowan county. R. R. Oct. 21, 1842

Thomasson, Nancy to Roycraft Kinchen, Oct., Wake county. R. R. Oct. 7, 1842

Thompson, Mary to William Tapp, My., Chatham county. R. R. My. 24, 1842

Thorowgood, Susan of Norfolk to James G. M'Pheeters of Raleigh, Mar. 3, Petersburg. R. R. Mar. 11, 1842

Thorp, Louis to Mildred Lewis, Oct., Oxford. R. R. Nov. 1, 1842
Thurston, Peter to Eleanor Elliott, Jan., Greensboro. R. R. Feb. 4, 1842
Tinnin, Theresa to John Newton Clark, Mar., Orange county. R. R. Mar. 15, 1842
Trice, Pleasant to Martha J. Atkins, Apr. 26, Orange county. R. R. My. 6, 1842
Troy, Mary N. to James F. Marsh, Feb., Randolph county. R. R. Feb. 22, 1842
Turner, Hezekiah of Rowan county to Carolina Foard, Feb., Davie county. R. R. Feb. 8, 1842.
Tyler, John to Clarissa Brooks, Jan., Washington, Beaufort county. R. R. Jan. 11, 1842
Upchurch, Bartlett to Jane Whitaker, Dec. 27, Raleigh. R. R. Dec. 30, 1842
Veach, Rachel to Charles Mendenhall, Aug., Guilford county. R. R. Aug. 30, 1842
Vick, Edward, Jr. to Martha Coatney, Jly., Anson county. R. R. Jly. 29, 1842
Waggoner, John of Cabarrus county to Margaret Earnheart, Feb., Rowan county. R. R. Feb. 18, 1842
Walker, Elizabeth P. to Walter A. Cameron of Hillsboro, Mar., Petersburg. R. R. Mar. 15, 1842
Walker, Dr. Jacob G. of Leasburg, Caswell county to Louisa E. Jones of Wake county, Jly. 12, White Plains, Wake county. R. R. Jly. 15, 1842
Walker, Jeremiah to Emily Edwards of Chatham county, Apr. 5, Guilford county. R. R. Apr. 29, 1842
Walker, Mary P. to Thos. H. Byrne, Jly., Fayetteville. R. R. Jly. 22, 1842
Wall, Jane to Franklin Dumas of Richmond county, Sept., Stanly county. R. R. Sept. 9, 1842
Wallace, James to Editha Duleena Hunter, Mar., Mecklenburg county. R. R. Mar. 15, 1842
Walton, J. B. to Ellen Gamble, Jan., Fayetteville. R. R. Feb. 4, 1842
Walton, Susan C. to Asa Ribelin, Apr. 7, Davidson county. R. R. My. 3, 1842
Ward, Henry Dana of New York to Charlotte Galbreath of Dublin, Ireland & Raleigh, My., Fairfax county, Virginia. R. R. Je. 3, 1842
Warren, William Henry to Mrs. Nancy Herring, Oct., Sampson county. R. R. Oct. 25, 1842
Warren, William W. to Charlotte Field, Jan., Guilford county. R. R. Feb. 4, 1842
Washington, Dr. James R. of Kinston, Lenoir county to Mary Lancaster Israel, Je., Philadelphia. R. R. Je. 10, 1842
Watson, Mary Jane to Richard Frazier, Dec., Chatham county. R. R. Dec. 9, 1842
Watts, Carmi Ann to Edward R. Hunter of this State, Sept., Portsmouth, Virginia. R. R. Sept. 27, 1842
Webb, Joseph B. Jr. of Hillsboro to Sarah Frances Cheshire, Mar., Edenton. R. R. Mar. 11, 1842
Webb, Susan to Saunders Flack, Feb., Guilford county. R. R. Feb. 11, 1842
Weddington, John R. of Cabarrus county to Narcissa Black, Sept., Mecklenburg county. R. R. Sept. 23, 1842

Weisiger, Marinda Virginia to Robert Cochran, Jr., Apr., Fayetteville. R. R. Apr. 19, 1842
Wetmore, Frances to William G. Broadfoot, Feb., Fayetteville. R. R. Feb. 8, 1842
Wheeler, Augusta of New York to William Locke, Apr. 30, Salisbury. R. R. My. 3, 1842
Wheless, Mildred to P. D. Terrell of Wake county, Feb. 8, Nash county. R. R. Feb. 18, 1842
Whitaker, Jane to Bartlett Upchurch, Dec. 27, Raleigh. R. R. Dec. 30, 1842
Whitaker, Samuel H. to Lydia A. Jones, Jly. 6, Wake county. R. R. Jly. 12, 1842
Whitaker, W. W. Jr. to Christian B. Wilson of Mecklenburg county, Virginia, Je. 16, Raleigh. R. R. Je. 21, 1842
Whitaker, William W. to Amelia Ann Jones, Dec., Wake county. R. R. Dec. 30, 1842
White, Col. James of Cabarrus county to Mrs. Mary C. Higginbotham, My., Charlotte. R. R. My. 24, 1842
White, Rhoda to Thomas Manning, Aug., Guilford county. R. R. Aug. 30, 1842
Whitecar, John G. to Susan B. Hardison, Jan., Plymouth, Washington county. R. R. Jan. 21, 1842
Whitenbury, Jane to A. V. W. Hewlett, Jan., Wilmington. R. R. Jan. 25, 1842
Whitfield, John H. of Duplin county to Nancy S. Clifton, Jan., Sampson county. R. R. Jan. 21, 1842
Whitfield, Mary to H. B. Clifton of Sampson county, Apr., Duplin county. R. R. Apr. 19, 1842
Whiting, Richard to Martha M. Murrell of Wake county, Jly., Tuscaloosa, Alabama. R. R. Jly. 12, 1842
Whitley, Mrs. Mary Ann to Tho. Edward Nelson, Dec. 15, Pitt county. R. R. Jan. 14, 1842
Whitson, Drucilla to Alney Burgin of Burke county, Feb., Buncombe county. R. R. Mar. 1, 1842
Williams, Miss A. E. of New Hanover county to Benjamin W. Berry of Wilmington, Oct. 13. R. R. Oct. 28, 1842
Williams, Elizabeth Kerr of Wake county to J. A. Lillington, Aug. 9, Surry county. R. R. Aug. 19, 1842
Williams, John D. to Caroline Liles, Oct., Anson county. R. R. Oct. 7, 1842
Williams, Joseph of Tennessee to Melinda R. Williams, My. 31, Raleigh. R. R. Je. 3, 1842
Williams, Melinda R. to Joseph Williams of Tennessee, My. 31, Raleigh. R. R. Je. 3, 1842
Williams, Rina to David Gregory, Dec., Fayetteville. R. R. Dec. 9, 1842
Williamson, Eliza to Warner Clarke, Je. 8, Salisbury. R. R. Je. 17, 1842
Wills, Alonzo J. to Ann Bradley, Jan., Newbern. R. R. Feb. 4, 1842
Wilson, Christian B. of Mecklenburg county, Virginia to W. W. Whitaker, Jr., Je. 16, Raleigh. R. R. Je. 21, 1842
Wilson, Rachel E. to Henry J. Jones, Jan. 15, Buncombe county. R. R. Feb. 1, 1842

Winchester, Pamela to William Hudson, Feb., Mecklenburg county. R. R. Feb. 22, 1842
Winfield, Jane to William Evans, Jan., Beaufort. R. R. Jan. 21, 1842
Wingard, Mary of Lexington, South Carolina to Rev. Paul Kissler of this State, Jan., South Carolina. R. R. Jan. 21, 1842
Withers, Dr. John of York District, South Carolina to Margaret A. Springs, Jly., Mecklenburg county. R. R. Aug. 2, 1842
Wolf, Sarah E. to Capt. P. Israel, Jan. 15, Buncombe county. R. R. Feb. 1, 1842
Woody, Robert to Frances Edwards, Jan., Chatham county. R. R. Feb. 4, 1842
Wright, Aaron to Jane Pool, Oct., Montgomery county. R. R. Oct. 28, 1842
Wright, Lucy Gillespie to Dr. Hugh A. Monroe of Unionville, South Carolina, Apr., Bladen county. R. R. My. 13, 1842
Yost, John to Sarah Safret, Feb., Rowan county. R. R. Feb. 18, 1842

1843

Abernathy, John C to Sarah S. Hutson, Je., Mecklenburg county. R. R. Je. 13, 1843
Adams, Lucy Ann to Henry Turner, Dec., Wake county. R. R. Dec. 29, 1843
Ainsley, Asa of Washington county to Margaret Wynn, Mar., Chowan county. R. R. Mar. 7, 1843
Albert, Mary to Johnston Underwood, Dec., Orange county. R. R. Dec. 29, 1843
Alexander, Leander D. of Mississippi to Margaret Parks, Aug., Mecklenburg county. R. R. Aug. 25, 1843
Allen, Elizabeth to John Mitchell, Oct., Granville county. R. R. Oct. 27, 1843
Alston, Louisa B. to Thos K. Thomas, Nov. 15, Louisburg. R. R. Nov. 21, 1843
Alston, Thomas N. F. of Warren county to Elizabeth Perry, Feb. 22, Franklin county. R. R. Mar. 3, 1843
Arendel, Dr. M. F. to Zilphia Ann Leecraft, Nov., Carteret county. R. R. Dec. 1, 1843
Arnold, Hezekiah to Miss Patrick, Mar., Washington county. R. R. Mar. 7, 1843
Austin, Elizabeth to Harrison Tyrrell, Nov., Caswell county. R. R. Nov. 3, 1843
Bailey, Frances C. to Maj. J. M. Hunt of Granville county, Oct., Person county. R. R. Oct. 27, 1843
Baker, Frances to Lieut. John Chambers of Wake county, Feb. 15, Franklin county. R. R. Feb. 21, 1843
Baker, Mary Ann to John W. Munroe of Cumberland county, Jly., Robeson county. R. R. Jly. 14, 1843
Balance, Mrs. Lavinia to John Ross, Apr., Washington, Beaufort county. R. R. Apr. 18, 1843
Baldwin, Agnes J. to James A. Smith of Robeson county, Feb., Wilmington. R. R. Feb. 3, 1843

Barrow, Ann to Robert T. D. Young of Louisburg, Jan. 18, Franklin county. R. R. Feb. 3, 1843

Barton, Harriet to Richard H. Lee, Dec., Hillsboro. R. R. Dec. 29, 1843

Baskerville, John to Sarah D. Young, Dec., Granville county. R. R. Dec. 8, 1843

Battle, Cornelia V. to John S. Dancy of Tarboro, Dec., Cool Springs, Edgecombe county. R. R. Dec. 22, 1843

Bennett, Francis S. to Benjamin S. Cox, Oct., Anson county. R. R. Oct. 17, 1843

Bettner, Charles of Newbern to Eliza Booth, Apr., Columbus, Mississippi. R. R. Apr. 21, 1843

Betts, Calvin of Wake county to Sarah Stone of Granville county, Sept. 20, Granville county. R. R. Sept. 29, 1843

Bishop, F. W. to Elizabeth Links, Feb., Washington, Beaufort county. R. R. Feb. 21, 1843

Bishop, Martha to Cullen Powell, Nov., Halifax county. R. R. Nov. 14, 1843

Blount, Alex C. to Julia E. Washington of Wayne county, Oct. 26, Newbern. R. R. Nov. 3, 1843

Blum, Alexander C. to Antionette M. Shultz, Je., Salem. R. R. Je. 2, 1843

Bogle, James of this State to Rebecca Riggs of Baltimore, Jan., New York. R. R. Jan. 10, 1843

Boger, Mathias of Salisbury to Sarah R. Derr, Je. 28, Lincoln county. R. R. Jly. 18, 1843

Boon, Dr. James H. of this State to Julia Smith of Philadelphia, Aug., Philadelphia. R. R. Aug. 4, 1843

Booth, Eliza to Charles Bettner of Newbern, Apr., Columbus, Mississippi. R. R. Apr. 21, 1843

Bowman, Margaret Hampton to Rev. John L. Moore of Germantown, Aug., Stokes county. R. R. Aug. 4, 1843

Brian, Hellen to Emeline G. Rumley, Dec. 22, Carteret county. R. R. Jan. 10, 1843

Briggs, Ann E. to Joseph C. Meador, My., Hertford county. R. R. My. 2, 1843

Briggs, Bradfoot to Darcas Elizabeth Hambleton, Apr., Washington, Beaufort county. R. R. Apr. 18, 1843

Briggs, William W. to Lucy Ochiltree, Mar., Fayetteville. R. R. Mar. 7, 1843

Brodie, Martha A. R. to Lieut. C. H. Kennedy of U. S. N., Oct. 11, Warren county. R. R. Oct. 17, 1843

Brown, Benjamin F. to Mary Jamison, Je., Mecklenburg county. R. R. Je. 13, 1843

Brown, Columbia A. to Frederick J. Lord, Dec. 13, Wilmington. R. R. Dec. 19, 1843

Brown, Laura to Joseph Chambers, Sept., Salisbury. R. R. Sept. 8, 1843

Brown, William H. to Mrs. Naomi Dancy, Feb., Iredell county. R. R. Feb. 14, 1843

Browning, Williamson to Sarah H. Eubanks of Virginia, Feb., Garysburg. R. R. Feb. 3, 1843

Bumpass, Rev. Sidney D. of Raleigh to Frances M. Webb, Dec. 27, Person county. R. R. Jan. 6, 1843

Burns, Sarah to Col. John C. Sosserman of Pontotoc, Mississippi, Feb., Cabarrus county. R. R. Feb. 28, 1843

Burwell, Blair of Staunton to Mary Ann Davis, Sept. 13, Franklin county. R. R. Sept. 29, 1843

Caddell, Presly to Hannah M'Crummen, Sept., Moore county. R. R. Sept. 15, 1843

Caldwell, James H. of Falkland, Alabama to Amelia Caroline Crenshaw of Wake Forest, Aug. 17. R. R. Aug. 29, 1843

Callum, James R. of Milton to Mary Clancy, Dec., Hillsboro. R. R. Dec. 12, 1843

Campbell, Archibald of Robeson county to Catharine Q. M'Neill, Jan. 19, Rockfish. R. R. Feb. 3, 1843

Campbell, Penelope of Norfolk to John Wilson of Milton, Oct., Philadelphia. R. R. Nov. 3, 1843

Carrington, Mary E. of Raleigh to Dr. Wm. C. Crump of Manchester, Virginia, Nov. 22, Greenville, Pitt county. R. R. Dec. 8, 1843

Carter, Adaliza to Zebulon English, Nov., Randolph county. R. R. Nov. 10, 1843

Chambers, Lieut John of Wake county to Francis Baker, Feb. 15, Franklin county. R. R. Feb. 21, 1843

Chambers, Joseph to Laura Brown, Sept., Salisbury. R. R. Sept. 8, 1843

Cheshire, Rev. Joseph B. to Elizabeth Parker, Feb., Tarboro. R. R. Feb. 17, 1843

Clancy, Mary to James R. Callum of Milton, Dec., Hillsboro. R. R. Dec. 12, 1843

Clapp, Wm. to Matilda Thomas, Nov., Anson county. R. R. Dec. 1, 1843

Clark, Mary Sumner to Dr. Wm. Geo. Thomas, Nov., Tarboro. R. R. Nov. 10, 1843

Clark, Rosannah C. to Archibald W. Hedgepeth, Oct., Hillsboro. R. R. Oct. 24, 1843

Clements, Mrs. Mary to Jeremiah G. Respass of Beaufort, Mar., Williamston, Martin county. R. R. Mar. 21, 1843

Coart, John C. to Margaret Templeton, Feb., Newbern. R. R. Feb. 7, 1843

Cobb, Miss H. E. A. to J. H. Peebles, Feb., Kinston, Lenoir county. R. R. Feb. 7, 1843

Coleman, Elizabeth Delight to James A. Rozier of Robeson county, Dec., Columbus county. R. R. Dec. 12, 1843

Collet, Samuel of Davidson county to Jane Frazer, Nov., Randolph county. R. R. Nov. 10, 1843

Collins, Ann of Edenton to Hon. William B. Shepard, Je. 8, Edenton. R. R. Je. 9, 1843

Conrad, Catharine to Dr. A. C. Wharton, Feb., Stokes county. R. R. Feb. 7, 1843

Conrad, Julia A. to Dr. Beverly Jones, Nov., Stokes county. R. R. Dec. 1st, 1843

Cooley, Tarmesia to Daniel D. Philips, Je., Hillsboro. R. R. Je. 13, 1843

Cooper, Laura Weston to George H. Tonnoffski, Mar. 16, Raleigh. R. R. Mar. 21, 1843

Cotfield, Margaret L. to Thomas D. Warren of Edenton, Je., Chowan county. R. R. Je. 9, 1843

Courts, Jane F. to James M. Moore, Feb., Rockingham county. R. R. Feb. 7, 1843
Cowan, Sally S. to Dr. James F. M'Ree, Jr., My. 9, Wilmington. R. R. My. 23, 1843
Cox, Benjamin S. to Francis S. Bennett, Oct., Anson county. R. R. Oct. 17, 1843
Cox, Jacob to Martha Walker, Nov, Randolph county. R. R. Dec. 1, 1843
Crabtree, Wesley to Elizabeth Gattis, Dec., Orange county. R. R. Dec. 12, 1843
Craven, George W. of Randolph county to Elizabeth Pharr, Feb., Cabarrus county. R. R. Feb. 7, 1843
Crenshaw, Amelia Carolina of Wake Forest to James H Caldwell of Falkland, Alabama, Aug. 17, Wake Forest. R. R. Aug. 29, 1843
Cromartie, Duncan to Mary A. Mckay, Dec., Bladen county. R. R. Dec. 22, 1843
Cromartie, Sophia C. of Bladen county to Lewis C. Oates of Sampson county, Nov. 1, Bladen county. R. R. Nov. 10, 1843
Crump, Dr. Wm. C. of Manchester, Virginia to Mary E. Carrington of Raleigh, Nov. 22, Greenville, Pitt rounty. R. R. Dec. 8, 1843
Dancy, John S. of Tarboro to Cornelia V. Battle, Dec., Edgecombe county. R. R. Dec. 22, 1843
Dancy, Mrs. Naomi to William H. Brown, Feb., Iredell county. R. R. Feb. 14, 1843
Davenport, Ephraim B. to Mary Speight, Mar., Edenton. R. R. Mar. 7, 1843
Davis, Geo. W. of Wilmington to Mary Adelaide Polk of Salisbury, Dec. 17, Rosedale, Fayette county, Tennessee. R. R. Jan. 10, 1843
Davis, Mary Ann to Blair Burwell of Staunton, Sept. 13, Franklin county. R. R. Sept. 29, 1843
Deems, Prof. to Anna Disosway of New York, Je. 29, Asbury, New Jersey. R. R. Jly. 11, 1843
Derr, Sarah R. to Mathias Boger of Salisbury, Je. 28, Lincoln county. R. R. Jly. 18, 1843
Dilworth, Richard of Caswell county to Lucy Ann Eskridge, Nov., Person county. R. R. Nov. 3, 1843
Disbrow, Rev. Charles H. to Mary E. B. Gordon, My., Gates county. R. R. My. 12, 1843
Disosway, Anna of New York to Prof. Deems of New York, Je. 29, Asbury, New Jersey. R. R. Jly. 11, 1843
Dobbin, Catharine L. to J. G. Shepherd, Apr., Fayetteville. R. R. Apr. 25, 1843
Donaho, Emily of Milton to Capt. Alfred Stanly of Louisiana, Sept., Milton. R. R. Sept. 29, 1843
Donnell, Malvina R. to Alexander M'Neely, Je., Guilford county. R. R. Je. 2, 1843
Douglas, Sarah L. to Emery M. West, Oct., Anson county. R. R. Oct. 17, 1843
Douglass, Dr. George B. to Mary Ellis, Dec., Davidson county. R. R. Dec. 8, 1843
Dowd, Elizabeth to Daniel M'Crummen, Nov. 2, Moore county. R. R. Nov. 14, 1843

Drake, Dr. John G. F. to Mary Ann Harrison, Oct. 24, Nash county. R. R. Nov. 7, 1843
Dudley, David C. of Raleigh to Carolina Shipp, Feb. 26, Wake county. R. R. Aug. 1, 1843
Dunn, John of Moore county to Jureah Haywood, Dec., Montgomery county. R. R. Dec. 8, 1843
Eberhart, Henry to Susanna Haywood of Northampton county, Feb., Gaston county. R. R. Feb. 28, 1843
Eliott, Elisha to Sarah Elliott, Mar, Edenton. R. R. Mar. 7, 1843
Elliott, Sarah to Elisha Elliott, Mar., Edenton. R. R. Mar. 7, 1843
Ellis, Mary to Dr. George B. Douglass, Dec., Davidson county. R. R. Dec. 8, 1843
Ellison, James, Jr. to Sarah Jane, Nov., Washington, Beaufort county. R. R. Nov. 3, 1843
English, Zebulon to Adaliza Carter, Nov., Randolph county. R. R. Nov. 10, 1843
Eppes, Miss H. P. to P. E. Hervey, Oct., Halifax. R. R. Oct. 6, 1843
Eppes, Dr. Willie I. to Temperance B. Joyner, Nov., Halifax county. R. R. Nov. 14, 1843
Ernul, Ann to Henry Whitehurst, Nov, Craven county. R. R. Dec. 1, 1843
Eskridge, Lucy Ann to Richard Dilworth of Caswell county, Nov., Person county. R. R. Nov. 3, 1843
Eubanks, Sarah H. of Virginia to Williamson Browning, Feb., Garysburg. R. R. Feb. 3, 1843
Evans, Dr. Augustus C. to Eliza C. W. Washington, Mar. 16, Waynesboro. R. R. Mar. 21, 1843
Evans, Catharine of Hillsborough to John Turner, My. 18, Fayetteville. R. R. My. 23, 1843
Everett, David B. to Sarah R. Rainey, My. 4, Wayne county. R. R. Je. 2, 1843
Fearrington, John J. to Elizabeth E. Mebane, Feb. 23, Pittsboro. R. R. Feb. 28, 1843
Fentress, Thomas R. to Margaret Johnson, Sept. 6, Raleigh. R. R. Sept. 8, 1843
Ferebee, Samuel to Mary Harrington, Nov., Currituck county. R. R. Nov. 14, 1843
Ferrill, Jane to William Patterson Montgomery of Guilford county, Aug. 3, Orange county. R. R. Aug. 29, 1843
Ficklen, Joseph B. of Falmouth, Va. to Ellen M'Gehee, Je. 22, Person county. R. R. Jly. 4, 1843
Flow, John to Jane Russel, Feb., Mecklenburg county. R. R. Feb. 28, 1843
Fotterall, Marlan to Samuel R. Potter of Wilmington, Oct. 18, Philadelphia. R. R. Oct. 31, 1843
Foust, Mrs. Rebecca C. to Daniel C. Harden, Feb., Orange county. R. R. Feb. 21, 1843
Franklin, Joseph R. to Henrietta Rowe, Aug., Newbern. R. R. Aug. 25, 1843
Frazer, Jane to Samuel Collett of Davidson county, Nov., Randolph county. R. R. Nov. 10, 1843

Gathings, Philip to Elizabeth White, Nov., Anson county. R. R. Dec. 1, 1843
Gattis, Elizabeth to Wesley Crabtree, Dec., Orange county. R. R. Dec. 12, 1843
Gillespie, Mary E. to Dr. Samuel D. Rankin, Nov., Rowan county. R. R. Dec. 1, 1843.
Gilliam, Robert B. of Oxford to Melissa Kittrell of Franklin, Dec. 27, Franklin county. R. R. Dec. 29, 1843
Glover, Edwin to Laura Smith, Sept., Fayetteville. R. R. Sept. 15, 1843
Gordon, Mary E. B. to Rev. Charles H. Disbrow, My., Gates county. R. R. My. 12, 1843
Graves, Mary U. to Col. Harrison M. Waught, Apr. 11, Surry county. R. R. Apr. 28, 1843
Green, Robert N. to Prudence N. Ward, Mar., Chatham county. R. R. Mar. 17, 1843
Greer, John F. of Ashe county to Martha C. Jones of Caldwell county, My. 16, 1843. R. R. Je. 9, 1842
Guion, Ferebe E. to Dr. John R. Justice, Dec., Newbern. R. R. Dec. 22, 1843
Hall, Frances E. to Rev. James Stacy, Jan., Fayetteville. R. R. Jan. 10, 1843
Hambleton, Darcos Elizabeth to Bradfoot Briggs, Apr., Washington, Beaufort county. R. R. Apr. 18, 1843
Hamilton, Hugh C. to Susan L. Massie of Virginia, Aug., Catawba county. R. R. Aug. 25, 1843
Harden, Daniel C. to Mrs. Rebecca C. Foust, Feb., Orange county. R. R. Feb. 21, 1843
Hargrove, Hamilton H. to Eliza E. Overman, Nov., Lexington. R. R. Nov. 10, 1843
Harper, James of Darke county, Ohio to Louisa C. M'Dowell of Caldwell county, Sept. 12, Caldwell county. R. R. Sept. 19, 1843
Harris, Stephen of Craven county to Mary E. White, Nov., Orange county. R. R. Nov. 3, 1843
Harrison, Mary Ann to Dr. John G. F. Drake, Oct. 24, Nash county. R. R. Nov. 7, 1843
Haywood, Jureah to John Dunn of Moore county, Dec., Montgomery county. R. R. Dec. 8, 1843
Haywood, Susanna to Henry Eberhart of Northampton county, Feb., Gaston county. R. R. Feb. 28, 1843
Hedgpeth, Archibald W. to Rosannah C. Clark, Oct., Hillsboro. R. R. Oct. 24, 1843
Henderson, Wm. A. to Mary A. Cooper, Dec., Mecklenburg county. R. R. Dec. 19, 1843
Hervey, P. E. to Miss H. P. Eppes, Oct., Halifax. R. R. Oct. 6, 1843
Hiatt, Col. Joab to Julia Sharpe, Feb., Rockingham. R. R. Feb. 7, 1843
Hicks, Thomas C. of Granville county to Susan Fenner Ligon, Oct. 12, Wake Forest. R. R. Oct. 13, 1843
Hill, Samuel of Randolph county to Maria Miller of Jones county, Feb. 4, Wayne county. R. R. Feb. 17, 1843
Hinard, Thomas to Louisa Wootten, Sept. 14, Johnston county. R. R. Sept. 29, 1843

Hinton, Salina to Wm. H. H. M'Cullers, Sept. 20, Johnston county. R. R. Sept. 29, 1843
Hogan, James to Catharine J. Strayhorn, Oct., Orange county. R. R. Oct. 24, 1843
Holland, Margaret M. to Col. Sam'l N. Stowe, Oct., Lincoln county. R. R. Oct. 31, 1843
Horton, Col. Samuel P. to Carolina C. Lee of Johnston county, Je. 22, Wake county. R. R. Je. 27, 1843
Hunt, Maj. J. W. of Granville county to Frances C. Bailey, Oct., Person county. R. R. Oct. 27, 1843
Hunt, William C. of Concord to Rosannah B. Potter, Dec., Charlotte. R. R. Dec. 8, 1843
Hunter, Henry F. of Mecklenburg county to Mary S. Neel, Apr., Cabarrus county. R. R. Apr. 14, 1843
Huston, Sarah S. to John C. Abernathy, Je., Mecklenburg county. R. R. Je. 13, 1843
Hybart, Tho. L. to Eliza Maffit, Feb., Fayetteville. R. R. Feb. 24, 1843
Irvine, Wm. of Bedford, Virginia to Mary Ann Lewis, Aug., Milton. R. R. Aug. 25, 1843
Iseley, Emily Ann to Ezekiel May, Apr., Guilford county. R. R. Apr. 18, 1843
Jamison, Mary to Benjamin F. Brown, Je., Mecklenburg county. R. R. Je. 13, 1843
Jane, Sarah to James Ellison, Je., Nov., Washington, Beaufort county. R. R. Nov. 3, 1843
Jeffreys, Adelaide of Franklin county to Noah Sessom, Apr., Marshall county, Mississippi. R. R. Apr. 18, 1843
Jeffreys, Robert J. to Miss M. P. Jenkins, Jly., Orange county. R. R. Jly. 11, 1843
Jenkins, Miss M. P. to Robert J. Jeffreys, Jly., Orange county. R. R. Jly. 11, 1843
Jewett, C. Adelaide to George P. Swift of Georgia, Apr., Robeson county. R. R. Apr. 28, 1843
Johnson, Louisa to Charles F. Jones, Aug., Randolph county. R. R. Aug. 4, 1843
Johnson, Margaret to Thomas R. Fentress, Sept. 6, Raleigh. R. R. Sept. 8, 1843
Jones, Rev. Amos W. of this State to Mary E. Womack, Oct. 4, Pittsboro. R. R. Oct. 10, 1843
Jones, Barnabas, Jr. to Martha Helen Stephenson, Oct. 26, Wake county. R. R. Oct. 31, 1843
Jones, Dr. Beverly to Julia A. Conrad, Nov., Stokes county. R. R. Dec, 1, 1843
Jones, Charles F. to Louisa Johnson, Aug., Randolph county. R. R. Aug. 4, 1843
Jones, Dr. Edmund A. of Caldwell county to Harriet N. Dunlap, Nov., Charlotte. R. R. Nov. 17, 1843
Jones, Martha C. of Caldwell county to John F. Greer of Ashe county, My. 16. R. R. Je. 9, 1843
Jones, Mary to Peter Brown Ruffin, Nov. 10, Hillsboro. R. R. Nov. 21, 1843

Joyner, Temperance B. to Dr. Willie I. Eppes, Nov., Halifax county. R. R. Nov. 14, 1843

Julian, Jesse B. to Isabella B. Troy, Dec. 5, Randolph county. R. R. Dec. 19, 1843

Justice, Dr. John R. to Ferebe E. Guion, Dec., Newbern. R. R. Dec. 22, 1843

Kelley, Wm. John to Lovedy M'Kethan, Oct. 4, Cumberland county. R. R. Oct. 17, 1843

Kennedy, Lieut. C. H. of U. S. N. to Martha A. R. Brodie, Oct. 11, Warren county. R. R. Oct. 17, 1843

Kerlock, Lydia to Albert Wallace of Mecklenburg county, Aug., Anson county. R. R. Aug. 25, 1843

Keton, William of Petersburg, Virginia to Mary A. C. White of Henderson, Granville county, Dec. 14. R. R. Dec. 22, 1843

Killough, David B. to Mary Rodgers, Apr., Cabarrus county. R. R. Apr. 18, 1843

Kingsbury, Elizabeth to Julius M. Love, Aug., Salisbury. R. R. Aug. 25, 1843

Kittrell, Melissa of Franklin county to Robert B. Gilliam of Oxford, Dec. 27, Franklin county. R. R. Dec. 29, 1843

Latimer, Z. to Elizabeth Savage, Jly., Wilmington. R. R. Jly. 14, 1843

Lee, Caroline C. of Johnston county to Col. Samuel P. Horton, Je. 22, Wake county. R. R. Je. 27, 1843

Lee, Richard H. to Harriet Barton, Dec., Hillsboro. R. R. Dec. 29, 1843

Lee, Thursday A. to David S. Mathias of Sampson county, Nov., New Hanover county. R. R. Dec. 1, 1843

Leecraft, Zilphia Ann to Dr. M. F. Arendel, Nov., Carteret county. R. R. Dec. 1, 1843

Lewis, Lucy Ann to Archibald Williams of Franklin, My., Oxford. R. R. My. 9, 1843

Lewis, Mary Ann to Wm. Irvine of Bedford, Virginia, Aug., Milton. R. R. Aug. 25, 1843

Ligon, Susan Fenner to Thomas C. Hicks of Granville county, Oct. 12, Wake Forest. R. R. Oct. 13, 1843

Lindeman, Elizabeth to Jeremiah Nixon of New Hanover county, Apr. 19, Raleigh. R. R. Apr. 21, 1843

Linke, Elizabeth to F. W. Bishop, Feb., Washington, Beaufort county. R. R. Feb. 21, 1843

Little, Martha A. to Thomas Respass, Apr., Washington, Beaufort county. R. R. Apr. 18, 1843

Locke, William to Jane A. Wheeler, Dec., Salisbury. R. R. Dec. 8, 1843

London, M. of Wilmington to Rachel Troy of Columbus, Jly., Columbus county. R. R. Jly. 21, 1843

Long, William J. of Randolph county to Mary Webb, Jly., Hillsboro. R. R. Jly. 11, 1843

Lord, Frederick J. to Columbia A. Brown, Dec. 13, Wilmington. R. R. Dec. 19, 1843

Love, Julius M. to Elizabeth Kingsbury, Aug., Salisbury. R. R. Aug. 25, 1843

Lumley, Mrs. Sarah to Capt. George W. Styron, Nov., Carteret county. R. R. Dec. 1, 1843

Lumpkin, Mrs. Mary to John Walters, Oct., Granville county. R. R. Oct. 27, 1843

M'Aulay, Martin A. to Adaline Scarbrough, Dec., Montgomery county. R. R. Dec. 8, 1843

M'Cormick, Anne to Arch'd M'Lauchlin, Mar., Robeson county. R. R. Mar. 31, 1843

M'Crummen, Daniel to Elizabeth Dowd, Nov. 2, Moore county. R. R. Nov. 14, 1843

M'Crummen, Hannah to Presley Caddell, Sept., Moore county. R. R. Sept. 15, 1843

M'Cullers, Wm. H. H. Sr. to Salina Hinton, Sept. 20, Johnston county. R. R. Sept. 29, 1843

M'Dowell, Louisa C. of Caldwell county to James Harper of Darke county, Ohio, Sept. 12, Caldwell county. R. R. Sept. 19, 1843

M'Gehee, Ellen to Joseph B. Ficklen of Falmouth, Virginia, Je. 22, Person county. R. R. Jly. 4, 1843

M'Ilhenny, Eliza C. to James Shines, Oct. 14, Wilmington. R. R. Oct. 27, 1843

M'Kay, Mary A. to Duncan Cromartie, Dec., Bladen county. R. R. Dec. 22, 1843

M'Kethan, Lovedy to John Wm. Kelley, Oct. 4, Cumberland county. R. R. Oct. 17, 1843

M'Lean, Hannah C. to Maj. Newton Wharton, Je., Guilford county. R. R. Je. 2, 1843

M'Leod, William to Martha Ann Vaughan, Aug. 17, Raleigh. R. R. Sept. 1, 1843

M'Millan, Dugald to Mary Wright, Oct. 15, New Hanover county. R. R. Oct. 31, 1843

M'Nair, Annabella to John M'Nair, Jly., Robeson county. R. R. Jly. 28, 1843

M'Nair, John to Annabella M'Nair, Jly., Robeson county. R. R. Jly. 28, 1843

M'Neely, Alexander R. Donnell, Je., Guilford county. R. R. Je. 2, 1843

M'Neill, Elizabeth to John C. Sinclair, Mar., Robeson county. R. R. Mar. 31, 1843

M'Neill, Harriet Almira to Duncan M'Kay, Jan. 8, Robeson county. R. R. Feb. 17, 1843

M'Kay, Duncan to Harriet Almira M'Neill, Jan. 8, Robeson county. R. R. Feb. 17, 1843

M'Lauchlin, Arch'd to Anne M'Cormick, Mar., Robeson county. R. R. Mar. 31, 1843

M'Rae, Almira A. to Green Williams, Mar., Montgomery county. R. R. Mar. 31, 1843

M'Ree, Dr. James F. Jr. to Sally S. Cowan, My. 9, Wilmington. R. R. My. 23, 1843.

M'Williams, William J. to Mary Ann Murch, Feb., Washington, Beaufort county. R. R. Feb. 21, 1843

Massie, Susan L. of Virginia to Hugh C. Hamilton, Aug., Catawba county. R. R. Aug. 25, 1843

Mathias, David S. of Sampson county to Thursday A. Lee, Nov., New Hanover county. R. R. Dec. 1, 1843

May, Ezekiel to Emily Ann Iseley, Apr., Guilford county. R. R. Apr. 18, 1843
Mebane, Capt. Morgan to Mary Morrow, Dec., Orange county. R. R. Dec. 29, 1843
Meacham, Elizabeth A. to Hampton R. West, My., Anson county. R. R. My. 12, 1843
Meador, Joseph C. to Ann E. Briggs, My., Hertford county. R. R. My. 2, 1843
Mebane, Elizabeth E. to John J. Fearrington, Feb., Pittsboro. R. R. Feb. 28, 1843
Miller, Maria of Jones county to Samuel Hill of Randolph county, Feb. 4, Wayne county. R. R. Feb. 17, 1843
Mitchell, John to Elizabeth Allen, Oct., Granville county. R. R. Oct. 27, 1843
Mixon, Charles W. to Anna Maria Underhill, Mar., Chowan county. R. R. Mar. 7, 1843
Maffitt, Eliza to Tho' L. Hybart, Feb., Fayetteville. R. R. Feb. 24, 1843
Montgomery, William Patterson of Guilford county to Jane Ferrill, Aug. 3, Orange county. R. R. Aug. 29, 1843
Moore, George I. of New Hanover county to Hulda Murray, Je., Duplin county. R. R. Je. 13, 1843
Moore, James M. to Jane F. Courts, Feb., Rockingham county. R. R. Feb. 7, 1843
Moore, Rev. John L. to Margaret Hampton Bowman of Germantown, Aug., Stokes county. R. R. Aug. 4, 1843
Moore, Martha A. to Stephen L. Tucker of Raleigh, Apr. 6, Franklin county. R. R. Apr. 14, 1843
Morrow, Mary to Capt. Morgan Mebane, Dec., Orange county. R. R. Dec. 29, 1843
Morton, Chambers to Eliza Ussery, Dec., Montgomery county. R. R. Dec. 22, 1843
Munroe, John W. to Mary Ann Baker of Cumberland county, Jly., Robeson county. R. R. Jly. 14, 1843
Murch, Mary Ann to William J. M'Williams, Feb., Washington, Beaufort county. R. R. Feb. 21, 1843
Murphy, Hamson F. to Elizabeth A. Simpson, Je., New Hanover county. R. R. Je. 13, 1843
Murray, Hulda to George I. Moore, of New Hanover county, Je., Duplin county. R. R. Je. 13, 1843
Neel, Mary S. to Henry F. Hunter of Mecklenburg county, Apr., Cabarrus county. R. R. Apr. 14, 1843
Newkirk, Ann J. to Dr. J. B. Seavey, Nov. 9, New Hanover county. R. R. Dec. 1, 1843
Nicholson, Rev. David B. to Zilphia Pearsall, Nov., Duplin county. R. R. Nov. 17, 1843
Nixon, Jeremiah of New Hanover county to Elizabeth Lindeman, Apr. 19, Raleigh. R. R. Apr. 21, 1843
Northcott, Queen to Joseph Owen of Moore county, My., Montgomery county. R. R. My. 12, 1843
Oates, Lewis C. of Sampson county to Sophia C. Cromartie of Bladen county, Nov. 1, Bladen county. R. R. Nov. 10, 1843

Oates, Nicey to Gideon A. Thompson, Sept. 5, Moore county. R. R. Sept. 15, 1843
Ochiltree, Lucy to William W. Briggs, Mar., Fayetteville. R. R. Mar. 7, 1843
Orrell, Major C. J. of Fayetteville to Mildred Eliza Watters, Feb., Clarendon, Brunswick county. R. R. Feb. 3, 1843
Overman, Eliza E. to Hamilton H. Hargrove, Nov., Lexington. R. R. Nov. 10, 1843
Owen, Joseph of Moore county to Queen Northcott, My., Montgomery county. R. R. My. 12, 1843
Paisley, William J. to Margaret J. Wiley, Feb. 1, Guilford county. R. R. Feb. 21, 1843
Parker, Caroline N. to Theophilus S. Underwood, Oct. 7, Sampson county. R. R. Feb. 17, 1843
Parker, Elizabeth to Rev. Joseph B. Cheshire, Feb., Tarboro. R. R. Feb. 17, 1843
Parks, Margaret to Leander D. Alexander of Mississippi, Aug., Mecklenburg county. R. R. Aug. 25, 1843
Patrick, Miss to Hezekiah Arnold, Mar., Washington county. R. R. Mar. 7, 1843
Patterson, Mariam G. to Peyton R. Tunstall, Dec. 13, Franklin county. R. R. Dec. 29, 1843
Pearsall, Zilphia to Rev. David Nicholson, Nov., Duplin county. R. R. Nov. 17, 1843
Peebles, J. H. to Miss H. E. A. Cobb, Feb., Kinston, Lenoir county. R. R. Feb. 7, 1843
Pender, Amarilla James to Robert H. Pender, Nov., Edgecombe county. R. R. Nov. 10, 1843
Pender, Robert H. to Amarilla James Pender, Nov., Edgecombe county. R. R. Nov. 10, 1843
Perkins, Ann G. to James P. Wood of this State, Feb., Brownsville, Tennessee. R. R. Feb. 3, 1843
Perry, Elizabeth to Thomas N. F. Alston of Warren county, Feb. 22, Franklin county. R. R. Mar. 3, 1843
Pharr, Elizabeth to George W. Craven of Randolph county, Feb., Cabarrus county. R. R. Feb. 7, 1843
Phifer, Louisa to Robert S. Young, Dec., Cabarrus county. R. R. Dec. 15, 1843
Philips, Daniel D. to Tarmesia H. Cooley, Je., Hillsboro. R. R. Je. 13, 1843
Philips, Mary to Emmanuel Whitfield, Aug., Washington. R. R. Aug. 29, 1843
Polk, Mary Adelaide of Salisbury to Geo. W. Davis of Wilmington, Dec. 17, Rosedale, Fayette county, Tennessee. R. R. Jan. 10, 1843
Potter, Henry H. of Fayetteville to Isabella C. Scott of Raleigh, Sept. 14, Raleigh. R. R. Sept. 15, 1843
Potter, Samuel R. of Wilmington to Marlan Fotterall, Oct. 18, Philadelphia. R. R. Oct. 31, 1843
Potter, Rosannah B. to William C. Hunt of Concord, Dec., Charlotte. R. R. Dec. 8, 1843
Powell, Cullen to Martha Bishop, Nov., Halifax county. R. R. Nov. 14, 1843

Primrose, John to Eliza Tarbox, Oct. 19, Raleigh. R. R. Oct. 24, 1843
Raboteau, Charles C. to Sarah A. Wynne, My. 2, Louisburg. R. R. My. 9, 1843
Rainey, Sarah R. to David B. Everett, My. 4, Wayne county. R. R. Je. 2, 1843
Rankin, Dr. Samuel D. to Mary E. Gillespie, Nov., Rowan county. R. R. Dec. 1, 1843
Ray, Charles to Elizabeth Smith, Feb., Davie county. R. R. Feb. 7, 1843
Reinhardt, Daniel F. of Lincolnton to Harriet E. Shuford, Nov., Lenoir, Caldwell county. R. R. Nov. 17, 1843
Respass, Thomas to Martha A. Little, Apr., Washington, Beaufort county. R. R. Apr. 18, 1843
Respass, Jeremiah G. of Beaufort to Mrs. Mary Clements, Mar., Williamston, Martin county. R. R. Mar. 21, 1843
Riggs, Rebecca of Baltimore to James Bogle of this State, Jan., New York. R. R. Jan. 10, 1843
Ringstaff, Susan to Merrel Utly, Nov., Hillsboro. R. R. Nov. 3, 1843
Robinson, John R. to Harriet A. Henderson, Dec., Mecklenburg county. R. R. Dec. 19, 1843
Rodgers, Mary to David B Killough, Apr., Cabarrus county. R. R. Apr. 18, 1843
Rogers, Thomas M. to Euphemia Brockett, Nov., Wilmington. R. R. Dec. 1, 1843
Ross, John to Mrs. Lavinia Balance, Apr., Washington, Beaufort county. R. R. Apr. 18, 1843
Rowe, Henrietta to Joseph R. Franklin, Aug., Newbern. R. R. Aug. 25, 1843
Royster, Marcus to Frances Webb, Oct., Granville county. R. R. Nov. 3, 1843
Rozier, James A. of Robeson county to Elizabeth Delight Coleman, Dec., Columbus county. R. R. Dec. 12, 1843
Ruffin, Peter Brown to Mary Jones, Nov. 10, Hillsboro. R. R. Nov. 21, 1843
Rumley, Emeline G. to Hellen Brian, Dec. 22, Carteret county. R. R. Jan. 10, 1843
Russel, Jane to John Flow, Feb., Mecklenburg county. R. R. Feb. 28, 1843
Sanders, Col. Jnō. F. of Johnston county to Emily J. Thompson, Jly. 4, Chatham county. R. R. Jly. 14, 1843
Sanders, Linn P. of Madison county, Virginia to Polly Ann Sanders, Nov., New Hanover county. R. R. Dec. 1, 1843
Sanders, Polly Ann to Linn P. Sanders of Madison county, Virginia, Nov., New Hanover county. R. R. Dec. 1, 1843
Savage, Elizabeth to Z. Latimer, Jly., Wilmington. R. R. Jly. 14, 1843
Scarbrough, Adaline to Martin A. M'Aulay, Dec., Montgomery county. R. R. Dec. 8, 1843
Scott, Isabella C. of Raleigh to Henry H. Potter of Fayetteville, Sept. 14, Raleigh. R. R. Sept. 15, 1843
Seavey, Dr. J. B. to Ann J. Newkirk, Nov. 9, New Hanover county. R. R. Dec. 1, 1843

Sessoms, Noah to Adelaide Jeffreys of Franklin county, Apr., Marshal county, Mississippi. R. R. Apr. 18, 1843
Sharpe, Julia to Col. Joab Hiatt, Feb., Rockingham. R. R. Feb. 7, 1843
Shephard, Hon. William B. to Ann Collins of Edenton, Je. 8, Edenton R. R. Je. 9, 1843
Shepherd, J. G. to Catharine L. Dobbin, Apr., Fayetteville. R. R. Apr. 25 1843
Shines, James to Eliza C. M'Ilhenny, Oct. 14, Wilmington. R. R. Oct. 27, 1843
Shipp, Caroline to David C. Dudley of Raleigh, Feb. 26, Wake county. R. R. Aug. 1, 1843
Shollington, Dr. Wm. E. J. to Sarah Barnes, Dec., Cool Springs, Edgecombe county. R. R. Dec. 22, 1843
Shuford, Harriet E. to Daniel F. Reinhardt of Lincolnton, Nov., Lenoir, Caldwell county. R. R. Nov. 17, 1843
Shultz, Antoinette M. to Alexander C. Blum, Je., Salem. R. R. Je. 2, 1843
Simpson, Elizabeth A. to Murphy Hansom F., Je., New Hanover county. R. R. Je. 13, 1843
Sinclair, John C. to Elizabeth M'Neill, Mar., Robeson county. R. R. Mar. 31, 1843
Smith, Caroline to Mumford D. Williams, Dec., Montgomery county. R. R. Dec. 22, 1843
Smith, Elizabeth to Charles Ray, Feb., Davie county. R. R. Feb. 7, 1843
Smith, Henderson to Gilly Taylor, Dec. 3, Raleigh. R. R. Dec. 8, 1843
Smith, James A. of Robeson county to Agnes J. Baldwin, Feb., Wilmington. R. R. Feb. 3, 1843
Smith, Julia of Philadelphia to Dr. James H. Boon of this State, Aug., Philadelphia. R. R. Aug. 4, 1843
Smith, Laura to Edwin Glover, Sept., Fayetteville. R. R. Sept. 15, 1843
Sosserman, Col. John C. of Pontotoc, Mississippi to Sarah Burns, Feb., Cabarrus county. R. R. Feb. 28, 1843
Speight, Mary to Ephriam B. Davenport, Mar., Edenton. R. R. Mar. 7, 1843
Stacy, Rev. James to E. Frances Hall, Jan., Fayetteville. R. R. Jan. 10, 1843
Stanly, Capt. Alfred of Louisiana to Emily Donaho of Milton, Sept., Milton R. R. Sept. 29, 1843
Stanly, Edward R. of Newbern to Harriet Elizabeth Tull, Nov., Lenoir county. R. R. Dec. 1, 1843
Stephenson, Martha Helen to Barnabas Jones, Jr., Oct. 26, Wake county. R. R. Oct. 31, 1843
Stone, Sarah of Granville county to Calvin Betts, Wake county, Sept. 20, Granville county. R. R. Sept. 29, 1843
Stowe, Col. Sam'l N. to Margaret M. Holland, Oct., Lincoln county. R. R. Oct. 31, 1843
Strayhorn, Catharine J. to James Hogan, Oct., Orange county. R. R. Oct. 24, 1843
Streather, E. J. to Elizabeth Wilson, Sept. 19, Anson county. R. R. Oct. 6, 1843
Styron, Capt. George W. to Mrs. Sarah Lumley, Nov., Carteret county. R. R. Dec. 1, 1843

Suit, John of Rolesville to Amanda C. Terrell of Wake county, My. 30. R. R. Je. 2, 1843
Summerrell, M. W. to Emily R. White, Dec., Newbern. R. R. Dec. 22, 1843
Sumner, Charles of York to Arabella W. Wynnter of Blairsville, Feb., Blairsville. R. R. Feb. 7, 1843
Swift, George P. of Georgia to Miss C. Adelaide Jewett, Apr., Robeson county. R. R. Apr. 28, 1843
Swim, William of Randolph county to Hannah M. Walker, Aug. 3, Orange county. R. R. Aug. 29, 1843
Tarbox, Eliza to John Primrose, Oct. 19, Raleigh. R. R. Oct. 24, 1843
Taylor, Gilly to Henderson Smith, Dec. 3, Raleigh. R. R. Dec. 8, 1843
Templeton, Margaret to John C. Coart, Feb., Newbern. R. R. Feb. 7, 1843
Terrell, Amanda C. of Wake county to John Suit of Rolesville, My. 30. R. R. Je. 2, 1843
Thomas, Matilda to Wm. Clapp, Nov., Anson county. R. R. Dec. 1, 1843
Thomas, Thos. K. to Mrs. Louisa B. Alston, Nov. 15, Louisburg. R. R. Nov. 21, 1843
Thomas, Dr. Wm. Geo. to Mary Sumner Clark, Nov., Tarboro. R. R. Nov. 10, 1843
Thompson, Emily J. to Col. Jno. F. Sanders of Johnston county, Jly. 4, Chatham county. R. R. Jly. 14, 1843
Thompson, Gideon A. to Nicy Oats, Sept. 5, Moore county. R. R. Sept. 15, 1843
Tonnoffske, George H. to Laura Weston Cooper, Mar. 16, Raleigh. R. R. Mar. 21, 1843
Toomer, Mary of Wilmington to Jonathan Whaley, Nov., Fayetteville. R. R. Dec. 1, 1843
Troy, Isabella B. to Jesse B. Julian, Dec. 5, Randolph county. R. R. Dec. 19, 1843
Troy, Rachael of Columbus county to M. London of Wilmington, Jly., Columbus county. R. R. Jly. 21, 1843
Tucker, Stephen L. of Raleigh to Martha A. Moore, Apr. 6, Franklin county. R. R. Apr. 14, 1843
Tull, Harriet Elizabeth to Edward R. Stanly of Newbern, Nov., Lenoir county. R. R. Dec. 1, 1843
Tunstall, Peyton R. to Mariam G. Patterson, Dec. 13, Franklin county. R. R. Dec. 29, 1843
Turner, Henry to Lucy Ann Adams, Dec., Wake county. R. R. Dec. 29, 1843
Turner, John of Hillsboro to Catharine Evans, My. 18, Fayetteville. R. R. My. 23, 1843
Tyrrell, Harrison to Elizabeth Austin, Nov., Caswell county. R. R. Nov. 3, 1843
Underhill, Anna Maria to Charles Mixson, Mar., Chowan county. R. R. Mar. 7, 1843
Underwood, Johnston to Mary Albert, Dec., Orange county. R. R. Dec. 29, 1843
Underwood, Theophilus S. to Caroline N. Parker, Oct. 7, Sampson county. R. R. Feb. 17, 1843
Ussery, Eliza to Chambers Morton, Dec., Montgomery county. R. R. Dec. 22, 1843

Utly, Merrel to Susan Ringstaff, Nov., Hillsboro. R. R. Nov. 3, 1843
Vanderford, Anderson of Raleigh to Virginia Waddell, Sept. 14, Franklin county. R. R. Sept. 19, 1843
Vaughan, Martha Ann to William M'Leod, Aug. 17, Raleigh. R. R. Sept. 1, 1843
Weddell, Virginia to Anderson Vanderford of Raleigh, Sept. 14, Franklin county. R. R. Sept. 19, 1843
Walker, Hannah M. to William Swim of Randolph county, Aug. 3, Orange county. R. R. Aug. 29, 1843
Walker, Martha to Jacob Cox, Nov., Randolph county. R. R. Dec. 1, 1843
Wallace, Albert of Mecklenburg county to Lydia Kerlock, Aug., Anson county. R. R. Aug. 25, 1843
Walters, John to Mrs. Mary Lumpkin, Oct., Granville county. R. R. Oct. 27, 1843
Ward, Prudence N. to Robert N. Green, Mar., Chatham county. R. R. Mar. 17, 1843
Warren, Thomas D. of Edenton to Margaret L. Cotfield, Je., Chowan county. R. R. Je. 9, 1843
Washington, Eliza C. W. to Dr. Augustus C. Evans, Mar. 16, Waynesboro. R. R. Mar. 21, 1843
Washington, Julia E. of Wayne county to Alex C. Blount, Oct. 26, Newbern. R. R. Nov. 3, 1843
Watters, Mildred Eliza to Major C. J. Orrell, Feb., Clarendon, Brunswick county. R. R. Feb. 3, 1843
Waugh, Col. Harrison M. to Mary U. Graves, Apr. 11, Surry county. R. R. Apr. 28, 1843
Webb, Frances to Marcus Royster, Oct., Granville county. R. R. Nov. 3, 1843
Webb, Frances M. to Rev. Sidney D. Bumpass of Raleigh, Dec. 27, Person county. R. R. Jan. 6, 1843
Webb, Mary to William J. Long of Randolph county, Jly., Hillsboro. R. R. Jly. 11, 1843
West, Emery M. to Sarah L. Douglas, Oct., Anson county. R. R. Oct. 17, 1843
West, Hampton R. to Elizabeth A. Meacham, My., Anson county. R. R. My. 12, 1843
Whaley, Jonathan to Mary Toomer of Wilmington, Nov., Fayetteville. R. R. Dec. 1, 1843
Wharton, Dr. A. C. to Catharine Conrad, Feb., Stokes county. R. R. Feb. 7, 1843
Wharton, Maj. Newton to Hannah C. McLean, Je., Guilford county. R. R. Je. 2, 1843
Wheeler, Jane A. to William Locke, Dec., Salisbury. R. R. Dec. 8, 1843
White, Elizabeth to Philip Gathings, Nov., Anson county. R. R. Dec. 1, 1843
White, Emily R. to W. W. Sumerrell, Dec., Newbern. R. R. Dec. 22, 1843
White, Mary A. C. of Henderson, Granville county to William Keton of Petersburg, Virginia, Dec. 14. R. R. Dec. 22, 1843
White, Mary E. to Stephen Harris of Craven county, Nov., Orange county. R. R. Nov. 3, 1843
Whitehurst, Henry to Ann Ernul, Nov., Craven county. R. R. Dec. 1, 1843

Whitfield, Emanuel to Mary Phillips, Aug., Washington. R. R. Aug. 29, 1843
Wiley, Margaret J. to William J. Paisley, Feb. 1, Guilford county. R. R. Feb. 21, 1843
Williams, Archibald of Franklin to Lucy Ann Lewis, My., Oxford. R. R. My. 9, 1843
Williams, Green to Almira A. M'Rae, Mar., Montgomery county. R. R. Mar. 31, 1843
Williams, Mumford D. to Caroline Smith, Dec., Montgomery county. R. R. Dec. 22, 1843
Wilson, Elizabeth to E. J. Streather, Sept. 19, Anson county. R. R. Oct. 6, 1843
Wilson, John of Milton to Penelope Campbell of Norfolk, Virginia, Oct., Philadelphia. R. R. Nov. 3, 1843
Womack, Mary E. to Rev. Amos W. Jones of this State, Oct. 4, Pittsboro. R. R. Oct. 10, 1843
Wood, James P. of this State to Ann G. Perkins, Feb., Brownsville, Tennessee. R. R. Feb. 3, 1843
Wootten, Louisa to Thomas Hinard, Sept. 14, Johnston county. R. R. Sept. 29, 1843
Wright, Mary to Dugald M'Millan, Oct. 15, New Hanover county. R. R. Oct. 31, 1843
Wynn, Margaret to Asa Ainsley of Washington county, Mar., Chowan county. R. R. Mar. 7, 1843
Wynne, Sarah A. to Charles C. Raboteau, My. 2, Louisburg. R. R. My. 9, 1843
Wynnter, Arabella W. of Blairsville to Charles Sumner of York, Feb., Blairsville. R. R. Feb. 7, 1843
Young, Robert S. to Louisa Phifer, Dec., Cabarrus county. R. R. Dec. 15, 1843
Young, Robert T. D. of Louisburg to Ann Barrow, Jan. 18, Franklin county. R. R. Feb. 3, 1843
Young, Sarah D. to John Baskerville, Dec., Granville county. R. R. Dec. 8, 1843

1844

Adams, Mary Ann to John Pratt, Mar., Anson county. R. R. Mar. 26, 1844
Albright, Mary Martha to J. W. Brower of Surry county, Apr., Greensboro. R. R. Apr. 12, 1844.
Alexander, Lee to Mary Johnson, Feb. 1, Mecklenburg county. R. R. Feb. 16, 1844
Allen, Alsey H. of Lowndes to Mary Cooper Stedman of Raleigh, Je. 18, Dallas county, Alabama. R. R. Sept. 13, 1844
Allen, Frances to Jas. M. Thompson, Jly. 18, Orange county. R. R. Jly. 30, 1844
Allen H. to Mary Williams, Mar., Anson county. R. R. Mar. 8, 1844
Allen, Nancy Jane to Dr. Lewis J. Dorton, Nov., Edgecombe county. R. R. Nov. 29, 1844
Allen, Wm. H. to Evelina L. Taylor, Feb. 8, Brunswick county. R. R. Feb. 20, 1844

Aldred, Sarah to Allen Osbern, Feb. 2, Randolph county. R. R. Feb. 13, 1844

Alston, Ann Lillington to Wiiilam H. Hester of Granville county, Jan., Wake county. R. R. Jan. 16, 1844

Anderson, Martha A. to James G. Tate, Sept., Orange county. R. R. Sept. 24, 1844

Ashby, Edmund J. of Robeson county to Ann M. Wooten of Bladen county, Apr. R. R. Apr. 19, 1844

Atkins, Edward N. to Sarah Currie, Dec., Wilmington. R. R. Dec. 31, 1844

Bagley, Thomas of Johnson county to Lucinda Pike of Wayne county, Jan. 21, Wayne county. R. R. Jan. 30, 1844

Baker, Rev. Archibald of Richmond county to Sarah E. James, Dec., Wilmington. R. R. Dec. 31, 1844

Baldwin, Mastin of Montgomery county to Annis Pankey, My. 30, Richmond county. R. R. Je. 11, 1844

Ballefant, John of Tennessee to Eliza Turner, Oct. 2, Hillsborough. R. R. Oct. 15, 1844

Banker, Jacob L. to Mary C. Yerbin, Oct., Mecklenburg county. R. R. Oct. 25, 1844

Barclay, Julia G. to James Cameron of Wilmington, Mar., Barclaysville. R. R. Mar. 15, 1844

Barnes, Wright to Mrs. Mary A. S. Sharpe, Feb. 13, Edgecombe county. R. R. Feb. 27, 1844

Barton, William to Hetty Crabtree, Apr., Orange county. R. R. Apr. 3, 1844

Baskersville, Betsey P. to James L. Duke, Je. 23, Warren county. R. R. Aug. 2, 1844

Bebee, Malinda to Joshua Carmon, My., Fayetteville. R. R. My. 17, 1844

Beckerdite, Mary Ann to Rev. John Rich of North Carolina Conference, Nov., Davidson county. R. R. Nov. 29, 1844

Bethune, Ann to Erwin Charlile, Mar., Robeson county. R. R. Mar. 26, 1844

Betts, Willy H. of Raleigh to Lucius Rand, Mar. 21, Wake county. R. R. Apr. 2, 1844

Bidwell, Mary to Daniel Johnson of Fayetteville, Sept., Middletown, Connecticut. R. R. Oct. 4, 1844

Bird, Rev. N. of Darlington District, South Carolina, to Eliza J. Steel, Jan. 20, Richmond county. R. R. Feb. 13, 1844

Bishop, Margaret Alice to Nash Creek, Sept., Orange county. R. R. Sept. 24, 1844

Black, Cresida to W. T. Newell, Jly. 25, Cabarrus county. R. R. Aug. 2, 1844

Black, Lorenzo to Malinda Weaver, Feb. 13, Lincoln county. R. R. Feb. 27, 1844

Blanton, Wm. J. to Miss A. C. Coward, Jan. 25, Rutherford county. R. R. Feb. 6, 1844

Blue, John M. to Margaret Camerett, Dec. 28, Moore county. R. R. Jan. 9, 1844

Bobbitt, Lucinda to Thomas H. Farthing, Je., Orange county. R. R. Je. 21, 1844

Bolton, Elizabeth H. of Philadelphia to Dr. Joseph Hollifield of Baltimore,

Feb. 1, Charlotte. R. R. Feb. 16, 1844

Bowden, J. O. to Sarah Amanda Collins, Mar., Weldon. R. R. Mar. 12, 1844

Bowers, Patsy to William Riley, Sept., Orange county. R. R. Oct. 1, 1844

Bradley, Lucy to Stephen Jewett, Jan., Wilmington. R. R. Feb. 2, 1844

Bream, Elizabeth A. of Stokes county to John Lewellin of Davie county, Nov., Salisbury. R. R. Nov. 19, 1844

Brewer, John M. of Nansemond county, Virginia to Ann Eliza Wait of Wake Forest, Nov., Wake Forest College. R. R. Nov. 19, 1844

Brewer, Capt. Thomas to N. Caroline Betty, Oct., Orange county. R. R. Oct. 22, 1844

Britain, William of Bertie county to Frances Ann Johnston, Jly. 17, Hillsboro. R. R. Jly. 30, 1844

Brock, Mary E. to George F. Kornegay, Jan. 2, Jones county. R. R. Jan. 16, 1844

Brower, J. W. of Surry county to Mary Martha Albright, Apr., Greensboro. R. R. Apr. 12, 1844

Brown, Columbia Annabella to Frederick J. Lord, Dec. 18, Wilmington. R. R. Jan. 2, 1844

Bruton, George M. to Martha Christian, Mar., Montgomery county. R. R. Mar. 19, 1844

Buffalo, Joseph G. M. to Marina Robbins, Jan. 9, Raleigh. R. R. Jan. 12, 1844

Caldwell, Susan A. to Dr. Howard Z. Cosby of Raleigh, Jan. 10, Greensborough. R. R. Jan. 16, 1844

Callais, Elizabeth W. to John W. Emmet of Salisbury. R. R. Mar. 26, 1844

Camerett, Margaret to John M. Blue, Dec. 28, Moore county. R. R. Jan. 9, 1844

Cameron, James of Wilmington to Julia G. Barclay, Mar., Barclaysville. R. R. Mar. 15, 1844

Carmon, Joshua to Malinda Bebee, My., Fayetteville. R. R. My. 17, 1844

Carney, Ann Lucas of Fayetteville to Frank Martin of Vermont, Feb., Franklinton, Ohio. R. R. Feb. 27, 1844

Carson, N. P. of Franklin county to Miss E. J. Hicks, Jly. 11, Wake county. R. R. Jly. 19, 1844

Carter, Augustus H. to Catharine J. Hartsfield, Dec., Wilmington. R. R. Dec. 31, 1844

Cawthorn, John V. to Mary H. Pope, Mar., Warrenton. R. R. Mar. 19, 1844

Charlile, Erwin to Ann Bethune, Mar., Robeson county. R. R. Mar. 26, 1844

Cheek, Nash to Margaret Alice Bishop, Sept., Orange county. R. R. Sept. 24, 1844

Christian, Martha to George M. Bruton, Mar., Montgomery county. R. R. Mar. 19, 1844

Clark, Mary Alethea of Scotland Neck to Dr. Wm. J. Hawkins of Franklin county, Jan. 9, Warren county. R. R. Feb. 16, 1844

Clary, Elizabeth to John S. Wise, Feb. 1, Randolph county. R. R. Feb. 13, 1844

Clingman, Laura M. to Major Thomas Forster of Raleigh, Sept. 24, Cincinnati. R. R. Oct. 8, 1844

Collins, Sarah Amanda to J. O. Bowden, Mar., Weldon. R. R. Mar. 12, 1844

Cook, Major John H. to Miss M. M. Starr, Dec., Fayetteville. R. R. Dec. 31, 1844
Cosby, Dr. Howard B. of Raleigh to Susan A. Caldwell, Jan. 10, Greensborough. R. R. Jan. 16, 1844
Costen, Mary E. to Peterson B. Satterfield of New Orleans, La., Aug., Gates county. R. R. Aug. 9, 1845
Council, Margaret to William Shaw, My., Rockfish, Cumberland county. R. R. My. 17, 1844
Coward, Miss A. C. to Wm. J. Blanton, Jan. 25, Rutherford county. R. R. Feb. 6, 1844
Crabtree, Hetty to William Barton, Apr., Orange county. R. R. Apr. 3, 1845
Craddock, Susan Catherine to Franklin Snead, Feb., Sampson county. R. R. Mar. 1, 1844
Craven, Rev. Braxton to Irene Leach, Oct., Randolph county. R. R. Oct. 22, 1844
Crawford, Harriet Ann to Walter Steel, Je. 27, Richmond county. R. R. Jly. 9, 1844
Crenshaw, Louisa to Wm. B. Norman of Granville county, Sept., Wake county. R. R. Sept. 24, 1844
Cromartie, Duncan to Mary A. McKay, Dec. 12, Bladen county. R. R. Jan. 2, 1844
Croom, John B. to Mrs. J. M'Alister, Mar., New Hanover county. R. R. Mar. 29, 1844
Cunningham, Solomon to Sarah S. Fletcher, Feb. 13, Buncombe county. R. R. Feb. 27, 1844
Currie, Sarah to Edward N. Atkins, Dec., Wilmington. R. R. Dec. 31, 1844
Custis, Peter to Sally A. Smith, Dec., Newbern. R. R. Dec. 20, 1844
Daniels, Hon. J. R. J. of Halifax District to Frances Stith of Raleigh, Aug. 29, Raleigh. R. R. Sept. 3, 1844
Darden, Joseph to Miss E. Hobbs, Mar. 14, Sampson county. R. R. My. 3, 1844
Davis, Dr. Adam C. of Lenoir county & Greenville to Aramita H. Moses, Jan. 11, Strawberry hill, Wayne county. R. R. Jan. 30, 1844
Davis, Anne Jane to David Melvin, Mar., Bladen county. R. R. Mar. 26, 1844
Davis, D. A. to Mary Elizabeth Horah, Nov., Salisbury. R. R. Nov. 19, 1844
Davis, Jane W. to James Murray, Mar., Pitt county. R. R. Mar. 5, 1844
Deweese, Major Wm. to Martha B. M'Cauley, Jan. 18, Mecklenburg county. R. R. Jan. 30, 1844
Dixon, George B. of Mississippi to Mary B. M'Donald, Mar., Edenton. R. R. Mar. 29, 1844
Dortch, Dr. Lewis J. to Nancy Jane Allen, Nov., Edgecombe county. R. R. Nov. 29, 1844
Dotson, George W. to Barbara Paterson, Jan. 24, Cabarrus county. R. R. Feb. 2, 1844
Duke, James L. to Betsey P. Baskerville, Je. 23, Warren county. R. R. Aug. 2, 1844
Duke, John T. to Tabitha C. Whitamore, Nov., Rockingham county. R. R. Nov. 29, 1844

Duskin, Sarah Jane to John C. Latta, Sept., Orange county. R. R. Oct. 1, 1844

Edwards, James to Gracey Teel, Oct., Chatham county. R. R. Oct. 22, 1844

Elliott, Exum of Perquimans county to Mrs. Isabella Elliott, Mar., Pasquotank county. R. R. Mar. 5, 1844

Elliott, Mrs. Isabella to Exum Elliott of Perquimans county, Mar., Pasquotank county. R. R. Mar. 5, 1844

Ellis, John of Rowan county to Mary P. White of Raleigh, Aug. 25, Philadelphia. R. R. Sept. 3, 1844

Emmet, John W. of Salisbury to Elizabeth W. Callais, Mar., Fayetteville. R. R. Mar. 26, 1844

Erwin, John of Rutherfordton to Louisa E. Gash, Oct., Buncombe county. R. R. Nov. 5, 1844

Farthing, Thomas H. to Lucinda Bobbitt, Je., Orange county. R. R. Je. 21, 1844

Fentress, John M. to Mary Kirkman, My., Guilford county. R. R. My. 21, 1844

Ferell, Emeline to Solomon Gooch, Je., Orange county. R. R. Je. 21, 1844

Fletcher, Sarah S. to Solomon Cunningham, Feb. 13, Buncombe county. R. R. Feb. 27, 1844

Flowers, David F. to Sarah Gillespie, Dec. 12, Bladen county. R. R. Jan. 2, 1844

Forster, Major Thomas of Raleigh to Laura M. Clingman of Cincinnati, Sept. 24, Cincinnati. R. R. Oct. 8, 1844

Foy, James H. to Catharine O. House, Dec. 19, Onslow county. R. R. Jan. 9, 1844

Fulton, Eliza G. to William F. Hester, Nov. 5, Raleigh. R. R. Nov. 12, 1844

Gaines, James to Mrs. Karah Kidd, Dec. 24, Moore county. R. R. Jan. 16, 1844

Gales, Weston R. of Raleigh to Mary Spies of New York City, Jan. 8, New York City. R. R. Jan. 16, 1844

Gash, Louisa E. to John Erwin of Rutherfordton, Oct., Buncombe county. R. R. Nov. 5, 1844

Gaskill, George of Orange county to Martha Tyre of Guilford county, Jan. 30, Guilford county. R. R. Feb. 6, 1844

Gauze, Melvina A. to Richard H. Grant, Apr., Wilmington. R. R. Apr. 30, 1844

Gibson, William to Sarah M'Nair, Feb., Laurel Hill, Richmond county. R. R. Feb. 16, 1844

Gillespie, Sarah to David F. Flowers, Dec. 12, Bladen county. R. R. Jan. 2, 1844

Godfrey, Joseph G. of Perquimans county to Margaret M. Haughton, Jan. 29, Edenton. R. R. Feb. 13, 1844

Gooch, Solomon to Emeline Ferell, Je., Orange county. R. R. Je. 21, 1844

Gorham, Thomas A. to Susan Z. Selby, Sr., Jan. 28, Greenville, Pitt county. R. R. Feb. 6, 1844

Grant, Richard H. to Melvina A. Gauze, Apr., Wilmington. R. R. Apr. 30, 1844

Graves, Major John K. of Caswell county to Laura A. Willis, Jan. 21, Yanceyville, Caswell county. R. R. Feb. 2, 1844

Green, Caroline C. to John C. Haigh of Fayetteville, Je., Wilmington. R. R. Je. 21, 1844

Green, James S. to Mrs. Caroline A. Holmes, Feb. 13, Wilmington. R. R. Feb. 20, 1844

Green, Richard F. to Eiza Bryan Huggins, Jan. 11, Trenton, Jones county. R. R. Jan. 30, 1844

Griffiths, Nancy to Weldon S. Hunter, Feb. 14, Tarboro. R. R. Feb. 27, 1844

Haigh, John C. of Fayetteville to Caroline C. Green, Je., Wilmington. R. R. Je. 21, 1844

Halsey, Sarah J. of Tyrrell county to W. H. Winn, M. D. of Charlottesville, Virginia. R. R. Nov. 29, 1844

Hamilton, Archibald C. of Rutherford county to Mrs. Charlotte C. Reinheardt, Oct., Caldwell county. R. R. Nov. 5, 1844

Harding, Margaret Jane to William M. Mebane of Orange county, Nov., Orange county. R. R. Nov. 29, 1844

Harrington, Lion to Susan Minter, Mar. 21, Chatham county. R. R. My. 3, 1844

Harris, Anna James to Richard Parker, Nov., Stanly county. R. R. Nov. 19, 1844

Harris, Elizabeth to Daniel Pharr, Feb. 8, Cabarrus county. R. R. Feb. 27, 1844

Harris, Leo to Arrena Lea, Sept. 10, Person county. R. R. Sept. 24, 1844

Hartsfield, Catharine J. to Augustus H. Carter, Dec., Wilmington. R. R. Dec. 31, 1844

Haughton, Margaret M. to Joseph G. Godfrey of Perquimans county, Jan. 29, Edenton. R. R. Feb. 13, 1844

Hawkins, Dr. Wm. J. of Franklin county to Mary Alethea Clark of Scotland Neck, Jan. 9, Warren county. R. R. Feb. 16, 1844

Hayes, John T. of Lincoln county to Cynthia J. Hutchison of Charlotte, Mar. Marengo county, Alabama. R. R. Mar. 8, 1844

Henly, Jane to Jonathan P. Winslow, Feb. 1, Randolph county. R. R. Feb. 13, 1844

Henly, Wm. Penn of Stokes county to Sarah S. Lindsay, Apr., Guilford county. R. R. Apr. 12, 1844

Henry, Carolina to John M. Manly, Nov. 27, Raleigh. R. R. Nov. 29, 1844

Herring, Rufus J. to Ann Moore, Mar., Sampson county. R. R. Mar. 29, 1844

Hester, William F. to Eliza G. Fulton, Nov. 5, Raleigh. R. R. Nov. 12, 1844

Hester, William H. of Granville county to Ann Linington Alston, Jan., Wake county. R. R. Jan. 16, 1844

Hill, Caroline of Wilmington to Hugh C. M'Lean, Nov., Moore county. R. R. Nov. 5, 1844

Hicks, Miss E. J. to N. P. Carson of Franklin county, Jly. 11, Wake county. R. R. Jly. 19, 1844

Hill, Elizabeth to William Pipkin, Oct. 24, Moore county. R. R. Nov. 15, 1844

Hill, Sion to Elizabeth Nance, Feb. 4, Randolph county. R. R. Feb. 13, 1844

Hillyard, Jane E. to B. B. Roberts of Davidson county, Apr. 5, Davidson county. R. R. Apr. 19, 1844

Hims, Rev. James S. of Fayetteville & Winsborough to Sarah C. McIver, Apr., Society Hill, South Carolina. R. R. Apr. 30, 1844

Holman, Sarah to Silas M. Link of Orange county, Sept., Person county. R. R. Oct. 1, 1844

Holmes, Mrs. Caroline A. to James S. Green, Feb. 13, Wilmington. R. R. Feb. 20, 1844

Hobbs, Miss E. to Joseph Darden, Mar. 14, Sampson county. R. R. My. 3, 1844

Hollifield, Dr. Joseph of Baltimore to Elizabeth H. Bolton of Philadelphia, Feb. 1, Charlotte. R. R. Feb. 16, 1844

Holt, Simon P. to Miss E. A. Stevens, Mar. 14, Sampson county. R. R. My. 3, 1844

Horah, Mary Elizabeth to D. A. Davis, Nov., Salisbury. R. R. Nov. 19, 1844

House, Catharine O. to James H. Foy, Dec. 19, Onslow county. R. R. Jan. 9, 1844

Houston, Jane to Robert A. Young, Jly. 25, Cabarrus county. R. R. Aug. 2, 1844

Huggins, Eliza Bryan to Richard F. Green, Jan. 11, Trenton, Jones county. R. R. Jan. 30, 1844

Humphrey, Indiana to Dr. John Shackelford, Dec. 26, Onslow county. R. R. Jan. 9, 1844

Hunter, Archibald C. to Eliza J. Strayhorn, Dec. 21, Orange county. R. R. Jan. 9, 1844

Hunter, Weldon S. to Nancy Griffiths, Feb. 14, Tarboro. R. R. Feb. 27, 1844

Hutchison, Cynthia J. of Charlotte to John T. Hayes of Lincoln county, Mar., Marengo county, Alabama. R. R. Mar. 8, 1844

James, Sarah E. to Rev. Archibald Baker of Richmond county, Dec., Wilmington. R. R. Dec. 31, 1844

Jarvis, Moses W. of Newbern to Mrs. Frances P. Waters, Oct., Brooklyn, New York. R. R. Oct. 29, 1844

Jewett, Stephen to Lucy Bradley, Jan., Wilmington. R. R. Feb. 2, 1844

Johnson, Arch'd A. to Emma Thompson, Apr., Cumberland county. R. R. Apr. 19, 1844

Johnson, Daniel of Fayetteville to Mary Bidwell, Sept., Middleton, Connecticut. R. R. Oct. 4, 1844

Johnson, Duncan to Mary M'Phatter, Mar., Robeson county. R. R. Mar. 26, 1844

Johnson, Dr. Joseph R. to Amanda M'Neily, Mar., Mocksville. R. R. Mar. 8, 1844

Johnson, Mary to Lee Alexander, Feb. 1, Mecklenburg county. R. R. Feb. 16, 1844

Johnson, Neill to Mrs. Benetta Pointer, Mar., Fayetteville. R. R. Mar. 19, 1844

Johnston, Frances Ann to William Britain of Bertie county, Jly. 17, Hillsboro. R. R. Jly. 30, 1844

Jones, Rev. C. C. to Sarah Jane M'Lauchlin, Mar. 24, Fayetteville. R. R. My. 3, 1844

Jones, Mrs. Elizabeth to Dr. Blake Little, Apr., Sumter county, Alabama. R. R. Apr. 12, 1844

Jones, Elizabeth M. to Dr. Rufus K. Speed of Gates county, Feb., Edenton. R. R. Feb. 27, 1844

Jordan, Calvin to Elizabeth Stevens, Jan. 14, Wake county. R. R. Jan. 30, 1844

Jordan, Samuel to Martha Ann Nichols, Oct., Orange county. R. R. Oct. 22, 1844

Kelly, Henry S. to Lucy Ann Turner, both formerly of New York, Nov., Wilmington. R. R. Dec. 6, 1844

Kelly, John B. to Isabella C. M'Lean, Nov., Washington hill, Moore county. R. R. Nov. 29, 1844

Kendall, Franklin to Margaret Moss, Nov., Stanly county. R. R. Nov. 19, 1844

Kerner, Israel to Elmira Perry, Nov., Stokes county. R. R. Nov. 26, 1844

Kilkelly, William Gray to Emeline Alston Murden, Apr. 18, Raleigh. R. R. Apr. 23, 1844

Kidd, Mrs. Karah to James Gaines, Dec. 24, Moore county. R. R. Jan. 16, 1844

King, Elizabeth to Daniel G. Schoolfield of Guilford county, Apr., Rockingham. R. R. Apr. 12, 1844

King, Jacob R. to Sarah White, Dec. 21, Onslow county. R. R. Jan. 9, 1844

Kirkman, Mary to John M. Fentress, My., Guilford county. R. R. My. 21, 1844

Kornegay, George F. to Mary E. Brock, Jan. 2, Jones county. R. R. Jan. 16, 1844

Lamb, Mary to Oliver L. Lindley of Chatham county, Sept. 12, Guilford county. R. R. Sept. 24, 1844

Lander, Margaret to Rev. Wm. J. Langdon of Raleigh, Dec., Lincolnton. R. R. Dec. 31, 1844

Langdon, Rev. Wm. J. of Raleigh to Margaret Lander, Dec., Lincolnton. R. R. Dec. 31, 1844

Langford, Robert to Ann Eliza Mullen, Sept., Granville county. R. R. Oct. 1, 1844

Latta, John C. to Sarah Jane Duskin, Sept., Orange county. R. R. Oct. 1, 1844

Latta, Nancy A. to Tyre Ray, My., Orange county. R. R. My. 17, 1844

Lea, Arrena to Lea Harris, Sept. 10, Person county. R. R. Sept. 24, 1844

Lea, Mary Jane of Chatham county to George W. Watson of Haywood county, Jan. 29. R. R. Mar. 22, 1844

Leach, Irene to Rev. Braxton Craven, Oct., Randolph county. R. R. Oct. 22, 1844

Le Bell, Durant H. to Frances V. Mauney of Carteret county, Dec. 18, Beaufort county. R. R. Feb. 6, 1844

Lewellin, John of Davie county to Elizabeth A. Bream of Stokes county, Nov., Salisbury. R. R. Nov. 19, 1844

Lindley, Oliver L. of Chatham county to Mary Lamb, Sept. 12, Guilford county. R. R. Sept. 24, 1844

Lindsay, Sarah S. to Wm. Penn Henly of Stokes county, Apr., Guilford county. R. R. Apr. 12, 1844

Link, Silas M. of Orange county to Sarah Holman, Sept., Person county. R. R. Oct. 1, 1844

Little, Dr. Blake to Mrs. Elizabeth Jones, Apr., Sumter county, Alabama. R. R. Apr. 12, 1844

Long, Capt. Anderson B. to Nancy Long, Jan. 30, Rutherford county. R. R. Feb. 13, 1844

Long, Nancy to Capt. Anderson B. Long, Jan. 30, Rutherfordton. R. R. Feb. 13, 1844

Lord, Frederick J. to Columbia Annabella Brown, Dec. 18, Wilmington. R. R. Jan. 2, 1844

Lowry, Allen of Stokes county to Lydia M'Knight of Guilford county, Feb., Guilford county. R. R. Feb. 16, 1844

Lucas, Effy Ann to James R. M'Laurin of Richmond county, Feb., Marlborough District, South Carolina. R. R. Feb. 16, 1844

Lumsden, Sarah of Johnston county to John P. Sandford of Goldsboro & Boston, Mass., Oct. 31, Fayetteville. R. R. Nov. 15, 1844

Lurry, Caswell to Sarah Roberts, Mar., Anson county. R. R. Mar. 8, 1844

M'Alister, Mrs. J. to John B. Croom, Mar., New Hanover county. R. R. Mar. 29, 1844

M'Cauley, Martha B. to Major Wm. Deweese, Jan. 18, Mecklenburg county. R. R. Jan. 30, 1844

M'Donald, Mary B. to George B. Dixon of Mississippi, Mar., Edenton. R. R. Mar. 29, 1844

M'Dougald, Col. to Lucy Sutton, Dec. 6, Bladen county. R. R. Feb. 20, 1844

M'Dugal, Major Dugald to Elizabeth Jane M'Neill, Nov., Moore county. R. R. Dec. 6, 1844

M'Ginnis, J. W. to Margaret Patterson, Sept., Mecklenburg county. R. R. Sept. 27, 1844

M'Iver, Sarah C. to Rev. James S. Hims of Fayetteville & Winsborough, Apr., Society hill, S. C. R. R. Apr. 30, 1844

M'Kay, Mary A. to Duncan Cromartie, Dec. 12, Bladen county. R. R. Jan. 2, 1844

M'Knight, Lydia of Guilford county to Allen Lowry of Stokes county, Feb., Guilford county. R. R. Feb. 16, 1844

M'Lauchlin, Mary to L. S. Tower of Pittsborough, Nov. 6, Fayetteville. R. R. Nov. 8, 1844

M'Lauchlin, Sarah Jane to Rev. C. C. Jones, Mar. 24, Fayetteville. R. R. My. 3, 1844

M'Laurin, James R. of Richmond county to Effy Ann Lucas, Feb., Marlborough District, S. C.: R. R. Feb. 16, 1844

M'Lean, Dr. Addison to Mary Purvines, Feb. 6, Cabarrus county. R. R. Feb. 27, 1844

M'Lean, Hugh C. to Caroline Hill of Wilmington, Nov., Moore county. R. R. Nov. 5, 1844

M'Lean, Isabella C. to John B. Kelly, Nov., Washington Hill, Moore county. R. R. Nov. 29, 1844

M'Nair, Sarah to William Gibson, Feb, Laurel Hill, Richmond county. R. R. Feb. 16, 1844

M'Namara, Anastasia of Salisbury to John Spaun of Sumpter District, S. C., Feb. 1, Cheraw, S. C. R. R. Feb. 13, 1844

M'Neill, Archibald of Robeson county to Isabella M'Neill, Dec. 28, Cumberland county. R. R. Jan. 16, 1844

M'Neill, Elizabeth Jane to Major Dugald M'Dugal, Nov., Moore county. R. R. Dec. 6, 1844

M'Neill, Isabella to Archibald M'Neill of Robeson county, Dec. 28, Cumberland county. R. R. Jan. 16, 1844.
M'Neill, Jane S. of Fayetteville to Col. John M. Rose of Greensborough, Mar. 25, Fayetteville. R. R. My. 3, 1844
M'Neily, Amanda to Dr. Joseph R. Johnson, Mar., Mocksville. R. R. Mar. 8, 1844
M'Phatter, Mary to Duncan Johnson, Mar., Robeson county. R. R. Mar. 26, 1844
Mailey, Charles E. to Nancy Richmond, Jly. 20, Washington. R. R. Aug. 20, 1844
Manly, Col. John M. to Carolina Henry, Nov. 27, Raleigh. R. R. Nov. 29, 1844
Manly, Hon. M. E. to Sarah Simpson, Je. 27, Newbern. R. R. Jly. 9, 1844
Martin, Frank of Vermont to Ann Lucas Carney of Fayetteville, Feb., Franklinton, Ohio. R. R. Feb. 27, 1844
Martin, Susan W. to Seaborn Williams of Raleigh, Feb. 8, Tuskegee, Alabama. R. R. Feb. 27, 1844
Martin, Thomas S. to Ann C. Poindexter, Nov., Surry county. R. R. Nov. 19, 1844
Mauney, Frances V. of Carteret county to Durant H. LeBell, Dec. 18, Beaufort county. R. R. Feb. 6, 1844
Maury, Mrs. Frances H. to Samuel Perry of Franklin county, Dec. 31, Elizabeth city. R. R. Jan. 9, 1844
Mebane, William M. of Orange county to Margaret Jane Harding, Nov., Orange county. R. R. Nov. 29, 1844
Melvin, David to Anne Jane Davis, Mar., Bladen county. R. R. Mar. 26, 1844
Michal, Susannah to Mr. Reinhardt, Jan. 28, Catawba county. R. R. Feb. 9, 1844
Milton, Mrs. Isaiah to Jesse Saunders, Dec. 28, Moore county. R. R. Jan. 5, 1844
Minter, Susan to Lion Harrington, Mar. 21, Chatham county. R. R. My. 3, 1844
Moore, Ann to Rufus J. Herring, Mar., Sampson county. R. R. Mar. 29, 1844
Morrow, Elizabeth to Joseph H. Pickett, Mar., Orange county. R. R. Mar. 5, 1844
Moses, Araminta H. to Dr. Adam C. Davis of Lenoir county and Greenville, Jan. 11, Strawberryhill, Wayne county. R. R. Jan. 30, 1844
Moss, Elizabeth to Samuel M. Wilkerson, Jly. 18, Orange county. R. R. Jly. 30, 1844
Moss, Margaret to Franklin Kendall, Nov., Stanly county. R. R. Nov. 19, 1844
Mullen, Ann Eliza to Robert Langford, Sept., Granville county. R. R. Oct. 1, 1844
Murden, Emeline Alston to William Gray Kilkelly, Apr. 18, Raleigh. R. R. Apr. 23, 1844
Murray, James to Jane W. Davis, Mar., Pitt county. R. R. Mar. 5, 1844
Nance, Elizabeth to Sion Hill, Feb. 4, Randolph county. R. R. Feb. 13, 1844

Newell, W. T. to Cresida Black, Jly. 25, Cabarrus county. R. R. Aug. 2, 1844
Newell Wm. T. to Susan Jane Swinson, Apr., Duplin county. R. R. Apr. 30, 1844
Newman, John to Timsy Woods, My., Hillsboro. R. R. My. 17, 1844
Nichols, Martha Ann to Samuel Jordan, Oct., Orange county. R. R. Oct. 22, 1844
Nixon, Chas. D. to Mary Louisa Wooten, Mar., Fayetteville. R. R. Mar. 8, 1844
Norman, Wm. B. of Granville county to Louisa Crenshaw, Sept., Wake county. R. R. Sept. 24, 1844
Osbern, Allen to Sarah Allred, Feb. 2, Randolph county. R. R. Feb. 13, 1844
Pankey, Annis to Mastin Baldwin of Montgomery county, My. 30, Richmond county. R. R. Je. 11, 1844
Parker, Richard to Anna James Harris, Nov., Stanly county. R. R. Nov. 19, 1844
Paschall, Sarah Jane A. to Burrell Taylor, Sept., Granville county. R. R. Oct. 1, 1844
Paterson, Barbara to George W. Dotson, Jan. 24, Cabarrus county. R. R. Feb. 2, 1844
Patterson, Nancy Ann to Porter Wharton, Apr., Guilford county. R. R. Apr. 12, 1844
Perry, Caleb G. of Pasquotank county to Eliza Perry, Sept. 12, Wake county. R. R. Sept. 13, 1844
Perry, Eliza to Caleb G. Perry of Pasquotank county, Sept. 12, Wake county. R. R. Sept. 13, 1844
Perry, Elmira to Israel Kerner, Nov., Stokes county. R. R. Nov. 26, 1844
Perry, Samuel of Franklin county to Mrs. Frances H. Maury, Dec. 31, Elizabeth City. R. R. Jan. 9, 1844
Petty, N Caroline to Capt. Thomas Brewer, Oct., Orange county. R. R. Oct. 22, 1844
Pharr, Daniel to Elizabeth Harris, Feb. 8, Cabarrus county. R. R. Feb. 27, 1844
Pickett, Joseph H. to Elizabeth Morrow, Mar., Orange county. R. R. Mar. 5, 1844
Pike, Lucinda of Wayne county to Thomas Bagley of Johnson county, Jan. 21, Wayne county. R. R. Jan. 30, 1844
Pipkin, William to Elizabeth Hill, Oct. 24, Moore county. R. R. Nov. 15, 1844
Poindexter, Ann C. to Thomas S. Martin, Nov., Surry county. R. R. Nov. 18, 1844
Pointer, Mrs. Benetta to Neill Johnson, Mar., Fayetteville. R. R. Mar. 19, 1844
Pope, Mary H. to John V. Cawthorn, Mar., Warrenton. R. R. Mar. 19, 1844
Powers, Mrs. Martha to Rev. Isaac W. West of Duplin county, Mar., New Hanover county. R. R. Mar. 5, 1844
Pratt, John to Mary Ann Adams, Mar., Anson county. R. R. Mar. 26, 1844
Purvines, Mary to Dr. Addison M'Lean, Feb. 6, Cabarrus county. R. R. Feb. 27, 1844

Rand, Lucius to Willy H Betts of Raleigh, Mar 21, Wake county. R. R. Apr. 2, 1844
Ray, Tyre B. to Nancy A. Latta, My., Orange county. R. R. My. 17, 1844
Reinhardt, Mr. to Susannah Michal, Jan. 28, Catawba county. R. R. Feb. 9, 1844
Reinheardt, Charlotte C. to Archibald C. Hamilton of Rutherford county, Oct., Caldwell county. R. R. Nov. 5, 1844
Rich, Rev. John of N. C. Conference to Mary Ann Beckerdite, Nov., Davidson county. R. R. Nov. 29, 1844
Richmond, Nancy to Charles E. Mailey, Jly. 20, Washington. R. R. Aug. 20, 1844
Riley, William to Patsey Bowers, Feb. 13, Orange county. R. R. Oct. 1, 1844
Roach, Eliza to Willis Smith, Feb. 13, Orange county. R. R. Feb. 20, 1844
Robbins, Julius C. to Susan E. Smithwick of Martin county, My., Washington. R. R. My. 17, 1844
Robbins, Marina to Joseph G. M. Buffalo, Jan. 9, Raleigh. R. R. Jan. 12, 1844
Roberts, B. B. of Davidson county to Jane E. Hillyard, Apr. 5, Davidson county. R. R. Apr. 19, 1844
Roberts, Sarah to Caswell Lurry, Mar., Anson county. R. R. Mar. 8, 1844
Roberts, Mrs. Sarah L. to John Walton of Gates county, Oct., Edenton. R. R. Oct. 18, 1844
Rogers, James to Partilda Buffalo, Jan. 4, Wake county. R. R. Jan. 30, 1844
Rose, Col. John M. of Greensborough to Jane S. M'Neill of Fayetteville, Mar. 25, Fayetteville. R. R. My. 3, 1844
Sandford, John P. of Goldsboro & Boston, Mass. to Sarah Lumsden of Johnston county, Oct. 31, Fayetteville. R. R. Nov. 15, 1844
Satterfield, Peterson B. of New Orleans, La. to Mary E. Costen, Aug., Gates county. R. R. Aug. 9, 1844
Saunders, Jesse to Mrs. Isaiah Milton, Dec. 28, Moore county. R. R. Jan. 5, 1844
Schoolfield, Daniel G. of Guilford county to Elizabeth King, Apr., Rockingham. R. R. Apr. 12, 1844
Selby, Susan Z. Sr. to Thomas A. Gorham, Jan. 28, Greenville, Pitt county. R. R. Feb. 6, 1844
Shackelford, Dr. John to Indiana Humphrey, Dec. 26, Onslow county. R. R. Jan. 9, 1844
Sharpe, rMs. Mary A. S. to Wright Barnes, Feb. 13, Edgecombe county. R. R. Feb. 27, 1844
Shaw, William to Margaret Council, My., Rockfish, Cumberland county. R. R. My. 17, 1844
Shepard, James B. of Raleigh to Francis Donnell, Apr. 25, Newbern. R. R. My. 7, 1844
Simpson, Sarah to Hon. M. E. Manly, Je. 27, Newbern. R. R. Jly. 9, 1844
Smith, William to Rebecca Stuart of Cumberland county, Mar. 19, Fayetteville. R. R. Mar. 26, 1844
Smith, Willis to Eliza Roach, Feb. 13, Orange county. R. R. Feb. 20, 1844
Smithwick, Susan E. of Martin county to Julius C. Robbins, My., Washington. R. R. My. 17, 1844

Snead, Franklin to Susan Catharine Craddock, Feb., Sampson county. R. R. Mar. 1, 1844

Somerville, Robert to Christiana Adaline Todd, Feb. 1, Mecklenburg county. R. R. Feb. 16, 1844

Spaun, John of Sumter District, S. C. to Anastasia Macnamara of Salisbury, Feb. 1, Cheraw, S. C. R. R. Feb. 13, 1844

Sparrow, Thomas Jr. to Ann Maria Blackwell, Apr. 24, Newbern. R. R. My. 7, 1844

Speed, Dr. Rufus K. of Gates county to Elizabeth M. Jones, Feb., Edenton. R. R. Feb. 27, 1844

Spies, Mary of New York City to Weston R. Gales of Raleigh, Jan. 8, New York City. R. R. Jan. 16, 1844

Stanly, Jas. G. of Craven county to Mary Wilkins, Dec., Newbern. R. R. Dec. 20, 1844

Starr, Miss M. M. to Major John H. Cook, Dec., Fayetteville. R. R. Dec. 31, 1844

Stedman, Mary Cooper of Raleigh to Alsey H. Allen of Lowndes, Je. 18, Dallas county, Ala. R. R. Sept. 13, 1844

Steel, Walter Leak to Harriet Ann Crawford, Je. 27, Richmond county. R. R. Jly. 9, 1844

Steel, Eliza J. to Rev. N. Bird of Darlington District, S. C., Jan. 20, Richmond county. R. R. Feb. 13, 1844

Steele, Elizabeth to R. J. Steele, Jr., Feb., Richmond county. R. R. Mar. 1, 1844

Steele, R. J. Jr. to Elizabeth Steele, Feb., Richmond county. R. R. Mar. 1, 1844

Stevens, Miss E. A. to Simon Holt, Mar. 14, Sampson county. R. R. My. 3, 1844

Stith, Frances of Raleigh to Hon. J. R. Daniel of Halifax District, Aug. 29, Raleigh. R. R. Sept. 3, 1844

Stone, Bethania to Wm. Wade, Apr. 27, Rockfish. R. R. My. 3, 1844

Stone, Lucinda to Jacob Williams, Mar., Cumberland county. R. R. Mar. 19, 1844

Strayhorn, Eliza J. to Archibald C. Hunter, Dec. 21, Orange county. R. R. Jan. 9, 1844

Strowd, Tabitha of Orange county to Mr. Quakinbosh of Chatham county, Dec. 12, Orange county. R. R. Jan. 9, 1844

Stuart, Rebecca of Cumberland county to William Smith, Mar. 19, Fayetteville. R. R. Mar. 26, 1844

Sutton, Lucy to Col. M'Dougald, Dec. 6, Bladen county. R. R. Feb. 20, 1844

Swinson, Susan Jane to Wm. T. Newell, Apr., Duplin county. R. R. Apr. 30, 1844

Taylor, Evelina L. to Wm. H. Allen, Feb. 8, Brunswick county. R. R. Feb. 20, 1844

Taft, William to Louisa Vannoorden, Feb., Pitt county. R. R. Mar. 5, 1844

Tate, James G. to Martha A. Anderson, Sept., Orange county. R. R. Sept. 24, 1844

Taylor, Burrell to Sarah Jane A. Paschall, Sept., Granville county. R. R. Oct. 1, 1844

Teel, Gracey to James Edwards, Oct., Chatham county. R. R. Oct. 22, 1844

Thompson, Emma to Arch'd A. Johnson, Apr., Cumberland county. R. R. Apr. 19, 1844
Thompson, Jas. M. to Frances Allen, Jly. 18, Orange county. R. R. Jly. 30, 1844
Todd, Christiana Adaline to Robert Somerville, Feb. 1, Mecklenburg county. R. R. Feb. 16, 1844
Tower, L. S. of Pittsborough to Mary M'Lauchlin, Nov. 6, Fayetteville. R. R. Nov. 8, 1844
Turner, Eliza to John Ballefant of Tennessee, Oct. 2, Hillsborough. R. R. Oct. 15, 1844
Turner, Lucy Ann to Henry S. Kelly both formerly of New York, Nov., Wilmington. R. R. Dec. 6, 1844
Tyre, Martha of Guilford county to George Gaskill of Orange county, Jan. 30, Guilford county. R. R. Feb. 6, 1844
Quakingbosh, Mr .of Chatham county to Tabitha Strowd of Orange county, Dec. 21, Orange county. R. R. Jan. 9, 1844
Vannoorden, Louisa to William Taft, Feb., Pitt county. R. R. Mar. 5, 1844
Wade, Wm. to Bethnia Stone, Apr. 27, Rockfish. R. R. My. 3, 1844
Wait, Ann Eliza of Wake Forest to John M. Brewer of Nansemond county, Va., Nov., Wake Forest College. R. R. Nov. 19, 1844
Walker, Col. James M. to Elizabeth J. Young, Apr., Rockingham. R. R. Apr. 12, 1844
Walton, John of Gates county to Mrs. Sarah L. Roberts, Oct., Edenton. R. R. Oct. 13, 1844
Warren, Wm. to Catharine Wright of Jamestown, Jan. 30, Guilford county. R. R. Feb. 6, 1844
Waters, Mrs. Frances P. to Moses W. Jarvis of Newbern, Oct., Brooklyn, N. Y. R. R. Oct. 29, 1844
Watson, George W. of Haywood county to Mary Jane Lea of Chatham county, Jan. 29. R. R. Mar. 22, 1844
Weaver, Malinda to Lorenzo Black, Feb. 13, Lincoln county. R. R. Feb. 27, 1844
West, Rev. Isaac W. of Duplin county to Mrs. Martha Powers, Mar., New Hanover county. R. R. Mar. 5, 1844
Wharton, Porter to Nancy Ann Patterson, Apr., Guilford county. R. R. Apr. 12, 1844
Whitamore, Tabitha C. to John T. Duke, Nov., Rockingham county. R. R. Nov. 29, 1844
White, Mary P. of Raleigh to John Ellis of Rowan county, Aug. 25, Philadelphia. R. R. Sept. 3, 1844
White, Sarah to Jacob R. King, Dec. 21, Onslow county. R. R. Jan. 9, 1844
Wilkerson, Samuel M. to Elizabeth Moss, Jly. 18, Orange county. R. R. Jly. 30, 1844
Wilkins, Mary to Jas. G. Stanly of Craven county, Dec., Newbern. R. R. Dec. 20, 1844
Williams, Casey to Joel Williams, Mar., Cumberland county. R. R. Mar. 19, 1844
Williams, Jacob to Lucinda Stone, Mar., Cumberland county. R. R. Mar. 19, 1844

Williams, Joel to Carey Williams, Mar., Cumberland county. R. R. Mar. 19, 1844
Williams, Mary to Mr. H. Allen, Mar., Anson county. R. R. Mar. 8, 1844
Williams, Seaborn to Susan W. Martin of Raleigh, Feb. 8, Tuskegee, Alabama. R. R. Feb. 27, 1844
Willis, Laura A. to Maj. John K. Graves of Caswell county, Jan. 21, Yanceyville, Caswell county. R. R. Feb. 2, 1844
Winn, W. H., M. D. of Charlottesville, Va. to Sarah J. Halsey of Tyrrell county. R. R. Nov. 29, 1844
Winslow, Jonathan P. to Jane Henly, Feb. 1, Randolph county. R. R. Feb. 13, 1844
Wise, John S. to Elizabeth Clary, Feb. 1, Randolph county. R. R. Feb. 13, 1844
Woods, Timsy to John Newman, My., Hillsboro. R. R. My. 17, 1844
Wooten, Ann M. of Bladen county to Edmund J. Ashby of Robeson county, Apr. R. R. Apr. 19, 1844
Wooten, Mary Louisa to Chas D. Nixon, Mar., Fayetteville. R. R. Mar. 8, 1844
Wright, Catharine of Jamestown to Wm. W. Warren, Jan. 30, Guilford county. R. R. Feb. 6, 1844
Yerbin, Mary C. to Jacob L. Banker, Oct., Mecklenburg county. R. R. Oct. 25, 1844
Young, Elizabeth J. to Col. James M. Walker, Apr., Rockingham. R. R. Apr .12, 1844
Young, Robert A. to Jane Houston, Jly. 25, Cabarrus county. R. R. Aug. 2, 1844

1845

Adams, Lynn to Mary M. Williams of Wake county, Jan. 29, Wake county. R. R. Feb. 7, 1845
Alexander, Orry Ann to Col. John Baxter of Hendersonville, My., Buncombe county. R. R. My. 23, 1845
Alexander, Sarah C. of Boxwood, Mecklenburg county, Virginia to Robert A. Hamilton of Granville county, Dec. 18, Boxwood, Mecklenburg county, Va. R. R. Jan. 7, 1845
Allen, Barbara to D. A. M'Millan, My., Kelley's Cove, Bladen county. R. R. My. 20, 1845
Allen, David to Isabella M'Knight, Dec., Mecklenburg county. R. R. Dec. 5, 1845
Allmand, Nancy to Daniel Myers, Jly., Cabarrus county. R. R. Jly. 4, 1845
Andres, Mary to Robert E. Troy of Lumberton, Jly., Bladen county. R. R. Jly. 8, 1845
Arendell, Mary E. to Benjamin Leecraft, Feb., Carteret county. R. R. Feb. 11, 1845
Ashe, Richard J. of Hillsboro to Mary P. Mitchell, Oct. 28, Chapel Hill. R. R. Nov. 4, 1845
Atkinson, William Rebecca Frances of Pitt county to Thaddeus E. Dillard of Sussex Court House, Virginia, Nov., Scotland Neck. R. R. Nov. 11, 1845
Bacon, Mary to Henry Woods, Mar., Orange county. R. R. Apr. 1, 1845

Ball, Mary E. of Richmond to Capt. James H. Davis of the State, Aug., Richmond, Va. R. R. Aug. 19, 1845
Barlow, John H. of Orange & Franklin counties to Caroline Gill, Jan. 2, Louisburg. R. R. Jan. 7, 1845
Barnum, Dr. Richard of Wake county to Elizabeth Ann Hurst, Apr., Baltimore. R. R. Apr. 29, 1845
Barrow, Joseph W. to Martha M. Ives, Nov., Perquimans county. R. R. Nov. 25, 1845
Battle, Mary E. of Nashville to Dr. Theophilus H. Scott of Raleigh. R. R. My. 23, 1845
Battle, William S. to Elizabeth M. Dancy, Jly., Tarboro. R. R. Jly. 8, 1845
Batts, Mary to William S. Long, Jan., Edgecombe county. R. R. Jan. 14, 1845
Bauman, John G. to Ellen Fitman, Feb., Wilmington. R. R. Feb. 21, 1845
Baxter, Col. John of Hendersonville to Orry Ann Alexander, My., Buncombe county. R. R. My. 23, 1845
Beard, Thomas to Elizabeth Gullett, Mar., Greensboro. R. R. Mar. 11, 1845
Becton, Mrs. Eliza A. G. to John E. Becton of Wayne county, Apr., Jones county. R. R. Apr. 8, 1845
Becton, John E. of Wayne county to Mrs. Eliza A. G. Becton, Apr., Jones county. R. R. Apr. 8, 1845
Bell, John of Tuscumbia, Alabama to Elizabeth Dunn of Wake Forest, Jly. 21, Wake Forest. R. R. Jly. 29, 1845
Benners, Edward G. to Helen Donaldson, Jan. 18, Mobile. R. R. Feb. 4, 1845
Bennett, Eliza Ann to Dr. C. C. M'Caskell, Apr. 24, Anson county. R. R. My. 9, 1845
Bernard, German of Pitt county to Juliet Gilliam of Surry county & Columbia, S. C., Sept. 24, Greensboro. R. R. Oct. 24, 1845
Bethune, Alexander to Amanda Bolton, My., Charlotte. R. R. My. 9, 1845
Bethune, Mary Jane to Neill M'Fayden, Mar., Cumberland county. R. R. Apr. 1, 1845
Betts, Albert C. of Fulton, Mississippi & Raleigh to Adelia A. Gregg, Mar. 13, Pontotoc, Mississippi. R. R. Apr. 4, 1845
Birdsall, Frances to F. A. S. Mathews, Nov. 3, Raleigh. R. R. Nov. 4, 1845
Bishop, James E. to Mary A. Canoway, Sept., Newbern. R. R. Sept. 16, 1845
Bishop, Mary to William H. Taylor, Oct., Newbern. R. R. Oct. 14, 1845
Black, Sarah to John R. Weddington, Sept., Cabarrus county. R. R. Sept. 5, 1845
Bledsoe, Moses A. to Martha G. Hunter, Sept. 25, Raleigh. R. R. Sept. 30, 1845
Blount, Joseph E. to Eveline S. M. Smith of Hyde county, Sept., Washington. R. R. Sept. 5, 1845
Blount, Polly Ann to Samuel C. Eborn, Nov., Washington, Beaufort county. R. R. Nov. 25, 1845
Blount, Susan S. to Frederick Grist of Beaufort, Aug. 13, Warrenton. R. R. Aug. 22, 1845
Blunt, John William to Louisa Wadkins, Je, Sampson county. R. R. Je. 10, 1845

Boggan, Louisa to Thomas B. Harrington of Montgomery county, Je., Anson county. R. R. Je. 10, 1845
Bolton, Amanda to Alexander Bethune, My., Charlotte. R. R. My. 9, 1845
Bolton, Caroline E. to Lewis L. Williams of Raleigh, Je. 25, Jefferson City, Mo. R. R. Jly. 29, 1845
Bond, Elizabeth A. to Addison W. Clayton, Feb., Edenton. R. R. Feb. 14, 1845
Boyce, Mrs. S. H. to Stanhope Hunter, Jly., Mecklenburg county. R. R. Aug. 1, 1845
Boyd, Susan E. to Henry B. Williams of Charlotte, Feb., Mecklenburg county. R. R. Feb. 7, 1845
Boyden, Nathaniel to Mrs. Jane Mitchell, Dec., Salisbury. R. R. Dec. 12, 1845
Boykin, William to Elizabeth Vaughan, Dec. 18, Raleigh. R. R. Dec. 23, 1845
Bradsher, Maretetia to Samuel H. Turrentine, Mar., Orange county. R. R. Apr. 1, 1845
Brantly, Rev. John J. to Delia Ann Smith, Nov., Fayetteville. R. R. Nov. 25, 1845
Bright, Eliza to John A. Parrott, My., Lenoir county. R. R. My. 13, 1845
Brinson, Fereba to Henry Parks of Wayne county, Sept., Jones county. R. R. Sept. 16, 1845
Broadhurst, Henry to Sarah A. Carr, Mar., Duplin county. R. R. Mar. 11, 1845
Bryan, Ann A. of Wilmington to David King of Bladen county, My., Wilmington. R. R. My. 16, 1845
Bryan, Elias of Chatham county to Sarah C. M'Kay, Dec., Cumberland county. R. R. Dec. 16, 1845
Bryan, Sarah to Dr. Franklin Hart, Nov., Edgecombe county. R. R. Nov. 25, 1845
Bunting, J. E. to Miss R. J. Jacobs, Oct., Wilmington. R. R. Oct. 28, 1845
Burge, James of Halifax county to Helen Strother, Dec. 31, Louisburg. R. R. Jan. 7, 1845
Burns, James E. of Chatham county to Mary Ann M'Iver, Je., Moore county. R. R. Je. 10, 1845
Burnsides, Elizabeth to John Sykes, Aug. 27, Orange county. R. R. Sept. 9, 1845
Busbee, Perrin to Annie E. G. Taylor, Jan. 1, Raleigh. R. R. Jan. 3, 1845
Caldwell, Elizabeth to Charles F. Fisher, Aug., Salisbury. R. R. Sept. 2, 1845
Callais, John D. to Sarah Mitchell, Je., Fayetteville. R. R. Je. 17, 1845
Calloway, Dr. J. W. of Rutherfordton to Anne Johnston, Nov., Lincoln county. R. R. Nov. 21, 1845
Cameron, Elia A. to Henry K. Witherspoon, Mar., Hillsboro. R. R. Mar. 4, 1845
Campbell, Carlton J. to Christian F. Gibbs, Je., Wilmington. R. R. Je. 17, 1845
Carell, Lemuel to Mrs. James King,, Mar., Orange county. R. R. Apr. 1, 1845
Carr, Hinton E. to Elizabeth Royal, Dec. 10, Sampson county. R. R. Dec. 30, 1845

Carr, Sarah A. to Henry Broadhurst, Mar., Duplin county. R. R. Mar. 11, 1845
Carraway, Mary A. to James E. Bishop, Sept., Newbern. R. R. Sept. 16, 1845
Carter, Mary E. J. to B. G. Worth, Jly. 3, Ashborough. R. R. Jly. 8, 1846
Carver, John M. to Elizabeth M'Neill Black, Apr., Fayetteville. R. R. Apr. 8, 1845
Chipman, Louisa A. to Dr. Jno. H. Sanders, My., Guilford county. R. R. My. 30, 1845
Chunn, Susan W. to William Murphy, Aug., Rowan county. R. R. Aug. 26, 1845
Clanton, Sarah Ann to Dr. William H. Joyner, Je. 7, Warren county. R. R. Je. 20, 1845
Clark, Ann O. to John D. Hawkins, Jr., Jly. 2, Warren county. R. R. Jly. 8, 1845
Clark, David to Anna M. Thorne, Oct., Halifax. R. R. Oct. 21, 1845
Clark, William to Miram H. Lewis, Sept., Union county. R. R. Oct. 3, 1845
Clayton, Addison W. to Elizabeth A. Bond, Feb., Edenton. R. R. Feb. 14, 1845
Coble, Samuel to Nelly Holt, Aug., Guilford county. R. R. Sept. 2, 1845
Compton, Martha Ann to P. H. Smith, Sept. 3, Granville county. R. R. Sept. 12, 1845
Cook, Thomas C. of Salisbury to Mrs. Harriet Stoll, Oct., Charleston. R. R. Oct. 24, 1845
Cooley, Henry D. to Eleanor Stuart, Nov. 19, Raleigh. R. R. Nov. 21, 1845
Cosby, Mary L. to Leopold E. Heartt, Dec. 3, Raleigh. R. R. Dec. 9, 1845
Covington, Thomas T. to Mary Jane Ellerbe, Jly., Richmond county. R. R. Jly. 25, 1845
Cowan, Mrs. Jane to Ex-Gov. Edward B. Dudley, Sept. 8, Wilmington. R. R. Sept. 16, 1845
Cowan, Robert Jr. to Eliza Dickinson, My. 14, Wilmington. R. R. My. 16, 1845
Craven, Elixa P. to Elisha J. Crowson, Apr. 10, Randolph county. R. R. Apr. 25, 1845
Crist, Jacob Rudolph to Miranda Rosalie Keehlen, Salem, Stokes county, Nov. 12, Salem, Stokes county. R. R. Nov. 18, 1845
Crocker, Eliza to Capt. Jesse S. Montford, Mar., Newbern. R. R. Mar. 25, 1845
Cromartie, Jane R. to Archibald Murphy of Sampson county, Oct., Bladen county. R. R. Nov. 4, 1845
Cromartie, Margaret Ann to Rev. Edgar L. Parkins of N. C. Conference, Mar., Bladen county. R. R. Apr. 8, 1845
Crowson, Elisha J. to Eliza P. Craven, Apr. 10, Randolph county. R. R. Apr. 25, 1845
Dalton, Miss M. G. to John P. Smith of Stokesburg, Mar., Stokes county. R. R. Mar. 11, 1845
Dancy, Elizabeth M. to William S. Battle, Jly., Tarboro. R. R. Jly. 8, 1845
Davidson, Wm. F. of Charlotte to Charlotte M. Gooch, Jly., Hopewell church, Chester District, S. C. R. R. Aug. 1, 1845
Davis, Eliza Ann to Rev. Wm. Robinson, Sept., Lenoir county. R. R. Sept. 19, 1845

Davis, Capt. James H. of this state to Mary E. Ball of Richmond, Aug., Richmond, Va. R. R. Aug. 19, 1845

Davis, Mary Eliza to Thomas S. D. M'Dowell, Oct., Bladen county. R. R. Oct. 28, 1845

Davis, Samuel to Martha Seely, Nov, Pasquotank county. R. R. Nov. 18, 1845

Dibble, Elizabeth C. to Dr. Walter Duffy of Rutherfordton, Apr., Craven county. R. R. Apr. 8, 1845

Dickinson, Eliza to Robert Cowan, Jr., My. 14, Wilmington. R. R. My. 16, 1845

Dickinson, P. K. to Alice London, Dec., Wilmington. R. R. Dec. 12, 1845

Dickson, Mrs. Elizabeth D. of York District, S. C. to Andrew O'Brien of Lincolnton, Sept., Yorkville. R. R. Sept. 5, 1845

Dickson, Dr. James H. to Margaret Owen, Mar., Wilmington. R. R. Mar. 11, 1845

Dickson, Dr. Robert D. to Mary M'Laurin, Nov., Wilmington. R. R. Nov. 11, 1845

Dilliard, Thaddeus E. of Sussex Court House, Virginia to William Rebecca Francis Atkinson of Pitt county, Nov., Scotland Neck. R. R. Nov. 11, 1845

Donaldson, Helen to Edward G. Benners, Jan. 18, Mobile. R. R. Feb. 4, 1845

Donnell, William A. to Mary Springs, Sept., Guilford county. R. R. Oct. 3, 1845

Dozier, Miss P. of Camden county to James T. Littlejohn of Oxford, Apr., Camden county. R. R. Apr. 8, 1845

Dudley, Edward B. Ex-Gov. to Mrs. Jane Cowan, Sept. 8, Wilmington. R. R. Sept. 16, 1845

Dudley, Jane to Lieut. Johnson, U. S. Army, Mar. 31, Wilmington. R. R. Apr. 11, 1845

Duffy, Dr. Walter of Rutherfordton to Elizabeth C. Dibble, Apr., Craven county. R. R. Apr. 8, 1845

Dunn, Elizabeth of Wake Forest to John Bell of Tuscumbia, Alabama, Jly. 21, Wake county. R. R. Jly. 29, 1845

Dunn, Eunice A. to David Gordon, Mar., Newbern. R. R. Mar. 25, 1845

Eborn, Samuel C. to Polly Ann Blount, Nov., Washington, Beaufort county. R. R. Nov. 25, 1845

Edmondson, Rufus W. of Stantonsburg, Edgecombe county to Caroline Wilder, Oct. 16, Wake county. R. R. Oct. 21, 1845

Edwards, John to Eliza Kirby, Apr. 22, Anson county. R. R. My. 9, 1845

Ellerbe, Mary Jane to Thomas T. Covington, Jly., Richmond county. R. R. Jly. 25, 1845

Elliott, Alice Ann to Samuel E. Moore, Jan., Tarboro. R. R. Jan. 17, 1845

Erwin, Catharine to Major Allen C. Jones of this State, Je., Greensborough, Alabama. R. R. Jly. 1, 1845

Featherstone, Edward to Mary Howett, Apr. 23, Edenton. R. R. My. 9, 1845

Fisher, Charles F. to Elizabeth Caldwell, Aug., Salisbury. R. R. Sept. 2, 1845

Fitman, Ellen to John G. Bauman, Feb., Wilmington. R. R. Feb. 21, 1845

Foster, Dr. Peter S. to Matilda K. Williams, Aug. 3, Louisburg. R. R. Sept. 30, 1845
Foust, Caroline M. to Dr. Calvin E. Graves, Mar., Orange county. R. R. Apr. 1, 1845
Freeland, Elizabeth C. to Dr. Samuel D. Schoolfield of Guilford county, Nov., Orange county. R. R. Nov. 14, 1845
Freeland, Mrs. Lucinda L. to James B. M'Dade of Chapel Hill, Sept., Orange county. R. R. Sept. 23, 1845
Garner, Margaret E. to Wm. D. Smith, Dec., Wilmington. R. R. Dec. 12, 1845
Garrard, Rev. Thompson of the Methodist Conference to Mrs. Martha A. M'Cullers, Dec. 9, Wake county. R. R. Dec. 16, 1845
Gaskill, Susan A. to Robert J. Mebane of Wadesborough, Feb., Orange county. R. R. Feb. 7, 1845
Gattis, Emily to Nathaniel King, Apr., Orange county. R. R. My. 2, 1845
Gault, Ann of Boston, Massachusetts to Thomas S. Hutchins of Newbern, Je., Boston, Mass. R. R. Jly. 1, 1845
Gay, Rev. John L. to Anne Eliza Parke of Wadesboro, Je., Barbour county, Alabama. R. R. Je. 3, 1845
Gibbs, Christian F. to Carlton J. Campbell, Je., Wilmington. R. R. Je. 17, 1845
Gill, Caroline to John H. Barlow of Orange & Franklin counties, Jan. 2, Louisburg. R. R. Jan. 7, 1845
Gillet, Charlotte M. of Jones county to William H. Wood of Craven county, Oct., Craven county. R. R. Oct. 14, 1845
Gilliam, Juliet of Surry county & Columbia, South Carolina, to German Bernard of Pitt county, Sept. 24, Greensboro. R. R. Oct. 24, 1845
Gooch, Charlotte M. to Wm. F. Davidson of Charlotte, Jly., Hopewell church, Chester District, South Carolina. R. R. Aug. 1, 1845
Goodlake, Thomas W. of Mecklenburg county to Elenor Willoughby of Wadesborough, Sept., Concord. R. R. Oct. 3, 1845
Gordon, David to Eunice A. Dunn, Mar., Newbern. R. R. Mar. 25, 1845
Gordan, Dickson P. of Anson county to Zilpha Ann Sellers of Chesterfield District, South Carolina, Je. 25. R. R. Jly. 4, 1845
Gordon, Elizabeth to William M'Comb of Mecklenburg county, Oct., Anson county. R. R. Oct. 24, 1845
Gorrall, Hannah to Jesse B. Holmes, My., Guilford county. R. R. My. 20, 1845
Govan, Eaton Pugh to Julia A. Hawks, Mar. 4, Marshall county. R. R. Apr. 15, 1845
Graham, Joseph Montrose of Lincoln county to Mary A G. Washington of Newbern, Mar. 12, Hillsboro. R. R. Mar. 25, 1845
Grant, Rev. William to Sarah J. Meador, Feb., Hertford. R. R. Feb. 14, 1845
Graves, Dr. Calvin E. to Caroline M. Foust, Mar., Orange county. R. R. Apr. 1, 1845
Gregg, Adelia A. to Albert C. Betts of Fulton, Mississippi & Raleigh, Mar. 13, Pontotoc, Mississippi. R. R. Apr. 4, 1845
Grist, Frederick of Beaufort to Susan S. Blount, Aug. 13, Warrenton. R. R. Aug. 22, 1845

Groves, Henry W. of St. Augustine, Florida to Julia A. Halsey, Nov., Wilmington. R. R. Nov. 18, 1845
Gullett, Elizabeth to Thomas Beard, Mar., Greensboro. R. R. Mar. 11, 1845
Halsey, Cullen to Charlotte Perry, Sept., Chowan county. R. R. Sept. 16, 1845
Halsey, Julia A. to Henry W. Groves of St. Augustine, Florida, Nov., Wilmington. R. R. Nov. 18, 1845
Hamilton, Jane to Dr. Laidsin Mills, Je., Rutherfordton. R. R. Je. 3, 1845
Hamilton, Robert A. of Granville county to Sarah C. Alexander of Boxwood, Mecklenburg county, Virginia, Dec. 18, Boxwood, Mecklenburg county, Va. R. R. Jan. 7, 1845
Hardie, Alexander to Elizabeth Woodward, Feb., Raleigh. R. R. Feb. 11, 1845
Hardie, Robert W. of Raleigh to Mary Ann Rhodes, Nov. 19, Fayetteville. R. R. Nov. 25, 1845
Hardison, Mary to James M. Tayman, Nov., Washington, Beaufort county. R. R. Nov. 25, 1845
Harrell, Dr. James to Sarah Ann Skinner, Feb., Chowan county. R. R. Feb. 21, 1845
Harrington, Thomas B. to Louisa Boggan of Montgomery county, Je., Anson county. R. R. Je. 10, 1845
Harris, Mary Eliza Thomas of Granville county to Ira D. Reid of Rockingham, Dec., Granville county. R. R. Dec. 12, 1845
Harriss, Elizabeth to James L. Tomlinson, Feb., Richmond county. R. R. Feb. 21, 1845
Harriss, Lucretia Jane to Joel Wooley, Je, Montgomery county. R. R. Je. 10, 1845
Hart, Dr. Franklin to Sarah Bryan, Nov., Edgecombe county. R. R. Nov. 25, 1845
Hatfield, Charles to Mrs. Deborah Pratt, Apr., Perquimans county. R. R. My. 9, 1845
Hawkins, John D. Jr. to Ann O. Clark, Jly. 2, Warren county. R. R. Jly. 8, 1845
Hawkins, Lucy of Warren county to Leonard Henderson of Granville county, My., 28, Raleigh. R. R. Je. 6, 1845
Hawks, Julia A. to Eaton Pugh Govan, Mar. 4, Mashall county. R. R. Apr. 15, 1845
Hawley, John to Lucinda Threalkil, Apr., Moore county. R. R. Apr. 11, 1845
Haynes, Charles to Sarah Walker, Nov., Rutherford county. R. R. Nov. 21, 1845
Hays, Wm. A. to Jane E. Womack, Sept., Pittsborough. R. R. Sept. 30, 1845
Hearne, Davidson of Stanly county to Leah Caroline Melchor, Sept., Cabarrus county. R. R. Sept. 30, 1845
Heartt, Leopold, E. to Mary L. Cosby, Dec. 3, Raleigh. R. R. Dec. 9, 1845
Henderson, Leonard of Granville county to Lucy Hawkins of Warren county, My. 28, Raleigh. R. R. Je. 6, 1845
Henderson, Dr. Pleasant of Salisbury to Rebecca Francis Wimbish of Halifax Court House, Virginia, Dec. 26. R. R. Jan. 7, 1845

Henry, Virginia to Duncan K. M'Rae, U. S. District Attorney, Oct. 8, Raleigh. R. R. Oct. 10, 1845
Hicks, Elizabeth T. to Robert A. Jenkins, Oct. 30, Granville county. R. R. Nov. 7, 1845
Hill, Cynthia C. to Rufus Page, Jly. 23, Raleigh. R. R. Jly. 25, 1845
Hill, Nancy to James E. Norfleet, Apr. 15, Edenton. R. R. My. 9, 1845
Hill, Dr. Nathan B. of Randolph county to Eliza L. Mendenhall of Guilford county, My. 14, Deep River. R. R. My. 20, 1845
Hinton, Martha Ann to Henry Mordecai, Sept. 3, Raleigh. R. R. Sept. 5, 1845
Hinton, Peter W. of Pasquotank county to Mrs. Sarah J. Wrighton, Jly., Edenton. R. R. Jly. 29, 1845
Holeman, Sarah H. to Calvin C. Strowd, Nov., Orange county. R. R. Nov. 14, 1845
Holmes, Jesse B. to Hannah Gorrall, My., Guilford county. R. R. My. 20, 1845
Hollister, Julia to Dr. J. B. Tull, Mar., Newbern. R. R. Mar. 25, 1845
Holt, Nelly to Samuel Coble, Aug., Guilford county. R. R. Sept. 2, 1845
Howard, J. C. to Elizabeth Williams, Dec., Sampson county. R. R. Dec. 9, 1845
Howett, Mary to Edward Featherstone, Apr. 23, Edenton. R. R. My. 9, 1845
Hughes, Gunnyadd to Lewis Wallace, Aug. 17, Johnston county. R. R. Aug. 26, 1845
Humphreys, Susan to David Weir, Oct., Greensboro. R. R. Oct. 24, 1845
Hunter, Martha G. to Moses A. Bledsoe, Sept. 25, Raleigh. R. R. Sept. 30, 1845
Hunter, Stanhope to Mrs. S. H. Boyce, Jly., Mecklenburg county. R. R. Aug. 1, 1845
Hurst, Elizabeth Ann to Dr. Richard Barnum of Wake county, Apr., Baltimore. R. R. Apr. 29, 1845
Hutchins, Thomas S. of Newbern to Ann Gault of Boston, Massachusetts, Je., Boston, Mass. R. R. Jly. 1, 1845
Ingole, Jesse A. to Elizabeth Rich of Guilford county, Feb. 28. R. R. Mar. 11, 1845
Iredell, Jane to Thomas D. Meares of Wilmington, Oct. 15, Raleigh. R. R. Oct. 17, 1845
Ives, Martha M. to Joseph W. Barrow, Nov., Perquimans county. R. R. Nov. 25, 1845
Ivey, Ann Eliza to David M'Duffie, Mar., Fayetteville. R. R. Mar. 11, 1845
Jacobs, Ann Eliza to David M'Duffie, Mar., Fayetteville. R. R. Mar. 11, 1845
Jacobs, Mrs. R. J. to J. E. Bunting, Oct., Wilmington. R. R. Oct. 28, 1845
Jenkins, Benjamin to Nancy Jones, Nov., Granville county. R. R. Nov. 25, 1845
Jenkins, Robert A. to Elizabeth T. Hicks, Oct. 30, Granville county. R. R. Nov. 7, 1845
Jewell, Nancy to Nathaniel G. Rand, Oct. 21, Wake county. R. R. Oct. 31, 1845
Johnson, Frances Ann to Wallace M. Reinhardt, Oct., Lincolnton. R. R. Oct. 31, 1845

Johnson, Dr. James of Northampton county to Miss E. J. Mason of Southampton, Virginia, Nov. 18, Washington. R. R. Dec. 2, 1845

Johnson, Lieut. U. S. Army to Jane Dudley, Mar. 31, Wilmington, R. R. Apr. 11, 1845

Johnston, Anne to Dr. J. W. Calloway of Rutherfordton, Nov., Lincoln county. R. R. Nov. 21, 1845

Jones, Major Allen C. of this State to Catharine Erwin, Je., Greensborough, Alabama. R. R. Jly. 1, 1845

Jones, J. Speed of Warren county to Lucy B. Petteway, Je. 16, Halifax county. R. R. Jly. 4, 1845

Jones, John V. to Mrs. Margaret S. Williams, My., Rockingham. R. R. My. 30, 1845

Jones, Nancy to Benjamin Jenkins, Nov., Granville county. R. R. Nov. 25, 1845

Joyner, Dr. William H. to Sarah Ann Clanton, Je. 7, Warren county. R. R. Je. 20, 1845

Keehlen, Miranda Rosalie to Jacob Rudolph Crist, Stokes county, Nov. 12, Salem, Stokes county. R. R. Nov. 18, 1845

King, David of Bladen county to Ann A. Bryan of Wilmington, My., Wilmington. R. R. My. 16, 1845

King, Mrs. James to Lemuel Carell, Mar., Orange county. R. R. Apr. 1, 1845

King, Nathaniel to Emily Gattis, Apr., Orange county. R. R. My. 2, 1845

Kirby, Eliza to John Edwards, Apr. 22, Anson county. R. R. My. 9, 1845

Lane, Margaret to Dr. Peter M. Walker, My., Wilmington. R. R. My. 6, 1845

Latta, Wm. S. of Fayetteville to Mary M. Pickett of Elizabeth City, Nov., Oxford. R. R. Nov. 18, 1845

Lee, Catharine to R. M. Powell, Je., Robeson county. R. R. Je. 10, 1845

Leecraft, Benjamin to Mary E. Arendell, Feb., Carteret county. R. R. Feb. 11, 1845

Lee, Susan to Nicholas Thompson, Aug. 19, Johnston county. R. R. Aug. 26, 1845

Leigh, William R. of Newbern to Jane P. Wood of Louisburg, Dec., Brownsville West Tennessee. R. R. Dec. 12, 1845

Lewis, Miram H. to William Clark, Sept., Union county. R. R. Oct. 3, 1845

Littlejohn, James T. of Oxford to Miss P. G. Dozier of Camden county, Apr., Camden county. R. R. Apr. 8, 1845

Lloyd, Mrs. Maria A. of Raleigh to Sidney A. Robertson of New Orleans, My. 5, Tallahassee, Florida. R. R. My. 27, 1845

Long, William S. to Mary Batts, Jan., Edgecombe county. R. R. Jan. 14, 1845

London, Alice to P. K. Dickinson, Dec., Wilmington. R. R. Dec. 12, 1845

Love, William, R. to Louisa Terry, Oct. 2, Raleigh. R. R. Oct. 7, 1845

M'Allister, Mrs. E. to Rev. R. M'Nabb, Sept., Fayetteville. R. R. Sept. 30, 1845

M'Bryde, Flora to William C. Watkins, My., Anson county. R. R. My. 27, 1845

M'Caskell, Dr. C. C. to Elixa Ann Bennett, Apr. 24, Anson county. R. R. My. 9, 1845

M'Clelland, Ceny to R. W. Martin, Jly., Cabarrus county. R. R. Aug. 1, 1845

M'Comb, William of Mecklenburg county to Elizabeth Gordon, Oct., Anson county. R. R. Oct. 24, 1845

M'Cotter, John T. B. to Narcissa E. M. Paul, Feb., Newbern. R. R. Feb. 11, 1845

M'Cullers, Mrs. Martha A. to Rev. Thompson Garrard of the Methodist Conference, Dec. 9, Wake county. R. R. Dec. 16, 1845

M'Dade, James B. of Chapel Hill to Mrs. Lucinda L. Freeland, Sept., Orange county. R. R. Sept. 23, 1845
M'Donald, Donald to Isabella Patterson, Feb., Moore county. R. R. Feb. 21, 1845
M'Dowell, Thomas S. D. to Mary Eliza Davis, Oct., Bladen county. R. R. Oct. 28, 1845
M'Duffie, David to Ann Eliza Ivey, Mar., Fayetteville. R. R. Mar. 11, 1845
M'Fayden, Neill to Mary Jane Bethune, Mar., Cumberland county. R. R. Apr. 1, 1845
M'Govern, Ann to Wm. Norris of New York, Je., Wilmington. R. R. Je. 3, 1845
M'Iver, Mary Ann to James E. Burns of Chatham county, Je., Moore county. R. R. Je. 10, 1845
M'Kay, Sarah C. to Elias Bryan of Chatham county, Dec., Cumberland county. R. R. Dec. 16, 1845
M'Kinnie, Henry of Alabama to Mary E. Vicke, of Hertford county, Je., Florida. R. R. Je. 10, 1845
M'Knight, Isabella to David Allen, Dec., Mecklenburg county. R. R. Dec. 5, 1845
M'Laurin, Mary to Dr. Robert D. Dickson, Nov., Wilmington. R. R. Nov. 11, 1845
M'Millan, D. A. to Barbara Allen, My., Kelley's Cove, Bladen county. R. R. My. 20, 1845
M'Millan, Daniel to Ann Elizabeth Patterson, Mar., Moore county. R. R. Apr. 8, 1845
M'Nabb, Rev. R. to Mrs. E. M'Allister, Sept., Fayetteville. R. R. Sept. 30, 1845
M'Neill, Elizabeth Black to John M. Carver, Apr., Fayetteville. R. R. Apr. 8, 1845
M'Phail, Isaiah to Ellen Sophia Parker, Feb., Sampson county. R. R. Feb. 21, 1845
M'Rae, Duncan K. U. S. District Attorney, to Virginia Henry, Oct. 8, Raleigh. R. R. Oct. 10, 1845
M'Rae, Philip of Robeson county to Ann Martin of Richmond county. R. R. My. 16, 1845
Marriott, Aley A. of Wake county to William D. Rice of Greene county, Alabama, Aug. 13, Raleigh. R. R. Aug. 15, 1845
Marsh, William to Rebecca Jane Young, Feb., Fayetteville. R. R. Feb. 7, 1845
Martin, Ann of Richmond county to Philip M'Rae of Robeson county, My., Richmond county. R. R. My. 16, 1845
Martin, R. W. to Ceny M'Clelland, Jly., Cabarrus county. R. R. Aug. 1, 1845
Martin, Mrs. Rebecca of Johnston county to William Mooneyham, Nov. 20, Wake county. R. R. Dec. 2, 1845
Mason, Miss E. J. of Southampton, Virginia to Dr. James Johnston of Northampton county, Nov. 18, Washington. R. R. Dec. 2, 1845
Mathews, F. A. S. of Elizabeth City to Frances Birdsall, Nov. 3, Raleigh. R. R. Nov. 4, 1845
Meador, Sarah J. to Rev. William Grant, Feb., Hertford. R. R. Feb. 14, 1845

Meares, Thomas D. of Wilmington to Jane Iredell, Oct. 15, Raleigh. R. R. Oct. 17, 1845

Mebane, Robert J. of Wadesborough to Susan A. Gaskill, Feb., Orange county. R. R. Feb. 7, 1845

Melchor, Leah Melchor to Davidson Hearne of Stanly county, Sept., Cabarrus county. R. R. Sept. 30, 1845

Mendenhall, Eliza L. of Guilford county to Dr. Nathan B. Hill of Randolph county, My. 14, Deep River. R. R. My. 20, 1845

Mendenhall, Nancy E. to David M. Osborne, Sept., Guilford county. R. R. Oct. 3, 1845

Mercer, James to Ketsey Regan, Je., Robeson county. R. R. Je. 17, 1845

Miller, Ivy to Elizabeth Parker, Jly., Rowan county. R. R. Jly. 4, 1845

Mills, Dr. Ladsin to Jane Hamilton, Je., Rutherfordton. R. R. Je. 3, 1845

Minor, Jno. J. to Mary S. Pearce, Dec., Fayetteville. R. R. Dec. 12, 1845

Mitchell, Mrs. Jane to Nathaniel Boyden, Dec., Salisbury. R. R. Dec. 12, 1845

Mitchell, Mary P. to Richard J. Ashe of Hillsboro, Oct. 28, Chapel Hill. R. R. Nov. 4, 1845

Mitchell, Sarah to John D. Callais, Je., Fayetteville. R. R. Je. 17, 1845

Mitchener, Festus to Mary Ann Wilder, Sept. 11, Johnston county. R. R. Sept. 19, 1845

Montford, Capt. Jesse S. to Eliza Crocker, Mar., Newbern. R. R. Mar. 25, 1845

Mooneyham, William to Mrs. Rebecca Martin of Johnston county, Nov. 20, Wake county. R. R. Dec. 2, 1845

Moore, Samuel E. to Alice Ann Elliott, Jan., Tarboro. R. R. Jan. 17, 1845

Mordecai, Henry to Martha Ann Hinton, Sept. 3, Raleigh. R. R. Sept. 5, 1845

Moseley, Jordan of Orange county to Mary Ann Patterson, Aug., Guilford county. R. R. Sept. 2, 1845

Mullen, Dr. Francis N. of Perquimans county to Mrs. Elizabeth Proctor, Nov., Camden county. R. R. Nov. 18, 1845

Murphey, Julia Ann to Capt Thomas Ray, Aug. 28, Orange county. R. R. Sept. 9, 1845

Murphy, Archibald of Sampson county to Jane R. Cromartie, Oct., Bladen county. R. R. Nov. 4, 1845

Murphy, David of Sampson county to Julia A. Whitaker of Raleigh, Je. 3, Raleigh. R. R. Je. 6, 1845

Murphy, Dr. W. Duke of Fayetteville to Lydia D. Thompson of Philadelphia, My., Grace church Philadelphia. R. R. My. 27, 1845

Murphy, Robert to Grissella Stewart, Nov., Cumberland county. R. R. Nov. 18, 1845

Murphy, William to Susan W. Chunn, Aug., Rowan county. R. R. Aug. 26, 1845

Myers, Daniel to Nancy Allmand, Jly., Cabarrus county. R. R. Jly. 4, 1845

Needham, Sarah F. to Samuel E. Northington, Sept., Greensboro. R. R. Oct. 3, 1845

Nichols, Sarah A. of Cuttingsville, Vermont to Julius Wilcox of Warrenton, Oct. 16, Warrenton Female Seminary. R. R. Oct. 28, 1845

Norfleet, James E. to Nancy Hill, Apr. 15, Edenton. R. R. My. 9, 1845

Norris, Wm. of New York to Ann M. Govern, Je., Wilmington. R. R. Je. 3, 1845
Northington, Samuel E. to Sarah F. Needham, Sept., Greensboro. R. R. Oct. 3, 1845
Nortwick, M. F. Van to Frances L. Oliver, Sept. 2, Washington. R. R. Sept. 19, 1845
O'Brien, Andrew of Lincolnton to Mrs. Elizabeth D. Dickson of York District, South Carolina, Sept., Yorkville. R. R. Sept. 5, 1845
Oliver, Frances L. to M. F. Van Nortwick, Sept. 2, Washington. R. R. Sept. 19, 1845
Osborne, David M. to Nancy E. Mendenhall, Sept., Guilford county. R. R. Oct. 3, 1845
Owen, Margaret to Dr. James H. Dickson, Mar., Wilmington. R. R. Mar. 11, 1845
Page, Rufus, to Cynthia C. Hill, Jly. 23, Raleigh. R. R. Jly. 25, 1845
Parish, Avazella to Charles Sugg, Nov 27, Wake county. R. R. Dec. 2, 1845
Parke, Anne Eliza of Wadesboro to Rev. John L. Gay, Je., Barbour county, Alabama. R. R. Je. 3, 1845
Parker, Elizabeth to Ivy Miller, Jly., Rowan county. R. R. Jly. 4, 1845
Parker, Ellen Sophia to Isaiah M'Phail, Feb., Sampson county. R. R. Feb. 21, 1845
Parker, Sarah E. to Charles A. Russ of Granville county, My., Orange county. R. R. My. 27, 1845
Parks, Henry of Wayne county to Feriba Brinson, Sept., Jones county. R. R. Sept. 16, 1845
Parrott, John A. to Eliza Bright, My., Lenoir county. R. R. My. 13, 1845
Patterson, Ann Elizabeth to Daniel M'Millan, Mar., Moore county. R. R. Apr. 8, 1845
Patterson, Elizabeth B. of Franklin county to James Turner of Greenville county, Virginia, Feb. 5, Louisburg. R. R. Feb. 11, 1845
Patterson, Isabella to Donald M'Donald, Feb., Moore county. R. R. Feb. 21, 1845
Patterson, Mary Ann to Jordan Moseley of Orange county, Aug., Guilford county. R. R. Sept. 2, 1845
Paul, Narcissa E. M. to John T. B. M'Cotter, Feb., Newbern. R. R. Feb. 11, 1845
Pearce, John W. of Halifax county to Sarah Williams of Warrenton, Je., Warren county. R. R. Je. 10, 1845
Pearce, Mary S. to Jno. J. Minor, Dec., Fayetteville. R. R. Dec. 12, 1845
Peltier, Virginia to James Watson, Aug. 13, Orange county. R. R. Sept. 5, 1845
Perkins, Rev. Edgar L. of N. C. Conference to Margaret Ann Cromartie, Mar., Bladen county. R. R. Apr. 8, 1845
Perry, Charlotte to Cullen Halsey, Sept., Chowan county. R. R. Sept. 16, 1845
Pettway, Lucy B. to J. Speed Jones of Warren county, Je. 16, Halifax county. R. R. Jly. 4, 1845
Pickett, Mary M. of Elizabeth City to Wm. S. Latta of Fayetteville, Nov., Oxford. R. R. Nov. 18, 1845

Pool, Thomas W. to Sarah Hicks, Oct. 30, Granville county. R. R. Nov. 7, 1845
Powell, Dr. Joseph W. to Martha B. Whitaker, Jan., Halifax county. R. R. Jan. 17, 1845
Powell, Mrs. Mary to John Watson of Warren county, Nov., Halifax county. R. R. Nov. 21, 1845
Powell, R. M. to Catharine Lee, Je., Robeson county. R. R. Je. 10, 1845
Pratt, Mrs. Deborah to Charles Hatfield, Apr., Perquimans county. R. R. My. 9, 1845
Proctor, Mrs. Elizabeth to Dr. Francis N. Mullen of Perquimans county, Nov., Camden county. R. R. Nov. 18, 1845
Rand, Nathaniel G. to Nancy Jewell, Oct. 21, Wake county. R. R. Oct. 31, 1845
Ray, Capt. Thomas to Julia Ann Murphey, Aug. 28, Orange county. R. R. Sept. 9, 1845
Read, John to Sally G. Sneed, Jly. 23, Granville county. R. R. Aug. 19, 1845
Regan, Kitsey to James Mercer, Je., Robeson county. R. R. Je. 17, 1845
Reid, Ira D. of Rockingham to Mary Eliza Thomas Harris of Granville county, Dec., Granville county. R. R. Dec. 12, 1845
Reinhardt, Wallace M. to Frances Ann Johnson, Oct., Lincolnton. R. R. Oct. 31, 1845
Rhodes, Mary Ann to Robert W. Hardie of Raleigh, Nov. 19, Fayetteville. R. R. Nov. 25, 1845
Rice, William D. of Greene county, Alabama to Aley A. Marriott of Wake county, Aug. 13, Raleigh. R. R. Aug. 15, 1845
Rice, Elizabeth to Jesse A. Ingole of Guilford county, Feb. 28. R. R. Mar. 11, 1845
Riddle, Spencer L. of Pittsborough to Mary T. White, Feb. 5, Wake county. R. R. Feb. 11, 1845
Robertson, A. Sidney of New Orleans to Mrs. Maria A. Lloyd of Raleigh, My. 5, Tallahassee, Florida. R. R. My. 27, 1845
Robinson, Rev. Wm. to Eliza Ann Davis, Sept., Lenoir county. R. R. Sept. 19, 1845
Ross, James N. to Laura Wilson, Dec., Mecklenburg county. R. R. Dec. 12, 1845
Royal, Elizabeth to Hinton E. Carr, Dec. 10, Sampson county. R. R. Dec. 30, 1845
Russ, Charles A. of Granville county to Sarah E. Parker, My., Orange county. R. R. My. 27, 1845
Sanders, Christiana to James M. Stephen, Feb., Wilmington. R. R. Feb. 11, 1845
Sanders, Edward W. to Alice Ann Ward, Oct., Onslow county. R. R. Nov. 7, 1845
Sanders, Dr. Jno. H. to Louisa A. Chipman, My., Guilford county. R. R. My. 30, 1845
Saunders, Camillus of Raleigh to Harriet Hamilton Taylor of Newport, Rhode Island, My. 8, Newport, R. I. R. R. My. 20, 1845
Schoolfield, Dr. Samuel D. of Guilford county to Elizabeth C. Freeland, Nov., Orange county. R. R. Nov. 14, 1845

Scott, Dr. Theophilus H. of Raleigh to Mary E. Battle of Nashville, My. 8, Nashville. R. R. My. 23, 1845
Seely, Martha to Samuel Davis, Nov., Pasquotank county. R. R. Nov. 18, 1845
Sellers, Zilphia Ann of Chesterfield District, South Carolina to Gordon P. Dickson of Anson county, Je. 25. R. R. Jly. 4, 1845
Shouse, William to Adeline M. Ziglar, Jly., Stokes county. R. R. Aug. 1, 1845
Skinner, Sarah Ann to Dr. James Harrell, Feb., Cabarrus county. R. R. Feb. 21, 1845
Smith, Adriadne E. to John Ruffin Williams, of Raleigh, Jly. 2, Raleigh. R. R. Jly. 4, 1845
Smith, Delia Ann to Rev. John J. Brantly, Nov., Fayetteville. R. R. Nov. 25, 1845
Smith, Evelina S. M. of Hyde county to Joseph E. Blount, Sept., Washington. R. R. Sept. 5, 1845
Smith, John P. of Stokesburg to Miss M. G. Dalton, Mar., Stokes county. R. R. Mar. 11, 1845
Smith, P. H. to Martha Ann Compton, Sept. 3, Granville county. R. R. Sept. 12, 1845
Smith, Wm. D. to Margaret E. Garner, Dec., Wilmington. R. R. Dec. 12, 1845
Sneed, Sally G. to John Read, Jly. 23, Granville county. R. R. Aug. 19, 1845
Springs, Mary to William A. Donnell, Sept., Guilford county. R. R. Oct. 3, 1845
Standlin, John to Mrs. Margaret White, Apr., Perquimans county. R. R. My. 9, 1845
Stedman, William to Clara H. White of Richmond, Virginia, Je. 19, near Pittsboro. R. R. Je. 24, 1845
Steen, Jacob to Elizabeth Terry, My. 1, Raleigh. R. R. My. 6, 1845
Stephen, James M. to Christiana Sanders, Feb., Wilmington. R. R. Feb. 11, 1845
Stewart, Grossella to Robert Murphy, Nov., Cumberland county. R. R. Nov. 18, 1845
Stoll, Mrs. Harriet to Thomas C. Cook of Salisbury, Oct., Charleston. R. R. Oct. 24, 1845
Strayhorn, Mary Jane to Wm. T. Tate, Aug. 28, Orange county. R. R. Sept. 9, 1845
Strother, Helen to James Burge of Halifax county, Dec. 31. R. R. Jan. 7, 1845
Strowd, Calvin C. to Sarah H. Holeman, Nov., Orange county. R. R. Nov. 14, 1845
Stuart, Eleanor to Henry D. Cooley, Nov. 19, Raleigh. R. R. Nov. 21, 1845
Sugg, Charles to Avazella Parish, Nov. 27, Wake county. R. R. Dec. 2, 1845
Swaim, Mrs. Anne to Abrather Vickery, Aug., Guilford county. R. R. Sept. 2, 1845
Sykes, John to Elizabeth Burnsides, Aug. 27, Orange county. R. R. Sept. 9, 1845

Tate, Wm. T. to Mary Jane Strayhorn, Aug. 28, Orange county. R. R. Sept. 9, 1845
Taylor, Annie E. G. to Perrin Busbee, Jan. 1, Raleigh. R. R. Jan. 3, 1845
Taylor, Harriet Hamilton of Newport, Rhode Island to Camillus Saunders of Raleigh, My. 8, Newport, R. I. R. R. My. 20, 1845
Taylor, William H. to Mary Bishop, Oct., Newbern. R. R. Oct. 14, 1845
Tayman, James M. to Mary Hardison, Nov., Washington, Beaufort county. R. R. Nov. 25, 1845
Terry, Elizabeth to Jacob Steen, My. 1, Raleigh. R. R. My. 6, 1845
Terry, Louisa to William R. Love, Oct. 2, Raleigh. R. R. Oct. 7, 1845
Terry, Sarah Ann to Morgan Williams, Feb. 4, Raleigh. R. R. Feb. 7, 1845
Thompson, Lydia of Philadelphia to Dr. W. Duke Murphy of Fayetteville, My., Grace church, Philadelphia. R. R. My. 27, 1845
Thompson, Nicholas to Susan Lee, Aug. 19, Johnston county. R. R. Aug. 26, 1845
Thorne, Anna M. to David Clark, Oct., Halifax. R. R. Oct. 21, 1845
Threalkil, Lucinda to John Hawley, Apr., Moore county. R. R. Apr. 11, 1845
Tomlinson, James L. to Elizabeth Harriss, Feb., Richmond county. R. R. Feb. 21, 1845
Troy, Robert E. of Lumberton to Mary Andres, Jly., Bladen county. R. R. Jly. 8, 1845
Tull, Dr. J. G. to Julia Hollister, Mar., Newbern. R. R. Mar. 25, 1845
Turner, James of Greenville county, Virginia to Elizabeth B. Patterson of Franklin county, Feb. 5, Louisburg. R. R. Feb. 11, 1845
Turrentine, Samuel H. to Maretetia T. Bradsher, Mar., Orange county. R. R. Apr. 1, 1845
Vicke, Mary E. of Hertford county to Henry M'Kinnie of Alabama, Je., Florida. R. R. Je. 10, 1845
Vickery, Abiather to Mrs. Anne Swaim, Aug., Guilford county. R. R. Sept. 2, 1845
Wadkins, Louisa to John William Blunt, Je., Sampson county. R. R. Je. 10, 1845
Walker, Dr. Peter M. to Margaret Lane, My., Wilmington. R. R. My. 6, 1845
Walker, Sarah to Charles Haynes, Nov., Rutherford county. R. R. Nov. 21, 1845
Wallace, Lewis to Gunnyadd Hughes, Aug. 17, Johnston county. R. R. Aug. 26, 1845
Ward, Alice Ann to Edward W. Sanders, Oct., Onslow county. R. R. Nov. 7, 1845
Washington, Mary A. G. of Newbern to Joseph Montrose Graham of Lincoln county, Mar. 12, Hillsboro. R. R. Mar. 25, 1845
Watkins, William C. to Flora M'Bryde, My., Anson county. R. R. My. 27, 1845
Watson, James to Virginia Peltier, Aug. 13, Orange county. R. R. Sept. 5, 1845
Watson, John of Warren county to Mrs. Mary Powell, Nov., Halifax county. R. R. Nov. 21, 1845
Weddington, John R. to Sarah Black, Sept., Cabarrus county. R. R. Sept. 5, 1845

Weir, David P. to Susan Humphreys, Oct., Greensboro. R. R. Oct. 24, 1845
Whitaker, Julia A. of Raleigh to David Murphy of Sampson county, Je. 3, Raleigh. R. R. Je. 6, 1845
Whitaker, Martha B. to Dr. Joseph W. Powell, Jan., Halifax county. R. R. Jan. 17, 1845
White, Clara H. of Richmond to William Stedman, Je. 19, near Pittsboro. R. R. Je. 24, 1845
White, Mrs. Margaret to John Standlin, Apr., Perquimans county. R. R. My. 9, 1845
White, Mary T. to Spencer L. Riddle of Pittsborough, Feb. 5, Wake county. R. R. Feb. 11, 1845
Wilcox, Julius of Warrenton to Sarah A. Nichols of Cuttingsville, Vermont, Oct. 16, Warrenton Female Seminary. R. R. Oct. 28, 1845
Wilder, Caroline to Rufus W. Edmonson of Stantonsburg, Edgecombe county to Caroline Wilder, Oct. 16, Wake county. R. R. Oct. 21, 1845
Wilder, Mary Ann to Festus Mitchener, Sept. 11, Johnston county. R. R. Sept. 19, 1845
Williams, Elizabeth to J. C. Howard, Dec., Sampson county. R. R. Dec. 9, 1845
Williams, Henry B. of Charlotte to Susan E. Boyd, Feb., Mecklenburg county. R. R. Feb. 7, 1845
Williams, Matilda K. to Dr. Peter S. Foster, Aug. 3, Louisburg. R. R. Sept. 30, 1845
Williams, Mary M. to Lynn Adams, Wake county, Jan. 29, Wake county. R. R. Feb. 7, 1845
Williams, John Ruffin to Ariadne E. Smith, Raleigh, Jly. 2, Raleigh. R. R. Jly. 4, 1845
Williams, Lewis L. of Raleigh to Caroline E. Bolton, Je. 25, Jefferson City, Missouri. R. R. Jly. 29, 1845
Williams, Mrs. Margaret S. to John V. Jones, My., Rockingham. R. R. My. 30, 1845
Williams, Morgan to Sarah Ann Terry, Feb. 4, Raleigh. R. R. Feb. 7, 1845
Williams, Sarah of Warrenton to John W. Pearce of Halifax county, Je., Warren county. R. R. Je. 10, 1845
Willoughby, Eleanor of Wadesborough to Thomas W. Goodlake of Mecklenburg county, Sept., Concord. R. R. Oct. 3, 1845
Wilson, Laura to James N. Ross, Dec., Mecklenburg county. R. R. Dec. 12, 1845
Wimbish, Rebecca Francis of Halifax Court House, Virginia to Dr. Pleasant Henderson of Salisbury, Dec. 26. R. R. Jan. 7, 1845
Witherspoon, Henry K. to Eliza A. Cameron, Mar., Hillsboro. R. R. Mar. 4, 1845
Womack, Jane E. to Wm. A. Hays, Sept., Pittsborough. R. R. Sept. 30, 1845
Wood, Jane P. of Louisburg to William P. Leigh of Newbern, Dec., Brownsville, West Tennessee. R. R. Dec. 12, 1845
Wood, William H. of Craven county to Charlotte M. Gillet of Jones county, Oct., Craven county. R. R. Oct. 14, 1845
Woods, Henry to Mary Bacon, Mar., Orange county. R. R. Apr. 1, 1845

Woodward, Elizabeth to Alexander Hardie, Feb., Raleigh. R. R. Feb. 11, 1845

Wooley, Joel to Lucretia Jane Harriss, Je., Montgomery county. R. R. Je. 10, 1845

Worth, B. G. to Mary E. J. Carter, Jly. 3, Asheborough. R. R. Jly. 8, 1845

Wrighton, Mrs. Sarah J. to Peter W. Hinton of Pasquotank county, Jly., Edenton. R. R. Jly. 29, 1845

Young, Rebecca Jane to William Marsh, Feb., Fayetteville. R. R. Feb. 7, 1845

Ziglar, Adeline M. to William Shouse, Jly., Stokes county. R. R. Aug. 1, 1845

PART II

DEATHS

1826

Abernathy, Ezekiel, Aug. 15, Charlotte. R. R. Sept. 1, 1826
Adkinson, Mrs. John, Je. 7, New Hanover county. R. R. Je. 30, 1826
Albertson, Joseph, Jan. 22, Perquimans county. R. R. Feb. 17, 1826
Albright, Mrs. Henry, Oct., Guilford county. R. R. Oct. 6, 1826
Alexander, Abigail, Aug. 28, Mecklenburg county. R. R. Sept. 15, 1826
Alexander, Eli, Sept. 5, Mecklenburg county. R. R. Sept. 22, 1826
Allen, Samuel of Wilmington, Jly. 29, Fayetteville. R. R. Aug. 4, 1826
Alsobrook, Mrs. Samuel E., Nov. 1, Hillsborough. R. R. Nov. 3, 1826
Amick, John, Aug. 21, Randolph county. R. R. Sept. 1, 1826
Anderson, Dr. Athelston, Aug. 17, Nashville. R. R. Sept. 8, 1826
Arrington, Mrs. Richard, Jly. 31, Nash county. R. R. Aug. 18, 1826
Baber, B. H. of Richmond, Va., Feb., Wilmington. R. R. Feb. 17, 1826
Bagge, Eliza, Apr. 31, Salem. R. R. Je. 9, 1826
Bane, Thomas, Oct. 31, Hillsborough. R. R. Nov. 7, 1826
Barnes, Mrs. Jacob, Jan. 26, Wake county. R. R. Mar. 10, 1826
Beard, Mrs. W. M., Sept. 18, Iredell county. R. R. Sept. 22, 1826
Beardown, John, Sept. 18, Mecklenburg county. R. R. Oct. 6, 1826
Bell, Zadock, Dec., Wake county. R. R. Dec. 15, 1826
Bennett, Mrs. William B. of Williamston, Feb. 1, Martin county. R. R. Feb. 17, 1826
Bennehan, Richard D., Jan., Orange county. R. R. Jan. 20, 1826
Bingham, Rev. Wm., Feb. 5, Orange county. R. R. Feb. 17, 1826
Bishop, Mrs. Hardiman, Sept. 7, Scotland Neck. R. R. Sept. 29, 1826
Black, Capt. Thos., My. 9, Mecklenburg county. R. R. Je. 9, 1826
Bledsoe, Allen of Raleigh, Oct. 8, Huntsville. R. R. Oct. 15, 1826
Blount, Mrs. John, Sept. 8, Edenton. R. R. Sept. 29, 1826
Bocciardi, Mrs. G., Dec. 24, Chapel Hill. R. R. Jan. 20, 1826
Boddie, Thomas of Nash county, Sept. 15, Madison county. R. R. Nov. 17, 1826
Bond, Edmond, Oct. 4, Chowan county. R. R. Oct. 20, 1826
Bond, John, Sept. 27, Bertie county. R. R. Oct. 20, 1826
Boney, John F., Aug. 20, South Washington. R. R. Sept. 8, 1826
Bowers, Mrs. Alexander, Jan. 7, Davidson county. R. R. Jan. 27, 1826
Boyd, Thomas D., Nov., Charlotte. R. R. Nov. 3, 1826
Bradford, Wm. of Hillsboro, Sept. 24, Norfolk. R. R. Oct. 6, 1826
Brainerd, Rev. C. C., Oct. 27, Warrenton. R. R. Nov. 3, 1826
Branch, Mrs. Joseph, Jan., Halifax county. R. R. Jan. 20, 1826
Branum, Mrs. Mary of this State, Aug. 12, Mississippi. R. R. Aug. 18, 1826
Brickell, Mrs. James, Feb., Hertford county. R. R. Mar. 3, 1826
Brown, Philip, Jan., Rowan county. R. R. Jan. 27, 1826
Brownrigg, Thomas, Aug. 1, Chowan county. R. R. Aug. 18, 1826
Bryan, Susan H. of Brunswick county, Je. 2, Wilmington. R. R. Je. 16, 1826
Bunn, Redmen, Sr., Aug. 19, Nash county. R. R. Aug. 25, 1826
Caldwell, Rev. Samuel G., Oct. 3, Charlotte. R. R. Oct. 20, 1826
Cameron, William of Fayetteville, Nov. 19, Orange county. R. R. Nov. 24, 1826
Campbell, Mrs. Daniel, Sept., Beaufort. R. R. Oct. 6, 1826

Campbell, Duncan, Oct., Charlotte. R. R. Oct. 27, 1826
Campbell, John Hume of Tennessee, Aug. 1, Lincoln county. R. R. Aug. 25, 1826
Card, Benson, Je. 21, Raleigh. R. R. Je. 23, 1826
Carrell, Capt. William of Virginia, Jan. 18, Burke county. R. R. Feb. 17, 1826
Carter, Francis, Je. 16, Stokes county. R. R. Jly. 14, 1826
Carter, William, Jly. 5, Bertie county. R. R. Jly. 7, 1826
Chambers, Mrs. Thos., Oct., Chowan county. R. R. Oct. 20, 1826
Chapman, Wm., My. 15, Salisbury. R. R. Je. 9, 1826
Charlton, Mrs. Thomas I., Oct. 24, Edenton. R. R. Nov. 10, 1826
Chopton, William P., Jly. 15, Halifax. R. R. Aug. 25, 1826
Clodfeller, John, Apr. 24, Davidson county. R. R. Je. 9, 1826
Cohen, Jonas of London, Sept. 3, Charlotte. R. R. Sept. 22, 1826
Cook, Mrs. Wm., Sept. 21, Franklin county. R. R. Sept. 29, 1826
Cooper, Mrs. Fleet, Mar. 15, Sampson county. R. R. Mar. 24, 1826
Copeland, James, Jly. 17, Hertford county. R. R. Jly. 28, 1826
Crowell, Maj. Samuel, My. 30, Halifax county. R. R. Je. 9, 1826
Crowell, William, Aug. 23, Halifax county. R. R. Sept. 22, 1826
Culpepper, Mason, Feb., Camden county. R. R. Feb. 24, 1826
Cummins, Mrs. Mary, Aug. 21, Wilmington. R. R. Sept. 8, 1826
Cuthbertson, David, Aug. 25, Mecklenburg county. R. R. Sept. 15, 1826
Daniel, Mrs. Chesley, Apr. 29, Springfield. R. R. My. 5, 1826
Davis, Mrs. Hannah, Jan. 6, Warren county. R. R. Mar. 10, 1826
Davis, Mrs. Jane, Aug. 6, Newbern. R. R. Aug. 18, 1826
Davis, Lucy, Nov. 2, Warren county. R. R. Nov. 10, 1826
Davis, Wm., Aug. 28, Hyde county. R. R. Sept. 29, 1826
Dawson, Mrs. William of Northampton county, Je. 18, Macon, Ga. R. R. Jly. 7, 1826
Denny, Wm., Aug. 30, Guilford county. R. R. Sept. 15, 1826
DeRosset, Dr., Jly., Wilmington. R. R. Jly. 14, 1826
Denny, Donnell, Aug. 2, Guilford county. R. R. Aug. 18, 1826
Denny, Thomas, Je. 26, Guilford county. R. R. Jly. 7, 1826
Dick, James, My. 17, Guilford county. R. R. Je. 2, 1826
Dixon, Capt. Geo., Apr., Newbern. R. R. Apr. 14, 1826
Dunn, Boling, Jan. 22, Wake county. R. R. Jan. 27, 1826
Dunn, Mrs. Boling, Jan. 24, Wake county. R. R. Jan. 27, 1826
Dunn, Mrs. Hardiman, My. 29, Wake county. R. R. Je. 2, 1826
Eason, Bennet B. of Edgecombe county, Nov. 2, Alabama. R. R. Dec. 15, 1826
Eddy, Jacob, Feb. 15, Fayetteville. R. R. Feb. 17, 1826
Edens, Mrs. Robert of Bertie county, Mar. 3, Norfolk, Va. R. R. Mar. 31, 1826
Edmonds, George, Feb. 18, Northampton county. R. R. Mar. 3, 1826
Elliott, George, Jly. 10, Cumberland county. R. R. Jly. 14, 1826
Evans, George Washington, Oct., Fayetteville. R. R. Oct. 6, 1826
Farrar, Maj. Peter, Jly. 4, Chatham county. R. R. Jly. 14, 1826
Ferebee, Mrs. Margaret, Feb. 23, Currituck county. R. R. Mar. 17, 1826
Ferguson, John of Scotland, Sept. 8, Plymouth. R. R. Sept. 29, 1826
Field, Mrs. Jesse, Aug. 9, Guilford county. R. R. Aug. 25, 1826
Fisher, Mrs. Thomas, Aug. 6, Lincoln county. R. R. Sept. 8, 1826
Flaniken, David, Sr. of Pennsylvania, Sept. 26, Mecklenburg county. R. R. Oct. 27, 1826
Floyd, William, Dec. 29, Granville county. R. R. Jan. 13, 1826

Flynt, Joseph M. of Stokes county, Je. 13. R. R. Jly. 14, 1826
Foster, Wm., Apr. 25, Buncombe county. R. R. Je. 9, 1826
Fry, Philip, Jan. 3, Lincoln county. R. R. Feb. 17, 1826
Fulenwider, John, Sr., Sept. 4, Lincoln county. R. R. Sept. 22, 1826
Fuller, Dempsey of Raleigh, Oct. 18, Alabama. R. R. Nov. 17, 1826
Garrett, Joseph, Jr. of Washington, Jly., Plymouth. R. R. Jly. 28, 1826
Gause, John, Jr., Feb., Brunswick county. R. R. Feb. 17, 1826
Gibson, John, Jr., Jan. 14, Rowan county. R. R. Feb. 3, 1826
Graham, Flora, Jly. 16, Robeson county. R. R. Aug. 4, 1826
Graham, Gen. Geo., Apr. 11, Mecklenburg county. R. R. Apr. 14, 1826
Granger, John P., Jan. 14, Bladen county. R. R. Jan. 27, 1826
Green, Elizabeth, Jan. 3, Jones county. R. R. Jan. 27, 1826
Green, Rebecca, Aug. 10, Orange county. R. R. Sept. 1, 1826
Gregory, Mrs. Wm., Mar., Elizabeth City. R. R, Mar. 31, 1826
Hall, Rev. Dr., Jly. 25, Iredell county. R. R. Aug. 18, 1826
Hall, Robert P. of this State, Jly. 7, Franklin, Tenn. R. R. Aug. 11, 1826
Hanner, Melinda, Jan., Guilford county. R. R. Jan. 27, 1826
Harris, Rev. Abner of Halifax county, Jly. 2, Montgomery county, Tenn. R. R. Aug. 11, 1826
Harris, Thos., Jan. 28, Pasquotank county. R. R. Feb. 17, 1826
Harris, Maj. Thomas, Jly. 31, Iredell county. R. R. Sept. 15, 1826
Harris, Col. West of this State & Virginia, Jly. 26, Montgomery county. R. R. Aug. 18, 1826
Harris, Mrs. West, Aug., Montgomery county. R. R. Sept. 8, 1826
Harvey, Joseph, Feb. 16, Raleigh. R. R. Feb. 17, 1826
Hassam, Mrs. John H., Dec. 14, Raleigh. R. R. Dec. 15, 1826
Hatch, Lemuel, Aug., Jones county. R. R. Aug. 18, 1826
Haywood, Mrs. Anna, Apr. 6, Raleigh. R. R. Apr. 14, 1826
Haywood, John, Jly. 21, Franklin county. R. R. Jly. 28, 1826
Heldebrand, Mrs. Catharine, My. 17, Salisbury. R. R. Je. 9, 1826
Higson, Willoughby, Aug. 28, Hyde county. R. R. Sept. 29, 1826
Hill, William Bennett, Sept. 1, Wake county. R. R. Sept. 8, 1826
Hill, William H. of Wilmington, Feb., Raleigh. R. R. Feb. 24, 1826
Hillman, Jesse, Sept. 15, Halifax county. R. R. Sept. 29, 1826
Hinton, Claudia, Nov., Wake county. R. R. Dec. 1, 1826
Hogg, John of London, Nov. 4, Fayetteville. R. R. Nov. 10, 1826
Holland, Col. James, Mar. 30, Lincoln county. R. R. Apr. 21, 1826
Holmes, Mrs. Lucien of Sampson county, Feb. 15, Fayetteville. R. R. Mar. 3, 1826
Holt, Alfred A., Aug. 2, Orange county. R. R. Aug. 18, 1826
Horn, Jacob, Sept. 22, Edgecombe county. R. R. Sept. 29, 1826
Hoskins, Lemuel, Feb., Chowan county. R. R. Feb. 24, 1826
Houston, James H. of Iredell county, Aug. 20, Fayetteville. R. R. Aug. 25, 1826
Howell, Jethro of Wayne county, Jan. 4, Raleigh. R. R. Jan. 6, 1826
Hubbard, Asa of Wadesborough to Sarah Ann Tryon of Connecticut, Nov. R. R. Dec. 1, 1826
Huggins, John, Jly. 1, Iredell county. R. R. Jly. 7, 1826
Huie, Pleasant M., Je. 4, Salisbury. R. R. Je. 23, 1826
Hunter, John Haywood, Nov., Wake county. R. R. Nov. 10, 1826
Hyson, John, Aug. 28, Hyde county. R. R. Sept. 29, 1826
Iredell, Hannah, Sept. 12, Chowan county. R. R. Sept. 29, 1826

Jackson, Isaac, Jly. 28, Orange county. R. R. Aug. 25, 1826
Jacobs, Benjamin, Sr., Jan. 16, Wilmington. R. R. Jan. 27, 1826
Jacobs, Mrs. Jonathan H., Feb. 23, Hertford. R. R. Mar. 17, 1826
Jarrol, Jacob, Je. 9, New Hanover county. R. R. Je. 30, 1826
Jarvis, Mary of Hyde county, Jan. 29, Washington, Beaufort county. R. R. Feb. 17, 1826
Jones, Mrs. David, Je. 19, Wilmington. R. R. Je. 30, 1826
Jones, Dr. H. of Newbern, Sept. 22, Pennsylvania. R. R. Oct. 15, 1826
Jones, Henry C. of Halifax, Oct. 29, Petersburg. R. R. Nov. 10, 1826
Jones, Capt. Josiah, Feb. 22, Perquimans county. R. R. Mar. 31, 1826
Jones, Mary of Pitt county, Aug., Washington. R. R. Aug. 18, 1826
Jones, Mrs. Roger, Aug. 29, Craven county. R. R. Sept. 1, 1826
Jones, Mrs. Tignal, Jly. 12, Raleigh. R. R. Jly. 14, 1826
Johnson, Mrs. Jno. M. of Warren county, My., Tennessee. R. R. Je. 2, 1826
Johnston, Col. Charles W. of Warren county, Sept. 8, Virginia. R. R. Oct. 15, 1826
Jordan, Keziah, Jly. 20, Wake Forest. R. R. Aug. 4, 1826
Kellogg, Joseph, Jly. 17, Wilmington. R. R. Jly. 28, 1826
Kendrick, Mrs. Martha, Dec. 24, Mecklenburg county. R. R. Jan. 13, 1826
Kirkpatrick, Anne, Aug. 28, Mecklenburg county. R. R. Sept. 15, 1826
Krider, Jacob, Jan. 8, Salisbury. R. R. Jan. 27, 1826
Lancaster, Rev. William, Sept. 16, Franklin county. R. R. Sept. 22, 1826
Lane, Martha, Sept. 15, Halifax county. R. R. Sept. 29, 1826
Lane, Mary, Nov., Cumberland county. R. R. Nov. 3, 1826
Lawrence, Joshua, Mar. 10, Northampton county. R. R. Mar. 31, 1826
Lawton, Mrs. Winborn A., Sept. 17, Wilmington. R. R. Oct. 6, 1826
Lee, Rebecca, Apr. 23, Jones county. R. R. My. 5, 1826
Lemay, Miles S., Sept. 22, Granville county. R. R. Oct. 13, 1826
Lewis, Capt. James, Sr., Dec. 23, Granville county. R. R. Feb. 3, 1826
Lewis, Melissa, Aug. 8, Halifax county. R. R. Sept. 8, 1826
Little, Mrs. Jane of Petersburg, Va., Feb. 1, Robeson county. R. R. Feb. 17, 1826
Little, John of Edenton, Feb. 3, Oxford. R. R. Feb. 17, 1826
Loftin, Mrs. Lewis, Sept. 22, Wilmington. R. R. Oct. 6, 1826
Long, Joshua, Jan., Elizabeth City. R. R. Jan. 27, 1826
Long, Littlebury, Mar. 13, Northampton county. R. R. Mar. 31, 1826
M'Cann, Mrs. Ann, Feb. 1, Wilmington. R. R. Feb. 17, 1826
M'Clenhan, John, Nov., Granville county. R. R. Dec. 1, 1826
M'Dougald, Rev. Allen, Je. 17, Cumberland county. R. R. Je. 30, 1826
M'Dowell, James R., Apr. 5, Burke county. R. R. My. 5, 1826
M'Farland, Neal of Laurel Hill, Je. 12, Columbia, S. C. R. R. Je. 27, 1826
M'Garty, J. of Baltimore, Oct. 28, Fayetteville. R. R. Nov. 3, 1826
M'Glohon, William, Mar. 1, Bertie county. R. R. Mar. 31, 1826
M'Kay, Caroline of Wilmington, Sept. 26, Rhode Island. R. R. Oct. 13, 1826
M'Kay, Dr. Edward, Apr., Davidson county. R. R. Je. 9, 1826
M'Leran, Catharine, Dec. 1, Fayetteville. R. R. Dec. 8, 1826
M'Lean, Levi H., Sept., Halifax county. R. R. Oct. 6, 1826
M'Millan, Mrs. Daniel, My. 12, Richmond county. R R. Je. 9, 1826
M'Nair, Mrs. Janet of Scotland, Oct., Fayetteville. R. R. Oct. 20, 1826
M'Neely, Robert, Je. 16, Iredell county. R. R. Jly. 21, 1826
M'Nider, John, Mar. 6, Perquimans county. R. R. Mar. 31, 1826

Maer, Samuel, Feb., Windsor. R. R. Feb. 24, 1826
Martin, Betsey, Aug. 22, Newbern. R. R. Aug. 25, 1826
Masters, Joseph, Aug. 9, Newbern. R. R. Aug. 18, 1826
Matthews, John, Jly. 16, Fayetteville. R. R. Jly. 21, 1826
Means, Jas. A. of Cabarrus county, My. 15, Concord. R. R. Je. 9, 1826
Miller, Ephraim, Sept. 14, Bertie county. R. R. Oct. 6, 1826
Miller, Col. Stephen, Mar. 23, Duplin county. R. R. Apr. 14, 1826
Moody, Jacob, Jly. 25, Lincoln county. R. R. Aug. 18, 1826
Moore, Maj. Thomas J. of Caswell county, Dec. 28, Georgia. R. R. Feb. 10, 1826
Morgan, Haynes, Oct. 18, Rowan county. R. R. Oct. 27, 1826
Morris, Mordecai, Jr., Jan., Pasquotank county. R. R. Jan. 27, 1826
Mulhollan, Col. Hugh, Apr. 17, Orange county. R. R. Apr. 28, 1826
Mullen, John, Jan., Pasquotank county. R. R. Feb. 3, 1826
Murphey, Mrs. William D., Nov. 2, Hillsborough. R. R. Nov. 3, 1826
Murray, Dr. John C. of Rockingham county, Nov. R. R. Nov. 10, 1826
Muse, Mrs. Richard, Aug., Pasquotank county. R. R. Sept. 1, 1826
Neal, Henry, Aug. 2, Orange county. R. R. Aug. 25, 1826
Neale, Moses, Feb. 23, Franklin county. R. R. Mar. 3, 1826
Newberry, Mrs. Jesse, Aug. 16, Cumberland county. R. R. Oct. 6, 1826
Newland, Capt. Hugh Tate, Oct. 5, Morganton. R. R. Oct. 27, 1826
Nixon, Mrs. Delight, Nov. 16, Chowan county. R. R. Dec. 15, 1826
O'Kelly, Rev. James, Oct. 16, Chatham county. R. R. Nov. 3, 1826
Owens, Baswell, Aug. 20, Rowan county. R. R. Sept. 22, 1826
Parker, Mrs. John, Sept., Tarborough. R. R. Sept. 22, 1826
Patterson, Mrs. Nathan, Sept. 21, Franklin county. R. R. Sept. 29, 1826
Patterson, Mrs. Tilman, Sept. 25, Franklin county. R. R. Sept. 29, 1826
Paxton, John of Virginia, Dec. 20, Warrenton. R. R. Dec. 22, 1826
Peck, Capt. Henry, Jan. 27, Beaufort. R. R. Feb. 17, 1826
Perry, Mrs. Green of Warren county, Aug. 23, Georgia. R. R. Sept. 29, 1826
Pierson, Rev. of Washington, Beaufort county, Sept., Washington, D. C. R. R. Oct. 6, 1826
Pippen, Mrs. Joseph, Aug. 30, Edgecombe county. R. R. Sept. 1, 1826
Plummer, Kemp, Jan., Warrenton. R. R. Jan. 27, 1826
Poindexter, Rev. Richard, Jan. 25, Windsor. R. R. Mar. 10, 1826
Pool, Mrs. David, My. 8, Rowan county. R. R. Je. 9, 1826
Porter, Col. Jas., Jan., Mecklenburg county. R. R. Jan. 13, 1826
Porter, Mrs. William B., Apr. 3, Mecklenburg county. R. R. Apr. 21, 1826
Potts, Dr. Tho' of South Carolina, Sept. 19, Statesville. R. R. Sept. 22, 1826
Powell, Richard of Pitt county, Aug. 25, Greene county. R. R. Sept. 15, 1826
Price, Mrs. Thomas, Feb., Wake county. R. R. Feb. 24, 1826
Reddick, Polly, Jr., Jan. 25, Martin county. R. R. Feb. 17, 1826
Reddick, Thomas, Jr., Jan. 20, Martin county. R. R. Feb. 17, 1826
Rhem, Mrs. Jno., Jly., Craven county. R. R. Aug. 18, 1826
Richardson, Joseph of Europe, Feb., Washington, Beaufort county. R. R. Mar. 10, 1826
Robinson, Ezekiel, Aug. 13, Mecklenburg county. R. R. Sept. 1, 1826
Robinson, John, Aug. 28, Mecklenburg county. R. R. Sept. 15, 1826
Robinson, Mrs. Peter of Bladen county, Oct. 29, Fayetteville. R. R. Nov. 3, 1826
Robson, John of this State, Aug. 16, Columbia, S. C. R. R. Sept. 8, 1826
Rogers, Willis of Raleigh, Feb. 28, Wake county. R. R. Mar. 3, 1826

Rounssaville, Charles M'Allister, Jly. 17, Lexington. R. R. Jly. 28, 1826
Ruffin, Wm. of Raleigh, Sept. 9, Philadelphia. R. R. Oct. 20, 1826
Sawyer, Mrs. Lemuel of this State, Jan. 28, Washington, D. C. R. R. Feb. 3, 1826
Sawyer, Mrs. Mathias E., Dec., Edenton. R. R. Dec. 15, 1826
Scott, Mrs. Elijah, Aug. 5, Newbern. R. R. Aug. 18, 1826
Scurlock, Mrs. Mary, Aug. 20, Halifax county. R. R. Sept. 8, 1826
Seaton, William, Sept., Washington, D. C. R. R. Sept. 29, 1826
Sharp, Richard, Oct. 19, Mecklenburg county. R. R. Nov. 3, 1826
Sharpe, Mrs. William, Je., Burke county. R. R. Je. 23, 1826
Sheldon, Mrs. Isreal of Hyde county, Aug., Newbern. R. R. Sept. 1, 1826
Simmons, Farnifold, Jan. 23, Jones county. R. R. Feb. 17, 1826
Simonton, Robert, Apr. 13, Statesville. R. R. My. 5, 1826
Slade, Elijah, Apr. 22, Caswell county. R. R. Je. 23, 1826
Slade, John M., Sept., Edenton. R. R. Sept. 22, 1826
Slatter, Capt. Solomon, Oct. 14, Scotland Neck. R. R. Nov. 17, 1826
Smallwood, Mrs., Apr. 13, Raleigh. R. R. Apr. 14, 1826
Smith, Gen'l Benjamin, Feb., Brunswick county. R. R. Feb. 17, 1826
Smith, James, Jan., Orange county. R. R. Feb. 3, 1826
Smith, Mary, Aug., Jones county. R. R. Aug. 18, 1826
Sneed, Mrs. Step, Aug. 3, Williamsborough. R. R. Aug. 25, 1826
Sossman, Henry, Jly. 31, Davidson county. R. R. Aug. 25, 1826
Speigh, Mrs. Jesse, Sept. 5, Greene county. R. R. Sept. 22, 1826
Spencer, Mrs. Ed., Oct., Hyde county. R. R. Oct. 6, 1826
Stallings, Meshack of Franklin county, Sept. 2, Duplin county. R. R. Sept. 15, 1826
Stevenson, Mary Ann, Mar. 30, Wake county. R. R. Apr. 14, 1826
Storke, Valentine, Aug. 20, Salisbury. R. R. Sept. 1, 1826
Sturdivant, William, My. 31, Wake county. R. R. Je. 2, 1826
Tate, Col. Jno. B., Je. 30, Burke county. R. R. Aug. 11, 1826
Taylor, John, Oct. 10, Chowan county. R. R. Oct. 27, 1826
Taylor, Richard, Jr., Sept. 29, Granville county. R. R. Oct. 15, 1826
Thomas, Elisha, Feb. 19, Bertie county. R. R. Mar. 31, 1826
Thompson, Mrs. Jos., Feb. 2, Orange county. R. R. Feb. 17, 1826
Thompson, William B., Aug., Guilford county. R. R. Sept. 8, 1826
Thorogood, John, Mar. 12, Tyrrell county. R. R. Mar. 31, 1826
Walker, Mrs. Jane, Jan. 27, Hillsborough. R. R. Feb. 3, 1826
Walker, Joel, Aug. 27, Wilmington. R. R. Sept. 8, 1826
Walkup, Mrs. Robert, Sept. 1, Mecklenburg county. R. R. Oct. 6, 1826
Walton, Itildia, Aug. 9, Person county. R. R. Aug. 18, 1826
Ward, Baker R., Sept. 7, Chowan county. R. R. Sept. 29, 1826
Ward, Dr. Thos. J., Apr. 31, Waynesboro. R. R. Je. 16, 1826
Watson, Arthur, Jan. 17, Martin county. R. R. Feb. 17, 1826
Watson, John, Aug. 21, Duplin county. R. R. Aug. 25, 1826
Wells, Jacob, Sr., Sept. 4, S. Washington. R. R. Sept. 15, 1826
White, Mrs. Richard, Dec. 18, Franklin county. R. R. Jan. 6, 1826
White,*Wm. M. formerly of Raleigh, Jly. 27, Craven county. R. R. Aug. 18, 1826
Williams, Gabriel Long, Feb. 16, Warren county. R. R. Mar. 10, 1826
Williams, Mrs. Nancy, Aug. 23, Warren county. R. R. Sept. 8, 1826
Williams, Mrs. William H., Apr. 25, Sampson county. R. R. My. 5, 1826

Wills, James, Aug. 7, Edenton. R. R. Aug. 18, 1826
Wilson, Mrs. Samuel, Jan., Rowan county. R. R. Jan. 27, 1826
Wooten, Peter, Aug., New Hanover county. R. R. Sept. 15, 1826
Worke, Capt. Robert, Mar. 21, Statesville. R. R. Apr. 14, 1826
Wortham, Elizabeth, Apr. 30, Warrenton. R. R. My. 5, 1826
Wynne, Eliza, Sept. 6, Chowan county. R. R. Sept. 29, 1826
Yellowley, Capt. Edward, Jan. 27, Martin county. R. R. Feb. 17, 1826
Yellowley, Samuel, Sept. 30, Williamston. R. R. Oct. 27, 1826
Zenely, Malvina, Aug., Salem. R. R. Sept. 8, 1826

1827

Abernathy, Mrs. Ezekiel, Aug. 6, Charlotte. R. R. Aug. 21, 1827
Adams, Martin, Feb. 17, Raleigh. R. R. Feb. 23, 1827
Alexander, Elam of Mecklenburg county, Feb. 2, Raleigh. R. R. Feb. 6, 1827
Alexander, Mrs. E., My. 21, Rutherford county. R. R. Je. 15, 1827
Alexander, Mrs. James, Jly. 16, Mecklenburg county. R. R. Jly. 31, 1827
Alexander, John Garrison, Nov. 6, Mecklenburg county. R. R. Nov. 20, 1827
Allen, Albert V. of Newbern, Aug. 20, St. Bartholemews. R. R. Sept. 4, 1827
Allen, Archibald, Feb. 24, Wilmington. R. R. Mar. 6, 1827
Allen, John, Apr. 24, Mecklenburg county. R. R. My. 15, 1827
Andrews, D. R., Sr. of Virginia, Mar. 29, Wake county. R. R. Apr. 6, 1827
Armstrong, John, Je. 30, Cumberland county. R. R. Aug. 7, 1827
Arrington, Dr. Joseph, Jly. 24, Nash county. R. R. Jly. 31, 1827
Arrington, Mrs. Joseph, Apr., Nash county. R. R. My. 1, 1827
Asking, Thomas, Je. 10, Fayetteville. R. R. Je. 15, 1827
Atkins, Lewis B. of Orange county, Jly. 18. R. R. Jly. 24, 1827
Bailey, Mrs. Ann, Oct. 7, Forks of the Yadkin. R. R. Dec. 18, 1827
Beatty, Mrs. William H., Apr. 3, Bladen county. R. R. Apr. 17, 1827
Beck, William, Mr. 14, Sampson county. R. R. Mar. 27, 1827
Bell, Edward, Aug. 17, Fayetteville. R. R. Aug. 28, 1827
Bell, Mrs. Mary, Jly. 3, Raleigh. R. R. Jly. 10, 1827
Bell, Reason W., Nov. 9, Edgecombe county. R. R. Dec. 4, 1827
Bennett, John N., Oct. 21, Nashville. R. R. Nov. 16, 1827
Berry, Mrs. Lemuel D. of Alabama, Jan., Pitt county. R. R. Feb. 2, 1827
Bethune, Elizabeth, My. 27, Richmond county. R. R. Je. 15, 1827
Bird, Valentine, Mar. 11, Rowan county. R. R. Mar. 27, 1827
Biset, Mrs. Judah, Jan. 17, Nash county. R. R. Feb. 2, 1827
Black, William, Sept. 14, Mecklenburg county. R. R. Oct. 16, 1827
Blair, Mrs. George, Oct. 22, Edenton. R. R. Dec. 18, 1827
Bowell, Abner F., Je. 5, Fayetteville. R. R. Je. 26, 1827
Boyd, Patrick, Sept. 10, Mecklenburg county. R. R. Sept. 25, 1827
Boykin, Hardy, Jan. 11, Nash county. R. R. Feb. 2, 1827
Bradford, Horace, Je. 27, Fayetteville. R. R. Jly. 3, 1827
Brainerd, Mrs. Elijah of Vermont, Apr. 10, Warrenton. R. R. My. 1, 1827
Branch, Joseph of this State, My. 24, Franklin, Tenn. R. R. Jly. 6, 1827
Brooks, John W., Feb. 23, Camden county. R. R. Mar. 20, 1827
Brown, Mrs. Robert T. of Ireland and Franklin county, Jly. 29, Duplin county. R. R. Aug. 3, 1827
Bryan, Christ, Sept. 18, Trenton. R. R. Oct. 5, 1827
Butler, Moses, My., Craven county. R. R. Je. 5, 1827

Butler, William C. of Elizabeth City, Oct. 30, Philadelphia, Pa. R. R. Nov. 20, 1827
Calder, John, Sept. 14, Charlotte. R. R. Oct. 2, 1827
Caldwell, Daniel, Sept. 15, Charlotte. R. R. Oct. 2, 1827
Campbell, Daniel A., Jan. 16, Richmond county. R. R. Jan. 30, 1827
Campbell, George of Bertie & Orange county, Sept. 1, Indiana. R. R. Oct. 23, 1827
Campbell, Robert, Mar. 1, Cumberland county. R. R. Mar. 13, 1827
Cannte, Mrs. Jane, Aug. 17, Fayetteville. R. R. Aug. 28, 1827
Casso, Francis P. of Raleigh, Jan. 1, Tuscaloosa, Ala. R. R. Feb. 6, 1827
Charles, Thomas of Wake county, Oct., City Point, Va. R. R. Nov. 2, 1827
Chauncey, Mrs. Miles, Aug. 1, Beaufort county. R. R. Aug. 17, 1827
Cheek, Jno., Jan. 20, Warren county. R. R. Jan. 30, 1827
Cherry, James P., Jly. 24, Pitt county. R. R. Jly. 27, 1827
Clark, Rev. Joseph of Randolph county, Oct. 9, Montgomery county. R. R. Oct. 26, 1827
Clinch, Capt. Joseph J. of this State, Oct. 4, Pensacola. R. R. Nov. 2, 1827
Coleman, James of Wadesboro, Aug. 19, Pilot Mountain. R. R. Oct. 2, 1827
Coleman, Thomas of Anson county, Feb. 26, Montgomery, Ala. R. R. My. 1, 1827
Cornick, Mrs. Mary Ann, Nov. 15, Elizabeth city. R. R. Nov. 20, 1827
Cotten, Roderick, Jly., Chatham county. R. R. Jly. 27, 1827
Covington, General Benjamin H., Oct., Rockingham, Richmond county. R. R. Oct. 23, 1827
Cowan, Col. John, Aug. 12, Wilmington. R. R. Aug. 17, 1827
Craig, James, Je. 21, Orange county. R. R. Jly. 10, 1827
Cress, Philip, Mar. 30, Concord. R. R. Apr. 24, 1827
Culpepper, Mrs. John of Montgomery county, Feb. 5, Cheraw, S. C. R. R. Mar. 27, 1827
Cunningham, Mrs. James, Jan. 17, Bertie county. R. R. Jan. 30, 1827
Daves, Mrs. John P., Je. 9, Newbern. R. R. Je. 22, 1827
Davis, Anthony, Jan. 6, Warren county. R. R. Jan. 19, 1827
Davis, Matthew, Dec. 23, Warren county. R. R. Jan. 2, 1827
Davis, Mrs. Stephen, Jan. 8, Warrenton. R. R. Jan. 19, 1827
Delon, Simeon, Je., Pasquotank county. R. R. Je. 15, 1827
Dilliard, Joseph, Mar. 24, Raleigh. R. R. Mar. 27, 1827
Dinkins, Mrs. Mary, Aug. 5, Mecklenburg county. R. R. Aug. 21, 1827
Dismukes, Geo., Aug. 12, Chatham county. R. R. Aug. 21, 1827
Divine, Thomas of Ireland, Aug., Warrenton. R. R. Aug. 10, 1827
Donoho, Archimedes, Aug. 19, Caswell county. R. R. Aug. 28, 1827
Downey, Mrs. Samuel, Aug. 20, Granville county. R. R. Sept. 4, 1827
Drew, Wm., My. 8, Halifax. R. R. My. 11, 1827
Dudley, Mrs. Christopher, Sept., Onslow county. R. R. Sept. 14, 1827
Dunn, Mrs. Bolling, Jan. 26, Wake county. R. R. Feb. 2, 1827
Dunn, Nathan of New Jersey, Oct. 19, Salisbury. R. R. Dec. 18, 1827
Eagles, Joseph, My. 21, Wilmington. R. R. Je. 26, 1827
Edey, "Granny", My. 22, Oxford. R. R. My. 29, 1827
Elliott, Thomas, Sept. 18, Mecklenburg county. R. R. Oct. 2, 1827
Ellis, Dr. James H., Aug., Tyrrell county. R. R. Sept. 4, 1827
Ellis, Samuel Sitgreaves, Oct. 19, Newbern. R. R. Dec. 18, 1827
Eppes, Richard, Oct., Halifax. R R. Oct. 2, 1827

Exum, Capt. James, Je. 27, Northampton county. R. R. Aug. 7, 1827
Faison, Henry, Jan. 15, Sampson county. R. R. Jan. 30, 1827
Falconer, Dr. R. F. of this State, Nov., New Orleans. R. R. Nov. 23, 1827
Farrar, Capt. Edward, Jan. 28, Chatham county. R. R. Feb. 16, 1827
Ferguson, Mrs. Susanna, Mar., Randolph county. R. R. Apr. 6, 1827
Forster, Mrs. Anthony of Charleston, S. C., Nov. 16, Raleigh. R. R. Nov. 20, 1827
Fulton, Capt. John of Ireland, Apr. 6, Salisbury. R. R. Apr. 17, 1827
Gallant, Daniel, Sept. 18, Mecklenburg county. R. R. Oct. 2, 1827
Gardner, Thomas, Oct. 15, Warren county. R. R. Oct. 19, 1827
Gee, Col. Neville, Sept., Halifax county. R. R. Oct. 2, 1827
Gillett, Mrs. Bazaleel of Raleigh, My., Cincinnati, Ohio. R. R. Je. 5, 1827
Gilliam, Wm., Aug., Bertie county. R. R. Aug. 17, 1827
Glenn, James A. of Caswell county, Aug. 9, Philadelphia. R. R. Aug. 28, 1827
Good, Mrs. Benjamin C., My. 29, Newbern. R. R. Je. 5, 1827
Goodman, Lemuel, Aug. 18, Gates county. R. R. Sept. 4, 1827
Graham, John of Anson county, Oct. 6, Tennessee. R. R. Nov. 20, 1827
Graves, Rev. Barzillai, Jly. 13, Caswell county. R. R. Jly. 24, 1827
Gray, William, Jan. 23, Pitt county. R. R. Jan. 30, 1827
Greear, Mrs. Thomas, Oct. 2, Guilford county. R. R. Dec. 18, 1827
Green, Mrs. James, My. 31, Jones county. R. R. Je. 5, 1827
Green, Mrs. Nathaniel T., Oct. 31, Warren county. R. R. Oct. 19, 1827
Guthrie, Mrs. of Washington, Beaufort county, Jly. 16, Raleigh. R. R. Jly. 20, 1827
Haley, William, Jan. 29, Raleigh. R. R. Feb. 2, 1827
Hall, William P. of Halifax county, Sept. 28, Milton. R. R. Oct. 16, 1827
Harris, Dr. Charles, Jly., Cabarrus county. R. R. Jly. 24, 1827
Harvey, William M., Apr. 16, Gates county. R. R. My. 1, 1827
Hawkins, Col. Joseph of Raleigh, Aug. 5, Brunswick Mineral Springs. R. R. Aug. 10, 1827
Hawkins, Mrs. Samuel, Aug. 6, Beaufort county. R. R. Aug. 17, 1827
Hawks, Mrs. Francis L. of Hillsborough, Jly. 12, New Haven, Conn. R. R. Jly. 31, 1827
Hawley, Daniel of Connecticut, Sept. 27, Raleigh. R. R. Oct. 5, 1827
Haywood, Benjamin Rush, Oct. 9, Raleigh. R. R. Oct. 12, 1827
Haywood, John, Nov. 18, Raleigh. R. R. Nov. 20, 1827
Hedrick, T. W., Sept. 28, Wilmington. R. R. Oct. 16, 1827
Hester, Robert, My. 8, Person county. R. R. Je. 5, 1827
Hicks, Capt. William, Oct. 18, Orange county. R. R. Nov. 13, 1827
Hill, Col. James J. of Franklin county, Jly., Henderson county, Tenn. R. R. Aug. 7, 1827
Hinton, Samuel, Je. 14, Richmond county. R. R. Je. 15, 1827
Holley, Thomas, Aug. 8, Bertie county. R. R. Sept. 4, 1827
Holmes, James, Oct. 13, Sampson county. R. R. Oct. 16, 1827
Holt, Mrs. John, Aug. 23, Orange county. R. R. Sept. 4, 1827
Horn, Thomas, Jan. 24, Nash county. R. R. Feb. 2, 1827
Horniblow, Mrs. Elizabeth, Aug. 30, Chowan county. R. R. Sept. 18, 1827
Houze, Duke W., Nov. 29, Louisburg. R. R. Dec. 14, 1827
Howard, Capt. John, Aug. 6, Rowan county. R. R. Aug. 21, 1827
Howey, Adeline, Mar., Wilmington. R. R. Mar. 13, 1827
Hunt, Abigail Caroline, Dec. 31, Guilford county. R. R. Jan. 30, 1827

Hunter, Dr. Benjamin B., Mar., Nashville, Nash county. R. R. Mar. 30, 1827
Hunter, Rev. Humphrey, Aug. 21, Mecklenburg county. R. R. Sept. 18, 1827
Ingram, Mrs. John, Sept. 10, Cumberland county. R. R. Sept. 11, 1827
Jarrott, John, My. 20, Fayetteville. R. R. Je. 26, 1827
Jeffreys, Mrs. Geo. W., Aug. 14, Person county. R. R. Aug. 21, 1827
Jenkins, Irwin, Jly. 16, Hertford county. R. R. Aug. 10, 1827
Jones, Mrs. Richard, Aug. 17, Edenton. R. R. Sept. 4, 1827
Jones, Timothy W., Raleigh, Apr. 15. R. R. Apr. 17, 1827
Jones, Rev. Wm., Jly. 29, Jones county. R. R. Aug. 10, 1827
Johnson, General Robert R., Mar. 19, Warren county. R. R. Mar. 23, 1827
King, Edward C. of Newbern, Sept. 11, New York. R. R. Nov. 6, 1827
King, George, Jly. 7, Chatham county. R. R. Jly. 31, 1827
Kennedy, Lydia, Sept. 15, Moore county. R. R. Sept. 25, 1827
Kittrell, Tabitha Ann, Oct. 16, Chapel Hill. R. R. Nov. 6, 1827
Krider, Margaret, Sept. 21, Rowan county. R. R. Nov. 6, 1827
Lanier, Betsey Jones, Jan. 15, Franklin county. R. R. Feb. 16, 1827
Lassiter, Mrs. Hance, Sept. 24, Wake county. R. R. Sept. 28, 1827
Lassiter, William, Nov., Granville county. R. R. Nov. 13, 1827
Leak, William P., Aug. 31, Richmond county. R. R. Sept. 11, 1827
Lindsay, Doctor Edumund S., Je., Currituck county. R. R. Je. 15, 1827
Linster, John W., Sr., Sept. 21, Rowan county. R. R. Oct. 16, 1827
Long, Daniel, Je., Elizabeth City. R. R. Je. 15, 1827
Long, Richard, Jly. 3, Northampton county. R. R. Aug. 3, 1827
Logan, Mrs. John M., Oct. 8, Greensborough. R. R. Oct. 19, 1827
Lovick, Mrs. James, Aug. 11, Slocumb's creek. R. R. Sept. 4, 1827
M'Aden, J. H., Mar. 4, Caswell county. R. R. Mar. 13, 1827
M'Bee, Silas L., Sept. 15, Lincolnton. R. R. Oct. 2, 1827
M'Cain, James M., Sept. 16, Mecklenburg county. R. R. Oct. 16, 1827
M'Cullough, Mrs. H., Jan. 21, Washington, Beaufort county. R. R. Feb. 16, 1827
M'Kay, Alfred, Jly., Salisbury. R. R. Jly. 27, 1827
M'Knight, James, Sr., Aug. 24, Mecklenburg county. R. R. Sept. 18, 1827
M'Queen, Dr. Arch'd, Jly., Moore county. R. R. Jly. 17, 1827
M'Ray, Ann Gilchrist, Oct. 7, Cumberland county. R. R. Oct. 23, 1827
Marks, Thomas B., Oct. 1, Tarborough. R. R. Oct. 2, 1827
Marshall, Mrs. Humphrey, Mar. 2, Salisbury. R. R. Mar. 27, 1827
Martin, Mrs. William John of Granville county, Nov. 10. R. R. Nov. 16, 1827
Masters, Mrs. Elizabeth, Je. 27, Newbern. R. R. Jly. 6, 1827
Maxwell, Mary, Jan. 18, Charlotte. R. R. Feb. 16, 1827
Mebane, Capt. Robert, Je. 5, Orange county. R. R. Je. 15, 1827
Milner, Mrs. Jacobina, Jly. 28, Person county. R. R. Aug. 10, 1827
Mitchell, Hutchins, Aug. 23, Caswell county. R. R. Aug. 24, 1827
Mitchell, Wm. of New Jersey, Jly. 11, Newbern. R. R. Jly. 13, 1827
Morrison, Mrs. W. J., Oct. 6, Mecklenburg county. R. R. Dec. 18, 1827
Morse, Rev. William B. of Randolph county, Je. 11. R. R. Je. 19, 1827
Moss, John B. of Randolph county, Aug. 31, Fayetteville. R. R. Sept. 11, 1827
Murchison, John, Jly. 15, Cumberland county. R. R. Jly. 24, 1827
Mure, John, Mar. 3, Wilmington. R. R. Mar. 13, 1827
Murphy, John, Jly., Burke county. R. R. Jly. 3, 1827
Nelson, Mrs. John S., Je. 22, Cedar Grove on the Neuse. R. R. Jly. 6, 1827
Nichols, Mrs. Sarah, Jan. 15, Nash county R. R. Feb. 2, 1827
Nott, Mrs. William, Oct. 3, Fayetteville. R. R. Oct. 16, 1827

Ogburn, Mrs. Nichols, Aug. 20, Guilford county. R. R. Aug. 31, 1827
Overman, Mrs. Isaac, Je., Pasquotank county. R. R. Je. 15, 1827
Park, John, Mar. 10, Davidson county. R. R. Mar. 27, 1827
Parker, Mrs. Jos., Mar., Pasquotank county. R. R. Mar. 20, 1827
Patterson, James A. of Raleigh, My. 6, New York. R. R. My. 29, 1827
Patton, Mrs. James, Nov. 25, Asheville. R. R. Dec. 14, 1827
Peabody, Mrs. Julia Ann, Sept. 16, Fayetteville. R. R. Sept. 18, 1827
Pearce, Abner, Aug. 4, Kinston. R. R. Aug. 10, 1827
Pearce, Oliver, Mar. 26, Wake county. R. R. Mar. 27, 1827
Philips, Ursula, Feb. 10, Wake county. R. R. My. 1, 1827
Pickens, Israel of this State, Apr. 23, Matanzas. R. R. Je. 5, 1827
Piggott, Mrs. Jeremiah, Je. 2, Chatham county. R. R. Je. 15, 1827
Pleasants, Mrs. Elvira, Sept. 28, Wake county. R. R. Oct. 2, 1827
Polk, Maj. Samuel of Mecklenburg county, Dec. 3, Columbia, Tenn. R. R. Dec. 14, 1827
Porter, Samuel, Aug. 27, Charlotte. R. R. Sept. 18, 1827
Potter, Miles, Sr. of Brunswick county, Aug. 17, Towns creek. R. R. Sept. 4, 1827
Ragsdale, Jane, Sept. 20, Raleigh. R. R. Sept. 25, 1827
Ramsey, Henry, Sept. 28, Hertford county. R. R. Nov. 6, 1827
Ransom, Priscilla J., Nov. 4, Warren county. R. R. Nov. 16, 1827
Reeves, Mrs. Hartwell, Jly., Raleigh. R. R. Jly. 10, 1827
Reeves, Sarah, Apr. 7, Orange county. R. R. Apr. 17, 1827
Rhodes, Wm. S., Feb. 10, Windsor, Bertie county. R. R. Feb. 16, 1827
Riddle, Maj. Charles M. of Chatham county, My. 8, Greene county, Ala. R. R. Je. 26, 1827
Ridley, Col. Howell L., Aug. 24, Granville county. R. R. Sept. 4, 1827
Robertson, Walter, Aug. 8, Raleigh. R. R. Aug. 10, 1827
Rodman, William W. of Washington, Beaufort county, Jan. 1, On Ship. R. R. Mar. 20, 1827
Rose, Charles G., Jan. 9, Granville county. R. R. Jan. 19, 1827
Ruffin, Mrs. William of Raleigh, Feb., New Hanover county, Va. R. R. Mar. 6, 1827
Salmon, Samuel J., Sept. 20, Fayetteville. R. R. Nov. 6, 1827
Samuel, Capt. Josiah, Apr. 10, Caswell county. R. R. Apr. 17, 1827
Sandford, Hezekiah, Jr. of New York, Aug. 28, Edenton. R. R. Sept. 11, 1827
Sauls, John, Sept., Rocky Point. R. R. Sept. 14, 1827
Sawyer, Enoch, Mar., Camden county. R. R. Mar. 27, 1827
Scott, Mrs. Thomas G., Sept. 16, Raleigh. R. R. Sept. 18, 1827
Sears, Mrs., Oct. 22, Fayetteville. R. R. Oct. 23, 1827
Seawell, Joseph, Jly. 8, Moore county. R. R. Jly. 17, 1827
Shearen, Lewis, Sept., Warren county. R. R. Sept. 25, 1827
Simmons, Mrs. James, Feb. 25, Halifax. R. R. Mar. 6, 1827
Simpson, Miss of Edenburgh, Dec. 10, Brunswick county. R. R. Jan. 2, 1827
Simpson, Mrs. Robin, Oct. 29, Pasquotank county. R. R. Nov. 20, 1827
Sinclair, John, Apr. 10, Anson county. R. R. Apr. 27, 1827
Singletary, John W., Jan. 24, Washington, Beaufort county. R. R. Feb. 16, 1827
Skinner, Dempsey, Sr., My. 14, Edgecombe county. R. R. Je. 1, 1827
Smart, William, Sept. 28, Rutherford. R. R. Oct. 23, 1827
Smith, Mrs. William, Jan., Averasborough. R. R. Jan. 30, 1827

Sneed, Jeremiah, Aug. 11, New Hanover county. R. R. Aug. 28, 1827
Sneed, Junius, My. 23, Salisbury. R. R. Je. 1, 1827
Sparrow, Eliza, Oct., Newbern. R. R. Oct. 12, 1827
Stephens, Mrs. Squires, Oct. 8, Mecklenburgh county. R. R. Dec. 18, 1827
Stone, Thomas, Jly. 24, Chatham county. R. R. Jly. 31, 1827
Strictland, Lazarus, Jan. 25, Nash county. R. R. Feb. 2, 1827
Sugg, Samuel, My. 18, Wake county. R. R. My. 22, 1827
Swinson, Mrs. Elizabeth, Je. 25, Duplin county. R. R. Jly. 6, 1827
Taylor, Mrs. James D. of Virginia, Nov. 29, Rockingham county. R. R. Jan. 2, 1827
Taylor, Mrs. John, Feb. 23, Granville county. R. R. Mar. 2, 1827
Taylor, Wilson, Jan., Nash county. R. R. Feb. 2, 1827
Terry, Rev. Wm. of this State, Apr. 16, Alabama. R. R. My. 11, 1827
Thorne, Mrs. Samuel, Apr. 8, Halifax. R. R. Apr. 20, 1827
Tillinghast, Cyrus P., Aug. 6, Fayetteville. R. R. Aug. 21, 1827
Tilman, Col. Benj. S. of Craven county, My. 18, Milton. R. R. Je. 26, 1827
Toole, Mrs. Garry, Aug. 2, Sampson county. R. R. Aug. 10, 1827
Townsend, Josiah of Perquimans county, Oct. 30, Philadelphia, Pa. R. R. Nov. 20, 1827
Tredwell, Samuel of Rhode Island, Jly. 29, Edenton. R. R. Aug. 10, 1827
Trewolla, Mrs. Henry, Oct. 2, Raleigh. R. R. Oct. 5, 1827
Trexler, Lawrence, Sept. 13, Rowan county. R. R. Oct. 2, 1827
Thompson, Thomas, Jly., Bertie county. R. R. Jly. 13, 1827
Tyson, John, Jr., Jly. 16, Moore county. R. R. Aug. 7, 1827
Vipon, James Stuart, Feb., Greenville, Pitt county. R. R. Feb. 16, 1827
Walker, Mrs. James, Oct. 22, Wilmington. R. R. Dec. 18, 1827
Walker, Julius H. of Wilmington, Je. 18, South Carolina. R. R. Aug. 7, 1827
Walker, Mrs. Samuel, Sept. 4, Randolph county. R. R. Sept. 14, 1827
Welborn, James, Nov., Wilkes county. R. R. Nov. 23, 1827
Wells, Henry of New York, Jly. 12, Edenton. R. R. Jly. 24, 1827
West, Mrs. Robert, Aug., Bertie county. R. R. Aug. 3, 1827
Williams, Mrs. Ann, Aug. 10, Warren county. R. R. Sept. 7, 1827
Williams, Col. Joseph of Va., Aug. 11, Surry county. R. R. Aug. 28, 1827
Whitner, Mrs. Daniel, Oct., Lincoln county. R. R. Oct. 30, 1827
Wilcox, Mrs. Littleberry, Sept., Halifax county. R. R. Sept. 25, 1827
Wills, Henry of New York, Jly. 12, Edenton. R. R. Jly. 27, 1827
Wood, Jane of Randolph county, Aug. 9, Orange county. R. R. Sept. 14, 1827
Wood, Mrs. Peter, Jly. 22, Granville county. R. R. Jly. 31, 1827
Wortham, Mrs. John, Sr. of Virginia, My. 13, Warren county. R. R. Je. 1, 1827
Wright, David, Mar. 15, Duplin county. R. R. Mar. 27, 1827
Wright, Duncan of Scotland, Sept., Cumberland county. R. R. Sept. 11, 1827
Wynns, Mrs. Benjamin, Aug. 11, Murfreesboro. R. R. Sept. 4, 1827
Yancey, Mrs. Jackson, Feb. 14, Oxford. R. R. Mar. 6, 1827
Yarborough, Mrs. E., Oct. 17, Salisbury. R. R. Oct. 30, 1827
Yeaman, George, Nov., Concord. R. R. Nov. 20, 1827
Young, John, Dec., Granville county. R. R. Jan. 2, 1827

1828

Adams, John, Dec. 27, Wake county. R. R. Jan. 14, 1828
Albright, Jacob, Apr. 29, Lexington, Davidson county. R. R. My. 13, 1828
Alexander, Joab, Oct. 18, Mecklenburg county. R. R. Nov. 4, 1828

Allen, Mrs. Reynolds, Feb. 4, Wake county. R. R. Feb. 15, 1828
Allston, Gideon, Jr., Mar. 27, Warren county. R. R. Apr. 11, 1828
Alsobrook, Samuel E. of Hillsborough, Sept. 5, Jackson, Missouri. R. R. Oct. 17, 1828
Alston, Wm. F. of Warren county, Oct. 13, Raleigh. R. R. Oct. 17, 1828
Andrews, William, Mar., Wake county. R. R. Mar. 21, 1828
Austin, Green Deberry, Sept. 17, Anson county. R. R. Oct. 10, 1828
Austin, Mrs. Jacob, Sept. 17, Montgomery county. R. R. Oct. 10, 1828
Baker, John C., Feb., Anson county. R. R. Feb. 26, 1828
Baker, Mrs. Nancy, Oct., Warren county. R. R. Oct. 7, 1828
Barclay, John, Sr. of Wilmington, My., Cumberland county. R. R. My. 25, 1828
Barnard, Libni of Nantucket, My. 14, Guilford county. R. R. Je. 13, 1828
Beeby, Robert of England, Jly. 6, Wilmington. R. R. Jly. 22, 1828
Bell, Mrs. Susannah, Aug. 7, Washington, Beaufort county. R. R. Aug. 29, 1828
Blackledge, Mrs. Wm., Oct. 26, Lenoir county. R. R. Nov. 7, 1828
Blackwood, John, Je., Orange county. R. R. Je. 6, 1828
Blount, John Gray of Tarborough, Sept. 4, Raleigh. R. R. Sept. 9, 1828
Blue, Duncan, Sept. 23, Cumberland county. R. R. Oct. 28, 1828
Borough, Bryan of Moore county, Feb. 19, Alabama. R. R. Mar. 25, 1828
Boylan, William, Oct. 15, Chatham county. R. R. Oct. 17, 1828
Bradshaw, Barney, Mar. 16, Duplin county. R. R. Apr. 8, 1828
Bragg, Margaret, Je. 3, Warrenton. R. R. Je. 13, 1828
Brainerd, Rev. Elijah, My. 23, Warrenton. R. R. My. 30, 1828
Bridges, Mrs. Wm. B., Nov. 31, Franklin county. R. R. Dec. 30, 1828
Britt, Col. William D., Mar., Hertford county. R. R. Mar. 28, 1828
Brown, Maso, Oct. 12, Greene county. R. R. Oct. 28, 1828
Brown, Jethro, Nov. 10, Caswell county. R. R. Nov. 21, 1828
Brown, Rev. William, Feb. 23, Person county. R. R. Mar. 14, 1828
Bryan, Cader of Sampson county, Nov. 24, Duplin county. R. R. Dec. 5, 1828
Burch, Thomas of Raleigh, Jan., Kentucky. R. R. Jan. 8, 1828
Byers, Joseph, Oct. 29, Iredell county. R. R. Nov. 25, 1828
Bush, Wm. L. of New Hanover county, Aug. 14, Georgia. R. R. Sept. 23, 1828
Callender, Thomas of Raleigh, Aug. 20, Smithville. R. R. Sept. 2, 1828
Campbell, Rev. John of Orange county, Apr. 19, Milton. R. R. Je. 6, 1828
Chalmers, Thomas of Salisbury, Je. 23, Wadesboro. R. R. Jly. 4, 1828
Chisholm, Mrs. Whitson H., Jly. 22, Montgomery county. R. R. Aug. 8, 1828
Clark, Mrs. David, Jan. 4, Scotland Neck. R. R. Jan. 22, 1828
Coleman, Mrs. Ann, Sept. 1, Washington, Beaufort county. R. R. Sept. 16, 1828
Colquhoun, Duncan, Jly., Richmond county. R. R. Jly. 18, 1828
Comer, Dr. John, Nov., Caswell county. R. R. Nov. 28, 1828
Cooper, Rev. Fleet, Jan. 28, Sampson county. R. R. Feb. 22, 1828
Council, Mrs. Eurydice, Aug. 2, Edgecombe county. R. R. Sept. 12, 1828
Coxe, Dr. Charles, Sept. 25, Davidson county. R. R. Oct. 17, 1828
Crugh, John of Germany, Sept. 12, Wrightsville Sound. R. R. Sept. 23, 1828
Daniel, Chesley of this State, Aug. 5, Abbeville District, S. C. R. R. Sept. 23, 1828
Daniel, John Beverly, Nov. 22, Granville county. R. R. Dec. 12, 1828
Daniel, Maria Josephine, Nov. 9, Halifax. R. R. Nov. 28, 1828
Davis, Mrs. Thomas F., Sept. 8, Wilmington. R. R. Sept. 9, 1828

Denion, William of Guilford county, Nov. 24. R. R. Dec. 5, 1828
Dickinson, Mrs. K. P., My. 5, Wilmington. R. R. My. 13, 1828
Dinkins, James, Jr., Sept. 31, Mecklenburg county. R. R. Oct. 10, 1828
Donoho, Charles D., Sept. 29, Milton Caswell county. R. R. Oct. 7, 1828
Dow, John, Apr. 21, Mecklenburg county. R. R. My. 13, 1828
Dowden, Mrs. William, Je. 4, Newbern. R. R. Je. 10, 1828
Dixon, Frederick H. of Greene county, Mar. 9, Onslow county. R. R. Mar. 21, 1828
Dixon, Mrs. Windsor, Nov. 14, Greene county. R. R. Nov. 25, 1828
Dudley, Col. Christopher, Nov. 9, Onslow county. R. R. Nov. 14, 1828
Dutch, Nathaniel of Boston, Sept. 12, Wilmington. R. R. Sept. 23, 1828
Edmonds, Col. Charles, Apr. 10, Halifax county. R. R. Apr. 25, 1828
Eure, Capt. Jos. W., Je. 19, Halifax county. R. R. Jly. 11, 1828
Evans, Mrs. Jonathan, Jr., My. 26, Fayetteville. R. R. Je. 13, 1828
Fenner, Dr. Richard of Franklin, My. 12, Jackson, Tenn. R. R. Je. 3, 1828
Fleming, Mrs. Moses, Oct. 2, Iredell county. R. R. Oct. 10, 1828
Fowler, Wm. B., Jly. 4, Wake county. R. R. Jly. 18, 1828
Franklin, Bernard, Jan. 2, Surry county. R. R. Jan. 22, 1828
Freeman, Kinchen, Je. 23, Wake county. R. R. Jly. 4, 1828
Freshwater, Mrs. Wm., Feb. 2, Pasquotank county. R. R. Feb. 12, 1828
Frilick, Mrs. Joseph of Newbern, Sept., Smithfield. R. R. Sept. 23, 1828
Gabard, John of London, Aug. 18, Rowan county. R. R. Sept. 2, 1828
Gardner, Dr. Stephen, Nov. 8, Guilford county. R. R. Nov. 28, 1828
Giles, John, Jly., Onslow county. R. R. Jly. 25, 1828
Gillespie, Daniel of Rowan county, Jan. 26, Charlotte. R. R. Feb. 12, 1828
Glisson, Major Daniel, Jan. 29, Duplin county. R. R. Mar. 18, 1828
Goodwin, Mrs. Robert T., Feb., Fayetteville. R. R. Feb. 26, 1828
Gould, Daniel, Sr., My. 1, Anson county. R. R. My. 25, 1828
Granbury, Thomas, Feb. 11, Hertford. R. R. Feb. 12, 1828
Greer, Thos., Jan. 20, Mecklenburg county. R. R. Feb. 12, 1828
Grier, Mrs. Andrew of Lincoln county, Oct. 14, Mecklenburg county. R. R. Nov. 11, 1828
Grimes, Mrs. Ann, Mar. 11, Washington, Beaufort county. R. R. Mar. 21, 1828
Haliday, David of Petersburg, Va., Sept. 8, Fayetteville. R. R. Sept. 12, 1828
Hall, Mrs. John, Feb. 18, Franklin, Macon county. R. R. Apr. 4, 1828
Halsey, Mrs. Frederick, My., Edenton. R. R. My. 27, 1828
Hambleton, Mrs. James, Aug., Wake county. R. R. Aug. 29, 1828
Harper, Delany, Mar. 4, Greene county. R. R. Mar. 28, 1828
Harrington, Mrs. Rosanna, Oct. 13, Wadesboro. R. R. Oct. 28, 1828
Harris, Mrs. Elizabeth, Jan. 24, Edgecombe county. R. R. Feb. 8, 1828
Harris, Mrs. J. W., Apr. 14, Wake county. R. R. Apr. 25, 1828
Harris, Wm., Feb. 15, Cabarrus county. R. R. Mar. 14, 1828
Harriss, Mrs. Eleazer, Dec. 28, Ebenezer Academy. R. R. Jan. 14, 1828
Hartman, Henry, Apr. 19, Salisbury. R. R. Apr. 29, 1828
Hilliard, Carter, Jan. 15, Nash county. R. R. Feb. 8, 1828
Havens, Jonathan of New York State, My. 12, Washington, Beaufort county. R. R. Je. 10, 1828
Hubbell, Ransom of New England, Jan., Oxford. R. R. Jan. 4, 1828

Hinton, Mrs. Joseph B., Sept. 2, Washington, Beaufort county. R. R. Sept. 16, 1828
Holmes, Gen. Hardy of Sampson county, Nov. 22. R. R. Dec. 5, 1828
Hooper, Thomas C. of Fayetteville, Nov. 22, Chapel Hill. R. R. Nov. 25, 1828
Howard, Mrs. Benjamin, Feb. 7, Rowan county. R. R. Mar. 4, 1828
Hunter, Mrs. Theophilus, Nov. 27, Wake county. R. R. Dec. 2, 1828
Hurdle, Hardy, Je., Orange county. R. R. Je. 27, 1828
Hutton, Jos. of Philadelphia, Feb. 7, Newbern. R. R. Feb. 8, 1828
Irwin, James of Ireland and this State, Apr. 3, Georgia. R. R. Apr. 25, 1828
Irwin, Robert, Dec., Guilford county. R. R. Dec. 30, 1828
Jelks, Jared M. of Wake county, Jan. 12, Tennessee. R. R. Mar. 21, 1828
Jennings, Mrs. Hiram, Jly. 23, Anson county. R. R. Aug. 19, 1828
Johnson, Jeremiah of London, Aug. 17, Fayetteville. R. R. Aug. 19, 1828
Jones, Benjamin, Aug. 10, Scotland Neck, Halifax county. R. R. Aug. 29, 1828
Jones, Mrs. Edmund, My. 13, Western District. R. R. Jly. 22, 1828
Jones, Frederick, Apr., Newbern. R. R. My. 2, 1828
Jones, Nathaniel, My., Wake county. R. R. My. 20, 1828
Jones, Mrs. Phebe, Dec., Wilkes county. R. R. Jan. 1, 1828
Lawrence, Jeremiah, Oct. 9, Fayetteville. R. R. Oct. 24, 1828
Lees, Hannah M. of Great Britain, Je. 10, Warrenton. R. R. Je. 17, 1828
Lees, William, Sr., Feb. 8, Mecklenburg county. R. R. Mar. 4, 1828
Lenox, William of Ireland, Aug. 30, Milton. R. R. Sept. 2, 1828
Liles, Thomas, Apr. 10, Franklin county. R. R. Apr. 18, 1828
Lloyd, Isaac, Jly. 20, Louisburg. R. R. Jly. 22, 1828
Logan, Euselius of this State, Aug. 14, Greenville, Va. R. R. Sept. 2, 1828
Lawrence, Abram, Sept. 9, Statesville. R. R. Oct. 10, 1828
M'Donald, Allen, Feb. 12, Moore county. R. R. Mar. 4, 1828
M'Kay, John, Aug. 20, Smithville. R. R. Sept. 2, 1828
M'Knight, Mrs. James, Sept. 31, Mecklenburg county. R. R. Oct. 10, 1828
M'Lean, Dr. William, Oct. 25, Lincoln county. R. R. Nov. 25, 1828
M'Leran, Margaret, My. 1, Fayetteville. R. R. My. 27, 1828
M'Neely, Andrew, Apr. 16, Mecklenburg county. R. R. Apr. 29, 1828
M'Neely, D. C. of Rowan county, Mar. 25, New Haven, Conn. R. R. Apr. 29, 1828
M'Phail, Malcom, Jly. 21, Cumberland county. R. R. Jly. 22, 1828
M'Rae, Roderick, Jly., Cumberland county. R. R. Jly. 22, 1828
Macon, Major John, of this State, Feb. 9, Tenn. R. R. Mar. 25, 1828
Maffitt, Mrs. William H., Mar. 24, Fayetteville. R. R. Mar. 25, 1828
Martin, Ailey, Feb., Salisbury. R. R. Mar. 18, 1828
Martin, Jane, Feb. 9, Duplin county. R. R. Mar. 18, 1828
Martin, Nancy, Feb., Salisbury. R. R. Mar. 18, 1828
Memath, Robert R., Apr. 24, Chatham county. R. R. Apr. 29, 1828
Mitchell, Mrs. Thomas, Feb. 5, Louisburg. R. R. Feb. 26, 1828
Moring, John, Jr., Feb. 29, Chatham county. R. R. Mar. 7, 1828
Moore, Dr. Robert, Jly. 11, Rowan county. R. R. Jly. 25, 1828
Mooreman, Lemuel, Sept. 13, Lincolnton. R. R. Oct. 10, 1828
Morehead, Samuel, Sept. 24, Guilford county. R. R. Sept. 26, 1828
Moseley, John W., Jan. 2, Warren county. R. R. Feb. 8, 1828
Nance, Mrs. James, Je. 3, Wake county. R. R. Jly. 18, 1828

Neely, Capt. Nathan, Apr. 12, Rowan county. R. R. Apr. 29, 1828
Neely, Wm. M., Sept. 2, Mecklenburg county. R. R. Oct. 10, 1828
Nelson, Capt. John, Dec., Wilmington. R. R. Dec. 23, 1828
Oliver, Mrs. Susannah, Nov., Newbern. R. R. Nov. 7, 1828
Pearsall, John of Wayne county, Je. 18, Salisbury. R. R. Jly. 11, 1828
Pearsall, Joseph D., Aug. 25, Duplin county. R. R. Sept. 9, 1828
Person, Gen. Benjamin, Dec. 10, Carthage, Moore county. R. R. Dec. 23, 1828
Philips, David, Sept. 8, Edgecombe county. R. R. Sept. 30, 1828
Picket, Col. Joseph, Jly. 2, Wadesborough. R. R. Jly. 15, 1828
Pigot, Joseph of this State, Mar., Georgetown, S. C. R. R. Mar. 21, 1828
Popelson, Samuel W., Nov., Edenton. R. R. Nov. 14, 1828
Porter, Mrs. James, Mar. 18, Mecklenburg county. R. R. Apr. 29, 1828
Porter, Thomas, Je. 5, Madeline near Vera Cruz. R. R. Jly. 18, 1828
Potts, Mrs. Pauline C., Je. 23, Washington, Beaufort county. R. R. Jly. 11, 1828
Price, Caswell, Oct. 27, Wake county. R. R. Oct. 31, 1828
Pullen, Mrs. Samuel, Jly. 22, Raleigh. R. R. Jly. 29, 1828
Ragsdale, Benjamin, Nov. 19, Raleigh. R. R. Nov. 21, 1828
Randolph, Mrs. Tarborough. R. R. Oct. 17, 1828
Reston, Mr., Dec. 20, Wilmington. R. R. Dec. 23, 1828
Robinson, Philip, Je. 20, On Board Brig. Amazon, Je. 20. R. R. Jly. 25, 1828
Roles, Mrs. William, Je., Wake county. R. R. Je. 20, 1828
Ross, Rev. Martin, Feb. 2, Perquimans county. R. R. Feb. 12, 1828
Ruffin, Lamon, My. 24, Edgecombe county. R. R. My. 30, 1828
Satterwhite, Franklin T., Granville county. R. R. Feb. 12, 1828
Shaw, Jas. of Scotland, Je. 11, Newbern. R. R. Je. 17, 1828
Shaw, William of Scotland, Dec. 27, Raleigh. R. R. Jan. 1, 1828
Shepherd, William, My., Fayetteville. R. R. My. 25, 1828
Simison, Feb. 9, Charlotte. R. R. Mar. 4, 1828
Smith, David, Sept. 6, Topsail sound. R. R. Sept. 23, 1828
Smith, Maximilian, My. 26, Hertford. R. R. Je. 6, 1828
Soverveil, Mrs. James, Feb. 8, Warrenton. R. R. Feb. 12, 1828
Stafford, Wm., Feb. 14, Cabarrus county. R. R. Mar. 4, 1828
Standley, Richard, Dec. 25, Charlotte. R. R. Jan. 14, 1828
Stedman, Winship, Mar. 4, Pittsborough, Chatham county. R. R. Mar. 18, 1828
Stone, Annie, Jan. 19, Bertie county. R. R. Feb. 1, 1828
Sugg, Major Joshua, Je., Wake county. R. R. Je. 6, 1828
Swain, Mary, Mar. 17, Asheville. R. R. Apr. 4, 1828
Taylor, Wm. A., Sept. 30, Halifax. R. R. Oct. 17, 1828
Thompson, Rev. Thomas, Oct., Rockingham county. R. R. Oct. 3, 1828
Tisdale, Mrs. Barney, Je., Elizabeth City. R. R. Je. 13, 1828
Townsend, Alexander, Dec., Robeson county. R. R. Dec. 23, 1828
Tucker, Hon., Thomas Tudor, My. 8, Washington, D. C. R. R. My. 9, 1828
Turner, James Porter of Connecticut, Aug. 16, Fayetteville. R. R. Aug. 19, 1828
Vokes, Abbey of Ireland, Je. 9, Warrenton. R. R. Je. 13, 1828
Walton, Timothy, Sr., Dec., Wake county. R. R. Dec. 12, 1828

Watson, Col. Wm. C. of this State, Oct. 27, Henry county, Alabama. R. R. Nov. 7, 1828
Watts, Rev. John, Dec. 26, Williamston. R. R. Jan. 8, 1828
Whitlock, Mrs. Solomon, Jan. 18, Caswell county. R. R. Feb. 1, 1828
Williams, Col. Benj., Feb. 14, Moore county. R. R. Feb. 22, 1828
Williams, Mrs. Godfrey of Beaufort county, Aug. 5, Pitt county. R. R. Aug. 29, 1828
Williams, Col. Henry Christmas, Aug. 16, Warren county. R. R. Sept. 9, 1828
Williams, Mrs. John, Je. 13, Person county. R. R. Jly. 11, 1828
Williams, Thomas A. of Cumberland county, Aug. 28, Clairborne, Alabama. R. R. Sept. 23, 1828
Wilkinson, John of Fayetteville, Oct. 9, Chesterville, S. C. R. R. Oct. 28, 1828
Williamson, Mrs. Nathan, of Caswell county, Nov. 14. R. R. Dec. 5, 1828
Wilson, Willis, Mar., Camden county. R. R. Apr. 1, 1828
Winstead, Alexander, Jan. 15, Caswell Court House. R. R. Jan. 22, 1828
Wiss, Lewis, M. of Wilmington, Oct. 27, New York. R. R. Nov. 21, 1828
Witherspoon, John, Nov. 4, Iredell county. R. R. Nov. 25, 1828˙
Wright, Abraham, Aug. 30, Caswell county. R. R. Sept. 2, 1828
Yancy, Bartlett, Aug. 30, Caswell county. R. R. Sept. 2, 1828
Yancey, Jechonias, Jan. 15, Granville county. R. R. Jan. 25, 1828

1829

Abingdon, Rev. Wm. N. of Henry county, Va., Sept. 15, Davidson county. R. R. Oct. 1, 1829
Adkins, Samuel, Nov. 10, Wilmington. R. R. Nov. 19, 1829
Albertson, Benj., Je., Perquimans county. R. R. Je. 12, 1829
Alexander, Abraham, Apr. 11, Iredell county. R. R. Apr. 17, 1829
Alexander, Mrs. Isaac F., Sept. 8, Mecklenburg county. R. R. Oct. 1, 1829
Allen, Gen. Vine, Jly., Craven county. R. R. Jly. 16, 1829
Armstrong, Mary., Mar. 10, Newbern. R. R. Mar. 27, 1829
Arnot, James P., Jan. 1, Halifax county. R. R. Jan. 30, 1829
Arrington, Charles, Jan. 18, Hertford, Perquimans county. R. R. Feb. 6, 1829
Atkinson, Mrs. Benashly, Sept. 27, Pitt county. R. R. Oct. 29, 1829
Baird, Maj. Mathew, Oct. 25, Burke county. R. R. Nov. 12, 1829
Bailey, Capt. Allen, Aug. 26, Buncombe county. R. R. Sept. 4, 1829
Baker, Mrs. Isaac, My. 6, Wilmington. R. R. My. 22, 1829
Ballard, William W., Je. 28, Fayetteville. R. R. Jly. 2, 1829
Banks, Redding of Elizabeth City, Mar. 10, Washington, D. C. R. R. Mar. 20, 1829
Barksdale, Elizabeth, Aug. 23, Halifax county. R. R. Sept. 10, 1829
Barnet, John, Sr., Aug. 29, Mecklenburg county. R. R. Sept. 17, 1829
Barnhill, John, Oct. 9, Mecklenburg county. R. R. Oct. 29, 1829
Barr, Mrs. John D. of Greensboro, Aug. 3, Alabama. R. R. Sept. 4, 1829
Barrow, Mrs. Thomas, Je., Beaufort county. R. R. Je. 5, 1829
Battle, Joel of Falls of Neuse, Aug., Edgecombe county. R. R. Sept. 4, 1829
Bebee, Mrs. Asa, Oct. 12, Fayetteville. R. R. Oct. 22, 1829
Bell, George, My. 12, Newberne. R. R. My. 29, 1829
Bell, Susan, Oct. 10, Fayetteville. R. R. Oct. 22, 1829
Belt, Thomas, Feb. 7, Iredell county. R. R. Mar. 27, 1829

Bishop, Thomas, Mar. 6, New Hanover county. R. R. Mar. 27, 1829
Black, Duncan, Mar. 14, Fayetteville. R. R. Mar. 27, 1829
Black, John, Aug. 29, Mecklenburg county. R. R. Sept. 17, 1829
Blackwood, Mrs. William, Aug. 25, Orange county. R. R. Sept. 10, 1829
Blount, Mrs. John, Jly. 31, Edenton. R. R. Aug. 13, 1829
Boon, Mrs. John, Aug. 25, Orange county. R. R. Sept. 10, 1829
Bradley, Capt. Increase of Newbern, Sept., Beaufort county. R. R. Oct. 1, 1829
Branson, Levi, Sept. 13, Randolph county. R. R. Oct. 15, 1829
Brevard, William S., My. 7, Iredell county. R. R. Aug. 6, 1829
Brickle, Joe, J. S. M., Dec. 22, Pitt county. R. R. Dec. 31, 1829
Bridges, Elizabeth, Dec. 31, Franklin county. R. R. Jan. 2, 1829
Brown, Robert A., Mar. 28, Caswell county. R. R. Apr. 17, 1829
Bryan, Rev. Jonathan, Mar. 29, Wilmington. R. R. Apr. 5, 1829
Buckingham, John C. of New Jersey, My. 10, Fayetteville. R. R. My. 29, 1829
Bullock, Wm. Sr., Oct., Granville county. R. R. Oct. 15, 1829
Bunting, David, Oct. 14, Duplin county. R. R. Oct. 29, 1829
Burt, Mrs. John, Sept. 13, Halifax county. R. R. Oct. 1, 1829
Busbee, Lucetta, Sept. 22, Wake county. R. R. Sept. 24, 1829
Butler, Reuben of this State, Jan. 20, King William county, Va. R. R. Feb. 6, 1829
Buie, Margaret, Sept. 21, Cumberland county. R. R. Oct. 8, 1829
Cade, Mrs. Waddle, Jly., Fayetteville. R. R. Jly. 30, 1829
Campbell, Asa, Sept. 6, Iredell county. R. R. Sept. 24, 1829
Campbell, Mrs. Asa, Sept. 5, Iredell county. R. R. Sept. 24, 1829
Campbell, Mrs. Kenneth, Aug. 5, Wilmington. R. R. Aug. 20, 1829
Carson, William, Sept. 6, Iredell county. R. R. Sept. 24, 1829
Carson, William, Sept. 6, Surry county. R. R. Oct. 1, 1829
Carter, David, Oct., Hyde county. R. R. Oct. 15, 1829
Carthy, Dr. Thomas L. of Newbern, Aug. 15, Louisiana. R. R. Sept. 24, 1829
Chambers, Mrs. Otho, Apr. 10, Rowan county. R. R. My. 1, 1829
Chamness, Mrs. Naoim, Sept. 19, Randolph county. R. R. Oct. 15, 1829
Chapman, Mrs. Samuel, Jan., Newbern. R. R. Jan. 30, 1829
Cherry, Mrs. Lunsford W., Sept., Edgecombe county. R. R. Sept. 10, 1829
Clark, David, Sept. 23, Scotland Neck. R. R. Oct. 1, 1829
Clitherall, Dr. George C. of the U. S. Army, Nov. 10, Smithville. R. R. Nov. 26, 1829
Cobb, Eliza, Oct., Granville county. R. R. Oct. 15, 1829
Coffield, Wm., Jan., Chowan county. R. R. Feb. 6, 1829
Collins, Mrs. Arch'd., Nov., Wilmington. R. R. Dec. 3, 1829
Collins, Major Brice, Jan. 15, Burke county. R. R. Apr. 10, 1829
Connelly, Caleb, Jan. 9, Lincoln county. R. R. Feb. 6, 1829
Cook, Alfred, Sept. 6, Surry county. R. R. Oct. 1, 1829
Cook, Isaac, Mar. 2, Guilford county. R. R. Mar. 27, 1829
Croom, Dr. Abraham, My. 8, Lenoir county. R. R. My. 22, 1829
Croom, Gen. W., My. 8, Lenoir county. R. R. My. 22, 1829
Davis, Mrs. Thos. F., Mar. 26, Washington, Beaufort county. R. R. Apr. 10, 1829
Davis, Mrs. John R., Sept. 5, Beaufort county. R. R. Oct. 1, 1829

Day, David, Sept. 16, Halifax county. R. R. Oct. 1, 1829
Deford, William of Norfolk, Feb., Elizabeth City. R. R. Feb. 20, 1829
Dennis, Zachariah, Aug. 9, Hillsboro R. R. Aug. 20, 1829
Dickey, Sarah, Je. 12, Salisbury. R. R. Je. 26, 1829
Dickson, Mrs. Joseph of Ireland, Dec. 19, Orange county. R. R. Dec. 24, 1829
Dobson, Dr. Wm., Aug. 29, Davidson county. R. R. Sept. 24, 1829
Dunn, Hardeman, Feb. 20, Wake county. R. R. Feb. 27, 1829
Dusenbury, Samuel, Oct. 10, Lexington, Davidson county. R. R. Oct. 29, 1829
Edwards, Joshua, Sept., Guilford county. R. R. Sept. 17, 1829
Egerton, Elizabeth, Sept., Warren county. R. R. Oct. 1, 1829
Elliott, Mrs. Peter, Sept., Elizabeth City. R. R. Oct. 8, 1829
Faddis, John, Nov., Hillsboro. R. R. Dec. 3, 1829
Filhoner, Nicholas of Germany, Jan. 3, Rowan county. R. R. Jan. 23, 1829
Fitzgerald, Mrs. Nancy, Aug. 23, Rockingham county. R. R. Sept. 17, 1829
Fort, Mrs. Wm., Wake county, Feb. 8. R. R. Feb. 13, 1829
Fowler, Stephen of Connecticut, Mar. 24, Craven county. R. R. Apr. 10, 1829
Freear, Henry, Aug. 28, Halifax county. R. R. Sept. 10, 1829
Fuller, Rev. Bartholomew, Sept. 25, Franklin county. R. R. Oct. 8, 1829
Gee, Jos., Sept., Halifax county. R. R. Sept. 10, 1829
Geer, Gilbert of Groton Connecticut and this State, Apr. 25, On the sound. R. R. My. 1, 1829
Geren, Miranda R., Sept. 22, Guilford county. R. R. Oct. 1, 1829
Gillaspie, Col. Daniel, Jan. 17, Guilford county. R. R. Jan. 30, 1829
Gillaspie, Robt., Sept. 25, Guilford county. R. R. Oct. 15, 1829
Gillespie, David, Sept. 28, Bladen county. R. R. Oct. 15, 1829
Glendening, Mrs. William, My., Wake county. R. R. My. 22, 1829
Gordon, Maj. Nathaniel, Feb. 1, Wilkes county. R. R. Feb. 27, 1829
Gowing, Mrs. John, Jan., Newbern. R. R. Jan. 30, 1829
Grady, Mrs. Henry, Nov. 10, Buncombe county. R. R. Dec. 31, 1829
Graham, Catherine, Nov. 21, Charlotte. R. R. Dec. 10, 1829
Gray, Elisha, M. of Randolph county, Aug. 25, Sumner county, Tenn., Oct. 15, 1829
Green, Solomon, Oct. 16, Warren county. R. R. Oct. 29, 1829
Grimes, Mrs. Bryan, Mar. 16, Pitt county. R. R. Mar. 20, 1829
Guion, Mrs. Isaac D., Jly. 16, Edgecombe county. R. R. Aug. 20, 1829
Guy, Mrs. Hinton, Oct. 6, Cumberland county. R. R. Oct. 8, 1829
Hacket, Levin, Sept. 29, Guilford county. R. R. Oct. 15, 1829
Hambleton, Eliza, Sept. 5, Wilmington. R. R. Sept. 24, 1829
Hamner, Mrs. James G., Apr. 14, Fayetteville. R. R. Apr. 24, 1829
Harden, John, My., Rockingham county. R. R. My. 8, 1829
Hare, John, Sept. 22, Warren county. R. R. Oct. 1, 1829
Harrell, Anna, Oct. 21, Washington. R. R. Oct. 29, 1829
Harris, Jas., Columbus, Aug. 12, Mecklenburg county. R. R. Sept. 24, 1829
Harris, Maj. Jonathan, Oct,, Mecklenburg county. R. R. Nov. 5, 1829
Harris, John B., Aug. 6, Wilmington. R. R. Aug. 20, 1829
Harris, Sophia S., Sept. 1, Mecklenburg county. R. R. Sept. 17, 1829
Harrison, John, Sr., Sept. 23, Wake county. R. R. Sept. 24, 1829
Harrison, Wm., Aug., Franklin county. R. R. Sept. 4, 1829

Hawkins, Rob't. of Warrenton, Nov. 14, Courtland, Alabama. R. R. Dec. 10, 1829
Hawley, Mrs. Samuel T., Sept. 8, Fayetteville. R. R. Sept. 10, 1829
Haywood, Sherwood of Newbern, Oct. 8, Raleigh. R. R. Oct. 8, 1829
Heath, Mrs. Delia, Sept. 27, Guilford county. R. R. Oct. 15, 1829
Hemphill, Mathew L. of Chester, S. C., Nov. 3, Mecklenburg county. R. R. Nov. 26, 1829
Henderson, Mrs. Jabes H. of Wilmington, Nov. 18, Tennessee. R. R. Dec. 31, 1829
Henderson, Mrs. Thomas of Raleigh, Aug. 8, Tennessee. R. R. Sept. 10, 1829
Hinton, Mrs. Ransom, My. 31, Wake county. R. R. Je. 5, 1829
Hodges, Col. Joseph, Aug. 4, Georgia. R. R. Sept. 10, 1829
Hogg, Richard, Dec. 27, Raleigh. R. R. Dec. 31, 1829
Hogg, Susan Edwards, My. 8, Raleigh. R. R. Aug. 6, 1829
Hollowell, Nathan, Sept. 20, Perquimans county. R. R. Oct. 8, 1829
Hollowell, Mrs. Wm., Sept., Pasquotank county. R. R. Oct. 8, 1829
Holmes, Gen. Gabriel, Sept. 26, Sampson county. R. R. Oct. 15, 1829
Holmes, Rev. Henry, Aug., Edenton. R. R. Aug. 6, 1829
Hood, Mrs. John H. of South Carolina, Sept. 20, Mecklenburg county. R. R. Oct. 15, 1829
Hoover, George, Sr., Jan. 11, Davidson county. R. R. Feb. 6, 1829
Hoover, Mrs., Jan. 9, Davidson county. R. R. Feb. 6, 1829
Howard, Mrs. Henry B., Mar. 14, Wilmington. R. R. Mar. 20, 1829
Howard, Mrs. John, Jly. 13, Rowan county. R. R. Jly. 30, 1829
Hoyle, Laban I. of Lincoln county, Feb. 24, University of Virginia. R. R. Mar. 27, 1829
Hudler, Mrs. Fred, Nov., Newbern. R. R. Nov. 26, 1829
Hughes, Mrs. Judith of this State, Dec. 24, Mecklenburg county, Va. R. R. Jan. 9, 1829
Hughes, Wm. C., Sept. 16, Warren county. R. R. Oct. 1, 1829
Hunt, Mrs. Nathan, Aug., Guilford county. R. R. Aug. 6, 1829
Hunter, Mrs. Jacob, Sept. 21, Wake county. R. R. Oct. 8, 1829
Hunter, William H., Nov. 9, Raleigh. R. R. Nov. 12, 1829
Huntington, Minor of Connecticut, Nov., Newbern. R. R. Nov. 26, 1829
Hyman, Samuel, Feb. 19, Williamston. R. R. Mar. 20, 1829
Irwin, John A., My. 8, Tarborough. R. R. My. 15, 1829
Irwin, Mrs. Robert, Dec., Guilford county. R. R. Jan. 2, 1829
Irwin, Mrs. Sarah, My. 13, Tarborough. R. R. My. 15, 1829
Jacobs, Benjamin, Je., Wilmington. R. R. Je. 12, 1829
Jacobs, Benj., Nov. 12, Wilmington. R. R. Nov. 26, 1829
Jacobs, Jos., of Wilmington & Massachusetts, Sept. 25, Cumberland county. R. R. Oct. 8, 1829
Johnson, Joshua, Aug., Guilford county. R. R. Aug. 6, 1829
Jones, Albrighton, My. 17, Wake county. R. R. My. 22, 1829
Jones, David, My., Bladen county. R. R. My. 22, 1829
Jones, Mrs. James, Jr., My. 30, Halifax county. R. R. Je. 12, 1829
Jones, Mrs. John, My. 10, Buncombe county. R. R. Je. 12, 1829
Joseph, Solomon M., Sept., Washington, Beaufort county. R. R. Oct. 1, 1829
Kilpatrick, Mrs. Elizabeth, My. 7, Rowan county. R. R. My. 22, 1829
Kilpatrick, Rev. Jos. D., Oct., Rutherford county. R. R. Oct. 8, 1829

Kirkpatrick, Hugh G., Aug. 29, Mecklenburg county. R. R. Sept. 17, 1829
Kirtland, Mrs. H. L., Oct., Edgecombe county. R. R. Nov. 12, 1829
Knox, Catharine, Sept., Camden county. R. R. Oct. 1, 1829
Knox, Elizabeth, Sept., Camden county. R. R. Oct. 1, 1829
Knox, LayFayette, Sept., Camden county. R. R. Oct. 1, 1829
Lain, Winston Asbury, Sept. 7, Fayetteville. R. R. Sept. 17, 1829
Legon, Mrs. Francis, Mar. 6, New Hanover county. R. R. Mar. 27, 1829
Leonard, Mrs. John P. of Fayetteville, Oct. 13, Bladen county. R. R. Oct. 29, 1829
Lewis, Francis, Feb. 24, New Hanover county. R. R. Mar. 27, 1829
Lilly, Wm., Apr. 26, Northampton county. R. R. My. 8, 1829
Little, William P., Jly. 19, Warren county. R. R. Jly. 30, 1829
Locke, Mrs. Richard, Mar. 6, Rowan county. R. R. Mar. 27, 1829
London, Rufus Marsden, Sept. 18, Wilmington. R. R. Oct. 1, 1829
Long, Mrs. Henry W., Oct. 2, Murfreesboro. R. R. Oct. 29, 1829
Long, John S., Dec., Rowan county. R. R. Jan. 9, 1829
Love, Maria Caroline, Sept. 5, South Washington. R. R. Sept. 24, 1829
Lovet, Joseph, Jr., Sept. 29, Guilford county. R. R. Oct. 15, 1829
Lowry, James, Feb. 6, Rowan county. R. R. Feb. 27, 1829
Lumsden, Mrs. John, Feb. 13, Fayetteville. R. R. Feb. 27, 1829
M'Cauley, Robert, Mar., Orange county. R. R. Mar. 13, 1829
M'Connaughey, Mrs. Ann, Je., Rowan county. R. R. Je. 12, 1829
M'Dade, Mrs. Willis, Apr. 1, Wake county. R. R. Apr. 17, 1829
M'Daniel, Malachi, Oct. 18, Orange county. R. R. Oct. 29, 1829
M'Intyre, James of Scotland, Sept., Fayetteville. R. R. Sept. 17, 1829
M'Laurin, Mrs. Mary, Feb. 25, Richmond county. R. R. Mar. 27, 1829
M'Lean, Mrs. John, Sept. 25, Lincoln county. R. R. Oct. 29, 1829
M'Lean, John Sr., Sept. 16, Iredell county. R. R. Oct. 15, 1829
M'Leod, Mrs. of this State, Oct. 7, Mobile, Alabama. R. R. Nov. 5, 1829
M'Leod, Nancy of this State, Oct. 8, Mobile, Alabama. R. R. Nov. 5, 1829
M'Nairy, Mrs. James, Sept., Guilford county. R. R. Sept. 17, 1829
M'Neill, Daniel, Mar., Moore county. R. R. Apr. 17, 1829
M'Neill, Alexander D., Sept. 12, Cumberland county. R. R. Sept. 17, 1829
M'Neill, Dr. Daniel of this State & Baltimore, Dec. 8, Bladen county. R. R. Jan. 9, 1829
M'Racken, Mrs. of Scotland, Oct. 3, Cumberland county. R. R. Oct. 8, 1829
Mallett, Mrs. C. P., Mar. 13, Fayetteville. R. R. Mar. 20, 1829
Martin, William J., Oct. 16, Wake county. R. R. Oct. 22, 1829
Menzies, Capt. Robert of Leaksville, Jan. 7, Wentworth. R. R. Jan. 30, 1829
Miller, James, Jan., Jones county. R. R. Jan. 23, 1829
Miller, Mrs. James, Dec., Rutherfordton. R. R. Jan. 9, 1829
Mitchell, Francis, of Milton, Sept. 10, Greensboro. R. R. Oct. 1, 1829
Moore, Alfred, Jan. 20, Hertford, Perquimans county. R. R. Feb. 6, 1829
Moore, W., Sept. 2, Franklin. R. R. Sept. 10, 1829
Murdock, William, Jly. 14, Iredell county. R. R. Aug. 6, 1829
Murphy, Mrs. A. D., Apr. 8, Orange county. R. R. Apr. 24, 1829
Neely, Francis, Nov., Rowan county. R. R. Nov. 26, 1829
Norman, George, My., Granville county. R. R. My. 8, 1829
Oakes, Thomas, Oct. 16, Rowan county. R. R. Nov. 5, 1829
Oates, Mrs. John, Oct. 9, Lincoln county. R. R. Oct. 29, 1829

O'Daniel, Henry, Sr., Oct. 16, Orange county. R. R. Oct. 29, 1829
Ogburn, Ch. P., of Guilford county, Sept. 18, Henry county, Va. R. R. Oct. 15, 1829
Olmsted, Mrs. of Chapel Hill, My. 4, New Haven. R. R. Jly. 9, 1829
Ormond, James, Mar. 3, Greene county. R. R. Mar. 20, 1829
Osborne, Dr. F. W. H. of North Carolina, Sept. 30, Mobile, Alabama. R. R. Nov. 12, 1829
Overman, Charles, Feb., Pasquotank county. R. R. Feb. 20, 1829
Parisho, Joshua, Apr., Elizabeth City. R. R. My. 1, 1829
Parker, Isaac, Apr. 18, Wilmington. R. R. My. 1, 1829
Parker, William, Aug. 14, Bladen county. R. R. Aug. 20, 1829
Parks, Martha, Nov. 29, Charlotte. R. R. Dec. 10, 1829
Parsons, Mrs. Thomas, Sept. 30, Guilford county. R. R. Oct. 15, 1829
Patrick, John Menan, My., Greene county. R. R. My. 22, 1829
Patterson, John, Jr., Aug. 29, Mecklenburg county. R. R. Sept. 17, 1829
Pearce, Jesse, My., Craven county. R. R. My. 15, 1829
Peebles, Geo., Sept., Halifax county. R. R. Oct. 1, 1829
Perry, Green of Franklin county, Oct. 14, Putnam county, Ga. R. R. Dec. 3, 1829
Phifer, John F., Dec. 27, Cabarrus county. R. R. Jan. 16, 1829
Pierret, John of France, Je., Warrenton. R. R. Je. 12, 1829
Pittman, Oliver, Sept., Edgecombe county. R. R. Oct. 1, 1829
Poitevent, Mrs. John, Je. 8, Brunswick county. R. R. Jly. 2, 1829
Pool, Solomon, Sr., Pasquotank county. R. R. Je. 12, 1829
Powell, John, Oct., Swansborough, Onslow county. R. R. Oct. 22, 1829
Powell, Mrs. John, Nov., Newbern. R. R. Nov. 26, 1829
Powell, Reuben of Halifax county, Aug. 27, Greensville county, Va. R. R. Sept. 10, 1829
Prevo, Thomas, Aug. 4, Randolph county. R. R. Aug. 13, 1829
Pyle, John S. of Chatham county, Sept., Fayetteville. R. R. Sept. 10, 1829
Raboteau, Mrs. John S. Sr., of Raleigh, Nov., Franklin county. R. R. Nov. 5, 1829
Rankin, Mrs. Jesse, Oct. 28, Salisbury. R. R. Nov. 12, 1829
Rankin, William G., Sept. 17, Guilford county. R. R. Oct. 1, 1829
Ravenscroft, Mrs. Sarah, Jan. 15, Bladen county. R. R. Aug. 20, 1829
Reaves, Edward, Aug. 3, Bladen county. R. R. Aug. 20, 1829
Reddit, Mrs. Alfred J., of Washington, Beaufort county, My. 11, Jackson, Tenn. R. R. Jly. 16, 1829
Reed, Mrs. Ellis Barbara, Oct. 18, Stokes county. R. R. Nov. 5, 1829
Reed, Mrs. Wm., Oct. 3, Perquimans county. R. R. Oct. 29, 1829
Reichel, Capt. Augustus of Charleston, S. C., Oct. 5, Wilmington. R. R. Oct. 15, 1829
Remoussian, Capt. Augustus of Charleston, S. C., Oct. 5, Wilmington. R. R. Oct. 15, 1829
Rice, Mrs. Thomas, Sept., Greensboro. R. R. Oct. 1, 1829
Rich, Mrs. Peter, Sept. 13, Randolph county. R. R. Oct. 15, 1829
Richardson, Rev. James of Bladen county, Sept. 5, Moulter, Alabama. R. R. Nov. 5, 1829
Ricks, Capt. David, My. 24, Nash county. R. R. Jly. 9, 1829
Ridley, Mrs. Thomas D., Nov. 1, Granville county. R. R. Nov. 12, 1829
Riley, Thomas of Orange county, Je. 13, Tenn. R. R. Sept. 10, 1829

Robbins, Mrs. Elizabeth Ann of Warrenton, Apr., New York. R. R. My. 8, 1829
Robinson, Pleasant of Guilford county, Sept. 5, Columbus, Ga. R. R. Oct. 8, 1829
Robertson, Capt. John of this State, Jan. 1, Madison county, Tenn. R. R. Feb. 6, 1829
Robinson, Mrs. George, Aug. 20, Rowan county. R. R. Sept. 4, 1829
Rouse, Alex, Sept. 7, Wilmington. R. R. Sept. 24, 1829
Rowland, Gen. Alfred, Apr. 4, Lumberton. R. R. Apr. 10, 1829
Ruffin, William of Raleigh, My., Hanover county, Va. R. R. My. 8, 1829
Ruffner, William H. of Pennsylvania, Nov. 8, Wilmington. R. R. Nov. 19, 1829
Rumley, Jane, Aug. 4, Beaufort. R. R. Aug. 20, 1829
Salmon, David D. Jr., Oct. 10, Fayetteville. R. R. Oct. 29, 1829
Sanders, Reuben of Johnston county, Dec. 28, Raleigh. R. R. Dec. 31, 1829
Sessoms, Isaac, Aug., Bladen county. R. R. Aug. 20, 1829
Settle, Mrs. Joseph, Oct. 7, Rockingham county. R. R. Nov. 19, 1829
Shaw, Mrs. A. of Newport, R. I., Aug., Tyrrell county. R. R. Aug. 13, 1829
Shaw, Daniel, Dec. 15, Cumberland county. R. R. Jan. 9, 1829
Sheppard, Dr. James H. of Orange county, Nov., Hardeman county, Tenn. R. R. Dec. 31, 1829
Sherley, James of Caswell county, My. 16, Natchez Mississippi. R. R. Jly. 23, 1829
Sherrill, Mrs. Jacob, Nov. 10, Lincoln county. R. R. Dec. 31, 1829
Skinner, Joshua, Sept. 20, Perquimans county. R. R. Oct. 8, 1829
Sims, Mrs. William, Feb. 28, Wake county. R. R. Mar. 6, 1829
Sloan, Capt. Robert, Feb. 20, Charlotte. R. R. Feb. 27, 1829
Sloan, Mrs., Jan., Hillsboro. R. R. Jan. 23, 1829
Smith, Charles of Virginia, Aug. 14, Surry county. R. R. Sept. 4, 1829
Smith, Mrs. James N., Jan. 16, Jones county. R. R. Jan. 30, 1829
Smith, Robert, Aug. 3, Raleigh. R. R. Aug. 6, 1829
Smith, Wm. of Virginia, Feb. 4, Chatham county. R. R. Feb. 13, 1829
Sneed, Maj. A. H. of Granville county, Sept. 19, Washington, Ga. R. R. Oct. 8, 1829
Snively, Jos., Je., Fayetteville. R. R. Je. 26, 1829
Snode, Mrs. Samuel, Sept., Washington. R. R. Sept. 17, 1829
Springs, Capt. William P., Nov. 29, Charlotte. R. R. Dec. 10, 1829
Stallings, William, Apr. 6, Duplin county. R. R. Apr. 24, 1829
Stanly, Mrs. Richard D., Jan. 5, Newbern. R. R. Jan. 18, 1829
Staton, Redding, Oct., Edgecombe county. R. R. Nov. 12, 1829
Stevens, Jos., Sept. 3, Sampson county. R. R. Sept. 17, 1829
Stevenson, Simon, My. 29, Wake county. R. R. Je. 5, 1829
Stewart Mrs. Maria Lee of Bladen county, Apr. 15, Chippola, Florida. R. R. My. 15, 1829
Stublefield, Carter, Je. 8, Rockingham. R. R. Je. 26, 1829
Sumner, Charles E. of Gates county, Mar. 15, Nansemond county, Va. R. R. Apr. 5, 1829
Tanner, Joseph of Warren county, Oct. 20, Anson county. R. R. Nov. 5, 1829
Taylor, Mrs. Ann of Scotland and Fayetteville, Nov. 27, Raleigh. R. R. Dec. 3, 1829

Taylor, Chief Justice John Louis, Jan. 29, Raleigh. R. R. Feb. 6, 1829
Taylor, Mrs. Kinchen, My. 27, Nash county. R. R. Je. 26, 1829
Tharp, Deborah, Sept. 11, Guilford county. R. R. Oct. 1, 1829
Thomas, James O. K., Aug. 22, Franklin county. R. R. Sept. 4, 1829
Thomas, John, Je., Iredell county. R. R. Je. 12, 1829
Thomas, Mrs. Norfleet H., Sept. 1, Halifax county. R. R. Sept. 10, 1829
Thomas, Rev. Christopher of Mathews county, Va., Nov. 14, Newbern. R. R. Nov. 26, 1829
Tomlinson, Mrs. James, Aug. 27, Johnston county. R. R. Sept. 10, 1829
Troy, Mrs. Matthew, Mar. 25, Salisbury. R. R. Apr. 17, 1829
Umstead, Dr. John of Pennsylvania, Apr. 4, Orange county. R. R. Apr. 5, 1829
Varden, Wilson, Jly. 25, Pasquotank county. R. R. Aug. 13, 1829
Waddell, Mrs. Hugh Y., Nov., Wilmington. R. R. Nov. 19, 1829
Wade, Mrs. Freeman, Nov., Newbern. R. R. Nov. 26, 1829
Wade, William, My. 26, Rutherford county. R. R. Je. 26, 1829
Wadsworth, Mrs. Thomas, Sept. 1, Craven county. R. R. Sept. 10, 1829
Walden, Mrs. Agnes, My., Elizabeth City. R. R. My. 22, 1829
Walker, Col. Hugh, Je. 12, Randolph county. R. R. Je. 26, 1829
Wallace, William, My. 21, Mecklenburg county. R. R. Je. 26, 1829
Wallace, William, My. 21, Salisbury. R. R. Jly. 2, 1829
Walton, Mrs. William, Jan. 29, Rowan county. R. R. Feb. 20, 1829
Ware, David of this State, Oct., Mobile, Alabama. R. R. Nov. 5, 1829
Watt, John, Oct. 20, Rockingham county. R. R. Nov. 12, 1829
Webb, William E., My. 30, Halifax county. R. R. Je. 12, 1829
White, Cynthia W. of this State, Feb., Knoxville, Tenn. R. R. Feb. 20, 1829
White, Mrs. Henry, Sept., Perquimans county. R. R. Oct. 8, 1829
White, Mrs. Joseph, Sept., Pasquotank county. R. R. Oct. 8, 1829
Whitesette, John of Rockingham county, Oct. 24, Jones county, Ga. R. R. Nov. 12, 1829
Williams, Benj., Oct. 22, Washington. R. R. Nov. 5, 1829
Williams, John A. of Raleigh, Jan. 9, Greene county, Alabama. R. R. Feb. 6, 1829
Williams, Mrs. Robert, Jr., Oct. 23, Pitt county. R. R. Nov. 12, 1829
Williams, Dr. Robt. J., Sept. 29, Warren county. R. R. Oct. 1, 1829
Williams, Gen. Wm., My. 3, Martin county. R. R. My. 22, 1829
Willis, Capt. Elijah, Mar. 10, Newbern. R. R. Mar. 27, 1829
Wilson, William, Sept., Camden county. R. R. Oct. 1, 1829
Winslow, Mrs. Edward L., Oct. 11, Fayetteville. R. R. Oct. 22, 1829
Wood, Daniel, Je., Rowan county. R. R. Je. 19, 1829
Woodward, Baker of Morganton, Feb., Covington, Tipton county, Tenn. R. R. Feb. 20, 1829
Wright, Dr. John Louis, Nov. 22, Wilmington. R. R. Dec. 3, 1829
Wright, William Grady, My. 10, Bladen county. R. R. My. 29, 1829
Yancey, Mrs. Charles, Je. 10, Chapel Hill. R. R. Je. 26, 1829
Yancey, Rufus A. of Caswell county, Oct., Richmond, Va. R. R. Nov. 12, 1829
Yancey, James, Oct. 27, Caswell Court House. R. R. Dec. 3, 1829

1830

Airey, John, Apr 29, Salisbury   R. R. My. 13, 1830
Alexander, Adam of this State, Nov., Georgia.   R. R. Dec. 2, 1830
Allen, Frances of Newbern, Je. 14, Raleigh.   R. R. Je. 17, 1830
Allen, Mary of Newbern, Je. 13, Raleigh.   R. R. Je. 17, 1830
Allison, Thomas, Sept. 13, Iredell county.   R. R. Sept. 30, 1830
Andrews, John, Apr., Rowan county.   R. R. Apr. 29, 1830
Bagge, Mrs. C. F., Oct. 14, Stokes county.   R. R. Oct. 28, 1830
Baker, Agatha, Aug. 11, Martin county.   R. R. Aug. 26, 1830
Baker, Blake, Je. 14, Warren county.   R. R. Jly. 29, 1830
Baker, Michael B., Dec., Rutherfordton.   R. R. Dec. 9, 1830
Ballinger, Temple of Guilford county, Mar. 25, Indiana.   R. R. Apr. 29, 1830
Barge, Lewis, Jly. 25, Robeson county.   R. R. Aug. 5, 1830
Barnet, Mrs. Jesse, Dec. 13, Granville county.   R. R. Jan. 28, 1830
Beard, Mrs. John, Jr., Oct. 6, Salisbury.   R. R. Oct. 14, 1830
Beatty, Thomas, Mar. 29, Wilmington.   R. R. Apr. 29, 1830
Bell, Marmaduke N., Feb. 22, Edgecombe county.   R. R. Mar. 18, 1830
Bell, Thomas, Sr., Sept. 18, Chatham county.   R. R. Sept. 30, 1830
Best, Benjamin, Jr., Nov., Wilmington.   R. R. Nov. 18, 1830
Blum, David, Aug. 7, Stokes county.   R. R. Oct. 7, 1830
Brackett, Adkins, Nov., Burke county.   R. R. Nov. 4, 1830
Buie, Archibald W. of Cumberland county, Je. 6, Hillsborough.   R. R. Jly. 31, 1830
Burgwin, George P. A., Jan. 26, Newbern.   R. R. Feb. 4, 1830
Burnham, Mrs. John, Nov. 1, Wake Forest.   R. R. Nov. 11, 1830
Burns, Mrs. Geo., Sept. 8, Granville county.   R. R. Oct. 21, 1830
Burns, John of Ireland, Feb. 10, Buncombe county.   R. R. Je. 3, 1830
Buxton, Mrs. James B., Nov. 25, Elizabeth City.   R. R. Dec. 9, 1830
Caldwell, Dr. of Charlotte, Nov., Lexington, Ky.   R. R. Nov. 18, 1830
Cameron, Mrs. Esther of Wilmington, Jly. 30, Raleigh.   R. R. Aug. 5, 1830
Chambers, Otho, Nov. 7, Salisbury.   R. R. Dev. 9, 1830
Cherry, Lemuel, Mar. 24, Washington, Beaufort county.   R. R. Apr. 15, 1830
Cheshire, John, Jan. 17, Edenton.   R. R. Mar. 1, 1830
Childs, Mrs. Eliza, Jly. 30, Raleigh.   R. R. Aug. 5, 1830
Clemmons, Mrs. James, Jan. 10, Guilford county.   R. R. Feb. 4, 1830
Clemmons, Mrs. Lydia, Jan. 10, Guilford county.   R. R. Jan. 28, 1830
Cluff, Mary, Mar., Elizabeth City.   R. R. Mar. 18, 1830
Connelly, Jacob S., Aug., Burke county.   R. R. Sept. 9, 1830
Cotton, Godwin, Je. 5, Hertford county.   R. R. Jly. 8, 1830
Cranford, Leonard, Apr. 13, Montgomery conty.   R. R. My. 13, 1830
Crosby, Tirza, Sept. 19, Rowan county.   R. R. Oct. 14, 1830
Crosby, Mrs. William, Sept. 13, Rowan county.   R. R. Oct. 14, 1830
Curtis, Anderson of Raleigh, Aug., Fayetevile.   R. R. Sept. 2, 1830
Drake, Mrs. N. J., Dec. 1, Greensboro.   R. R. Dec. 9, 1830
Dudley, William, Mar. 16, Newbern.   R. R. Mar. 23, 1830
Dunbibin, Mrs. Julius C., Mar. 18, Wilmington.   R. R. Apr. 1, 1830
Eaton, Major John R., Je., Granville county.   R. R. Je. 24, 1830
Ellison, Mrs. Henry, Nov., Washington, Beaufort county.   R. R. Nov. 11, 1830

Erwin, Elam Alphonso, Nov. 7, Morganton. R. R. Dec. 2, 1830
Ferrand, Dr. Stephen L., Nov. 15. R. R. Dec. 9, 1830
Fields, David L. of Guilford county, Sept. 11. R. R. Sept. 16, 1830
Fleming, Thomas, Mar., Warren county. R. R. Apr. 1, 1830
Ford, Mrs. Frederick, Apr., Rowan county. R. R. Apr. 29, 1830
Fuller, Mary, Jan. 16, Franklin county. R. R. Jan. 28, 1830
Graham, Andrew of Rowan, Sept., Athen, Ga. R. R. Sept. 23, 1830
Graham, Capt. Richard, Aug. 12, Rowan county. R. R. Sept. 9, 1830
Hamilton, Mrs. James, Mar. 27, Granville county. R. R. Apr. 1, 1830
Hargrave, Jesse, Jly. 23, Lexington. R. R. Aug. 12, 1830
Harris, Mrs. Sam'l S., Feb. 26, Cabarrus county. R. R. Mar. 18, 1830
Harrison, John W., Oct., Northampton county. R. R. Oct. 28, 1830
Harvey, Mrs. Edmond B., Aug. 14, Hertford county. R. R. Oct. 7, 1830
Haskell, John of New York, Mar., Wilmington. R. R. Mar. 18, 1830
Hearsey, Mrs. George T. of Fayetteville, Mar. 9, New Orleans. R. R. Apr. 15, 1830
Heath, Major Chapel, Dec., Halifax. R. R. Dec. 9, 1830
Helfer, Capt. Daniel, Nov., Rowan county. R. R. Dec. 2, 1830
Helme, Dr. R. H. Feb. 23, Smithfield. R. R. Mar. 1, 1830
Helper, Daniel, Nov. 5, Rowan county. R. R. Nov. 18, 1830
Henderson, Rich'd B., Feb. 15, Williamsborough. R. R. Feb. 25, 1830
Hill, Jordan, Aug. 15, Louisburg. R. R. Aug. 26, 1830
Hillyard, Elizabeth W., Aug. 4, Granville county. R. R. Sept. 23, 1830
Hogg, Mrs. Gavin, Dec. 3, Raleigh. R. R. Dec. 9, 1830
Holmes, Thomas of Salisbury, Je., Tuscaloosa, Ala. R. R. Je. 17, 1830
Hooks, Eveline Jane Amanda, Je. 25, Johnston county. R. R. Jly. 15, 1830
Hutchinson, Mrs. George, Sept. 15, Mecklenburg county. R. R. Oct. 21, 1830.
Jenkins, Mrs. Frances, Aug., Pitt county. R. R. Sept. 9, 1830
Jones, David, Mar. 1, Wilmington. R. R. Mar. 18, 1830
Jones, George, Apr. 26, Wilkesboro. R. R. My. 27, 1830
Jones, Nicholas, My. 18, Orange county. R. R. Je. 10, 1830
Jordan, Rev. John, Aug., Chowan county. R. R. Aug. 19, 1830
Johnson, Charles of Warren county, Aug 12, West Hill, Wake county. R. R. Aug. 19, 1830
Justice, John, Je., Buncombe county. R. R. Je. 10, 1830
Kerner, Joseph, Je. 9, Stokes county. R. R. Je. 31, 1830
Kerr, Mrs. George of Hillsborough, Je., Tuscaloosa, Ala. R. R. Je. 17, 1830
King, Catharine of New York, Jan. 18, Moore county. R. R. Jan. 28, 1830
Kirkpatrick, Rev. Josiah James, Jly. 25, Fayetteville. R. R. Aug. 5, 1830
Knight, Andrew, Apr., Caswell county. R. R. Apr. 15, 1830
Lewis, Hart of Connecticut, Dec., Orange county. R. R. Dec. 9, 1830
Lewis, Major John E., Aug. 31, Caswell county. R. R. Sept. 9, 1830
Lewis, Col. Willis of Granville county, Nov. 19, Bolivar, Tenn. R. R. Dec. 2, 1830
Lloyd, Richard, Je., Wilmington. R. R. Jly. 31, 1830
Locke, Matthew, Jan. 7, Salisbury. R. R. Jan. 28, 1830
Love, Capt. Joseph of Macon county, Jly., Madison county, Tenn. R. R. Jly. 15, 1830
Lowrance, Sarah, Jan. 28, Iredell county. R. R. Feb. 25, 1830

M'Allister, Mrs. Charles, Aug., Bladen county. R. R. Sept. 2, 1830
M'Arn, Archibald, Jan. 11, Richmond county. R. R. Jan. 28, 1830
M'Aulay, Dr. John of Moore county, Mar. 16, Fayetteville. R. R. Mar. 22, 1830
M'Cain, Joseph, Aug. 26, Rockingham county. R. R. Apr. 29, 1830
M'Coy, Alexander of Scotland, Sept., Iredell county. R. R. Sept. 23, 1830
M'Donald, Alexander of Scotland, Jan., Fayetteville. R. R. Feb. 4, 1830
M'Entire, Mrs. Nancy of Ireland, Je. 12, Morganton. R. R. Je. 31, 1830
M'Ilhenny, Elizabeth, Nov., Wilmington. R. R. Nov. 18, 1830
M'Kay, Neill, Sept., Cumberland county. R. R. Sept. 9, 1830
M'Lean, Dan'l, Je., Cumberland county. R. R. Je. 17, 1830
M'Millan, John, Aug., Richmond county. R. R. Sept. 2, 1830
M'Neil, James, My. 16, Cumberland county. R. R. My. 27, 1830
M'Rae, Mrs. Daniel, Jan., Fayetteville. R. R. Jan. 28, 1830
Mahan, John E., Aug. 26, Concord, Cabarrus county. R. R. Sept. 9, 1830
Marsh, Sarah, Jan. 8, Cumberland county. R. R. Feb. 4, 1830
Mallett, Peter James, Apr. 26, Raleigh. R. R. Apr. 29, 1830
Matthews, Major Mussendine, Mar. 17, Iredell county. R. R. Apr. 1, 1830
Miall, Thomas, Je., Wake county. R. R. Jly. 1, 1830
Miles, Mrs. W. H. of Raleigh, Sept., Spartanburg, S. C. R. R. Sept. 16, 1830
Moore, Mrs. James, Aug. 15, Halifax county. R. R. Sept. 2, 1830
Moore, James of Granville county, Nov. 1, Bedford county, Tenn. R. R. Dec. 9, 1830
Morris, Col. Aquilla, Mar. 15, Halifax county. R. R. Mar. 23, 1830
Moss, Robert, Apr. 4, Montgomery county. R. R. My. 13, 1830
Neily, Mrs. Thomas J. of Northampton county, Jly. 27, Fayette county, Tenn. R. R. Sept. 16, 1830
Newberry, Isaac, Jan., Fayetteville. R. R. Jan. 28, 1830
Oakes, Pleasant, Aug. 30, Rowan county. R. R. Sept. 23, 1830
Odeneal, Mrs. John, Apr., Rockingham county. R. R. Apr. 15, 1830
Osborne, Mrs. Adley, Sept. 23, Iredell county. R. R. Oct. 28, 1830
Paisley, Mary Ann, Jly. 23, Greensborough. R. R. Aug. 12, 1830
Parker, Elisha, Apr. 30, Chowan county. R. R. My. 13, 1830
Parks, Capt. Hugh, Jan. 12, Mecklenburg county. R. R. Jan. 28, 1830
Pettigrew, Mrs. Ebenezer, Jly. 1, Tyrrell county. R. R. Jly. 15, 1830
Pinkston, Wm. Sr., Aug. 23, Rowan county. R. R. Sept. 9, 1830
Pinkston, Mrs. William, Oct. 7, Rowan county. R. R. Oct. 14, 1830
Polk, Col. William, Sept. 9, Raleigh. R. R. Sept. 16, 1830
Poor, Edwin, Dec., Morganton. R. R. Dec. 9, 1830
Price, Thomas, Dec., Wake county. R. R. Dec. 16, 1830
Pugh, Mrs. Jane, Aug. 19, Randolph county. R. R. Sept. 16, 1830
Ravenscroft, Rt. Rev. John Stark, Mar. 5, Raleigh. R. R. Mar. 11, 1830
Rea, Patsey, Aug., Chowan county. R. R. Aug. 19, 1830
Robards, Lawrence, Nov., Rowan county. R. R. Dec. 2, 1830
Sanders, Col. John, Nov., Johnston county. R. R. Nov. 25, 1830
Satterfield, Henry B., Nov., Edenton. R. R. Nov. 11, 1830
Sharpe, James of Scotland, Je., Anson county. R. R. Je. 17, 1830
Sims, Allen, Feb. 4, Raleigh. R. R. Feb. 11, 1830
Slater, Mary, Jly., Scotland Neck. R. R. Jly. 8, 1830
Smith, David, Jly., Fayetteville. R. R. Jly. 8, 1830
Smith, David, Jr., Aug. 23, Wilmington. R. R. Sept. 2, 1830

Smith, Michael, Oct. 8, Rowan county. R. R. Oct. 14, 1830
Sneed, Dudley M., of Granville county, Sept. 19, Burke county. R. R. Oct. 21, 1830
Southall, Rev. Daniel of Murfreesborough, Nov., Washington, D. C. R. R. Nov. 11, 1830
Stanly, Jonathan, Nov., Wilmington. R. R. Nov. 18, 1830
Stewart, David, Apr., Rowan county. R. R. Apr. 29, 1830
Southerland, Jenny, Mar. 22, Fayetteville. R. R. Mar. 25, 1830
Taylor, Col. James, Feb. 24, Pittsborough. R. R. Mar. 11, 1830
Taylor, Reuben, Apr., Caswell county. R. R. Apr. 15, 1830
Terrell, Henry, Jan. 30, Wake county. R. R. Feb. 4, 1830
Thompson, Beverly J., Jly. 20, Lincolnton. R. R. Aug. 12, 1830
Thompson, Mrs. Henry, Dec., Hillsborough. R. R. Dec. 9, 1830
Thompson, John, Dec. 19, Guilford county. R. R. Jan. 7, 1830
Towns, Mrs. Joseph H. of Wilmington, Apr., Cheraw, S. C. R. R. Apr. 29, 1830
Turner, Mrs. James, Sept. 7, Wake county. R. R. Sept. 23, 1830
Tuten, James of Fayetteville, Sept., Robeson county. R. R. Sept. 9, 1830
Vines, Col. William, Oct. 6, Beaufort county. R. R. Oct. 21, 1830
Wagner, Mrs. William, Nov., Cabarrus county. R. R. Nov. 11, 1830
Wallace, Horatio, Oct. 2, Ocracoke. R. R. Oct. 14, 1830
Watt, Thompson, Aug. 5, Rockingham county. R. R. Aug. 19, 1830
Williams, Mrs. John, Feb. 16, Rowan county. R. R. Mar. 18, 1830
Williams, John, Sept. 3, Wake county. R. R. Sept. 9, 1830
Williams, Mrs. Wm., Jly. 8, Martin county. R. R. Jly. 15, 1830
Wilson, Sarah, Aug., Cabarrus county. R. R. Sept. 9, 1830
Wingate, Mrs. Jesse, Jan. 19, Wilmington. R. R. Jan. 28, 1830
Winston, Mrs. George of Franklin county, Jan., York District, S. C. R. R. Mar. 11, 1830
Worth, Mrs. Judith of Nantucket, Oct. 25, Guilford county. R. R. Nov. 11, 1830
Wright, Dr. William W. of Nansemond county, Va., Feb. 24, Pasquotank county. R. R. Mar. 18, 1830
Yancey, Mrs. Charles, Je., Granville county. R. R. Je. 24, 1830
Zink, Jacob, Aug. 9, Lexington. R. R. Sept. 9, 1830

1831

Adams, John Meredith, Jly 15, Hillsboro. R. R. Aug. 4, 1831
Alston, Gen. John, Mar. 21, Halifax county. R. R. Apr. 14, 1831
Armistead, Anthony, Feb. 26, Plymouth. R. R. Mar. 24, 1831
Arnot, David of Scotland, Mar., Halifax county. R. R. Mar. 31, 1831
Avera, Alexander of Cumberland county, Jan., Wake county. R. R. Jan. 20, 1831
Avera, Moses, Oct., Averasborough, Cumberland county. R. R. Oct. 13, 1831
Baker, Lawrence of Halifax county, Sept. 5. R. R. Sept. 15, 1831
Barge, Mrs. Lewis, Apr. 19, Robeson county. R. R. Apr. 21, 1831
Belden, Simeon, Je., Fayetteville. R. R. Je. 9, 1831
Birdsall, Stephen, Sept. 18, Raleigh. R. R. Sept. 29, 1831
Bozman, James, Mar. 9, Edenton. R. R. Mar. 31, 1831

Branson, Henry, Sr., of Randolph county, Oct., Fayetteville. R. R. Oct. 27, 1831
Brock, John H. Oct. 9, Craven county. R. R. Nov. 3, 1831
Buffalow, William, Aug. 26, Raleigh. R. R. Sept. 1, 1831
Buie, Capt. Alex, My. 1, Cumberland county. R. R. My. 5, 1831
Bunn, Willie, Nov., Nash county. R. R. Nov. 10, 1831
Burney, Mrs. James of Columbus county, My. 3, Raleigh. R. R. My. 5, 1831
Burton, Mrs. Robert, Jan. 31, Granville county. R. R. Feb. 10, 1831
Calhorda, John P. of Portugal, Sept., Wilmington. R. R. Oct. 6, 1831
Cannon, Dr. Wm. B. of Cabarrus county, Jly., Missouri. R. R. Jly. 21, 1831
Carter, William, Sept., Chatham county. R. R. Sept. 29, 1831
Chamness, Mrs. John, Oct. 21, Greensborough. R. R. Nov. 3, 1831
Chandler, Rev. Stephen, Jly. 31, Caswell county. R. R. Aug. 25, 1831
Coman, Mrs. James, Aug. 9, Raleigh. R. R. Aug. 11, 1831
Cowan, Col. Thomas of Maryland, Apr., Wilmington. R. R. Apr. 21, 1831
Crawford, Wm. of Moore county, Feb., Wilmington. R. R. Feb. 24, 1831
Daniel, Mrs. R. J. J., Aug., Halifax. R. R. Aug. 11, 1831
Davis, Imri, Oct. 4, Raleigh. R. R. Oct. 13, 1831
Devanne, Thomas, Jan. 27, New Hanover county. R. R. Mar. 17, 1831
Devereux, Susan Edwards, My. 25, Raleigh. R. R. Je. 2, 1831
Digges, Marshall, Sr., of Virginia, My. 3, Anson county. R. R. My. 5, 1831
Dilliard, Lydia, Jly. 17, Orfange county. R. R. Jly. 21, 1831
Donnell, Mrs. John R., Sept. 3, Newbern. R. R. Sept. 15, 1831
Drake, Dr. Nicholas, Jan. 15, Nash county. R. R. Jan. 27, 1831
Edmondson, Bryan, Oct. 22, Newbern. R. R. Nov. 3, 1831
Ellis, Col. John S. of Raleigh, Oct., Newbern. R. R. Oct. 13, 1831
Ellis, Mrs. John, Jr., Aug. 23, Johnston county. R. R. Sept. 1, 1831
Ellis, Rufus, My. 13, Rowan county. R. R. Je. 9, 1831
England, Mrs. William of Fayetteville, Apr. 4, Moore county. R. R. Apr. 21, 1831
Fearing, Sarah Frances, Jan., Elizabeth City. R. R. Jan. 20, 1831
Fleming, Mrs. James, My. 3, Wilmington. R. R. My. 25,.1831
Flury, Henry, My., Edenton. R. R. My. 25, 1831
Gibson, Dr. William M., Aug. 14, Germantown, Stokes county. R. R. Aug. 25, 1831
Goneke, Mrs. John F., of Raleigh, Jly., Columbia, Tenn. R. R. Aug. 4, 1831
Gianople, Mrs. John E., Feb., Wilmington. R. R. Feb. 24, 1831
Graton, Col. Isaac, Apr. 19, Rutherfordton. R. R. My. 5, 1831
Gunter, Elder, Oct. 22, Chatham county. R. R. Oct. 27, 1831
Hall, Almond, Feb. 4, Rowan county. R. R. Feb. 24, 1831
Hall, George A., Apr. 26, Newbern. R. R. My. 5, 1831
Hall, John, Jr., Sept. 9, Rutherfordton. R. R. Sept. 15, 1831
Harris, Mrs. John of Core creek, Oct. 13, Bertie county. R. R. Oct. 20, 1831
Henderson, Dr. James M. of Raleigh, Jly. 21, Carroll county, Tenn. R. R. Sept. 15, 1831
Higgs, Mrs. Joseph, Nov., Halifax county. R. R. Nov. 3, 1831
Higgs, Mrs. Willie, Je. 16, Halifax county. R. R. Jly. 28, 1831
Hill, Rev. Charles A., Jly. 17, Franklin county. R. R. Jly. 28, 1831
Hinton, Lewis, Oct. 21, Chatham county. R. R. Nov. 3, 1831
Hinton, Mrs. William, Sept., Wake county. R. R. Sept. 15, 1831

Hodge, Capt. Arthur, Jly., Newbern. R. R. Jly. 14, 1831
Hodges, Geo., Apr. 23, Averasborough. R. R. My. 5, 1831
Hollowell, Eli., Nov., Edgecombe county. R. R. Nov. 3, 1831
Holmes, Mrs. Henry, Aug. 7, Craven county. R. R. Aug. 25, 1831
Hunter, Isaiah of Swift creek, Oct., Wake county. R. R. Oct. 13, 1831
Hunter, Joseph of Swift creek, Oct., Wake county. R. R. Oct. 13, 1831
Ingram, Capt. Alexander H., Apr. 7, Mecklenburg county. R. R. My. 5, 1831
Justice, John of Newbern, Oct. 13, Bertie county. R. R. Oct. 20, 1831
Jones, Robert Allen, Sept. 20, Raleigh. R. R. Sept. 29, 1831
Kerr, Mrs. William, Oct. 19, Greensborough. R. R. Nov. 3, 1831
Lacy, Theophilus, Sr. of Rockingham county, Oct., Morgan county, Ala. R. R. Oct. 13, 1831
Lamb, Isaac N., Jan., Elizabeth City. R. R. Jan. 20, 1831
Lankford, John, Jan., Rutherford county. R. R. Feb. 3, 1831
Laroque, Mrs. J. B., Oct. 21, Trenton, Jones county. R. R. Nov. 3, 1831
Lea, Rev. James Madison of Caswell county, Nov. 7, Wake county. R. R. Nov. 10, 1831
Leak, Mrs. F. T., Sept., Rockingham. R. R. Sept. 15, 1831
Lewellen, William of Edgecombe county, Nov., Greenville, Pitt county. R. R. Nov. 3, 1831
Long, Mrs. Elizabeth, Jan., Halifax. R. R. Jan. 13, 1831
Lord, John of Wilmington, Aug. 28, Smithville. R. R. Sept. 1, 1831
Lowe, Anderson of Randolph county, Oct. 8, Camden, S. C. R. R. Oct. 20, 1831
Lumpkin, Mrs. Fleming, Oct. 13, Granville county. R. R. Nov. 3, 1831
M'Daniel, William, Jan., Caswell county. R. R. Jan. 13, 1831
M'Donald, Duncan, Apr. 1, Raleigh. R. R. Apr. 7, 1831
M'Donald, Kenneth, Oct., Fayetteville. R. R. Oct. 13, 1831
M'Dougald, Arch'd., Oct., Robeson county. R. R. Oct. 6, 1831
M'Gehee, Joseph of Milton, Caswell county, Oct. 8, Gates county. R. R. Oct. 27, 1831
M'Knight, Rev. James, Oct., Mecklenburg county. R. R. Oct. 6, 1831
M'Nair, Duncan, Oct., Robeson county. R. R. Oct. 6, 1831
M'Queen, Mrs. Archibald, My. 3, Robeson county. R. R. My. 25, 1831
M'Rae, Mrs. Alexander, Aug. 25, On the sound. R. R. Sept. 1, 1831
M'Ree, Dr. Griffith J., Feb., Wilmington. R. R. Mar. 3, 1831
Manly, Edward Dudley, Aug. 17, Raleigh. R. R. Aug. 18, 1831
Manly, Julia Ann, Aug. 27, Chatham county. R. R. Sept. 1, 1831
Mastin, Mrs. Jeremiah, Aug., Newbern. R. R. Aug. 25, 1831
Meenan, Daniel of Ireland, Sept. 29, Raleigh. R. R. Oct. 13, 1831
Meenan, Hugh of Charlotte, Mar. 16, St. Augustine, Fla. R. R. Apr. 28, 1831
Mendenhall, James, Oct. 28, Guilford county. R. R. Nov. 10, 1831
Miller, Major Alexander C., My., Bladen county. R. R. My. 25, 1831
Moseley, William, Apr. 10, Lenoir county. R. R. My. 5, 1831
Murphey, William D., Je. 26, Hillsborough. R. R. Jly. 7, 1831
Neill, Capt. William of Iredell county, Mar., Henderson county. R. R. Mar. 17, 1831
Nelson, Mrs. Frederick B. of Washington, Beaufort county, Jly., Alabama. R. R. Jly. 28, 1831

Nixon, Col. Richard of this State, Jan. 25, Haywood county, Tenn. R. R. Mar. 17, 1831
O'Fairhill, Dr. Barnabas Basil of Ireland, Feb., Hillsborough. R. R. Feb. 24, 1831
Parker, Elizabeth, Jly. 17, Montgomery county. R. R. Aug. 25, 1831
Patton, Col. John, Apr., Buncombe county. R. R. Apr. 14, 1831
Peacock, Mrs. Catharine, Jan. 4, Moore county. R. R. Jan. 20, 1831
Pemberton, Samuel, Oct., Lawrence, Montgomery county. R. R. Oct. 13, 1831
Perry, Mary of Wake county, Aug. 10, Catawba county. R. R. Oct. 6, 1831
Phifer, Mrs. Caleb, Apr., Cabarrus county. R. R. Apr. 28, 1831
Philpot, Col. John W. of Nash county, Oct. 2, Tennessee. R. R. Nov. 3, 1831
Polk, Marshall T., Apr. 15, Charlotte. R. R. Apr. 28, 1831
Powell, Dempsey, Jly. 29, Wake Forest. R. R. Aug. 4, 1831
Prince, Dr. Sidney S. of Chatham county, My., Alabama. R. R. My. 5, 1831
Pugh, Mrs. Lethe, Apr. 17, Granville county. R. R. Apr. 28, 1831
Rhem, Mrs. Joseph, My. 11, Jones county. R. R. Je. 9, 1831
Roane, Thomas, Oct. 23, Moore county. R. R. Nov. 3, 1831
Robason, Jesse, Je., Beaufort county. R. R. Jly. 7, 1831
Rogerson, Mrs. Isaiah, Jan., Perquimans county. R. R. Jan. 20, 1831
Ross, Joseph of Ireland, Apr. 14, Raleigh. R. R. Apr. 21, 1831
Rountree, Jesse, Apr. 12, Pitt county. R. R. My. 5, 1831
Russel, Mark, Sr., Apr. 22, Anson county. R. R. My. 5, 1831
Scott, Elijah, Jly., Craven county. R. R. Jly. 14, 1831
Sears, Mrs. John, Oct. 16, Newbern. R. R. Oct. 27, 1831
Sheppard, Major James, Jan., Pitt county. R. R. Jan. 13, 1831
Smallwood, Mrs. Samuel, Feb., Beaufort county. R. R. Mar. 3, 1831
Smith, Mrs. Peter, Jly., Davidson county. R. R. Jly. 21, 1831
Spaight, Charles G., Aug. 25, Newbern. R. R. Sept. 1, 1831
Stark, Rev. A. G. of Germany, Mar. 27, Rowan county. R. R. Apr. 21, 1831
Stith, Mrs. Bassett, Oct. 21, Halifax. R. R. Nov. 3, 1831
Stone, Mrs. Thomas G., Jly. 19, Nashville. R. R. Aug. 4, 1831
Suddereth, Mrs. John, Mar. 31, Burke county. R. R. My. 5, 1831
Tate, James, Je., Orange county. R. R. Je. 9, 1831
Telfair, Dr. David A., Feb. 9, Bath. R. R. Mar. 3, 1831
Thomas, Oliver of Raleigh, Nov., Wake county. R. R. Nov. 3, 1831
Thompson, Samuel of Orange county, Apr. 10, Covington, Tenn. R. R. Apr. 21, 1831
Tillman, Clara, Oct. 16, Newbern. R. R. Oct. 27, 1831
Toms, Col. Francis, Dec. 24, Perquimans county. R. R. Jan. 13, 1831
Tripp, Mrs. Sally, Jly., Beaufort county. R. R. Jly. 14, 1831
Vannoy, Mrs. Joel, Feb. 10, Wilkesboro. R. R. Mar. 17, 1831
Vanstory, John, Oct. 17, Guilford county. R. R. Nov. 3, 1831
Waddell, Mrs. John, Jr., Feb. 21, New Hanover county. R. R. Mar. 17, 1831
Waddell, John, Sr., Dec. 20, Pittsborough, Chatham county. R. R. Jan. 6, 1831
Wall, Henry, Je., Rockingham. R. R. Jly. 7, 1831
Wall, John Sr. of Virginia, Feb. 26, Richmond county. R. R. Mar. 24, 1831

Watson, John of Northampton county, Jan., Halifax county. R. R. Jan. 20, 1831
Wilkes, James, Oct. 7, Bertie county. R. R. Oct. 20, 1831
Williams, Col. Daniel of Sampson county, Aug. 16, Tenn. R. R. Sept. 1, 1831
Wilson, John of Pennsylvania, My. 28, Lincoln county. R. R. Je. 9, 1831
Wilson, Rev. John M., Aug., Mecklenburg county. R. R. Aug. 11, 1831
Wright, Dr. John B., Mar., Duplin county. R. R. Mar. 17, 1831

1832

Allen, Col. Richard of Maryland, Nov., Wilkes county. R. R. Nov. 15, 1832
Bolthrop, Wm. of Raleigh, Nov. 14, Warren county. R. R. Dec. 7, 1832
Bondurant, H. M. of Alabama, Nov., Salisbury. R. R. Nov. 15, 1832
Boyd, Margaret, Oct. 20, Mecklenburg county. R. R. Nov. 15, 1832
Caldwell, Rev. Robert L., Oct. 17, Statesville, Iredell county. R. R. Dec. 7, 1832
Click, Nicholas, Sr. of Germany, Oct. 22, Forks of the Yadkin. R. R. Nov. 23, 1832
Dodson, Robert J., Nov., Rockingham county. R. R. Nov. 15, 1832
Graham, Alexander of Cumberland county, Nov. 15, Georgia. R. R. Dec. 7, 1832
Green, Mrs. Elizabeth, Oct. 25, Rowan county. R. R. Nov. 23, 1832
Green, Maj. William, Nov. 6, Rutherford county. R. R. Nov. 23, 1832
Goodloe, Mrs. Ann, Oct. 28, Franklin county. R. R. Nov. 23, 1832
Hart, Samuel, Nov., Green county. R. R. Dec. 7, 1832
Hinton, Mrs. Charles, Dec. 22, Wake county. R. R. Dec. 28, 1832
Hubbard, Frances, Nov., Caswell county. R. R. Nov. 15, 1832
Hunter, Mrs William, Dec, Martin county R. R. Dec. 21, 1832
Jones, Duponseau, Nov. 11, Pittsborough, Chatham county. R. R. Nov. 30, 1832
Lewis, Philip J., Nov. 15, Granville county. R. R. Nov. 30, 1832
Lewis, Mrs. Warner M., Dec. 14, Caswell county. R. R. Dec. 28, 1832
London, John R., Dec. 15, Wilmington. R. R. Dec. 21, 1832
Martin, Mrs. Jas., Oct. 21, Rockingham county. R. R. Nov. 30, 1832
Palmer, Martin, Oct. 31, Hillsborough. R. R. Nov. 15, 1832
Rounsaville, Benjamin of Raleigh, Nov. 7, Lexington. R. R. Nov. 15, 1832
Royal, Mrs. Hardy, Oct. 21, Sampson county. R. R. Nov. 30, 1832
Shine, William E., Nov. 24, Halifax county. R. R. Dec. 7, 1832
Smith, William, Nov. 3, Charlotte. R. R. Nov. 15, 1832
Smith, David of Wilmington, Nov., Fayetteville. R. R. Nov. 15, 1832
Stanly, Mrs. Alex H., Nov. 29, Newbern. R. R. Dec. 7, 1832
Thomas, Joel, Nov. 6, Caswell county. R. R. Dec. 7, 1832
Tulke, J. of Germany, Nov. 13, Newbern. R. R. Dec. 7, 1832
Washington, Sarah H., Nov. 15, Wayne county. R. R. Dec. 7, 1832

1833

Alexander, Isaac, Sr., Sept. 2, Mecklenburg county. R. R. Sept. 17, 1833
Barge, Mrs. George K., Jly., Fayetteville. R. R. Jly. 16, 1833
Bell, Mrs. David H., Feb. 14, Bogue Sound, Carteret county. R. R. Mar. 12, 1833
Bird, Jehu, Major Gen'l. Oct. 16, Orange county. R. R. Oct. 29, 1833
Blacknall, Thomas, Jr., Nov., Granville county. R. R. Nov. 12, 1833
Blount, John Gray, Jan. 4, Washington. R. R. Jan. 11, 1833

Boon, Daniel of Johnston county, Aug. 2, Tipton county, Georgia. R. R. Oct. 8, 1833
Boon, Mrs. Mary G., Aug. 22, Tipton county, Tenn. R. R. Oct. 1, 1833
Bowden, Mrs. Sarah, Nov., Newbern. R. R. Nov. 12, 1833
Bradford, Henry, Mar. 14, Halifax county. R. R. Mar. 26, 1833
Brenon, Mrs. James G., Mar. 30, Warrenton. R. R. My. 7, 1833
Brower, Mrs. Alfred, Sept., Randolph county. R. R. Sept. 3, 1833
Brown, Mrs. Anderson of this State, Feb. 7, Virginia. R. R. Feb. 26, 1833
Brown, Mrs. Jeremiah, Apr. 2, Salisbury. R. R. Apr. 16, 1833
Brown, Mrs. Robert, Dec. 7, Wilmington. R. R. Dec. 17, 1833
Browne, Peter, Oct. 26, Raleigh. R. R. Oct. 29, 1833
Bryan, James, Feb. 9, Edgecombe county. R. R. Mar. 12, 1833
Bullock, Richard H., Apr. 9, Warren county. R. R. My. 21, 1833
Burne, Thomas, Feb. 24, Chatham county. R. R. Mar. 12, 1833
Caldcleugh, A. R., Apr. 12, Lexington. R. R. Apr. 30, 1833
Cannon, Robert, Jly., Raleigh. R. R. Jly. 9, 1833
Card, Benson, Je., Raleigh. R. R. Jly. 4, 1833
Card, Mrs. Dec. 9, Raleigh. R. R. Dec. 10, 1833
Carmichael, Gilbert, Mar. 11, Cumberland county. R. R. Mar. 26, 1833
Carter, Charles, Nov., Newberne. R. R. Dec. 3, 1833
Cash, F. A. of Anson county, Jly., Florida. R. R. Jly. 23, 1833
Christmas, Capt. Richard, Mar. 18, Haw River. R. R. Apr. 16, 1833
Christmas, Richard, Mar. 18, Orange county. R. R. Mar. 26, 1833
Cooke, Mrs. Henry M., Nov., Beaufort. R. R. Dec. 3, 1833
Corbin, Octavius N. of Virginia, Oct., Wilmington. R. R. Oct. 29, 1833
Covington, Mrs. Benjamin C., Oct., Richmond county. R. R. Oct. 29, 1833
Cowan, Mrs. Thomas J., Aug. 8, Wilmington. R. R. Aug. 27, 1833
Davidson, Mrs. Ephraim, Aug. 28, Iredell county. R. R. Oct. 15, 1833
Downey, Mrs. James, Nov., Granville county. R. R. Nov. 12, 1833
Drummond, Wm. H., My. 2, Raleigh. R. R. My. 7, 1833
Dryman, Henry of Macon county, Nov. 22, New Mexico, Ga. R. R. Dec. 31, 1833
Dunbibin, Dr. Junius C., Sept. 18, Wilmington. R. R. Oct. 8, 1833
Eaton, Mrs. William, Jan. 20, Warren county. R. R. Jan. 25, 1833
Eccles, John, Sept., Fayetteville. R. R. Oct. 1, 1833
Ellenwood, Henry S., Apr. 2, Wilmington. R. R. Apr. 9, 1833
Ellis, Mrs. Amaryllis, Oct. 5, Newbern. R. R. Oct. 15, 1833
Espie, Rev. Thos. of Salisbury, Apr. 24, Lincoln county. R. R. Apr. 30, 1833
Findlay, John, Apr. 6, Orange county. R. R. My. 21, 1833
Fitzpatrick, Polly, Jan. 21, Salisbury. R. R. Jan. 25, 1833
Fox, Lark of Franklin county, Aug. 22, Clinton, Mississippi. R. R. Sept. 10, 1833
Freeman, Mrs. Elizabeth of Raleigh, Mar. 12, Plymouth, Mass. R. R. Apr. 9, 1833
Gerock, Samuel, Sept., Trenton, Jones county. R. R. Oct. 1, 1833
Glenn, Mrs., Wake county, Jan. R. R. Jan. 25, 1833
Graham, Andrew of Scotland, Aug. 15, Raleigh. R. R. Aug. 20, 1833
Graham, Edward, Mar. 21, Newbern. R. R. Mar. 26, 1833
Grant, Col. John, Apr. 5, Onslow county. R. R. Apr. 23, 1833
Grice, Charles, Sept., Elizabeth City. R. R. Sept. 10, 1833

Hairston, Maj. Peter, Dec. 1, Stokes county. R. R. Jan. 25, 1833
Hall, Hon. John, Jan. 29, Warrenton. R. R. Feb. 8, 1833
Harper, Mrs. James, Dec. 21, Greene county. R. R. Dec. 31, 1833
Haslen, Mrs. Thomas of Newbern, Mar. 8, Granville county. R. R. My. 8, 1833
Hawkins, Col. Joseph, My. 10, Halifax. R. R. My. 14, 1833
Hawkins, C. L. Philemon, Jan. 28, Warren county. R. R. Feb. 8, 1833
Haywood, Dr. Lewis G., Mar. 29, Lenoir county. R. R. Apr. 9, 1833
Henderson, Leonard, Aug. 13, Granville county. R. R. Aug. 20, 1833
Henderson, Mark M. of Chapel Hill, Oct. 8, Huntington, Tenn. R. R. Nov. 5, 1833
Henderson, Dr. Samuel, Mar. 11, Charlotte. R. R. Mar. 26, 1833
Hill, Jane, Dec. 23, Randolph county. R. R. Jan. 18, 1833
Hill, Mrs. William, Feb. 14, Raleigh. R. R. Feb. 22, 1833
Hinton, Sidney R. of Wake county, Jly., Greensboro, Alabama. R. R. Jly. 16, 1833
Hogan, Wm. of this State, Jly., Georgia. R. R. Aug. 6, 1833
Holmes, Mrs. James H., Sept. 5, Currituck county. R. R. Oct. 1, 1833
Horton, Mrs. Wm., Mar. 14, Hillsboro. R. R. My. 7, 1833
Hughes, Mrs. Whitmel, Mar. 17, Bertie county. R. R. My. 7, 1833
Hunt, Col. Wm., Mar. 8, Granville county. R. R. Mar. 26, 1833
Hutchings, Cecilia, Sept. 4, Raleigh. R. R. Sept. 10, 1833
Irwin, Mrs. John, Apr. 6, Charlotte. R. R. Apr. 23, 1833
Jennings, Lemuel, Jan., Pasquotank county. R. R. Feb. 1, 1833
Jones, Mrs. Burwell P., Apr. 14, Wake county. R. R. My. 21, 1833
Jones, John H., Mar. 11, Newbern. R. R. Mar. 19, 1833
Jones, Margaret, Apr., Wilmington. R. R. Apr. 23, 1833
Jones, Mrs. Walter G., Apr. 16, Wadesboro, Anson county. R. R. Je. 4, 1833
Jordan, Edmond, Jan. 12, Wake county. R. R. Feb. 1, 1833
Kincey, Stephen, Oct., Newbern. R. R. Oct. 15, 1833
Kyle, Hazlett, Je. 5, Raleigh. R. R. Jly. 9, 1833
Langley, Mrs. Sarah, Sept. 30, Raleigh. R. R. Oct 1, 1833
Lenoir, Mrs. Wm., Oct. 9, Wilkes county. R. R. Oct. 22, 1833
Lewis, Malachi S., Je., Camden county. R. R. Je. 18, 1833
Lockhart, Maj. Adam, Feb. 11, Anson county. R. R. Mar. 12, 1833
Lowndes, Rawlins, W., Dec. 21, Greenville. R. R. Jan. 18, 1833
Lumsden, Mrs. William, Jly., Fayetteville. R. R. Jly. 23, 1833
M'Coll, Duncan, Oct., Fayetteville. R. R. Oct. 29, 1833
M'Farland, Tryam, Nov. 9, Richmond county. R. R. Nov. 19, 1833
M'Kethan, Dr. John H. of Raleigh, Aug. 23, New Orleans. R. R. Sept. 10, 1833
M'Rae, Alexander, Aug. 6, Montgomery county. R. R. Sept. 3, 1833
M'Rae, Duncan, Sept., Richmond county. R. R. Sept. 3, 1833
Marling, Jacob, Dec. 18, Raleigh. R. R. Dec. 24, 1833
Martin, John, Feb. 17, Raleigh. R. R. Feb. 22, 1833
Martin, John, Feb. 16, Wake county. R. R. Mar. 5, 1833
Martin, John, Apr. 8, Raleigh. R. R. Apr. 9, 1833
Matthews, Mrs. Mussendine, Aug. 6, Iredell county. R. R. Aug. 27, 1833
Meilan, Mrs. Anthony, Sept., Wilmington. R. R. Sept. 17, 1833
Mims, Britton of Johnston county, Sept. 8, Augusta, Ga. R. R. Oct. 1, 1833

Moore, Mrs. Elizabeth, Feb. 1, Pitt county. R. R. Feb. 8, 1833
Moore, Julia R., Feb. 24, Wilmington. R. R. Mar. 12, 1833
Moring, Mrs. John, Apr. 25, Chatham county. R. R. Je. 4, 1833
Mulhollon, Col. Hugh, Jly. 1, Orange county. R. R. Jly. 16, 1833
Neville, Mrs. Thomas, Aug. 31, Halifax county. R. R. Oct. 15, 1833
Norment, Mrs. John H., Dec., Athens Tenn. R. R. Dec 17, 1833
Ochitree, Archibald, Dec. 28, Fayetteville. R. R. Jan. 18, 1833
Oliver, Mrs. Thomas, Nov., Newbern. R. R. Nov. 12, 1833
Parker, John of England, Dec. 15, Raleigh. R. R. Dec. 24, 1833
Parks, Nancy Elvita, Je. 9, Wilkes county. R. R. Jly. 23, 1833
Perry, Susan M. of Virginia, Sept. 23, Raleigh. R. R. Oct. 1, 1833
Pettegrew, Mrs. Charles, Aug. 4, Washington county. R. R. Aug. 20, 1833
Philips, Albert G., Feb. 17, Raleigh. R. R. Feb. 22, 1833
Picot, Gen. P. O. of Plymouth, Sept. 3. R. R. Oct. 1, 1833
Pipkin, Jethro, Dec. 20, Gates county. R. R. Dec. 31, 1833
Potter, Ann Eliza of South Carolina, Jly., Fayetteville. R. R. Aug. 6, 1833
Powell, Mrs. Elizabeth, Apr., Newbern. R. R. Aug. 9, 1833
Ratican, Mrs. Michael, Mar. 1, Warrenton. R. R. Mar. 12, 1833
Ray, David, Apr. 8, Orange county. R. R. Apr. 16, 1833
Read, Dr. Thomas H. of Granville county, Aug. 10, Pittsylvania county, Va. R. R. Aug. 27, 1833
Reddick, Mills, Dec. 22, Gates county. R. R. Dec. 31, 1833
Rhodes, Mrs. John, Oct. 22, Wake county. R. R. Nov. 5, 1833
Roberts, Mrs. Sarah, Mar. 15, Jones county. R. R. Apr. 23, 1833
Roberts, infant daughter of Richard Roberts, Aug. 16, Raleigh. R. R. Aug. 20, 1833
Robins, Mrs. Anne, Je. 14, Wilkes county. R. R. Jly. 23, 1833
Shephard, Mrs. Charles, Nov., Newbern. R. R. Dec. 3, 1833
Sills, David, Je. 13, Nash county. R. R. Je. 25, 1833
Sink, Mrs. Joseph, Apr. 11, Lexington. R. R. Apr. 30, 1833
Smart, Maj. Thomas B., Aug. 20, Mecklenburg county. R. R. Oct. 8, 1833
Smith, James T. of Anson county, Oct., Chapel Hill. R. R. Oct. 15, 1833
Smith, Rev. James of Granville county, Nov., Knoxville, Tenn. R. R. Nov. 12, 1833
Smith, Jane C., Apr. 1, Averasborough. R. R. Apr. 16, 1833
Smith, William, Oct., Averasborough. R. R. Oct. 29, 1833
Speller, Thomas, Sr., Aug. 25, Bertie county. R. R. Sept. 10, 1833
Springs, Eli., Mar. 14, Charlotte. R. R. Mar. 26, 1833
Staley, Conrad of Randolph county, Mar. 6, Hillsborough. R. R. Mar. 26, 1833
Stanback, Mary J., Jly. 31, Richmond county. R. R. Aug. 20, 1833
Stanford, Rev. Samuel, Je., Duplin county. R. R. Je. 18, 1833
Stanly, George Badger, Aug. 29, Newbern. R. R. Oct. 8, 1833
Stanly, John, Aug. 2, Newbern. R. R. Aug. 13, 1833
Steiner, Rev. Abraham, Sr., My. 22, Salem. R. R. Je. 4, 1833
Strong, Mrs. W. H., Feb. 3, Pittsborough. R. R. Feb. 15, 1833
Spooner, Emma of Petersburg, Va., Aug. 17, Shoco Springs. R. R. Aug. 27, 1833
Sumner, Col. Jethro, Sept., Gates county. R. R. Sept. 10, 1833
Swain, infant son of Governor Swain, Aug. 16, Raleigh. R. R. Aug. 20, 1833

Swift, William R., Oct. 9, Washington, Beaufort county. R. R. Oct. 15, 1833
Tandy, Mrs. William H. of New York, Apr. 16, Newbern. R. R. Apr. 23, 1833
Taylor, Mrs. William G., Sept., Newbern. R. R. Oct. 1, 1833
Thomas, Maj. Samuel, Je. 12, Franklin county. R. R. Je. 25, 1833
Thompson, Duncan, Jly., Fayetteville. R. R. Jly. 23, 1833
Usher, William of Ireland, Aug. 31, Wilmington. R. R. Sept. 17, 1833
Vaughan, Mrs. Ann C., Jan. 8, Williamsborough, Granville county. R. R. Feb. 15, 1833
Waddell, Edmond, Jan. 6, Brunswick county. R. R. Jan. 25, 1833
Ward, Col. Eli. W. of Onslow county, Sept. 17, Fayette county, Arkansas. R. R. Nov. 5, 1833
Washington, Sarah H., Nov. 15, Wayne county. R. R. Jan. 11, 1833
Webb, Mrs. William S., Nov., Newbern. R. R. Nov. 12, 1833
West, Robert Johnson, Je. 24, Raleigh. R. R. Je. 25, 1833
Whitfield, Julia Bryan of Wayne county, Aug. 2, Tipton county, Georgia. R. R. Oct. 8, 1833
Whitfield, Mrs. J. O. of Wayne county, Nov. 22, Tipton county, Georgia. R. R. Dec. 17, 1833
Williams, Joseph John, Mar. 13, Halifax county. R. R. My. 7, 1833
Winn, Stephen W., Feb. 23, Craven county. R. R. Mar. 12, 1833
Wood, Newton, Mar., Wake county. R. R. Mar. 26, 1833
Woodruff, Mrs. John, Apr. 19, Charlotte. R. R. Apr. 30, 1833
Wright, Jas. N. of Bladen county, Oct., Clinton, Mississippi. R. R. Oct. 29, 1833
Wyatt, John of England, Oct. 22, Charlotte. R. R. Nov. 5, 1833

1834

Adam, John R. of Fayetteville, Mar., Island of Jamaicai. R. R. Apr. 1, 1834
Alsobrook, Lemuel, Oct. 14, Anson county. R. R. Nov. 4, 1834
Alston, Erasmus G., Aug. 29, Halifax. R. R. Sept. 9, 1834
Alston, Jos. I. of Franklin county, Aug. 4, Richmond, Tenn. R. R. Sept. 9, 1834
Ballard, Capt. Kedar, Jan. 16, Gates county. R. R. Feb. 18, 1834
Barham, Benjamin, Aug. 25, Wake county. R. R. Sept. 2, 1834
Beasly, Mary, Aug. 12, Wake county. R. R. Aug. 19, 1834
Beckwith, Col. John of this State, Oct., Poughkeepsie, N. Y. R. R. Nov. 4, 1834
Bethel, Gen. William of Rockingham county, Apr., Natchez, Mississippi. R. R. Jly. 15, 1834
Birdsall, Col. Jesse of Fayetteville & New York, Apr., Fayetteville. R. R. Apr. 8, 1834
Boylan, Alexander H. of Raleigh, Oct., Tenn. R. R. Nov. 4, 1834
Bracken, Mrs. A. F., Oct., Rockingham county. R. R. Nov. 11, 1834
Bradley, Richard, Mar. 28, Wilmington. R. R. Apr. 8, 1834
Bragg, Mrs. Thomas, Sr., Jan. 8, Warrenton. R. R. Jan. 21, 1834
Brown, David, Je., Rowan county. R. R. Je. 17, 1834
Brown, Hardy of Jones county, Feb., Twiggs county, Ga. R. R. Feb. 18, 1834
Brown, Mrs. Jethro, Sept. 17, Caswell county. R. R. Sept. 30, 1834

Brown, Captain John of Birmingham, England, Feb. 7, Wilmington. R. R. Feb. 11, 1834
Bruer, Nathaniel of Edenton, Feb., Norfolk. R. R. Feb. 11, 1834
Buffalow, Mrs. John, Apr. 18, Raleigh. R. R. Apr. 22, 1834
Burlingham, Capt. William of Windsor, Bertie county, My. 29, Franklin county. R. R. Je. 10, 1834
Burton, John F., Sept. 4, Beatties Ford, Lincoln county. R. R. Sept. 23, 1834
Cain, William, Sr., Jly. 28, Orange county. R. R. Aug. 12, 1834
Campbell, Mrs. Isabella, Sept. 24, Cumberland county. R. R. Oct. 14, 1834
Cheek, James, Sept., Orange county. R. R. Sept. 23, 1834
Clark, Dr. Archibald A., Sept. 26, Elizabethtown, Bladen county. R. R. Oct. 14, 1834
Click, Mrs. Rebecca, Oct. 13, Rowan county. R. R. Nov. 4, 1834
Cobb, John, Je., Lenoir county. R. R. Je. 17, 1834
Cooke, Thos. H., Mar. 30, Raleigh. R. R. Apr. 1, 1834
Cox, Williams of Onslow county, Nov. 11, Sampson county. R. R. Dec. 9, 1834
Craig, Mrs. Ellen, Sept. 17, Chapel Hill. R. R. Sept. 23, 1834
Curtis, Mrs. Anderson, Oct., Fayetteville. R. R. Oct. 14, 1834
Danvers, George of Connecticut, Apr. 23, Wilmington. R. R. My. 13, 1834
Dillon, Samuel, Oct., Murfreesboro. R. R. Oct. 28, 1834
Dismukes, Dr. George W. of Chatham county, Aug. 12, Autauga county, Ala. R. R. Sept. 16, 1834
Doane, Augustus of Wilmington, Oct., Moore county. R. R. Oct. 28, 1834
Donlop, Mrs. David of Franklin county, Aug. 7, Marengo county, Ala. R. R. Sept. 30, 1834
Dow, Lovenzo, Feb. 2, Georgetown, D. C. R. R. Feb. 11, 1834
Dowd, Mrs. Cornelius, Mar. 29, Moore county. R. R. Apr. 15, 1834
Dozier, Col. Thos., Mar. 9, Camden county. R. R. Apr. 1, 1834
Drake, Mrs. Silas A., Sept., Ellerbe Mineral Springs, Richmond county. R. R. Sept. 9, 1834
Ecklin, Mrs. Joshua, Sept., Beaufort county. R. R. Sept. 30, 1834
Edwards, Theophilus, Sept. 6, Greene county. R. R. Oct. 14, 1834
Ellis, Miss P., Nov. 1, Chatham county. R. R. Dec. 2, 1834
Ellison, Thomas, Sept., Beaufort county. R. R. Sept. 30, 1834
Evans, Josiah, Sept. 29, Cumberland county. R. R. Oct. 14, 1834
Evans, Mary, Aug. 24, Cumberland county. R. R. Aug. 26, 1834
Evans, Morris, Aug. 25, Wake county. R. R. Sept. 2, 1834
Ferebee, Thomas, Apr., Currituck county. R. R. Apr. 22, 1834
Flewellen, Capt. William of Halifax county, Sept. 23, Carroll county, Tenn. R. R. Oct. 28, 1834
Forbes, Mrs. John, Apr. 25, Elizabeth City. R. R. My. 13, 1834
Forney, Gen. Peter, Feb. 1, Lincoln county. R. R. Feb. 25, 1834
Foy, Maj. Thomas, Sept. 4, Onslow county. R. R. Sept. 16, 1834
Franklin, Mrs. Jesse, Feb. 20, Surry county. R. R. Mar. 11, 1834
Galloway, Robert, Mar. 27, Rockingham. R. R. Apr. 8, 1834
Gardner, Mrs. Wm., Oct. 16, Guilford county. R. R. Nov. 4, 1834
Gee, Capt. James, Apr. 13, Scotland Neck. R. R. My. 13, 1834
Gould, Rev. Daniel of New Hampshire & this State, Apr. 29, Statesville,

Iredell county. R. R. My. 20, 1834
Grant, Col. James, Oct. 23, Raleigh. R. R. Nov. 11, 1834
Green, William T., Oct., Halifax. R. R. Oct. 28, 1934
Griffin, Andrew, Oct., Rowan county. R. R. Oct. 28, 1834
Guffie, Mrs. Martha of Wake county, Apr. 12, Paris, West Tennessee. R. R. Je. 3, 1834
Gully, Eder John, Apr., Wake county. R. R. Apr. 22, 1834
Gunter, Isham, Jly. 28, Chatham county. R. R. Aug. 12, 1834
Hall, George C. of Connecticut, Oct., Fayetteville. R. R. Oct. 28, 1834
Halsey, William H., Apr. 10, Wilmington. R. R. Apr. 22, 1834
Hamilton, Alexander of Scotland & Granville county, Jan., Williamsboro, Granville county. R. R. Jan. 21, 1834
Hancock, Richard G., Sept., Newbern. R. R. Sept. 16, 1834
Harrison, Benjamin, Dec., Camden county. R. R. Dec. 9, 1834
Hawley, William I., Je. 26, Fayettevile. R. R. Jly. 1, 1834
Henderson, Alexander Hamilton of Rockingham county, Aug. 18, Sumpter county, Ala. R. R. Sept. 16, 1834
Herbin, Thomas, Apr. 27, Rockingham county. R. R. My. 13, 1834
Holder, Melinda, Je. 24, Milton. R. R. Jly. 15, 1834
Howard, Benjamin, Oct., Rowan county. R. R. Oct. 28, 1834
Howie, Samuel, Sept. 26, Cumberland county. R. R. Oct. 14, 1834
Humphrey, Catharine S., Oct., Fayetteville. R. R. Oct. 14, 1834
Isler, Jos. B., Dec. 19, Oxford. R. R. Jan. 21, 1834
Ivey, Mrs. John, Oct. 17, Halifax county. R. R. Nov. 4, 1834
Jasper, Elizabeth Ann B. of Hyde county, Jan. 30, Franklin county. R. R. Feb. 11, 1834
Johnson, George M. of Wake county, Sept. 4, Greensborough, Alabama. R. R. Sept. 30, 1834
Johnson, Robert, Aug. 7, Bladen county. R. R. Sept. 9, 1834
Jones, Henry L. of Fayetteville, Jly., Smithville. R. R. Jly. 29, 1834
Jones, Rowan, Feb., Salisbury. R. R. Feb. 11, 1834
Jones, Col. William, Je. 11, Bladen county. R. R. Jly. 1, 1834
Joyner, Mrs. Andrew, Mar. 8, Halifax county. R. R. Mar. 18, 1834
Kenneday, James A., Apr. 16, Mecklenburg county. R. R. My. 13, 1834
Knight, Isaac of Guilford county, Nov. 11, Rowan county. R. R. Dec. 2, 1834
Kyle, Wm. of Ireland, Jly. 27, Onslow county. R. R. Aug. 12, 1834
Lawrence, Mrs. A. S. of Raleigh, My. 17, Elmira, N. Y. R. R. Je. 3, 1834
Lea, Gabriel, Sr., Jly. 28, Caswell county. R. R. Aug. 12, 1834
Lee, Mrs. Leroy M., Dec., Elizabeth City. R. R. Dec. 9, 1834
Leroy, Louis, Jly. 5, Washington, Beaufort county. R. R. Jly. 8, 1834
Loftin, Joseph, Oct., Lenoir county. R. R. Oct. 28, 1834
Love, Mrs. Thomas, Nov. 3, Franklin, Macon county. R. R. Dec. 9, 1834
Lyde, Rev. Augustus Foster of Wilmington, Nov. 19, Philadelphia. R. R. Dec. 9, 1834
Mabry, David, Jly. 12, Wake county. R. R. Jly. 29, 1834
M'Clelland, Dr. Hugh, Mar. 17, Iredell county. R. R. Apr. 1, 1834
M'Kerall, Capt. John, Sept. 17, Hillsboro. R. R. Sept. 23, 1834
Macnamara, Mrs. Robert, Nov. 27, Salisbury. R. R. Dec. 9, 1834
Martin, Dr. William of Elizabeth City, Oct., Norfolk, Va. R. R. Oct. 21, 1834

Miller, Frederick, Aug. 11, Bladen county. R. R. Sept. 9, 1834
Miller, John, Je. 1, Raleigh. R. R. Je. 3, 1834
Miller, Mary Anne of Jones county, Dec., Twiggs county, Ga. R. R. Dec. 9, 1834
Miller, Rev. Robert, Je., Mary's Grove, Burke county. R. R. Je. 3, 1834
Murchison, Kenneth of Scotland, Jly. 7, Moore county. R. R. Jly. 29, 1834
Myatt, Mrs. Mark, Jly., Wake county. R. R. Jly. 15, 1834
Nichols, Benajah, Nov. 13, Bertie county. R. R. Dec. 2, 1834
Nichols, Caleb, Apr. 26, Wilmington. R. R. My. 13, 1834
Oliver, Samuel M., Aug. 30, Elizabethtown, Bladen county. R. R. Sept. 16, 1834
Parker, Gabriel G. of Lenoir county, Apr. 11, Lee county, Ga. R. R. My. 13, 1834
Pearson, Hon. Joseph, Oct. 27, Raleigh. R. R. Nov. 11, 1834
Pickard, Henry, Jan., Lawrence county, Tennessee. R. R. Jan. 14, 1834
Pickett, Martin, Apr., Pee Dee. R. R. Apr. 22, 1834
Pipkin, Mrs. John D., Dec. 25, Gates county. R. R. Jan. 14, 1834
Polk, Col. William, Jan. 14, Raleigh. R. R. Jan. 21, 1834
Potter, Mrs. Nathaniel, Sept., Smithville, Brunswick county. R. R. Sept. 16, 1834
Pugh, Dr. Whitmel H. of Bertie county, Nov. 1, Louisiana. R. R. Dec. 30, 1834
Ragsdale, Elizabeth of Tarborough, Aug. 30, Raleigh. R. R. Sept. 2, 1834
Reichel, Rev. Benjamin, Jan., Salem. R. R. Jan. 7, 1834
Rhodes, Charles of New Jersey & this State, Oct., Fayetteville. R. R. Nov. 11, 1834
Rhodes, John, Oct. 23, Wake county. R. R. Nov. 18, 1834
Salmon, Mrs. David D., Oct. 18, Cumberland county. R. R. Nov. 11, 1834
Sanders, Mrs. Ransom, My. 29, Johnston county. R. R. Je. 10, 1834
Saunders, James, Je., Rockingham county. R. R. Je. 17, 1834
Simpson, George Winston, Sept. 11, Raleigh. R. R. Sept. 16, 1834
Sleighter, David of Germany & this State, Je., Rowan county. R. R. Je. 17, 1834
Smith, A. D. of Granville county, Jan. 22, Iredell county. R. R. Feb. 11, 1834
Smith, James W. of Newbern, Sept. 1, Swansborough. R. R. Sept. 16, 1834
Smith, Capt. John, Nov., Wake county. R. R. Nov. 18, 1834
Stanford, Jonathan D. of Duplin county, Je. 10, Fayetteville. R. R. Jly. 1, 1834
Stuart, John of Ireland & this State, Oct. 3, Raleigh. R. R. Oct. 7, 1834
Sumner, Mrs. Jethro, Sept. 22, Gates county. R. R. Oct. 14, 1834
Swinson, Jesse, Apr. 17, Duplin county. R. R. My. 13, 1834
Taylor, Col. Richard, Mar., Granville county. R. R. Mar. 4, 1834
Terry, James of England & this State, Apr. 14, Chatham county. R. R. Apr. 22, 1834
Thompson, James W. of Raleigh, Jly. 29, Illinois. R. R. Jly. 23, 1834
Thompson, Rev. Jehu S., Dec. 2, Orange county R. R. Dec. 30, 1834
Thompson, Thomas of Pittsborough, Chatham county, Nov., Petersburg, Va. R. R. Nov. 4, 1834
Tuton, Mrs. Oliver of Fayetteville, Sept. 27, Robeson county. R. R. Oct. 14, 1834

Vanhook, Robert, Oct. 21, Person county. R. R. Nov. 4, 1834
Vestal, Nathan, Oct. 25, Chatham county. R. R. Nov. 11, 1834
Wall, Jesse, Feb. 2, Wake county. R. R. Feb. 25, 1834
Ward, Gen. Edward, Aug. 16, Onslow county. R. R. Sept. 2, 1834
Ward, Dr. John F. of Tarborough, Feb. 25, Madison County, Tenn. R. R. Apr. 1, 1834
Weaver, Benjamin, Sept., Edgecombe county. R. R. Sept. 16, 1834
West, Michael, Mar. 6, Lincoln county. R. R. Apr. 1, 1834
Whitaker, Mrs. Robt. L. of Franklin county, Sept. 2, Halifax. R. R. Sept. 16, 1834
Whitehead, Williamson, Aug. 10, Fayetteville. R. R. Aug. 12, 1834
Whitesides, Duncan of Hilslborough, Mar. 22, Marion, Alabama. R. R. Apr. 1, 1834
Williamson, James, Sr. of Scotland & this State, Nov. 20, Person county. R. R. Dec. 9, 1834
Wilson, Mrs. Joseph, Oct., Charlotte. R. R. Oct. 21, 1834
Wilson, Mrs. Napier of Raleigh, Sept. 7, Columbia, Tenn. R. R. Oct. 21, 1834
Womack, Sarah Ann, Aug. 17, Pittsborough. R. R. Aug. 26, 1834
Wood, George F., Sept. 12, Louisburg, Franklin county. R. R. Sept. 16, 1834
Wood, Dr. John E., Nov. 13, Bertie county. R. R. Dec. 2, 1834
Woodall, Absalom of Johnston county, Feb. 4, Greene county, Alabama. R. R. My. 13, 1834
Woodall, Jas., Aug. 19, Johnston county. R. R. Sept. 23, 1834

1835

Adams, Mrs. Rachel, Oct. 2, Washington, Beaufort county. R. R. Oct. 27, 1835
Albright, Susannah, Aug. 29, Lexington, Davidson county. R. R. Sept. 22, 1835
Allen, Jennings, Jan. 3, Fairfield District, S. C. R. R. Mar. 3, 1835
Allen, Capt. Young, Sept. 5, Wake county. R. R. Sept. 22, 1835
Archer, David, Sept. 5, Guilford county. R. R. Sept. 29, 1835
Armistead, Stark, Mar., Bertie county. R. R. Mar. 17, 1835
Armstrong, Mrs. Farquhar C., Jly., Cumberland county. R. R. Jly. 21, 1835
Armstrong, Thomas, Apr., Chapel Hill. R. R. Apr. 14, 1835
Arnold, Essek of Fayetteville, Jly. 8, Salem. R. R. Aug. 18, 1835
Ashe, Col. Samuel, Nov. 3, Fayetteville. R. R. Nov. 10, 1835
Badger, Mrs. George E., Mar. 1, Raleigh. R. R. Mar. 10, 1835
Baker, Sophia, Je., Fayetteville. R. R. Je. 23, 1835
Barclift, Thomas J. of Elizabeth City, Nov. R. R. Nov. 10, 1835
Baskerville, Charles, Mar. 21, Mecklenburg, Va. R. R. Apr. 14, 1835
Beard, Mrs. Anthony, Sept. 13, Fayetteville. R. R. Sept. 15, 1835
Beard, John, Jly., Bladen county. R. R. Jly. 21, 1835
Beatty, Mrs. Henry B., Feb., Cumberland county. R. R. Feb. 17, 1835
Beckwith, Mary Badger, My. 5, Raleigh. R. R. My. 12, 1835
Bevele, Armsworthy, Feb., Stokes county. R. R. Feb. 17, 1835
Birth, William W. of Raleigh, Jan., Washington, D. C. R. R. Jan. 20, 1835

Biwighaus, Mrs. Christiana, Oct. 12, Salem. R. R. Nov. 3, 1835
Blount, Mrs. William A., Aug., Washington, Beaufort county. R. R. Sept. 1, 1835
Blount, Hon. Willie, Governor of this State, Sept., Tennessee. R. R. Oct. 6, 1835
Bond, Edwin, Jly. 3, Edenton. R. R. Aug. 4, 1835
Bradford, Richard H. of this State, Mar. 30, Washington, D. C. R. R. Apr. 7, 1835
Brown, Mrs. Abigail, Mar. 15, Hillsboro. R. R. Apr. 7, 1835
Brown, Caroline Isabella, Aug. 29, Wake county. R. R. Sept. 8, 1835
Brown, Catharine, My. 14, Wake county. R. R. My. 19, 1835
Brown, Eliza Ann, Aug. 27, Wake county. R. R. Sept. 8, 1835
Brown, Mrs. Jas. W., Oct., Caswell county. R. R. Oct. 20, 1835
Bruce, Abner B., Apr., Hillsboro. R. R. Apr. 14, 1835
Buie, Effie of Moore county, Oct., Raleigh. R. R. Oct. 20, 1835
Caldwell, Mrs. David F., Apr. 16, Salisbury. R. R. Apr. 21, 1835
Caldwell, Joseph, Jan. 27, Chapel Hill. R. R. Aug. 4, 1835
Callaway, Thomas, Jly. 24, Ashe county. R. R. Aug. 25, 1835
Campbell, Emeline, Jly. 28, Raleigh. R. R. Aug. 4, 1835
Campbell; Mrs. Mary, Dec. 23, Warrenton. R. R. Jan. 6, 1835
Carpenter, Thomas, Jly., Rockingham county. R. R. Jly. 14, 1835
Carr, Lucy Jane, Sept. 28, Sampson county. R. R. Oct. 27, 1835
Carraway, Archibald, Sept. 18, Wadesboro, Anson county. R. R. Oct. 27, 1835
Carrington, Col. Paul of Milton, Aug. 19, White Sulphur Springs, Va. R. R. Sept. 8, 1835
Carter, Jesse, Aug. 3, Chatham county. R. R. Aug. 25, 1835
Clemmons, James, Jan., Friendship, Guilford county. R. R. Jan. 20, 1835
Cole, Mrs. Frances, Sept. 23, Granville county. R. R. Oct. 6, 1835
Collier, Probert of Lenoir county, Feb., Wayne county. R. R. Feb. 17, 1835
Cook, Henry M. of Beaufort, Mar., Randolph, Tipton county, Tennessee. R. R. Mar. 31, 1835
Cotterell, Elizabeth Lewis, Sept. 30, Salisbury. R. R. Oct. 20, 1835
Covington, Benjamin L., Aug. 24, Richmond county. R. R. Sept. 15, 1835
Crause, Andrew, Feb., Stokes county. R. R. Feb. 17, 1835
Crawford, Samuel, Oct., Orange county. R. R. Oct. 6, 1835
Crawford, William, Sept. 30, Richmond county. R. R. Oct. 20, 1835
Crossland, Alexander, Aug., Warrenton. R. R. Sept. 1, 1835
Crump, Col. John, Feb., Montgomery county. R. R. Feb. 17, 1835
Cruse, John, Mar. 23, Raleigh. R. R. Mar. 24, 1835
Culbertson, James, Aug. 6, Chatham county. R. R. Aug. 25, 1835
Culbertson, David, Sept., Anson county. R. R. Nov. 3, 1835
Dameron, Mrs. Joseph, Sept., Caswell county. R. R. Oct. 13, 1835
Dane, Hon. Nathan, Mar., Beverly, Massachusetts. R. R. Mar. 10, 1835
Daniel, James W. of Person county, Sept. 5, Fayetteville. R. R. Sept. 15, 1835
Davis, Mrs. Archibald H., My. 8, Franklin county. R. R. My. 26, 1835
Davis, Mrs. Margaret, Jly. 28,, Elizabeth City. R. R. Aug. 18, 1835
Debnam, Mrs. Bartholomew Y., Apr. 7, Franklin county. R. R. Apr. 14, 1835
Devereux, Fanny Pollock, My. 24, Raleigh. R. R. Je. 2, 1835

Dewey, Mrs. Charles, Nov. 17, Raleigh. R. R. Nov. 24, 1835
Downing, Edward of Ireland, Sept. 22, Craven county. R. R. Nov. 10, 1835
Dupuy, Louisa Matilda, Jly. 21, Raleigh. R. R. Jly. 28, 1835
Elks, Elias, Sept. 3, Pitt county. R. R. Sept. 15, 1835
Etchison, Mrs. Mary, Mar. 12, Rowan county. R. R. Apr. 7, 1835
Evans, Mrs. Deborah, Sept. 2, Guilford county. R. R. Sept. 29, 1835
Evans, Phineas, Jly. 28, Perquimans county. R. R. Aug. 18, 1835
Faucette, Rufus Wall, Feb. 7, Haywood, Chatham county. R. R. Feb. 24, 1835
Fletcher, Rev. Thomas, Mar. 18, Wilkes county. R. R. Apr. 21, 1835
Foggle, Christian, Sept. 7, Stokes county. R. R. Oct. 20, 1835
Fonville, Bruce, Sept. 22, Craven county. R. R. Nov. 3, 1835
Fort, Frederick M., Dec. 30, Wake county. R. R. Jan. 13, 1835
Freeland, Thomas, Mar. 25, Orange county. R. R. My. 19, 1835
Freeman, Mrs. Edmund B., Jan. 28, Raleigh. R. R. Feb. 3, 1835
Freeman, Rev. Jonathan Otis, Nov. 2, Washington, Beaufort county. R. R. Nov. 17, 1835
Gale, Mrs. Enoch R., Sept. 23, Elizabeth City. R. R. Oct. 13, 1835
Gales, Weston (Infant), My. 12, Raleigh. R. R. My. 19, 1835
Ganilt, Joseph, Jly. 4, Washington county. R. R. Jly. 14, 1835
Gardner, Ambrose, Jly. 25, Pasquotank county. R. R. Aug. 18, 1835
Gibson, Mrs. Francis, Sept. 12, Rowan county. R. R. Oct. 6, 1835
Gibson, Mrs. James, Sept., Fayetteville. R. R. Sept. 8, 1835
Godbey, George, Jan. 28, Rowan county. R. R. Mar. 3, 1835
Goodwin, Thomas, Sept. 23, Newbern. R. R. Nov. 10, 1835
Gordon, Alexander, Jly. 25, Camden county. R. R. Aug. 18, 1835
Graham, Alex of Mecklenburg county, Jan. 31, Augusta, Ga. R. R. Feb. 17, 1835
Graham, Col. William, My. 3, Rutherford county. R. R. My. 19, 1835
Grant, John of Connecticut, Jly. 1, Salem. R. R. Aug. 18, 1835
Grigg, Rev. Jacob, Sept. 28, Greensville county, Va. R. R. Oct. 6, 1835
Guion, Martha, Jly. 20, Raleigh. R. R. Jly. 28, 1835
Gullett, Ann, Sept. 7, Greensboro. R. R. Sept. 29, 1835
Halliday, Robert J. of Fayetteville, Oct. 11, Philadelphia. R. R. Nov. 3, 1835
Hamilton, Elizabeth, Je. 11, Wilmington. R. R. Je. 23, 1835
Hancock, Rev. John, Feb., Montgomery county. R. R. Feb. 17, 1835
Hardie, Henry of Scotland, Nov. 7, Raleigh. R. R. Nov. 10, 1835
Hargrove, Israel, My. 3, Granville county. R. R. My. 26, 1835
Harper, Mrs. James, Oct. 4, Green county. R. R. Oct. 13, 1835
Harrington, Mrs. Wm. D. of Moore county, Oct. 12, Narrow Point. R. R. Nov. 3, 1835
Harris, Warren, Sr., Nov., Halifax county. R. R. Nov. 3, 1835
Hart, Mrs. John Graves, Jan. 12, Granville county. R. R. Mar. 3, 1835
Hathaway, Burton, Aug. 25, Tyrrell county. R. R. Sept. 22, 1835
Henderson, Mrs. David, Apr., Mecklenburg county. R. R. Apr. 14, 1835
Higgins, Capt. Lucius M. of Maine & Newbern, Aug., Newbern. R. R. Aug. 25, 1835
Hill, Mrs. Green, My. 5, Raleigh. R. R. My. 12, 1835
Hogg, Gavin of Raleigh, Oct. 28, New York City. R. R. Nov. 10, 1835

Holmes, Mrs. Caroline G. of Wilmington, Aug. 30, Philadelphia. R. R. Aug. 11, 1835
Hooks, Col. David of Duplin county, Jly. 22, West Tennessee. R. R. Sept. 22, 1835
Hopkins, Mrs. A. B. W. of Wake county, Jly. 8, Greene county, Alabama. R. R. Aug. 4, 1835
Hotchkiss, H. S., Sept. 16, Wilmington. R. R. Sept. 29, 1835
Houston, George W., Jan. 25, Mecklenburg county. R. R. Feb. 17, 1835
Houston, Dr. Wm. of Guilford county, Mar. 9, Orange county. R. R. Apr. 7, 1835
Howell, Jordan, Mar. 30, Fayetteville. R. R. Apr. 14, 1835
Humphreys, Mrs. Henry, Jly. 25, Greensboro. R. R. Aug. 18, 1835
Hutchings, James, Aug. 28, Raleigh. R. R. Sept. 1, 1835
Hutchinson, Mary Ann, Sept., Caswell county. R. R. Nov. 10, 1835
James, John H. of Wilmington, Sept. 22, Charleston. R. R. Oct. 6, 1835
Jeffreys, Candace H., Aug. 7, Person county. R. R. Aug. 11, 1835
Jones, infant daughter of Benson F. Jones, My. 21, Oxford. R. R. My. 26, 1835
Jones, Capt. Ethelred, Oct. 2, Wake county. R. R. Oct. 13, 1835
Jones, Mrs. John D., Mar., Wilmington. R. R. Mar. 10, 1835
Jones, Tignal of Morgan county to Susan King of Lawrence county both formerly of Wake county, Je. 28, Alabama. R. R. Jly. 7, 1835
Joy, Louisa, Jly. 27, Rutherfordton. R. R. Sept. 8, 1835
Joyner, Thomas B., Sept. 2, Scotland Neck, Halifax county. R. R. Oct. 13, 1835
Keith, William, Sept. 7, New Hanover county. R. R. Sept. 29, 1835
Kerr, N. W. W. Apr. 19, Macon county. R. R. My. 19, 1835
King, Benjamin S. of Raleigh, Sept. 29, Greensboro, Alabama. R. R. Oct. 20, 1835
Krause, Samuel, Oct. 22, Bathabara, Stokes county. R. R. Nov. 3, 1835
Lamb, Mrs. Moses, Sept., Rowan county. R. R. Nov. 3, 1835
Latham, Mrs. Elbanon, Sept. 13, Beaufort county. R. R. Oct. 13, 1835
Lawrence, Waldemar, Jly. 17, Raleigh. R. R. Jly. 21, 1835
Lea, James, Sr., Je. 30, Caswell county. R. R. Jly. 14, 1835
Lemay, Mrs. Lewis, Sept. 7, Granville county. R. R. Oct. 20, 1835
Lenoir, Eliza Mira, Aug. 15, Fort Defiance, Wilkes county. R. R. Sept. 15, 1835
Lineback, Mrs. Christian, Feb., Stokes county. R. R. Feb. 17, 1835
Little, John of this State, Aug. 10, Philadelphia. R. R. Aug. 25, 1835
Littleberry, Gary, Nov., Halifax county. R. R. Nov. 3, 1835
Long, Mrs. Daniel, Aug. 22, Elizabeth City. R. R. Sept. 15, 1835
Mabry, Green, Nov., Halifax county. R. R. Nov. 3, 1835
M'Cain, Mrs. Tillotson, Sept., Caswell county. R. R. Oct. 13, 1835
M'Connaughey, Elizabeth Harris, Sept. 23, Charlotte. R. R. Oct. 20, 1835
M'Cracken, Thomas, Apr., Chapel Hill. R. R. Apr. 14, 1835
M'Dowell, Hugh, Jly., Mecklenburg county. R. R. Aug. 4, 1835
M'Iver, Duncan of this State, Sept. 22, Tallahatchee, Mississippi. R. R. Nov. 3, 1835
M'Kee, Rankin, Aug., Orange county. R. R. Aug. 18, 1835
M'Keithan, Charlotte, Jly. 6, Wilmington. R. R. Aug. 4, 1835

McKenzie, Hector of Robeson county, Oct. 13, Sumpter county, Alabama. R. R. Nov. 3, 1835
McPherson, Colin, Aug., Cumberland county. R. R. Sept. 8, 1835
M'Pherson, Joseph, Feb., Stokes county. R. R. Feb. 17, 1835
M'Queen, Neil, My. 5, Queensdale, Robeson county. R. R. My. 26, 1835
Manly, Mrs. Matthias E., Mar. 16, Newbern. R. R. Mar. 24, 1835
Manning, Lieut. David A. of Edenton, Jly. 21, Key West, Florida. R. R. Sept. 1, 1835
Matthews, Dr. Thomas C., Pasquotank county, Aug., Elizabeth City. R. R. Sept. 1, 1835
Mixson, Mrs. Charles W., Aug. 14, Edenton. R. R. Sept. 1, 1835
Moore, Mrs. Cornelius of Anson county, Sept., Autauga county, Alabama. R. R. Sept. 22, 1835
Moore, Lavinia, Oct. 9, Pitt county. R. R. Oct. 27, 1835
Moore, Maurice, Sept. 14, New Hanover county. R. R. Sept. 29, 1835
Moore, Samuel, Sept. 13, Sampson county. R. R. Oct. 6, 1835
Morgan, Acrill, Oct. 20, Raleigh. R. R. Oct. 27, 1835
Moseley, Wm., Aug. 20, Halifax county. R. R. Sept. 8, 1835
Mull, Capt. Thomas, Jan. 24, Salisbury. R. R. Feb. 17, 1835
Nixon, Mrs. James M. of Duplin county, Aug. 23, Quincey, Florida. R. R. Sept. 1, 1835
Nobles, Mrs. Luke, Sept. 1, Pitt county. R. R. Sept. 15, 1835
Norfleet, Dr. Thomas of Person county, Sept., Rutherford county, Tennessee. R. R. Oct. 13, 1835
Norris, Peyton, Oct. 21, Wake county. R. R. Oct. 27, 1835
Northington, Mrs. Jesse, Sept. 20, Cumberland county. R. R. Oct. 13, 1835
Oliver, Nathaniel J., Oct., Washington, Beaufort county. R. R. Oct. 27, 1835
Osborne, Mrs. H. H. of New York, Je. 11, Raleigh. R. R. Je. 16, 1835
Owen, Mrs., Jly. 29, Bladen county. R. R. Aug. 18, 1835
Owen, Charles P. of Bladen county, Aug. 13, Hillsboro. R. R. Aug. 25, 1835
Parham, Lucy, Feb., Granville county. R. R. Feb. 17, 1835
Parham, Samuel R., Feb., Granville county. R. R. Feb. 17, 1835
Parsley, Robert, Jly. 13, Bladen county. R. R. Jly. 21, 1835
Partee, George, Oct. 30, Rowan county. R. R. Nov. 3, 1835
Paschall, Rev. Wesley W., Mar. 27, Granville county. R. R. Apr. 14, 1835
Patterson, Mann, My. 28, Chapel Hill. R. R. Je. 23, 1835
Phifer, Mrs. William of Concord, Jly., Cabarrus county. R. R. Jly. 14, 1835
Pickett, Mrs. Joseph, Feb. 2, Wadesborough, Anson county. R. R. Feb. 24, 1835
Piper, John, Apr. 25, Orange county. R. R. My. 19, 1835
Pleasants, Micajah, Sr., Jly. 31, Caswell county. R. R. Aug. 18, 1835
Potter, Mrs. Henry, Aug. 26, Beaufort county. R. R. Sept. 15, 1835
Potter, Robert, Mar., Smithville. R. R. Mar. 10, 1835
Potts, Dr. John W. of Tarborough, Aug., Little Rock, Arkansas. R. R. Aug. 18, 1835
Potts, Maj. Wm., Oct. 13, Iredell county. R. R. Nov. 3, 1835
Powell, Mrs. Robert, Sept. 21, Richmond county. R. R. Oct. 6, 1835
Pridgen, Mrs. Hardy, Sept. 25, Nash county. R. R. Oct. 20, 1835

Purify, Ann, Aug., Cumberland county. R. R. Sept. 1, 1835
Quince, Mrs. Elizabeth, Sept. 23, New Hanover county. R. R. Nov. 10, 1835
Ragan, William, Feb. 23, Raleigh. R. R. Mar. 3, 1835
Ragsdale, Mrs. Benjamin, Jly. 7, Wake county. R. R. Jly. 14, 1835
Raiford, Mrs. Philip, Jly. 9, Johnston county. R. R. Aug. 4, 1835
Raiford, Robert of Fayetteville, Oct. 14, Augusta, Georgia. R. R. Nov. 3, 1835
Ramsey, Mrs. Ann of Chatham county, Sept., Marengo county, Alabama. R. R. Aug. 4, 1835
Reeves, Margaret, Sept. 17, Raleigh. R. R. Sept. 29, 1835
Reid, Mrs. Lucy T., Oct. 23, Wake Forest. R. R. Oct. 27, 1835
Rhodes, Cornelius, Sept., Elizabeth City. R. R. Nov. 10, 1835
Richardson, Mrs. J. J., Oct. 26, Lincolnton. R. R. Nov. 17, 1835
Rogers, Shadrack, Oct. 15, Pitt county. R. R. Oct. 27, 1835
Ross, John D., Sept. 26, Franklin county. R. R. Oct. 27, 1835
Rush, John G. of Montgomery county, Jly., Richmond county. R. R. Jly. 28, 1835
Salmon, Mrs. Francis, Sept. 22, Duplin county. R. R. Oct. 13, 1835
Sasser, Dallas of Wayne county, Aug. 22, Raleigh. R. R. Sept. 1, 1835
Sawyer, Dr. Matthias E., Apr. 27, Edenton. R. R. My. 19, 1835
Scales, Daniel of Rockingham county, Jly., Williamson county, Tennessee. R. R. Aug. 4, 1835
Scott, Joseph, Aug. 3, Caswell county. R. R. Sept. 22, 1835
Seawell, Hon. Henry, Oct. 6, Raleigh. R. R. Oct. 13, 1835
Shaw, Mrs. John of Orange county, Aug., Somerville, Tennessee. R. R. Aug. 18, 1835
Shaw, Matthew, Jly. 27, Raleigh. R. R. Aug. 4, 1835
Shaw, Murdock of Fayetteville, Sept., Quincey, Florida. R. R. Oct. 6, 1835
Sheperd, Penelope S., Aug. 29, Newbern. R. R. Sept. 15, 1835
Shepperd, Carter Peyton, Jly., Stokes county. R. R. Jly. 14, 1835
Shober, Mrs. Gotlieb, Je. 13, Salem, Stokes county. R. R. Je. 23, 1835
Simms, Burwell, Jan. 14, Wake county. R. R. Feb. 3, 1835
Simonton, Absalom K., Jan. 18, Statesville. R. R. Feb. 17, 1835
Slade, Henry, Oct. 10, Martin county. R. R. Nov. 3, 1835
Smith, Christian E., Sept. 17, Onslow county. R. R. Nov. 3, 1835
Smith, Col. Maurice, Je., Granville county. R. R. Je. 23, 1835
Smith, Reliance H. of Harwick, Massachusetts, Feb., Washington, Beaufort county. R. R. Feb. 17, 1835
Sneed, Mrs. James, Sept., Milton. R. R. Sept. 8, 1835
Somerville, Robert D., Aug. 12, Warrenton. R. R. Aug. 25, 1835
Southerland, Robert, Aug. 25, Duplin county. R. R. Sept. 22, 1835
Speight, Capt. James, Nov. 5, Wake county. R. R. Nov. 17, 1835
Speire, Samuel, Oct. 8, Pitt county. R. R. Oct. 27, 1835
Stephens, Godfrey of Newbern, Sept. 25, Florida. R. R. Oct. 27, 1835
Swann, Mary Green, Sept., Chatham county. R. R. Sept. 29, 1835
Swindall, Lucy Matilda, Sept. 23, Columbus county. R. R. Nov. 3, 1835
Taylor, Harriet B., Sept. 24, Pittsboro, Chatham county. R. R. Oct. 13, 1835
Taylor, William, Oct. 20, Newbern. R. R. Nov. 3, 1835
Taylor, Mrs. Wm. A. of Granville county, Dec. 27, Tipton county, Tenn. R. R. Feb. 17, 1835

Tench, Martha Ann Elizabeth, Dec. 18, Raleigh. R. R. Dec. 29, 1835
Teworthy, Samuel of England, Jly. 25, Mecklenburg county. R. R. Aug. 18, 1835
Thompson, Robert Montgomery, My. 18, Raleigh. R. R. My. 26, 1835
Trotter, Thomas of Scotland & this State, Dec. 24, Beaufort. R. R. Jan. 6, 1835
Tutenton, Benjamin, Sept. 6, Orange county. R. R. Sept. 29, 1835
Unthank, Jesse A. of Surry county, Aug. 28, Lincoln county, Tennessee. R. R. Oct. 6, 1835
Waddill, Hiram G., Aug. 23, Salisbury. R. R. Sept. 8, 1835
Walker, George W., Sept. 28, Scotland Neck, Halifax county. R. R. Oct. 13, 1835
Walker, Mrs. James, Jly. 18, Orange county. R. R. Aug. 4, 1835
Wall, Elder William of Johnston county, Dec. 22, Wake county. R. R. Feb. 3, 1835
Wallace, Hugh, Aug. 2, Wilmington. R. R. Aug. 18, 1835
Warren, John H. of Wake county, Aug. 20, Fayette county, Tennessee. R. R. Oct. 27, 1835
Watts, Thomas D. of Orange county, Apr., Chapel Hill. R. R. Apr. 14, 1835
Weaver, Richard H., Je. 13, Northampton county. R. R. Je. 23, 1835
Westcoat, Arthur, Aug. 25, Brunswick county. R. R. Sept. 22, 1835
White, Hannah Elizabeth, My. 13, Raleigh. R. R. My. 19, 1835
Whitfield, Mary, Oct. 19, Raleigh. R. R. Oct. 20, 1835
Williams, David, Sept. 28, Martin county. R. R. Oct. 13, 1835
Williams, Henry G., Jan. 16, Warren county. R. R. Mar. 3, 1835
Williams, Mrs. John, Feb., Louisburg. R. R. Feb. 17, 1835
Williams, Mrs. William W., Sept. 24, Warren county R. R. Oct. 13, 1835
Winston, Hon. Fountain of Stokes county, Jan., Natchez, Mississippi. R. R. Jan. 27, 1835
Wolff, Ann P., Aug. 29, Stokes county. R. R. Sept. 22, 1835
Wood, Mrs. Joshua of Nixton, Oct. 15, Pasquotank county. R. R. Nov. 3, 1835
Woolard, Rufus, Oct., Washington, Beaufort county. R. R. Oct. 27, 1835
Wooten, John, Sr., Sept. 25, Wayne county. R. R. Oct. 20, 1835
Wright, Rev. Thomas of Wilmington, My., Memphis, Tennessee. R. R. Je. 2, 1835
Yarbrough, Mrs. Martha, Nov., Halifax. R. R. Nov. 3, 1835
Young, James, Mar., Mecklenburg county. R. R. Mar. 10, 1835

1836

Abernathy, David, Je., Lincoln county. R. R. Je. 28, 1836
Albritton, Mrs. Martha, Jan. 30, Greene county. R. R. Mar. 1, 1836
Alexander, Albert Munroe, Dec. 16, Mecklenburg county. R. R. Jan. 5, 1836
Alexander, Mrs. Ezra, Sept. 20, Mecklenburg county. R. R. Oct. 25, 1836
Allen, Major Alexander, Dec. 29, Hawfields. R. R. Jan. 26, 1836
Anderson, Eliza Jane, Sept. 7, Newbern. R. R. Sept. 27, 1836
Anderson, Mrs. Quinton, Jan. 19, Caswell county. R. R. Feb. 2, 1836
Anderson, Robert, Irwin, Sept. 7, Newbern. R. R. Sept. 27, 1836

Applewhite, Mrs. Henry, Sept. 22, Scotland Neck, Halifax county. R. R. Oct. 11, 1836
Arrington, Jas., Mar. 12, Nash county. R. R. Apr. 5, 1836
Ashburn, Henry of Bertie county, Sept. 30, Norfolk, Va. R. R. Oct. 4, 1836
Austin, Capt. Samuel of Maryland, Apr. 8, Forks of the Yadkin. R. R. My. 10, 1836
Avery, John, Oct. 12, Chowan county. R. R. Nov. 1, 1836
Backhouse, Benjamin W. of Newbern, Jly. 30, Newbern. R. R. Aug. 2, 1836
Badger, Mrs. Thomas of Raleigh, My. 11, Newbern. R. R. My. 17, 1836
Baker, Zaddock of this State, Apr. 1, Greene county, Alabama. R. R. My. 10, 1836
Barr, Mrs. Thomas of this State, Oct. 27, Selma, Alabama. R. R. Nov. 22, 1836
Battle, Zilphia, Oct., Onslow county. R. R. Oct. 11, 1836
Belden, Mrs. Simeon, Je., Fayetteville. R. R. Je. 21, 1836
Bell, Mrs. Elizabeth, Oct. 9, Newbern. R. R. Oct. 25, 1836
Bellamy, Mrs. William, Sept., Nash county. R. R. Oct. 11, 1836
Bennett, Eliza C., Aug. 10, Anson county. R. R. Nov. 8, 1836
Benton, Wm. H., Oct. 14, Charlotte. R. R. Nov. 8, 1836
Bissell, Mrs. Nathaniel, Nov., Edenton. R. R. Nov. 22, 1836
Blake, Mrs. B. T., Jan. 22, Wake county. R. R. Feb. 2, 1836
Blake, Mrs. Isham, Jr., Jan., Fayetteville. R. R. Feb. 2, 1836
Boger, Mrs. George, Apr. 28, Cabarrus county. R. R. My. 17, 1836
Bonner, Joshua, Sr., Apr., Stokes county. R. R. Apr. 19, 1836
Booker, Daniel of this State, Sept., Greensboro, Alabama. R. R. Oct. 18, 1836
Boswell, Reuben, Oct. 16, Mecklenburg county. R. R. Nov. 8, 1836
Brandon, William of Rowan county, Nov. 6, Smith county, Tenn. R. R. Nov. 22, 1836
Brewster, Mrs. J. H., Nov. 4, Wilmington. R. R. Nov. 22, 1836
Brickhouse, Elsbury, Dec. 21, Tyrrell county. R. R. Jan. 5, 1836
Brown, Napoleon B., Oct. 22, Smithville, Brunswick county. R. R. Nov. 8, 1836
Brown, Samuel, Jan. 29, Person county. R. R. Mar. 1, 1836
Bryan, Felix of Wilkes county, Oct., Madison, Ga. R. R. Nov. 8, 1836
Buffalo, John O., Oct. 9, Middleton, Hyde county. R. R. Oct. 25, 1836
Buie, Mrs. Sarah of Argyleshire, Scotland, Jan. 11, Cumberland county. R. R. Mar. 1, 1836
Bullock, Lucy Ann, Oct., Chowan county. R. R. Nov. 1, 1836
Burch, Joel H., Apr. 2, Surry county. R. R. My. 10, 1836
Burges, Thomas, Apr., Halifax. R. R. Apr. 26, 1836
Burton, Hutchins G., Apr. 21, Lincoln county. R. R. Apr. 26, 1836
Butler, John, Jan. 19, Wake county. R. R. Mar. 29, 1836
Bynum, Mrs. Jesse A., Sept. 15, Halifax. R. R. Sept. 27, 1836
Cairns, Mrs. C., Sept. 7, Newbern. R. R. Sept. 27, 1836
Callaway, Samuel, Jan. 30, Surry county. R. R. My. 10, 1836
Camp, John C., Jan. 27, Northampton county. R. R. Feb. 9, 1836
Carigan, James, Jr., Jan. 1, Cabarrus county. R. R. Jan. 26, 1836
Carson, Dr. John W. of Burke county, Jly. 12, Knoxville, Tenn. R. R. Aug. 2, 1836
Carver, William, Sr., Apr., Cumberland county. R. R. Apr. 19, 1836
Catlett, B., Je. 7, Camden county. R. R. Jly. 5, 1836

Chalmers, Charles of Fayetteville & Chapel Hill, Jan. 7, Chapel Hill. R. R. Feb. 2, 1836
Charles, G. W. of this State, Jly. 25, Terry county, Alabama. R. R. Aug. 23, 1836
Charles, Mildred S. of Wake county, Sept., Tuscaloosa, Alabama. R. R. Oct. 18, 1836
Clark, John M., Apr. 18, Cumberland county. R. R. Apr. 26, 1836
Cobb, Edward, Apr., Edgecombe county. R. R. Apr. 19, 1836
Cobb, Mrs. Thomas R., Sept. 21, Elizabeth City. R. R. Oct. 18, 1836
Cochran, Col. Joshua W., Oct. 6, Wilmington. R. R. Oct. 18, 1836
Collins, James, Oct., Wilmington. R. R. Oct. 18, 1836
Condry, Prussia E., Apr. 4, Beaufort county. R. R. Apr. 26, 1836
Cooke, Mrs. Thomas, Aug. 23, Raleigh. R. R. Aug. 30, 1836
Cooper, Capt. Jno., Feb. 27, Waughtown, Stokes county. R. R. Mar. 15, 1836
Cowan, John, Oct. 6, Charlotte. R. R. Nov. 8, 1836
Cox, Mrs. John, Oct. 9, Anson county. R. R. Nov. 8, 1836
Cox, Mrs. John, Oct. 15, Anson county. R. R. Nov. 1, 1836
Cox, Thomas, Feb., Scotland Neck, Halifax county. R. R. Feb. 16, 1836
Creecy, Mrs. Charles, Dec. 21, Chowan county. R. R. Jan. 5, 1836
Crowell, John, Apr. 17, Halifax. R. R. My. 31, 1836
Crump, Conrad, Sept. 1, Burke county. R. R. Sept. 27, 1836
Dalton, Mrs. Samuel, Mar. 17, Rockingham county. R. R. Je. 28, 1836
Daniel, Beverly, My., Raleigh. R. R. My. 31, 1836
Daniel, Mrs. J. J., Feb. 28, Raleigh. R. R. Mar. 8, 1836
Davis, Joseph, Apr. 3, Elizabeth City. R. R. My. 3, 1836
Davis, Margaret, Mrs., Mar. 29, Beaufort county. R. R. Apr. 26, 1836
Dent, Jas., Jan. 20, Franklin county. R. R. Feb. 2, 1836
Devereux, Mrs. Thomas P. of Raleigh, Jly. 18, White Sulphur Springs, Greenbrier county, Va. R. R. Aug. 2, 1836
Dewey, Ann Laetitia, Sept. 9, Raleigh. R. R. Sept. 13, 1836
Dismukes, George A. of Anson county, Jan. 4, Autauga county, Alabama. R. R. Mar. 1, 1836
Downs, Leven, My. 14, Milton. R. R. My. 17, 1836
Duguid, Edward G., Oct. 7, Newbern. R. R. Oct. 25, 1836
Dulany, Mrs. Daniel M., Oct., Onslow county. R. R. Oct. 11, 1836
Dunn, Bolling of Wake county, Jly. 21, La Grange, Alabama. R. R. Aug. 16, 1836
Dunn, John, Oct. 17, Wake Forest. R. R. Nov. 15, 1836
Ehringhaus, Mrs. J. C. B., Oct., Elizabeth City. R. R. Nov. 1, 1836
Elliot, Nixon of Guilford county, Oct. 7, Orange county. R. R. Oct. 25, 1836
Ellis, Charles, Jan. 6, Mecklenburg county. R. R. Feb. 2, 1836
Epps, Mrs. Harriet D., Jly., Halifax. R. R. Jly. 19, 1836
Etheredge, Mrs. Geo. W., Oct. 21, Camden county. R. R. Nov. 22, 1836
Evans, Alexander, Jan. 24, Pitt county. R. R. Mar. 1, 1836
Evans, John, Oct. 9, Cumberland county. R. R. Oct. 25, 1836
Farrett, Mary Delah of Edgecombe county, Sept., Marrengo county, Alabama. R. R. Oct. 18, 1836
Fishel, Jacob, Jly., Stokes county. R. R. Jly. 26, 1836
Fleming, Samuel, Sept. 19, Rowan county. R. R. Oct. 4, 1836

Flowers, Hardy, Nov., Edgecombe county. R. R. Nov. 15, 1836
Foster, Anderson E., My. 11, Forks of the Yadkin, Rowan county. R. R. My. 31, 1836
Frost, Ezekiel, Dec. 21, Stokes county. R. R. Jan. 5, 1836
Frost, James B., Apr., Stokes county. R. R. Apr. 19, 1836
Gallagher, Mrs. Ann M. of England, Oct. 27, Washington, Beaufort county. R. R. Nov. 8, 1836
Gatlin, John, Je. 20, Kinston, Lenoir county. R. R. Jly. 12, 1836
Gilchrist, Thomas, Je. 12, Salisbury. R. R. Je. 28, 1836
Glenn, Patrick M. of Person county, Je., Missouri. R. R. Je. 21, 1836
Gorman, John S. of Raleigh, Sept. 24, Tuscaloosa, Alabama. R. R. Oct. 18, 1836
Gray, Margaret, Apr. 7, Clemonsville, Davidson county. R. R. My. 3, 1836
Green, John R., Je., Milton. R. R. Je. 28, 1836
Hales, Chapman, Sept. 16, Johnston county. R. R. Oct. 4, 1836
Hallowell, Mrs. Meriam, Dec. 27, Pasquotank county. R. R. Jan. 5, 1836
Hanner, Alfred E., Aug. 25, Wentworth, Rockingham county. R. R. Sept. 6, 1836
Hardin, Mrs. William H., My. 24, Pittsborough. R. R. My. 31, 1836
Harper, John, Oct. 21, Halifax. R. R. Nov. 1, 1836
Harrington, Mrs. James, Oct. 16, Anson county. R. R. Oct. 25, 1836
Haughton, Mrs. Deborah, Oct., Edenton. R. R. Oct. 18, 1836
Haywood, Dr. John Lee of Raleigh, Feb. 26, Smithfield, Johnston county. R. R. Mar. 8, 1836
Haywood, William Henry, Je. 30, Raleigh. R. R. Je. 28, 1836
Henderson, Mrs. John, My. 30, Lincoln county. R. R. Je. 28, 1836
Henderson, Col. Thomas of Rockingham county, Je. 22, Alabama. R. R. Aug. 2, 1836
Herndon, Mrs. John R., Feb. 25, Perquimans county. R. R. Mar. 15, 1836
Hilliard, Dr. John T., Sept. 9, Halifax county. R. R. Sept. 27, 1836
Hilman, Col. Sam'l, Mar. 6, Rutherfordton. R. R. Mar. 22, 1836
Hobbs, Mr., Mar. 11, Sampson county. R. R. Mar. 29, 1836
Hogan, Col. William, Dec. 12, Randolph county. R. R. Dec. 27, 1836
Holcombe, George, Apr., Caswell county. R. R. Apr. 19, 1836
Holmes, Mrs. James of Sampson county, Oct., Fayetteville. R. R. Oct. 8, 1836
Hooks, Mrs. Curtis, Jan. 16, Wayne county. R. R. Feb. 2, 1836
Hoskins, Mrs. Joseph N., Nov., Edenton. R. R. Nov. 22, 1836
Houston, Mrs. Owen, Jan. 9, Fayetteville. R. R. Mar. 1, 1836
Howard, James, Sept. 13, Newbern. R. R. Sept. 27, 1836
Huggins, Isaac R., Sept., Onslow county. R. R. Sept. 27, 1836
Hunt, Mrs. Daniel, Dec. 29, Jonesville, Surry county. R. R. Jan. 5, 1836
Hunter, Isaac N., Oct. 16, Chatham county. R. R. Nov. 15, 1836
Hunter, Virginia, Dec. 8, Newbern. R. R. Jan. 26, 1836
Hutcheson, Mrs. James, Apr. 2, Mecklenburg county. R. R. Apr. 26, 1836
Ingram, John, Fayetteville. R. R. Feb. 2, 1836
Jackson, Mrs. Eliza Ann, Nov. 16, Scotland Neck. R. R. Feb. 2, 1836
Jacobs, Mrs. Nancy, Je. 4, Person county. R. R. Je. 28, 1836
Jones, Alfred T., Dec. 7, Newbern. R. R. Jan. 26, 1836
Jones, Gideon of Craven county, Jan. 14, Tennessee. R. R. Mar. 1, 1836
Jones, Geo. O., Jan. 27, Stokes county. R. R. Feb. 2, 1836

Jones, Emma Elizabeth, Jly. 21, Salisbury. R. R. Aug. 2, 1836
Jones, Isaac N. of Granville county, Jly. 15, Arkansas. R. R. Sept. 27, 1836
Jones, Mrs. Sarah, Oct. 7, Newbern. R. R. Oct. 25, 1836
Jordan, Mrs. Dillon, Sr., Apr. 3, Fayetteville. R. R. Apr. 19, 1836
Judkins, Joseph B., Nov., Greenville, Pitt county. R. R. Nov. 22, 1836
King, Mrs. Martha R. of East Tennessee, Jan. 28, Stokes county. R. R. Feb. 2, 1836
Kingsbury, Mrs. R., Oct. 15, Oxford. R. R. Nov. 1, 1836
Kirkland, William, Je. 21, Orange county. R. R. Je 28, 1836
Kitrell, Margaret A. of Chapel Hill, Oct., Greensboro, Alabama. R. R. Nov. 22, 1836
Knox, Robert M., Je. 9, Elizabeth City. R. R. Je. 28, 1836
Latta, Mrs. W. S. of Fayetteville, Sept., Oxford. R. R. Sept. 27, 1836
Lee, Tempy Maria Theresa, Je. 24, Gates county. R. R. Jly. 19, 1836
Lewelling, Dr. Elijah, Apr. 23, Hillsboro. R. R. My. 3, 1836
Litchford, Ambrose A. of Raleigh, Jan. 22. Halifax. R. R. Feb. 2, 1836
Little, Edward, Oct. 13, Rowan county. R. R. Nov. 8, 1836
Lobb, William of England, Aug. 30, Raleigh. R. R. Sept. 6, 1836
Lockhart, Eliza T., Sept. 7, Newbern. R. R. Sept. 27, 1836
Lockheart, Elder Nathaniel, Dec. 21, Pitt county. R. R. Feb. 2, 1836
Luton, Henry, Je., Edenton. R. R. Je. 21, 1836
M'Auley, Ann, Oct. 9, Montgomery county. R. R. Nov. 22, 1836
M'Auley, George, Oct. 10, Montgomery county. R. R. Nov. 22, 1836
M'Auley, Mrs. Margaret, Oct. 9, Montgomery county. R. R. Nov. 22, 1836
M'Cauley, James C., Oct., Wilmington. R. R. Oct. 18, 1836
M'Cord, John, Jly. 22, Mecklenburg county. R. R. Aug. 16, 1836
M'Iver, Mrs. Alexander, Oct. 6, Duplin county. R. R. Nov. 1, 1836
M'Kinnon, John, Nov. 4, Montgomery county. R. R. Nov. 22, 1836
M'Leod, Mrs. Catharine, Jly. 11, Fayetteville. R. R. Jly. 19, 1836
M'Leod, Norman, Oct. 9, Fayetteville. R. R. Oct. 25, 1836
M'Lure, Cyrus, Je. 3, Mecklenburg county. R. R. Je. 28, 1836
M'Masters, Robert C. of Montgomery county, Jly. 5, Cumberland county. R. R. Jly. 12, 1836
M'Pheeters, David Brainard, Oct. 17, Raleigh. R. R. Oct. 25, 1836
M'Pherson, Willie of Camden county, Dec. 19, Norfolk. R. R. Jan. 12, 1836
M'Rackan, Mrs. Robert M., Apr., Brunswick county. R. R. Apr. 26, 1836
Mallett, Mrs. Peter, Apr. 2, Fayetteville. R. R. Apr. 19, 1836
Martin, James H., Je. 1, Anson county. R. R. Je. 28, 1836
Mathews, Mrs. Thos. C., Feb., Elizabeth City. R. R. Mar. 15, 1836
Miller, Mrs. Alexander C., Oct. 12, Bladen county. R. R. Nov. 8, 1836
Miller, Geo., Apr., Cabarrus county. R. R. Apr. 19, 1836
Mitchell, Mrs. Leroy, Sept., Franklin county. R. R. Oct. 11, 1836
Mitchener, Samuel, Sr., Apr. 18, Johnson county. R. R. My. 3, 1836
Moderwell, Robert, Nov. 5, Greensborough. R. R. Nov. 22, 1836
Montague, Hieronymus, Sept. 5, Wake county. R. R. Sept. 13, 1836
Moore, Alanson W., Mar. 18, Rutherfordton. R. R. Apr. 5, 1836
Morehead, Abraham, Mar. 11, Greensboro, Guilford county. R. R. My. 3, 1836
Morgan, Miles, Oct. 16, Camden county. R. R. Oct. 8, 1836

Moring, Christopher, Aug. 27, Greensboro, Guilford county. R. R. Sept. 6, 1836
Mullen, Elizabeth, Apr. 3, Murfreesborough. R. R. My. 3, 1836
Murray, Obed E. of New Hanover county, Apr., Columbus, Ga. R. R. Apr. 19, 1836
Newton, Mrs. Margaret, Oct., Onslow county. R. R. Oct. 11, 1836
Nickolson, Alexander, Apr. 3, Richmond county. R. R. Apr. 26, 1836
Nixon, John, Sept. 23, Perquimans county. R. R. Oct. 11, 1836
Noel, Mrs. Barbara, Mar., Stokes county. R. R. My. 3, 1836
Norwood, Augustus, Apr. 25, Wake county. R. R. My. 3, 1836
O'Bryan, Caledonia, Jly. 4, Warren county. R. R. Jly. 19, 1836
Oliver, Samuel, Jr., Newbern. R. R. Sept. 27, 1836
Outlaw, Frances E. of Bertie county, My. 16, Mount Pleasant. R. R. Je. 28, 1836
Outlaw, Ralph, Oct. 26, Bertie county. R. R. Nov. 15, 1836
Overman, Charles B., Jan. 9, Elizabeth City. R. R. Mar. 1, 1836
Pate, James, Apr., Beaufort county. R. R. Apr. 26, 1836
Pelt, Simon Van., Jan., Pasquotank county. R. R. Mar. 1, 1836
Perkins, Peter of Surry county, Dec. 2, Stokes county. R. R. Jan. 5, 1836
Philips, Gen. Abram, Mar. 23, Rockingham county. R. R. Mar. 3, 1836
Plummer, John, Apr., Davidson county. R. R. Apr. 19, 1836
Polk, Gilbert, Je. 15, Salisbury. R. R. Je. 28, 1836
Pollock, Mrs. H. M., Mar. 2, Onslow county. R. R. Apr. 26, 1836
Pollock, Mrs. John, Mar. 23, Onslow county. R. R. Apr. 26, 1836
Price, Mary L., Oct. 10, Mecklenburg county. R. R. Nov. 8, 1836
Price, Dr. Thomas P., Sept. 11, Caswell county. R. R. Sept. 27, 1836
Pugh, Tho's., Je. 8, Martin county. R. R. Je. 28, 1836
Purdie, Sarah Ann, Oct. 19, Elizabeth, Bladen county. R. R. Oct. 8, 1836
Reid, Margaret B. of Chatham county, Apr. 15, Oxford. R. R. My. 10, 1836
Reston, Duncan F., Oct., Fayetteville. R. R. Nov. 1, 1836
Richardson, Bryan of Johnston county, Mar. 19, Sumter county, Alabama. R. R. My. 3, 1836
Richardson, Mrs. John S., Oct. 19, Bladen county. R. R. Oct. 8, 1836
Richardson, Stephen Chipley of this State, Sept., Lexington, Ky. R. R. Sept. 27, 1836
Ricks, Edmond, Nov., Pitt county. R. R. Nov. 22, 1836
Ripple, Henry, Dec. 19, Stokes county. R. R. Jan. 5, 1836
Robinson, Mrs. John, Jly. 7, Cabarrus county. R. R. Aug. 16, 1836
Robinson, William, Oct., Montgomery, Alabama. R. R. Oct. 18, 1836
Rutland, Benjamin H. of this State, Oct. 8, Montgomery, Alabama. R. R. Nov. 22, 1836
Rutledge, Enos, Jan. 6, Surry county. R. R. Mar. 1, 1836
Ryan, John B. of Windsor, Apr. 17, New York. R. R. My. 10, 1836
Salter, Mrs. John, Sept., Washington, Beaufort county. R. R. Oct. 4, 1836
Sanders, Amanda, Oct. 7, Newbern. R. R. Oct. 25, 1836
Saunders, Dr. William of Warren, R. I. & Newbern, Oct. 22, Newbern. R. R. Nov. 8, 1836
Saunier, Mrs. Francis, Jan. 3, Charlotte. R. R. Mar. 1, 1836
Scarborough, Mrs. Margaret, Sept. 7, Newbern. R. R. Sept. 27, 1836
Shaw, Mary Catharine, Sept., Washington, Beaufort county. R. R. Oct. 11, 1836
Shepard, Mrs. Wm. B. of this State, Mar. 23, Alexandria, D. C. R. R. Apr. 5, 1836

Shine, Philip, Oct. 4, Cabarrus county. R. R. Nov. 8, 1836
Shirly, Jno., Jly., Pasquotank county. R. R. Jly. 19, 1836
Shober, Mary Ann, Apr. 25, Salem, Stokes county. R. R. My. 17, 1836
Shuford, Martin P., My., Rutherford county. R. R. My. 17, 1836
Shultz, Mrs. Jacob, Mar. 8, Stokes county. R. R. My. 3, 1836
Smimous, James, Apr. 9, Halifax county. R. R. Apr. 26, 1836
Simpson, Gen. Samuel, Oct. 24, Fort Barnwell, Craven county. R. R. Oct. 8, 1836
Skinner, Henry, Sept. 22, Perquimans county. R. R. Oct. 11, 1836
Slater, Fielding, Sept. 22, Salisbury. R. R. Oct. 4, 1836
Slater, John, Jan. 9, Stokes county. R. R. Jan. 26, 1836
Smith, Mrs. Caspar, Dec. 22, Rowan county. R. R. Jan. 5, 1836
Smith, Major Robt. W., Sept. 21, Cabarrus county. R. R. Oct. 4, 1836
Sneed, Americus J. of Person county, Je. 15. R. R. Jly. 12, 1836 (Suicide)
Snowden, Mrs. Ann, Dec. 11, Elizabeth City. R. R. Jan. 5, 1836
Sparrow, Mary Eliza, Sept. 25, Newbern. R. R. Oct. 25, 1836
Speight, William Vines, Oct. 31, Greene county. R. R. Nov. 22, 1836
Starkie, Jonathan, Apr. 2, Caswell county. R. R. Apr. 26, 1836
Stedman, Emily Euphania, Sept., Pittsboro. R. R. Sept. 27, 1836
Stedman, Robert P., Aug. 13, Pittsboro. R. R. Sept. 13, 1836
Stedman, W. W., Feb., Gates county. R. R. Feb. 9, 1836
Stuart, Charles of Raleigh, My. 28, Fayeteville. R. R. Je. 7, 1836
Sullivan, Martha H. of Robeson county, Jan. 4, Duplin county. R. R. Mar. 1, 1836
Tate, Col. David, My., Burke county. R. R. My. 31, 1836
Taylor, Mrs. Martha, Jan. 24, Louisburg. R. R. Feb. 2, 1836
Templeton, John, Oct. 9, Newbern. R. R. Oct. 25, 1836
Tench, Mrs. Archer, Dec. 14, Raleigh, Dec. 20, 1836
Thompson, Mrs. David, Jan. 3, Smithfield, Johnston county. R. R. Mar. 1, 1836
Tinnin, Robert, Dec. 31, Orange county. R. R. Jan. 26, 1836
Trotter, Mrs. Jane, Jly. 4, Salisbury. R. R. Jly. 19, 1836
Turner, Capt. James R., Jly. 20, Halifax county. R. R. Aug. 16, 1836
Underwood, Nancy, Mar. 17, Wake Forest. R. R. Mar. 29, 1836
Vokes, George, Oct. 9, Warrenton. R. R. Oct. 25, 1836
Wadsworth, Mrs. W. D., Feb. 1, Craven county. R. R. Mar. 1, 1836
Watkins, John, Sept., Rolesville. R. R. Sept. 13, 1836
Watson, James M., Mar. 19, Duplin county. R. R. My. 3, 1836
Walton, Jesse W., Nov. 6, Rowan county. R. R. Nov. 22, 1836
Ward, Eli S., Oct., Onslow county. R. R. Oct. 25, 1836
Warren, Mrs. Henry, Jly. 20, Wake county. R. R. Aug. 2, 1836
Watters, Dr. Thomas, Apr. 21, Wilmington. R. R. Apr. 26, 1836
Weems, Capt. Elijah of Raleigh, Feb. 8, Vicksburg, Miss. R. R. Mar. 22, 1836
Wilkins, Mrs. John, Jan. 8, Beaufort county. R. R. Mar. 1, 1836
Williams, Mrs. Lewis A., Oct. 16, Martin county. R. R. Nov. 8, 1836
Williams, William C. of Raleigh, Oct. 19, Wilmington. R. R. Nov. 8, 1836
Wills, James, Je., Edenton. R. R. Je. 28, 1836
Wilson, Jesse of Hertford, Perquimans county, Oct., Winton. R. R. Oct. 18, 1836
Winfrey, John, Dec., Surry county. R. R. Jan. 5, 1836

Woody, Mrs. Robert of Chatham county, My. 21. R. R. Je. 7, 1836
Yoder, Capt. John, Dec. 30, Lincoln county. R. R. Mar. 1, 1836
Young, Joseph, Dec. 28, Cabarrus county. R. R. Jan. 26, 1836
Young, William, Dec. 14, Hyde county. R. R. Dec. 20, 1836

1837

Aaron, Henry, Nov., Halifax county. R. R. Nov. 27, 1837
Alford, Madison S., Sept. 29, Franklin county. R. R. Oct. 9, 1837
Alston, Frances, Apr., Wake Forest. R. R. Apr. 25, 1837
Alston, Hon. Willis, Apr. 19, Halifax county. R. R. My. 2, 1837
Ambrose, Wm. W., Jan. 22, Onslow county. R. R. Feb. 21, 1837
Arnold, Mrs. Whitlock, Je., Randolph county. R. R. Je. 13, 1837
Arrington, Mourning R., Je., Halifax county. R. R. Je. 13, 1837
Arrington, Peter, Sr., Jly. 3, Nash county. R. R. Jly. 17, 1837
Ashe, Mrs. Samuel P. of Fayetteville, Feb., Brownsville, Tennessee. R. R. Feb. 21, 1837
Avera, Hardy, Apr., Smithfield. R. R. My. 2, 1837
Avery, Rev. John of this State, Jan. 17, Green county, Alabama. R. R. Feb. 14, 1837
Bagge, Charles F., Aug., Salem. R. R. Aug. 28, 1837
Baker, Mrs. Cornell, Jly. 14, Raleigh. R. R. Jly. 17, 1837
Barbee, Gilly, Aug. 6, Orange county. R. R. Sept. 18, 1837
Barnett, Mrs. Robert S., Oct., Granville county. R. R. Oct. 9, 1837
Beggs, James of Scotland, Nov., Cumberland county. R. R. Nov. 27, 1837
Bell, Nancy Gibbons, Mar., Beaufort county. R. R. Mar. 21, 1837
Bellamy, Alexander, My. 18, Florida. R. R. Je. 19, 1837
Bellamy, Mrs. Samuel C. of Lenoir, My. 11, Florida. R. R. Je. 19, 1837
Billings, Mrs. Ann, Jan. 23, Edenton, Chowan county. R. R. Feb. 21, 1837
Blackman, Col. Calvin R. of Wayne county, Je., Sumpter county, Alabama. R. R. Je. 19, 1837
Blalack, Millington, Nov., Granville county. R. R. Nov. 20, 1837
Blackwood, Samuel P., Nov., Hillsboro. R. R. Nov. 20, 1837
Boon, John, Dec., Burke county. R. R. Dec. 18, 1837
Bowell, Mrs. Abner, F., Oct., Fayetteville. R. R. Oct. 9, 1837
Braswell, Jacob, Aug. 1, Edgecombe county. R. R. Aug. 7, 1837
Brazier, R. H. B., Jan. 5, Raleigh. R. R. Jan. 10, 1837
Bridges, Joseph, Apr., Chatham county. R. R. Apr. 18, 1837
Brooks, Larkin, Sept., Chatham county. R R. Sept. 25, 1837
Brown, Mrs. Absalom, Jly. 12, Lincoln county. R. R. Jly. 24, 1837
Brown, Thomas Cowan, Oct., Salisbury. R. R. Oct. 23, 1837
Brownrigg, Mrs. Treacy, My. 30, Waynesborough. R. R. Je. 19, 1837
Bryan, Green, Jly. 7, Newbern. R. R. Jly. 24, 1837
Bryan, Needham, G., Mar. 4, Smithfield, Johnson county. R. R. Mar. 21, 1837
Cain, Mrs. William, Je. 24, Hillsboro. R. R. Jly. 10, 1837
Cameron, Robert W., Nov., Fayetteville. R. R. Nov. 27, 1837
Campbell, James, Je. 6, Statesville, Iredell county. R. R. Je. 19, 1837
Campbell, Mrs. John of Fayetteville, Feb., Nashville, Tenn. R. R. Feb. 21, 1837
Canady, Elijah, Feb. 7, Beaufort. R. R. Feb. 21, 1837

Carpenter, Henry, Nov., Lincoln county. R. R. Nov. 27, 1837
Carraway, Charles, Mar., Craven county. R. R. Mar. 21, 1837
Chaffin, Mrs. W. O., Je. 25, Davie county. R. R. Jly. 24, 1837
Charles, Stephen, Mar., Elizabeth City. R. R. Mar. 7, 1837
Chelton, Stephen, Apr. 19, Surry county. R. R. My. 16, 1837
Cherry, Roderick, Je., Pitt county. R. R. Je. 13, 1837
Christian, Thomas of Wilmington, Sept., Columbus, Mississippi. R. R. Oct. 2, 1837
Clark, Nancy, Jan., Edenton. R. R. Jan. 31, 1837
Clements, Woodson, Nov. 26, Wake county. R. R. Nov. 27, 1837
Cloud, Mrs. Ann, Je., Orange county. R. R. Je. 13, 1837
Close, F. C. of Guilford county, Sept. 17, New Orleans. R. R. Oct. 30, 1837
Coart, John, Mar., Newbern. R. R. Mar. 21, 1837
Cochran, Margery Jane, Nov., Mecklenburg county. R. R. Nov. 20, 1837
Cochran, Mrs. R. M., Nov., Mecklenburg county. R. R. Nov. 20, 1837
Collins, James, Mar., Beaufort county. R. R. Mar. 7, 1837
Cook, Mrs. John P., Jly. 6, Wake county. R. R. Jly. 24, 1837
Cornell, Ann Eliza, Aug., Raleigh. R. R. Aug. 14, 1837
Cothran, Jesse, Jan. 22, Person county. R. R. Feb. 21, 1837
Cotten, Spencer D. of Tarboro, Aug. 28, Hot Springs, Va. R. R. Oct. 9, 1837
Coughenour, Mrs. Jacob, Mar., Salisbury. R. R. Mar. 28, 1837
Cowan, John, My. 2, Rowan county. R. R. My. 16, 1837
Craige, Mary Elizabeth, Oct., Salisbury. R. R. Oct. 23, 1837
Creecy, Mrs. James R. of Edenton, Nov., Manchester, Mississippi. R. R. Nov. 27, 1837
Crossland, Martha Ann Elizabeth of Warrenton, Aug. 29, Greensborough, Alabama. R. R. Sept. 18, 1837
Crowell, Newsom, Mar., Edgecombe county. R. R. Mar. 21, 1837
Davenport, Mira A. of Wilkes county, Jly. 3. R. R. Jly. 31, 1837
Davis, James, Sept. 1, Mecklenburg county. R. R. Sept. 25, 1837
Delacy, John D. of Raleigh, Apr. R. R. Apr. 25, 1837
Depoe, Joseph Lawrence, Nov., Fayetteville. R. R. Nov. 6, 1837
DeRossett, Mrs. A. J., Sr., Mar. 9, Wilmington. R. R. Mar. 21, 1837
Dewey, Catharine, Oct., Newbern. R. R. Oct. 23, 1837
Dewey, Elizabeth, Oct., Newbern. R. R. Oct. 23, 1837
Dillen, Dolla, Sept. 27, Guilford county. R. R. Oct. 30, 1837
Dobbin, John M., Apr., Fayetteville. R. R. Apr. 25, 1837
Dougall, Capt. Wm., Apr., Wilmington. R. R. Apr. 25, 1837
Douglass, Rev. James W., Sept. 5, Fayetteville. R. R. Sept. 11, 1837
Duke, James W., Mar., Camden county. R. R. Mar. 7, 1837
Dukes, James R., Mar., Beaufort county. R. R. Mar. 7, 1837
Dunn, Mrs. M. C. of Franklin county, My., Weakly county, Tennessee. R. R. My. 16, 1837
Durham, William W., Oct. 29, Caswell county. R. R. Nov. 20, 1837
Dutter, Mrs. Nicholas, Je., Lincolnton. R. R. Je. 19, 1837
Everett, Thomas, Feb. 6, Richmond county. R. R. Feb. 21, 1837
Exum, William, Sr. of Wayne county, Jly. 30, Rockingham Springs. R. R. Aug. 14, 1837
Farley, Mrs. Andrew, Mar., Milton. R. R. Mar. 28, 1837
Faust, Mrs. Elenor, Sept. 12, Salisbury. R. R. Sept. 18, 1837

Ferrell, Ephraim, Jan. 28, Wake county. R. R. Feb. 14, 1837
Fisher, Susan Elizabeth, Dec. 27, Salisbury. R. R. Jan. 24, 1837
Foster, Edmund, Aug. 5, White-Oak-mountain. R. R. Aug. 28, 1837
Fullenwider, Jacob, Lincoln county, Apr. R. R. Apr. 25, 1837
Fuller, Mrs. Sarah B., Apr., Edenton. R. R. Apr. 18, 1837
Gaston, Mrs. Alex F., Mar. 16, Lincoln county. R. R. My. 9, 1837
Giles, Rev. John of Johnson county, Mar., Hyde county. R. R. Mar. 7, 1837
Gillespie, Mrs. Richard, Jan. 24, Rowan county. R. R. Feb. 21, 1837
Grady, Mrs. John, Sr., Mar. 23, Anson county. R. R. Apr. 25, 1837
Graham, Col. Joseph, of Lincoln county, Oct., Memphis, Tennessee. R. R. Oct. 9, 1837
Graham, Locke, Nov., Rowan county. R. R. Nov. 6, 1837
Graham, Mrs. Purvis, Sept. 28, Rowan county. R. R. Oct. 9, 1837
Graves, Azariah, My., Caswell county. R. R. My. 16, 1837
Gregory, Henry, Mar., Camden county. R. R. Mar. 7, 1837
Green, Mrs. Gideon M., Apr., Warren county. R. R. Apr. 18, 1837
Grier, Mrs. Wm. M. of Lincoln county, Je., Mecklenburg county. R. R. Je. 13, 1837
Griffin, Allen, Feb. 17, Wake county. R. R. Mar. 7, 1837
Hardee, Mrs. Nancy, Feb. 5, Lenoir county. R. R. Feb. 21, 1837
Hare, Richard, Jan. 18, Warren county. R. R. Feb. 14, 1837
Harper, Mrs. Charles H., Apr., Greene county. R. R. My. 9, 1837
Harris, Sarah of Rowan county, Je., Cabarrus county. R. R. Je. 13, 1837
Harrison, Wyatt of this county, Oct. 21, Little Rock, Arkansas. R. R. Nov. 27, 1837
Harvey, Mrs. John C., My. 12, Guilford county. R. R. Je. 13, 1837
Hatcher, Timothy, Sept., New Hanover county. R. R. Oct. 2, 1837
Henderson, Hugh L. of Rutherfordton, d. at Sea. Jan. 26. R. R. Mar. 21, 1837
Henderson, Mary E., Sept. 4, Mecklenburg county. R. R. Sept. 25, 1837
Henderson, Pleasant of this State, Je. 28, McMinnville. R. R. Jly. 24, 1837
Heptinstall, Asa A., Jan. 17, Enfield. R. R. Jan. 31, 1837
Hicks, Mrs. Edward B. of this State, Feb. 12, Lawrenceville, Brunswick county, Va. R. R. Feb. 21, 1837
Hicks, Henry, Je., Iredell county. R. R. Je. 13, 1837
Higgs, Mrs. Sarah, Apr. 1, Halifax county. R. R. Apr. 18, 1837
Hines, Mrs. Peter R., Nov., Edgecombe county. R. R. Nov. 6, 1837
Hinton, Henry, Oct. 16, Wake county. R. R. Oct. 23, 1837
Hobbs, Jonathan, Aug. 10, Orange county. R. R. Aug. 21, 1837
Holden, Louisa, Jly. 28, Orange county. R. R. Aug. 14, 1837
Holland, William, Nov., Rutherford county. R. R. Nov. 6, 1837
Hoskins, James H., Apr., Edenton. R. R. Apr. 18, 1837
Hoyle, Mrs. Eli, Nov., Lincoln county. R. R. Nov. 20, 1837
Huckaby, Mrs. Robert A., Jly., Mecklenburg county. R. R. Jly. 31, 1837
Irwin, Francis, Oct., Charlotte. R. R. Oct. 9, 1837
Jenkins, Mrs. Joseph F., Jly. 22, Edgecombe county. R. R. Aug. 7, 1837
Jones, Martha Ann, Nov., Warren county. R. R. Nov. 27, 1837
Jones, William, Jly. 9, Onslow county. R. R. Jly. 24, 1837
Jones, Willie W., Nov. 3, Raleigh. R. R. Nov. 27, 1837
Jinkins, Sanford, Je. 11, Chatham county. R. R. Jly. 17, 1837
Johnson, Randal, Apr. 29, Greensboro. R. R. My. 16, 1837

Jordan, Dillon, Sr., Oct. 11, Fayetteville. R. R. Oct. 16, 1837
Jordan, Thomas, Mar., Beaufort county. R. R. Mar. 7, 1837
Kenan, Major Tho. H. of this State, Mar., Milledgeville, Ga. R. R. Apr. 18, 1837
Kincaid, Capt. John, Oct., Lincoln county. R. R. Oct. 30, 1837
King, Benjamin S. of Raleigh, Aug. 30, Greene county, Alabama. R. R. Sept. 25, 1837
King, Joseph W. of Fayetteville, Oct. 31, Chattahoochee, Florida. R. R. Nov. 27, 1837
Kelly, John of Bladen county, Aug. 9, Columbus county. R. R. Oct. 2, 1837
Kersey, Samuel, Oct. 10, Guilford county. R. R. Oct. 30, 1837
Kesler, Eleanor, Oct., Salisbury. R. R. Oct. 23, 1837
Kittrell, Bryant of Chapel Hill, Sept. 21, Greensborough, Alabama. R. R. Oct. 23, 1837
Knight, William, Mar., Edgecombe county. R. R. Mar. 21, 1837
Knox, Mrs. J. R. of Fayetteville, Mar., Carlisle, Pa. R. R. Mar. 28, 1837
Krider, Mary M., Dec., Rowan county. R. R. Dec. 23, 1837
Lamb, Mrs. James, Sept., Guilford county. R. R. Sept. 25, 1837
Lane, David, Oct. 2, Tarboro, Edgecombe county. R. R. Oct. 16, 1837
Lanthary, John, Mar., Iredell county. R. R. Mar. 28, 1837
Latta, James, Nov., Iredell county. R. R. Nov. 20, 1837
Laughter, William of Warren county, Sept. 28, La Grange, Tenn. R. R. Oct. 16, 1837
Lazenby, Lurana, Mar., Iredell county. R. R. Mar. 28, 1837
Leach, John, Mar. 10, Johnston county. R. R. Mar. 21, 1837
Ledbetter, Mrs. Isaac, Sept., Buncombe county. R. R. Sept. 25, 1837
Lewis, Mrs. Willis of Granville county, Sept. 17, Hardeman county, Tenn. R. R. Nov. 13, 1837
Ligon, Green W., Feb. 22, Raleigh. R. R. Feb. 28, 1837
Lindsay, Daniel, Jr., Mar., Currituck county. R. R. Mar. 21, 1837
Lister, Nathan, Jly. 24, Guilford county. R. R. Aug. 31, 1837
Long, Thomas, Mar., Perquimans county. R. R. Mar. 21, 1837
M'Cain, Mrs. John, Feb. 1, Caswell county. R. R. Feb. 21, 1837
M'Connaughey, John Howard, Aug. 18, Rowan county. R. R. Sept. 18, 1837
M'Dowell, Joseph, Jan. 29, Milton, Caswell county. R. R. Feb. 21, 1837
M'Iver, Mrs. Effie, Jan., Moore county. R. R. Jan. 3, 1837
M'Kay, Mrs. Wm., My. 5, Clinton, Sampson county. R. R. My. 9, 1837
M'Laughlin, Mrs. Rebecca, Sept. 28, Rowan county. R. R. Oct. 9, 1837
M'Lean, Christiana, Apr., Robeson county. R. R. My. 9, 1837
M'Nab, Mrs. Robt., Apr. 11, Duplin county. R. R. My. 9, 1837
M'Rae, Duncan, Feb., Fayetteville. R. R. Feb. 21, 1837
M'Rum, Rachel Elizabeth, Jly., Mecklenburg county. R. R. Jly. 31, 1837
M'Williams, John, Je., Beaufort county. R. R. Je. 13, 1837
Macon, Nathaniel, Jly., Warren county. R. R. Jly. 3, 1837
Marley, Mrs. Rachael, Sept., Chatham county. R. R. Sept. 25, 1837
Martin, William C., Jly., Surry county. R. R. Jly. 31, 1837
Mason, Mary H., Oct. 26, Raleigh. R. R. Nov. 6, 1837
Mebane, Col. John, Sept. 13, Chatham county. R. R. Oct. 16, 1837
Merrill, Mrs. Daniel, Apr. 22, Randolph county. R. R. My. 16, 1837

Merriman, Charles Rollin of Vermont, Apr. 9, Wake Forest. R. R. My. 2, 1837
Midgett, Sparrow, Mar., Hyde county. R. R. Mar. 7, 1837
Miller, John, Oct., Davidson county. R. R. Oct. 9, 1837
Miller, Mrs. John, Jly. 13, Davidson county. R. R. Jly. 17, 1837
Minnis, Mrs. John R., Mar. 9, Orange county. R. R. Mar. 21, 1837
Minor, Mrs. Randal, Oct., Granville county. R. R. Oct. 9, 1837
Minter, Richard of Chatham county, Jly., Jasper county, Ga. R. R. Jly. 17, 1837
Mitchell, General David, Apr., Milledgeville, Ga. R. R. My. 9, 1837
Monroe, Woodson, Mar., Rowan county. R. R. Mar. 28, 1837
Montgomery, Gen. Bridger I., Apr., Hertford county. R. R. My. 9, 1837
Montgomery, Geo. W., Jan. 4, Hertford county. R. R. Jan. 10, 1837
Montgomery, Mrs. James, Nov., Caswell county. R. R. Nov. 13, 1837
Moore, Alfred, Jly. 25, Orange county. R. R. Aug. 7, 1837
Moore, Romulus L. of Chatham county, Oct. 28, Washington, D. C. R. R. Nov. 6, 1837
Mordecai, Mary, Nov., Raleigh. R. R. Nov. 13, 1837
Morris, Sarah J., My. 7, Raleigh. R. R. My. 16, 1837
Morrow, Mrs. David, Sept. 6, Mecklenburg county. R. R. Sept. 25, 1837
Morrow, Sarah Frances, Nov., Orange county. R. R. Nov. 20, 1837
Murphy, Henrietta of Wilmington, Feb. 7, Salisbury. R. R. Feb. 21, 1837
Murr, Mrs. Esther, Oct., Salisbury. R. R. Oct. 23, 1837
Murry, Kettura, Apr. 22, Raleigh. R. R. Apr. 25, 1837
Neagle, Mrs. John, Apr., Lincoln county. R. R. My. 9, 1837
Neale, John, Jan., Newbern. R. R. Jan. 31, 1837
Neel, Mrs. Samuel, Nov., Mecklenburg county. R. R. Nov. 6, 1837
Nixon, Dr. Phineas, Nov. 24, Randolph county. R. R. Dec. 23, 1837
Norfleet, Elisha B., Dec., Hertford county. R. R. Dec. 4, 1837
Odom, Mrs. Charles of Wake county, My. 6, Limestone county, Alabama. R. R. Jly. 24, 1837
Oliver, John, Oct., Newbern. R. R. Oct. 23, 1837
Page, Mrs. Mary M. C. of Chowan county, Dec., Richmond, Va. R. R. Dec. 4, 1837
Parham, Avery, Je. 25, Wake county. R. R. Jly. 10, 1837
Pasteur, Edward G. of Newbern, Nov., Green county, Alabama. R. R. Nov. 27, 1837
Patridge, Wiatt Booker, Oct. 3, Haywood, Chatham county. R. R. Oct. 23, 1837
Patton, Mrs. J. W., My., Asheville. R. R. My. 16, 1837
Patton, Robert of this State, Apr., Milledgeville, Georgia. R. R. My. 9, 1837
Pearce, Samuel of Providence, R. I., Jan., Fayetteville. R. R. Jan. 3, 1837
Pearsall, Henry Clay, My. 25, Duplin county. R. R. Je. 13, 1837
Pearsall, Mrs. James, Nov. 4, Duplin county. R. R. Nov. 27, 1837
Peoples, Mrs. N. M., Oct., Lincolnton. R. R. Oct. 23, 1837
Perry, Mr., Jly. 23, Wilmington. R. R. Aug. 7, 1837
Phifer, Col. Martin, Nov., Cabarrus county. R. R. Nov. 27, 1837
Phillips, Mrs. J. J., Apr., Columbus county. R. R. My. 9, 1837
Philips, Frederic, Oct. 1, Tarboro, Edgecombe county. R. R. Oct. 16, 1837
Pickett, Hon. William D. of this State, Dec., Montgomery, Alabama. R. R. Dec. 18, 1837"

Pinkston, Hampton, Dec. 9, Rowan county. R. R. Dec. 23, 1837
Pittman, Arthur, Dec. 21, Halifax county. R. R. Jan. 31, 1837
Pool, James M. Jr. of Elizabeth City, Feb. 21, Baltimore. R. R. Mar. 28, 1837
Poole, Mrs. Theophilus, Mar. 29, Johnston county. R. R. My. 9, 1837
Powell, Kedar, Sept., Wake county. R. R. Sept. 25, 1837
Powell, Mrs. Mary, Jly. 17, Halifax county. R. R. Aug. 7, 1837
Powell, Thomas, Jan., Halifax. R. R. Jan. 31, 1837
Prescott, Austin, Jly. 7, Craven county. R. R. Jly. 24, 1837
Price, William H., Je., Pitt county. R. R. Je. 13, 1837
Pritchett, Mrs. Mary, Dec., Greensboro. R. R. Dec. 18, 1837
Ragland, Thomas, Je. 27, Chatham county. R. R. Jly. 17, 1837
Raney, William, Mar. 6, Rowan county. R. R. Mar. 21, 1837
Reinhardt, Col. John, Dec., Lincoln county. R. R. Dec. 13, 1837
Rencher, Mrs. D. G. of Wake county, Dec. 12. R. R. Feb. 21, 1837
Rendleman, Mrs. John L., Nov., Rowan county. R. R. Nov. 6, 1837
Respess, Richard, Mar., Beaufort county. R. R. Mar. 7, 1837
Ridley, Col. of Granville county, Je. 27, Washington, D. C. R. R. Jly. 10, 1837
Ridley, Maj. J. C. of Granville county,, Je., Washington, D. C. R. R. Jly. 3, 1837
Rigsbe, Mrs. James, Jan. 27, Wake county. R. R. Feb. 14, 1837
Riley, Rachel, Jly. 23, Orange county. R. R. Aug. 14, 1837
Roberts, Peregrine, Nov. 21, Lincolnton. R. R. Dec. 18, 1837
Roberson, William, Je., Edgecombe county. R. R. Je. 13, 1837
Ross, Jack, F. of this State, Nov., Mobile, Alabama. R. R. Nov. 13, 1837
Rush, Mrs. James, Sept. 28, Davidson county. R. R. Oct. 30, 1837
Sanders, Mrs. Brittain of this State, Mar., Madison county, Va. R. R. Mar. 21, 1837
Sassnett, Zachariah, Oct. 2, Tarboro, Edgecombe county. R. R. Oct. 16, 1837
Satterfield, Mrs. Edward H. of Alexandria, La., Aug., Edenton. R. R. Sept. 4, 1837
Satterwaite, John, Mar., Beaufort county. R. R. Mar. 7, 1837
Sawyer, Dr. Matthias E., Dec. 5, Chowan county. R. R. Dec. 18, 1837
Scarlette, John, Je., Orange county. R. R. Je. 13, 1837
Schenk, Mrs. D. W., Oct. 21, Lincolnton. R. R. Nov. 6, 1837
Schoolfield, Agnes, Mar., Guilford county. R. R. Mar. 21, 1837
Sellers, Elizabeth, Oct., Cumberland county. R. R. Oct. 16, 1837
Sessums, Mrs. Isaac T., Aug. 5, Nashville. R. R. Aug. 7, 1837
Sharpe, Major Amos, Mr., Iredell county. R. R. Aug. 7, 1837
Shaw, James, Mar. 7, Rolesville. R. R. Mar. 21, 1837
Shaw, John A. of Newport, R. I., Mar., Currituck county. R. R. Mar. 7, 1837
Shearin, Zachariah, Apr., Warren county. R. R. Apr. 18, 1837
Shores, Simeon, Jly., Wilkes county. R. R. Jly. 31, 1837
Smith, Benedicte, Apr., Edenton. R. R. Apr. 18, 1837
Smith, Margaret, Sept. 18, Mecklenburg county. R. R. Sept. 25, 1837
Smith, Samuel C., Nov. 13, Wake county. R. R. Nov. 20, 1837
Sneed, Samuel F. of Granville county, Aug. 12, La Grange, Tennessee. R. R. Sept. 18, 1837

Spurgin, Wm., Dec., Waughtown, Stokes county. R. R. Dec. 18, 1837
Stevelie, Dr. John H. of Switzerland, Jan. 29, Morganton. R. R. Jan. 31, 1837
Stevenson, Josiah, Jan., Halifax county. R. R. Jan. 31, 1837
Strayhorn, William, Jly. 8, Orange county. R. R. Jly. 31, 1837
Suttle, Mrs. George, Jly. 7, Island Ford on Main Broad River. R. R. Jly. 31, 1837
Swan, Alexander D., Dec. 5, Pittsborough. R. R. Dec. 23, 1837
Swink, Mrs. Peter J., Jly. 3, Rowan county. R. R. Jly. 17, 1837
Swoner, Ann Eliza, Nov., Washington. R. R. Nov. 20, 1837
Taylor, Mrs. Henry of Wilmington, Sept., Liverpool, England. R. R. Oct. 2, 1837
Taylor, John, Apr. 23, Granville county. R. R. My. 16, 1837
Taylor, Mrs. John of Chapel Hill, Apr., Hillsborough. R. R. Apr. 18, 1837
Thompson, Joshua, Jly. 27, Orange county. R. R. Aug. 14, 1837
Toland, Rachael, Nov., Beaufort. R. R. Nov. 20, 1837
Troy, Mrs. John, Jan. 23, Randolph county. R. R. Jan. 31, 1837
Tucker, Edith, Nov., Iredell county. R. R. Nov. 27, 1837
Tucker, Rev. Robert, Je., Lincoln county. R. R. Je. 13, 1837
Vaughan, Maj. Truitt, Mar. 30, Wake Forest. R. R. My. 2, 1837
Waddell, Mrs. John of Brunswick county, Je. 7, Pittsborough. R. R. Je. 19, 1837
Ward, Cicero S., Nov. 10, Newbern. R. R. Nov. 27, 1837
Washington, John, Aug. 21, Newbern. R. R. Sept. 4, 1837
Webb, John, Apr. 27, Bertie county. R. R. My. 16, 1837
Webster, William D. of Milton, Jly. 23, Athens, Alabama. R. R. Aug. 21, 1837
Wedding, Henry, My. 12, Raleigh. R. R. My. 16, 1837
Welch, Rev. Miles, Jan., Chowan county. R. R. Jan. 31, 1837
White, Mrs. Miles, Mar., Elizabeth City. R. R. Mar. 7, 1837
Whitaker, Laura, Jly. 18, Raleigh. R. R. Jly. 24, 1837
Whitaker, Rebecca, Mar., Davie county. R. R. Mar. 28, 1837
Wilkins, Mrs. Samuel of Newbern, Jan. 8, Mobile, Alabama. R. R. Jan. 31, 1837
Wilkins, Winslow S., Nov., Wilmington. R. R. Nov. 6, 1837
Williford, O. K., Jly. 27, Wilmington. R. R. Aug. 7, 1837
Willis, Spence P., Feb. 6, Newbern. R. R. Feb. 21, 1837
Wilkings, Edward, Nov., Fayetteville. R. R. Nov. 20, 1837
Wilson, Mrs. William, Oct., Wilmington. R. R. Oct. 9, 1837
Winburn, Mrs. Henry G., Nov. 10, Edgecombe county. R. R. Nov. 27, 1837
Wood, Charles, Aug. 7, Orange county. R. R. Aug. 14, 1837
Woodburen, Watson W., Sept., Greensboro. R. R. Sept. 25, 1837
Woolworth, Susan, Oct., Salisbury. R. R. Oct. 23, 1837
Yarbrough, Thomas of Franklin county, Je. 13, Fayette county, Tenn. R. R. Jly. 17, 1837
Yates, Matthew, Oct., Wake county. R. R. Oct. 16, 1837
Young, Rev. John, Jly. 21, Franklin county. R. R. Aug. 7, 1837
Young, Laura Ann, Jan., Salisbury. R. R. Jan. 31, 1837
Zimmerman, Mrs. Sarah, My., Lincolnton. R. R. My. 16, 1837

1838

Ashe, Mrs. Thomas of this State, Dec., Greensboro, Alabama. R. R. Dec. 31, 1838
Boddie, Mrs. W. W., Oct. 25, Ashe county. R. R. Nov. 5, 1838
Bower, Col. George, Jly. 27, Ashe county. R. R. Nov. 5, 1838
Byrd, Mrs. Thomas, Nov. 9, Orange county. R. R. Nov. 19, 1838
Cook, Mark, Nov., Raleigh. R. R. Nov. 12, 1838
Cotten, Mrs. Lydia, Dec. 7, Wadesboro. R. R. Dec. 24, 1838
Dunn, Lucinda, Nov., Wake county. R. R. Nov. 12, 1838
Harris, Mrs. Daniel, Dec. 18, Montgomery county. R. R. Dec. 31, 1838
M'Pherson, Gen. James T., Nov. 12, Camden county. R. R. Dec. 3, 1838
Martin, Mrs. Dianah, Oct. 1, Wilkes county. R. R. Nov. 5, 1838
Midyett, John, Dec., Tyrrell county. R. R. Dec. 24, 1838
Norcom, Dr. Benjamin R., Dec., Edenton. R. R. Dec. 24, 1838
Perry, Col. Jeremiah, Oct. 17, Franklin county. R. R. Nov. 5, 1838
Reid, David of Cumberland county, Nov. 28, Madison, Tennessee. R. R. Dec. 31, 1838
Scott, Dr. John of Rowan county, Dec., LaGrange. R. R. Dec. 24, 1838
Thomas, Mrs. Jas., Dec. 5, Richmond county. R. R. Dec. 31, 1838
Turner, John, Sr., Dec., Rowan county. R. R. Dec. 24, 1838
Weant, Jacob, Dec., Rowan county. R. R. Dec. 24, 1838

1839

Alston, Mrs. Thos. W., Jly. 7, Warren county. R. R. Jly. 20, 1839
Anderson, Col. Ruel, Sept., Pitt county. R. R. Sept. 28, 1839
Anderson, Mrs. Wm. E., Oct. 31, Hillsboro. R. R. Nov. 23, 1839
Ayer, General Henry W., Jly. 27, Fayetteville. R. R. Aug. 3, 1839
Bailey, Alston of New York, Jan., Cumberland county. R. R. Feb. 4, 1839
Bassinger, Mrs. Samuel, Dec., Salisbury. R. R. Dec. 7, 1839
Benners, Mrs. Fanny, My. 13, Weldon. R. R. Je. 29, 1839
Benson, Thomas, Nov., Salisbury. R. R. Nov. 23, 1839
Blake, Mrs. James H., Apr., Charlotte. R. R. Apr. 6, 1839
Blackman, Mrs. Job, Apr., Johnston county. R. R. Apr. 13, 1839
Brehon, Dr. James G., Oct. 2, Warrenton. R. R. Oct. 5, 1839
Brely, Mrs. William R., Je. 3, Anson county. R. R. Je. 15, 1839
Brown, Edward A., Jly. 9, Bladen county. R. R. Jly. 27, 1839
Brown, James, Sept., Rowan county. R. R. Sept. 21, 1839
Brown, Mrs. Joel, Apr. 21, Raleigh. R. R. Apr. 27, 1839
Brown, Mrs. Neal, Je. 7, Raleigh. R. R. Je. 15, 1839
Brown, Samuel C., Aug., Salisbury. R. R. Aug. 31, 1839
Buchett, Col. Theodore F., Apr. 27, White Sulphur Springs, Rutherford county. R. R. My. 11, 1839
Buffalow, Henry, Sept. 5, Wake county. R. R. Sept. 14, 1839
Buie, Mrs. J. R., Aug. 26, Laurel Hill, Richmond county. R. R. Sept. 14, 1839
Burkett, Daniel, Dec., Ashe county. R. R. Dec. 14, 1839
Burns, Mrs. Otway, Nov., Portsmouth, Carteret county. R. R. Nov. 23, 1839
Cameron, Mrs. Catharine of Chatham county, Sept. 15, Cumberland county. R. R. Sept. 28, 1839
Cameron, Mrs. John A., Sept., Cumberland county. R. R. Sept. 21, 1839
Cameron, Mary Ann, Jly. 22, Raleigh. R. R. Jly. 27, 1839

Cameron, Rebecca, Sept. 14, Raleigh. R. R. Sept. 21, 1839
Campbell, Alexander, Dec. 14, Raleigh. R. R. Dec. 21, 1839
Campbell, Mrs. John, My. 13, Weldon. R. R. Je. 29, 1839
Campbell, Joseph Outlaw, Mar. 29, Raleigh. R. R. Apr. 6, 1839
Cansler, Mrs. Philip, Je., Lincoln county. R. R. Je. 29, 1839
Carrington, William C. G., Feb. 20, Raleigh. R. R. Feb. 25, 1839
Cattanach, Mrs. Thomas of England, Je. 6, Raleigh. R. R. Je. 15, 1839
Clark, Mrs. John, Sept., Lincolnton. R. R. Sept. 14, 1839
Cline, Mrs. Henry, Sept., Lincolnton. R. R. Sept. 14, 1839
Collins, Josiah, Jan., Edenton. R. R. Feb. 25, 1839
Daniel, Mrs. Lewis of Person county, Je. 12. R. R. Jly. 6, 1839
Dixon, Mrs. Willis, Aug., Craven county. R. R. Aug. 17, 1839
Donnell, John S. of Guilford county, Feb. 20, Buchanan county, Mo. R. R. Mar. 23, 1839
Donnel, Mrs. William, Mar. 18, Guilford county. R. R. Mar. 23, 1839
Drake, Capt. Mathew of Chatham county, Aug., Savannah, Ga. R. R. Aug. 31, 1839
Dunn, Chas., Sept., Salisbury. R. R. Sept. 21, 1839
Fry, Abel, Sept., Lincolnton. R. R. Sept. 21, 1839
Gales, Mrs. Joseph of this State & England, Je. 26, Washington, D. C. R. R. Jly. 6, 1839
Glover, Chas., Nov., Rowan county. R. R. Nov. 23, 1839
Gorman, Mrs. Henry, Jly. 31, Raleigh. R. R. Aug. 3, 1839
Gorman, Lycurgus Hannibal, Sept. 19, Raleigh. R. R. Sept. 21, 1839
Green, Col. Lewis, Sept., Granville county. R. R. Sept. 28, 1839
Green, Thomas, Nov., Guilford county. R. R. Nov. 9, 1839
Guion, Mrs. E. P., Jly. 19, Raleigh. R. R. Jly. 27, 1839
Gully, Nathan, Jan. 5, Wake county. R. R. Jan. 21, 1839
Hague, Mrs. Thomas A., Mar. 7, Salisbury. R. R. Mar. 23, 1839
Hall, Sidney, Nov., Newbern. R. R. Nov. 23, 1839
Halliday, James of Scotland, Je. 4, Halifax. R. R. Je. 29, 1839
Halsey, Mrs. Ellen P., Sept. 5, Wilmington. R. R. Sept. 14, 1839
Hampton, Mrs. William, Jan., Salisbury. R. R. Jan. 21, 1839
Harden, Capt. Mark, Aug. 12, Rockingham county. R. R. Aug. 17, 1839
Harris, William, Sr., Jly., Caswell county. R. R. Jly. 27, 1839
Harriss, Dr. Wm. J., Jly. 9, Wilmington. R. R. Jly. 20, 1839
Harrison, Andrew, Jly., Caswell county. R. R. Jly. 27, 1839
Harvey, Mrs. John, Jan., Newbern. R. R. Feb. 4, 1839
Hawkins, Mrs. R. J., Sept., Halifax. R. R. Sept. 21, 1839
Henderson, Lawson, Jr., Aug. 21, Lincolnton. R. R. Sept. 7, 1839
Henderson, Sarah, Je. 12, Vineville. R. R. Jly. 13, 1839
Hicks, Rev. Berryman of Rutherford county, Je. 11, Spartanburgh District, S. C. R. R. Aug. 17, 1839
Hill, Harmon, Sept., Beaufort county. R. R. Sept. 28, 1839
Hill, Mrs. Samuel, Mar., Randolph county. R. R. Mar. 30, 1839
Hobbs, Mrs. Jesse, Je., Iredell county. R. R. Je. 29, 1839
Hines, Mrs. Brian of Holeysville, Lincoln county, Feb., Green county, Alabama. R. R. Mar. 4, 1839
Holt, Mrs. Rachael, Oct. 30, Orange county. R. R. Nov. 9, 1839
Howell, William, Dec., Ashe county. R. R. Dec. 14, 1839
Irwin, Dr. R. C., Aug., Cabarrus county. R. R. Aug. 31, 1839

Jarvis, Mrs. Moses W. of Newbern, Aug., White Plains, N. Y. R. R. Aug. 31, 1839
Johnston, Henry, Jly. 1, Tarboro. R. R. Jly. 13, 1839
Jones, Edmund, Dec. 30, Palmyra, Wilkes county. R. R. Feb. 4, 1839
Kelly, Oliver L., Apr. 3, Wilmington. R. R. Apr. 13, 1839
Kerr, Mrs. Joseph, Aug. 24, Rowan county. R. R. Sept. 7, 1839
Kirkland, Mrs. Wm., Jly. 6, Hillsborough. R. R. Jly. 27, 1839
M'Allister, David of this State, Mar., Philadelphia. R. R. Mar. 23, 1839
M'Cauley, Andrew, Jr. of Orange county, Je. R. R. Jly. 6, 1839
M'Racken, Mrs. Robert, Sept., Brunswick county. R. R. Sept. 28, 1839
Martin, Col. John, Sr., Feb. 15, Wilkes county. R. R. Mar. 11, 1839
Maxwell, James of Raleigh, Jan., Warrenton. R. R. Jan. 21, 1839
Metts, Craven, Nov., Lenoir county. R. R. Nov. 23, 1839
Middleton, Robert, Nov., Duplin county. R. R. Nov. 23, 1839
Mordecai, Laura, Jly. 4, Richmond, Va. R. R. Jly. 13, 1839
Morphess, Mrs. Alexander, Je. 15, Raleigh. R. R. Je. 29, 1839
Moore, Mrs. Gideon E., Jan. 26, Stokes county. R. R. Feb. 4, 1839
Morphis, William F., Jly. 19, Raleigh. R. R. Jly. 27, 1839
Moody, Capt. Wm., Sept. 17, Northampton county. R. R. Sept. 28, 1839
Moses, Joseph C. of Louisburg, Sept. 11, Clinton, Alabama. R. R. Sept. 28, 1839
Moore, Col. Maurice of New Hanover county, Aug., Louisiana. R. R. Aug. 17, 1839
Mungar, Mrs. Nelson H. of Granville county, Je. 29, Benton, Mississippi. R. R. Aug. 10, 1839
Myrover, Mrs. Celia, Apr., Fayetteville. R. R. Apr. 6, 1839
Nicholson, John Anderson, Jly. 18, Raleigh. R. R. Jly. 20, 1839
Oates, Agnes Louisa, Sept., Charlotte. R. R. Sept. 14, 1839
Outland, Edward G., Je. 7, Halifax. R. R. Je. 29, 1839
Osborne, Col. Adam J. of this State, Je. 1, Linden, Maringo county, Alabama. R. R. Jly. 27, 1839
Parker, Mrs. David, Sept. 18, Hillsboro. R. R. Sept. 21, 1839
Pearsall, Hugh, Apr. 13, Duplin county. R. R. Sept. 7, 1839
Perry, Capt. Burnwell, Oct., Wake county. R. R. Oct. 5, 1839
Perry, Mrs. Sam'l, My. 26, Franklin county. R. R. Je. 29, 1839
Pharr, Mrs. Walter S., Sept., Mecklenburg county. R. R. Sept. 14, 1839
Pickett, Margaret Ann of Wadesborough, Anson county, Apr., Marengo county, Ala. R. R. Apr. 13, 1839
Poston, William, Nov., Rowan county. R. R. Nov. 23, 1839
Reed, John, Nov., Rowan county. R. R. Nov. 23, 1839
Respass, Langley, Sept., Washington, Beaufort county. R. R. Sept. 28, 1839
Riley, Elizabeth, Apr. 8, Orange county. R. R. Apr. 20, 1839
Robertsson, Willie, Sept. 14, Wake county. R. R. Sept. 28, 1839
Robinson, Robin, Sept., Cabarrus county. R. R. Sept. 14, 1839
Roper, William, Aug. 6, Wilmington. R. R. Aug. 10, 1839
Salmon, Mrs. Richard, Aug., Sampson county. R. R. Aug. 17, 1839
Saunders, Mrs. Angelina of this county, Jly. 14, Fayette county, Tennessee. R. R. Aug. 17, 1839
Sellars, James Thompson, Apr. 2, Wilmington. R. R. Apr. 13, 1839
Shuford, Mrs. Thos. R., Aug., Lincolnton. R. R. Aug. 17, 1839
Smith, Catharine Elizabeth, Apr., Cumberland county. R. R. Apr. 6, 1839

Smith, Duncan, Mar., Fayetteville. R. R. Mar. 23, 1839
Smith, John, Dec., Davie county. R. R. Dec. 14, 1839
Smith, Mrs. John W. of Williamston, Oct., Greene county, Alabama. R. R. Oct. 5, 1839
Tanner, John Rex, Jan. 23, Raleigh. R. R. Feb. 4, 1839
Taylor, Samuel B. of Hillsboro, Aug. 27, Lawrenceville, S. C. R. R. Sept. 28, 1839
Taylor, Dr. Thomas B., Nov. 20, Granville county. R. R. Nov. 30, 1839
Waddell, Maurice, Sept., Brunswick county. R. R. Sept. 28, 1839
Walker, Andrew of Orange county, Sept., Sumpter county, Alabama. R. R. Sept. 28, 1839
Walters, Mrs. Archibald, Jly., Caswell county. R. R. Jly. 27, 1839
Watson, Elizabeth O., Dec. 7, Wilmington. R. R. Dec. 14, 1839
Whitaker, Calvin J., Aug. 13, Raleigh. R. R. Aug. 17, 1839
Williams, Mrs. S. A., Je., Warren county. R. R. Je. 29, 1839
Williams, William, Jan., Snow Hill, Greene county. R. R. Feb. 4, 1839
Worke, A. J. of Iredell county, Je., Mecklenburg county. R. R. Je. 15, 1839
Wright, Mrs. William B., Sept. 15, Cumberland county. R. R. Sept. 21, 1839

1840

Adams, George, Aug. 31, Hyde county. R. R. Sept. 11, 1840
Adams, Philip, Apr., Wake county. R. R. Apr. 7, 1840
Adams, Philip, Sr., Mar. 31, Wake county. R.␣My. 22, 1840
Alexander, James Graham, Oct. 8, Mecklenburg county. R. R. Oct. 23, 1840
Andres, Col. Samuel, Apr. 14, Bladen county. R. R. Apr. 21, 1840
Austin, Dr. Benjamin of New York, Aug. 10, Salisbury. R. R. Aug. 25, 1840
Barr, James H. of Raleigh, Apr., Houston, Texas. R. R. Apr. 28, 1840
Beach, Barnum of Bridgeport, Conn., Jan. 23, Fayetteville. R. R. Jan. 28, 1840
Beckwith, Nathaniel, Nov. 14, Plymouth. R. R. Nov. 24, 1840
Bigham, Joseph, Sept. 15, Mecklenburg county. R. R. Oct. 9, 1840
Blue, William, Nov. 1, Cumberland county. R. R. Nov. 17, 1840
Braddy, Elizabeth, Nov., Newbern. R. R. Nov. 27, 1840
Brooks, Wm. C., Nov. 20, Elizabeth City. R. R. Dec. 1, 1840
Brower, William of England, Sept. 10, Newbern. R. R. Sept. 18, 1840
Brown, Mrs. Amabella, Jan., Wilmington. R. R. Jan. 7, 1840
Brown, Maj. Thos., Jan., Bladen county. R. R. Jan. 7, 1840
Brownrigg, Dr. John H. of Edenton, Apr., West Port, Mississippi. R. R. My. 5, 1840
Bryan, John, Feb. 8, Sampson county. R. R. Feb. 25, 1840
Bryan, Gen. Joseph H. of Granville county, Jan., La Grange, Tenn. R. R. Jan. 24, 1840
Buck, Absalom, Sept. 11, Washington, Beaufort county. R. R. Sept. 22, 1840
Buffaloe, William Embry, Jly. 23, Wake county. R. R. Jly. 31, 1840
Buie, Neill, Mar., Cumberland county. R. R. Apr. 3, 1840
Bullock, Dr. Benjamin of Granville county, Jly. 4, Mississippi. R. R. Aug. 21, 1840
Burgess, Laura M. of Raleigh, Dec. 16, Memphis, Tenn. R. R. Jan. 14, 1840
Butner, Mrs. John, Feb. 1, Rowan county. R. R. Feb. 21, 1840
Bynum, Mark, Mar., Chatham county. R. R. Mar. 27, 1840
Bynum, infant son of Col. J. G. Bynum of Rutherfordton, Apr., Burke county. R. R. Apr. 14, 1840

Cameron, Ann Owen, Mar. 27, Raleigh. R. R. Mar. 31, 1840
Campbell, Mrs. Archibald, Oct. 14, Wilmington. R. R. Oct. 27, 1840
Campbell, Mrs. Donald, Jan. 14, Raleigh. R. R. Jan. 21, 1840
Campbell, Edward, Oct. 14, Wilmington. R. R. Oct. 27, 1840
Caruthers, Mrs. John, Aug., Greensboro. R. R. Aug. 28, 1840
Cavin, Miles of Iredell county, Nov. 1, Marengo county, Alabama. R. R. Nov. 27, 1840
Certain, Mrs. Emanuel, Sept. 11, Newbern. R. R. Sept. 18, 1840
Clark, Mrs. Eleanor, Jan., Greensboro. R. R. Jan. 3, 1840
Clark, Jonathan P., Apr., Guilford county. R. R. Apr. 21, 1840
Click, Mrs. Daniel, Feb., Davie county. R. R. Feb. 4, 1840
Cline, Col. Michael, Jan., Lincoln county. R. R. Jan. 31, 1840
Cobbs, Thomas, Sept. 14, Wake county. R. R. Sept. 15, 1840
Collier, Mrs. Obedieus of Orange county, Aug. 2, Perry county, Alabama. R. R. Aug. 18, 1840
Cook, Col. Henry H., Dec. 7, Raleigh. R. R. Dec. 8, 1840
Cooke, Mrs. Mark, Aug. 5, Raleigh. R. R. Aug. 7, 1840
Crawford, Mrs. Joel of Halifax county, Oct. 29, Sparta, Georgia. R. R. Nov. 13, 1840
Cutler, Mrs. H. G., Nov., Newbern. R. R. Nov. 27, 1840
Dancy, Wm., Sept. 23, Edgecombe county. R. R. Sept. 25, 1840
Daniel, Beverly, Sept. 14, Raleigh. R. R. Sept. 15, 1840
Daniel, Mrs. Cornelia A. of this State, Crownswick, Tennessee. R. R. Jly. 17, 1840
Devane, James, Mar. 13, New Hanover county. R. R. My. 15, 1840
Dewey, Mrs. Mary, Dec. 30, Raleigh. R. R. Jan. 3, 1840
Denson, Mrs. Martha, My., Franklin county. R. R. Jly. 17, 1840
Dinkins, Col. Samuel of this State, Jly. 22, Tennessee. R. R. Aug. 18, 1840
Dixon, William, Sept. 14, Portsmouth, of this State. R. R. Sept. 29, 1840
Donnell, Levi, Jan., Greensboro. R. R. Jan. 3, 1840
Drew, Joshua, Je. 7, Scotland Neck. R. R. Aug. 28, 1840
Dudley, Ann Hatridge, Jan., Wilmington. R. R. Jan. 14, 1840
Dudley, Major Christopher, Oct. 14, Wilmington. R. R. Oct. 27, 1840
Dudley, Edward B., Jr., Aug. 3, Wilmington. R. R. Aug. 11, 1840
Dudley, Mrs. Edward B., Oct. 14, Raleigh. R. R. Oct. 16, 1840
Dunn, Mrs. Ann C. of Mecklenburg county, Dec., Mississippi. R. R. Dec. 8, 1840
Durham, Caswell, Je., Hillsboro. R. R. Je. 23, 1840
Ellington, Mrs. Frances, Jan., Wentworth, Rockingham county. R. R. Jan. 24, 1840
Ellison, Shadrack Allen, Dec., Beaufort county. R. R. Dec. 8, 1840
Everett, Harriet Ann, Jan., Wilmington. R. R. Jan. 7, 1840
Forman, Boyd A. of Rutherford, Feb., San Jacinto Bay, Texas. R. R. Feb. 4, 1840
Franklin, Abner of Statesville, Iredell county, Jan., Gainesville, Ala. R. R. Jan. 28, 1840
Franklin, Hon. Meshack, Dec. 18, Surry county. R. R. Jan. 3, 1840
Frilick, James of Raleigh, Mar. 6, Mississippi. R. R. Apr. 3, 1840
Fulenwider, Mrs. John, Apr. 8, Lincoln county. R. R. Apr. 21, 1840
Gardner, Mrs. Mary Ann, Aug. 6, Guilford county. R. R. Aug. 28, 1840
Gee, Mrs. George of Virginia, Mar., Chatham county. R. R. Mar. 27, 1840

Gill, Mrs. John N., Nov. 17, Granville county. R. R. Nov. 24, 1840
Godley, Marshall, Sept. 24, Pitt county. R. R. Sept. 29, 1840
Goor, Mrs. Isaac, Jr., Jan. 9, Duplin county. R. R. Jan. 24, 1840
Gorman, Henry of Ireland, Nov. 4, Raleigh. R. R. Nov. 6, 1840
Gray, Anna Jane, Jan., Randolph county. R. R. Jan. 21, 1840
Green, Mrs. Edward, Jly. 23, Guilford county. R. R. Aug. 4, 1840
Green, John B. of Richmond, Va., Aug. 24, Franklinton. R. R. Aug. 28, 1840
Green, Mrs. Simon W. of Warren county, Sept. 18, Tennessee. R. R. Oct. 9, 1840
Grimes, Maj. William H. of Raleigh, Apr., Austin, Texas. R. R. Apr. 28, 1840
Grist, David C., Dec., Beaufort county. R. R. Dec. 8, 1840
Guion, John W., Jly. 17, Newbern. R. R. Jly. 24, 1840
Hall, Mrs. Joseph, Sr., Dec. 14, Davie county. R. R. Dec. 22, 1840
Hall, Salmon of Connecticut and this State, Apr. 25, Newbern. R. R. Je. 5, 1840
Hamilton, Wm. A. of Scotland, Dec., Granville county. R. R. Dec. 22, 1840
Hanks, Mrs. Benjamin F., Nov., Newbern. R. R. Nov. 27, 1840
Harris, Benjamin of this State, Sept. 25, Norfolk, Va. R. R. Oct. 9, 1840
Harris, Rev. Samuel J., Oct. 16, Granville county. R. R. Nov. 6, 1840
Harrison, Elisha of Johnston county, Jly. 23, Raleigh. R. R. Jly. 28, 1840
Harriss, Mrs. Nancy, Aug. 13, Raleigh. R. R. Aug. 21, 1840
Hawkins, Mrs. William, Mar. 5, Somerville, Morgan county, Alabama. R. R. Apr. 7, 1840
Hayes, Ann, Franklin county. R. R. Jly. 17, 1840
Hays, John, Sr., Aug. 5, Wake county. R. R. Aug. 11, 1840
Hellen, Isaac R. of Beaufort, Jan., Mobile, Alabama. R. R. Jan. 17, 1840
Henderson, Mrs. P. of Chapel Hill, Nov. 25, Huntington, Tennessee. R. R. Dec. 11, 1840
Herndon, Edmund, My. 10, Orange county. R. R. My. 19, 1840
Hollingsworth, Col. Stephen, Sept. 14, Cumberland county. R. R. Sept. 18, 1840
Holmes, Owen, Je. 6, Wilmington. R. R. Je. 12, 1840
Holmes, Walker Davis, Jan. 21, Wilmington. R. R. Jan. 28, 1840
Hoskins, Eliza Theresa, My. 29, Wilmington. R. R. Je. 12, 1840
Howard, William, Nov. 4, Edgecombe county. R. R. Nov. 24, 1840
Huffines, John, Oct. 18, Guilford county. (Suicide). R. R. Nov. 10, 1840
Harvey, Mrs. John, Nov. 5, Newbern. R. R. Nov. 6, 1840
Humphreys, Henry, Mar. 26, Greensboro. R. R. Mar. 31, 1840
Hunter, Mrs. John, Apr., Davie county. R. R. Apr. 14, 1840
Hutchins, Mrs. John of Onslow county, Jly. 21, Mississippi. R. R. Sept. 18, 1840
Ingles, Mrs. John of Wake county, Jly. 19, Granville county. R. R. Jly. 28, 1840
Jeffreys, Robert N., Mar. 15, Wake county. R. R. My. 22, 1840
Johnson, John, Aug. 22, Randolph county. R. R. Sept. 8, 1840
Joiner, Col. Daniel, Oct., Masonboro sound, New Hanover county. R. R. Oct. 27, 1840
Jones, Asa, Feb. 8, Newbern. R. R. Feb. 21, 1840
Jones, Henrietta M. of Fayetteville, Nov., Pittsborough. R. R. Nov. 6, 1840
Jones, John, Jan., Newbern. R. R. Jan. 14, 1840
Jones, J. T. of this State, Dec., New Haven, Connecticut. R. R. Dec. 25, 1840

Julian, Joseph, Jan., Randolph county. R. R. Jan. 7, 1840
Kewell, Capt. Charles S., Sept. 21, Washington, Beaufort county. R. R. Sept. 22, 1840
Lamb, C. G. H., Sept. 8, Hyde county. R. R. Sept. 18, 1840
Lane, Col. Isaac, Je., Randolph county. R. R. Je. 23, 1840
Laughinghouse, Mrs. William, Jan. 2, Pitt county. R. R. Jan. 17, 1840
Lawrence, William, Mar. 27, Granville county. R. R. Mar. 31, 1840
Lewelling, Mrs. Ann M., Apr., Hillsboro. R. R. Apr. 14, 1840
Lewis, Mrs. Hannah of New Haven, Connecticut, Nov. 28, Raleigh. R. R. Dec. 1, 1840
Lewis, Mrs. Richard H. of Edgecombe county, Sept. 24, Greensboro, Alabama. R. R. Oct. 13, 1840
Lewis, Mrs. Winny, Jly. 2, Raleigh. R. R. Jly. 7, 1840
Lippitt, Caroline Wright, Je. 1, Wilmington. R. R. Je. 12, 1840
Littlejohn, Mrs. Joseph B. of Granville county, Sept. 16, Tennessee. R. R. Oct. 20, 1840
Lowry, David, Oct. 15, Chapel Hill. R. R. Oct. 20, 1840
Mann, William, Mar., Tyrrell county. R. R. Mar. 31, 1840
Mason, John, Feb. 24, Mecklenburg county. R. R. Mar. 3, 1840
M'Alpin, Daniel Logan, Dec., Yanceyville, Caswell county. R. R. Dec. 8, 1840
M'Cord, Mrs. John, Mar., Mecklenburg county. R. R. Mar. 31, 1840
M'Cray, Mrs. Bedford, Jly. 9, Orange county. R. R. Jly. 28, 1840
M'Donald, Archibald, Mar., Richmond county. R. R. Mar. 6, 1840
M'Kinlay, Mrs. James, Oct. 5, Newbern. R. R. Oct. 23, 1840
M'Kinne, Michael of this State, Sept. 9, Hardeman county, Tennessee. R. R. Oct. 27, 1840
M'Lauchlin, Mrs. Mary, Jan., Robeson county. R. R. Jan. 24, 1840
M'Laurin, Hugh, Je., Fayetteville. R. R. Je. 12, 1840
M'Leod, Mrs. Ellen, Je., Salisbury. R. R. Je. 12, 1840
M'Leon, John of Montgomery county, Nov., Shelby county, Alabama. R. R. Nov. 6, 1840
M'Leod, Mrs. John of Montgomery county, Nov., Shelby county, Alabama. R. R. Nov. 6, 1840
M'Nairy, James, Sr., Oct., Guilford county. R. R. Oct. 23, 1840
M'Neill Dr. Hector, Mar. 1, Cumberland county. R. R. Mar. 6, 1840
M'Pherson, John, Nov. 1, Fayetteville. R. R. Nov. 6, 1840
M'Ree, Mrs. Ann, Apr., Bladen county. R. R. Apr. 10, 1840
M'Rorie, Martha Ann, Jan., Statesville. R. R. Jan. 17, 1840
M'Taggart, Alexander, Oct. 14, Wilmington. R. R. Oct. 27, 1840
Mault, Mrs. William, Mar., Rowan county. R. R. Mar. 17, 1840
Meadors, Mrs. Edward, Jan., Newbern. R. R. Jan. 14, 1840
Miles, Eliza Catharine, Sept. 30, Yanceyville. R. R. Oct. 9, 1840
Miller, Jesse, Feb., Orange county. R. R. Mar. 3, 1840
Moore, Elam, Feb., Mecklenburg county. R. R. Feb. 21, 1840
Morgan, Mrs. James of Hertford county, Dec., New Washington, Texas. R. R. Dec. 22, 1840
Motz, John M., Mar. 9, Lincolnton. R. R. Mar. 17, 1840
Mullen, Hugh, Apr., Randolph county. R. R. Apr. 21, 1840
Mullinix, Mrs. Jesse, Aug. 25, Randolph county. R. R. Sept. 1, 1840
Murphy, Robert, Oct., Masonboro Sound, New Hanover county. R. R. Oct. 27, 1840

Myrover, James H., Mar., Fayetteville. R. R. Mar. 27, 1840
Nott, William of Middletown, Connecticut, Nov. 20, Fayetteville. R. R. Nov. 27, 1840
O'Bryan, Tillotson, Jly. 11, Richmond county. R. R. Aug. 4, 1840
Osborne, Jesse, Sept. 1, Randolph county. R. R. Sept. 8, 1840
Palmer, James B. of Orange county, Jly. 30, Perry county, Alabama. R. R. Aug. 18, 1840
Palmer, Mrs. Mary A., Jan., Hillsborough. R. R. Jan. 14, 1840
Peterson, Peter, Oct. 21, Newbern. R. R. Nov. 6, 1840
Poindexter, David, Feb., Stokes county. R. R. Feb. 21, 1840
Pritchett, William, Oct. 13, Newbern. R. R. Oct. 23, 1840
Ray, Maj. John, Apr., Orange county. R. R. Sept. 7, 1840
Reancy, William Shadrack Allen, Je., Washington, Beaufort county. R. R. Je. 23, 1840
Rives, Edward, Feb. 2, Chatham county. R. R. Mar. 6, 1840
Roberts, David of Granville county, Apr., Shelby county, Tenn. R. R. My. 1, 1840
Robeson, Mrs. Marion of Scotland, Nov., Bladen county. R. R. Nov. 6, 1840
Robinson, John, Aug. 23, Halifax. R. R. Aug. 28, 1840
Robinson, John, Jan. 31, Montgomery county. R. R. Feb. 28, 1840
Rucks, Capt. John, Jan. 11, Granville county. R. R. Jan. 24, 1840
Salls, Mary, Feb., Hillsboro. R. R. Mar. 3, 1840
Saunders, Richard, Feb. 3, South Washington. R. R. Feb. 28, 1840
Scott, Caroline Winslow, Aug. 7, Raleigh. R. R. Aug. 21, 1840
Scott, Thomas W., Oct. 23, Wake county. R. R. Oct. 27, 1840
Shuman, Mrs. John, Feb., Salisbury. R. R. Feb. 4, 1840
Simmons, Col. Jesse H., Jan. 25, Halifax. R. R. Feb. 4, 1840
Simmons, Mrs. John, My. 13, Caswell county. R. R. My. 22, 1840
Simmons, Maj. John W. of Halifax, Feb., Columbus, Mississippi. R. R. Feb. 21, 1840
Singletary, John, Je., Beaufort county. R. R. Je. 23, 1840
Slater, Mrs. Sarah H., Jan., Rockingham county. R. R. Jan. 3, 1840
Slocumb, Col. Ezekiel, Jly. 4, Wayne county. R. R. Jly. 10, 1840
Smith, Mrs. Charity, Je. 27, Raleigh. R. R. Jly. 3, 1840
Smith, Mrs. Reuben, Sept., Granville county. R. R. Sept. 8, 1840
Smith, Samuel, Jly. 15, Davie county. R. R. Aug. 4, 1840
Smith, Hon. Wm. of this State, Je. 26, Huntsville, Alabama. R. R. Jly. 17, 1840
Smoot, Alexander, Apr., Davie county. R. R. Apr. 14, 1840
Southall, James, Oct. 20, Henderson. R. R. Nov. 24, 1840
Spencer, John, Feb., Surry county. R. R. Feb. 4, 1840
Stedman, Edward of Chatham county, Je. 19, Spring Hill, Alabama. R. R. Jly. 17, 1840
Stephens, Martha L., Feb., Elizabeth City. R. R. Feb. 4, 1840
Stewart, Virginia Carolina, Je., Washington, Beaufort county. R. R. Je. 23, 1840
Street, Hon. W. B. of Hillsborough, Je. 20, Greensborough, Alabama. R. R. Jly. 17, 1840
Swann, Elizabeth, Jan. 8, Wilmington. R. R. Jan. 24, 1840
Taylor, Miles, Je. 11, Williamsborough, Granville county. R. R. Je. 23, 1840
Walker, Carlton, Oct. 12, Hillsborough. R. R. Oct. 20, 1840

Wall, Arthur, Oct., Wake county. R. R. Oct. 20, 1840
Weaver, Jacob, Jan., Salisbury. R. R. Jan. 14, 1840
Whitesides, Thomas, Feb., Rutherford county. R. R. Feb. 4, 1840
Whitfield, Miss Ruth A. T. of Nashville, Sept., Gainesville, Alabama. R. R. Sept. 23, 1840
Wiley, Claudia, Mar. 23, Wadesborough. R. R. Apr. 3, 1840
Wiley, Rev. Philip B., Aug. 20, Pittsborough, Chatham county. R. R. Aug. 25, 1840
Wilkins, William U., Gaston county, Oct., Bertie county. R. R. Oct. 27, 1840
Williams, Mrs. Ann, Montgomery county, Alabama, Nov., Shelby county, Alabama. R. R. Nov. 6, 1840
Williams, Mrs. Elizabeth, Je., Hillsboro. R. R. Je. 23, 1840
Williams, Major Joseph, Oct. 5, Surry county. R. R. Oct. 16, 1840
Williams, Dr. Robert, Oct. 12, Pitt county. R. R. Oct. 16, 1840
Williamson, Mrs. Robert, Sept. 8, Lincoln county. R. R. Sept. 11, 1840
Willis, Mrs. E., Feb., Greensborough. R. R. Feb. 21, 1840
Winfield, Mrs. Thomas B., Feb., Beaufort county. R. R. Feb. 4, 1840
Wood, Ellis, Aug. 19, Randolph county. R. R. Sept. 1, 1840
Wood, William, Jly. 14, Halifax county. R. R. Aug. 28, 1840
Wooten, Caleb, Jan., Newbern. R. R. Jan. 14, 1840
Wright, Col. James, Apr., Duplin county. R. R. My. 1, 1840
Young, Elijah, Mar. 11, Raleigh. R. R. Mar. 13, 1840
Young, Mrs. Eliza, Oct. 6, Raleigh. R. R. Oct. 13, 1840

1841

Adams, Margaret, Dec., Greensboro. R. R. Dec. 31, 1841
Adams, Zachariah, My., Beaufort county. R. R. My. 25, 1841
Alexander, Col. Evan, Apr., Mecklenburg county. R. R. Apr. 27, 1841
Alexander, Dr. Joseph McKnitt, Oct. 17, Charlotte. R. R. Oct. 26, 1841
Alsobrook, Mrs. Alexander P., Oct. 5, Halifax. R. R. Oct. 15, 1841
Alston, Joseph John, Sr., My., Chatham county. R. R. My. 14, 1841
Alston, Mrs. Samuel, Aug. 24, Wake Forest. R. R. Sept. 3, 1841
Ames, Mrs. Lucinda J., Sept., Salisbury. R. R. Sept. 14, 1841
Armstrong, Mrs. Mary, Mar. 26, Raleigh. R. R. Mar. 30, 1841
Avery, Charles T. of Raleigh, Oct., St. Augustine, Florida. R. R. Oct. 15, 1841
Baker, Abraham, Oct., Wilmington. R. R. Oct. 26, 1841
Baker, George W. of Fayette county, Alabama, Nov., Salisbury. R. R. Nov. 9, 1841
Ball, Ann, Jan. 10, Orange county. R. R. Jan. 26, 1841
Ball, James, Dec. 29, Orange county. R. R. Jan. 26, 1841
Ball, Willie, Jan. 10, Orange county. R. R. Jan. 26, 1841
Barnard, Col. Carter, Mar., Pasquotank county. R. R. Apr. 2, 1841
Barrow, Frederick D., Je., Beaufort county. R. R. Je. 29, 1841
Baynor, Richard W., Aug., Beaufort county. R. R. Aug. 24, 1841
Beard, Michael, Apr., Anson county. R. R. Apr. 27, 1841
Beasley, Mrs. Fielding, Oct., Cumberland county. R. R. Je. 25, 1841
Beatty, Henry B., Nov., Bladen county. R. R. Nov. 19, 1841
Bell, Caleb C. of Newbern, Jly., Beaufort, Carteret county. R. R. Jly. 13, 1841
Boddie, Willis H. of Northampton county, Aug., Mt. Pleasant, Tennessee. R. R. Aug. 10, 1841

Bolton, Jeremiah H. of Philadelphia, Oct. 8, Charlotte. R. R. Oct. 22, 1841
Borden, A. J. of Fall River, Massachusetts, Oct. 5, Goldsboro, Wayne county. R. R. Oct. 26, 1841
Borroughs, Mrs. Allen, Je., Rowan county. R. R. Je. 18, 1841
Bostwick, Maj. Wm. M. of Mecklenburg county, Nov., Lamar, Mississippi. R. R. Nov. 23, 1841
Bouchelle, Dr. Thomas, Dec. 14, Morganton. R. R. Dec. 25, 1841
Boyd, Mrs. Disa, Jan., Montgomery county. R. R. Feb. 2, 1841
Brannock, Henry, Sr., Je., Orange county. R. R. Je. 25, 1841
Brent, Dr. Thomas S., Mar., Rockingham. R. R. Mar. 26, 1841
Bridges, Joseph, Jly. 24, Louisburg. R. R. Sept. 3, 1841
Brinkley, Mrs. Josiah, Sept., Halifax county. R. R. Sept. 28, 1841
Brown, Sophia of Columbus, Mississippi, Oct., Bladen county. R. R. Oct. 26, 1841
Brummell, Elvira, Dec., Davidson county. R. R. Dec. 31, 1841
Brummell, Jacob, Oct., Davidson county. R. R. Oct. 15, 1841
Bruner, Mrs. Elizabeth, Je. 2, Salisbury. R. R. Je. 15, 1841
Burch, Mary Eliza, Oct. 6, Wilmington. R. R. Oct. 26, 1841
Burton, Col. Edward of Virginia, Apr. 13, Oxford. R. R. Apr. 20, 1841
Butler, Sarah Frances, Mar., Granville county. R. R. Mar. 9, 1841
Caldwell, G. W. (infant), Jly. 3, Charlotte. R. R. Jly. 16, 1841
Campbell, Laura Alexandriana, Jly. 22, Raleigh. R. R. Jly. 27, 1841
Campbell, Mary, Mar., Guilford county. R. R. Mar. 16, 1841
Capehart, Mrs. Cullen, Nov., Bertie county. R. R. Nov. 19, 1841
Caraway, Tristram T., Aug., Anson county. R. R. Aug. 24, 1841
Carbry, Thomas of Greensborough, Oct. 1, Coffeeville, Mississippi. R. R. Oct. 22, 1841
Carpenter, Israel H., Oct., Wilmington. R. R. Oct. 26, 1841
Carr, Jonas J. of Sparta, Oct., Nash county. R. R. Oct. 8, 1841
Carr, Mrs. Jonas J., Dec. 25, Edgecombe county. R. R. Jan. 8, 1841
Carr, Thomas, Sr., Jan. 23, Stokes county. R. R. Feb. 5, 1841
Carr, William, Je., Duplin county. R. R. Je. 22, 1841
Carraway, Henry Clay, Aug., Lenoir county. R. R. Aug. 24, 1841
Carrigan, Mrs. William A., Apr., Orange county. R. R. Apr. 13, 1841
Casper, Mrs. Jacob, My., Salisbury. R. R. My. 25, 1841
Castle, Samuel of Connecticut, Oct., Wilkes county. R. R. Nov. 5, 1841
Cauble, Henry, My. 6, Lincoln county. R. R. My. 25, 1841
Cays, Robert L. of Norfolk, Jan. 7, Raleigh. R. R. Jan. 8, 1841
Causey, Joseph M., Sept. 30, Guilford county. R. R. Oct. 8, 1841
Chaffin, Nathan, Je. 11, Davie county. R. R. Je. 25, 1841
Cheek, Robt. T., My. 10, Warren county. R. R. My. 21, 1841
Cheshire, Mrs. Tennison, My., Davie county. R. R. My. 11, 1841
Clark, Mrs. William of Greenville, Oct. 27, Jackson, Mississippi. R. R. Nov. 19, 1841
Clemmons, Benton, Aug., Mocksville. R. R. Sept. 3, 1841
Cobb, Mrs. Wm., Aug., Lincolnton. R. R. Sept. 3, 1841
Cochran, Mrs. Joseph, Jly., Cabarrus county. R. R. Jly. 6, 1841
Cohoon, Mrs. P. A. R. C., Dec. 21, Tarborough. R. R. Jan. 8, 1841
Coleman, Mrs. Daniel, Sept. 25, Concord, Cabarrus county. R. R. Nov. 5, 1841
Collins, John W., Oct. 2, Beaufort county. R. R. Oct. 12, 1841

Congleton, Samuel Gregory, Sept., Washington, Beaufort county. R. R. Sept. 21, 1841
Connors, James, Mar., Beaufort county. R. R. Mar. 16, 1841
Conrad, Laura, Jan., Stokes county. R. R. Jan. 29, 1841
Cook, Mrs. Henry, Apr. 9, Raleigh. R. R. Apr. 13, 1841
Cooper, Henderson of this State, Nov. 5, Lynchburg. R. R. Nov. 16, 1841
Cooper, William of North Carolina, Mar., Baker county, Georgia. R. R. Mar. 26, 1841
Covington, Mrs. Nancy, Nov. 5, Richmond county. R. R. Nov. 23, 1841
Cowan, Rev. James of Belfast, Ireland, Sept. 19, Wayne county. R. R. Oct. 26, 1841
Cowell, William, Jan., Washington, Beaufort county. R. R. Jan. 15, 1841
Crabtree, Henry Jones, Oct., Wake county. R. R. Oct. 19, 1841
Crawley, Benjamin, Je., Halifax county. R. R. Je. 18, 1841
Crenshaw, Mrs. Frederic B., My. 13, Forestville. R. R. My. 21, 1841
Crenshaw, William Daniel Lumus, Jly., Forestville, Wake county. R. R. Jly. 27, 1841
Cromartie, Richard W., Oct., Bladen county. R. R. Oct. 8, 1841
Croom, Isaac, Aug., Lenoir county. R. R. Aug. 27, 1841
Dalrymple, Mrs. Alexander, My., Newbern. R. R. My. 28, 1841
Davidson, Robert H. M. of Mecklenburg county, Oct. 25, Quincey, Florida. R. R. Nov. 23, 1841
Davis, Mrs. Archibald of Wayne county, Jly., Chapel Hill. R. R. Jly. 16, 1841
Davis, Martha Caroline, Jan. 12, Waxhaw settlement. R. R. Jan. 22, 1841
Davis, Mrs. John S., My., Hyde county. R. R. My. 25, 1841
Dilliard, Joseph John of Raleigh, Je., Marshall county, Mississippi. R. R. Je. 25, 1841
Dorsey, Elizabeth of Wilmington, Mar., Guilford county. R. R. Mar. 16, 1841
Drake, Edwin, Jly. 14, Nash county. R. R. Jly. 23, 1841
Draughon, Hardy, Apr., Sampson county. R. R. Apr. 30, 1841
Dudley, Mrs. Christopher, Sept., Wilmington. R. R. Sept. 10, 1841
Dunlap, George T. of Anson county, Je., Mobile, Alabama. R. R. Je. 18, 1841
Dupree, Lavinia, Feb., Beaufort county. R. R. Feb. 23, 1841
Eaton, Mrs. Christiana B., Apr., Granville county. R. R. Apr. 23, 1841
Edgerton, Hiram, Oct., Bath, Beaufort county. R. R. Oct. 19, 1841
Elliott, Eleanor Adeline, Aug., Lincoln county. R. R. Aug. 10, 1841
Elliott, Benjamin, Mar., Elizabeth City. R. R. Mar. 9, 1841
Eppes, John W., Je., Halifax. R. R. Je. 29, 1841
Evans, Josiah, Oct., Cumberland county. R. R. Oct. 15, 1841
Falls, Naoma, Apr., Lincoln county. R. R. Apr. 16, 1841
Farrar, Col. John, Oct., Haywood, Chatham county. R. R. Oct. 15, 1841
Farrow, Sarah Ann, Sept., Washington, Beaufort county. R. R. Sept. 21, 1841
Ferrill, Anadella, Aug., Granville county. R. R. Aug. 3, 1841
Ferris, Walton, Oct., Mecklenburg county. R. R. Oct. 22, 1841
Fisher, Mrs. John, Jly. 6, Davidson county. R. R. Jly. 16, 1841
Fleming, Robert N., Oct. 29, Rowan county. R. R. Nov. 9, 1841
Foard, William, Je. 4, Salisbury. R. R. Je. 18, 1841
Folger, Adolphus Jefferson, Aug., Stokes county. R. R. Aug. 24, 1841
Folks, Jona, Dec. 6, Robeson county. R. R. Dec. 17, 1841
Fooshe, Mrs. Ambrose, Dec., Chatham county. R. R. Dec. 17, 1841
Fortiscue, Mary Eliza, Oct., Bath, Beaufort county. R. R. Oct. 19, 1841

Fox, Mrs. Lark of this State, Je. 17, Louisville, Kentucky. R. R. Oct. 8, 1841
Freeman, Elder James, Feb. 8, Wake county. R. R. Feb. 26, 1841
Frick, George, My., Rowan county. R. R. My. 25, 1841
Gaither, Burgess A., Oct. 15, Iredell county. R. R. Oct. 26, 1841
Gales, Joseph, Sr., Aug. 24, Raleigh. R. R. Aug. 27, 1841
Gardner, Mrs. James H. of Philadelphia, Oct., Halifax. R. R. Oct. 15, 1841
Garner, Mrs. Burgess, Mar., Davie county. R. R. Mar. 5, 1841
Garrett, Mrs. N. B., Oct., Beaufort county. R. R. Oct. 12, 1841
Garrison, Thomas, Je., Duplin county. R. R. Je. 22, 1841
Geffroy, Felix, Je., Elizabeth City. R. R. Je. 25, 1841
George, Mrs. St., Nov., Wilmington. R. R. Nov. 9, 1841
Gholson, Ann Yates, Feb. 28, Petersburg. R. R. Mar. 5, 1841
Gill, Mrs. Wm. A., Jly. 27, Granville county. R. R. Aug. 6, 1841
Givhan, Mrs. William of Raleigh, Apr. 19, Dallas county, Alabama. R. R. My. 14, 1841
Gorrell, Robt. D., Nov., Guilford county. R. R. Nov. 9, 1841
Grady, John, Sr. of Wake county, Aug. 24, Chambers county, Alabama. R. R. Sept. 28, 1841
Graham, Hamilton C., Aug. 30, Raleigh. R. R. Aug. 31, 1841
Green, Mrs. Arthur, Sept., Halifax county. R. R. Sept. 28, 1841
Greenlee, Mrs. J. M., Dec. 14, Burke county. R. R. Jan. 5, 1841
Grier, Mrs. John H., Nov., Mecklenburg county. R. R. Nov. 16, 1841
Grist, Mrs. Mary, Je., Washington, Beaufort county. R. R. Je. 22, 1841
Hall, Elisha, Aug., Montgomery county. R. R. Sept. 3, 1841
Hall, Mrs. Mary, Aug., Montgomery county. R. R. Sept. 3, 1841
Halliburton, John C., My. 23, Morganton. R. R. Je. 4, 1841
Hammond, William L., Oct., Bath, Beaufort county. R. R. Oct. 19, 1841
Hampton, Mrs. Joseph W., Je. 15, Cabarrus county. R. R. Jly. 2, 1841
Hampton, Mrs. Nancy, Apr., Iredell county. R. R. Apr. 16, 1841
Hancock, Thomas, Mar., Randolph county. R. R. Mar. 16, 1841
Hardie, Mrs. W. H., Dec., Halifax county. R. R. Dec. 17, 1841
Hargrave, John S. of Davidson county, Oct., Lexington. R. R. Oct. 19, 1841
Harmon, Mrs. A., Jan. 28, Stokes county. R. R. Feb. 5, 1841
Harris, Mary Roxanna of La Grange, Tennessee, Mar., Salisbury. R. R. Mar. 5, 1841
Harvey, Dr. Edmund B., Je. 18, Edenton. R. R. Je. 29, 1841
Hatter, Roger Fitch of Connecticut, Dec. 20, Raleigh. R. R. Dec. 25, 1841
Hattridge, Mrs. Anna B. of Wilmington, Nov. 29, Lincolnton. R. R. Dec. 17, 1841
Headen, Andrew, Dec. 10, Chatham county. R. R. Jan. 1, 1841
Henderson, Mrs. Alexander M., Jly., Edenton. R. R. Jly. 2, 1841
Hiatt, Sarah Jane, Je., Guilford county. R. R. Je. 25, 1841
Holdshouser, Andrew, Mar., Salisbury. R. R. Mar. 5, 1841
Holland, Sarah Oliver, Nov. 25, Kinston, Lenoir county. R. R. Dec. 17, 1841
Holloway, John, Mar., Raleigh. R. R. Mar. 19, 1841
Horah, Robert M., Sept., Salisbury. R. R. Sept. 14, 1841
Hooper, Col. James D., Je., Fayetteville. R. R. Jly. 2, 1841
Hoskins, Mrs. Ann, Sept., Wilmington. R. R. Sept. 10, 1841
Howarth, Dr. Henry C., Je., Franklin, Macon county. R. R. Je. 11, 1841
Hunt, Zebulon, Oct., Davidson county. R. R. Oct. 15, 1841
Huntington, Mrs. J., Nov., Wilmington. R. R. Nov. 23, 1841

Huske, John W., Oct. 6, Fayetteville. R. R. Oct. 8, 1841
Inge, Dr. Richard of Franklin county, Aug., Greene county, Alabama. R. R. Aug. 17, 1841
Inge, Col. William W. of Granville county, Dec., Livingston, Alabama. R. R. Dec. 31, 1841
Ingram, Mrs. Joseph, Jan., Anson county. R. R. Jan. 22, 1841
Ives, Mrs. Zadoc, Mar., Beaufort county. R. R. Mar. 16, 1841
Jarvis, Joseph, Je., Washington, Beaufort county. R. R. Je. 22, 1841
Jarvis, Mrs. W. B., My., Washington, Beaufort county. R. R. My. 18, 1841
Jenkins, Mary Frances, Jan., Tarboro. R. R. Jan. 29, 1841
Johnson, Eleanora, Sept. 10, Halifax county. R. R. Sept. 24, 1841
Johnson, Rev. Wm. S., Sept. 20, Springhill, Wake county. R. R. Sept. 21, 1841
Johnson, Henry M., Oct., Fayetteville. R. R. Oct. 29, 1841
Johnston, Jane C. of Lincoln county, Aug., Greensboro. R. R. Sept. 3, 1841
Johnston, Joshua, Jly. 30, Northampton county. R. R. Aug. 10, 1841
Jones, Nathaniel, Aug. 31, Wake county. R. R. Sept. 10, 1841
Jones, William Henry, Oct., Bath, Beaufort county. R. R. Oct. 19, 1841
Jordan, Josiah, Mar., Pasquotank county. R. R. Apr. 2, 1841
Jordan, Thomas, My., Pitt county. R. R. My. 18, 1841
Julian, Mrs. Jacob, Oct., Mecklenburg county. R. R. Oct. 22, 1841
Kenan, Col. Daniel L. of Duplin county, Dec. R. R. Jan. 1, 1841
Kestler, Sarah Cornelia, Jly. 3, Charlotte. R. R. Jly. 16, 1841
King, Benjamin, Je., Flat Rock, Henderson county. R. R. Je. 4, 1841
Lain, Fountain, Sept. 18, Fayetteville. R. R. Sept. 24, 1841
Lane, Hardy B., Jly., Newbern. R. R. Jly. 13, 1841
Lane, Joseph, Mar., Halifax county. R. R. Mar. 26, 1841
Lasater, John, Apr. 13, Chatham county. R. R. Apr. 16, 1841
Laughinghouse, John Edward, Feb., Pitt county. R. R. Feb. 23, 1841
Lazarus, Aaron of Wilmington, Oct. 2, Petersburg. R. R. Oct. 5, 1841
Leonard, Capt. Jacob of Brunswick county, Dec., Mobile. R. R. Dec. 17, 1841
Lewis, Martha Seawell, Dec., Milton. R. R. Dec. 25, 1841
Lewis, Warner, Dec., Milton, Caswell county. R. R. Dec. 31, 1841
Lewis, William of Greene county, Oct., Cumberland county. R. R. Oct. 15, 1841
Lindsay, William, Oct. 3, Guilford county. R. R. Oct. 15, 1841
Lineback, Joseph, Jan., Forsyth county. R. R. Feb. 2, 1841
Littlejohn, John W., Aug., Edenton. R. R. Aug. 10, 1841
Lloyd, Joseph R., Feb., Tarboro. R. R. Feb. 12, 1841
Lockhart, Col. Wm. B., Jan. 7, Northampton county. R. R. Feb. 9, 1841
Lounce, William, Nov., Washington, Beaufort county. R. R. Nov. 16, 1841
M'Cauley, Mrs. Andrew, Sr., My., Orange county. R. R. Je. 1, 1841
M'Cullouch, Miss Elizabeth, Apr., Lincoln county. R. R. Apr. 16, 1841
M'Farlane, Mrs. Mary Ann, Nov., Wilmington, On the Sound. R. R. Nov. 9, 1841
M'Gary, Elizabeth of Fayetteville, Oct., Wilmington. R. R. Oct. 19, 1841
M'Guffie, Jane, Aug. 8, Raleigh. R. R. Aug. 10, 1841
M'Kay, John Lloyd, Jan. 12, Bladen county. R. R. Jan. 22, 1841
M'Knight, Robert, Feb., Guilford county. R. R. Feb. 2, 1841
M'Laughlin, Alexander W. of Richmond county, Jan., South Carolina. R. R. Jan. 22, 1841
M'Laughlin, James of Ireland, Jan. 1, Raleigh. R. R. Jan. 5, 1841
M'Laurin, John, Sr., Je. 18, Fayetteville. R. R. Je. 25, 1841

M'Lean, Archibald Neal, Jan., Fayetteville. R. R. Feb. 5, 1841
M'Lean, Mrs. David, Aug., Greensboro. R. R. Sept. 3, 1841
M'Lead, Willis H., Dec. 22, Johnston county. R. R. Dec. 31, 1841
M'Nair, John, Sr., Apr., Richmond county. R. R. Apr. 30, 1841
M'Neely, Albert C., Oct. 5, Mocksville. R. R. Oct. 19, 1841
M'Neill, Mrs. George C. of Fayetteville, Jan., New Orleans. R. R. Feb. 2, 1841
M'Williams, Elizabeth, Je., Washington, Beaufort county. R. R. Je. 29, 1841
M'Williams, John, Nov., Beaufort county. R. R. Nov. 16, 1841
Madra, R. H. of this State, Aug. 5, Florence, Alabama. R. R. Aug. 27, 1841
Mahoney, Samuel, Nov. 5, Wilmington. R. R. Nov. 9, 1841
Mann, Capt. Thomas, Mar. 11, Edenton. R. R. Mar. 23, 1841
Marsh, Mary Ann, Oct., Cumberland county. R. R. Oct. 15, 1841
Marshall, Alexander P., Nov., Mecklenburg county. R. R. Nov. 23, 1841
Marshall, John G., Mar. 27, Raleigh. R. R. Mar. 30, 1841
Marshall, Thomas, Dec. 31, Halifax. R. R. Jan. 8, 1841
Mason, Henry of Halifax, Jan. 8, Scotland. R. R. Mar. 23, 1841
Matthew, Mrs. H. H., Oct. 4, Mecklenburg county. R. R. Oct. 22, 1841
Matthews, Jane E., Oct. 3, Mecklenburg county. R. R. Oct. 19, 1841
Meekins, Mrs. Benjamin, My., Washington, Beaufort county. R. R. Je. 1, 1841
Mendenhall, Nathan, Oct. 17, Guilford county. R. R. Nov. 2, 1841
Meredith, Milton A., Oct. 5, Guilford county. R. R. Oct. 15, 1841
Miller, Henrietta, Aug. 8, Newbern. R. R. Aug. 13, 1841
Miller, Gen. Stephen of Duplin county, Apr., Tallahassee, Florida. R. R. Apr. 13, 1841
Mitchell, Abram, Je., Onslow county. R. R. Je. 25, 1841
Mitchell, John, Oct. 5, Guilford county. R. R. Oct. 15, 1841
Mobley, Major Ollen, Feb., Sampson county. R. R. Feb. 26, 1841
Montgomery, Mrs. Jas. C., Apr., Mecklenburg county. R. R. Apr. 27, 1841
Moore, John, Apr., Rutherford county. R. R. Apr. 16, 1841
Moore, Lodowick, Sr. of Person county, Dec., Sumpter county, Alabama. R. R. Dec. 17, 1841
Morrow, Mrs. William, Jr., Nov., Orange county. R. R. Nov. 16, 1841
Mulhollon, John, Jan. 3, Hawfields, Orange county. R. R. Jan. 15, 1841
Munn, Mrs. James, Jan., Montgomery county. R. R. Feb. 9, 1841
Munro, Mrs. Robert, My., Cumberland county. R. R. My. 7, 1841
Neely, Washington, Oct., Rowan county. R. R. Oct. 15, 1841
Nichols, James, Jly. 16, Wake county. R. R. Jly. 23, 1841
Nicholls, Mrs. Penelope A., Aug. 5, Windsor, Bertie county. R. R. Aug. 24, 1841
Nicholson, John, Jan., Richmond county. R. R. Feb. 2, 1841
Nicks, Geo., Nov., Guilford county. R. R. Nov. 9, 1841
Norris, John of Wake county, Aug. 20, Tuscaloosa, Alabama. R. R. Sept. 17, 1841
Oates, Jethro, Oct., Sampson county. R. R. Oct. 15, 1841
O'Bryan, John Ingles of this State, Sept. 28, Weakly county, Tennessee. R. R. Oct. 29, 1841
Oliver, Susan P., Aug. 8, Newbern. R. R. Aug. 13, 1841
Opits, Charles G., Dec. 14, Salem. R. R. Dec. 25, 1841
Outland, Thos. N., Nov., Halifax. R. R. Nov. 19, 1841
Owen, Mrs. James, Apr., Wilmington. R. R. Apr. 13, 1841
Owen, Hon. John, Oct. 6, Pittsboro. R. R. Oct. 19, 1841

Parker, Col. David, Nov. 9, Hillsboro. R. R. Nov. 16, 1841
Patton, Benjamin Francklin of Asheville, Jan. 1, Clarkesville, Alabama. R. R. Jan. 8, 1841
Pearce, Polly, Mar., Beaufort county. R. R. Mar. 16, 1841
Person, Mary Ann of Carthage, Nov. 19, Moore county. R. R. Jan. 1, 1841
Purnell, Adelaide, Nov., Wilmington. R. R. Nov. 9, 1841
Purnell, David, Oct., Halifax county. R. R. Oct. 15, 1841
Rattedge, James, Aug. 1, Davie county. R. R. Aug. 10, 1841
Ransom, William, Je. 22, Franklin county. R. R. Je. 29, 1841
Rawlins, Mary Eppes of Norfolk, Va., My. 22, Oxford. R. R. My. 28, 1841
Reed, Mrs. Henry, Nov., Greensboro. R. R. Nov. 9, 1841
Rencher, Mary Jones, Oct., Pittsborough. R. R. Oct. 15, 1841
Ridley, William J., Sept. 23, Warren county. R. R. Oct. 8, 1841
Roberts, Mrs. Wm. B., My., Davidson county. R. R. My. 11, 1841
Robertson, Nicholas C., Oct. 3, Raleigh. R. R. Oct. 5, 1841
Robinson, James F., Apr., Lincoln county. R. R. Apr. 16, 1841
Rodgers, Hugh, Oct. 25, Mecklenburg county. R. R. Nov. 23, 1841
Rotan, Mrs. Nancy, Je. 6, Salisbury. R. R. Je. 18, 1841
Russell, John Council, Oct., Fayetteville. R. R. Oct. 29, 1841
Ryan, George of Bertie county, Jan. 21, Wake county. R. R. Jan. 26, 1841
Satchwell, Mrs. John E., Aug., Beaufort county. R. R. Aug. 24, 1841
Satterthwaite, William S., My., Beaufort county. R. R. Je. 1, 1841
Schardle, Mrs. Peter, Oct. 18, Raleigh. R. R. Oct. 19, 1841
Scott, Mrs. Eliza, Mar., Wilmington. R. R. Mar. 19, 1841
Searcy, Thomas, Aug. 11, Rockingham county. R. R. Sept. 3, 1841
Shankle, Rev. George, Nov., Stanly county. R. R. Nov. 9, 1841
Shaw, Willie, Sr. of Orange county, Mar., Somerville, Tennessee. R. R. Mar. 19, 1841
Singletary, Adelaide, Oct. 1, Washington, Beaufort county. R. R. Oct. 12, 1841
Smith, Mrs. Catharine, Sept., Salisbury. R. R. Sept. 14, 1841
Smith, Mrs. Casper, Je. 13, Rowan county. R. R. Jly. 2, 1841
Smith, George Freeman, Jan. 1, Raleigh. R. R. Jan. 5, 1841
Smith, Mrs. Jonathan of Averasborough, Feb. 3, Wake county. R. R. Feb. 19, 1841
Smith, Robert H., Nov., Washington, Beaufort county. R. R. Nov. 16, 1841
Snead, James M., Aug. 8, Newbern. R. R. Aug. 13, 1841
Sneed, James, Oct., Orange county. R. R. Nov. 2, 1841
Sneed, Jonathan R. of Hillsborough, Sept. 9, Lafatte county, Mississippi. R. R. Sept. 24, 1841
Sneed, Stephen K. of Granville county, Apr., La Grange, Tennessee. R. R. Apr. 13, 1841
Somervel, Mrs. James, Nov. 26, Mecklenburg county, Va. R. R. Jan. 1, 1841
Southerland, Dr. Samuel N. of this State, Apr. 30, Gainesville, Alabama. R. R. Je. 4, 1841
Stanly, George, My., Newbern. R. R. My. 14, 1841
Starling, Robert, Apr., Johnston county. R. R. Apr. 23, 1841
Strayhorn, Mary, Jan. 15, Orange county. R. R. Jan. 26, 1841
Stubblefield, John Wyatt, Oct., Rockingham. R. R. Oct. 15, 1841
Sturdivant, James, Sr., Nov. 24, Dinwiddie county, Va. R. R. Jan. 1, 1841
Sturdivant, Robert, Apr. 27, Halifax. R. R. My. 7, 1841
Stewart, Charles, Nov. 29, Newbern. R. R. Dec. 10, 1841

Sugg, Reddin, Je. 26, Edgecombe county. R. R. Jly. 2, 1841
Swain, George Franklin, Aug., Guilford county. R. R. Aug. 24, 1841
Swaine, John, Oct. 3, Guilford county. R. R. Oct. 8, 1841
Swaim, Mrs. Rachael, Mar. 3, Asheboro. R. R. Mar. 16, 1841
Taylor, Alfred Moore, Apr., Hillsboro. R. R. Apr. 27, 1841
Taylor, Elizabeth, Jan., Cumberland county. R. R. Feb. 5, 1841
Taylor, Mrs. John C., Dec., Granville county. R. R. Dec. 17, 1841
Telfair, Paulina, My. 7, Smithfield. R. R. My. 14, 1841
Tharpe, Mrs. Noah, My., Guilford county. R. R. My. 21, 1841
Thompson, Mrs. Isabella, Nov. 23, Orange county. R. R. Jan. 1, 1841
Thompson, Rev. John C., Apr. 19, Granville county. R. R. Apr. 27, 1841
Tomerson, John, Oct., Bath, Beaufort county. R. R. Oct. 19, 1841
Transu, Mrs. Abraham, Jly., Stokes county. R. R. Jly. 16, 1841
Transu, John, Jly. 7, Bethania. R. R. Jly. 16, 1841
Turner, Mrs. John D., Sept., Halifax county. R. R. Sept. 28, 1841
Tyson, Jas., Mar., Moore county. R. R. Mar. 26, 1841
Vickery, Rev. Christopher of Va., Apr., Randolph county. R. R. Apr. 16, 1841
Vinson, Peter, Sept. 6, Halifax county. R. R. Sept. 28, 1841
Vinson, Robert, Sept. 6, Halifax county. R. R. Sept. 28, 1841
Wallace, Christopher, Sept., Wilmington. R. R. Oct. 10, 1841
Wallace, Eliza, Oct., Bath, Beaufort county. R. R. Oct. 19, 1841
Wallace, Elizabeth, Apr., Cabarrus county. R. R. Apr. 27, 1841
Wallace, Mrs. Hunter, Oct., Bath, Beaufort county. R. R. Oct. 19, 1841
Wallace, Matthew, Aug., Mecklenburg county. R. R. Aug. 24, 1841
Wallace, Willie, Oct., Bath, Beaufort county. R. R. Oct. 19, 1841
Watson, Israel S., Feb. 3, Hyde county. R. R. Feb. 12, 1841
Wayne, Mrs. Mary, Apr., Orange county. R. R. Apr. 27, 1841
Webb, Ann Elizabeth, My., Halifax. R. R. My. 21, 1841
Welch, William, Jan. 1, Raleigh. R. R. Jan. 5, 1841
Whitehead, Henry A., Je., Halifax. R. R. Je. 29, 1841
Weddifield, William of Philadelphia, Apr., Fayetteville. R. R. Apr. 30, 1841
Wier, James of Ireland, Aug. R. R. Aug. 3, 1841
Wilkinson, Jesse, Je., Washington, Beaufort county. R. R. Je. 15, 1841
Williams, Dr. William H. of Berkshire county, Massachusetts, Je. 19, Pasqoutank county. R. R. Je. 29, 1841
Windley, Mrs. William W., Oct., Bath, Beaufort county. R. R. Oct. 19, 1841
Ward, Henry of Chatham county, Sept. 22, Mobile. R. R. Oct. 8, 1841
Waters, Mrs. Mary, Aug., Washington, Beaufort county. R. R. Sept. 3, 1841
Weatherly, James Daniel Webster, Aug., Greensborough. R. R. Aug. 24, 1841
Wheeler, Charles K. of Massachusetts, Oct., Salisbury. R. R. Oct. 22, 1841
White, Dr. Willie N., My. 16, Hillsboro. R. R. My. 25, 1841
Whitley, Sarah A., Oct., Bath, Beaufort county. R. R. Oct. 19, 1841
Wilkinson, Elizabeth A., Dec. 28, Raleigh. R. R. Dec. 31, 1841
Wilkes, Mrs. James of Granville county, Oct., Maury county, Tennessee. R. R. Oct. 26, 1841
Wingate, Cornelia, Nov. 23, Wilmington. R. R. Dec. 7, 1841
Woodfin, Mary Adelaide, Mar., Macon county. R. R. Mar. 16, 1841
Yokely, Mrs. Samuel, Oct., Davidson county. R. R. Oct. 15, 1841
Yarbrough, David of Hillsboro, Sept. 23, Marion, Alabama. R. R. Oct. 12, 1841
Yarbrough, Dr. Henry of Hillsboro, Sept. 8, Marion, Alabama. R. R. Oct. 12, 1841

Young, Archibald of Statesville, Aug., Lawrence District, S. C. R. R. Sept. 3, 1841
Young, Miss Thomas H. of Iredell county, Jan., Canton. R. R. Jan. 29, 1841

1842

Abernathy, Smith, Jan. 23, Wake Forest. R. R. Feb. 11, 1842
Alexander, Elias, Oct., Mecklenburg county. R. R. Oct. 4, 1842
Alexander, Francis M. of this State, Oct., Mobile, Alabama. R. R. Oct. 21, 1842
Allen, John M. of Montgomery county, Oct., Stanly county. R. R. Oct. 28, 1842
Alston, John J., Sept. 18, Chatham county. R. R. Sept. 30, 1842
Anderson, Robert, Apr. 15, Williamsborough, Granville county. R. R. Apr. 26, 1842
Armfield, William, Feb., Greensboro. R. R. Feb. 18, 1842
Armstrong, Mrs. Thomas D. of Orange county, Dec., Montgomery county, Alabama. R. R. Dec. 2, 1842
Atkins, Mrs. John, Feb., Cumberland county. R. R. Feb. 8, 1842
Backhouse, Allen, Oct., Newbern. R. R. Oct. 14, 1842
Backhouse, Mrs. Allen, Apr., Newbern. R. R. Apr. 8, 1842
Baker, Mary Louisa, Apr., Salisbury. R. R. My. 3, 1842
Beard, Mary E., Aug., Salisbury. R. R. Aug. 30, 1842
Beattie, Cummins M., Oct. 4, Greensboro. R. R. Oct. 14, 1842
Beebe, Asa of Connecticut, Apr., Fayetteville. R. R. Apr. 26, 1842
Belden, Lewis S., Oct. 29, Fayetteville. R. R. Nov. 4, 1842
Betts, Col. William of this State, Dec., Montgomery county, Alabama. R. R. Dec. 2, 1842
Blackburn, Robert, Oct., Stokes county. R. R. Nov. 8, 1842
Blair, George of Edenton, Dec. 10, New Orleans. R. R. Feb. 4, 1842
Blanchard (infant), Jan., Newbern. R. R. Jan. 18, 1842
Blake, Emma Jane, Mar., Fayetteville. R. R. Mar. 18, 1842
Blakeney, Mrs. Jas. W., Oct., near Cheraw. R. R. Oct. 14, 1842
Bland, Ann Eliza, Oct., Orange county. R. R. Nov. 1, 1842
Blount, Mrs. Frederick, Sept. 18, Newbern. R. R. Sept. 30, 1842
Blount, John Gray, Apr., Washington, Beaufort county. R. R. Apr. 8, 1842
Boddie, George, Dec. 12, Nash county. R. R. Dec. 30, 1842
Boger, Daniel M., Oct., Salisbury. R. R. Oct. 21, 1842
Bottom, William, Je. 27, Northampton county. R. R. Aug. 5, 1842
Bowen, Mrs. Frances of Fayetteville, Oct. 2, Camden, Wilcox county, Alabama. R. R. Oct. 28, 1842
Boylan, James of Raleigh, Nov., Somerville, Tennessee. R. R. Nov. 29, 1842
Bradley, John, Oct. 14, Onslow county. R. R. Oct. 25, 1842
Bradley, John A. (son), Oct. 5, Onslow county. R. R. Oct. 25, 1842
Branch, Mrs. Joseph, Aug. 13, Halifax. R. R. Aug. 23, 1842
Branch, Joseph, Aug. 16, Halifax. R. R. Aug. 30, 1842
Brantley, James, Oct. 3, Halifax. R. R. Oct. 21, 1842
Brevard, Alexander J. M. of Lincoln county, Je., Columbia, South Carolina. R. R. Je. 10, 1842
Brevard, Samuel R., Oct., Lexington. R. R. Oct. 14, 1842
Brickell, William Stuart, Oct., Halifax county. R. R. Oct. 25, 1842
Brickell, Susan Caroline, Lafayette, Sept., Halifax. R. R. Sept. 23, 1842
Brickell, Capt. William, Oct. 1, Enfield, Halifax county. R. R. Oct. 21, 1842
Brooks, Mrs. J. H., Apr. 26, Edenton. R. R. My. 6, 1842

Brown, Andrew H., Jly., Mecklenburg county. R. R. Aug. 2, 1842
Brown, Mrs. J. M., Apr., Salisbury. R. R. My. 3, 1842
Brown, Mrs. Michael, Oct., Rowan county. R. R. Oct. 14, 1842
Brown, Moses, Sr., Jan., Rowan county. R. R. Jan. 11, 1842
Bruce, Lucian, Sept. 2, Carthage, Moore county. R. R. Sept. 9, 1842
Bryan, John, Jan. 31, Wilkes county. R. R. Mar. 1, 1842
Bryan, Lewis, Feb., Newbern. R. R. Feb. 8, 1842
Burgwyn, J. Collinson, Nov., Northampton county. R. R. Nov. 18, 1842
Burt, James Battle, Jly. 6, Wake county. R. R. Jly. 8, 1842
Burton, Robert H., Feb. 26, Lincoln county. R. R. Mar. 8, 1842
Burton, Jane, Jan., Mecklenburg county. R. R. Jan. 21, 1842
Byrne, Thomas H. of Bladen county, Sept., Fayetteville. R. R. Sept. 23, 1842
Caldwell, Dr. Alfred W., Sept., Welch's Mill, Cabarrus county. R. R. Oct. 4, 1842
Caldwell, William Lowndes of this State, Feb., Washington, D. C. R. R. Feb. 11, 1842
Cameron, Jane of Orange county, Oct. 7, Raleigh. R. R. Oct. 14, 1842
Campbell, Frances, Aug. 15, Warrenton. R. R. Aug. 23, 1842
Cannon, David of this State, Oct., Lauderdale county, Alabama. R. R. Oct. 21, 1842
Carney, Mrs. James, Apr. 20, Newbern. R. R. Apr. 29, 1842
Chambers, Robert E., Oct., Anson county. R. R. Oct. 21, 1842
Chapman, Elizabeth, Jly. 14, Newbern. R. R. Jly. 29, 1842
Charles, Benjamin H., Jan., Pasquotank county. R. R. Jan. 25, 1842
Charles, Mrs. Benjamin H., Feb., Pasquotank county. R. R. Feb. 22, 1842
Chears, V. T. of Anson county, Dec. 12, La Grange, Tennessee. R. R. Jan. 25, 1842
Clark, George of Massachusetts, Oct., Washington, Beaufort county. R. R. Nov. 1, 1842
Clark, Mrs. James, Jan. 14, Orange county. R. R. Feb. 1, 1842
Close, Mrs. John, Jan., Stokes county. R. R. Jan. 21, 1842'
Coles, Fanny, Feb., Rowan county. R. R. Feb. 18, 1842
Collins, Robert, Aug., Charlotte. R. R. Aug. 9, 1842
Coman, James of Ireland, Jan. 9, Raleigh. R. R. Jan. 11, 1842
Conrad, Peter, Oct., Lexington. R. R. Oct. 14, 1842
Cook, William, Sr., Jan., Franklin county. R. R. Jan. 21, 1842
Copeland, William, Apr., Moore county. R. R. Apr. 26, 1842
Couch, Jabez, Sept. 27, Guilford county. R. R. Oct. 4, 1842
Cowan, John Loudon, Aug. 22, Smithville. R. R. Sept. 9, 1842
Crain, Thomas D., Apr., Hillsboro. R. R. Apr. 19, 1842
Cromartie, Miriam of Bladen county, Nov., Fayetteville. R. R. Nov. 18, 1842
Cronin, Rev. Timothy J., Oct., Salisbury. R. R. Nov. 1, 1842
Crowder, Thomas, Je., Wake county. R. R. Je. 10, 1842
Crowder, Mrs. Thomas of Orange county, My., Georgia. R. R. My. 31, 1842
Cumming, Mary Lavinia, My., Greensboro. R. R. My. 20, 1842
Custis, Peter of Newbern, Apr., Accomac county, Virginia. R. R. Apr. 8, 1842
Daniel, Moore of Orange county, Feb., Greensboro. R. R. Feb. 8, 1842
Davidson, Gen. Ephraim, Feb. 25, Iredell county. R. R. Mar. 18, 1842
Davis, Evan, Jan., Davidson county. R. R. Jan. 21, 1842
Dennis, Joseph H., Sept. 25, Guilford county. R. R. Oct. 4, 1842
Denny, James, Aug., Guilford county. R. R. Aug. 30, 1842

Dicken, Mrs. Lewis B. K., Oct., Halifax. R. R. Oct. 21, 1842
Dicken, Mecom, Oct., Halifax. R. R. Oct. 21, 1842
Dismukes, Mrs. George, Apr., Chatham county. R. R. Apr. 29, 1842
Doak, Roddy, Jly. 17, Guilford county. R. R. Aug. 2, 1842
Dobbin, Margaret, Apr., Fayetteville. R. R. Apr. 26, 1842
Dobbins, Joseph, Jan., Rowan county. R. R. Jan. 11, 1842
Douthit, David, Oct. 28, Davidson county. R. R. Nov. 8, 1842
Drake, William Franklin, Apr. 21, Nashville, Nash county. R. R. My. 13, 1842
Dunn, Mrs. Elizabeth J., Sept., Mecklenburg county. R. R. Sept. 23, 1842
Eaton, Mrs. John R., Jly. 11, Granville county. R. R. Jly. 22, 1842
Elam, Alexander G. of Raleigh, Nov., Fayetteville. R. R. Nov. 18, 1842
Elliott, Col. Benjamin, Mar., Randolph county. R. R. Mar. 18, 1842
Elliott, Willis J., Feb., Edenton. R. R. Feb. 8, 1842
Eppes, Mrs. Wilie J. of Buckingham county, Jan., Chowan county. R. R. Feb. 4, 1842
Erambert, Abram, Oct. 29, Fayetteville. R. R. Nov. 4, 1842
Evans, Sherwood, Apr. 23, Franklin. R. R. My. 17, 1842
Fannin, Mrs. John H. of this State, Oct., Alabama. R. R. Oct. 28, 1842
Faucette, Chesley Farrar, Aug. 1, Haywood, Chatham county. R. R. Aug. 9, 1842
Favor, G. K. of Portland, Maine, Sept. 16, Greensboro. R. R. Sept. 30, 1842
Fentress, Thomas, Je. 30, Randolph county. R. R. Jly. 22, 1842
Ferrall, Mrs. Elizabeth of Langford, Ireland, Sept., Halifax. R. R. Sept. 23, 1842
Fillhour, Adam, Jan., Rowan county. R. R. Jan. 11, 1842
Finch, Nancy A. M., Aug., Davidson College. R. R. Aug. 9, 1842
Forrest, Mrs. James, Nov., Orange county. R. R. Nov. 22, 1842
Foy, Enoch, Oct., Jones county. R. R. Oct. 14, 1842
Gales, Mrs. Weston R., Jan. 24, Raleigh. R. R. Jan. 25, 1842
Galloway, Mrs. F., Oct., Cabarrus county. R. R. Oct. 21, 1842
Gary, Mrs. Henry, Mar., Halifax. R. R. Mar. 15, 1842
Geer, Catharine Stanly, Jly., Wadesboro. R. R. Jly. 8, 1842
Gheen, James, Apr., Salisbury. R. R. My. 3, 1842
Gheen, Mrs. Sarah Susannah, Sept., Salisbury. R. R. Sept. 23, 1842
Gholson, Mrs. Mary, Jan. 28, Brunswick county. R. R. Feb. 11, 1842
Gilliam, Mrs. Robert B. of Oxford, Oct. 8, Danville, Virginia. R. R. Oct. 28, 1842
Gilmer, Euphemia Jane, My. 14, Greensboro. R. R. My. 20, 1842
Gilmer, Wm. Paisley, Feb., Greensboro. R. R. Feb. 18, 1842
Gordon, Mrs. Sarah of Fredericksburg, Virginia, Mar., Wilkes county. R. R. Apr. 1, 1842
Gorrell, Mrs. Robert, Sept., Guilford county. R. R. Oct. 4, 1842
Green, Mrs. James S., Je. 3, Wilmington. R. R. Je. 10, 1842
Gretter, George K., Sept., Greensboro. R. R. Sept. 9, 1842
Griffiths, Edmund, Jan., Washington. R. R. Jan. 21, 1842
Hadlock, James of Connecticut, Oct. 31, Fayetteville. R. R. Nov. 11, 1842
Hall, Mrs. Albert, Sept., South Washington, New Hanover county. R. R. Sept. 6, 1842
Hall, Robert, Sept., Guilford county. R. R. Oct. 4, 1842
Hampton, Dr. James A. of Iredell county, Oct., Yorkville, South Carolina. R. R. Oct. 21, 1842

Happoldt, Mrs. J. M. H., Jan. 6, Charlotte. R. R. Jan. 21, 1842
Harding, Robert Hollister, Dec. 23, Milton. R. R. Dec. 30, 1842
Harrison, Elisha, Sept. 3, Smithfield, Johnston county. R. R. Sept. 9, 1842
Harty, Benjamin, Oct., Charlotte. R. R. Oct. 4, 1842
Hawkins, Dr. Joseph, Aug. 5, Warren county. R. R. Aug. 9, 1842
Hawley, Mrs. Isaac, Feb., Fayetteville. R. R. Apr. 26, 1842
Hayward, John, Jly. 14, Newbern. R. R. Jly. 29, 1842
Henderson, Calvin Jones of Jackson, Tennessee and this State, Oct. 11, On the Mississippi. R. R. Nov. 18, 1842
Henderson, Harriet Caroline, Jan., Lincolnton. R. R. Jan. 11, 1842
Henry, Philip J. of Beaufort, My. 19, Charleston, South Carolina. R. R. My. 31, 1842
Henshaw, Benjamin, Apr. 15, Chatham county. R. R. Apr. 29, 1842
Hicks, Joseph T. of Granville county, Je. 15, Warren county, Mi. R. R. Jly. 12, 1842
Hill, Nathaniel, Feb., Rocky Run, Wilmington. R. R. Feb. 15, 1842
Hinton, James, My. 13, Wake county. R. R. My. 20, 1842
Hinton, James, Aug. 7, Greensboro. R. R. Aug. 12, 1842
Hinton, Indiana, Apr. 27, Wake county. R. R. Je. 3, 1842
Hinton, John H. of this State, Aug. 28, Carrollton, Greene county, Illinois. R. R. Nov. 25, 1842
Hinton, Mrs. P. W., Apr., Pasquotank county. R. R. Apr. 8, 1842
Hinton, Dr. Thomas Prince, Mar., Pasquotank county. R. R. Mar. 15, 1842
Holden, John, Oct., Orange county. R. R. Nov. 1, 1842
Holland, Dr. William, Dec., Kinston, Lenoir county. R. R. Dec. 30, 1842
Holloman, Mrs. Lewis, Feb. 25, Raleigh. R. R. Mar. 4, 1842
Holt, Michael, Apr. 27, Orange county. R. R. Apr. 29, 1842
Hoover, Gen. George, Je. 25, Ashborough, Randolph county. R. R. Jly. 1, 1842
Horn, Mary E., Sept. 10, Snow Hill, Greene county. R. R. Sept. 30, 1842
Horn, Mrs. Wm. H., Sept. 10, Snow Hill, Greene county. R. R. Sept. 30, 1842
Horney, Mrs. John C., Sept., Greensboro. R. R. Sept. 9, 1842
Hoskins, Mrs. Mary, Sept. 13, Guilford county. R. R. Sept. 23, 1842
Howard, Mrs. Barnett of Granville county, Jan. 8, Henry county, Tennessee. R. R. Apr. 1, 1842
Howard, Mrs. Thomas, Jly. 31, Newbern. R. R. Aug. 19, 1842
Howard, Wm., Oct. 22, Statesville. R. R. Nov. 1, 1842
Hubbard, Frances, Jan. 11, Milton. R. R. Jan. 14, 1842
Husted, Charles Manly, Sept. 6, Smithfield. R. R. Sept. 13, 1842
Husted, Fitz Green Halleck, Oct. 4, Smithfield. R. R. Oct. 21, 1842
Husted, John MacLeod, Oct. 16, Smithfield. R. R. Oct. 21, 1842
Hutchison, John of England, Dec., Newbern. R. R. Dec. 30, 1842
Hutchison, Mrs. Thomas L., Feb., Mecklenburg county. R. R. Feb. 8, 1842
Jarvis, Mrs. James, Oct. 19, Stokes county. R. R. Nov. 8, 1842
Jarvis, Lieut. Joseph W., U.S.N. of Newbern, Sept., Portsmouth, Carteret county. R. R. Sept. 30, 1842
Jarvis, Mary, Apr., Newbern. R. R. Apr. 29, 1842
Jeffreys, Simon of Franklin county, My. 6, Fayetteville. R. R. My. 13, 1842
Jenkins, Mrs. James, Apr., Cumberland county. R. R. Apr. 29, 1842
Jewett, Mrs. S. of Wilmington, Je. 13, Moore county. R. R. Je. 24, 1842
Johnson, Edward, Jan., Dinwiddie Court House, Virginia. R. R. Feb. 4, 1842
Johnson, Neill, Sept., Fayetteville. R. R. Sept. 23, 1842

Johnson, Sarah, My. 7, Raleigh. R. R. My. 10, 1842
Johnson, Willie, My. 29, Raleigh. R. R. Je. 3, 1842
Johnston, Mrs. Amos, My. 29, Edgecombe county. R. R. Je. 10, 1842
Johnston, Helen S., Oct., Edenton. R. R. Nov. 1, 1842
Jones, Benj. George, Nov. 2, Granville county. R. R. Nov. 8, 1842
Jones, Matthew, Oct., Salisbury. R. R. Oct. 21, 1842
Jones, Nathan, Dec., Richmond county. R. R. Dec. 2, 1842
Jones, Thos. S., Oct., Fayetteville. R. R. Oct. 28, 1842
Jordan, Burwell P. of Franklin county, Sept. 20, Alabama. R. R. Sept. 23, 1842
Jordan, William, Jan., Washington. R. R. Jan. 21, 1842
Joseph, Mrs. Solomon M., Oct., Washington, Beaufort county. R. R. Nov. 1, 1842
Kelly, John of Dublin, Ireland, Aug. 24, Fayetteville. R. R. Aug. 26, 1842
Kelly, Mrs. John B., Feb. 2, Moore county. R. R. Feb. 22, 1842
Kennedy, Capt. Marcus T. C., Oct., Mecklenburg county. R. R. Oct. 4, 1842
Kerby, James, Sr., Jly. 5, Chatham county. R. R. Jly. 12, 1842
Kirkland, Thomas (infant), Nov. 15, Orange county. R. R. Nov. 22, 1842
Kirkman, Rebecca, Sept., Greensboro. R. R. Oct. 4, 1842
Kirr, Melinda, Feb., Guilford county. R. R. Feb. 11, 1842
Kirsey, Alex, Jan. 13, Milton. R. R. Jan. 14, 1842
Knowles, L. B., Sept., Greensboro. R. R. Oct. 4, 1842
Kornegay, Thomas W. of Jones county and Tuscaloosa, Alabama, Jly., Philadelphia, Pa. R. R. Jly. 26, 1842
Lamb, Josiah, Apr. 18, Chatham county. R. R. Apr. 29, 1842
Lane, Mrs. Isaac, Jly., Guilford county. R. R. Aug. 2, 1842
Latham, Maria Lucy, Sept., Craven county. R. R. Sept. 23, 1842
Latham, Mrs. Thomas, Nov. 12, Beaufort. R. R. Nov. 22, 1842
Laughinghouse, James E. of Pitt county, Nov. 7, Wake Forest. R. R. Nov. 11, 1842
Lemay, Harriet P. of Granville county, Je. 20, Marshall county, Mi. R. R. Jly. 29, 1842
Lennon, Rev. Dennis, Jly. 16, Columbus county. R. R. Aug. 5, 1842
Lessesne, Caroline, Aug., Elizabethtown, Bladen county. R. R. Aug. 23, 1842
Lewis, Henry, Dec. 26, Milton. R. R. Jan. 14, 1842
Lewis, Dr. John Wesley, Nov. 22, Raleigh. R. R. Nov. 25, 1842
Lewis, Orrin of Connecticut & Chapel Hill, Aug. 3, Marion, Alabama. R. R. Aug. 19, 1842
Lewis, Warner M., Dec. 22, Milton. R. R. Jan. 14, 1842
Lindeman, D. of Raleigh, Sept., Mobile, Alabama. R. R. Sept. 30, 1842
Linder, Angelina, Jly., Rockingham. R. R. Aug. 2, 1842
Linthicum, Diana, Sept. 18, Greensboro. R. R. Sept. 30, 1842
Locke, Major John, Oct. 24, Davie county. R. R. Nov. 1, 1842
Locke, Mrs. William, Oct. 16, Salisbury. R. R. Oct. 28, 1842
London, John Lord, Nov. 11, Wilmington. R. R. Nov. 22, 1842
Long, Stephen B., Aug., Perquimans county. R. R. Aug. 19, 1842
Lougee, Olivia Burch, Aug. 20, Raleigh. R. R. Aug. 23, 1842
Mabry, Mrs. Alfred, Sept. 10, Halifax. R. R. Sept. 23, 1842
M'Alister, Flora, Jly., Cumberland county. R. R. Jly. 12, 1842
M'Clelland, Mrs. Jane, Feb., Iredell county. R. R. Feb. 8, 1842
M'Coy, Mrs. Hugh, Oct., Mecklenburg county. R. R. Oct. 4, 1842

M'Cracken, Mrs. Thomas of Guilford county, Nov. 22, Randolph county. R. R. Nov. 29, 1842
M'Geachy, Alex'r, Jr., Sept., Robeson county. R. R. Sept. 23, 1842
M'Intosh, Mrs. Duncan, Nov., Moore county. R. R. Nov. 8, 1842
M'Innis, Murdock of Scotland, Feb., Robeson county. R. R. Feb. 8, 1842
M'Iver, Evander, Je. 2, Chatham county. R. R. Je. 24, 1842
M'Keown, William Henry, Sept., Fayetteville. R. R. Sept. 9, 1842
M'Leod, Mrs. Ann, Apr., Moore county. R. R. Apr. 26, 1842
M'Morine, John, Mar., Pasquotank county. R. R. Mar. 15, 1842
M'Nair, Edmund D., Dec. 7, Tarboro. R. R. Dec. 30, 1842
M'Quay, William, Oct., Mecklenburg county. R. R. Oct. 4, 1842
M'Rae, Mrs. Alexander, Oct. 17, Wilmington. R. R. Nov. 1, 1842
M'Ree, Mrs. Ann F., Aug. 8, Wilmington. R. R. Aug. 23, 1842
M'Pheeters, Rev. William, Nov. 7, Raleigh. R. R. Nov. 8, 1842
Markland, Nathaniel, Jan. 20, Davie county. R. R. Feb. 8, 1842
Marsh, John B., Nov., Fayetteville. R. R. Nov. 11, 1842
Marlin, Jesse, Aug., Rowan county. R. R. Aug. 30, 1842
Martin, Robert, Oct., Wilkes county. R. R. Oct. 21, 1842
Mathews, Tandy, Jr., Jly., Stokes county. R. R. Jly. 22, 1842
Matthes, Mrs. David S., Apr., Sampson county. R. R. Apr. 26, 1842
Meares, Wm. B., Mar. 17, Warren county. R. R. Mar. 22, 1842
Melwean, Nancy, Apr., Newbern. R. R. Apr. 29, 1842
Mills, John, Jan., Rutherford. R. R. Jan. 11, 1842
Miller, Mrs. Henry M., Feb. 1, Raleigh. R. R. Feb. 4, 1842
Mixon, Charles, Oct., Wilmington. R. R. Oct. 25, 1842
Moore, Sarah, Sept., Guilford county. R. R. Sept. 9, 1842
Moore, Betsey Turner, Jly. 27, Raleigh. R. R. Jly. 29, 1842
Moore, Mary Elizabeth, Je. 11, Edenton. R. R. Jly. 1, 1842
Moorman, John, Sr., Oct., Richmond county. R. R. Oct. 25, 1842
Mundy, Henry H. of Franklin county, Oct., Pickens, Alabama. R. R. Oct. 21, 1842
Northam, Sarah Jane, Oct. 19, Smithfield. R. R. Oct. 25, 1842
Norwood, Hon. William, Jan. 29, Hillsborough. R. R. Feb. 8, 1842
Noyes, Capt. John M. of Massachusetts & Rhode Island, Nov., Wilmington. R. R. Nov. 8, 1842
Nixon, Charles, Oct. 18, Wilmington. R. R. Oct. 28, 1842
Orr, Dr. J. T. J., Jan. 16, Mecklenburg county. R. R. Feb. 1, 1842
Overdier, Mrs. David of Fayetteville, Mar. 5, Columbus, Ohio. R. R. Mar. 18, 1842
Owens, Christopher, Sept., Halifax. R. R. Sept. 23, 1842
Owen, Joseph Washington, Aug., Charlotte. R. R. Aug. 30, 1842
Palmer, Mary Ann, Mar., Milton. R. R. Mar. 11, 1842
Parker, Mrs. Jonathan, Sr., Jly. 22, Greensboro. R. R. Aug. 2, 1842
Peace, Joseph, Dec. 3, Raleigh. R. R. Dec. 6, 1842
Pearson, Mrs. John G., Oct., Stokes county. R. R. Oct. 4, 1842
Pearson, Mrs. Richmond, Dec., Fayetteville. R. R. Dec. 30, 1842
Peebles, Peterson T., Je. 11, Northampton county. R. R. Je. 21, 1842
Pinkston, Mrs. Susannah, Oct., Davidson county. R. R. Oct. 14, 1842
Poindexter, Gabriel, Feb., Stokes county. R. R. Feb. 25, 1842
Powell, Mrs. Avery M. of Iredell county, My. 19, Lenoir, Caldwell county. R. R. Je. 3, 1842

Powell, Jessie, Oct. 7, Wake Forest. R. R. Oct. 14, 1842
Primm, John D., Oct., Mecklenburg county. R. R. Oct. 4, 1842
Prince, Mrs. Harriet of Salisbury, Feb., Charleston, South Carolina. R. R. Feb. 18, 1842
Proctor, Albert G., Mar., Pasquotank county. R. R. Mar. 15, 1842
Pulliam, Sarah, Dec. 1, Raleigh. R. R. Dec. 2, 1842
Quince, Nathaniel Hill, Oct. 26, Wilmington. R. R. Nov. 8, 1842
Ramsour, David, Mar., Lincolnton. R. R. Mar. 15, 1842
Rankin, Joseph, Sept. 10, Greensboro. R. R. Sept. 23, 1842
Rascoe, Mrs. William D., Oct., Edenton. R. R. Nov. 1, 1842
Reynolds, Jeremiah, Sept., Guilford county. R. R. Sept. 9, 1842
Rhodes, Mrs. Charles, Nov. 10, Fayetteville. R. R. Nov. 18, 1842
Robards, Col. William, Je. 17, Granville county. R. R. Je. 24, 1842
Robbins, Mrs. Ahi, Sept. 6, Randolph county. R. R. Oct. 4, 1842
Robeson, Mrs. Bartram, Je. 26, Prospect place, Bladen county. R. R. Jly. 12, 1842
Roberts, Charles L. formerly of Raleigh & Green county, Alabama, Jly. 22, Eutaw, Alabama. R. R. Jly. 26, 1842
Roberts, Martha Ann of Raleigh, Oct. 28, Gainesville, Alabama. R. R. Nov. 8, 1842
Robinson, Alice, Apr. 23, Fayetteville. R. R. Apr. 26, 1842
Rodday, Nancy, Feb., Edenton. R. R. Feb. 8, 1842
Rogers, Green, Jly. 22, Wake county. R. R. Jly. 26, 1842
Rogers, Sarah Frances, Sept. 13, Wake county. R. R. Sept. 23, 1842
Roland, Lewis, Je., Wake county. R. R. Je. 10, 1842
Rothaas, Mrs. Ann Elizabeth, Oct., Salem. R. R. Nov. 1, 1842
Sanders, Penny Louisa, Sept. 9, Johnston county. R. R. Sept. 13, 1842
Sasser, Margaret, Jly. 8, Wayne county. R. R. Jly. 12, 1842
Satterfield, Henry N., Aug., Chatham county. R. R. Aug. 19, 1842
Satterfield, John, Aug. 29, Mount Tirza, Person county. R. R. Sept. 9, 1842
Savage, Mrs. M. D., Jly. 18, Windsor. R. R. Aug. 23, 1842
Scott, Mrs. David, Oct., Greensboro. R. R. Oct. 21, 1842
Scott, John of Hillsboro, Je. 3, Houston, Texas. R. R. Jly. 8, 1842
Shaw, Col. Wm., Oct., Orange county. R. R. Oct. 4, 1842
Shufford, Mrs. A., Je., Lenoir, Caldwell county. R. R. Je. 24, 1842
Simpson, William Henry Harrison, Aug. 24, Wilmington. R. R. Sept. 9, 1842
Singletary, Mrs. John, Sept. 19, Washington, Beaufort county. R. R. Sept. 27, 1842
Skinner, Mrs. Jas. B., Oct., Edenton. R. R. Nov. 1, 1842
Skinner, Joseph B., Mar., Pasquotank county. R. R. Mar. 15, 1842
Slater, Elisha, Oct., Stokes county. R. R. Nov. 8, 1842
Smith, Charles, Sept., Fayetteville. R. R. Sept. 9, 1842
Snow, Mary, Apr. 26, Raleigh. R. R. Apr. 29, 1842
Southall, N. N., Dec. 30, Henderson, Granville county. R. R. Jan. 4, 1842
Spencer, I. H. of Hillsborough, Mar. 1, Hyde county. R. R. Mar. 11, 1842
Stanback, Thomas F. of Richmond county, Jly. 9, Marshall county, Mississippi. R. R. Aug. 26, 1842
Stanly, Mrs. James G., Jly. 17, Newbern. R. R. Jly. 29, 1842
Steele, Mrs. William F., Je. 4, Iredell county. R. R. Je. 24, 1842
Stewart, Capt. Arch'd, Sept., Robeson county. R. R. Sept. 23, 1842
Stewart, Calvin H. of New York City, Mar., Salisbury. R. R. Mar. 15, 1842

Stilwell, Mrs. Catharine, Aug., Mecklenburg county. R. R. Aug. 9, 1842
Stokes, Ex. Governor Montford of this State, Nov. 4, Fort Gibson, Arkansas.
R. R. Dec. 13, 1842
Streater, James, Nov. 4, Richmond county. R. R. Dec. 2, 1842
Stuart, Hector, Sept., Cumberland county. R. R. Sept. 9, 1842
Sugg, John, Jan. 15, Wake county. R. R. Jan. 18, 1842
Sullivan, Joel, Sept., Guilford county. R. R. Oct. 4, 1842
Swain, Eleanor (infant), Oct. 13, Chapel Hill. R. R. Oct. 25, 1842
Tartt, Thomas E. of Edgecombe county, My. 6, Mobile, Alabama. R. R. My. 20, 1842
Taylor, Dr. George H., Jly. 31, Newbern. R. R. Aug. 19, 1842
Taylor, Mary Pugh (infant), Oct., Washington, Beaufort county. R. R. Nov. 1, 1842
Terrell, Pleasant Dempsey, My. 9, Rolesville. R. R. Je. 21, 1842
Thomasson, Needham, Mar., Mecklenburg county. R. R. Mar. 15, 1842
Thompson, Elizabeth, Sept., Salisbury. R. R. Sept. 23, 1842
Thompson, Wilson (alias Bunge), Apr. 7, Montgomery county. R. R. Apr. 26, 1842
Thomson, Mrs. William, Sept. 13, Wilmington. R. R. Sept. 23, 1842
Tisdale, William D. of Nash county, Feb., Livingston, Alabama. R. R. Feb. 15, 1842
Todd, Mrs. William, Jly. 27, Charlotte. R. R. Aug. 9, 1842
Tooley, Mrs. John M. of this State, Feb., Montgomery county. R. R. Feb. 22, 1842
Tucker, Mrs. Stephen L., Aug. 12, Raleigh. R. R. Aug. 16, 1842
Tye, John, Sept. 9, Mecklenburg county. R. R. Sept. 23, 1842
Tyre, Duncan C., Oct. 6, Greensboro. R. R. Oct. 14, 1842
Tyre, Washington, Oct. 2, Greensboro. R. R. Oct. 14, 1842
Vann, John, Sr., Apr., Sampson county. R. R. Apr. 26, 1842
Wall, John, Sr., Jly., Rockingham. R. R. Aug. 2, 1842
Wall, Mrs. John L. of Anson county, Sept., Cumberland county. R. R. Sept. 23, 1842
Wallace, Jeremiah, Apr., Wilmington. R. R. Apr. 26, 1842
Wallace, Jeremiah, Jr., Feb., Wilmington. R. R. Feb. 15, 1842
Weant, Susannah Eugenia, Oct., Charlotte. R. R. Oct. 4, 1842
Weathers, Adeline Christiana, Oct. 14, Wake county. R. R. Oct. 21, 1842
Webb, Mrs. Creecy, Apr. 29, Franklin. R. R. My. 17, 1842
Weber, Margaret, Je., Iredell county. R. R. Je. 24, 1842
Weir, Mrs. D. P., My. 11, Greensboro. R. R. My. 20, 1842
White, Addison, Mar., Pasquotank county. R. R. Mar. 15, 1842
White, Mrs. Burton, Sept. 24, Guilford county. R. R. Oct. 4, 1842
White, Eliza, Sept. 23, Guilford county. R. R. Oct. 4, 1842
White, Isaac, Sept., Guilford county. R. R. Oct. 4, 1842
White, Dr. William of Davidson College, Jan., Mecklenburg county. R. R. Jan. 4, 1842
Wilkerson, Daniel, Feb. 7, Orange county. R. R. Feb. 8, 1842
Wilkerson, Mrs. Daniel W., Feb., Orange county. R. R. Feb. 8, 1842
Williams, Andrew Marshall, Sept. 9, Mecklenburg county. R. R. Sept. 23, 1842
Williams, Hon. Lewis, Feb., Washington. R. R. Mar. 1, 1842
Williams, Mrs. Robert, Oct. 14, Raleigh. R. R. Oct. 18, 1842
Williamson, James, Jan., Fayetteville. R. R. Jan. 21, 1842

Williamson, Rev. John, Sept. 14, Mecklenburg county. R. R. Sept. 30, 1842
Wills, Mrs. Henry of Edenton, Oct., Petersburg, Va. R. R. Nov. 1, 1842
Wilson, Mrs. Claudia, Feb. 24, Randolph county. R. R. Mar. 11, 1842
Wilson, Frances Amy, Sept. 23, Greensboro. R. R. Sept. 30, 1842
Wilson, Mrs. John of Milton, Caswell county, Mar. 28, Raleigh. R. R. Apr. 1, 1842
Wilson, Mrs. Wesley D., Sept. 23, Davidson county. R. R. Oct. 7, 1842
Winborne, Cornelius, Feb., Greensboro. R. R. Feb. 11, 1842
Wood, George, Jan., Newbern. R. R. Jan. 18, 1842
Woodburn, Alphens Leroy, Oct. 2, Greensboro. R. R. Oct. 14, 1842
Wright, Mrs. Susan, Feb., Wilmington. R. R. Feb. 8, 1842
Yarbrough, Archibald, Nov. 1, Franklin county. R. R. Nov. 11, 1842
Young, Mrs. John H., Apr., Orange county. R. R. Apr. 19, 1842
Young, Mrs. Levi W. of Hillsboro, Feb., Demopolis, Alabama. R. R. Feb. 18, 1842

1843

Adams, Cornelia, Feb., Greensboro. R. R. Feb. 7, 1843
Alexander, Mrs. Elizabeth, Nov. 26, Cabarrus county. R. R. Dec. 15, 1843
Alford, James Jordan, Sept. 19, Alfordsville. R. R. Oct. 6, 1843
Allen, Mrs., Oct. 10, Washington, Beaufort county. R. R. Oct. 17, 1843
Alston, Major John, Nov., Halifax county. R. R. Nov. 3, 1843
Armistead, Cullen C., Sept. 11, Washington county. R. R. Oct. 17, 1843
Armistead, Starke, Aug. 21, Warrenton. R. R. Sept. 12, 1843
Arms, Mrs. Oliver of Massachusetts, Nov., Mecklenburg county. R. R. Nov. 10, 1843
Armstrong, Catharine, Apr., Cumberland county. R. R. Apr. 21, 1843
Arrington, Richard, Nov. 14, Nash county. R. R. Nov. 21, 1843
Avery, Louisa Harriet, Feb., Morganton, Burke county. R. R. Feb. 28, 1843
Baily, Richard T., Sept., Halifax county. R. R. Oct. 6, 1843
Baker, Mrs. Simmons J., My. 4, Raleigh. R. R. My. 5, 1843
Ball, Clifford, Sept. 3, Beaufort, Carteret county. R. R. Sept. 15, 1843
Ballard, Martha, Nov., Oxford. R. R. Nov. 21, 1843
Bangle, Mrs. John, Nov., Cabarrus county. R. R. Dec. 15, 1843
Barger, Mrs. John, Nov., Cabarrus county. R. R. Dec. 15, 1843
Barker, Lewis, Apr. 19, Wake county. R. R. My. 26, 1843
Barnes, Major Edwin, Oct., Edgecombe county. R. R. Oct. 17, 1843
Batchelor, Mary, Mar., Heathville, Halifax county. R. R. Mar. 3, 1843
Beasly, Ann, Apr. 20, Raleigh. R. R. Apr. 21, 1843
Beatty, Mrs. H. W., Mar. 5, Fayetteville. R. R. Mar. 7, 1843
Becton, Frederick I., Apr., Jones county. R. R. Apr. 21, 1843
Bellamy, James H., Sept. 23, Nash county. R. R. Oct. 17, 1843
Bennett, Major John D., Jan., Plymouth. R. R. Jan. 6, 1843
Bethune, Mrs. Alex of Fayetteville, Sept., Charlotte. R. R. Sept. 15, 1843
Betts, William, Oct. 31, Cumberland county. R. R. Nov. 10, 1843
Biddle, Mrs. Samuel S. of Beaufort county, Oct., Fort Barnwell, Craven county. R. R. Oct. 17, 1843
Black, Thomas O., Dec., Mecklenburg county. R. R. Dec. 8, 1843
Blake, Sarah Elizabeth, Je., Charlotte. R. R. Je. 13, 1843
Bledsoe, Solomon, Nov. 16, Wake county. R. R. Dec. 1, 1843-

Blount, Mrs. Ann, Apr. 19, Albemarle Sound. R. R. My. 2, 1843
Blount, Mrs. Annis, Aug., Newbern. R. R. Aug. 25, 1843
Blount, Clement H., Apr., Chowan county. R. R. My. 2, 1843
Blount, James Blakemore, Oct., Washington, Beaufort county. R. R. Oct. 10, 1843
Blum, Lavinia, Sept. 18, Salem. R. R. Oct. 17, 1843
Bond, Anne Cannon, Oct., Halifax. R. R. Oct. 31, 1843
Bond, Mary Eliza, Nov., Lenoir. R. R. Dec. 1, 1843
Boon, Samuel, Je., Fayetteville. R. R. Je. 2, 1843
Bowman, Rich'd, Oct. 5, Guilford county. R. R. Oct. 17, 1843
Branch, Samuel, Sr., Feb., Halifax. R. R. Feb. 7, 1843
Brandon, John P., Nov., Iredell county. R. R. Nov. 10, 1843
Briggs, John J., Apr. 24, Goldsboro. R. R. My. 2, 1843
Briggs, Wm. H., Oct., Masonborough Sound, New Hanover county. R. R. Oct. 17, 1843
Bruin, Jesse, Aug., Washington. R. R. Aug. 29, 1843
Brothers, John Thomas, Oct., Washington, Beaufort county. R. R. Oct. 10, 1843
Brown, Ann Maria, Aug. 19, Salisbury. R. R. Sept. 1, 1843
Brown, Daniel, Nov., Robeson county. R. R. Nov. 17, 1843
Brown, John, Oct. 6, Randolph county. R. R. Oct. 17, 1843
Brown, Joseph, Nov., Wake county. R. R. Nov. 17, 1843
Brown, Mrs. Thomas of Bladen county, Oct. 7, Wrightsville. R. R. Oct. 17, 1843
Burton, Col. Frank, N. W. of Granville county, Jly., Tennessee. R. R. Jly. 11, 1843
Burns, Geo. of Scotland, Oct. 14, Granville county. R. R. Oct. 24, 1843
Burrows, Mrs. John S., My., Hyde county. R. R. My. 23, 1843
Cabaniss, Eliza Bridgeforth, Sept., Cleveland county. R. R. Sept. 15, 1843
Cameron, Mrs. Duncan, Oct. 6, Raleigh. R. R. Nov. 10, 1843
Campbell, Duncan, Mar., Fayetteville. R. R. Mar. 31, 1843
Carr, Jonas J., My. 16, Edgecombe county. R. R. Je. 2, 1843
Carrigan, Mrs. Peter, Sept. 28, Orange county. R. R. Oct. 10, 1843
Carter, Cornelia Caroline, Sept. 27, Guilford county. R. R. Oct. 17, 1843
Chambers, Mrs. Joseph, Nov., Iredell county. R. R. Nov. 10, 1843
Charles, Stephen, Dec., Elizabeth City. R. R. Dec. 8, 1843
Clark, Maj. James W., Dec., Tarboro. R. R. Dec. 22, 1843
Clark, William, Aug. 6, Pitt county. R. R. Aug. 25, 1843
Clements, Capt. George W., Oct., Washington, Beaufort county. R. R. Oct. 10, 1843
Clemmons, Mrs. John, Nov., Clemmonsville, Davidson county. R. R. Nov. 17, 1843
Coble, Eli, Nov., Randolph county. R. R. Nov. 7, 1843
Coffield, James, My., Edenton. R. R. My. 26, 1843
Cogdell, Susan, Dec., Wayne county. R. R. Dec. 12, 1843
Copeland, William C., Oct. 12, Washington, Beaufort county. R. R. Oct. 17, 1843
Corum, Major Columbus, Jly. 12, Cabarrus county. R. R. Jly. 25, 1843
Coughenour, John, Apr. 16, Rowan county. R. R. Apr. 28, 1843
Courts, Mrs. Daniel W., Jan. 15, Rockingham county. R. R. Feb. 3, 1843
Cowan, Abel, Feb., Rowan county. R. R. Feb. 7, 1843
Cowan, Mrs. David, Apr., Mecklenburg county. R. R. Apr. 18, 1843

Cowan, Nancy, Je., Wilmington. R. R. Je. 13, 1843
Cowan, William, Sept. 23, Mobile. R. R. Oct. 6, 1843
Cov, Mrs. Jacob, Oct., Randolph county. R. R. Oct. 27, 1843
Cox, Lucinda, Oct. 15, Randolph county. R. R. Oct. 27, 1843
Crawford, Col. C. P., Nov., Union county. R. R. Nov. 10, 1843
Creekman, Mrs. Charity, Nov., Henderson. R. R. Dec. 1, 1843
Currie, Joseph, Nov., Leasburg. R. R. Nov. 7, 1843
Currie, Randal, Sept. 23, Randalsville, Robeson county. R. R. Oct. 17, 1843
Cutts, William, Nov., Wake county. R. R. Dec. 5, 1843
Dail, Mrs. Thomas, My., Perquimans county. R. R. My. 9, 1843
Davis, Mrs. D. A. of Anson county, Nov., Salisbury. R. R. Nov. 10, 1843
Dean, Capt. Stewart, Oct., Edenton. R. R. Oct. 17, 1843
Davis, Wilson, Oct., Newbern. R. R. Oct. 17, 1843
Dicks, Peter, Feb. 10, Randolph county. R. R. Feb. 21, 1843
Douglass, Joseph, Apr., Edenton. R. R. My. 2, 1843
Draughon, Mrs. Catharine, My., Sampson county. R. R. My. 12, 1843
Dudley, Eliza, Mar., Wilmington. R. R. Apr. 4, 1843
Eccles, Edward J. of Fayetteville, Aug. 26, On board Ship. R. R. Sept. 8, 1843
Ehringhaus, Adolph C., Feb., Elizabeth City. R. R. Feb. 28, 1843
Elliott, Mrs. Kinchen, My., Salisbury. R. R. My. 12, 1843
Elliott, Mrs. Mary, Apr. 22, Cumberland county. R. R. Apr. 28, 1843
Emery, Eliza Jane, Oct., Newbern. R. R. Oct. 17, 1843
Everest, Mrs. Charles W. of Fayetteville, Jly., Hamden, Connecticut. R. R. Jly. 14, 1843
Fairly, Mrs. Robert, Oct. 13, Robeson county. R. R. Oct. 27, 1843
Farrar, John, Apr. 6, Raleigh. R. R. Apr. 7, 1843
Faulcon, Jesse N., Mar., Halifax county. R .R. Mar. 3, 1843
Featherston, Rev. Chapel, Sept., Washington, Beaufort county. R. R. Sept. 15, 1843
Ferrand, Mrs. W. P., Apr. 1, Swansboro. R. R. Apr. 18, 1843
Ferrell, Jonathan, Mar. 30, Wake county. R. R. Apr. 7, 1843
Fisher, David, My., Hyde county. R. R. My. 23, 1843
Foreman, Martha E., Oct. 24, Pitt county. R. R. Nov. 3, 1843
Fort, Foster, Nov. 9, Wake Forest. R. R. Dec. 1, 1843
Fort, John Talbot, Sept. 25, Wake county. R. R. Oct. 6, 1843
Fort, William, Sr., Je. 21, Wake county. R. R. Je. 27, 1843
Fowle, Mrs. S. R., Oct., Washington, Beaufort county. R. R. Oct. 10, 1843
Fox, Dr. Stephen, Dec., Mecklenburg county. R. R. Dec. 19, 1843
Foy, Mrs. Charles H., Jly. 30, Newbern. R. R. Aug. 15, 1843
Fraley, T. G., Nov., Wilmington. R. R. Nov. 10, 1843
Freeman, William W., Dec., Charlotte. R. R. Dec. 8, 1843
Frink, Mrs. Samuel, Sept. 19, Brunswick county. R. R. Oct. 6, 1843
Fullwood, John L., Nov., Mecklenburg county. R. R. Nov. 10, 1843
Fullwood, John M., Nov., Mecklenburg county. R. R. Nov. 10, 1843
Furr, Paul, Jr., Oct. 17, Cabarrus county. R. R. Dec. 1, 1843
Furr, Mrs. Paul, Sr., Oct. 16, Cabarrus county. R. R. Dec. 1, 1843
Gaines, Mrs. Jas. L., Apr., Montgomery county. R. R. Apr. 21, 1843
Garey, Thomas, Mar., Halifax county. R. R .Mar. 3, 1843
Garrett, Mrs. Alfred F., Aug. 15, Plymouth. R. R. Aug. 29, 1843
Gatlin, Mrs. John of Kinston, Mar. 13, Wayne county. R. R. Mar. 17, 1843
Gause, Benjamin, Sept. 12, Wilmington. R. R. Oct. 6, 1843

Gause, Martha Judith, Sept. 15, Wilmington. R. R. Oct. 6, 1843
Gause, Mary Durant, Sept. 14, Wilmington. R. R. Oct. 6, 1843
Geffy, Elizabeth of this State, Je. 8. R. R. Je. 13, 1843
Getty, Henry W., Nov. 21, Hyde county. R. R. Dec. 19, 1843
Gibbs, Haywood of Hyde county, Oct., On board ship. R. R. Oct. 10, 1843
Gibbs, Henry W., Nov. 21, Hyde county. R. R. Dec. 22, 1843
Gilbreath, Mrs. Wm., Apr., Guilford county. R. R. Apr. 7, 1843
Giles, Henry Bradley, Mar., Wilmington. R. R. Apr. 4, 1843
Glover, Mrs. James D., My., Salisbury. R. R. My. 12, 1843
Gordon, Robert G. of Richmond county, Jly., Wilcox county. R. R. Jly. 21, 1843
Gorman, Thomas M. of Raleigh, Sept. 13, Wilmington. R. R. Sept. 19, 1843
Gorrell, Ralph C., Feb., Greensboro. R. R. Feb. 17, 1843
Green, Col. Charles P., Nov. 17, Warren county. R. R. Nov. 24, 1843
Gregory, Harvey, Oct., Washington, Beaufort county. R. R. Oct. 10, 1843
Gregory, John, My., Perquimans county. R. R. My. 9, 1843
Grier, Rev. Isaac, Nov., Mecklenburg county. R. R. Nov. 17, 1843
Griffis, Capt. John, Sept. 24, Orange county. R. R. Oct. 10, 1843
Grist, Mrs. Frederick, Aug., Beaufort county. R. R. Aug. 25, 1843
Guthrie, Mrs. Lidea, Oct., Washington, Beaufort county. R. R. Oct. 10, 1843
Hanrahan, Catharine, Aug. 6, Greenville. R. R. Aug. 25, 1843
Harris, Mary Anna, Aug. 24, Raleigh. R. R. Aug. 29, 1843
Harvey, Thomas B., Dec., Pasquotank county. R. R. Dec. 22, 1843
Harris, Robert Houston, Dec., Charlotte. R. R. Dec. 8, 1843
Harrison, Mrs. Margaret L., Dec. 7, Washington county. R. R. Dec. 22, 1843
Hathaway, Mrs. Jas., My., Perquimans county. R. R. My. 9, 1843
Havens, Sarah Smith, Oct., Washington, Beaufort county. R. R. Oct. 17, 1843
Hawks, Samuel C. of Newbern, Mar., Flushing, New York. R. R. Mar. 3, 1843
Hawkshurst, James W., Oct. 10, Greensboro. R. R. Oct. 17, 1843
Hawley, Dr. Samuel of New York, Sept. 16, Wilmington. R. R. Sept. 19, 1843
Henderson, Mrs. Andrew, Apr., Mecklenburg county. R. R. Apr. 14, 1843
Henderson, John L. of Salisbury, Jly., Raleigh. R. R. Jly. 14, 1843
Henderson, Major Lawson, Nov. 21, Lincolnton. R. R. Dec. 5, 1843
Henderson, Major Pleasant of Chapel Hill, Dec. 10, Huntington, Tennessee. R. R. Jan. 13, 1843
Hendon, Mrs. Mary H. of Franklin county, Aug., Somerville, Tennessee. R. R. Aug. 29, 1843
Hicks, Amanda I., Jly. 26, Granville county. R. R. Aug. 8, 1843
Hill, Hinton, Nov., Randolph county. R. R. Nov. 17, 1843
Hill, John M., Feb., Chatham county. R. R. Feb. 3, 1843
Hill, Mrs. Thomas of New Hanover county, My. 23, Pittsboro, Chatham county. R. R. My. 30, 1843
Hinton, Emma Adelaide, Jly., Chatham county. R. R. Jly. 25, 1843
Hodges, Joseph, Sept. 22, Wilmington. R. R. Oct. 6, 1843
Hollister, William, Aug., Newbern. R. R. Aug. 18, 1843
Holloway, Franklin, Oct., Washington, Beaufort county. R. R. Oct. 10, 1843
Hooks, Col. Phillip, Nov. 8, Waynesboro. R. R. Dec. 1, 1843
Hooks, Mrs. Phillip, Nov. 11, Waynesboro. R. R. Dec. 1, 1843
Horn, Henry W. of Fayetteville, Sept. 28, Mobile, Alabama. R. R. Oct. 17, 1843
Hoskins, Mrs. Edmund of Edenton, Feb., Mississippi. R. R. Feb. 7, 1843
Hoskins, Sally, Jly., Guilford county. R. R. Jly. 28, 1843

Houston, Archibald, Oct., Cabarrus county. R. R. Oct. 31, 1843
Howell, Rev. John, Mar. 16 ,Wayne county. R. R. Mar. 31, 1843
Hudson, Henry of Wake Forest, Nov. 5, Wayne county. R. R. Dec. 12, 1843
Hughes, Mrs. Isaac W., Feb., Newbern. R. R. Feb. 24, 1843
Hughes, Mrs. Nelson B., My. 25, Raleigh. R. R. My. 30, 1843
Huie, Mary Ann of Salisbury, Nov., Autauga county, Alabama. R. R. Nov. 10, 1843
Hunt, Mrs. Andrew, Nov., Lexington. R. R. Nov. 7, 1843
Hunter, Ephraim, Nov., Anson county. R. R. Dec. 1, 1843
Hunter, Mrs. Mary, Aug. 4, Newbern. R. R. Aug. 18, 1843
Hussey, Stephen, Aug., Guilford county. R. R. Aug. 4, 1843
Hutchings, Alpheus, Jly. 14, Raleigh. R. R. Jly. 18, 1843
Hutchings, Priscilla Macon, Dec. 25, Raleigh. R. R. Dec. 29, 1843
Hyman, Samuel, Aug., Newbern. R. R. Sept. 1, 1843
Isehour, Solomon, Dec., Mecklenburg county. R. R. Dec. 19, 1843
Ingram, Capt. Edwin, My. 12, Montgomery county. R. R. My. 26, 1843
Ingram, John Steele, Nov., Montgomery county. R. R. Nov. 17, 1843
Jeffreys, Dr. Simon, Mar. 27, Franklin county. R. R. Apr. 21, 1843
Johnson, Caroline Isabel, Oct., Davidson College. R. R. Oct. 31, 1843
Johnson, Robert P., Dev., Charlotte. R. R. Dec. 8, 1843
Johnson, William, Oct. 10, Anson county. R. R. Oct. 27, 1843
Johnson, Wm. of Weathersfield, Connecticut, Sept. 28, Wilmington. R. R. Oct. 17, 1843
Jones, Barnabas, Nov. 20, Wake county. R. R. Dec. 5, 1843
Jones, George of Wilkes county, My. 12, Rutherford county. R. R. Je. 2, 1843
Jones, Hugh Campbell, Dec., Wilmington. R. R. Dec. 8, 1843
Jones, Margaret A., Mar. 17, Wilmington. R. R. Mar. 21, 1843
Jones, Mrs. Nicey of Martin county, Oct., Washington, Beaufort county. R. R. Oct. 10, 1843
Jones, Rebecca Caldwaller, Jly. 19, Hillsboro. R. R. Jly. 25, 1843
Jordan, Mrs. Daniel of Stokes county, Dec., Rockingham. R. R. Dec. 8, 1843
Justice, Mrs. John, My. 29, Newbern. R. R. Je. 2, 1843
Keahey, William H., My. 18, Charlotte. R. R. Je. 2, 1843
Kemp, Mrs. Drury, My. 14, Wake county. R. R. My. 23, 1843
Kenan, Col. Thomas of this State, Oct. 22, Selma, Alabama. R. R. Nov. 10, 1843
Kennedy, William, Jr., Nov., Davidson county. R. R. Nov. 10, 1843
Killian, Dr. Leander, Decv., Salisbury. R. R .Dec. 19, 1843
King, Asa of Newbern, Apr. 16, Greensborough, Alabama. R. R. My. 5, 1843
Kirby, Wm., Oct., Sampson county. R .R. Oct. 17, 1843
Kirkland, Alexander M., My. 4, Hillsborough. R. R. My. 23, 1843
Kirkpatrick, Capt. John, Apr., Wilmington. R. R. Apr. 25, 1843
Lamb, Isaac, Aug., Guilford county. R. R. Aug. 4, 1843
Lambert, Mrs. William, Oct. 6, Guilford county. R. R. Oct. 17, 1843
Lane, Mrs. Wm. B. of Randolph county, Nov., Lenoir, Caldwell county. R. R. Nov. 7, 1843
Lawrence, Joshua, Feb., Edgecombe county. R. R. Feb. 3, 1843
Lea, Major William A., Sept., Leasburg, Caswell county. R. R. Oct. 3, 1843
Ledbetter, Mrs. Hellen, Dec., Davidson county. R. R. Dec. 8, 1843
Lee, Edmund Hatch, Feb., Newbern. R. R. Feb. 7, 1843
Lefler, Henry, My., Salisbury. R. R. My. 12, 1843

Leroy, Christopher N., Sept. 7, Washington, Beaufort county. R. R. Sept. 15, 1843
Lewis, Mrs. Exum, Nov. 16, Edgecombe county. R. R. Dec. 29, 1843
Lipe, Mrs. Godfrey, Nov. 29, Cabarrus county. R. R. Dec. 15, 1843
Liles, Lydia, Oct., Nortmampton county. R. R. Oct. 17, 1843
iLndsay, Annie W., Oct., Greensboro. R. R. Oct. 27, 1843
Lindsay, James B., My., Anson county. R. R. My. 23, 1843
Little, Ann, Apr. 9, Raleigh. R. R. Apr. 11, 1843
Lumsden, John, Apr., Fayetteville. R. R. Apr. 28, 1843
Lyde, George of Wilmington, Dec., New Orleans. R. R. Dec. 29, 1843
Lynch, Mrs. James, Dec., Lawrenceville. R. R. Dec. 22, 1843
M'Aden, Catharine Ann, Nov., Caswell county. R. R. Nov. 7, 1843
M'Bride, A. W., Nov., Cheraw, South Carolina. R. R. Nov. 17, 1843
M'Cauley, Andrew, Sr., Sept. 26, Orange county. R. R. Oct. 10, 1843
M'Comb, Mrs. Samuel of Charlotte, Jly. 22, Lee county, Georgia. R. R. Aug. 25, 1843
M'Comb, Mrs. William, Mar. 14, Mecklenburg county. R. R. Mar. 28, 1843
M'Common, Anne Ephna, Aug. 3, Waxhaw settlement. R. R. Aug. 29, 1843
M'Common, John Milton, Aug. 3, Waxhaw settlement. R. R. Aug. 29, 1843
M'Common, Viney, Jly. 30, Waxhaw settlement. R. R. Aug. 29, 1843
M'Common, Wade, Aug. 3, Waxhaw settlement. R. R. Aug. 29, 1843
M'Corkle, John, Dec. 2, Union county. R. R. Dec. 8, 1843
M'Coy, Theodore, Aug., Newbern. R. R. Sept. 1, 1843
M'Cuiston, Col. Jesse, Apr., Greensboro. R. R. Apr. 7, 1843
M'Curdy, Arch'd, Nov. 12, Cabarrus county. R. R. Dec. 8, 1843
M'Donald, Mrs. Alex'r, My., Fayetteville. R. R. My. 2, 1843
M'Dowell, John, Dec., Mecklenburg county. R. R. Dec. 19, 1843
M'Dugald, Hugh of Scotland, Dec., Bladen county. R. R. Dec. 29, 1843
M'Eachin, Mrs. James, Apr., Robeson county. R. R. Apr. 21, 1843
M'Iver, Mrs. Kenneth, Aug., Moore county. R. R. Aug. 4, 1843
M'Kay, Murdock, Jly. 21, Wilmington. R. R. Jly. 28, 1843
M'Kethan, Nathan K., Aug., Cumberland county. R. R. Aug. 4, 1843
M'Kinnon, Mrs. A. C., My. 22, Richmond county. R. R. Je. 2, 1843
M'Lean, Mrs. John, Jly., Robeson county. R. R. Jly. 14, 1843
M'Lelland, Alexander W., Nov., Bladen county. R. R. Nov. 7, 1843
M'Lure, Thomas, Nov., Cabarrus county. R. R. Nov. 10, 1843
M'Millan, Mrs. Daniel, Dec., Moore county. R. R. Dec. 22, 1843
M'Neely, Alexander, Nov., Guilford county. R. R. Dec. 1, 1843
M'Pheeters, Mrs. James G., My. 7, Raleigh. R. R. My. 9, 1843
M'Pherson, Alexander Telfair, Oct. 24, Smithfield. R. R. Nov. 7, 1843
M'Pherson, Benjamin Franklin, Oct. 25, Smithfield. R. R. Nov. 7, 1843
M'Ree, Mrs. John, Dec., Iredell county. R. R. Dec. 8, 1843
Macnamara, Col. Robert, Apr. 30, Rowan county. R. R. My. 2, 1843
Marriott, Ann E., Jly. 1, Wake county. R. R. Jly. 7, 1843
Mason, Teressa Elixa and John Hicks (twins), Je., Hillsboro. R. R. Je. 27, 1843
Masters, Mrs. Samuel, Oct., Newbern. R. R. Oct. 17, 1843
Mendenhall, Mrs. Elisha, My. 3, Greensborough. R. R. My. 5, 1843
Miles, Rev. R. B. of Greensboro, Aug., Amherst county, Virginia. R. R. Sept. 8, 1843
Miller, James, Nov. 28, Cabarrus county. R. R. Dec. 15, 1843

Montague, John C. of Virginia, Dec. 12, Wayne county. R. R. Dec. 22, 1843
Montgomery, Dr. William, Dec., Orange county. R. R. Dec. 12, 1843
Moore, Mrs. Alfred L. of Duplin county, Nov., New Hanover county. R. R. Nov. 10, 1843
Moore, Augustus of Northampton county, Jly., Marshall county, Mississippi. R. R. Jly. 28, 1843
Moore, John L. of Washington, Jan. 31, Stokes county. R. R. Feb. 17, 1843
Moore, Mary Louisa, Dec., Halifax. R. R. Dec. 22, 1843
Moore, Robert G., Dec. 4, Newbern. R. R. Dec. 8, 1843
Mordecai, Capt. Alfred, Jly. 24, Washington, D. C. R. R. Aug. 4, 1843
Morphess, Alexander of Raleigh, Nov., Orange county. R. R. Nov. 3, 1843
Munroe, John, Dec., Fayetteville. R. R. Dec. 12, 1843
Murphy, Mrs. Thomas, Jly., Fayetteville. R. R. Jly. 28, 1843
Murray, Mrs. Eli, Nov., Orange county. R. R. Nov. 7, 1843
Newbell, John, Sept., Milton. R. R. Sept. 29, 1843
Norcom, Mrs. James, Jr., Dec. 14, Chowan county. R. R. Dec. 22, 1843
O'Bryan, Dennis Giraldus, Nov. 13, Warren county. R. R. Dec. 1, 1843
O'Hanlon, Elizabeth Myers, Je., Fayetteville. R. R. Je. 16, 1843
O'Neal, Mrs. Jane, My. 16, Wilmington. R. R. Je. 2, 1843
Orr, James, Apr., Mecklenburg county. R. R. Apr. 18, 1843
Outlaw, George B., Mar., Windsor, Bertie county. R. R. Mar. 28, 1843
Owens, Elizabeth, Oct., Halifax. R. R. Oct. 10, 1843
Palmer, James, Mar., Windsor, Bertie county. R. R. Mar. 28, 1843
Parham, Mrs. Elizabeth G., Je. 30, Raleigh. R. R. Jly. 7, 1843
Parker, Jonathan, Apr., Greensboro. R. R. Apr. 18, 1843
Parks, Joseph Y., Dec., Mecklenburg county. R. R. Dec. 19, 1843
Patterson, Mrs. Joseph, Aug., Mecklenburg county. R. R. Aug. 25, 1843
Patterson, Lawrence D., Aug., Mecklenburg county. R. R. Aug. 25, 1843
Patterson, Smith, Aug. 1, Louisburg. R. R. Aug. 15, 1843
Pearce, Peleg of Providence, R. I., Oct. 6, Fayetteville. R. R. Oct. 17, 1843
Pell, Irvine Atkinson, Aug., Newbern. R. R. Sept. 1, 1843
Pendergrass, Franklin M., Nov., Iredell county. R. R. Nov. 10, 1843
Pendleton, Mrs. M. C. of Lynchburg, Virginia, Oct., Salisbury. R. R. Nov. 3, 1843
Perry, Mrs. Joshua, Nov. 17, Franklin county. R. R. Nov. 24, 1843
Phillips, Martin, Oct., Newbern. R. R. Oct. 17, 1843
Phillips, Capt. William, Nov., Davidson county. R. R. Nov. 17, 1843
Pittman, Mrs. Graham C., My., Edgecombe county. R. R. My. 2, 1843
Pittman, Sarah Elizabeth, Aug. 4, Newbern. R. R. Aug. 18, 1843
Poisson, John, Apr., Wilmington. R. R. Apr. 18, 1843
Polk, Rufus K. of Raleigh, Feb. 25, Nashville, Tennessee. R. R. Mar. 14, 1843
Polk, Mrs. Thos. R., Je. 18, La Grange, Tennessee. R. R. Jly. 14, 1843
Polk, Mrs. William of Warren county, Dec. 10, Raleigh. R. R. Dec. 19, 1843
Pope, Benjamin A., Nov. 8, Halifax. R. R. Nov. 14, 1843
Pope, Mrs. William H., Dec. 11, Halifax. R. R. Dec. 15, 1843
Porter, Ely, Feb. 13, Tarboro. R. R. Feb. 17, 1843
Porter, Dr. James Green, Apr., Mecklenburg county. R. R. Apr. 18, 1843
Powell, John S. of Smithfield, Oct., Waynesborough. R. R. Oct. 27, 1843
Power, Eliza C., Sept. 24, Wilmington. R. R. Oct. 6, 1843
Pratt, Mrs. Edith, Sept., Anson county. R. R. Oct. 6, 1843
Pritchett, Mrs. Wm., Apr., Greensboro. R. R. Apr. 7, 1843

Pugh, Dr. Jesse C., Oct. 7, Washington, Beaufort county. R. R. Oct. 17, 1843
Radcliffe, T. D., Apr. 1, Wilmington. R. R. Apr. 18, 1843
Rambaut, William of Raleigh, Dec., Cumberland county. R. R. Dec. 8, 1843
Ray, Mrs. Mary Ann, Aug. 5, Wake county. R. R. Sept. 5, 1843
Rayner, Amos, My. 4, Hertford county. R. R. My. 19, 1843
Reavis, Lewis, Dec. 6, Henderson. R. R. Dec. 8, 1843
Redding, Jonathan, Nov., Randolph county. R. R. Dec. 1, 1843
Redding, Joseph S. T., Oct., Washington, Beaufort county. R. R. Oct. 10, 1843
Reed, Mrs. John, Sr., Nov., Cabarrus county. R. R. Dec. 15, 1843
Reed, Joseph, Jly. 7, Mecklenburg county. R. R. Jly. 18, 1843
Reinhardt, John Q. A., Jly., East Florida. R. R. Jly. 21, 1843
Rice, Mrs. Amos R., Nov., Iredell county. R. R. Nov. 10, 1843
Richards, John B., Oct., Washington, Beaufort county. R. R. Oct. 10, 1843
Robbins, Mrs. Thomas, Oct., Washington, Beaufort county. R. R. Oct. 10, 1843
Robinson, Mrs. Martha, Nov. 28, Cabarrus county. R. R. Dec. 15, 1843
Rogerson, Mrs. Susan B. of Elizabeth City, Oct., New Orleans. R. R. Oct. 31, 1843
Roseman, John, Apr. 25, Rowan county. R. R. My. 2, 1843
Sallard, Capt. Charles, Nov., Person county. R. R. Nov. 7, 1843
Sanders, Mrs. John, My., Johnston county. R. R. My. 2, 1843
Satterwhite, Hanson P., Mar. 7, Burke county. R. R. Apr. 11, 1843
Saunders, Benj. R., My., Hyde county. R. R. My. 23, 1843
Sears, Mrs. Henrietta S. of Raleigh, Sept. 19, Mobile. R. R. Oct. 17, 1843
Seawell, Mary B., Oct. 3, Raleigh. R. R. Oct. 6, 1843
Settle, Maj. Benjamin, Aug., Rockingham county. R. R. Aug. 25, 1843
Sharpe, Col. Benjamin, My., Edgecombe county. R. R. My. 2, 1843
Shepard, Hon. Charles, Oct. 24, Newbern. R. R. Oct. 31, 1843
Shuman, Jacob, Dec., Mecklenburg county. R. R. Dec. 8, 1843
Sims, Col. Herbert, Je., Orange county. R. R. Je. 27, 1843
Slocumb, Eliza G., Oct. 22, Waynesboro. R. R. Oct. 31, 1843
Slocumb, Mary G., Oct. 10, Waynesboro. R. R. Oct. 31, 1843
Small, Malcolm, Nov. 23, Cumberland county. R. R. Dec. 15, 1843
Smith, Albert, Aug., Davidson county. R. R. Aug. 25, 1843
Smith, Henry, Apr. 9, Edenton. R. R. My. 2, 1843
Smith, Dr. James C., Apr. 15, Fayetteville. R. R. Apr. 21, 1843
Smith, Jane, Jly., Fayetteville. R. R. Jly. 14, 1843
Smith, John, My., Perquimans county. R. R. My. 9, 1843
Smith, John, Oct. 24, Wake Forest. R. R. Nov. 3, 1843
Smith, John B. of Granville county, Aug. 23, Burnsville, Yancey county. R. R. Sept. 15, 1843
Smith, Malcom L., Dec., Rockfish factory. R. R. Dec. 8, 1843
Smith, Mrs. Samuel E. of Newbern, Aug., Gates county. R. R. Sept. 1, 1843
Smith, Mrs. Susannah, Oct., Newbern. R. R. Oct. 17, 1843
Sneed, Mrs. Jonathan P. of Hillsboro, My. 2, LaFayette county, Mississippi. R. R. Je. 2, 1843
Sneed, Major Junius, Je. 26, Salisbury. R. R. Jly. 7, 1843
Spears, William Wallace, Nov. 18, Cabarrus county. R. R. Dec. 15, 1843
Spencer, Jack, My., Hyde county. R. R. My. 23, 1843
Spruill, Mrs. Samuel B. of Northampton county, Mar. 29, Raleigh. R. R. Mar. 31, 1843
Stallings, Isaac, Aug. 22, Johnston county. R. R. Sept. 1, 1843

Stanly, James G., Jr., Nov., Henderson. R. R. Dec. 1, 1843
Stanly, Mrs. John of this State, Aug. 30, Farquier county, Va. R. R. Sept. 8, 1843
Stansell, Captain William, Oct., Pitt county. R. R. Oct. 17, 1843
Stark, Sarah Eliza, Nov., Fayetteville. R. R. Nov. 17, 1843
Steele, Mrs. Mary N., Aug. 19, Salisbury. R. R. Sept. 1, 1843
Stone, Lucy E., Apr. 8, Granville county. R. R. Apr. 18, 1843
Stough, Mrs. Martin, Nov. 27, Cabarrus county. R. R. Dec. 15, 1843
Stow, Capt. Cyrus, Oct. 23, Wilmington. R. R. Oct. 31, 1843
Strayhorn, John, Sr., Je., Orange county. R. R. Je. 16, 1843
Stricklin, Lot of Johnston county, Je. 1, Richmond county. R. R. Aug. 4, 1843
Swaim, Jesse, Oct. 9, Guilford county. R. R. Oct. 17, 1843
Tate, Lemuel S., Oct., Orange county. R. R. Oct. 24, 1843
Taylor, Wesley Coke, Dec., Oxford. R. R. Dec. 19, 1843
Temple, Mrs. Allen, My., Chatham county. R. R. My. 30, 1843
Thames, Mrs. David, Sept. 16, Cumberland county. R. R. Oct. 6, 1843
Thomas, Mrs. Jas. I., Dec. 14, Oxford. R. R. Dec. 29, 1843
Thompson, John, Aug., Orange county. R. R. Aug. 29, 1843
Thompson, Mrs. Phoebe, Je. 22, Raleigh. R. R. Je. 27, 1843
Thompson, Mrs. Susan, My., Salisbury. R. R. My. 12, 1843
Turner, Joseph, My., Hyde county. R. R. My. 23, 1843
Tyre, Mrs. Council, Oct., Greensboro. R. R. Oct. 27, 1843
Vaughan, Mrs. Geo. W. of this State, Feb. 24, Columbus, Mississippi. R. R. Mar. 21, 1843
Vokes, Joseph of Warrenton, Sept. 18, Mobile. R. R. Oct. 6, 1843
Wadsworth, Edward, Mar., Petersburg. R. R. Mar. 31, 1843
Walker, John, Sept. 27, Orange county. R. R. Oct. 10, 1843
Wallace, Dr. Rufus A. of Charlotte, Dec. 15, Raleigh. R. R. Dec. 19, 1843
Ward, Mary, Apr. 17, Fayetteville. R. R. Apr. 21, 1843
Warne, Mrs. Joseph B. of Boydton, Virginia, Oct. 7, Salisbury. R. R. Oct. 24, 1843
Washington, Mrs. George of Kinston, Aug. 21, New York. R. R. Sept. 12, 1843
Watson, Mrs. David, My., Chatham county. R. R. My. 5, 1843
Watson, E. J. of Chatham county, Aug., Somerville, Tennessee. R. R. Aug. 29, 1843
Watson, Gen. James C. of Cumberland county, My., Mount Meigs, Alabama. R. R. My. 2, 1843
Watt, James F., Mar., Rockingham. R. R. Mar. 24, 1843
Weathers, Rev. James, Apr., Granville county. R. R. Apr. 18, 1843
Weddington, Joseph Y. ,Oct., Mecklenburg county. R. R. Oct. 31, 1843
Weddington, Capt. Samuel, Nov. 1, Cabarrus county. R. R. Dec. 1, 1843
White, Mrs. Esther, Nov. 24, Cabarrus county. R. R. Dec. 15, 1843
White, Thomas, Sept. 5, Raleigh. R. R. Sept. 8, 1843
Whittier, John of Amesbury, Massachusetts and this State, Apr. 18, Wilmington. R. R. My. 5, 1843
Wilkins, Mrs. Mary of Sussex county, Virginia and Wake county, Jly. 2. R. R. Jly. 7, 1843
Williams, Mrs. Alexander, Oct. 15, Cumberland county. R. R. Oct. 27, 1843
Williams, Gen. James O. K., Oct., Washington, Beaufort county. R. R. Oct. 10, 1843
Williamson, Alice, My., Hyde county. R. R. My. 23, 1843

Williamson, Mrs. Godfrey, Jly., Mecklenburg county. R. R. Jly. 18, 1843
Wilson, Margaret of Milton, Mar., Norfolk, Virginia. R. R. Mar. 3, 1843
Wilson, Maj. Samuel, Feb., Mecklenburg county. R. R. Feb. 28, 1843
Wilson, William, Oct. 8, Union county. R. R. Oct. 31, 1843
Winborne, Micajah T. of Hertford county, Sept. 19, Mobile. R. R. Oct. 6, 1843
Winslow, Mrs. Warren of Fayetteville, My. 28, Smithville. R. R. My. 30, 1843
Wright, William, Mar. 22, Sloop Point. R. R. Apr. 25, 1843
Wright, Wm., Mar. 25, On the Sound, Wilmington. R. R. Apr. 18, 1843
Yarbrough, Mrs. Mildred, Jly. 18, Louisburg. R. R. Jly. 28, 1843
Yarborough, Mr., Nov. 25, Concord. R. R. Dec. 15, 1843

1844

Adams, Elizabeth E., Jan. 17, Beaufort. R. R. Feb. 9, 1844
Alexander, Mrs. Silas, Jly. 31, Mecklenburg county. R. R. Aug. 20, 1844
Alexander, Wm. B., Jan. 23, Mecklenburg county. R. R. Feb. 9, 1844
Allison, Capt. Robert, Jan. 21, Cabarrus county. R. R. Feb. 2, 1844
Anderson Alexander, Nov. 21, Wilmington. R. R. Nov. 29, 1844
Anderson, David of Scotland, Apr. 9, Fayetteville. R. R. Apr. 19, 1844
Anderson, George of Warrenton, Jan., La Grange, Tennessee. R. R. Feb. 6, 1844
Anderson, Mrs. Mary R. of Petersburg, Virginia, Je., Wilmington. R. R. Jly. 2, 1844
Armstrong, Anderson, Feb. 4, Orange county. R. R. Feb. 13, 1844
Atkins, John C. of Montgomery county, Feb., Fayetteville. R. R. Feb. 27, 1844
Avera, Richard of Averasborough, Mar. 22, Fayetteville. R. R. Mar. 26, 1844
Ball, Daniel, Sept. 29, Flat creek, Buncombe county. R. R. Oct. 22, 1844
Ball, Mrs., Feb. 24, Davidson county. R. R. Mar. 8, 1844
Barksdale, John Nash, Nov., Rutherford county ,Tennessee. R. R. Nov. 29, 1844
Barringer, Gen. Paul M., Je. 20, Lincolnton. R. R. Jly. 2, 1844
Barringer, Mrs. Paul, Oct. 22, Cabarrus county. R. R. Dec. 3, 1844
Batley, Thomas, Mar. 31, Fayetteville. R. R. Apr. 5, 1844
Battle, Isaac L. of Edgecombe county, Jan., Mariama, Florida. R. R. Jan. 12, 1844
Beard, Mrs. Elizabeth, Oct. 16, Guilford county. R. R. Nov. 29, 1844
Beaty, Moses, Feb. 2, Mecklenburg county. R. R. Feb. 27, 1844
Bechtler, Augustus of Germany, Dec. 21, Rutherfordton. R. R. Jan. 9, 1844
Belden, Mrs. Robert of Fayetteville, Je. 11, Bladen county. R. R. Je. 21, 1844
Belk, Joab M. G. of Lancaster, South Carolina, Oct. 26, Davidson county. R. R. Nov. 29, 1844
Bell, Capt. Wm. P. of Beaufort, Apr., Columbus, eGorgia. R. R. Apr. 5, 1844
Berry, Mrs. Catharine A., Aug. 20, Smithville. R. R. Sept. 6, 1844
Black, Mrs. Catharine, Jan. 10, Moore county. R. R. Jan. 19, 1844
Blackledge, Alice, Sept., Lenoir county. R. R. Oct. 15, 1844
Blackledge, Caroline M., Mar., Newbern. R. R. Mar. 22, 1844

Blackwelder, Capt. Chas., Jan. 22, Cabarrus county. R. R. Feb. 2, 1844
Blackwelder, Mrs. Isaac, Jan. 29, Cabarrus county. R. R. Feb. 13, 1844
Blackwell, Thomas, Dec. 25, Henderson county. R. R. Jan. 19, 1844
Bond, Mrs. Margaret, Feb. 1, Greenville, Pitt county. R. R. Feb. 13, 1844
Bost, Mrs. John D., Jan. 25, Cabarrus county. R. R. Feb. 2, 1844
Boyden, Mrs. Nathaniel, Aug. 10, Salisbury. R. R. Aug. 20, 1844
Bransom, Mrs. Henry, Nov., Fayetteville. R. R. Nov. 29, 1844
Brewster, Jacob H. of Connecticut, Nov. 6, Wilmington. R. R. Nov. 29, 1844
Brietz, Samuel E., Aug., Salem. R. R. Aug. 16, 1844
Britt, Mrs. W. A., Apr., Orange county. R. R. Apr. 3, 1844
Broadnax, Sally of Rockingham county, Oct. 30. R. R. Nov. 29, 1844
Brock, Mrs. Lewis, Mar., Hailsville, Duplin county. R. R. Mar. 5, 1844
Brown, Allen, Aug., Salisbury. R. R. Sept. 6, 1844
Brown, Mrs. Joseph, Nov. 6, Marion District, South Carolina. R. R. Nov. 29, 1844
Brown, Samuel of Stockridge, Massachusetts, Je. 9, Nashville. R. R. Je. 14, 1844
Brummell, Charles, Aug. 10, Davidson county. R. R. Aug. 20, 1844
Bruton, Mrs. Wm., Mar., Montgomery county. R. R. Mar. 8, 1844
Bryan, Mrs. James, Sr., Dec. 22, Bladen county. R. R. Jan. 9, 1844
Burr, John Andrew, Feb., Wilmington. R. R. Mar. 1, 1844
Bushell, Joseph, Oct., Edenton. R. R. Oct. 18, 1844
Caldwell, Mrs. Green W., Sept. 22, Charlotte. R. R. Sept. 27, 1844
Caldwell, Martha Ann, Nov. 11, Burke county. R. R. Nov. 29, 1844
Calloway, Mrs. Elijah, Dec. 17, Walnut Cove, Ashe county. R. R. Jan. 2, 1844
Cameron, Duncan, Apr. 14, Richmond county. R. R. Apr. 30, 1844
Cameron, William Owen, Oct., Hillsboro. R. R. Oct. 22, 1844
Campbell, Addison of Guilford county & Choctaw county ,Mississippi, Oct. 22, Pittsborough, Chatham county. R. R. Nov. 12, 1844
Carpenter, Mrs. Mary, Jan. 1, Lincoln county. R. R. Jan. 12, 1844
Carter, John, Sr., Oct., Chatham county. R. R. Oct. 18, 1844
Chambers, Mrs. David, Jan. 11, Iredell county. R. R. Feb. 9, 1844
Chambers, Mrs. Joseph P., Aug., Salisbury. R. R. Aug. 16, 1844
Cheek, Mrs. John, Sept., Warren county. R. R. Sept. 24, 1844
Childs, Ann E., Nov. 15, Fort Johnson. R. R. Nov. 29, 1844
Clark, James, Apr., Orange county. R. R. Apr. 23, 1844
Clark, Capt. William, Nov. 10, Raleigh. R. R. Nov. 12, 1844
Clark, Mrs. Wm. W., Dec., Newbern. R. R. Dec. 31, 1844
Clemmons, Harvey, Jly., Wake county. R. R. Jly. 30, 1844
Cline, Henry, Dec. 24, Lincolnton. R. R. Jan. 12, 1844
Coppedge, William, Sr., Dec. 17, Franklin county. R. R. Jan. 5, 1844
Couch, Samuel, Je., Orange county. R. R. Je. 14, 1844
Crawford, William D. of Salisbury, Jan. 22, Montgomery county. R. R. Feb. 2, 1844
Crawley, John of Norfolk, Virginia, Aug., Edenton. R. R. Aug. 9, 1844
Davidson, Mrs. W. S. M., Dec., Mecklenburg county. R. R. Dec. 31, 1844
Davis, Joseph E., Aug. 20, Wilmington. R. R. Sept. 3, 1844
Deaver, Mrs. R., Apr. 6, Sulphur Springs, Buncombe county. R. R. Apr. 19, 1844
Desmond, Mrs. Lewis C., Oct., Lenoir county. R. R. Oct. 22, 1844

Devereux, John, Sr., Jly. 1, Raleigh. R. R. Jly. 4, 1844
Dewese, Isaiah, Sr., Jan. 23, Cabarrus county. R. R. Feb. 2, 1844
Dodd, Parmela B., Oct., Orange county. R. R. Nov. 5, 1844
Donnell, Mrs. Erwin, Apr., Guilford county. R. R. Apr. 12, 1844
Donnell, Dr. Washington, Apr. 17, Greensboro. R. R. Apr. 23, 1844
Draughon, Mrs. Geo., Nov., Sampson county. R. R. Nov. 12, 1844
Dudley, Mrs. David C., Jan. 6, Raleigh. R. R. Jan. 9, 1844
Dudley, Mary, My. 14, Raleigh. R. R. My. 21, 1844
Dumas, Henry D., Nov., Richmond county. R. R. Nov. 5, 1844
Eagles, Mrs. Sarah, Dec. 17, Wilmington. R. R. Dec. 31, 1844
Edmunds, Etheldred of Halifax county, Sept., Littleton Depot. R. R. Sept. 24, 1844
Edney, Rev. Samuel of Pasquotank county, Sept. 19,, Henderson county. R. R. Oct. 15, 1844
Edwards, Mrs. Catharine, Feb. 10, Rowan county. R. R. Feb. 27, 1844
Edwards, Mrs. Henry, Jr., My., Orange county. R. R. My. 17, 1844
Elam, James, Mar. 18, Fayetteville. R. R. Mar. 29, 1844
Eller, John, Feb. 25, Rowan county. R. R. Mar. 8, 1844
Elliott, Jno of Greensboro, Oct., Wythe, Virginia. R. R. Nov. 29, 1844
Ellis, Mrs. George, Oct. 2, Orange county. R. R. Oct. 22, 1844
Ellis, Mrs. John, Oct. 19, Davidson county. R. R. Nov. 1, 1844
Eubank, Levi, Jan. 19, Jones county. R. R. Feb. 9, 1844
Evans, Sarah Jane, Apr. 12, Hillsboro. R. R. Apr. 23, 1844
Everitt, Lawrence C., Sept. 1, Richmond county. R. R. Nov. 5, 1844
Farmer, Moses, Nov., Edgecombe county. R. R. Dec. 6, 1844
Faucett, Mrs. David A. of Orange county, My., Memphis, Tennessee. R. R. My. 17, 1844
Foreman, Mary Louisa, Oct. 18, Green Wreath, Pitt county. R. R. Oct. 25, 1844
Foster, Peter, Je. 1, Franklin county. R. R. Je. 7, 1844
Franklin, Henry, Sept. 23, Chatham county. R. R. Oct. 1, 1844
Freeland, John Sr., Dec. 24, Orange county . R. R. Jan. 9, 1844
Freeman, Mrs. Jonathan, Otis, My. 27, Raleigh. R. R. My. 28, 1844
Gardner, Anna, Nov. 10, Wilmington. R. R. Nov. 29, 1844
Gaston, William, Jan. 23, Raleigh. R. R. Jan. 26, 1844
Gatewood, Gen. Williamson of this State, Apr., Equality, Illinois. R. R. Apr. 12, 1844
Goodwin, Lemuel, Feb. 5, Granville county. R. R. Feb. 13, 1844
Gorham, George F., Aug., Greenville. R. R. Mar. 5, 1844
Gorham, Mrs. George F. of Pitt county, Sept. 8, Warrenton. R. R. Sept. 29, 1844
Graham, Mrs. Hamilton, Feb. 2, Warren county. R. R. Feb. 9, 1844
Grunway, Col. William of Caldwell county, Aug. 1, Lenoir. R. R. Sept. 3, 1844
Guy, Capt. Wm. Henry, Jan. 25, Smithfield. R. R. Jan. 26, 1844
Hackney, James Addison, Je. 27, Chatham county. R. R. Jly. 12, 1844
Hackney, Mrs. Polly, Je. 30, Chatham county. R. R. Jly. 12, 1844
Hall, Wm., Feb. 28, Rowan county. R. R. Mar. 8, 1844
Hall, Wm. H., Mar., Weldon. R. R. Mar. 12, 1844
Hancock, Roger, Je., Orange county. R. R. Je. 21, 1844
Harbin, Mrs. William, Feb. 9, Statesville. R. R. Feb. 27, 1844

Hardin, Sally, Oct., Orange county. R. R. Nov. 5, 1844
Hargrove, Mrs. William, Oct. 10, Granville county. R. R. Nov. 1, 1844
Harper, James, Aug. 21, Greene county. R. R. Sept. 17, 1844
Harrington, Abner, Feb. 15, Chatham county. R. R. Mar. 1, 1844
Harris, Emily A., Aug., Rockingham. R. R. Aug. 30, 1844
Harris, Dr. Samuel S., Mar., Mecklenburg county. R. R. Mar. 19, 1844
Harrison, Mrs. William A., Nov. 10, Raleigh. R. R. Nov. 12, 1844
Hartman, Mrs. Otho, Nov., Rowan county. R. R. Nov. 26, 1844
Havener, Martin, Dec. 30, Lincoln county. R. R. Jan. 12, 1844
Hayes, Robert, Jan. 27, Charlotte. R. R. Feb. 9, 1844
Henderson, Logan B. of Lincoln county, Jly. 23, Marshall, Harrison county Texas. R. R. Sept. 24, 1844
Hervey, Edwin (infant) Nov., Fayetteville. R. R. Nov. 15, 1844
Heyl, Eli, Dec., Hoylsville. R. R. Dec. 20, 1844
Hill, Eugenia Ann, My. 11, Franklin county. R. R. My. 21, 1844
Hilliard, Mrs. James of Edgecombe, Dec. 11, Nash county. R. R. Jan. 12, 1844
Hinds, Wm. of Newbern, Jan. 16, Trenton. R. R. Jan. 30, 1844
Hinton, John, Dec. 13, Oakland (his residence). R. R. Dec. 10, 1844
Hoke, Frederick of York county, Pennsylvania, Jan. 1, Catawba county. R. R. Jan. 12, 1844
Hoke, Col. Michael, Sept. 9, Charlotte. R. R. Sept. 17, 1844
Hollum, Sturdivant, Oct. 2, Wake county. R. R. Oct. 8, 1844
Holt, James, Mar. 28, Johnston county. R. R. Apr. 12, 1844
Holt, Jesse, Aug. 28, Johnston county. R. R. Sept. 3, 1844
Hopkins, Joseph of Wake county, Jan. 5, Greene county, Alabama. R. R. Feb. 13, 1844
Horne, James J., Sept. 3, Pittsborough. R. R. Sept. 27, 1844
Horner, Thomas Sr., My. 10, Orange county. R. R. Je. 14, 1844
Hoyl, Rev. Abel of South Carolina Conference, Sept. 8, Union county. R. R. Sept. 24, 1844
Hoyle, Eli, Sept. 12, Lincoln county. R. R. Nov. 5, 1844
Hughes, Joseph, Je., Orange county. R. R. Je. 21, 1844
Humphrey, Edgar, Jan. 8, Onslow county. R. R. Jan. 30, 1844
Humphreys, Absalom T., Nov. 6, Greensboro. R. R. Nov. 19, 1844
Huntington, Duke H. of Hillsboro, Sept. 6, Marion, Alabama. R. R. Oct. 22, 1844
Hutchins, Isaac, Sept., Wake county. R. R. Oct. 1, 1844
Jackson, Clotilda, Mar., Pasquotank county. R. R. Mar. 5, 1844
Jackson, Giles Kelly of Greensborough, Alabama, Oct., Fayetteville. R. R. Oct. 18, 1844
Jarvis, Moses, Apr., Newbern. R. R. Apr. 30, 1844
Jeffreys, Mrs. Gray, Jly. 23, Wake county. R. R. Aug. 30, 1844
Johnson, Smith of Connecticut, Feb., Fayetteville. R. R. Feb. 27, 1844
Jones, Chas B. of Fayetteville, Jly. 30, Marengo county, Alabama. R. R. Aug. 30, 1844
Jones, Francis, Mar. 1, Hillsboro. R. R. Mar. 5, 1844
Jones, James C. of Wake county, Jan. 25, Franklin county. R. R. Feb. 2, 1844
Jones, John W. of Moore county, Oct., La Grange. R. R. Nov. 5, 1844

Jones, Mrs. R. D. of Bladen county, Nov. 3, Wilmington. R. R. Nov. 15, 1844
Jones, Sarah Louisa, Dec. 28, Rutherford county. R. R. Jan. 9, 1844
Jones, Mrs. Thos. D., Apr. 26, Newbern. R. R. My. 7, 1844
Jones, Mrs. William, Dec., Newbern. R. R. Dec. 10, 1844
Jordan, Iredell S. of this State, My. 6, Dallas county, Alabama. R. R. My. 7, 1844
Kelly, Sarah, Feb. 27, Rowan county. R. R. Mar. 8, 1844
Kerner, Mrs. Jos., Jan. 19, Kernersville, Stokes county. R. R. Feb. 9, 1844
Kimball, Mrs. Amos, Nov., Fayetteville. R. R. Dec. 6, 1844
Knight, Mrs. Peter E., Feb. 6, Edgecombe county. R. R. Feb. 16, 1844
Knox, Emma White, Mar. 8, St. Louis, Missouri. R. R. Mar. 26, 1844
Kyle, David Sr., Nov. 1, Rockingham county. R. R. Nov. 15, 1844
Lash, Christian, Jan. 12, Bethania, Stokes county. R. R. Feb. 9, 1844
Lillington, Mrs. John of Wilmington, Oct. 10, Raleigh. R. R. Oct. 15, 1844
Lindsay, Andrew, Nov. 2, Greensboro. R. R. Nov. 19, 1844
Little, Mrs. William, Nov., Edgecombe county. R. R. Dec. 6, 1844
Loftin, Mrs. Wm. C., Feb. 11, Lenoir county. R. R. Mar. 5, 1844
Long, John Sr., Sept., Orange county. R. R. Oct. 1, 1844
Love, Jane M'Kay, Nov. 2, Wilmington. R. R. Dec. 6, 1844
Love, Mrs. John D., Nov., Wilmington. R. R. Dec. 6, 1844
M'Caskill, Alexander, Dec. 10, Montgomery county. R. R. Jan. 19, 1844
M'Cauley, Andrew, Oct. 4, Raleigh. R. R. Oct. 15, 1844
M'Corkle, Mathew, Sept., Catawba county. R. R. Sept. 27, 1844
M'Dade, Mrs. James, Dec. 28, Chapel Hill. R. R. Jan. 9, 1844
M'Donald, Mrs. Thales, Nov., Davidson county. R. R. Nov. 26, 1844
M'Dougald, Rev. Allen, Oct. 17, Cumberland county. R. R. Nov. 5, 1844
M'Eachin, Edward, Mar., Robeson county. R. R. Apr. 2, 1844
M'Geachy, Alexander, Apr., Robeson county. R. R. Apr. 5, 1844
M'Iver, John Williams, Sept., Clemmonsville. R. R. Oct. 1, 1844
M'Kay, Mrs. Ann, My., Fayetteville. R. R. My. 17, 1844
M'Lester, Mrs. Nelson of Hillsborough, Je., Columbus, Ga. R. R. Je. 14, 1844
M'Neill, John, Sr., Dec. 31, Cumberland county. R. R. Jan. 16, 1844
M'Neill, Neill, Nov. 23, Moore county. R. R. Dec. 6, 1844
M'Pherson, Mrs. Duncan, Feb., Smithfield. R. R. Feb. 16, 1844
M'Rae, John, Mar., Robeson county. R. R. Mar. 26, 1844
Manning, Mrs. Joseph, Feb. 1, Edenton. R. R. Feb. 13, 1844
Martin, Mrs. William K., Je. 10, Franklin county. R. R. Jly. 10, 1844
Martindale, Stephen, Mar., Hailsville Duplin county. R. R. Mar. 5, 1844
Mebane, David, Mar., Orange county. R. R. Mar. 5, 1844
Michal, Major John, Apr., Lincolnton. R. R. Apr. 5, 1844
Miller, Mrs. Ivey, Nov., Rowan county. R. R. Nov. 26, 1844
Mills, Dr. Otis P., Mar. 4, Rutherford. R. R. Mar. 19, 1844
Missillier, Mrs. Rachel C., My. 4, Trenton. R. R. My. 7, 1844
Mitchell, Nathan, My., Fayetteville. R. R. My. 17, 1844
Mollan, Mrs. Stuart of Edenton, Mar. 12, New York. R. R. Apr. 5, 1844
Montague, James Y., Sept., Granville county. R. R. Sept. 24, 1844
Montgomery, Mary Ann, My., Orange county. R. R. My. 17, 1844
Monteith, Mrs. Abner, Jan. 4, Iredell county. R. R. Jan. 30, 1844
Montieth, William, Aug., Mecklenburg county. R. R. Sept. 6, 1844
Mooney, Mrs. James, Feb. 8, Rockingham county. R. R. Feb. 9, 1844

Moore, John, Jly. 19, Pitt county. R. R. Jly. 30, 1844
Moore, Junius Alex of Wilmington, Je., Tuscaloosa, Alabama. R. R. Jly. 2, 1844
Moore, Mrs. Maurice of Wilmington, My. 5, New York. R. R. My. 17, 1844
Morgan, Green, Nov., Guilford county. R. R. Nov. 29, 1844
Moring, John, Sept. 21, Chatham county. R. R. Oct. 1, 1844
Murphy, Mrs. David of Raleigh, Sept. 18, Sampson county. R. R. Sept. 27, 1844
Murphy, Eleanor, Feb. 3, Salisbury. R. R. Feb. 27, 1844
Nelson, Mrs. John, My., Orange county. R. R. My. 17, 1844
Norfleet, Isaac of Edgecombe county, Oct., Philadelphia, Pennsylvania. R. R. Nov. 5, 1844
Norment, Albert, Jan. 27, Mecklenburg county. R. R. Feb. 9, 1844
Northington, Mrs. Samuel E., Mar. 12, Raleigh. R. R. Mar. 19, 1844
Nunnery, Carter, Je. 2, Warrenton. R. R. Je. 14, 1844
Oliver, James A., Aug. 10, Duplin county. R. R. Aug. 16, 1844
Paisley, Mrs. James, Apr. 14, Guilford county. R. R. Apr. 23, 1844
Parker, Mrs. Weeks, Jan. 23, Edgecombe county. R. R. Feb. 2, 1844
Patton, Mrs. Thos T. of Morganton, Nov., Buncombe county. R. R. Nov. 29, 1844
Peacock, Robert W., Nov., Montgomery county. R. R. Nov. 5, 1844
Pearce, Mrs. J. Wesley of Franklin county, Je. 5, Fayetteville. R. R. Je. 14, 1844
Pearsall, Iantha, Oct. 30, Duplin county. R. R. Nov. 8, 1844
Pearson, Mrs. Asa, Apr. 12, Wake county. R. R. My. 3, 1844
Pearson, Mrs. John Stokes, Feb., Fayetteville. R. R. Mar. 1, 1844
Pearson, Mary, Apr. 17, Wake county. R. R. My. 3, 1844
Pearson, Mrs. Stephen, Apr. 25, Wake county. R. R. My. 3, 1844
Peebles, Harriet (infant) Aug. 3, Harmony Grove, Lenoir county. R. R. Aug. 9, 1844
Pitt, Eliza Jane, Feb., Wilmington. R. R. Mar. 1, 1844
Polk, Richard Trotter of this State, My., New Orleans. R. R. My. 17, 1844
Popelston, John, Oct., Edenton. R. R. Oct. 18, 1844
Potts, Isaac C., Feb. 24, Mecklenburg county. R. R. Mar. 19, 1844
Price, Mrs. Wm. J., Feb. 6, Wilmington. R. R. Feb. 20, 1844
Pullen, Ann Eliza, Jly. 13, Wake county. R. R. Jly. 19, 1844
Pulliam, Martha Helen of Wake county, Aug. 10, Somerville, Tennessee. R. R. Sept. 13, 1844
Ramsay, James, Feb. 7, Guilford ocunty. R. R. Feb. 9, 1844
Rayner, Elijah of Bertie county, Oct., Tennessee. R. R. Nov. 1, 1844
Reaves, Mrs. John, Sept. 2, Sampson county. R. R. Sept. 24, 1844
Rendleman, Mrs. Catharine, Jan. 23, Rowan county. R. R. Feb. 9, 1844
Rice, Mrs. Martha A., Mar. 6, Princeton, New Jersey. R. R. Apr. 5, 1844
Rich, Carey, Jan. 10, Greensboro. R. R. Feb. 6, 1844
Riley, William, Dec. 26, Orange county. R. R. Jan. 9, 1844
Rimer, Nicholas, Feb. 24, Rowan county. R. R. Mar. 8, 1844
Roberts, Richard H. of Raleigh, Sept. 1, Gainesville, Alabama. R. R. Sept. 17, 1844
Roberts, Roberts, Jr. of Raleigh, Sept., Gainesville, Alabama. R. R. Oct. 4, 1844
Rogers, Mrs. Benjamin of Wake county, Mar. 13. R. R. Mar. 29, 1844

Rollins, Frederick, Dec. 27, Wake county. R. R. Feb. 23, 1844
Rods, Lavin, Apr., Guilford county. R. R. Apr. 12, 1844
Russell, Joseph, Mar., Orange county. R. R. Mar. 22, 1844
Rutledge, Major Henry M., Mar., Nashville, Tennessee. R. R. Mar. 5, 1844
Sales, Rev. Anthony of Granville county, Je., Williamsborough. R. R. Je. 28, 1844
Satterwaite, James Edward, My., Pitt county. R. R. My. 17, 1844
Saunders, Louis M'Lane of Raleigh, Nov. 19, Rockhill Institute Elkridge, Maryland. R. R. Dec. 6, 1844
Saunders, Sarah E., Dec. 19, Raleigh. R. R. Dec. 24, 1844
Shaw, Mrs. David, Nov. 12, Fayetteville. R. R. Nov. 29, 1844
Shephard, Richard M. of Newbern, Jan. 11, New Orleans. R. R. Jan. 30, 1844
Sherrod, Ann Amanda B., Aug. 20, Greenville, Pitt county. R. R. Aug. 27, 1844
Shipley, Enoch T. of Washington county, Tennessee, Oct. 23, Greensboro, Guilford county. R. R. Nov. 8, 1844
Shipman, Daniel, Oct. 24, Columbus county. R. R. Nov. 29, 1844
Shipman, James, Jan. 4, Bladen county. R. R. Jan. 19, 1844
Shuford, Jacob, Apr., Catawba county. R. R. Apr. 12, 1844
Sikes, Enoch, Sept. 3, Union county. R. R. Sept. 24, 1844
Simonton, Gilbraith of Iredell county, Mar. 3, Monticello, Georgia. R. R. Mar. 29, 1844
Simpson, Exum, Aug., Chowan county. R. R. Aug. 9, 1844
Sinclair, Peter, Dec. 25, Moore county. R. R. Jan. 19, 1844
Slaughter, Christian, Sept. 24, Charlotte. R. R. Sept. 27, 1844
Sledge, Mrs. Joel of Franklin county, My. 11, Holly Springs, Mississippi. R. R. Je. 7, 1844
Smaw, Thomas, Sept., Newbern. R. R. Oct. 1, 1844
Snipes, Thomas, Mar., Chatham county. R. R. Mar. 22, 1844
Southgate, Rev. Frederick formerly of Wilmington, Apr., Quincey, Illinois. R. R. Apr. 30, 1844
Speck, Rev. Henry R., Oct. 6, Davidson county. R. R. Oct. 22, 1844
Stamey, John R., Sept. 14, Lincoln county. R. R. Nov. 5, 1844
Stanly, Mrs. Alexander H., Sept. 18, Newbern. R. R. Sept. 24, 1844
Stanton, Samuel, Oct., Randolph county. R. R. Oct. 18, 1844
Stanton, Mrs. Samuel, Oct., Randolph county. R. R. Oct. 18, 1844
Stowe, Mrs. Larkin of Mecklenburg county, Oct., Lincoln county. R. R. Oct. 25, 1844
Strickland, Joseph, Jan. 6, Sampson county. R. R. Feb. 6, 1844
Sutherland, James D., Oct. 10, Kenansville, Duplin county. R. R. Nov. 5, 1844
Swaim, Benjamin of Randolph county, Dec. 23, Raleigh. R. R. Dec. 24, 1844
Swaim, Thomas C., Mar. 1, Ashboro. R. R. Mar. 12, 1844
Swink, Augustus, Feb. 26, Rowan county. R. R. Mar. 8, 1844
Tate, Elizabeth, Feb. 29, Morganton. R. R. Mar. 12, 1844
Taylor, Anderson, Je. 3, Raleigh. R. R. Je. 7, 1844
Taylor, Martha, Aug. 10, Wake county. R. R. Aug. 13, 1844
Taylor, Col. Thomas, Dec. 26, Orange county. R. R. Jan. 9, 1844
Thompson, Anthony, Oct., Guilford county. R. R. Nov. 29, 1844

Thomson, Rev. David, Sept. 2, Smithfield, Johnson county. R. R. Sept. 13, 1844
Thomson, Lucy Ann, Sept. 2, Smithfield, Johnson county. R. R. Sept. 13, 1844
Thomson, Sally, Sept. 2, Smithfield, Johnson county. R. R. Sept. 13, 1844
Torrence, Mrs. Alex, Jr., Sept. 2, Iredell county. R. R. Oct. 25, 1844
Torrence, Mrs. Charles L., Nov. 18, Salisbury. R. R. Dec. 6, 1844
Urquhart, Mrs. Anna, Dec. 17, Wilmington. R. R. Dec. 31, 1844
Usher, Thomas of this State, Aug. 14, Holly Springs, Missouri. R. R. Sept. 17, 1844
Vance, Capt. David, Jan. 14, Buncombe county. R. R. Feb. 27, 1844
Vines, Samuel, Nov. 17, Greene county. R. R. Dec. 6, 1844
Waddill, Mrs. James M., Jan. 23, Wadesborough. R. R. Feb. 2, 1844
Waddill, Mary Emily, Mar., Anson county. R. R. Mar. 8, 1844
Waddill, Thomas, Sr. of Chatham county, Dec. 27, Stanly county. R. R. Jan. 16, 1844
Wadsworth, Mrs. William B., Mar., Craven county. R. R. Mar. 22, 1844
Walker, Dr. Levi, Sept. 1, Caswell county. R. R. Sept. 13, 1844
Wall, Frederick Anderson, My. 28, Wake county. R. R. Je. 7, 1844
Warren, Mrs. Nathaniel of Wake county, Nov. 6, Davidson county. R. R. Nov. 15, 1844
Watters, Mrs. Elizabeth of Hillsboro, Je. 30, Charleston, Massachusetts. R. R. Jly. 30, 1844
Wedding, Shadrack, My. 28, Raleigh. R. R. Je. 4, 1844
Weddington, Mrs. John R. of Cabarrus county, Oct., Mecklenburg county. R. R. Oct. 25, 1844
West, Thomas L., Jly. 10, Raleigh. R. R. Jly. 12, 1844
White, Mrs. William R. of Raleigh, Mar. 4, Zebulon Pike county, Georgia. R. R. My. 3, 1844
Whitfield, Elizabeth, Sept. 21, Lenoir county. R. R. Oct. 15, 1844
Whitley, Kedar, Aug. 10, Johnston county. R. R. Aug. 16, 1844
Wiley, John, Apr., Guilford county. R. R. Apr. 12, 1844
William, Eleanor E. of Warren county, Mar. 31, Raleigh. R. R. Apr. 2, 1844
Williams, Mrs. H. B., Feb. 9, Charlotte. R. R. Feb. 27, 1844
Williams, Nancy, Apr., Orange county. R. R. Apr. 5, 1844
Williams, Mrs. Robt., Sept. 22, Falkland, Pitt county. R. R. Oct. 4, 1844
Williams, Dr. Samuel H. of Danville, Virginia, Aug., Salisbury. R. R. Sept. 6, 1844
Wilson, James, Aug., Mecklenburg county. R. R. Sept. 6, 1844
Worth, Dr. David, Aug., Guilford county. R. R. Aug. 6, 1844
Wright, John Sr., Oct. 4, Sampson county. R. R. Oct. 18, 1844
Wright, Sarah J., Oct., Sampson county. R. R. Oct. 18, 1844
Yount, John, Jan. 14, Catawba county. R. R. Jan. 26, 1844

1845

Adams, Louisa M., Oct., Hillsboro. R. R. Oct. 17, 1845
Adams, Thomas, My., Salisbury. R. R. My. 20, 1845
Albright, Jesse, Feb. 16, Greensboro. R. R. Feb. 18, 1845
Alexander, Mrs. Charles, Aug., Mecklenburg county. R. R. Aug. 15, 1845

Alexander, Harriet Elizabeth, Oct., Charlotte. R. R. Oct. 24, 1845
Alexander, Dr. M. Winslow, Feb. 27, Mecklenburg county. R. R. Mar. 7, 1845
Alexander, Major Thomas, Jan., Mecklenburg county. R. R. Jan. 24, 1845
Amason, Roderick, Jan., Edgecombe county. R. R. Jan. 10, 1845
Ashford, Street, Nov., Clinton, Sampson county. R. R. Nov. 25, 1845
Atwell, Mrs. Thomas S., Jly., Rowan county. R. R. Jly. 4, 1845
Austin, Henry, Feb., Tarboro. R. R. Feb. 21, 1845
Bailey, Yancy, Apr. 18, Raleigh. R. R. Apr. 22, 1845
Baker, Mrs. Malcom, Je. 6, Robeson county. R. R. Je. 27, 1845
Ballenger, Beverly D., Aug. 19, Smithfield. R. R. Aug. 26, 1845
Baring, Mrs. Charles, Sept. 5, Mountain Lodge. R. R. Sept. 26, 1845
Barnes, Washington, Mar. 21, Warren county. R. R. Apr. 4, 1845
Barnes, Mrs. Washington, Apr. 1, Warren county. R. R. Apr. 4, 1845
Barry, Jonathan A., My., Wilmington. R. R. My. 20, 1845
Bartlett, Mrs. Elizabeth, Aug. 31, Newbern. R. R. Sept. 12, 1845
Basinger, Joseph, My., Rowan county. R. R. My. 20, 1845
Beard, John Sr., Jly., Salisbury. R. R. Jly. 4, 1845
Bell, Barthena, Je., Tarboro. R. R. Je. 24, 1845
Bell, Joseph of Beaufort, Carteret county, Feb. 20, Greensboro. R. R. Feb. 18, 1845
Bell, Col. Thomas, Oct., Pasquotank county. R. R. Oct. 24, 1845
Bethune, David, Feb., Robeson county. R. R. Feb. 7, 1845
Biggs, Kader of Windsor, Je. 18, Bertie county. R. R. Jly. 8, 1845
Biles, James of Salisbury, Je. 22, Morganton, Burke county. R. R. Jly. 4, 1845
Bird, Emily Lew, Aug. 22, Orange county. R. R. Sept. 12, 1845
Birkhead, E. R., Apr. 6, Mocksville. R. R. Apr. 22, 1845
Bissell, J. Humphrey of Charlotte, Mecklenburg county, Mar. 18, Philadelphia. R. R. Apr. 4, 1845
Bitting, Mrs. Anthony, Jan. 27, Stokes county. R. R. Mar. 14, 1845
Bivens, Nathaniel of Richardson's creek, Nov. 14, Union county. R. R. Dec. 12, 1845
Blackwell, Rebecca, Feb. 20, Rockingham county. R. R. Feb. 28, 1845
Bobo, Mrs. C. D. of Catawba county, Feb. 22. Mar. 7, 1845
Borden, Arnold of Fall River Massachusetts & Goldsboro, Wayne county, Mar. 7, Goldsboro, Wayne county. R. R. Mar. 18, 1845
Boyd, Mathew of Scotland and Chatham counties, Aug. 23, Pittsboro. R. R. Aug. 29, 1845
Boyd, Mrs. Thomas, Dec., Charlotte. R. R. Dec. 12, 1845
Brame, Rev. John Todd, Sept., Washington, Beaufort county. R. R. Sept. 16, 1845
Bray, Henry of Chatham county, My., Oketibbeha, Mississippi. R. R. My. 9, 1845
Brown, Col. John of Lewiston, Mifflin county, Pa., Oct., Buncombe county. R. R. Oct. 24, 1845
Brown, Mrs. Peter, My. 10, Salisbury. R. R. My. 20, 1845
Bucklin, Mrs. William, Je. 1, Newbern. R. R. Je. 10, 1845
Bunting, Mrs. Thomas, Nov. 1, Clinton, Sampson county. R. R. Nov. 18, 1845
Burton, Mary Amanda, Nov., Orange county. R. R. Nov. 25, 1845

Caldwell, Mrs. D. T., Jly. 4, Charlotte. R. R. Jly. 15, 1845
Calloway, Martha L., Jly. 22, Wilkesboro. R. R. Aug. 19, 1845
Cameron, John of Fayetteville, Je. 28, New Orleans. R. R. Jly. 11, 1845
Campbell, Catlett of Virginia, Jan. 18, Hillsborough. R. R. Jan. 28, 1845
Carloss, Maj. Archelaus, Apr. 11, Deep River, Chatham county. R. R. Apr. 18, 1845
Carney, John of Newbern, Oct., Fayetteville. R. R. Oct. 28, 1845
Caruthers, Julia Ann (infant), Sept., Newbern. R. R. Oct. 7, 1845
Caskill, Mrs. John M., Mar., Fayetteville. R. R. Apr. 1, 1845
Cherry, Jeremiah, Sept., Washington, Beaufort county. R. R. Sept. 5, 1845
Chinn, John H., Jly., Farmington, Davie county. R. R. Jly. 4, 1845
Clancy, Thomas, Apr. 28, Hillsboro. R. R. Apr. 29, 1845
Clark, Thomas S. of Virginia & North Carolina, Aug. 15, Lenoir county. R. R. Aug. 26, 1845
Clegg, Mrs. Isaac, Apr. 23, Chatham county. R. R. My. 2, 1845
Clement, John, Aug. 30, Mocksville. R. R. Sept. 12, 1845
Clingman, Peter, Feb. 16, Huntsville, Surry county. R. R. Mar. 7, 1845
Cooper, Capt. George, Oct. 12, Nashville. R. R. Oct. 24, 1845
Cotten, John W., My. 16, Tarboro. R. R. Je. 3, 1845
Cowan, Robert, My. 5, Wilmington. R. R. My. 9, 1845
Craige, Margaret, My. 27, Catawba county. R. R. Je. 13, 1845
Cress, Tobias, Sr., Aug. 12, Cabarrus county. R. R. Sept. 5, 1845
Culbertson, Gillespie, Apr. 4, Rowan county. R. R. Apr. 22, 1845
Cuthbert, Green M., Apr., Newberne. R. R. Apr. 11, 1845
Daniels, James, Jly., Cabarrus county. R. R. Jly. 4, 1845
Davidson, Mrs. Wm. Lee, My., Mecklenburg county. R. R. My. 9, 1845
Davidson, Wm. Lee, My., Mecklenburg county. R. R. My. 9, 1845
Davis, Abijah, Apr., Newbern. R. R. Apr. 8, 1845
Davis, Mrs. Charlotte, Je., Tarboro. R. R. Je. 24, 1845
Davis, Mrs. Peter R., Jr., Feb. 10, Warrenton. R. R. Feb. 14, 1845
Davis, Mrs. Thomas I., Nov. 25, Rock Hill near Wilmington. R. R. Dec. 12, 1845
Davison, Richard of England and this State, Aug., Warrenton, Warren county. R. R. Aug. 22, 1845
Dawson, John B. of Craven county, Feb., Newbern. R. R. Feb. 11, 1845
Devane, Mrs. John, Mar., New Hanover county. R. R. Mar. 11, 1845
Devane, Julia Eliza, Mar., New Hanover county. R. R. Mar. 11, 1845
Dicken, Dr. Ephraim, Dec., Tarborough. R. R. Dec. 16, 1845
Dilliard, Mrs. Merrit of Raleigh, Jly. 2, Carrollton, Miss. R. R. Jly. 25, 1845
Dismukes, Martha Felicia, Feb. 9, Palermo, Rowan county. R. R. Mar. 11, 1845
Dismukes, Dr. R. T., Feb. 29, Palermo, Rowan county. R. R. Mar. 11, 1845
Doak, Col. William, My. 27, Guilford county. R. R. Je. 13, 1845
Douglass, Mrs. George B., Apr. 4, Rowan county. R. R. Apr. 22, 1845
Duke, August William of Virginia and this State, Aug. 29, Granville county. R. R. Sept. 12, 1845
Dunn, Mrs. Wm., Aug. 18, Franklin county. R. R. Aug. 26, 1845
Dupree, Allen, Dec., Edgecombe county. R. R. Dec. 9, 1845
Duval, Rev. Dr., Apr. 13, Trenton, Jones county. R. R. Apr. 22, 1845

Eastwood, Margaret of Raleigh, Dec. 4, Cumberland county. R. R. Jan. 14, 1845
Ellen, Lydia F., Mar. 5, Wake county. R. R. Mar. 21, 1845
Elliott, Stephen, Oct. 10, Edenton. R. R. Oct. 21, 1845
Ellis, Sarah, Apr. 14, Davidson county. R. R. Apr. 29, 1845
Ennett, Thos., Nov. 25, Onslow county. R. R. Dec. 12, 1845
Erwin, Col. Leander Arthur of Burke county, Dec., Caddo Parish Louisiana. R. R. Dec. 16, 1845
Estes, Mrs. Elizabeth, Apr. 16, Hillsboro. R. R. Apr. 29, 1845
Exum, Mrs. Joseph J. of Murfreesboro & Northampton county, Jly. 23, Philadelphia. R. R. Aug. 8, 1845
Ferrebee, Samuel, Nov. 7, Currituck county. R. R. Dec. 12, 1845
Fisher, Mrs. Lewis, Oct., Cabarrus county. R. R. Oct. 3, 1845
Ford, Mrs. Osborne G. of Jersey settlement, Davidson county, Apr. 13, Rowan county. R. R. Apr. 29, 1845
Fraley, Alexander, My. 29, Salisbury. R. R. Je. 13, 1845
Fry, Matilda C., Jly., Stokes county. R. R. Jly. 4, 1845
Garver, Sally Caroline, My., Rowan county. R. R. My. 20, 1845
Gash, Reuben, J., Oct., Henderson county. R. R. Oct. 24, 1845
German, William of Queen Ann county, Maryland, My. 16, Anson county. R. R. Je. 13, 1845
Gibbs, M. Sophia, Mar., Wilmington. R. R. Mar. 11, 1845
Gibbs, Susan B., Mar., Wilmington. R. R. Mar. 11, 1845
Gibson, Mrs. James, My. 29, Rowan county. R. R. Je. 13, 1845
Gregory, Nathan, Apr. 19, Edenton. R. R. My. 9, 1845
Gregory, Gen. William, Nov., Elizabeth City. R. R. Nov. 11, 1845
Gretter, Thomas Chalmner (infant), Jly., Greensboro. R. R. Jly. 4, 1845
Grier, Mrs. Thomas I., Dec., Mecklenburg county. R. R. Dec. 12, 1845
Grissom, Capt. Thomas, Nov., Granville county. R. R. Nov. 25, 1845
Grist, James R. of Beaufort county, Feb., Brunswick county. R. R. Feb. 14, 1845
Guion, Isaac, My., Newbern. R. R. My. 13, 1845
Halsey, Henry, Aug. 28, Chowan county. R. R. Sept. 19, 1845
Hanrahan, Walter, Jan., Greenville, Pitt county. R. R. Jan. 10, 1845
Happoldt, Mary Lydia, Jly., Charlotte. R. R. Aug. 1, 1845
Hargrave, Franklin G., Oct., Lexington, Davidson county. R. R. Oct. 24, 1845
Hargrove, Col. Wm. T., Oct. 5, Granville county. R. R. Oct. 14, 1845
Harper, Gizeal, Mar., Randolph county. R. R. Mar. 11, 1845
Harrington, George of Richmond county, Aug. 15, Johnson county, Tennessee. R. R. Mar. 25, 1845
Harris, Mrs. C. W., Apr. 17, Mill Grove, Cabarrus county. R. R. My. 2, 1845
Harris, Littleton, Nov., Montgomery county. R. R. Nov. 4, 1845
Harris, Mary Lydia, Jly., Cabarrus county. R. R. Aug. 1, 1845
Hartsell, Mrs. Geo., Aug. 31, Cabarrus county. R. R. Sept. 9, 1845
Hatch, Durant of Craven & Jones county, Dec., Memphis, Tenn. R. R. Dec. 16, 1845
Hauner, Mrs. Sarah, Oct., Greensboro. R. R. Nov. 7, 1845
Hawkins, Mrs. M. T., Je. 27, Warren county. R. R. Jly. 4, 1845
Hawkins, Mrs. P. M., Je. 27, Warren county. R. R. Jly. 25, 1845

Headen, Isaac, Jan. 30, Chatham county. R. R. Feb. 21, 1845
Heflin, Mrs. R. T., Je. 10, Granville county. R. R. Je. 20, 1845
Henderson, Mrs. Richard, Sept. 16, Granville county. R. R. Oct. 3, 1845
Herring, James Sr., Sept. 3, Wayne county. R. R. Sept. 19, 1845
Herron, John W., Sept., Mecklenburg county. R .R. Oct. 3, 1845
Hill, Joseph Green, (infant) of Wake county, Jly. 6, Raleigh. R. R. Jly. 8, 1845
Hinton, Addison C. of Wake county, Apr., Cedar Bluff, Alabama. R. R. Apr. 11, 1845
Hinton, Alfred, Je. 27, Wake Forest. R. R. Jly. 8, 1845
Hinton, Mrs. James, Je. 24, Wake county. R. R. Jly. 4, 1845
Hogg, Christian of Raleigh, Feb. 18, Greensboro. R. R. Feb. 21, 1845
Holley, Margaret Ann, Dec., Bertie county. R. R. Dec. 12, 1845
Holloway, Sarah E., Je., Orange county. R. R. Jly. 1, 1845
Hopkins, Mrs. Tempe, Oct., Orange county. R. R. Oct. 17, 1845
Horton, Constant W., Feb. 17, Wake county. R. R. Feb. 21, 1845
Horton, Gen. William of Ashe county & Wilkes, Dec., Wilkes county. R. R. Dec. 16, 1845
House, Mrs. Elizabeth, Oct. 17, Wake county. R. R. Oct. 24, 1845
House, Geo., Mar., Rowan county. R. R. Apr. 1, 1845
House, Mrs. Geo., Mar., Rowan county. R. R. Apr. 1, 1845
Houston, Thomas, Oct., Mecklenburg county. R. R. Oct. 24, 1845
Howcott, Charles R., Apr. 13, Chowan county. R. R. My. 9, 1845
Huie, Dr. William L., Nov., Concord. R. R. Nov. 21. 1845
Hunt, Mrs. Enoch B., Apr. 22, Surry county. R. R. Je. 6, 1845
Huntington, James R., Dec., Milton. R. R. Dec. 12, 1845
Hutchings, Jno. A., Oct. 5, Granville county. R. R. Oct. 14, 1845
Irwin, Mrs. James, Jly., Mecklenburg county. R. R. Aug. 1, 1845
Irwin, Mrs. Mary Ann of Milton, Aug. 20, Lynchburg, Va. R. R. Sept. 9, 1845
Jamieson, Mrs. James of this State, My. 28, Halifax county, Va. R. R. Je. 20, 1845
Jeffreys, Dr. J. H., Apr. 10, Raleigh. R. R. Apr. 15, 1845
Jeffreys, William A., Oct. 3, Franklin county. R. R. Oct. 7, 1845
Jessup, Mrs. Isaac, Dec., Bladen county. R. R. Dec. 12, 1845
Johnson, Ann, Nov. 21, Cabarrus county. R. R. Dec. 5, 1845
Johnson, Dugald, Feb., Robeson county. R. R. Feb. 7, 1845
Johnson, Joseph G., My. 17, Raleigh. R. R. My. 20, 1845
Johnson, Mary Louisa, Mar., Fayetteville. R. R. Mar. 11, 1845
Johnston, Mary Reid, Oct., Lincoln county. R. R. Oct. 31, 1845
Jones, Arete, Sept. 12, Craven county. R. R. Oct. 7, 1845
Jones, Dr. Edmund H. of Wilkes county, Nov. 18, Lenoir, Caldwell county. R. R. Dec. 9, 1845
Jones, George L. of Newbern, Nov., Perry county, Alabama. R. R. Dec. 5, 1845
Jones, Dr. H. Pride, My. 15, Hillsborough. R. R. My. 27, 1845
Jones, John, Sept. 23, Craven county. R. R. Oct. 7, 1845
Jones, William, Apr. 23, Hertford. R. R. My. 9, 1845
Julian, David, Aug. 29, Caldwell county. R. R. Sept. 19, 1845
Kernutt, Dr. Jacob, Jly. 24, Lexington. R. R. Aug. 1, 1845
Kinney, Charles R., Oct., Hertford, Perquimans county. R. R. Oct. 21, 1845

Kirby, Mrs. Benjamin, D., Dec., Anson county. R. R. Dec. 16, 1845
Kirkland, Mrs. David of Orange county, Oct., Somerville, Tennessee. R. R. Oct. 24, 1845
Kittrell, Solomon, L., Oct. 18, Granville county. R. R. Oct. 24, 1845
Knox, Reuben, Mar. 30, St. Louis, Missouri. R. R. Apr. 18, 1845
Lane, Edmond, Mar. 29, Raleigh. R. R. Apr. 1, 1845
Latta, Mrs. John, Oct., Orange county. R. R. Oct. 17, 1845
Lea, Mrs. James K., Sept., Caswell county. R. R. Sept. 5, 1845
Leathers, James, Apr. 17, Orange county. R. R. My. 2, 1845
Lee, Rebecca Osby, Jly. 8, Raleigh. R. R. Jly. 11, 1845
Leonard, Major John of Brunswick county & Montgomery, Alabama, Mar., Bladen county. R. R. Apr. 1, 1845
Lindley, Thomas, Aug. 10, Chatham county. R. R. Aug. 26, 1845
Lindsay, Mrs. Andrew, Apr. 12, Guilford county. R. R. Apr. 25, 1845
Lindsay, Mrs. Wm. R. D., Feb. 17, Greensboro. R. R. Feb. 18, 1845
Little, George Washington, Oct. 20, Raleigh. R. R. Oct. 24, 1845
Logan, Mrs. John M., Mar. 29, Greensborough. R. R. Apr. 11, 1845
Long, James A. to Agnes Caldcleugh, Dec. 9, Lexington. R. R. Dec. 23, 1845
Long, Capt. Wm. A., My., Cabarrus county. R. R. My. 20, 1845
Longmire, Samuel H., Jly., Warrenton. R. R. Jly. 4, 1845
Lord, John Bradley, Aug., Warm Springs. R. R. Aug. 8, 1845
Love, Col. Robert, Jly. 17, of this State & Virginia. R. R. Aug. 1, 1845
Lucas, Margaret N., My. 20, Raleigh. R. R. My. 23, 1845
Lumsden, Mrs. William, Je. 28, Raleigh. R. R. Jly. 1, 1845
Lytaker, Mathias, Nov. 22, Cabarrus county. R. R. Dec. 5, 1845
McCord, Thomas, Dec., Mecklenburg county. R. R. Dec. 5, 1845
M'Cord, Wm., Nov., Mecklenburg county. R. R. Dec. 5, 1845
M'Crummen, Mrs. Jennet, My. 17, Sampson county. R. R. Je. 10, 1845
M'Cullers, Mrs. William, Aug. 2, Johnston county. R. R. Sept. 12, 1845
M'Gahey, Mrs. Milton, My., Mecklenburg county. R. R. My. 9, 1845
M'Kay, Archibald, My. 23, Cumberland county. R. R. Je. 10, 1845
M'Kimmon, Hugh, Apr. 28, Raleigh. R. R. My. 2, 1845
M'Knight, Mrs. Thomas, My., Mecklenburg county. R. R. My. 9, 1845
M'Laurin, Mrs. Thomas M., Nov., Cumberland county. R. R. Nov. 11, 1845
M'Lean, Angus, Sr., Dec., Robeson county. R. R. Dec. 12, 1845
M'Lean, Elizabeth, Feb., Guilford county. R. R. Feb. 18, 1845
M'Lean, Col. Giles S., Mar., Robeson county. R. R. Apr. 1, 1845
M'Lean, Maj. Henry of New York, Oct., Fayetteville. R. R. Oct. 28, 1845
M'Lean, Mrs. Joel, Apr. 22, Guilford county. R. R. My. 9, 1845
M'Leod, Murdock, My. 15, Cumberland county. R. R. Je. 10, 1845
M'Leod, Mrs. Murdock, My. 23, Cumberland county. R. R. Je. 10, 1845
M'Rae, Cameron, Farquhar, My. 18, Warrenton. R. R. My. 27, 1845
M'Rae, Moreaux, Sept. 12, Wadesborough. R. R. Sept. 26, 1845
M'Rae, Sarah, My., Warrenton. R. R. My. 13, 1845
Martin, Hon. James of this State, Feb., Mobile. R. R. Feb. 14, 1845
Martin, J. Logan, Jly., Charlotte. R. R. Jly. 15, 1845
Matthews, Dr. Samuel H., Elizabeth City, My. 4. R. R. My. 9, 1845
Metts, Mary Ann (infant) Sept., Kinston. R. R. Oct. 7, 1845
Mhoon, William S. of Bertie county, Dec. 25, Alabama. R. R. Jan. 24, 1845
Mitchell, Mrs. Nancy, Apr. 27, Raleigh. R. R. Apr. 29, 1845

Moore, Camm, Jly., Guilford county. R. R. Jly. 4, 1845
Moring, Christopher, Mar. 4, Wake county. R. R. Apr. 4, 1845
Moring, Dr. H. C., Oct., Greensboro. R. R. Nov. 7, 1845
Morrison, Mrs. Rufus W., My. 18, Rowan county. R. R. Je. 13, 1845
Morrow, Mrs. Benj., Oct., Charlotte. R. R. Oct. 31, 1845
Mullen, George, Sept. 26, Perquimans county. R. R. Oct. 14, 1845
Murphy, John, Sept., Cumberland county. R. R. Sept. 30, 1845
Neely, Archibald, Sept., Rutherford county R. R. Oct. 3, 1845
Neely, Col. James, Feb., Guilford county. R. R. Feb. 11. 1845
Newlon, James of Raleigh, Nov., Columbus Mississippi. R. R. Nov. 28, 1845
Nichols, Mrs. Mary of Orange county, Je., Norfolk, Virginia. R. R. Je. 20, 1845
Nixon, Peter, Sept. 13, Tarboro. R. R. Sept. 19, 1845
Nixon, Phineas, My. 16, Randolph county. R. R. My. 20, 1845
Orr, James H., Mar. 24, Charlotte. R. R. Apr. 8, 1845
Owen, Martha J., Sept. 9, Wilmington. R. R. Sept. 16, 1845
Paisley, John, My. 25, Guilford county. R. R. Je. 13, 1845
Paisley, Rev. John, Aug. 12, Orange county. R. R. Aug. 26, 1845
Patrick, Mrs. Edward, Mar. 27, Lenoir county. R. R. Apr. 22, 1845
Patterson, Mrs. Nathan of Franklin county, Feb. 15. R. R. Feb. 21, 1845
Pearce, Rev. John H., Dec., Fayetteville. R. R. Dec. 30, 1845
Peltier, Anthony, Je. 18, Chapel Hill. R. R. Jly. 1, 1845
Peltier, Mrs. Jeremiah B., Apr., 3, Beaufort, Carteret county. R. R. Apr. 22, 1845
Pender, Dr. Joshua, Dec., Edgecombe county. R. R. Dec. 9, 1845
Person, Presley C., Feb. 28, Franklin county. R. R. Mar. 14, 1845
Person, Mrs. Tabitha, Dec., Moore county. R. R. Dec. 9, 1845
Petersilie, Mrs. Charles, Dec., Bladen county. R. R. Dec. 9, 1845
Phifer, John, Oct. 18, Cabarrus county. (Long write up) R. R. Oct. 31, 1845
Poindexter, Mrs. Raleigh of Person county, Oct., Somerville, Tenn. R. R. Oct. 24, 1845
Powe, Wm. E., Apr. 4, Rowan county. R. R. Apr. 22, 1845
Presho, Mrs. Sarah, Aug., Beaufort, Carteret county. R. R. Aug. 22, 1845
Price, Moses, Aug., Edgecombe county. R. R. Aug. 26, 1845
Pugh, Mrs. Eaton of Roanoke this State, Aug. 16, Marshall county, Mississippi. R. R. Sept. 5, 1845
Puttick, Mrs. James, Apr. 2, Raleigh. R. R. Apr. 4, 1845
Puttick, Susan (infant), Sept. 13, Raleigh. R. R. Sept. 16, 1845
Ramsey, Mrs. Richard H., Dec. 15, Pasquotank county. R. R. Dec. 19, 1845
Rascoe, Wm. D., Nov. 12, Edenton. R. R. Nov. 25, 1845
Ray, Robert, of Sussex county, Virginia, Je., Wake county. R. R. Je. 10, 1845
Respass, Richard, My., Beaufort. R. R. My. 9, 1845
Ribelin, Samuel, Mar. 31 of Rowan & Davie county. R. R. Apr. 22, 1845
Richardson, Allen of Johnston county, Sept., Pickens county, Alabama. R. R. Sept. 19, 1845
Ridenhour, Mrs. Nicholas, Sr., Jly., Cabarrus county. R. R. Jly. 4, 1845
Rinehart, Christopher, Nov. 20, Cabarrus county. R. R. Dec. 5, 1845
Ritchie, Mrs. George, Nov. 16, Cabarrus county. R. R. Dec. 5, 1845
Rives, John J., Nov., Farmington, Moore county. R. R. Nov. 14, 1845
Scott, Mrs. John D., My. 14, Guilford county. R. R. My. 30, 1845

Sellers, Mrs. John, Jly., Sampson county. R. R. Jly. 8, 1845
Sewall, Dr. Thomas, Apr. 10, Washington, D. C. R. R. Apr. 15, 1845
Shepard, Mrs. James B., of Newbern, Jly. 11, Raleigh. R. R. Jly. 15, 1845
Shepard, Mrs. Thomas, My. 1, Duplin county. R. R. Je. 13, 1845
Sherwood, Hugh of Guilford county, Sept. 5, Washington county, Indiana. R. R. Oct. 31, 1841
Simmons, Elijah, Jr., Sept. 23, Jones county. R. R. Oct. 7, 1845
Singletary, Rev. John, Je. 21, Henderson county. R. R. Jly. 1, 1845
Sloan, John, Nov., Mecklenburg county. R. R. Dec. 5, 1845
Sloane, Mrs. Dixon, Nov., Kenansville, Duplin county. R. R. Nov. 18, 1845
Smith, Mrs. John A., Mar., Guilford county. R. R. Mar. 11, 1845
Smith, Peter, of Ireland, Feb., Wilmington. R. R. Feb. 14, 1845
Snead, Franklin, My. 24, Sampson county. R. R. Je. 10, 1845
Southall, Jesse, Oct. 6, Enfield. R. R. Oct. 21, 1845
Southerland, Jeremiah, Sept. 6, Duplin county. R. R. Sept. 19, 1845
Springs, Mrs. Mary, Jly., Guilford county. R. R. Jly. 4, 1845
Spruill, George E., Apr. 25, Warren county. R. R. My. 6, 1845
Spruill, Mary, Apr. 4, Warren county. R. R. Apr. 22, 1845
Spruill, Thomas H., My. 6, Warren county. R. R. My. 13, 1845
Stanford, Mrs. Richard A., Aug. 17, Orange county. R. R. Aug. 26, 1845
Steely, Mrs. E., Nov., Fayetteville R. R. Nov. 4, 1845
Stephens, Lott, My. 27, Fayetteville. R. R. Je. 13, 1845
Strange, Mrs. Robert of Hillsborough, Oct., Fayetteville. R. R. Oct. 28, 1845
Stricker, Daniel, Nov. 18, Cabarrus county R. R. Dec. 5, 1845
Sugg, Richard, H., Mar. 12, Wake county. R. R. Mar. 21, 1845
Sumner, Mrs. David E. of Hertford county, My. 4, Carter county, Tennessee. R. R. My. 23, 1845
Suter, Mrs. Alexander F., Mar. 18, Fort Johnston, Smithville. R. R. Apr. 8, 1845
Syme, Rev. Andrew, Oct. 26, Petersburg. R. R. Oct. 31, 1845
Taylor, Mrs. John, Apr. 17, Hilslboro. R. R. Apr. 29, 1845
Taylor, Mrs. John Louis, Jly. 1, Raleigh. R. R. Jly. 4, 1845
Thomas, Maria C., Je., Tarboro. R. R. Je. 24, 1845
Thorp, Mrs. Thomas, Mar. 4, Johnston county. R. R. Mar. 14, 1845
Tuton, William C. of Belfast Ireland, Apr. 12, Raleigh. R. R. Apr. 15, 1845
Vaneaton, Samuel, Mar., Davie county. R. R. Apr. 1, 1845
Vick, Samuel W., Je. 9, Nash county. R. R. Je. 24, 1845
Wallace, John, Dec., Iredell county. R. R. Dec. 12, 1845
Wallace, Dr. Joseph G., Feb., Onslow county. R. R. Feb. 11, 1845
Ward, Mrs. Solomon G., My., Warren county. R. R. My. 9, 1845
Watt, Mary Baily, Mar., Rockingham county. R. R. Mar. 11, 1845
Westbrooks, Amanda Caroline (infant) Jly., Guilford county. R. R. Jly. 4, 1845
Wheeler, Edward, Sept. 9, Salisbury. R. R. Sept. 19, 1845
Whitaker, John Wesley, Jly. 2, Raleigh. R. R. Jly. 4, 1845
Whitaker, Robert L., Sept. 18, Halifax. R. R. Sept. 19, 1845
White, Mrs. of Hyde county, Jan., Wake county. R. R. Jan. 24, 1845
White, William W. of Hyde county, Jan., Wake county. R. R. Jan. 24, 1845

Whitfield, Allen, Sept. 17, Wayne county. R. R. Oct. 7, 1845
Whitfield, William Howard of Granville county, Nov. 7, Wake Forest College. R. R. Nov. 14, 1845
Whitney, Adelaide Williard, Jly., Lexington. R. R. Aug. 1, 1845
Whitney, Reuben, M., My. 15, Washington. R. R. My. 20, 1845
Williams, Mary Lewis.of Surry county, Oct. 17, Greensboro. R. R. Oct. 24, 1845
Williams, Robert Edward, Je. 22, Pitt county. R. R. Je. 27, 1845
Williamson, Rosannah of Lincoln county, Jly., Charlotte. R. R. Jly. 4, 1845
Wilson, Mrs. Joseph H., Aug., Charlotte. R. R. Aug. 15, 1845
Wilson, Mrs. W. J., My., Mecklenburg county. R. R. My. 9, 1845
Wilson, William F., Jly., Mecklenburg county. R. R. Aug. 1, 1845
Winslow, Hardy G. Jr., Oct. 17, Randolph county. R. R. Oct. 31, 1845
Wooten, Robert, Nov., Bladen county. R. R. Nov. 4, 1845
Wright, Alice, Nov., Wilmington. R. R. Nov. 4, 1845
Wright, Bryant, Sept., Cumberland county. R. R. Sept. 30, 1845
Wright, William A., My., Wilmington. R. R. My. 16, 1845
Wyche, James of Granville county, Mar. 28, Raleigh. R. R Apr. 1, 1845
Yarborough, Mrs. Edward, Aug. 3, Salisbury & Raleigh. R. R. Aug. 5, 1845
Young, Mrs. Susan, Apr. 16, Wake Forest. R. R. Apr. 29, 1845

www.ingramcontent.com/pod-product-compliance
Lightning Source LLC
Chambersburg PA
CBHW052338230426
43664CB00041B/2193